Classroom Management in Lang

Research and Practice in Applied Linguistics

General Editors: **Christopher N. Candlin**, Macquarie University, Australia and the Open University, UK and **David R. Hall**, Macquarie University, Australia.

All books in this series are written by leading researchers and teachers in Applied Linguistics, with broad international experience. They are designed for the MA or PhD student in Applied Linguistics, TESOL or similar subject areas and for the language professional keen to extend their research experience.

Titles include:

Richard Kiely and Pauline Rea-Dickins
PROGRAM EVALUATION IN LANGUAGE EDUCATION

Cyril J. Weir
LANGUAGE TESTING AND VALIDATION

Tony Wright
CLASSROOM MANAGEMENT IN LANGUAGE EDUCATION

Forthcoming titles:

Martin Bygate and Virginia Samuda
TASKS IN LANGUAGE LEARNING

Francesca Bargiela, Catherine Nickerson and Brigitte Planken
BUSINESS DISCOURSE

Sandra Gollin and David R. Hall
LANGUAGE FOR SPECIFIC PURPOSES

Sandra Hale
COMMUNITY INTERPRETING

Geoff Hall
LITERATURE IN LANGUAGE EDUCATION

Marilyn Martin-Jones
BILINGUALISM

Martha Pennington
PRONUNCIATION

Devon Woods and Emese Bukor
INSTRUCTIONAL STRATEGIES IN LANGUAGE EDUCATION

Research and Practice in Applied Linguistics
Series Standing Order ISBN 1–4039–1184–3 hardcover
Series Standing Order ISBN 1–4039–1185–1 paperback
(*outside North America only*)

You can receive future titles in this series as they are published by placing a standing order. Please contact your bookseller or, in case of difficulty, write to us at the address below with your name and address, the title of the series and one of the ISBNs quoted above.

Customer Services Department, Macmillan Distribution Ltd, Houndmills, Basingstoke, Hampshire RG21 6XS, England

---

Classroom Management in Language Education

Tony Wright

First published 2005 by
PALGRAVE MACMILLAN
Houndmills, Basingstoke, Hampshire RG21 6XS and
175 Fifth Avenue, New York, N.Y. 10010
Companies and representatives throughout the world

PALGRAVE MACMILLAN is the global academic imprint of the Palgrave Macmillan division of St. Martin's Press, LLC and of Palgrave Macmillan Ltd. Macmillan® is a registered trademark in the United States, United Kingdom and other countries. Palgrave is a registered trademark in the European Union and other countries.

ISBN-13: 978–1–4039–4088–9 hardback
ISBN-10: 1–4039–4088–6 hardback
ISBN-13: 978–1–4039–4089–6 paperback
ISBN-10: 1–4039–4089–4 paperback

This book is printed on paper suitable for recycling and made from fully managed and sustained forest sources.

A catalogue record for this book is available from the British Library.

Library of Congress Cataloging-in-Publication Data
Wright, Tony, 1948 Feb. 18–
     Classroom management in language education / Tony Wright.
        p.   cm. — (Research and practice in applied linguistics)
     Includes bibliographical references and index.
     ISBN 1–4039–4088–6 (cloth) — ISBN 1–4039–4089–4 (pbk.)
     1. English language—Study and teaching.   2. English language—Study and teaching—Foreign speakers.   3. Classroom management. I. Title. II. Series.
     LB1576.W732 2005
     428′.007′1—dc22   2005043361

10   9   8   7   6   5   4   3   2   1
14   13   12   11   10   09   08   07   06   05

Printed and bound in Great Britain by
Antony Rowe Ltd, Chippenham and Eastbourne

To Linda, Tim and Liz

Contents

General Editors' Preface

Research and Practice in Applied Linguistics is an international book series from Palgrave Macmillan which brings together leading researchers and teachers in Applied Linguistics to provide readers with the knowledge and tools they need to undertake their own practice-related research. Books in the series are designed for students and researchers in Applied Linguistics, TESOL, Language Education and related subject areas, and for language professionals keen to extend their research experience.

Every book in this innovative series is designed to be user-friendly, with clear illustrations and accessible style. The quotations and definitions of key concepts that punctuate the main text are intended to ensure that many, often competing, voices are heard. Each book presents a concise historical and conceptual overview of its chosen field, identifying many lines of enquiry and findings, but also gaps and disagreements. It provides readers with an overall framework for further examination of how research and practice inform each other, and how practitioners can develop their own problem-based research.

The focus throughout is on exploring the relationship between research and practice in Applied Linguistics. How far can research provide answers to the questions and issues that arise in practice? Can research questions that arise and are examined in very specific circumstances be informed by, and inform, the global body of research and practice? What different kinds of information can be obtained from different research methodologies? How should we make a selection between the options available, and how far are different methods compatible with each other? How can the results of research be turned into practical action?

The books in this series identify some of the key researchable areas in the field and provide workable examples of research projects, backed up by details of appropriate research tools and resources. Case studies and exemplars of research and practice are drawn on throughout the books. References to key institutions, individual research lists, journals and professional organizations provide starting points for gathering information and embarking on research. The books also include annotated lists of key works in the field for further study.

The overall objective of the series is to illustrate the message that in Applied Linguistics there can be no good professional practice that isn't based on good research, and there can be no good research that isn't informed by practice.

Christopher N. Candlin
Macquarie University, Sydney
and Open University, UK

David R. Hall
Macquarie University, Sydney

Acknowledgements

Many people have knowingly and unknowingly contributed to writing this book. The series editors, Chris Candlin and David Hall, for inviting me to write it in the first place and for their ever-helpful editorial advice throughout the writing period. Their timely knowledge and expertise have been invaluable.

Joanna Haynes, Tony Brown and Ian Collingwood, who introduced me to new perspectives on learning and education beyond English language teaching in our long conversations while working together in Swaziland.

My colleagues, Hazel Sales and Boon Hua Lee, for patiently reading early drafts of parts of this book and providing valuable feedback and encouragement. My colleagues and friends Gabi Matei, Uwe Pohl, Ross Lynn, Liz Robbins and Sarah Rich for their support and timely talk.

Paul Gentle, for his unstinting support and creation of time and space for me to pull the work together.

Julian Edge and his colleagues at LSU in Aston University, The British Council Mexico and the organisers of Best of British 2003, and the PELLTA conference organising committee in Penang for providing me with opportunities to air my ideas on classroom management in public.

Joan Kelly Hall, Fred Erickson, Srikant Sarangi, Robin Goodfellow, Jonathan Crichton and Ou Yang Huhua for so generously assisting me with references and papers.

The many teachers and teacher educators who have followed MEd and PhD programmes with me over the past decade and more, at home in Plymouth, and away in Mexico, Swaziland and Namibia. Their contribution to my thinking and practice is inestimable.

Linda, above all, who has put up with my long periods of absence and supported me unfailingly through the inevitable ups and downs of a project like this one.

All mistakes and errors in this book are entirely mine.

Introduction

Classroom management is the central element of every teacher's daily professional experience, but it is a neglected topic in debates on language education. Its relative unimportance in Applied Linguistics literature is far outweighed by its significance for teachers and students in classrooms. As a consequence, there has been a tendency to reduce classroom management to a series of procedures and techniques teachers use for 'managing' their classroom groups and lessons, part of the craft knowledge and skills of the profession. However, there are signs that a correction of this imbalance is both possible and necessary. Recent research in language education, accompanied by shifts in thinking about language teaching practice, have made it possible; the intense contemporary debate and speculation about the purposes and role of education in all societies have made it necessary.

In the field of language education, two linked contemporary trends have been particularly influential in prompting a reassessment of classroom management. The first is the rise and subsequent questioning of communicative language teaching as the canon for language teaching. This is connected to and fuelled by a second trend: research on the actual practices of language education in a wide range of contexts internationally. Such research has served to emphasise both the diversity and intricacy of classroom life, and to reinforce perceptions that the classroom is the true centre of the educational experience, and confirm that it is here, through the teaching-and-learning process, that education 'happens'. The experience of practitioners innovating in non-Western contexts, typically drawing from, but also indigenising practice, research and theory originating in the West, has demonstrated that classroom management practices in different places have deep cultural roots, and that, while formal classroom education is a universal feature of the twenty-first-century world, its local variations are manifold. Thus, we increasingly debate 'post-communicative' or 'post-method' language teaching, with a focus on what is possible in our local classrooms rather than what is prescribed, and perhaps move closer to the types of practice envisaged by Breen and

1

Candlin (1980). The ways in which we manage classrooms are thus open to renewed debate and discussion, and the lived experience of practitioners and learners needs to be acknowledged as a part of this dialogue. In English language education, the current international dominance of English is the background against which classroom teaching-and-learning unfolds. While English may not retain this dominant position in the future (Graddoll 1997, 2004), its current role as a global medium of communication means that it is taught worldwide. As a result, the means by which it is taught are very influential; ongoing debate about technological transfer is sharpened by casting language teaching methodology itself as a 'technology' (Holliday 1994: 93). Ideas about teaching-and-learning invariably carry with them implications for managing classrooms, both directly, for example, through something as fundamental as seating arrangements, and indirectly, through implied participation opportunities in classroom activities, and teaching materials. These trends are unfolding against a background of technological change which directly impinges upon education and language education. The 'digital revolution' which has driven exponential growth in the use of information and communications technology – from mobile phones to the Internet – has enabled people to communicate more rapidly and to generate information more copiously than ever before. These technologies also suggest viable alternatives to formal classroom education, and are already being employed in programmes worldwide. However, like all technologies, they have an amplifying force, and may serve to reinforce the status quo that exists in classrooms around the world, rather than enabling more people to learn. Currently, new technologies are also deeply inequitable both in terms of access and also in terms of users' communicative capacities. A discussion of how classrooms are currently managed is therefore vital in order to maximise the positive potential of new technology in education; otherwise we run the risk of replicating practices which might limit learning opportunities.

The purposes of education have always been contested by societies; today, much debate revolves around such issues as 'choice', 'opportunity', 'lifelong learning' and 'widening access'. All of these have implications for how classrooms are managed, especially for the growing field of post-compulsory education in countries like Britain, Germany and the United States, and in basic education in the non-industrialised countries, where choice and necessity are in sharp conflict for a large proportion of the population. The broader social, economic and political trends in specific societies and internationally also influence policy in education and thus directly affect the lives of teachers and students – the influence of these broad trends on classroom management practices, while difficult to measure, is none the less profound, and very much a factor in prompting a reassessment of the notion of classroom management. Classroom management is then about both local activity in classrooms and also wider 'external' forces.

For many reasons, then, it is an opportune moment to bring classroom management to the centre of debate about language education. By providing a new conceptualisation of what it means, this book aims to make a contribution to enhanced understanding of language education. It will explore what teachers and students actually experience in managing classrooms, in terms of an understanding of professional practice – what teachers do together with their students, and why. In keeping with the book's focus on professional practice, it also looks at how teachers learn and the contribution of teacher education to professional learning. It also aims to raise awareness and increase knowledge of language teaching-and-learning practices in formal settings by synthesising research, theory and practice in classroom management from a variety of sources. Several themes are thus developed in the book:

- The importance of human relations and the emotional dimensions of teaching-and-learning in classroom management.
- The concept of participation in classroom life, and how management practices contribute to participation patterns.
- How the ever-present factors of time and space which define formal education influence management practices.

Together these form a basic framework for understanding classroom management, and enable discussion of issues such as the value of collaborative learning, of classroom climate, and managing the 'virtual classroom' of online learning. The active notion of 'managing' is preferred to the better known term 'management', as I believe it better captures the dynamic and unfolding nature of classroom life, and how ongoing activities contribute to both the present business of classroom groups and also become part of the history of learning groups. The 'survival' side of classroom life is also inherent in the idea of 'managing' – a lot of classroom life is a matter of 'getting by'. The character of classrooms is thus an outcome of the interaction between the countless in-time 'managing' activities of teachers and learners in lessons which draw on tacit knowledge of the context and intentional managing activity – or 'management' – and their emotional responses to these situations. 'Management' is just one type of classroom activity with overtones of control and intentionality, and must be viewed in relation to the emergent activities of classroom life.

This book is also a modest contribution to the debate about the nature of Applied Linguistics and its relationship with language education. As such it regards Applied Linguistics as a means of understanding professional practice and teaching-and-learning contexts. Classrooms are complex and not easily reducible, although an understanding does require a consideration of ideas in the form of 'models' of practice, and thus theories of pedagogy. It also entails a discussion of ideologies that influence formal education. The proposed reframing of classroom management raises questions for both research and practice, and the relationship between them. The type of research featured in the book is essentially classroom-focused and features contextually rich descriptions of practice. In this way the discussion highlights the specifics of classroom encounters. Research on classroom management additionally attempts to develop understanding by referring to wider social and cultural influences. Teachers themselves have done much of this research, either in inquiry, exploratory or action modes, or combinations of these. The aim of this research is to contribute to our understanding of classroom practices as they exist and how changes in practice are experienced. In this way, free from the potentially repressive dogmas of 'methodology' and 'method', students and teachers can together use inquiry as a means of seeking ways of creating better learning opportunities in classrooms. The additional focus on teacher education raises questions about the nature of the pedagogic knowledge base and the contribution of research activity to teacher education. It thus hints at ways of closing the gap between research and practice in language teacher education.

This is not a 'how to' book for teachers, offering suggestions or prescriptions on how to manage classrooms. There are many excellent resources which do this, and some are listed in Part 4. Its primary aim is to raise awareness, offer thinking frameworks and seed debate on classroom life. It suggests ways of inquiring into these issues as a means of informing ourselves – for example, about the conditions under which new classroom practices flourish. Research would in such cases inform strategies for introducing new ideas in classroom teaching by grounding decisions to innovate in reflection and understanding of existing realities.

The book is divided into four parts. Part 1 outlines the conceptual framework for understanding how classrooms are managed. Part 2 considers research on classroom life in terms of participation, engagement, and time and space. Part 3 outlines ways in which research on classroom management can be designed and conducted, and invites challenge or corroboration of some of the issues raised in Parts 1 and 2 in new contexts. It contains a review of useful research procedures and describes a number of research projects which readers may wish to use or to adapt to their own particular needs. Part 4 lists resources to facilitate further research and practice.

Part 1

Issues and Themes in Classroom Management

Introduction

Part 1 analyses classroom management from different perspectives – by examining the function and nature of classrooms, and by exploring classroom management practices and the role of teaching as a central classroom activity. I aim to address the following questions:

1. What is the character of the formal classroom learning context? What are the discoursal implications of formal classroom teaching-and-learning?
2. How do the institutional factors of the enclosure in space and time-boundedness of formal education affect classroom management practices?
3. How are classrooms portrayed in research and what is the nature of the dialectical relationship between their nature and classroom management practices?
4. What are the central concerns of classroom management? What discourses do they predicate?
5. What is the influence of the affective domain of classrooms – or engagement – to classroom management?
6. What are the patterns of participation in classrooms? And how are these managed?
7. What models of pedagogy are there and what influence do they have on classroom management?
8. How do teachers learn about teaching? How do they refine and develop their skills and knowledge?

Responses to these questions deal with different strands of the practices of classroom management and enable us to construct a rich picture of the influences on, and practices of, classroom management.

1
Towards an Agenda for Understanding Classroom Management

Managing classrooms is normally something we do rather than analyse. Like many teachers I have spent the bulk of my waking life in and around classrooms, as a teacher and as a student, and the classroom has become my natural habitat. One consequence of this is that much of my knowledge – both active and stored – about classrooms is tacit. This accumulated knowledge enables me to manage my classroom without too much conscious thought. A lot of my practice is thus routine and automated, even instinctive and intuitive. It is how I handle the complex reality of the classroom world I work in – if I paused during teaching to consciously address what I was doing, and everything that was at that time involved, I would probably be overwhelmed. Therefore, in order to comprehend the classroom fully or to articulate my experience to others, I have to make a particular effort to detach myself sufficiently from the everyday reality of classrooms. Without this distancing, the classroom can appear too 'obvious' and even humdrum for all of us who spend long periods of time there. By detaching myself, I hope to make sense of my experience, to understand better why classrooms are like they are. This process is akin to untying a very complex knot with many strands. The knot is classroom management itself. As a teacher, any insights I gain from this type of inquiry can positively affect the quality of classroom life both for myself and my students working with me.

1.1 Looking at classrooms

Understanding classroom management begins with an investigation of the observable events and activities of any classroom. To do this, we shall analyse three classrooms as described in writing by their teachers. The classrooms have not been chosen as exemplars of the contexts from which they are drawn, but are simply those of the teachers who described them. As you read, you might like to identify what is common to all of them and what seem to be obvious differences between them.

Data 1.1   Classroom learning contexts: teachers' descriptions

1. An English Lesson in Malaysia

A teacher walks into a class of 40 active pupils, boys and girls, aged eight. The teacher has a big book with her, with beautiful and colourful illustrations. She calls the pupils to sit around her at the front of the class. Everyone rushes to sit as close as possible to where the teacher is sitting. The pupils are pushing and squabbling amongst themselves. The teacher has to bring them under control. When everyone has sat quietly around her she begins her story. She starts by asking questions. 'Have you seen this before?' 'Have you read this story before?' The immediate response from the pupils is a drawn out 'ye-e-e-s' and 'no-o-o'. She then reads the story slowly and clearly, pointing her finger to every word so the children can see. When she's finished, she asks: 'Do you like the story?' A few enthusiastic pupils answer positively and the rest stay quiet. The teacher then instructs the group to return to their desks and complete a task she has set earlier. The task is based on the story, with true/false questions, matching questions and rearranging sentences, which the pupils complete at home.

2. An English Lesson in Mozambique

There are about 40 students, girls and boys in their early teens, sitting in pairs. They are copying a dialogue from the blackboard. The teacher reads the dialogue aloud line by line and the students read it after him. The teacher tells each student to be either A or B. He tells them to practise the dialogue as A and B. While the students are practising, the teacher moves about the classroom listening. There is quite a lot of noise. The teacher asks them to stop. He then asks two students to act out the dialogue in front of the class. Two or three pairs do this. The teacher then tells the pairs to write a similar dialogue. The pairs spend a few minutes writing and then present their dialogues to the class until the bell goes at end the lesson.

3. An English Lesson in China

Forty-one young adults, mixed, students sit in rows. The teacher stands in front of the blackboard and behind the teacher's desk. On the teacher's desk lies his copy of the textbook, teaching notes and teaching aids such as a tape recorder and headphones. After exchanging greetings with the students the teacher begins his lecture. The teacher writes the title of the text he is going to teach on the blackboard and the key points of his lecture as well. While the teacher is giving the lecture, students sit and listen and take notes. Around 5 to 10 minutes before the class ends, the teacher stops his lecture and gives the students a chance to ask questions about what he has been teaching. After answering the students' questions, the teacher gives students an assignment for reviewing the lesson and previewing the next. The class then ends.

The 'observables'

Our three sample classrooms illustrate the following facts about classrooms (these are summarised in Table 1.1).

Good list of some important parameters.

Table 1.1   Analysis of sample classrooms

Place	Use of space	Use of time	Language Data	Resources	Interactions	Atmosphere
Malaysian Example	Students sitting at front of class by teacher, also sitting; Children move to individual desks	Organising children; eliciting from children and focusing on story; reading of story; completing exercises on story + homework when lesson finishes	Story + exercises + interaction T/S	Story book including pictures; Ss previous knowledge	T/Ss to control Ss; T elicits from Ss; T/Ss to change seating and do exercises	Excited students; focused on tasks; 'business-like'
Mozambican Example	Students sitting in pairs; teacher at front of class and then moving around class	Copying dialogue from board; reading dialogue aloud; Ss practice dialogue privately; 2 Ss act dialogue out; Ss write new dialogue in pairs; Ss present dialogues to class	Sample dialogue; Ss' dialogues	Sample dialogue; Ss dialogue, Board	T gives instructions to Ss re tasks; Ss in pairs and to whole class	Orderly, controlled; 'business-like'
Chinese Example	Students in rows; teacher stands at front	T gives lecture – Ss make notes; Ss ask teacher questions for 5/10 minutes Homework task set	Text	Textbook, teaching aids	T exchanges greetings with Ss; question/answer session; T speaks to Ss	Cordial; 'business-like'

Use of classroom space

The students and teachers occupy a classroom space, or location, shared by the whole group. The students are seated in different configurations – in pairs, or singly, in rows. They may be facing each other or their teacher. They might already have occupied the space before their teacher arrived. The teacher changes the students' positions in the room during the lesson so that they can be close to her for a particular activity (Malaysian classroom) or so that they can jointly participate in different activities (pairs in the Mozambican classroom). We thus see whether or not pupils move during lessons, and how movement might have an effect such as a temporary breakdown in order, which the teacher has to restore. The teacher also moves about the classroom or stays in one place (the Mozambican classroom compared with the Chinese classroom). The spatial dimension of two of the lessons is further extended with homework.

Use of time

There is a sense of a purposive sequence of activity through time in the lessons, and of progression from one type of activity to another. There is also a clear sense that the students and teachers are busy, doing various things. We do not know exactly how long each lesson lasts, but we can see that a teacher has the option of allocating time for specific activities in a lesson (Chinese classroom). A bell signals the end of the Mozambican lesson. Homework extends the time-frames of two of the lessons.

Learning and teaching activity

In these classrooms, various types of language 'data' are presented to students – a storybook which the teacher reads to the children; a dialogue on the blackboard; the teacher's text. The storybook, the board and other texts, and the audiovisual aids in the Chinese classroom, are all integrated into the activities. The activities themselves appear to be based on these samples. The students may have been exposed to similar data on previous occasions – the data and the different ways it is presented and processed seem to pose few problems for the students. There are chances in all the lessons for the students to practise or consolidate their grasp of the data through classroom activities and homework that the teacher sets. We can't 'see' any learning happening in these lessons. We can only see the way the classroom encounters unfold through the sequences of activity.

Communication/interaction

There are various types of communication between the teacher and the students, and among the students during the course of the activities. These classrooms are not silent places. There is a lot of talking of different types by different participants, although in the Chinese classroom, it appears that the teacher speaks most of the time, while in the others, students have more opportunities to contribute verbally. We note, for example, the teacher asking the students questions and inviting them to take other opportunities to engage with the data through activities, attempted individually and collectively. Communication and interaction is also channelled through the teaching materials and other means of signalling meaning – gesture, for example (although it does not appear in any of the descriptions).

Atmosphere

It is very difficult to read descriptions like these and not have a sense of the emotional tenor of events. We thus gain some insights into the atmosphere of each classroom and learn more about the social nature of each classroom, and gain a sense of the relative closeness of the teacher/student relationship. We have already noted their 'busy-ness'. There are greetings exchanged; we sense how keen the Malaysian children are to hear the story, what the quality of their responses is like and whether or not they appeared to enjoy the story. We sense how they feel 'released' by moving to the front of the class to hear the story. We see them responding to the teacher's calls for calm and order. We might infer, perhaps erroneously, whether the students are happy, bored or excited in any of the classes. It is a sign of our knowledge of the emotional dimension of classroom activity.

Artefacts

We glimpse various artefacts in these classrooms – furniture such as a blackboard, teachers' table and students' desks, paper material such as teachers' notes and books, equipment like 'teaching aids', writing implements.

A picture of some complexity emerges from the analysis. The descriptions are, however, inevitably partial and the writers are naturally selective in what they present to their readers. We see only those surface features, or 'observables', selected by the three authors as 'typical' of their classrooms as requested at the time of writing. Other observables are 'missing': for instance, there is no mention of any of the other physical features of the classrooms – walls, windows, doors, lighting, floor, ceiling and so on – or the temperature or humidity. Periods of silence are not noted. There is little hard information about the ways in which participants move about or use gesture. There is also relatively little information offered about the atmosphere in two of the classrooms. More texture can be provided by detailed observations (Field Note 1.1). Here, we glimpse the close relationship between teaching-and-learning activity and social relationships and social activity. We gain a strong impression of the atmosphere in which these activities are carried out. There is information about movement and time, too.

Field Note 1.1   Classroom life in action (Kindergarten – Mexico)

The children (18 of them, four years old or so) are spread out round the room. Some are lying on the floor on their fronts, reading or drawing. One or two are talking quietly to each other. Other children are sitting individually at desks, also reading and drawing. The teacher is sitting at a desk, reading a story to two children. The walls are decorated with children's work, pictures, posters. There are boxes of toys and Lego bricks. A small classroom library, where one child is looking through the books, is in the corner. There is a hum of activity and busy noise coming from the children. The teaching assistant is looking after a child who has broken his pencil. The teacher finishes her story and stands up. She claps. Five minutes more and then we do maths, she says. She moves to the blackboard and writes some sums there.

We can create even more finely-grained pictures of classroom management in action by focusing more closely on specific aspects of classroom activity. One way we can do this is by recording and transcribing and analysing what teachers and students say (Extract 1.1).

Extract 1.1   Classroom talk

```
 1  T   she would / OK here it is / what do you want to do outside – go and come back
         quickly / OK here it is you see that the er / the er/ personal pronoun has changed –
         OK (T. cleans B/B: 20 secs) who has a car in this class
     Ss  Edward
 5       Edward
     T   who has a car in this class
     Ss  (inaudible)
     S #1   my grandpa
     Ss  (inaudible)
10   T   I didn't / I didn't ask you whether your father has a car / I asked you whether
     S #2   I have a Mazda
     T   nobody asked you that
     Ss  (inaudible) (general noise)
     T   excuse me / let's take for instance
15   S #3   ssh
     T   let's take for instance / that er – you – let's take for instance / that you had a car /
         if you had a car / where would you park it
```

In the example, the teacher asks an apparently straightforward question (line 3). What follows is far from orderly. Students answer (lines 4 and 5). The teacher repeats the question – has he heard the responses, or has he decided not to respond to them? A student answers (line 8) in the midst of more disordered responses from the class. The teacher rejects the answer (line 10) and is interrupted by a different student with an answer (line 11). This is rejected (line 12). The group all talk at once. The teacher begins to rephrase the question (line 14) and a student appeals for calm (line 15). In lines 16/17, the teacher reformulates the question.

The account of what happens in this classroom incident illustrates how the educational dialogue between teachers and students progresses. It does not, however, describe the classroom atmosphere or include any information about how teachers and learners move in the classroom space, or how they use materials like books or the board during the incident. It does provide a window onto how this teacher and his students manage their classroom. Why events proceed in the way they do is less clear, however. To understand this further we have to penetrate below the surface of activity, to explore the 'hidden' aspects of classroom life.

Hidden dimensions of classroom management – 'inner domains'

The three portrayals of the surface features of classrooms in different contexts have revealed their inherent complexity. However, in order to understand better how these and other classrooms are managed, we need to go beyond observable activity into the cultural, social, psychological and emotional worlds of classrooms, or to the 'inner' dimensions. Individual group members are thinking different thoughts and experiencing different emotional states, which may fluctuate considerably during classroom encounters. The social-psychological states and relationships within the three learning groups are also in flux. Gaining access to these 'inner' domains is, however, notoriously difficult. On the other hand, without these perspectives it is difficult to reach beyond our personal inferences and prejudices, and our understandings will be impoverished as a consequence.

One way of understanding how classroom management practices 'work' is to gain access to individuals' subjective experience of classroom life. For example, teachers' metaphors offer rich insights into how they experience and conceptualise classroom life. Analysis and exploration of these metaphors provides access to the thinking and beliefs behind what teachers do when they are in the classroom. For instance, they reveal attitudes towards teacher–learner relationships: priest–worshipper, teacher as 'place to shelter', teacher as salesperson, and so on. We also see traces of the ways in which teaching and learning are managed – as a business transaction, as a religious ceremony, as horticulture (Data 1.2).

Data 1.2   Classroom learning contexts

Teachers' metaphors for the classroom (a selection)

A classroom is...

A greenhouse ('protected environment'; careful husbandry'; 'teacher is gardener, students are plants')

A wrestling ring ('struggle for knowledge'; 'ideas fight for attention'; 'teacher as referee'; students as audience')

A market place ('noisy, active'; 'place for exchange of goods'; 'teacher as seller, student as buyer'; bargaining for the best price, or conditions for exchange')

A temple ('place to sit peacefully'; 'rituals'; 'teacher as priest, students as worshippers')

A hospital ('treatment of patients'; 'teacher–doctor, students–patients'; organised, systematic prescription)

A tree ('teacher is the tree and therefore the classroom'; 'students are birds and animals which shelter in the branches'; 'teacher sustains and nurtures and provides'; parasites and creepers – troublesome students)

We can look still further in seeking an understanding of classroom management by examining some of the hidden influences from 'outside' the classroom on teachers' and learners' classroom behaviour. A unique characteristic of classrooms as learning contexts results from the special functions they have been designed to fulfil. Classrooms are the essential locus of formal education, where many social and cultural influences intersect. The purposes of classrooms have themselves emerged from cultural, social, political and economic life and their associated discourses through history in particular contexts (Data 1.3). In contrast with less formal learning contexts, classrooms are permeated by the *educational* goals of formalised learning that led to their creation. The classroom is only one of a multitude of contexts in which people can learn, but it differs in significant ways from other learning contexts like the home, the workplace, play or everyday social interaction, notably the degree to which it is 'designed' and institutionalised. The nature of any classroom is thus an amalgam of local in-time activities and psychological and social processes on the one hand, and 'external' influences, on the other, adding further layers of complexity. These observable and unobservable features are schematised in Figure 1.1. Managing classrooms means managing this complexity, simultaneously contributing to the moment-by-moment unfolding of classroom life, and the longer story of formal education.

Data 1.3   Interview with a teacher

Two teachers are describing some of the extra-classroom influences in Cameroon:

We were trained in the lesson concept by the British. That meant revision to begin the lesson, new material and then practice to finish the lesson. Practice was always written for reinforcement. – ANF

There has to be some order. My students, even in the Upper Sixth, stand when I enter the class, and clear their desks of all previous lesson material when I enter the class… Children are not as regimented these days. – SK

ACTIVITIES, ACTION

What teachers and learners say and do.
Includes: TALK, MOVEMENT, GESTURE, USE
OF SPACE, POSTURE, FACIAL EXPRESSIONS.
OBSERVABLES   FIXED FEATURES of CLASSROOM, FURNITURE,
WALLS etc.

INDIVIDUAL FACTORS
AFFECTIVE domain—engagement, mood, emotional   **UNOBSERVABLES**
states
COGNITIVE domain—real time thinking
Previous experience and knowledge
Values, attitudes, beliefs

GROUP FACTORS
Social psychological factors

WIDER SOCIAL, CULTURAL and other influences

Figure 1.1   Observables and unobservables in classroom life

1.2   Core elements of classroom management

A number of interconnecting themes have emerged from the preceding analysis of the nature of classrooms which suggest a systemic framework for analysing language classroom management which reflects the experience of teaching-and-learning. Classroom management is concerned with four main strands of classroom life – space, time, participation and engagement.

The classroom context is at its most 'live' in the local action of managing participants' engagement and participation, and their use of resources such as language and content with which to participate and engage. Local action is best understood with reference to the delicate web of factors that influence each participant's contributions to teaching-and-learning. Classroom activity can also realise the national discourse of state education systems. Thus all teachers and learners participate in this wider discourse, which is interwoven with classroom discourse. Classroom life thus emerges from a variety of interacting external influences and internal or local processes (Figure 1.2). Managing classrooms is centrally concerned with reconciling and exploiting these influences with a view to promoting learning. It is a complex and demanding business, as multi-faceted as classrooms themselves: classroom management is complexity management.

Time and space

These are the two elements which most clearly define the basis of formal education, and which, although present in all human learning, are not specified or controlled as they are in formal contexts. Time and space

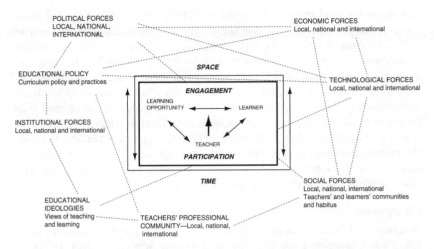

Figure 1.2 The language classroom: Internal processes and relationships, and external forces

NOTE: The classroom is shown at the centre of the complex of forces, time- and space-bound. Some of the interrelationships between the external forces are indicated, and the complete picture would show how they were all interrelated.

constraints are typically defined by larger institutions and authorities, and have a powerful influence on classroom life. The effect of ignoring them or of challenging them is profound. They overlap in teachers' plans for classroom activity and in the ongoing management of lessons. They literally and metaphorically constitute the *boundaries* of formal education, but are at the same time porous. Homework is one of the most obvious transfers of classroom time and space to another location, and an example of the connectedness of classroom contexts. Alternatively, the use of the Internet and other aspects of information technology to create virtual learning environments online challenges these boundaries in a more fundamental way.

Engagement

The affective domain, the territory of engagement, is at the very heart of the classroom management process. Engagement is a precondition of learning (van Lier 1996) and helps define the strength of motivation and individuals' approaches to learning. How we feel during a learning experience, short- or long-term, colours the experience and can block or accelerate learning. How participants engage with each other and the learning activities is thus a central process of the classroom. 'People management' is an overt manifestation of this; for a teacher, managing people in formal learning contexts is central. It also involves order and 'discipline'. Classrooms are also contexts in which various types of power are exercised and also, from time to time, challenged.

This more political form of engagement adds to the complexity of the class-room management task in the same way as emotional factors such as individuals' transitory moods. Self-management is a key issue too, particularly a student's capacity and willingness to take responsibility for learning, and a teacher's husbandry of their emotional resources. Hargreaves (1998) has gone as far as saying that emotional issues are the most important in teaching, and presumably learning too. Other elements of people management may be linked to the age and gender characteristics of a learning group. Engagement is not managed in isolation, however. There is a clear connection between the management of engagement and the management of space and time, as teachers and students make decisions about where to sit or stand, and who with, in what sorts of grouping, during lessons.

Participation

Teachers and learners participate in the lives of classroom learning com-munities. Classrooms are thus social discourse worlds (Mercer 1995), or communities of practice (Wenger 1998); they are also defined by the way in which social and cultural practices contribute to cultural and intellectual development in the widest sense. The social life of a learning group is initiated, maintained and extended by the multitude of interactions that take place between its members during lessons and outside the classroom too – the most obvious are the verbal interactions, subject of many studies. But there are also 'hidden' aspects of the social and psychological interactions among a group of people. They may be the outcome of 'chemistry' between group members, and therefore connected to the affective domain. Decisions made about interaction – with whom and about what – are both consciously and unconsciously mediated. Interactions are the basis of all the different types of information processing that classrooms initiate. They bring the inanimate alive as time and space are utilised, as learners and teachers engage, and lessons are 'done'. This perspective also enables us to examine non-participation or the role of silence in lessons.

Managing language classrooms is a multi-dimensional activity with the personal and pedagogic interwoven. Classrooms are environments where participants through engagement and participation, use and produce resources – social, intellectual and emotional. Material resources such as texts are processed, and personal resources such as resilience are brought into play during activity. In language classrooms, language itself is a resource, and in the foreign language classroom a problematically dual-natured one if it is both the target and the medium of instruction.

The four dimensions of classroom management that I have identified provide a means of understanding the classroom life is experienced. Their origins and their workings are examined further in Part 1.

2
Classrooms as Formal Contexts for Learning

2.1 Defining and analysing learning contexts

In simple terms a learning context occurs when a person encounters a learning opportunity in the course of everyday life. This definition does not assume success in learning, merely that there is an opportunity that may or may not be acted upon. When a person makes a commitment to learn, the opportunity becomes a goal. The analysis of any learning context must first, therefore, account for the relationships between learners and learning opportunities. However, as we have seen in Chapter 1, teachers are major players in classrooms learning contexts, and the full picture will also include teachers' contributions. The relationships between learners, teachers and learning opportunities together constitute the basis of classroom management practices.

Quote 2.1   Lantolf on activity theory

Activity in Leontiev's (1978) theory is not merely doing something, it is doing something that is motivated either by a biological need, such as hunger, or a culturally constructed need, such as the need to be literate in certain cultures. Needs become motives once they become directed at a particular object. Thus hunger does not become a motive until people decide to seek food; similarly, literacy does not become a motive for activity until people decide to learn to read and write. Motives are only realised in specific *actions* that are goal-directed (hence intentional and meaningful) and carried out under particular temporal and spatial conditions (or what are referred to as *operations*) and through appropriate *mediational means*. Thus an activity comprises three levels: the level of motivation, the level of action and the level of means.

(2000: 8, author's emphases)

A generative way of accounting for the relationships in a classroom or any other any learning context is through an application of 'activity theory'

(Quote 2.1). Activity theory enables us to look at fundamental relationships in any learning context, between learners, learning opportunities or goals, and any 'helpers' who may be present in the activity, thus accounting for 'mediated action' between learners and learning opportunities, and learners and helpers, using cultural tools such as language (Quote 2.2). The social, cultural and historical context of the activity in which a learning opportunity occurs, and which defines the role of any helper in learning, must also be included in any substantive analysis. Learners, too, are members of particular socio-cultural groups for whom specific learning goals may have value and meaning, which create an extra dimension of classroom life.

Quote 2.2   Wells and Claxton on the use of 'tools' in learning

As people work, play and solve problems together, so their spontaneous ways of thinking, talking and acting – the ideas that come to mind, the words they choose and the tools they make use of – embody an accumulated set of cultural values and beliefs that have been constructed and refined over previous generations. And, as they 'get things done' together, so younger or less experienced people pick up these habits and attitudes from their more experienced friends, relatives, teachers and colleagues.

...all joint activity requires...tools in order to coordinate participants' actions and to construct and pass on their understanding of the principles involved. Chief among these 'psychological' tools' is...language in all its modes...

(2002: 3–4)

Wright (1990) outlines a framework for analysing the relationship between learning, teaching and learning goals in order to understand better classroom role relationships between teachers and students. The framework is developed further in this section as a way of analysing different learning contexts, both informal ones and classrooms, in order to understand how they are managed. Definitions of the elements and the potential relationships between them appear in Concept 2.1.

Figure 2.1 is a schematic representation of the basic relationships between the elements. This framework reveals two key characteristics of learning contexts. First, how and by whom a learning goal is defined is significant. The relationship between people and learning opportunities is more direct when a person has identified an opportunity and chooses to learn. The person has potentially greater levels of emotional investment in learning in such a case. The relationship is less direct if another person has created or even imposed the learning opportunity on the learner. This is a form of intervention in the relationship between learners and learning goals, and is symbolised by the heavy arrow in the diagram. Thus the degree of

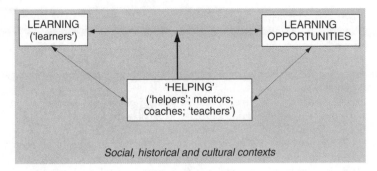

Figure 2.1   Relationships in learning contexts (after Wright 1990)

directness/indirectness in any classroom learner's relationship with a learning opportunity can affect their commitment to learning. The relationship suggests important connections between motivation and learning and the emotional domain, both of which have a strong influence on how we manage engagement in learning contexts.

Concept 2.1   Elements and relationships in contexts of learning

Elements
1. LEARNING OPPORTUNITY – What a person may consciously or unconsciously encounter. It may be natural or imposed or prescribed. It can consist of 'facts' or a form of abstract knowledge, skills (e.g. kinaesthetic, interpersonal, mental, etc.) or combinations of these. Learning opportunities always occur in social and cultural contexts. Even if people are alone while learning, they always represent particular socio-cultural groups, or are seeking membership of others.

2. LEARNING – What learners do – behaviourally, and cognitively – as they internalise new knowledge and skills. It is also influenced by learners' transitory emotional states. Learning is also collective, social (learning in the company of others), cultural (learning in and about culture) and organisational (as part of participation in organisational/institutional life).

3. HELPING – What another person can do to assist another engaged in learning. Help may be conscious and offered, or incidental, occurring through everyday social interaction; it may be solicited or unsolicited. It may also be prescribed or imposed.

Relationships
1. **Between learners and learning opportunities.** From the individual learner's point of view this is the most central relationship among the three elements. It varies in directness and distance relative to the learner.

Concept 2.1   (Continued)

- Intentionality – how deliberately a learning opportunity is sought, or whether it is random, accidental or incidental. The greater the level of the learner's intention to learn, the more an opportunity becomes a goal. This has implications for managing a learning encounter.
- Choice and Agency – whether or not the learning opportunity has been imposed on the person by society or other agencies external to the learner.
- Source – the extent to which a learning opportunity emerges in the course of experience, or whether it is designed and prescribed for the learner by others either inside or outside the immediate context of learning. It is not necessarily the case that designs for learning are imposed on learners if they have chosen to make a learning opportunity for themselves.

2. **Between learners and helpers.** There are many variations of the helper/learner relationship depending on factors such as:

- Whether the helper enters the relationship with the intention of deliberately initiating learning activity
- The social relationship between learner and helper (e.g. relative intimacy, status, power balance between helpers and learners, respective levels of responsibility for the occurrence of learning). The nature of the social relationship is likely to be influenced by many other factors, such as the specific context – a teacher can become a learner at home when she is helped to use a piece of computer software by another family member. In formal education the learner/helper relationship is institutionalised to varying degrees.
- The extent to which help is solicited by the learner or offered, unsolicited, is significant, depending on whether the context is designed or naturally-occurring.
- The helper's views on how people learn. These views will have an influence on how they choose to help, for example, by direct instruction or by watching and advising.

3. **Between 'helpers' and learning opportunities.** This relationship depends on:

- Whether or not the helper has imposed the learning opportunity on a person. For example, if the 'helper' has imposed a learning task, the relationship is more direct for the helper and less for the learner who has decided to seize a particular opportunity.
- Whether helpers have knowledge, expertise or special skills in the learning area, to the extent that they personify the model outcome of learning in some way.
- Helpers' views on the nature of the learning opportunity and whether or not learners are capable of meeting the challenge of learning.
- As a consequence, learners can be positioned by helpers in terms of the perceived level of difficulty of the learning task – they can be seen as either 'helpless' or capable.

An examination of an example classroom will illustrate the framework in action (Field Note 2.1).

Field Note 2.1   Classroom learning contexts

Secondary English Lesson – Malaysia
Students from 5UK1 are working in groups of five. There are eight groups, and they have chosen their groups by choosing a resort/tourist spot in the locality that they'd like to discuss and write a short piece on for a class brochure on local tourist spots. From the previous lesson they have prepared draft 1 and are now improving their drafts to draft 2. The teacher (Cik Z) has given them instructions (written on the board) to list places of interest someone might want to visit in their chosen resort/tourist spot and other activities that could be carried out there while on holiday. Students can be heard discussing the tourist spots in Malay (national language) and translating this information and opinion into English. They have English-English dictionaries and occasionally look up words. They also have bilingual dictionaries to help. Busy, noisy atmosphere. Everyone working.

Occasionally, they raise their hands or get the teacher's attention for some help. The teacher moves around from one group to another, and occasionally calls a group to the front where she works with them, either at the board or at the teacher's table. At the end of the lesson – bell (50 minutes), she asks if any group has finished their drafts. Two have some work to do and she asks them to have this done for tomorrow's lesson. She asks the group to read a passage in the textbook ready for later in the week.

There is a helper – a teacher – who has a leading role in mediating the activities and who further represents a form of institutionalised help provided by the school. Learning opportunities have been designed for classroom use, rather than chosen by the learners. This inevitably influences the nature of the social and psychological relationships between teachers and learners. The example classroom is orderly and businesslike. There is thus likely to be a certain degree of emotional distance between teachers and learners 'built in' to the classroom relationship. The teacher also defines various aspects of the learning encounter, providing a specific set of learning experiences and learning content. The teacher organises space and time for the students and models target language behaviour in various ways. Finally, there appears to be little opportunity for the students directly to influence the course of events, apart from pacing themselves in the tasks.

Formal and informal learning contexts

There are several ways in which learning contexts can be differentiated:

- By examining whether or not a learner seeks particular learning opportunities.
- By assessing the degree of choice exercised by the learner over what specifically is learned and how.
- By examining the ways in which any helpers provide assistance to learners.

Learning contexts display these and other features in different ways. This helps determine the relative level of formality of a classroom. For example, in many school classrooms, learners are not able to choose learning content (although they can and do choose whether or not to engage with what teachers present). In classrooms learning is the primary focus of activity, unlike informal contexts, in which the real activity itself (or 'doing') is central (Wenger 1998: 8). Wenger further points out that people are only positioned as *learners* by formal or 'designed' learning contexts, because there is specific learning to be accomplished, mandated by the context (Quote 2.3). In less formal contexts, people are people first and learners second. Wenger (1998: 8) also draws a useful comparison between the conscious and natural learning people do when they learn a new job, where learning is the outcome of engagement with the challenges of the new task, and the specific job-related training opportunity. In the latter, there is a shift from the self and cooperative management of the learning that 'on-the-job' learning entails to a greater degree of direct control of all aspects of the learning encounter by the helper (trainer).

Quote 2.3   Wenger on people becoming learners

There are . . . times when society explicitly places us in situations where the issue of learning becomes problematic and requires our focus: we attend classes, memorise, take exams, and receive a diploma.

Although learning can be assumed to take place, modern societies have come to see it as a topic of concern – in all sorts of ways and for a whole host of reasons. We develop national curricula, ambitious corporate training programmes, complex schooling systems. We wish to cause learning, to take charge of it, direct it, accelerate it, demand it, or even simply stop getting in the way of it. In any case we want to do something about it.

(1998: 7–8)

Purposes of formal learning

In order to understand classroom learning contexts, it is essential that we examine the educational designs which they realise. Learning goals and teachers are typically prescribed in classrooms. Society's specification of essential learning in formal education changes over time in accordance with the values that society, and particularly those people with the power and authority to influence decisions, accords particular types of knowledge and skill, and the ways in which and from whom these are acquired. All societies have a learning agenda which might be summarised as 'learning the salient aspects of the culture to perpetuate the society and possibly to advance it.' How this is accomplished varies considerably.

The biologist Richard Dawkins (1976) has likened the process of cultural reproduction to the replication of genes in the biological world (Concept 2.2).

Dawkins also alludes to the social nature of meme replication – a process of 'imitation'. This may be a simplification of human learning as a social process, but captures both the informal process and the more formal 'passing on' process. It is also significant that Dawkins portrays culture as dynamic and changing – popular tunes come and go, in the same way as new ideas or fashions.

Concept 2.2 Memes and cultural replication

Richard Dawkins, the evolutionary biologist, has postulated 'the law that all life evolves by the differential survival of replicating entities' (1976: 206). He identifies the DNA molecule as the prevailing replicating entity on Earth. He also identifies what he sees as a new type of cultural replicator as having recently (in evolutionary terms) evolved on Earth. He describes the new replicator – the **meme** – in the following way:

It is still in its infancy, still drifting clumsily about in its primeval soup...the new soup is the soup of human culture....the new replicator [is] a unit of cultural transmission, or a unit of *imitation*....Examples of memes are tunes, ideas, catch-phrases, clothes fashions, ways of making pots or building arches. Just as genes propagate themselves in the gene pool by leaping from body to body via sperms or eggs, so memes propagate themselves in the meme pool by leaping from brain to brain via a process which, in the broad sense, can be called imitation. If a scientist hears, or reads about, a good idea, he passes it on to his colleagues and students. He mentions it in his articles and lectures. If the idea catches on, it can be said to propagate itself, spreading from brain to brain.
(1976: 206)

Quote 2.4 Contrasting views of education (after Serpell)

The Bases of Western Education
Education in Western culture, whatever its socioeconomic functions, has from its earliest philosophical origins expressed a preoccupation with promoting cognitive growth, the expansion of knowledge and understanding. Cognition, in post-Renaissance Western thought, has been persistently conceived as private, transcendental, absolute and independent of will. (1993: 79)

The Chewa Perspective on Child Development and Intelligence
Serpell's (1993) study grounds the ways the Chewa conceptualise children's intellectual development in the cultural practices of everyday relations between adults and children, outside formal schooling.

Main Dimensions of Intelligence and its Development

1. 'Nzelu' – covering wisdom, cleverness and responsibility. Nzelu (or 'cognitive capacity') combines cognitive alacrity with social responsibility and cooperativeness.
2. Cognitive alacrity without social responsibility is viewed as a negative social force.

Quote 2.4   (Continued)

3. Shared responsibility among adult members of the community for socialising children.
4. Set of assumptions about how children's minds work stimulated or enabled by various types of adult intervention (e.g. demonstration leading to expertise; story-telling contributing to wisdom; sending children on errands leading to responsibility) and likely, desirable outcomes over various periods of time. Educational function built into everyday adult-child interactions.
5. A range of elaborate and unsupervised play activities in which social and cognitive skills are practised (e.g. model-making, board games).
   (1993: 60 and 73–4)

In a study of the responses of a traditional society – the Chewa of Eastern Zambia – to British education in Central Africa, Serpell (1993) identifies the driving forces of individualism in Western views of education (Quote 2.4) in contrast to the equally sophisticated and regulated collectivist and socially oriented traditional education Chewa society provides its children. In Chewa society, any adult is potentially a helper in the child's learning, but the process is not formalised in the sense of being programmed or located in a particular place. Culture is learned through participation, with guidance. The analysis demonstrates how the Western and the Chewa views of the purposes of education represent opposite poles of the formal–informal continuum of educational practice. This distinction, as we shall see, is useful in analysing classroom and other learning contexts, and how they are managed.

Views of formal education in the West

In order to see how the purposes of formal education influence its content and process, and therefore classroom management practices, we shall examine the ebb and flow of 'big ideas' in the framing of the purposes and scope of formal schooling in the West. These views are significant not only in the West, but also globally, as Western models of education have spread around the world. These views are likely to be as contested internationally as they are in the West (Quote 2.5).

Educational debate in the Anglo-Saxon world (Britain, North America, Australasia) is pervaded by an underlying conflict between the notions of education as cultural reproduction and education as acquiring the means to face the future (Wells 1993). In other words, education is either about learning the 'culture' where you happen to live, or it is about the acquisition of specific skills to enhance individual advancement often in the context of problem solving, for example, the economy. Olson (1996) argues that Western education, as well as being a medium of cultural reproduction, is also 'scientific', either through content or ways of thinking. Radical theorists like Giroux (1981), in contrast, argue that schooling is either hegemonic – imposing an agenda of cultural reproduction on learners – or counter-hegemonic – liberating learners and transforming their worlds for the better. Social critics like Bourdieu and Passeron (1990) further argue that many learners are distanced from the content of formal education because of the way a particular dominant social class defines it, or their *habitus*. In this way they see the classroom as a context in which social identity is reproduced and inequalities maintained.

However, political power shifts from group to group over time, and the economic goals of societies change. Consequently, views regarding the purpose and nature of formal education as the primary avenue for culture learning have been contested for as long as there have been schools. For example, in a period in which authority was consistently challenged, Illich (1971) famously advocated the abolition of schools, arguing that 'school is obligatory and becomes schooling for schooling's sake: an enforced stay in the company of teachers' (1971: 17). Holt (1964) too, in the same era, had similar ideas about schooling: 'Schools should be a place where children learn what they most need to know instead of what we think they ought to know' (1964: 289). Holt's ideas were to a considerable extent grounded in his pioneering work in observing children rather than teachers. Olson (1996), however, noting the trend towards 'child-centredness' in the West, criticises the extremes of the child-centred movement in education, ridiculing the notion 'that children are already competent theory formulators and inference makers and equipped by nature with the very concepts educators have traditionally thought it their duty to impart' (1996: 4). He goes on to identify problems associated with the trend towards 'critical thinking' in the West which operates in a cooperative, collaborative, narrative mode, rather than the traditional acquisition of formal paradigmatic knowledge. He wonders if the contradictory goals of truth and consensus can be reconciled, let alone achieved (1996: 9). Giroux (1981) has similar criticisms of radical educational goals.

Quote 2.5 The goals of formal education – a collection of views from the Anglo-Saxon world

[T]he responsibility of educational institutions for cultural reproduction and for ensuring that students appropriate the artefacts and practices that embody the solutions to problems encountered in the past. Indictments (of this position) tend to occur in texts which are more concerned with the responsibility of educational institutions for cultural renewal and for the formation and empowerment of its individual members to deal with future problems.
(Wells 1993: 3)

The theory and practice of education 'tends to oscillate between social concerns with mastery of a fixed curriculum and humane concerns with the mental lives of children.
(Olson 1996: 4)

Quote 2.5   (Continued)

The cognitive and cultural significance of a scientific mode of thought warrants much of the educational effort in both developed and developing countries. Its significance is seen both in the traditional focus on teaching academic disciplines and in more recent concerns with fostering critical thinking.
(Olson 1996: 3–4)

'The school is an entry into the life of the mind. One seeks to equip the child with deeper, more gripping, and subtler ways of knowing the world and himself.
(Bruner 1979: 118)

The goal of education is disciplined understanding; that is the process as well.
(Bruner 1979: 122)

Education, in its deepest sense and at whatever age it takes place, concerns the opening of identities – exploring new ways of being that lie beyond our current state.
(Wenger 1998: 263)

Culture is constantly in process of being recreated as it is interpreted and renegotiated by its members . . . a culture is a much a forum for negotiating and renegotiating meaning and for explicating action as it is a set of rules for action. . . . every culture maintains specialised institutions or occasions for this forum-like feature. Storytelling, theatre, science, even jurisprudence are all techniques for intensifying this function – ways of exploring possible worlds out of the context of immediate need. Education is one of the principle forms for exploring this function – though it is often timid in doing so.
(Bruner 1986: 123)

In a stable society, yesterday's education, if it were well designed originally, will do for the citizens of tomorrow. But if a culture is undergoing radical change, the demands of the future cannot be clearly predicted, and a different kind of pre-paration is required. . . . the key responsibility of the educator is not to give young people tools that may be out of date before they have been fully mastered, but to help them become confident and competent designers and makers of their own tools as they go along.
(Claxton 2002: 23)

A theory that can provide for educational change must recognise the extent to which it is bound by real constraints, both within and outside school settings. 'Radical' educational prescriptions that call for teachers and students to reassert their individuality, to criticise existing definitions of knowledge, to defy determinism with freedom, actively to construct their own lived reality and true humanity tend to go up in metaphysical smoke if they do not speak concretely to the existential reality of schooling.
(Giroux 1981: 104–5)

Bruner (1979) acknowledges the potential of education to open up life beyond the learner's present state, as does Wenger (1998), although for Wenger the explicit focus on the learner's identity is more crucial than the life of the mind, so prized by Bruner. Bruner (Quote 2.6) has lately modified his position and argued that education has a central function in exploring alternative forms of culture.

Quote 2.6   Bruner on the purposes of education

The language of education is the language of culture creating, not of knowledge consuming or knowledge acquisition alone.
   Culture is constantly in the process of being recreated as it is interpreted and negotiated.
. . . Every culture maintains specialised institutions or occasions for intensifying this function – ways of exploring possible worlds out of the context of immediate need. Education is (or should be) one of the principal forms for performing this function – though it is often timid in doing so.
(1986: 123)

A contemporary educational idea in the West (Claxton 2002, for example) is that education in the twenty-first century should aim to equip individuals with the skills for lifelong learning, and that educational practices need to change in order to help people cope with change and uncertainty, particularly because the future has never been more uncertain. Opponents of global capitalism (e.g. Gray 1998) would argue that these uncertain conditions have been created by particular economic practices, and that a return to a more protected and regulated world might serve to reduce uncertainty and presumably the need for market-driven lifelong learning. Regardless of the political arguments, lifelong learning might in itself be an intrinsically worthwhile goal for other reasons, including the fuller realisation of individual and social potential beyond the acquisition of the skills for earning a living. Advocates of education which is grounded in a focus on *learning* rather than teaching *per se* (Quote 2.7) form a strong alliance with lifelong learning advocates, and are contributing to the current redefinition of the curriculum and schooling in the West.

Quote 2.7   Changing schools and education

One of the most significant challenges facing those responsible for the future direction of the schooling system in this country [UK] is the conceptual relationship between learning and teaching. Learning has been seen as the product of teaching – a passive process of receiving and assimilating. We need to develop a new understanding of this relationship

---

Quote 2.7   (Continued)

in which learning is the active and dynamic force at work, and teaching is the means by which the appropriate support and guidance for that process can be provided.
(Whitaker 1998: 172)

Schools must change from places predominantly concerned with teaching, to institutions of learning.
(Whitaker 1998: 174)

Our institutions, to the extent that they address issues of learning explicitly, are largely based on the assumption that learning is an individual process, that it has a beginning and an end, that it is best separated from the rest of our activities, and that it is the result of teaching. Hence we arrange classrooms where students – free from the distractions of participation in the outside world – can pay attention to a teacher or focus on exercises.... As a result, much of our institutionalized teaching and training is perceived by would-be learners as irrelevant, and most of us come out of this treatment feeling that learning is boring and arduous, and that we are not really cut out for it.
(Wenger 1998: 3)

Consequences for foreign language teaching

Foreign language teaching currently faces unique challenges which impinge on classroom management. Global trends such as large-scale population movements and the increasing use of the Internet for communications and information management, among others, are increasingly seen as the background for a reshaping of the curriculum goals and teaching/learning processes of foreign language education (Quote 2.8). The dominant discourse of English language education in the early part of the twenty-first century is concerned, as a consequence, as much with responding to these 'external

---

Quote 2.8   Candlin on Including and Acknowledging External Influences on Foreign Language Education

. . . the curriculum, in its content and its processes, needs to achieve a balance between factors which are external to the learner and his life outside the school, and those factors internal to learners that govern, among others, their commitment and motivation.'
. . . the curriculum needs to be contextualised and interpreted in relation to the socio-political conditions, values and practices outside the school, characterised through particular ratified discursive practices of society at large, but it also has to be contextualised through the lived experiences of the participants within the school, and equally characterised by the frequently unratified discursive practices of the learners.
(2001: xiv)

forces' as it is about 'methodology' or teaching procedures (Concept 2.3). Issues related to the complexities of classroom learning and the wider contexts of this endeavour now appear to have as much, if not more, influence as more traditional concerns such as teaching methodology, which themselves have had to be reframed as a result of external forces. Language education has also had to respond to new ideas which advocate 'more learner-centredness' in the same way as other curriculum areas.

Concept 2.3   Some key contemporary issues in English language teaching

Views of language teaching are changing in the early part of the twenty-first century. Many of the changes result from a focus on learning and the contexts of learning. All have consequences for local classroom management practices, either directly or indirectly.

- Interculturality and conflict internationally and locally in classrooms. Increasing importance of English as 'cultural goods' (Canagarajah 1993).
- Increased concern with social values of English as an international language.
- Increased concern with 'appropriacy' of methodology (Holliday 1994).
- Focus on quality of life in classrooms and classroom health (Allwright 2002).
- Increased authenticity of language learning experience (van Lier 1996a).
- Increasing informality and use of resources from outside the classroom (Kohonen 2001).
- Increasing learners' awareness: of language, and of learning (van Lier 1996; Bolitho et al. 2003).
- Increased autonomy of learners (Benson 2001).
- Changed views of motivation (Dornyei 2001).
- Increased negotiation with learners and learner involvement in classroom decision-making (Breen and Littlejohn (2000).
- Decline of 'methods' and 'methodology' – renewed interest in pedagogy (Kumara-vadivelu 2001).

Defining curriculum in formal learning contexts

In practice, during the design and delivery of schooling, the broad learning goals of formal education are translated into curricular specifications. How a curriculum defines learning, the content of learning and the roles of teachers strongly influence the design for formal classroom learning. Different curricular models invariably realise different 'philosophies' and ideologies of formal learning, and competition between models is the norm rather than the exception. Fashions in curriculum tend to follow broad political, economic and social trends, reflecting the values of dominant groups in society (Giroux 1981; Bourdieu 1991). They also reflect intellectual fashions and trends. Consequently, the various major positions on curriculum design tend to adhere to one or more of the following broad conceptions of formal schooling (Concept 2.4):

- Education is about distributing and/or reproducing knowledge or acquiring skills to develop knowledge.
- Education is either about the culture or the individual.
- Formal learning is about preserving the socio-political status quo, or changing it.
- Social and cultural value systems are either open or closed to change and development.
- The quality of individual experience in formal learning is either paramount or irrelevant.

Concept 2.4   Educational value systems and conceptions of the curriculum

1. Reproductionist (distributing rather than manufacturing knowledge – Stenhouse 1975: 10)
'Classical Humanist' (Clark 1987 after Skilbeck 1982); Academic Rationalism (Eisner and Vallance 1974)
Focus on acquiring the tools to participate in the dominant cultural tradition of a society. Knowledge-oriented, with high importance of intellectual values and preserving cultural values.
See also Eisner and Vallance (1974) Curriculum as Development of Cognitive Processes (sharpening generally applicable intellectual processes) and Curriculum as Technology (focusing on technologies of instruction 'efficiently packaging and presenting material to students')

2. Reconstructionist (socially reforming – Illich 1971)
Social reconstructionist and socially relevant (Eisner and Vallance 1974)
Socially-oriented, promoting agreed social goals to the betterment of social conditions.

3. Progressive (Clark 1987) (developing individuals and valuing diversity)
Self-actualising (Eisner and Vallance 1974) 'Research-based' (Stenhouse 1975)
'School-based' (Skilbeck 1984)
Providing personally satisfying consummatory experience for individuals. The curriculum fully enters all aspects of a child's life.

Eisner and Vallance (1974) identify three 'fallacies' of curriculum theory, and each has been prominent at different periods in the history of formal education in different countries:

1. Formalism – the fallacy that curriculum can be specified with little reference to 'content', thus avoiding the requirement to answer the question 'what's significant and important enough to be taught?'

2. Content – the erroneous position that focuses only on the content of formal learning and fails to address key issues in how learning processes work.
3. Universalism – content (and indeed process) is taught regardless of contexts and students in the belief that there is a 'best' curriculum. The universalist fallacy militates against change in educational practices.

Eisner and Vallance's insights help us to make sense of the ebbs and flows of educational fashion and to see how these influence prescriptions for classroom teaching-and-learning and specifications for the content and/or process of formal education.

Classroom teachers deal with the often difficult task of interpreting and mediating different interpretations of curriculum goals and the relationships between learners, helpers and learning opportunities they imply or state. This struggle is reflected in approaches to the fundamental activity of classroom management, as changing definitions of the nature of the content of learning, and thus redefinitions of teachers' knowledge and expertise and learners' contributions to learning, reposition teachers relative to learners. A shift in emphasis from learning outcomes to learning process has a similar repositioning effect on teachers, and learners, too. Historically, these changes result in a process of continuous reconstruction of roles and identities in the classroom.

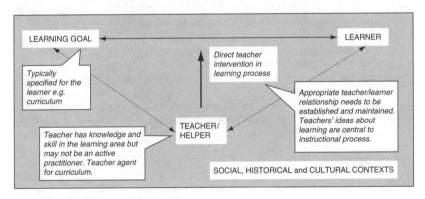

Figure 2.2   Relationships in formal classroom instruction

The relationships in formal contexts are schematised in Figure 2.2. The heavy arrow indicates *designed* and deliberate teacher intervention in contrast to less formal learning contexts. Learning goals are typically specified *for* the learner. The teacher possesses knowledge and skill in the learning area, but may not be an active practitioner – teaching itself is a 'specialised' occupation. Teachers have to establish and maintain social relationships with their students, while at the same time putting into practice a view of learning itself, often unaware of the assumptions they are making or the model they are following.

Greater informality: a contemporary educational issue

The distinction between formal and informal/everyday learning, or in-and-out of school learning, has strong implications for classroom management practices. Advocates of 'learning from experience' and 'learning by doing' (Concept 2.5) – Askew and Carnell (1998), Kohonen (2001), Sutherland et al. (2003), for example – emphasise the inherent value of 'everyday' learning and argue that classroom learning can be made more effective by adopting some of the practices of informal learning. Such a development has major implications for formal classroom learning contexts, indicating changed roles for teachers and learners, as well as potentially greater learner choice in learning processes. Because it focuses on some of the perceived shortcomings of formal classroom learning, the discussion also enables us to identify more features of classrooms as formal learning contexts, and thus to identify implications for classroom management.

Concept 2.5   Learning from experience

Theories of learning from *situated experience* emphasise the interactions between people and their environment, and how learning emerges from these interactions through improvisation, and above all action. These theories are both individual and also interpersonal and show how action in day-to-day encounters leads to significant learning. In this way, significant learning is grounded in experience. There is a long tradition of advocacy of this position (for example, Rousseau and Dewey).

Experiential learning involves both observing the phenomenon and doing something meaningful with it through active participation.
(Kohonen 2001: 23)

Learning from experience also involves collaboration and cooperation with significant others. Shared activities and conversations are the means through which much of learning from life occurs. 'Learning as participation', embedded in shared culture and history, both reproduces and transforms social life.
(Wenger 1998: 13)

The Value of 'Everyday' Learning from Experience
Proponents of an 'experiential' view of learning emphasise the effectiveness of 'real life' or informal learning:

'Everyday' learning has many of the features which promote effective learning. It focuses on the experiences of learners and has the potential for bringing about individual change in order to bring about social change.
(Askew and Carnell 1998: 99)

Learning is a continuous process that is grounded in experience. Thus knowledge and skill gained in one situation become instruments of understanding and dealing with situations that follow.

Learning is a holistic process of relating to the world.

Learning is active and self-directed and continues throughout life.
(Kohonen 2001: 30)

Across the world, the aims, organisation, institutions and processes of schooling reflect many differences – but they also face many of the same challenges. Amongst the most significant is how to manage the interface of the formal education that takes place in schools and the informal learning that occurs as part of diverse other activities of life . . . what if, instead of conceptualising schooling as some form of transmission, we tried to draw more fully on the cultural resources that are associated with informal learning? After all, such processes of learning powered human development . . . before the introduction of formal education. What if we could draw more fully on the experiences of learning that occur daily in homes, playgrounds, streets and workplaces – and on the expertise of parents, siblings, peers, mentors and others? In principle, it might be possible to harness the energy and high motivation that is often apparent in such settings, and off levels of support for new learning that would be impossible within schools.
(Sutherland, Claxton and Pollard 2002: 175)

The argument for more informal or 'experiential' learning is premised on the idea that most learning in an individual's life occurs in the normal process of living, away from formal educational settings such as schools and universities. As Wenger (1998: 8) notes, learning 'is not something we do when we do nothing else or stop doing something else'. Many learning experiences are natural or inevitable because people are cultural beings and learning culture by living in it is a defining quality of being human (Quote 2.9) – for example, learning to speak one's mother tongue. Other learning consists of 'personal discoveries', emerging from life experiences and encounters with cultural objects. These encounters are a form of 'cultural apprenticeship, as the child learns to use various cultural 'tools' such as language to appropriate cultural objects and means of mediating in learning contexts (Mercer 2000).

Quote 2.9   Mercer on the cultural experience of learning

. . . because humans are essentially cultural beings, even children's initial encounters with objects may be cultural experiences, and so their initial understandings may be culturally defined. In this sense, (their) appropriation is concerned with what meanings children may take from encounters in cultural contexts.
(1994: 104)

Many childhood learning events, such as learning appropriate mealtime behaviour, are initiated by older family members. Learning in life is also triggered by moments of crisis or change, as we adapt to difficult or new circumstances. All of these are often referred to as 'informal' or 'natural' learning experiences, characterised by a close learner–helper relationship, a strong commitment to goals, with learning opportunities appearing in the context of cultural life, and integrated into other aspects of culture learning.

People are naturally adept at learning informally, and do not seem to suffer from the problems of motivation or social and cognitive distancing, or external imposition that characterise formal education. Many educationalists believe that these can be replicated in formal settings, or that formal settings can even be abolished, and they have seized on the distinction between formal and informal learning, or 'in and out of school learning' as a set of principles for educational design (Resnick 1987, in Watkins et al. 1996) (Concept 2.6). Learning 'out of school' is portrayed as occurring in 'real contexts', in which the immediate transfer of new learning into purposeful action assures successful transfer of knowledge and skills (e.g. learning about car maintenance in a garage), a problem that has continually hampered the success of formal education (Bransford et al. 2000: 73–7). Informal learning is also associated with the first-hand experience and knowledge of a helper, a skilled and successful exemplar or model of performance or skill. Apprenticeship (Lave and Wenger 1991), or a 'master–pupil' relationship, is often cited as an efficient way of enabling young people to learn essential skills in their communities. These encounters are also characterised by the immediate economic or social importance of the learning opportunity, as in Chewa society referred to above. Learners may not have a choice about whether or not they learn, however – many trades are passed down through families, or the activity may be so important that as many as possible are made to learn it (e.g. agricultural practices in agrarian communities). Figure 2.3 summarises the elemental relationships in informal learning.

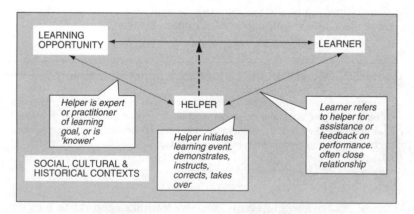

Figure 2.3   Informal learning encounters initiated by a 'helper'

Informal learning involving a skilled helper manifests some of the features of an apprenticeship situation. Any helper is typically a practitioner or expert. The helper generally initiates learning events, demonstrating and instructing, even taking over the task if necessary. The learner refers to the helper for assistance and feedback. The learner/helper relationship is often close, even one of dependency, with consequences for the discourses of formal education, to be examined in Section 3.

Concept 2.6   Learning in and out of school

Features	Learning in School	Learning out of School
Transfer of learning	Decontextualised	Has 'real' context
Source of learning	Second-hand	Is first-hand
Learner motivation	Needs motivating	Does not need motivating
Relative difficulty	Can be 'difficult'	Tends to come 'naturally' and enjoyably
Social Conditions	Tends to be individualistic	Is cooperative/shared
Assessment	Assessed by others	Self-assessed
Formality	Formal structure (time and space)	Few structures (not usually time-bound)

(after Resnick 1987, in Watkins et al. 1996)

Quote 2.10   Wenger on the separation of teachers from practice

If the pedagogical and institutional functions of educators completely displace their ability to manifest their identities as participants in their communities of practice, they lose their most powerful teaching asset. For instance, in many schools, the separation from mature practice is exacerbated by the roles of teachers as managers of large classrooms. In such a role, teachers do not have much opportunity to act as themselves – as adults, and thus as doorways into the adult world. Rather, they constantly have to act as teachers – that is, as representatives of the institution and upholders of curricular demands, with an identity defined by an institutional role.
(1998: 276)

In contrast to informal learning of trades or traditional skills in rural communities, formal school learning is 'second hand' (Quote 2.10). Learner motivation is a problem in many formal learning contexts like schools because learners are there under duress, and are not necessarily learning what they want to learn. In informal contexts, people are learning what they want to, but would probably need motivating from time to time even if they have selected the learning goal, or are doing it as part of their life in a community, as the desire to engage in learning inevitably waxes and wanes. Learning in school is also 'difficult' because the subject matter is often quite distant from learners' experience, whereas learning is seen as 'natural' and 'enjoyable' in informal contexts, as people engage with immediately relevant knowledge and skills.

Concept 2.7   Informal learning contexts – key features

Economic Imperatives

[The] expectations [of formal learning] contrast with those in household economic activity, where the emphasis is on error-free performance since the tasks and chores involved contribute to the smooth running of the household economic system. If members of a household raise livestock to supply their own food, caring for this livestock is an activity in which flawless task performance is valued over learning for learning's sake. This does not mean that learning does not occur or is discouraged; it simply means that a learner's performance is monitored closely and that independent functioning is not encouraged until it is likely to be error-free.
(Wertsch, Minick and Arus 1984: 155)

The activity of learning is inextricably linked to productive or economic activity.
(Wertsch, Minick and Arus 1984: 169)

Cultural Psychology – Apprenticeship and Other Studies
Cultural psychologists' work has examined how informal learning happens in field situations cross-culturally and also experimentally.

Examples:

1. **Greenfield** (1984) studied how practices of weaving are learnt in Chiapas, Mexico. Close relationships between helpers and learners. Helpers take over the task when they see learners making errors. Direct demonstration and modelling is combined with direction:
. . . relatively errorless learning' results 'because, in principle, just the right type and amount of help are provided at each point for the pupil to succeed.
(1984: 136)

2. **Lave** (1988) studied how tailoring is learnt in Liberia. Learners begin practising with scraps of cloth under close supervision of tailors. Focuses on the economic pressures not to waste material (therefore cutting out not attempted while learning). Lave notes how the activity itself structures an informal 'curriculum' for the apprentices.

3. **Wertsch, Minick and Arus** (1984) experimented with two groups: six mothers and their children of the same age and six teachers with children of similar age in rural and urban Brazil. All pairs were given the same task to perform in different locations. Mothers 'tended to perform the task behaviours and use direct forms of regulation more frequently than the teachers did' (1984: 163). Mothers carried out the difficult strategic steps and delegated only those aspects of the task which could be completed relatively efficiently and effectively. More of the children from these pairs could perform the task without errors than the 'taught' group, in which children were allowed a lot more freedom to experiment.

> These expectations (in formal learning) contrast with those in household economic activity, where the emphasis is on error-free performance since the tasks and chores involved contribute to the smooth running of the household economic system. If members of a household raise livestock to supply their own food, caring for this livestock is an activity in which flawless task performance is valued over learning for learning's sake. This does not mean that learning does not occur or is discouraged; it simply means that a learner's performance is monitored closely and that independent functioning is not encouraged until it is likely to be error-free.
>
> (Wertsch, Minick and Arus 1984: 155)

Informal learning, according to cross-cultural studies (Concept 2.7), is more often than not successful – especially if survival is at stake, as in learning how to earn a living. On the other hand, in formal contexts, the combination of the emotional or intellectual distance of learners from the learning opportunity, the lack of choice of learning opportunity, the lack of concrete opportunities to use new knowledge and skills, and a potentially problematical relationship in which teachers often have to coerce unmotivated learners to engage with learning goals, all amplify the difficulty of in-school learning. Furthermore, formal classroom learning is usually accomplished in large gatherings of people, but has a tendency to be individualistic because of the ways in which success in learning is judged; learners tend to be evaluated on an individual basis and ranked according to various criteria. Out-of-school learning is, by contrast, collective, cooperative and shared, the outcome of mutually beneficial social interaction, and also self-assessed. It often, however, includes long periods of solitary practice, a point overlooked by many of the studies. Learning in school is formally structured in time, whereas it is not usually so strictly time-bound out of school. Finally, in formal educational contexts, learning is located in a classroom, a space designed only for the business of teaching-and-learning. Out-of-school learning typically takes place in real contexts of activity – the basic skills of agriculture are perhaps most appropriately learnt on a farm, for example. These relationships do not preclude the learner interacting naturally with the imposed learning goals, or taking advantage of other incidental learning opportunities in classrooms, but the teacher usually aims to manage the conditions of the encounter (Chapter 1 and Field Note 2.1).

Although the 'informalist' analysis has revealed a number of negative features of the formal classroom context, it also has limitations. It does not provide a satisfactory account of how particular specialised types of knowledge and skills such as mathematics, science and literacy skills could be learnt informally. Because learning is 'enclosed' inside a building called a school in a classroom does not automatically mean that it is 'unnatural', desocialised and out of learners' control, or any less important and effective than everyday learning. It is *different*. There are several other ways in which the in/out dichotomy oversimplifies the formal learning context. For example:

- Motivation is seen as primarily context-dependent, but even out-of-school learning is subject to fluctuations in mood and energy levels over time (Dornyei 2000: 82ff). People are often asked to learn material which they find difficult, distasteful or demeaning in their work, as well.
- Learning can be 'difficult' in any setting: it can take time to attain mastery wherever and whatever one is learning.
- A child's encounter with a laboratory in school is as 'first hand' an experience of the world of science as a child's experimentation with matches in a forest is of fire. Not all school learning is decontextualised and much is learnt informally simply by observation and through participation.
- Classrooms are social contexts within the larger social context of the school. Schools themselves are social worlds – every day in schools there are countless social interactions, all shared, some cooperative, others conflictive These encounters are also reflective of wider social processes. Canagarajah's (1995) study of code-switching between Tamil and English in Sri Lankan classrooms provides excellent evidence for the porosity of classroom walls and the influence of the wider social world on the immediate classroom world (Quote 2.11).

Quote 2.11   Canagarajah on code-switching in Sri Lanka

. . . while English is used for interactions strictly demanded by the textbook and lesson, for all other interactions, Tamil is used; that is, Tamil is used for interactions that are considered, personal, personalised, unofficial or culturalised.

. . . English use in the in the ESL class is framed as strictly pedagogical, formal and 'official'. For all other extra-pedagogical purposes, Tamil, or a Tamil mixed with English . . . is preferred. This highly routinised or formulaic or formal use of English is influenced by the socio-political conditions in the Jaffna speech community.
(1995: 190, 191)

- When we learn something informally we tend to want some sort of feedback from others as well as engaging in self-assessment. To seek feedback on performance is a 'given' of learning.

Although formal learning contexts like classrooms are designed for very specific purposes, various types of learning happen there. As Wenger notes:

teaching does not cause learning: what ends up being learned may or may not be what was taught, or more generally what the institutional organization of instruction intended. Learning is an emergent, ongoing process, which may use teaching as one of its many structuring resources. (1998: 267)

Learning also emerges from the formal classroom process through joint activities and talk between teachers and learners. The nature of the formal encounter is different from the informal one because of different elemental relationships between learner and helper in terms of distance or imposition of help, for example. What is important about Wenger's insights about learning is that learning about context, human nature and oneself is eminently possible in any context, through engagement with and participation in that context.

Rather than thinking about learning contexts in terms of 'in or out of school', it may be more productive to see them as more or less formal, the degree of formality dependent on the way the design of the learning context positions learners and teachers socially, allows for choice of learning opportunity and how it specifies learning goals. Learning contexts are mapped onto a continuum of formal/informal contexts in Figure 2.4. They are distinguished by:

- The origin of help – incidental, solicited, imposed.
- The degree of structure – by activity or time.
- Choice of learning goal – learners' or outside agency's.
- The degree of institutionalisation.
- The degree of management by the learner.

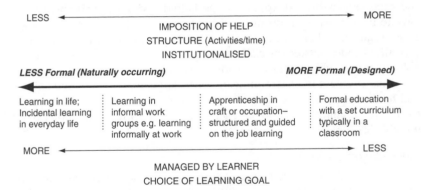

Figure 2.4   Continuum of formal and non-formal learning contexts

2.3   Discoursal issues in formal education

The analysis in sections 2.1 and 2.2 has revealed features of formal education which have consequences for the character of the discourses of formal education.

1. Classrooms have been created as dedicated locations for cultural reproduction and production (see Wells and Olson in Quote 2.5).
2. Teachers have a unique responsibility in helping learners to gain access to valued and often reified 'cultural goods' (Bourdieu 1991).

3. Teachers teach 'second-hand knowledge': they are not normally recognised as members of the communities of practice whose knowledge they attempt to pass on (Wenger, Quote 2.10), although for language teachers this is likely to be a contentious issue. Many language teachers are active users of the target language, and in their wider communities are models of expertise as 'linguists'.
4. Teachers are granted special responsibilities and authority by dint of their roles within educational institutions.

One of the overriding concerns of formal education has always been cultural reproduction. Although challenges to this position are motivated by a desire to alter the conditions of learning, or from reconceptualisations of knowledge itself, the 'deep' discourse of formal teaching-and-learning is intimately bound up with the transfer of special and valued knowledge from knower to non-knower. Thus, as Bernstein states, 'Pedagogic practice [is] a fundamental social context through which cultural reproduction-production takes place.' (1996: 17). Bernstein, like many other theorists, regards education as a process of transmission of the accumulated cultural resources of a community (Quote 2.5). In earlier work (e.g. 1971) Bernstein argues that the process is unequal because of the way knowledge is encoded in the classroom in spoken and especially written discourses – specialised codes – which themselves have to be learned as means of acquisition and reproduction of knowledge. Thus certain members of the community who do not have access to these specialised codes outside the classroom – in the home or community – are at a disadvantage when faced with formal learning. This is one aspect of the perennial problem of classroom learning in large groups of 'mixed ability' and has consequences for classroom management practices, as teachers are faced with dilemmas of how to encourage participation from potentially less able learners.

The pedagogic device

The roots of difficulty in formal learning can, to a degree, be traced to the nature of what Bernstein terms the pedagogic device (Concept 2.8). The pedagogic device has a knowledge component which influences *what* can be taught (content) and a regulatory component which governs *how* it can be taught (process). Bernstein argues that knowledge itself is subject to 'distributive' rules. These determine who has ownership of particular types of knowledge and therefore the power and status that knowledge confers on them. What tends to be taught in formal classrooms is 'specialist' knowledge, encoded in special ways, often far removed from everyday 'common sense' or 'mundane' knowledge. In engineering classes, for example, bridges are often imagined; the class rarely takes place on the site of a bridge. This affects the discourse in a number of ways. One major discoursal constraint it places on teachers is the need to 'translate' or 'recontextualise' specialised knowledge into a more accessible form, and in so doing, potentially distort or dilute it. This process of discoursal transformation by teaching broadly accounts for the perceived 'second-handedness' of formal education in terms of the teacher's knowledge. The actual experience of formal education is not second-hand though. This tends to be forgotten in discussions of educational discourse and is better accounted for by reference to informal activities. The pedagogic device also sets up its own evaluation criteria, as practices of teaching model criteria for judgement and success in learning. Notions of 'right/wrong' are thus implicit in what teachers teach, and how they present new knowledge.

Concept 2.8   The pedagogic device

The pedagogic device is the means for regulating pedagogic meanings, or what can be taught – in other words, how it is taught. It operates according to three hierarchically related contextual sets of *rules*:

1. *Distributive* – these rules enable different social groups to specialize in knowledge and practice because the rules distinguish between 'specialist' (or 'unthinkable') and 'mundane' knowledge. This gives specialist groups relative power and prestige, for example, doctors.
2. *Recontextualising* – these rules regulate the creation of specific pedagogic discourse in particular subjects, and how knowledge is taught. Pedagogic knowledge in subject fields is 'recontextualised' or made more accessible. Its subjects are simplified versions of the reality: school chemistry is imaginary and differs profoundly for example from pharmacology as practiced by a dispensing chemist, for example.
3. *Evaluative* – pedagogic practices model and transmit criteria for judgement of success in formal learning. Evaluative rules are a filter determining whether what has been 'transmitted' has been acquired. Examinations activate evaluative rules.

(after Bernstein 1996)

This adds to the 'distancing' effect produced by teachers not being practising representatives of their communities of practice – physicists, for example. As we have seen, one of the main arguments against formal education is that teachers are not usually practitioners in their specialised areas. What they are teaching is 'recontextualised', or a codified version of a real practice or knowledge field. This is a crucial difference between informal and formal learning. Informal learning as we have seen is generally embedded in contexts and cultures of practice. A key issue for language teachers in this respect is thus the extent to which they are active users of the target language. For teacher trainers, the same might be said about their continued capacity to teach – a common criticism from trainees is that teacher trainers are 'too theoretical', or 'divorced from practice'. Student teachers thus tend to be distanced from the everyday 'real' world of the classroom in training which is dominated by abstractions and specialised codes.

In any classroom, there are thus two discourses at work – horizontal and vertical (Bernstein 1996) (Concept 2.9). Much of everyday knowledge and experience is mediated through horizontal discourse, or 'natural', 'everyday' discourses. Both teachers and learners are likely to be at ease in this mode, as they have access to a wide range of discourse strategies, which are both classroom specific (teacher's and course book instructions, for example) and, more importantly from an educational point of view, ways of making connections with everyday events and more abstract knowledge fields. In linguistic terms, horizontal discourse draws on the resources of everyday communication and familiarity with different discourse types.

Concept 2.9   Horizontal and vertical discourses

Horizontal discourse is 'usually typified as everyday, oral or common-sense knowledge' (1996: 170). Horizontal discourses are acquired tacitly and are not always transferable to other contexts. They begin with mother/child interaction, and develop in all aspects of collective social life, including classrooms. These discourses include the notion of 'common-sense' and lived experience. Horizontal discourse thus encodes 'mundane' knowledge or everyday experience.

Vertical discourse, on the other hand, is a series of specialized languages with specialized modes of inquiry and rules for the production of especially written texts (1996: 171). The major difference between this discourse type and horizontal discourse is that its acquisition does not have to occur in its field of use. For example, we can learn about physics away from the research laboratory.

(after Bernstein 1996)

Vertical discourses, in contrast, encode concepts and experience in abstract terms, the most obvious example being the discourse of empirical science, but other more modern discourses, such as 'management' have also tended to render the everyday discourses of working together with people less comprehensible as they are invaded by abstract categories and concepts. A problem for learners and teachers is that horizontal and vertical discourses are intertwined in classroom encounters, and learners have to learn how to distinguish them. A core aspect of classroom management activity is to make decisions about which to foreground. There may be tendencies to shift towards a more vertical discourse when there is a content focus, and horizontally on occasions in which the social world of a group is the focus. Learners learn how to recognise these shifts are signalled as part of the task of classroom learning.

The example from an English lesson below illustrates the horizontal discourse of inviting learners to make a contribution, interwoven with the vertical discourse of linguistic description. The incident is also infused with the evaluative aspect of the pedagogic device as teacher and students evaluate the correctness of contributions.

Extract 2.1 Classroom talk

    T John broke the window / somebody to try putting / it in the passive / like Kathy did / John broke the window -- yes --
    S #5 John broke the window
    T is that right
5 Ss no
    T why / tell me why / it is not right -- first thing / yes --
    S #6 it is not in the passive tense
    T why is it not in the passive tense -- I just told you now that / something has been minimised / to make the passive tense / yes --
10 S #7 eh – the / verb is not / in the tense
    T that's one thing -- but
    S#8 he has used John 3
    T he has used John again / John broke the window / somebody put it in the passive -- yes
15 S #9 the window was broken by John –

Reference to the metalanguage of 'verbs' in the 'passive tense [*sic*]' is the main learning focus in the extract, the vertical discourse of the extract. In line 8, the teacher simplifies the grammatical idea by referring to how 'something has been minimised', an example of an immediate recontextualisation. Throughout, the teacher uses a horizontal discourse of elicitation and invitation in managing students' participation during the exchange.

Because horizontal and vertical discourses are interconnected as in the example, there are naturally tendencies towards conflict or harmony in classroom life, with consequences for classroom management. A tendency towards verticality can exclude learners, who may respond by withdrawing or contesting an activity. A teacher with the ability to recontextualise knowledge effectively may have the effect of lessening the vertical tendency. This helps classroom learners gain access to new concepts and knowledge fields, and maintains engagement.

In language teaching, the relationship between the vertical discourses of grammatical description and its specific metalanguage and the more horizontal discourses of everyday communication is important in making grammar accessible to students. If the discourse is too vertical and learners lack the linguistic resources to cope with this, it is likely that there will be difficulty or even conflict. This may lead to the exclusion of learners or refusal to participate. The choice of more 'experiential' modes of learning in grammar teaching (for example, language awareness activities (Bolitho et al. 2003) may also bring the vertical and horizontal into conflict, as the abstract world of grammatical description may be challenged and disturbed by the 'looseness' of everyday description. Much depends on the teacher being able to assist learners in gaining access to the vertical discourse of linguistic description, or enabling transformation from the horizontal into a more vertical discourse of rules and principles. Both are instances of teachers intervening in learning.

2.4   Implications of formal education for institutional and professional life

Most formal teaching and learning is 'enclosed' in schools, and this has further discoursal consequences. Because classroom management practices are embedded in wider institutional discourses, or the official agencies of education – schools, colleges, universities – which provide the authority for formal education, inevitably these practices are entwined with the discoursal practices of the institutions in which they exist. This is significant in teachers' working lives, affecting issues such as 'privacy' in classroom life, the extent of teachers' professional latitude in decision-making, and the ways in which they draw on the institution's authority for both legitimacy and support in the ways they manage classrooms. Institutional discourses constrain or attempt to regulate teaching-and-learning activity in the classroom. Schools bring together teachers and learners – they are the institutional agents of the professional's relationship with the client – the student (Quote 2.12). Because of this relationship, they have a powerful influence on the discourse of teaching-and-learning in a number of ways, most obviously by providing teachers and learners with their 'educational identities'.

Quote 2.12   Drew and Heritage on institutional discourses

. . . interaction is institutional insofar as participants' institutional or professional identities are somehow made relevant to the work activities in which they are engaged.

[Institutional discourses focus on] conduct that is in various ways shaped or constrained by the participants' orientation to social institutions either as their representatives or, in various senses, as their 'clients'.

(1992: 3–4, 5)

Drawing on Levinson (1992) and a discussion of activity types in social interaction, Drew and Heritage propose that institutional discourse has three main features (Concept 2.10):

- An institutional discourse specifies responses to institutional goals, rather than individual learners' or teachers' goals, constraints on what participants can contribute.
- It also specifies ways in which teachers and learners can interpret each other's contributions to discourse in institutional terms – inferencing procedures.
- The additional dimension of formality and informality in institutional discourse also has implications for classroom management; the more formal (or ritualised and reified, or vertical) the institutional discourse, the more likely that deviations from the norm will invite sanctions (Drew and Heritage 1992: 27). As Sarangi and Roberts (1999: 4) point out, 'Institutional rules and procedures partly derive their legitimacy through participants' recognition of and willingness to abide by a set of institutional routines'.

However, boundaries between formal and informal participation in classroom discourse are becoming blurred because of an increasing tendency in some societies towards less vertical discourse in public and educational life, and a greater overt advocacy of more informal learning through conversational and collaborative modes – a 'horizontalising' effect on the classroom discourse. The shift from a concern with classroom teaching to classroom learning (Quote 2.5) advocated by many educationalists threatens the old certainties of 'traditional' education. Local differences between classrooms have been foregrounded by the globalisation of communications, and a more pluralistic educational world is emerging in some contexts. Here, local horizontal rules of discourse appear to be challenging the traditional universal vertical discourse of education. This has the potential for creating difficulties in classroom management unless institutional goals are redefined and a weakening of certain institutional constraints such as time and space definition is sanctioned.

Concept 2.10   Institutional discourses – some patterns

1. **Goal-orientation** – participation in institutional life is oriented with reference to the goals of participants, both expert and non-expert. At least one participant must personify the goal through their conduct. Realising institutional goals to the satisfaction of 'clients' is the central discoursal goal.
2. **Constrained** – participation is constrained by the ways in which participants read the relative formality or informality of the setting. Institutional discourses both shape and are shaped by participant contributions: the greater the perceived formality, the less potential there is for shaping, and the stronger the tendency to ritual.

Concept 2.10   (Continued)

3. **Institutional inferencing** – various institutional activity types exhibit different institutionally-bound inferencing conventions. For example, professionals may feel bound by the context of 'consultation' not to express surprise or sympathy their clients' contributions. Alternatively, inserting 'conversational' remarks into more formal activity types such as meetings may create difficulties.

In all three patterns, participation is rendered more complex cross-culturally and cross-linguistically.
(after Drew and Heritage 1992, and Levinson 1992)

The vertical nature of much of classroom discourse ensures that classrooms are inherently asymmetrical in terms of knowledge and roles. The teacher's role automatically confers a degree of authority, and teachers are assumed to be more knowledgeable than the learners in the subject area. The professionalism of teachers is thus grounded in the asymmetry which confers status with knowledge. Institutions can enforce this asymmetry through various modes of control, both overt and covert. However, asymmetry is continuously open to challenge as knowledge is redistributed through the educational process. Teachers' professionalism may also be threatened by more overtly egalitarian approaches to teaching-and-learning, such as 'experiential' learning (e.g. Kohonen 1992; Kohonen et al. 2001) or transformational learning (Askew and Carnell 1998; Concept 2.5). This constrains classroom management practice and teachers' capacity to convert experiential knowledge into less mundane forms, to render it more conceptual, or 'vertical' in discoursal terms. A further issue is the extent to which participation patterns are managed in particular ways to enable transformations of horizontal discourse to occur successfully so that evaluative criteria, which exist in the vertical dimension, continue to be met. The regulatory power of testing and assessment systems invariably constrains changes in classroom management and discourse in this way, and more 'horizontal' educational practices, such as 'discovery', may ultimately be resisted because they do not meet the residual vertical evaluation system's requirements.

Different societies have met these challenges in different ways. For example, teachers may be required to learn ever more subject knowledge (Shulman 1986) in order to maintain the basic asymmetry. A common pattern in authoritarian contexts is to give institutions greater power to maintain control of students' behaviour while introducing more 'participative' forms of classroom activity. This avoids any basic change to the preferred modes of discourse in classroom management. By contrast, in more liberal contexts, the task of acquiring knowledge and its management is increasingly handed over to learners themselves, often in conjunction with highly sophisticated uses of information technology.

Professional, institutional and personal discourses

A further layer of understanding of contemporary educational discourse comes from Sarangi and Roberts (1999) who distinguish between 'professional', 'institutional' and 'personal' modes of talk (Concept 2.11). This distinction assists in locating authority and control, which are both important in classroom management, and the extent to which teachers draw their sense of authority from either their professional (knowledge-based) or institutional (systems-grounded) allegiances, and also how their practices are infused with personal talk which enables them to make 'horizontal connections' with students.

Concept 2.11   Institutional, professional and personal modes of talk

Professional Modes of Talk – 'what the professionals routinely do as a way of accomplishing their duties and responsibilities' (Sarangi and Roberts 1999: 15). Based on a sense of vocation and definable 'professional knowledge'. Characterised by vertical discourses which position 'clients' asymmetrically in terms of knowledge. 'Professional' characterised by formation of cultures and communities. Teachers explaining a point or correcting a student are operating in classroom mode.

Institutional Modes of Talk – characterised by 'regulating discourses' – rational and legitimate, backed up by the authority of an institution. Institutional discourses position clients in ways that meet institutional goals. Institutional discourses are a mix of vertical (institutional rules and procedures e.g. regulations for examinations) and horizontal (everyday relationships between members). Teachers typically revert to institutional modes of talk when referring to rules and regulations or procedures, including those relating to time and space use (what behaviour is permitted and not permitted in a classroom, for example).

Personal Experience Modes of Talk – 'the lifeworld voice...of personal experience' (Sarangi and Roberts 1999: 480; after Mischler 1984). Professionals refer to personal experiences in their professional talk. These are used to 'deal with uncertainties and back up claims' (1999: 480). Reminiscences and anecdotes are typical examples. The discourse mode is predominantly horizontal. An example is when a teacher refers to her own learning difficulties during a lesson.

In education, as in other activities such as medicine and law, professional and institutional discourses interact. For example, teachers create narratives about 'classes' and 'courses', display their special knowledge in classroom and other settings, and have the authority to evaluate learners' performance. The institutional discourses include gatekeeping – which govern selection for, training for and the evaluation of teaching – the management of schools and other institutions, and the institution's public face. Sarangi and Roberts (1999: 16) argue that workplace studies demonstrate 'the dominance of the institutional order over professional discourses'.

> ## Quote 2.13   Sarangi and Roberts on the 'new work order'
>
> ...a discourse which constitutes emergent work-related positions and identities... based on the ideas of new capitalism and the need to constantly change products and customise them as the only way to survive in the over-competitive marketplace. . . . this has meant pushing down responsibility to the workers and 'empowering' them to work. This is done by creating a core vision or culture which is shared by the managers and the workers alike. The shared rhetoric plays down the discourse of profit-making, and instead highlights those aspects of work ethics which will motivate the workers to take on extra responsibility.
> (1999: 9)

This conceptualisation of professional practice enables us to examine how institutions treat their 'clients' in the contemporary 'new work order' (Quote 2.13). The emergence of the 'new work order' has had the effect of changing teacher–learner relationships at the classroom level. Classrooms are the main locus of teachers' lives in the workplace – it is natural therefore for them to regard the professional privacy and autonomy which classrooms afford teachers as central to the construction of their professional identities. At stake is the concept of teachers' autonomy – teachers' practices for managing local classroom participation patterns may be threatened by institutional discourses which conflict with the professional discourses of practice. As education has become increasingly market-oriented, the learner (client) has become a 'customer', and the teacher and learner are repositioned as the traditional hierarchy is superseded. Institutions thus create regulatory frameworks which apparently protect the client, but may also act as a means of controlling and covertly undermining professional autonomy (Quote 2.14).

In a 'customer-centred' milieu teachers can easily find themselves grappling with a conflict between what learners demand (which may be a form of coaching to pass examinations) and their own professional values and standards. This is a position which is reached only slowly, and by the time it is apparent, it may be too late to change. With teachers risking the loss of their jobs as a penalty for failure to 'satisfy' customers in this sort of milieu, the way they manage events in and out of the classroom is likely to become survivalist rather than professional if they fail in their struggle. Many teachers will feel a sense of 'deprofessionalisation' as a result.

> ## Quote 2.14   Crichton on the effects of the 'New Capitalism' on institutional discourse
>
> The dominant discourse in the colleges...constructs the identities of and relationships between teachers, managers and students as 'communities of consumption' in which

teachers are operatives, responsible for carrying out tasks and procedures but not for deciding or questioning their purposes. This is the role of the college, identified with managers who...determine the purposes of teaching by supervising teachers to meet the commercial priority of creating and maintaining the 'happiness' of the students. In the process, the task for which teachers are held responsible is the 'repayment' of the debt owed to students by 'providing' them with learning, a 'consumption process' in which teaching is constructed as enabling students to meet their aspirations without effort, disappointment or imposition.

(2004: 374; from a study on private ESL colleges in Australia)

Certainly, the basis of teachers' expertise is challenged by the shift of emphasis in formal education from teaching to learning. However, the motives for institutions embracing this new discourse are more often commercial than educational. For example, Sarangi and Roberts (1999: 16) argue that new discourses of education which reposition students as 'independent learners' and courses as 'student-centred' have profound effects on teachers' employment prospects as redundancies are justified by increasing use of IT-based learning 'packages'.

Professional cultures

Professional discourse shapes and maintains professional cultures – of teachers, doctors and lawyers, among others. Teachers' cultures have emerged in formal education which is managed by institutions at an intermediate level between primary authorities like the state and the corporation and the micro level of the classroom. The ways in which institutions themselves are managed in turn affect what happens in the classrooms within them. Institutional practices in education grow up around the delivery of the curriculum over time periods, and the location of teaching and learning activity in institutional space. An administrative decision as apparently banal as allocating 'subject classrooms' will have profound effects on classroom management. The teachers are, in this instance, given 'home territory'. Here they have more influence over how space is used, on the availability of material resources for learning, and of local 'rules' for classroom conduct than the peripatetic teacher who works on learning groups' home territories.

At the same time, the working practices of teachers create different 'cultures' of teaching. These are influenced in turn by institutional constraints of spatial configuration and time structures in educational settings. Teacher cultures, which emerge from the shared experience of teaching, develop through interaction between classroom teaching experience and shared out-of-class encounters, most commonly staff room interaction (Richards 1997). Teacher cultures influence the quality of peer group relationships, levels of support among colleagues, and shared professional ethos and working practices. All of these (typically behind the scenes) practices influence ways in which teachers interact with students in and out of the classroom, and thus their classroom management practices.

Concept 2.12 Cultures of teaching

...*cultures of teaching* comprise beliefs, values, habits and assumed ways of doing things among communities of teachers who have had to deal with similar demands and constraints over many years.
(Hargreaves 1994: 165)

Individualism: the norm in most contexts. Teachers work privately behind closed doors. Can be interpreted as a psychological state – of the individual; an ecological state – physical separation; and isolation – a strategic means by which teachers conserve resources such as time.

Collaboration: teachers learn from each other in a supportive, spontaneous, voluntary atmosphere which encourages risk-taking and experimentation. Shared decision-making and staff consultation by authorities seen as central. Characterised by informality and shared unregulated practices.

Contrived Collegiality: A bureaucratically-imposed collaboration – administratively regulated, compulsory, fixed, formal and instrumentally-oriented, with the agenda imposed from outside a working group. This can be a stepping stone to true collegiality if managed effectively.

'Fragmented': small sub-groups of teachers within institutions. Strong insulation of sub-groups from each other. Individuals strongly identify with the culture of their group, e.g. departmental group. Practices and values are broadly shared. Politically-motivated and oriented: essentially defensive.

(after Hargreaves 1994)

Hargreaves (1994) identifies four broad cultures of teaching (Concept 2.12) which 'provide a context in which particular strategies of teaching are developed, sustained and preferred over time' (1994: 165). Thus, teachers of different age groups have different practices, and teachers of different subjects collectively invest in common practices and discourses; these are interpreted in different ways in different locations globally. The sharing of values, beliefs and practices is at the heart of the development of a 'culture' in this sense. Hargreaves argues that, while teachers are physically alone in classrooms (there are rarely other teachers present) they are never psychologically alone (Quote 2.15).

Quote 2.15　Hargreaves on the connections between teachers

What they [teachers] do [in classrooms] is powerfully affected by the outlooks and orientations of the colleagues with whom they work now and with whom they have worked in the past. In this respect, teacher cultures, the relationships between teachers and their colleagues, are among the most educationally significant aspects of teachers' lives and work. They provide a vital context for teacher development and for the ways that teachers teach. What goes on inside a teacher's classroom cannot be divorced from the relations that are forged outside it.

(1994: 165)

Hargreaves' analysis has many implications for understanding classroom management practices. Far from each classroom being an island, each with an entirely unique character, each is connected by invisible social, cultural and psychological threads to other classrooms, through the collective nature of teacher culture. These connections can extend across cultural and national boundaries, too. Scollon and Scollon (1995) analyse the culture of ESL teachers and find it differs from that of other teacher subject groups in several ways (Concept 2.13). This type of study demonstrates that the development of teacher culture is more than a matter of what happens in particular locations. It is the accumulation of shared knowledge and also attitudes, values and beliefs held in common. How teachers handle classroom management locally will be influenced by these 'universals' across different subject groups locally, nationally and internationally, and age groups, and different societies.

Concept 2.13　ESOL teachers' cultures

TESOL teachers fall into two broad groups – **BANA** (Britain, Australasia and North America) and non-BANA **TESEP** (Tertiary, Secondary, Primary) (Holliday 1994) Their experiences and working histories are very different in the following ways:

BANA is characterised by job mobility and travel, membership of international organisations like TESOL and IATEFL, reading journals like *ELT Journal*, native speaker intuition (but often little formal knowledge about language)
TESOL teachers are characterised by feeling of being 'non-traditional' in their own societies, generally outwardly-oriented culturally, tendency be well-educated, good knowledge of English in a formal sense, but still work within TESEP institutions.

Scollon and Scollon's (1995) study concentrates on the BANA (or ESL) teachers' culture which is highly individualised, with networks to support individual career development, a degree of shared insecurity, and more in common with other ESL teachers internationally than teachers from other subject groups in the same institution. Tendency to a relativistic stance and isolation from other teacher groups in their institution, and constantly their

Concept 2.13   (Continued)

discourse tends to 'cut across' the culture of the institutions they work for. Despite overtly anti-ideological and anti-universalist beliefs, there is still a strong affiliation with the individualistic and 'creative' canon of communicative language teaching. This can result in an assumption of an equal set of teacher/learner relationships in the classroom. A number of recent studies (e.g. Canagarajah 1993) have explored this conflict in terms of classroom management and discoursal difficulties. In contrast, modern language teachers in state systems – teachers of English in France or teachers of French in the UK – tend to belong to much the same types of professional cultures that teachers of other curriculum subjects do, and are, in this sense, closer to TESEP teachers in their attitudes and practices.

(after Scollon and Scollon 1995)

Summary

Learning occurs in a variety of contexts, emergent and designed, informal and formal. The levels of design and formality vary according to relationships between people, their learning goals and any helpers who are present in the learning context. Classrooms are the essential locus of formal education, and are open to a wide variety of social, economic and political influences because the purposes of formal education are open to change and are frequently contested. Classroom management involves mediation of these 'external' or 'hidden' influences as well as the day-to-day management of immediate encounters. Finally, formal schooling has discoursal consequences which affect classroom management practices in fundamental ways.

Further reading

Askew and Carnell (1998) argue for 'transformational learning'.
Bransford et al. (2000) is a useful introduction to various issues in learning.
Claxton (1999) contains a wide-ranging model of human learning in the context of 'lifelong learning'.
Drew and Heritage (1992) is a 'technical' collection of papers on institutional talk.
Hargreaves (1994) is an account of teachers' responses to change in their working practices.
Kohonen (2001) makes the case for 'experiential learning' in language education.
Lantolf (2000) is a good introduction to activity theory in second language learning.
Lave and Wenger (1991) is a useful study and conceptualisation of apprenticeship models of learning.
Wells and Claxton (2002) is a collection which makes the case for more informal language learning.
Wenger (1998) is a theorised account of learning in 'real world' contexts, with important implications for education.

3

Institutional Aspects of Classroom Management

A consequence of formal learning is that classrooms are invariably located in institutions, and their fundamental characteristics flow from this fact:

- Institutions designate classrooms as 'spaces' which offer opportunities for, and at the same time, constrain learning and professional activity. Classroom learning is 'enclosed'.
- Institutional time envelops classroom space, and is a significant influence on professional discourse, both in the classroom and in the lives of teachers and students outside the classroom.
- Institutional and professional discourses intertwine in spatial and temporal aspects of formal education.

The basic character of formal education is shaped by the ways in which teachers and learners experience and manage spatial and temporal features of the educational environment. The management of time and space affects both classroom relationships and learning opportunity. Traditionally, the management of both was regarded as primarily a teacher's responsibility; however, contemporary developments in pedagogy and technology serve to challenge this state of affairs. Additionally, there is evidence that time and space are experienced in different ways in different contexts. Time and space are thus subject to cultural relativities.

3.1 The spatial dimension

Formal education at any level is essentially *classroom* learning, the creation of 'pedagogic space' (Bourdieu and Passeron 1990: 120) through which the tasks of formal learning are mediated. The most common portrayal of a classroom is probably 'a room with classroom furniture', located in a school, or a space dedicated to pedagogic purposes, even outside a building – for example, under a shady tree. Classroom furniture can include some or all the following: desks, tables, benches (places for students), a 'teacher's table', blackboard or some other visual display and 'vertical' writing space, 'visual aids' such as an overhead projector, teaching aids such as realia, and computers (Field Notes 3.1). All of these physical manifestations of the educational process are essential resources for conveying meaning in educational encounters, and contribute to what Kress et al. (2001) call the 'multimodality' of teaching and learning. They also amplify any mediating activity in the classroom. How teachers and learners position themselves or are positioned relative to the furniture and other parts of the classroom are important – whether students and teachers are standing or sitting for example, and why. Classroom space is thus both horizontally *and* vertically arranged (Concept 3.2). How people and objects are positioned in classroom space and the parts they play are integral to classroom teaching-and-learning encounters and their management.

Field Notes 3.1   Classroom space and time

A Secondary School English Lesson – Cameroon
There are 42 students, seated two and three at a bench, in five rows. They are mid-teens and one or two older. (08:20) Lesson starts. The teacher (Mrs N.) mainly stands in front of the class and sometimes walks up and down the aisles. A student is told to stand up and read the first paragraph from a text in the course book. The other students follow the reading in their own books – some are sharing – many mouthing the words as they go. After the student finishes reading the teacher begins to explain the meaning of each sentence of this paragraph through paraphrasing, while the students make notes. When a particular phrase or sentence structure the teacher offers one or two sample sentences for illustration of how it might be used, written on the board. Students copy these down. Then students are asked in turn to stand and repeat the examples. After finishing this paragraph, they carry on with the rest of the text in the same way until the end of the lesson. The bell rings. (08:50) The teacher tells the group to answer the questions set on the text for homework.

B Primary Science Lesson – Swaziland
At the beginning of the lesson, the class assembled in its room and received instructions on the activity – lasted about 6 minutes. Class knows their teams from before it seems. They rushed off outside. There are now 51 students, aged approx. 10–11 working in groups of four and five. They are combing the space around the school for examples of insects and other living creatures, and identifying different plants. The teacher (Mr WN.) moves from group to group, asking questions and offering encouragement. He occasionally points something out. After 25 minutes, T. reminds students that they will have to return to classroom in 5 minutes, and to finish what they are doing.

Concept 3.2 Multimodality in classroom learning

Kress et al. note that there is a 'multiplicity of modes of communication that are active in the classroom' (2001: 1) rather than only speech. In their analysis of science lessons, they focus on speech, images, gesture, action with models, writing and movement. They argue that understanding teaching and learning requires us to understand how these modes interact in teaching and learning encounters.

Managing the classroom space is one of the central tasks of teachers and students. It is not only a question of allocating use and occupation of the physical space, but also use of pedagogic space, or the psychological channel of the learning purpose of any classroom, which includes the various modalities of communication. The classroom space symbolises educational purpose, and what happens in the space realises the purpose. A teacher and students are also typically placed together, face to face, in classroom space (Quote 3.1). Thus, a space occupied by a teacher and students under a tree, lacking physical boundaries, is a classroom as long as there are teacher and students have gathered there facing each other for the purposes of teaching-and-learning. The functional classroom space and its arrangement are together the most basic realisation of formal education, in contrast to the less deliberately structured physical spaces of more informal learning settings, where learning is done in the context of the activity or in an everyday setting such as the home, and where specialised educational resources are not needed. Figure 3.1 shows some of the many possible layouts of classroom furniture.

In Goffman's (1974) terms, the classroom is a social and psychological 'frame' for formal education (Concept 3.3). Immediately teacher and students gather and face each other, the frame is established, and participants can expect certain things to occur. Even if the students are working outside the physical walls of the classroom they are still in the frame, which sets up shared expectations of what can or cannot occur there. Outside in our example science classroom (Field Notes 3.1B) the frame shifts subtly from schoolchild to 'nascent naturalist'; during the language lesson, (Field Notes 3.1A) the frame of 'understanding a text in English' is activated. Frames can shift within lessons, and are signalled by changes in activity, thus influencing time use and possibly use of space in different student groupings.

Instances of movement, like students standing up to answer questions, or the teacher moving to and fro monitoring group discussion, signal changes in footing (Concept 8.8), or the ways in which people align themselves to each other in terms of interactive roles, or physically in an activity. All are significant ways in which teachers and learners manage classroom time and space, and are woven into the management of teaching-and-learning activities.

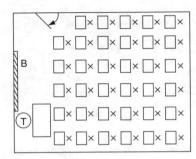

1. 'Traditional': Individual desks in rows.

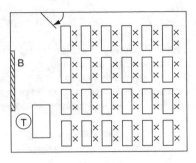

2. 'Traditional': Benches for 2 or more students. Often fixed to the floor.

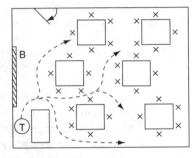

3. 'Restaurant': Random clusters, often permanent or semi-permanent.

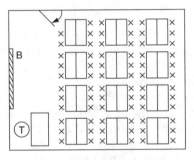

4. 'Islands': Regular groupings. Can be created by modifying 'benches' so that students on odd-numbered benches can turn to face those behind them.

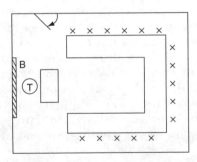

5. 'Horseshoe': Popular in Higher Education.

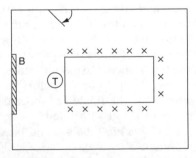

6. 'Seminar': A variant is when the teacher sits on the long side of the table, or 'cabinet meeting'.

Figure 3.1   Classroom layouts – a selection

NOTE: The figure depicts layouts I have seen in classrooms around the world, and is based on my field notes. It is, however, by no means definitive, and there are sure to be other layouts. The 'board' position is marked 'B', and the typical 'teacher base' is marked 'T'.

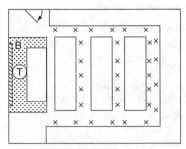

7. 'Laboratory': Layout determined by fixed installations of equipment.

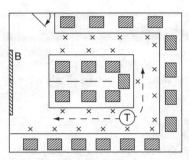

8. 'Looking Out': Typically a configuration in computer rooms, where access to power sources dictates layout.

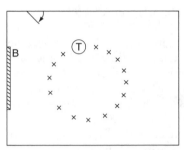

9. 'Circle': Typically chairs only or standing.

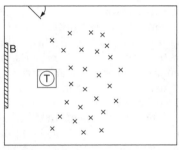

10. 'Story': Semi-circles of listeners surround the story teller, who is typically seated.

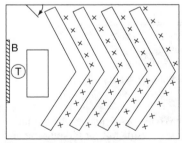

11. 'Chevrons': Occasionally seen in lecture theatres or laboratories.

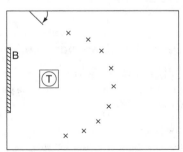

12. 'Semi-circle': Normally found in small classes. Individuals gather round the teacher.

Figure 3.1 (Continued)

Concept 3.3   Frames

Frames – are entailed by social interaction. They comprise a set of expectations shared among participations as to what the interaction ought to entail. Frames cover a range of contexts, from institutional to specific activities.

'The definition which participants give to their current social activity – to what is going on, what the situation is, and the roles the interactants adopt within it.' Thus behaviour is interpreted in the context of participants' current understanding of what frame they are in.

In language classes, 'group discussion' may be interpreted as a frame by participants. Our understandings of different frames enable us to see when there have been violations of 'frame space' (Goffman 1981: 230) and to effect appropriate repair strategies. (Goffman 1974)

For some commentators like Jackson (Quote 3.1), the classroom space is emblematic of its 'special' function, and endowed with almost spiritual significance. This may reflect either the origins of classrooms in religious teaching and practice (churches, mosques, temples all have the same basic elements of enclosure and face-to-face positioning of protagonists as classrooms) or the passionate views of educationalists like Jackson and Bruner, who believe in the elevated cultural purposes of schools (Quote 2.5, Chapter 2) as 'an entry into the life of the mind' (1979: 118). For Bruner, as for Jackson, the classroom space thus epitomises and realises the higher purposes of education. In reality, for most teachers and learners, the classroom is the place where they anchor their activities, a place which has to be managed on a moment-by-moment basis for a variety of reasons. However, space carries hidden messages which classroom participants respond to in subtle but significant ways.

Quote 3.1   Classrooms and space

. . . classrooms are special places. The things that happen there and the ways in which they happen combine to make these settings different from all others.
(Jackson 1968: 9)

The language classroom: . . . the gathering, for a given period of time, of two or more persons, (one of whom generally assumes the role of instructor) for the purpose of language learning.
(van Lier 1988: 47)

A classroom, like a church auditorium, is rarely seen as being anything other than that which it is. No one entering either place is likely to think that he is in a living room, or a grocery store, or a train station. Even if he entered at midnight or at some other time

> when the activities of the people would not give the function away, he would have no difficulty understanding what was **supposed** to go on there. Even devoid of people, a church is a church and a classroom, a classroom.
> (Jackson 1968:6)

1.1 Educational space

Doyle (1986: 397) identifies 'the physical milieu' as one of four 'scene coordinates' (after Burnett 1973: 293) that comprise the classroom context (Quote 3.2). He also points out that relatively little systematic research has been done on the physical design of classroom settings, and their effect on classroom management practices and teaching and learning in more general terms (1986: 402). This is a view shared by Hitchcock and Hughes (1989: 171), who note that 'as a topic of research interest, space allows us to ask a series of important, but often neglected questions', such as:

- How do people make sense of space?
- How do people conduct themselves in space?

Quote 3.2   Scene coordinates of classrooms

1. Temporal boundaries or duration.
2. The physical milieu, that is the shape of the site in which it occurs, the number and type of participants, the arrangement of participants in the available space, and the props or objects available to the participants.
3. The behaviour format or programme of action for the participants (e.g. maths or language).
4. The focal pedagogic content or concern of the segment (e.g. spelling test or writing lesson).

(after Burnett 1973, in Doyle 1986: 397)

Research on the effects of classroom space on classroom activity (Concept 3.4) mainly attempts to correlate physical conditions with student achievement and student behaviour. A common theme is that the configuration and use of classroom space has a strong influence on the quality of classroom activity. For example, the type of activity and the physical arrangements of the setting directly influence the amount of time teachers spend on organising students, working with individual students and dealing with inappropriate behaviour. An important conclusion is that the greater the amount of student choice and mobility, the greater the need for teachers to manage and control activity (Doyle 1986).

Concept 3.4   Research on the effects of physical design & space use on classroom life

1. Different designs of classrooms and furniture arrangements have relatively little effect on verbal interaction, but some effect on attitudes and conduct. Decreased 'density' and carefully designed 'traffic avenues', combined with clearly defined special purpose areas contribute to increased attentiveness and decreased distraction levels.

2. When students' seating was arranged in 'traditional rows', an 'action zone' directly in front of the teacher and at the centre of the room emerged. In the action zone, interaction was more personalised and conversational, and semi-private, whereas students in the 'public zone' (in the middle and back of the room) received more lecturing and one-way communication. If students are provided with a choice of where to sit, it is observed that some will sit where they can most easily participate.

3. Students appeared to improve in behaviour if sitting in rows, but complained of a loss of work space when in rows.

4. Open school spaces led to more disruption and distraction. Hitchcock and Hughes report a study which showed teachers creating 'boundaries' between areas and classes in open plan schools in order to cope with these types of difficulty, and promote a calmer and more peaceful environment for learning in 'home bases'. The findings confirmed other research which noted that teachers were more concerned about noise than students. However, they also report that the open plan layout led to changes in practice. Some research on open plan schooling noted a greater degree of informality and spontaneity in open plan schools. Additionally, in open plan classrooms teachers spent more time interacting with groups and individuals than traditional classrooms in which there was more lecturing and disciplinary action taken.

5. Alternative classroom layouts imply different learning and teaching types. For example, a rectangular arrangement of fixed desks with a teacher in front implies an empty learner waiting to be filled with knowledge. Changing configurations can aid different teaching strategies.

(after Doyle 1986; Hitchcock and Hughes 1989; Lambert 1994)

Hitchcock and Hughes (1989: 172) further argue that 'space and learning are linked' (Quote 3.3). However, they also remark that it is difficult to systematically investigate the effects of space because people draw on tacit and symbolic forms of knowledge in their use of space. In other words, implicit in school and the design of classroom space are messages about the purposes of education and how it is to be conducted. For example, whole group instruction is the outcome of the institutionalisation of education (Erickson and Shultz 1992) and consists of 'the scene of teaching...in which large numbers of students are involuntarily gathered in a setting apart from everyday life' (1992: 472). Erickson and Shultz go on to point out that this arrangement leads to an 'essentially adversarial relationship between teacher and students' (1992: 472). One of the great challenges in classroom management is to address the social and pedagogic difficulties inherent in the adversarial positioning of teachers and learners. Two educational trends directly address these issues, and challenge traditional assumptions about space use in ways that are as profound as open-plan, 'classroom-less' schooling:

- the growth of alternatives to traditional face-to-face classroom instruction like online and distance learning, which repositions teachers and learners physically, and therefore symbolically;
- the increasing importance of 'lifelong learning', and growth of adult learning, which also extends education into new time zones (e.g. evenings). This trend brings together adults in learner and teacher roles, with the potential difficulties in status relationships that are implied.

Quote 3.3   Hitchcock and Hughes on 'arenas of interaction'

Schools and classrooms may be conceived of as 'arenas of interaction'. School buildings, classrooms, areas and locations in school are interpreted and identified by different people in different ways. Teachers and pupils routinely cope with and manage the physical arrangements in schools. . . . The ways in which objects and classrooms are organized and arranged is not arbitrary; indeed the organization of a classroom often reflects the kind of spirit in which learning can take place and can furthermore be said to reflect conceptions of knowledge. The organisation and layout of a school or classroom tells as much about the character of the school and orientations of participants. . . . The spatial organisation of a school or classroom provides possibilities for learning but at the same time constraints. The school buildings and classrooms themselves express and embody conceptions of teaching and learning.
(1989: 172–3)

In summary, an understanding of the management of educational space accounts for the following:

1. The constraints and opportunities for learning that different space management practices create.
2. The symbolic meanings of educational space and their effect on learning.
3. The connections between time and space use in classrooms and their effects on learning opportunity.
4. The dynamics of space management inside the classroom, and the effects of 'breaking the boundaries' of classroom space both in traditional activities such as 'homework' to more radical developments such as computer-mediated communication in teaching and learning. For example, the relative 'privacy' of space use, from the public and semi-public classroom to the more private out-of-classroom management of educational space.

The meaning and use of classroom space

Classroom space is utilised in a multitude of different ways, which entail different groupings of students, different uses of wall space, different patterns of movement and different 'densities of population'. The 'geography' of classrooms has significant psychological and social effects on teachers and learners.

Proxemics and the design of spaces

Space is a constant in human social and cultural life. At the physical level, for example, how close we stand or sit next to strangers, or how we arrange the furniture in living and working spaces are significant. How we use and interpret the meanings of space and its physical features is a key part of social interaction. In their work, architects, town planners and landscape architects, among others, draw on knowledge of human response to space – from needs for security and safety to aesthetic considerations of harmony and pleasure, to satisfy human needs for privacy and for territoriality, to provide opportunities for gathering and shared experience. One wonders whether the designers of classroom space draw from the same knowledge base. Studies of these aspects of human life provide a basic conceptual map for understanding the influence of space and its management in educational settings.

Concept 3.5   Proxemics

Hall's most influential work, *The Hidden Dimension* (1966), argued that although humans share sensory means of experiencing space, these are moulded by culture. All cultural groups define and organise space, and these definitions are internalised at an unconscious level.

'Proxemics' is the study of how individuals and groups define the spaces that surround them. There are four levels of space:

1. *Intimate space* – entry into this very close bubble is acceptable only for intimates and close friends.
2. *Personal space* – this ranges from touching to just out of touching ranges.
3. *Social and consultative space* – this is the space in which people feel comfortable in normal social interaction with acquaintances and strangers.
4. *Public space* – the spatial area in which people interpret interactions as impersonal and therefore relatively anonymous.

Territory is also an important concept in proxemics. These range from personal territories or spaces, through to informal action territories, to 'home' territories where entrance may be restricted, to unrestricted public territories.
(after Hall 1966, and Bowers and Flinders 1990)

The social anthropologist E. T. Hall's (1966, 1984) work on proxemics (Concept 3.5) was concerned with how people used space in social interaction and in particular the fixed and semi or non-fixed features of any space. Hall saw that we have varying abilities to influence social interaction depending on the levels of control which we are able to exert over semi-fixed features of space. An example concerns the proximity and relative positioning of two chairs in a space. This has profound effects on the interaction between two people using them. People from many communities would find it difficult to initiate conversation if they were seated in two chairs fixed to the floor, for example. If, on the other hand, the chairs were moveable, two people would find a way of positioning them to 'play by the rules' of corporeal proximity and directness of eye contact favoured by their local cultural practices.

The design of office workspaces provides further evidence of the importance of the management (or manipulation) of people's responses to spatial arrangements. (Hubiak and Banning 1994). All these uses of space are designed to promote particular types of communication or activity.

In office workspaces, spatial issues can include:

1. the size and juxtaposition of personal workspaces relative to the perceived status of a member of an organisation. If the leader of an organisation sits among or apart from their employees is seen as significant, for example;
2. whether or not individuals have private spaces in which to work;
3. whether desks have access from both in front and behind;
4. access to working tools such as computers;
5. whether or not there is any plant material in the space;
6. tidiness and availability of storage facilities;
7. flexibility of space use. Unlike educational institutions, commercially oriented workspaces can change regularly, for example, from open-plan to 'island' layouts;
8. use of colour and lighting. For example, soft colours and spotlighting, have a softening and calming effect on workspaces.

These factors will all have a bearing on how teachers and learners manage and experience a classroom space. Bowers and Flinders (1990: 67) note how spatial distance, combined with positioning – for example, whether the teacher is standing or seated, standing over a seated person, or behind a large desk – conveys significant messages about teachers' status. (Quote 3.4) They point out how gaze and voice projection can also 'close' distance and have the effect of transforming intimate, private student behaviour in small groups into public zone behaviour.

Quote 3.4   Bowers and Flinders on teachers' social use of classroom space

Example 1

...a teacher sits at her desk (closely situated in relation to students) when eliciting ideas from students and when engaging them in a discussion that often became a genuine dialogue. However, when giving directions or otherwise assuming a more directive role, the teacher stands at the centre of the room. We have observed other teachers who signal the transition from a mutual discussion to a more directive and hierarchical relationship by positioning themselves behind their desk. This transition may also be signalled by moving to the front of the classroom.

Example 2

'Okay I'm going to ask you to work on your own today,' the teacher announces. 'Either read or study your spelling, but please work quietly.' The students open their notebooks or paperback novels and bend their heads over their desks. The teacher picks up his role book, sits down in a swivel chair with casters, and pushes himself down the first row of desks, stopping to talk briefly with each individual student. Because the student desks are set front-to-back with no space in between, the teacher must manoeuvre his chair to the side of each student so they are sitting shoulder-to-shoulder rather than face-to-face. The oblique positioning helps make their interaction less of a confrontation. Also, the fact that the teacher is sitting down, physically on a level with students, relaxes their talk.

(1990: 78)

Front and back stage – social and psychological regions in the classroom

Goffman's (1969) notion of front and back stage 'regions' (1969: 109) adds a further psychological dimension to the discussion of classroom space (Quote 3.5). People 'perform' in the front region, or front stage. In a classroom, the teacher typically occupies the front region, and in traditional classroom settings, is expected to do so according to particular norms and conventions of behaviour. The act of inviting students to perform in the front zone has both social and psychological significance. Normally, students are in the back region, and classroom convention stipulates that only the teacher can allow them access to the front zone. Erickson and Schultz (1992) use a spotlight metaphor for the process of bringing students into the front region in a psychological sense. The teacher's attention sweeps around the room like a lighthouse (1992: 470) and 'fixes' students in their beam. For the rest of the time in such classrooms, the students are effectively in the back region ('classroom underlife' as Erickson and Shultz 1992: 470 refer to it) or 'hiding'.

Quote 3.5   Goffman on front region and backstage performances

Classrooms are 'front regions' in a broad sense, while staff rooms are 'backstage'.

'front region'... the place where the performance is given. The performance of an individual in the front region may be seen as an effort to give the appearance that his activity in the region maintains and embodies certain standards (of treating the audience and personal 'decorum').

A back region or backstage may be defined as a place, relative to a given performance, where the impression fostered by the performance is knowingly contradicted as a matter of course. (Typically it is physically separated from the front region.)
(1969: 109–10 and 114)

The significance of spatial arrangements in classrooms is further enshrined in our informal language. We refer instinctively to 'the front' of the class (the teacher's zone, or near there), 'the back' of the class (furthest from the teacher's space). The language we use appears to reinforce the apparent 'givenness' of this arrangement. This is typified in many contexts where the teacher and students rarely, if ever, have any choice about the organisation of classroom furniture and use of space. How permanently classroom furniture is positioned is significant. Whether people are permitted by local institutional conventions to move classroom furniture into different configurations is an important classroom management issue. Classroom space does not have to be fixed – it can be reorganised to distance people from each other, to signal formality and to prevent spontaneous conversation; or alternatively to encourage proximity and informality, thus facilitating different types of social activity.

Institution-wide practices or even government regulations can specify whether a student always occupies the same place in a classroom – their 'territory'; or further determine whether or not the same group of students occupies the classroom for all of their school time, and a succession of teachers come to teach their subjects; or whether the classroom is dedicated to one teacher or a 'subject', like 'the English Room', and various groups of students attend subject classes there. In the latter there may be more latitude for the teacher to create a context reflecting their subject, using the wall space, for example, to display student work, pictures, posters and other material like maps, or charts which can provide a unique, dedicated and permanent context or world for a subject.

Space, teachers and teaching

The configuration of classroom space tends to constrain what teachers can do and therefore limits the uses of pedagogic space. Discussing the tendency for classroom experience to be fairly constant and predictable, Denscombe (1982) identifies the pressures forcing teachers to manage classrooms on the basis of interpersonal techniques, with a focus on people management. The pressures, he maintains, derive from a shortage of resources in most classrooms (Quote 3.6). The difficulties are exacerbated by the isolation of teachers from each other created by the 'cellular patterns of organisation' of classrooms in schools (Hargreaves 1994: 170).

Paradoxically these conditions contribute to teachers' feelings of autonomy, as they work 'alone' in their own classroom spaces or 'territories'. This is further amplified by the existence of teacher's 'home classrooms'. These factors become the basis of what Denscombe calls 'the hidden pedagogy' (Chapter 9), the informal, tacit 'rules' governing the behaviour of experienced teachers, and which are passed on to new entrants to the profession on entry to school life. As a consequence, unspoken conventions exist for managing classroom space at the school level as well as at the classroom.

Quote 3.6   Denscombe on the structure of school experience

Like all social situations the classroom involves a number of complex expectations about appropriate behaviour which have to be learned, negotiated and reinforced, but what is important about the classroom is the degree to which these expectations are inescapable. The participants are not at liberty to leave the arena of interaction and, for the time span of each lesson, both teacher and pupils find themselves the captive audience of the other.

Limited resources . . . are a fact of life in the classroom.

1. Lack of materials – teachers therefore are forced to rely on their own resources.
2. Lack of time . . .
3. Large numbers of pupils – affecting both quality of teaching and learning.

(1982: 255)

The crowdedness of classrooms, combined with shortages of material and time, forces teachers to adopt particular management practices to make the task easier. These practices are handed on between generations of teachers. It is not surprising therefore that there is opposition to the introduction of new patterns of classroom organisation and novel uses of space and time with computers, for example. Teachers invest a great deal in existing routines and unconsciously subscribe to the hidden pedagogy. This may assist us in further understanding why the contemporary trend towards the use of classrooms for learning (rather than instruction) is likely to have a destabilising effect on many teachers worldwide, as it challenges existing uses of space and their associated classroom management practices.

Figure 3.2 summarises the various themes developed in this section. The central zone of the diagram shows the aspects of classroom space use affecting classroom management. The outer 'ring' depicts the movement of learning and teaching beyond the classroom walls and school, from the public and semi-public domain of the classroom, to private control of educational space.

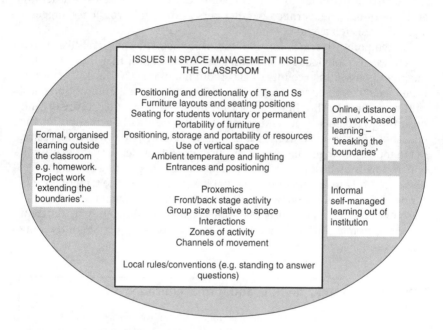

Figure 3.2   Themes in managing classroom space

3.2   The temporal dimension

Unlike informal learning, time in formal education is structured, at all levels, from the allocation of time to an activity to the length of a course or stage of educational experience such as Primary education. Formal education is time-bound as well as spatially enclosed. Unlike informal learning which proceeds according to its own natural rhythms and trajectories, formal learning is clock-bound (Lemke 2002b). Divisions of educational time, typically imposed by institutions from government to school or even academic departments within institutions, affect the educational enterprise at all levels from the classroom to the curriculum, and beyond into the more politically-driven time-frames of governments and other bodies which fund formal education. This section focuses on the way in which educational time is managed, particularly at the classroom level, and how the management of educational time is influenced by larger temporal structures. We shall also examine the ways in which teachers experience time. Teachers are the primary agents in managing time in the classroom in the majority of educational contexts, working in time from minute-to-minute classroom events to the management of larger units from 'lessons' to curricula lasting four years or more. All the issues raised in this chapter derive from studies of teaching and schooling. The learner's parallel perspective and experience suggests a parallel research agenda.

The temporal structures (or 'frames') of formal education are, like spatial structures, also 'obvious'. In fact, they are so humdrum that they are infrequently discussed in accounts of classroom life. Breen (2001a: 132) reminds us, for example, that 'how long a lesson should last' is a 'significant practice' in the classroom. The time frames of formal learning contexts are central organising elements in its management. They are the 'punctuation' of the education process (Engeström et al. 2002: 214). Studies, like Engeström et al.'s, of attempts to change educational practices provide evidence that the ways in which time is divided and used in formal education are obstacles to change. There are likely to be more fundamental issues at stake in the temporal structuring of formal education, which does not, at present, match the rhythms of learning. What is important is that time is construed differently by different players in formal education, with consequences for the processes of teaching and learning (Quote 3.7).

Quote 3.7   Lemke on time and formal education

Organizationally, schools minimise the opportunity for long-term intellectual development by severing the bonds between teacher and student every several months, disconnecting the study of each subject from the others, and even dividing the day into periods defined by the clock rather than learning. The whole point of intellectual and identity development is to learn to integrate experience over progressively longer time-scales, but the institutional arrangements of schooling seem designed to thwart that effort.

(2002a: 44)

Time also influences classroom life in other covert ways. Contemporary debate about the future of formal education refers regularly to the 'rapidly-changing world', 'ever-increasing pace of life', exponential technological change' (Wells and Claxton 2002b) as the background to educational change and reform. There is pressure on students and teachers to learn more, at a faster rate, in order to cope with the changing world, and to change their practices in order to accommodate change. This debate impinges directly on the lives of teachers and students engaged in formal learning. Teachers are pressured to change their practices (Claxton 2002) by moves to change the curriculum and the organisation of schooling. We shall examine below the sig of time in teachers' lives more generally.

Quote 3.8   Hargreaves on teachers and time

Time is a fundamental dimension through which teachers' work is constructed and interpreted by themselves, their colleagues and those who administer and supervise them. Time for the teacher is not just an objective, oppressive constraint but also a subjectively defined horizon of possibility and limitation. . . . Time structures the work of teaching and is in turn structured by it. Time is therefore more than a minor organisational contingency, inhibiting or facilitating management's attempts to bring about change. Its definition and imposition form part of the very core of teachers' work and of the policies and perceptions of those who administer it.
(1994: 95)

How teachers allocate time for different classroom learning and teaching tasks, for example, and how time pressures influence teachers' decision-making is one of many temporal factors to consider in understanding classroom life, as Hargreaves (1994) points out (Quote 3.8). New ways of teaching-and-learning typically suggest different ways of using time which conflict with students' and teachers' experience of 'what is best', or most convenient. They can also disturb established routines and hard-won normality because psychologically, new teaching procedures present new frames for teaching-and-learning which disturb the status quo. A further issue is that major parts of the educational process are conducted outside classroom time – planning, 'homework' or 'private study' are notionally outside the control of either teacher or institution. All these issues influence classroom management practices.

Educational time

Concept 3.6   Students' perception of educational time

'Class time is different from other time. In class time we do things to prepare for the exams. Out of class we learn different things for our own interest'. (Student quoted in Razianna's (2003) study of students' experience of learning English at Malaysian secondary schools). The study elicited this and similar comments from students regarding 'learning time'. They regarded class time as very different in nature and use from their learning time out of class.

How do students and teachers experience educational time? Estimates of the amount of time young people spend in education vary, but assuming that a person was to spend the bulk of their lives between the ages of 5 and 16 in

...hat person would experience something like 15,000 ...ontact, plus a great deal of time outside the classroom ...ich continue the processes begun in 'lessons'. This ...half the time of a young person's waking life. It is ..., that there are comparatively few studies which ...ers experience educational time. On the other hand, a fairly compre...... body of research examining the temporal dimension of classroom education from the teacher's perspective is emerging. The example cited from a study of students' perceptions of their language learning experience in schools (Concept 3.7) identifies a distinction which these students make between teaching time and learning time: classroom time is *teaching time* when they work to teachers' and the authorities' agendas, whereas *learning* time with personal significance is more likely to occur outside the classroom. The first significant issue regarding educational time is thus that teaching time and learning time are qualitatively and possibly chronologically different.

Concept 3.7   Educational time units

Educational time can be seen in different ways:

LESSONS – (also known colloquially as 'periods' and 'sessions') the basic administrative temporal and organisation unit. Lengths of periods vary from 30 minutes up to 120 minutes, longer for 'practical sessions' such as laboratory time. Teachers plan periods within time limits set by institutions and authorities. They tend to be divided into stages or 'segments' (Doyle 1986: 397) with correspond to different **activities**. Planned time allocation may be changed during periods in response to events. Students influence the course of events at period level.

Periods may be arranged on a weekly schedule, with regular timed slots for particular activities (e.g. Wednesday – project work)

'STUDY TIME' – planned or unplanned, but still managed, and both directly (set tasks) and indirectly (unfinished learning) influenced by classroom management practices. Classrooms are extended temporally. Study time can be spent in or out of school on 'homework tasks' or similar.

COURSE/PROGRAMME – a macro-unit of management, but of varying lengths. Often with a set curriculum to complete and assessment of aims/objectives. This rhythm is likely to influence time management indirectly at the period level, and especially in the sequencing of learning activities. Assessment periods normally come at particular points in the middle and end of courses.

TERM/SEMESTER – administrative units that may or may not directly influence classroom activity at the lesson level, but may influence staging of courses and indirectly lesson content and focus. These units are more likely to be tied to the need for rest from educational activity than to learning needs. Holidays mark interruptions in term schedules.

STAGE – stages of education for children and young people tend to correspond to biological age, although not always. Primary, secondary and tertiary are typical educational stages, each lasting for as long as six years in the case of primary education.

Educational time units: managing teaching and learning time

A primary characteristic of formal education is that it is organised on the basis of units of time (Concept 3.6), as Doyle (1986: 397 and Quote 3.2) has observed. The temporal experience of formal education is one of punctuated blocks of time of contact between teachers and students. Educational time is thus organised on the basis of time-bound *teaching* tasks, the largest one being completion of a stage of education. Educational time moves inexorably forwards at the macro level: lessons accumulate into courses, and courses into 'years' of study (or educational years) and so on. These are both sequential – for example, a day of 'lessons' in different areas of the curriculum in school – and interrupted – by breaks for meals or rest, or longer periods away from education itself. Because of the 'stop-start' nature of the educational process, teachers and students have to provide continuity, as well as initiation and closure, through the management of *transitions* and *interruptions* (Concept 3.8). Transitions are signalled at macro- and micro-temporal levels – the beginnings of 'academic years' or semesters; courses, lessons and activities in lessons. Transitions are important framing devices, and are marked discoursally either by specific verbal reference, rituals and ceremonies for the larger frames or simply by a bell between lessons. These are all devices for managing the passage of educational time.

Concept 3.8   Interruptions and transitions in educational time

Interruptions in educational time: holidays, weekends, public holidays, breaks for meals and play or rest. Interruptions are signalled in calendar time and often marked by rituals such as 'final assembly' or 'prize-givings'.

'**Transitions** are points in social interaction when contexts change' (Doyle 1986: 406).

Doyle notes major (between lessons and class meetings, or phases and activities of lessons) and minor transitions (between speaking turns in lessons). These are managed at the micro-level with elaborate signalling devices (see 7.2).

There are also periods of transition from non-educational to educational activity, a change of macro-context, again frequently marked by rituals.

The strategic management of transitions endows the longer-term aspects of the process with a sense of rhythm and even season (in Europe and North America for example, the academic year is broadly the same as that followed in medieval Europe, anchored to religious festivals and the seasonal working patterns of agriculture, despite the subsequent industrial and information ages) marking the progression through major stages of the educational process. Prabhu (1992: 226) comments that 'in designing educational activity, [this] concept of psychological progress [of the learner] is translated into one of curricular progression, the metaphor of a journey being equally applicable to both.' As we have seen it is a journey that is more like a rural bus ride than a long-haul flight, with frequent stops, and sometimes the need to refuel, or change drivers.

The ends of longer term periods of educational activity are often signalled by formal assessment and examination periods. The schedules of public examinations also influence the activities of whole societies. For children and adolescents in full-time primary and secondary education, these temporal rhythms define their lives, and those of their parents and guardians who arrange their lives around these rhythms. Changes in these macro-rhythms such as 'the school year' have an enormous impact on the structure of the working day, 'holiday periods' for people in employment and so on. Educational time is organised monochronically (Concept 3.9) – the central organising features of the timetable, or the semester system, are broadly fixed structures within which teachers and learners go about the business of formal education. Because these are defined end points and very often there are curricular completion 'targets' to meet, there is an inbuilt sense of progression and achievement in educational time frames. There is also the sense of being 'pulled' towards end points, and of the underlying imperative to complete tasks within time frames. There are, however, potential tensions between time as an opportunity for learning and development, or time for play, or, on the other hand, being constrained by time, of being driven by time limits and specific time frames.

Concept 3.9   How time is experienced

Hall (1984) observes that cultures tend to be either monochromic or polychronic in their attitudes towards time.

Monochronic: Tasks are clearly defined and done sequentially according to a set timetable. Thus there is time spent on and off task in the school or workplace. Targets and goals are often stated in temporal terms and success is measured by the achievement of goals within time frames. Also seen as 'masculine', Anglo-Saxon and Northern European and technical rationalist (Schon 1983).

Polychronic: Multi-tasking is common, with tasks being done in parallel. Deadlines are flexible and there is considerable blurring of social and task-related activities. Successful completion of tasks implies meeting original expectations and goals, provided that social cohesion is maintained. Also seen as 'feminine', 'southern hemisphere'.

The learning process is not, by its very nature, time-bound, however. As Brookfield (1990) points out, based on his own students' experience (Concept 3.10), learning has common rhythms and 'turning points' (1990: 43) which cannot be predicted by pre-packaged curricula or assessment schemes, and which are more polychronic in nature, defying the imposition of strict boundaries. Teaching which is truly sensitive to learning rhythms is thus likely sit uneasily with monochromic educational time (Quote 3.9). Furthermore, success in teaching comes about because of students' non-active time between lessons (Woods 1996: 112). This is time when students presumably are able to digest or ruminate on new information or follow lesson material up in their own time.

Quote 3.8   Lemke on the problems of monochronic time in education

We originally separated age groups in schools out of eighteenth century fears that older students would morally corrupt younger ones, but we continue today to rationalise this separation by the doctrine that there must be some ideal method of teaching that is specific to each small range of ages and radically distinct from those appropriate to other age groups. We ground this notion of linear developmental change in a highly implausible model that maps linear notions of clock time onto complex, multiple timescale, developmental processes.
(2002b: 80)

Concept 3.10   The rhythms of learning

Brookfield analysed learning logs and critical incidents from many of his tertiary level learners and discovered their experience was characterised by the following:

1. Learners feel insecure (the 'imposter syndrome' 1990: 44).
2. Learning is experienced emotionally.
3. Learning is often challenging (both positively and negatively).
4. Many learners complain that learning is not deep enough – it tends to be broad and rapidly moving from topic to topic.
5. Learning fluctuates and learners experience going backwards as well as forwards.
6. Significant episodes are unexpected.
7. A supportive learning community is important to survival as well as success.

Concept 3.10   (Continued)

While acknowledging the limitations of his research, Brookfield outlines how teaching might adapt itself to the sorts of experiences outlined above. To do so implies leaving the monochronic curriculum and spending time attending to learning.

The character of learning
Lemke makes the following observation about learning which concurs with Brookfield's:

If we teach something, and the student learns it, does it stick? How do we know? All teachers realize that change in beliefs and identities, and the acquisition of persistent skills, takes time; more time than any one interaction or lesson. There may be 'break-through' moments, critical points on the pathway of development, and the pathway itself extends over a longer stretch of time. Each breakthrough has been prepared by many prior experiences, and the effects of that special moment can easily fade, or even be erased or reversed by other later events. It is only over the long haul that serious change happens.
(2002a: 39)

(after Brookfield 1990: 43–56)

Classroom management is in dialectical relationship with both monochromic and polychronic 'streams' of time, simultaneously directing its use and responding to its use. A socio-cultural view of learning and teaching also alerts us to longer-term temporal issues. A socio-cultural view emphasises aspects of learning which have temporal influences well beyond the time structures of formal education:

- the gradual nature of learning as we become members of communities;
- the 'history' of the culturally significant activities in which we learn to participate, and our part in their continuation and adaptation to changed circumstances;
- the concomitant development of individual and collective identities from the accumulation of learning over the course of countless events.

As Lemke observes, contemporary schooling pays 'too much attention to what we study and not enough to what we become' (2002a: 35). He criticises schools and curricula for not attending to identity development and for segmenting time in such a way that experience is fragmented. He comments on the episodic and frequently punctuated nature of educational time, with interruptions such as transitions between stages of education. Under such circumstances it is left largely up to the individual student to make sense of the various fragments of their experience and to provide continuity (Quote 3.9).

Quote 3.9   Lemke on time and schooling

Organizationally, schools minimise the opportunity for long-term intellectual and identity development by severing the bonds between teacher and student every few months, disconnecting the study of each subject from all the others, and even dividing the day into periods defined by a clock rather than by the needs of learning. The whole point of intellectual and identity development is to learn to integrate experience over progressively longer time scales, but the institutional arrangements of schooling seem deliberately designed to thwart this effort.

(2002a: 44)

Teaching that is sensitive to the rhythms of learning has to be responsive to the particular vagaries of learning in time – this invariably creates dilemmas and tensions that affect classroom practice. For example, teachers who attempt to provide continuity and coherence to student experience risk failing to satisfy the 'completion imperative' (Concept 3.10) because they devote time to assisting students to synthesise learning on their own terms, rather than obeying monochronic trajectories. They also have to spend time liaising with colleagues who may be providing a radically different learning experience to the same group of students in order to manage continuity across different courses and programmes.

Concept 3.10   The completion imperative

In a study of classroom discoursal practices in Cameroon, Wright (1992) analysed the behaviour of teachers and students during what were termed 'Critical moments' – when the lesson went wrong for one reason or another – most typically due to student error. The analysis focused on what teachers and learners did by way of 'repair' at these crucial junctures, obeying what Wright termed the 'Correction Imperative'. Very often, however, teachers terminated repair sequences abruptly and either gave a correct answer or simply moved on to the next activity.

The second imperative suggested was the 'Completion Imperative' which derived from administrative pressure to complete the syllabus in a given time (syllabus meant course book in the location being studied). The Completion Imperative pushed teachers to proceed through lessons despite critical moments not having been fully resolved.

Critical moments disturbed the convenient time frames of lessons, but the completion imperative created tension between lesson as content (must complete) and lesson as time frame (unrealistic as lessons rarely if ever followed the lesson plan's route). There was thus tension between lesson goals and the more local moment-by-moment goals of repair as well as the broader tension created by completion and correction imperatives.

Teachers' local discourse management practices were, in terms of time management, influenced strongly by the higher-order imperatives driving from institutional and systemic

---

Concept 3.10   (Continued)

practices (see section 3.3). Correction and completion imperatives can be in conflict where the teacher takes time to treat error which occurs during a lesson, sometimes at the expense of completing a lesson plan. Such incidents can lead in the longer term to the 'loss' of substantial amounts of planned teaching time.

Teachers and time

To understand teachers' time management practices, again we need to see these in the context of their professional lives. Hargreaves (1994) has demonstrated time's definitive role in structuring teachers' work (Quote 3.10). In a socio-political analysis of the influence of time in teachers' lives (Concept 3.12), Hargreaves argues that conflict is the norm for teachers as they struggle to reconcile objective, externally imposed, and subjective, personal, conceptions of time. The core of a teacher's work in the classroom (or front-stage) is contrasted with other aspects of their work and lives in which administrators take decisions which impinge on teachers' 'down time' or traditionally private unstructured time use in back stage regions. Hargreaves also notes how teachers tend to perceive classroom time polychronically. This creates dissonance during periods of innovation because administrators and planning processes tend to be monochronic. They see innovations as relatively clear-cut, single issues whereas for classroom teachers working and thinking polychronically, innovations have to be accommodated among all the other conflicting events and processes that they are managing. Hargreaves observes that teachers tend to slow down the pace of change under these conditions.

Quote 3.10   Hargreaves on teachers and time

Time is a fundamental dimension through which teachers' work is constructed and interpreted by themselves, their colleagues and those who administer and supervise them. Time for the teacher is not just an objective, oppressive constraint but also a subjectively defined horizon of possibility and limitation. Teachers can take time and make time, just as much as they are likely to see time schedules and time commitments as fixed and immutable. Through the prism of time we can therefore begin to see ways in which teachers construct the nature of their work at the same time as they are constrained by it. Time, that is, is a major element in the *structuration* of teachers' work. Time structures the work of teaching and is in turn structured through it.

(1994: 95, author's emphasis)

Concept 3.12   Dimensions of time in teachers' work

Hargreaves distinguishes between four interconnected dimensions of time:

1. **Technical-Rational Time**. Time is viewed as a finite resource or means: it is spent rather than passed. Time can thus be 'managed' and manipulated. This view is ends or objectives driven and lies behind timetable creation, for example.
2. **Micropolitical Time**. How time is measured and divided up in education reflects dominant configurations of power and status. For example, the status of different areas of the curriculum is reflected in the amounts of time they are provided. The distribution of time among teachers is an indication of relative status and seniority, as is time spent doing non-teaching jobs. This varies across stages in education – for example, in Canada, primary school teaching is done mainly by women who spend the great proportion of their time in classrooms, whereas secondary education tends to be male-dominated. This reinforces the fact that secondary school teachers tend to have fewer contact hours.
3. **Phenomenological Time**. Time is experienced subjectively. Classroom time tends to be polychronic (see Concept 7.3) whereas administrative time is monochromic. Classroom time management tends to be sensitive to unpredictability and contingencies and is very much focused on immediate activity and resolution of difficulties.
4. **Sociopolitical Time**. 'The way in which particular views of time come to be administratively dominant' (1994: 107). Hargreaves identifies the separation of administrative and teacher time and the 'colonisation' of teachers' back region' by administrators, through the requirement for non-contact time to become accountable to authority, and, in effect, to become more monochromic.

(after Hargreaves 1994: 96–114)

Teachers have to manage time at several levels at any one time, from the multidimensional 'moment' in a lesson, to the daily and weekly rhythms of working with groups and juggling non-contact time for reading students' work and preparing lessons, to the institutional rhythms and to their own lives. The pressures exerted by the wider time issues such as institutional schedules and personal lives are not constant, and teachers find themselves having to balance competing interests at more or less every juncture of their lives in and out of the classroom. Furthermore, all this must be seen in the context of a teacher's career. Studies of teachers' 'professional life cycles' (Concept 3.13) show how teachers' capacity for, interest in and commitment to their work fluctuates through their lives. Teacher development, growth and change, and the 'stage' at which any individual teacher happens to be, influence their approach to classroom management. In the early stages of a teacher's career, for example, their struggles with classroom control are well documented.

Concept 3.13   A teacher's professional life cycle

STAGE 1 – EXPLORATION 'Beginning' or 'Survival' – characterised by difficulties with classroom control, conflict between ideals or theories and management of complexity and uncertainty in real classrooms, typically leading to 'discovery' of a teacher persona that 'fits'.

STAGE 2 – STABILISATION 'Consolidation' – characterised by movement away from self-concern to concern for students. Routines are developed and mastered, and teacher is more able to manage complexity and uncertainty. Difficult experiences can lead, however, to a degree of self-doubt and reassessment.

STAGE 3 – DIVERSIFICATION 'Experimentation' – characterised by a 'development' or 'innovation' spurt where teachers try out new ideas. Alternatively, teachers could be led into a period of reassessment and self-doubt, brought on by the dullness of classroom teaching or poor working conditions. Commitment can be challenged by disillusionment created by failure of experiments or reforms in which a teacher has participated.

STAGE 4 – SERENITY 'Coming To Terms' – characterised by decline in commitment professionally, but at the same time greater flexibility, tolerance and spontaneity in the classroom. Could be followed by a period of conservatism and rejection of change, aggravated by sense of failure of let-down (can affect young as well as old teachers)

STAGE 5 – DISENGAGEMENT 'Career twilight' – characterised by serene or bitter withdrawal and reinvestment of energies.

NB Stages are not linear and not necessarily age-related. Studies of teachers' lives (e.g. Goodson 1992) have shown that life events are unpredictable and personal experience, social and cultural environments have a great deal of influence on the shaping of a teacher's identity and professional persona.

(after Huberman 1993)

Teaching as a profession has to deal in equal measure with certainties and uncertainties. By structuring time in a timetable, institutions aim to provide a management framework for teachers' and students' classroom time. However, far from providing a teacher with a framework of certainty, the timetable can create as many problems as it solves because time is always scarce, a 'limited resource' (Denscombe 1982) (Quote 3.11). The timetable is a particular case in point: it is out of a teacher's control – a teacher has to take the slots as listed and live with the consequences, which are quite unpredictable (Quote 3.13).

Quote 3.11   Denscombe on limited time

Time is another resource which, as in most organisations, is a scare commodity. Teachers' activity in classrooms needs to take into account the time-span of the lesson, the frequency of meetings and the duration of the course – each of which provides a practical

constraint on the approach to the job which affects virtually all situations. And, although there have been concerted attempts to break the tyranny of lesson periods especially in the primary schools, the influence of the time-table continues to have a characteristically pervasive effect on teachers' perception of their job.
(1982: 256)

Quote 3.12   Lack of control over time at school

There is so much teachers have no control over: timetables, rooms, books, etc. It has been shown that often it is the most trivial constraints imposed by the institution and the situation that exert a powerful influence on what happens in the classroom. Practitioners warn the beginner that things like the timetable may make their lives a misery: 'A class may be angelic at 9.30 am, can be restive by 2 pm and positively murderous by 3.30 pm.'
(Francis 1975: 73–4, in Appel 1995)

Grade 10: 'They are timetabled for three lessons a week, one at the end of the afternoon after a PE lesson, one just before lunch, one very early in the morning.'
(Appel 1995: 13)

Further issues resulting from a consideration of the spatial and temporal dimensions of formal education are explored in section 3.3.

3.3   Managing classrooms without walls

Classroom time has always 'spilled' out of pedagogic space through homework and activities like project work. These activities may best be regarded as 'extensions' of classroom time and space. The homework type of activity is quite different in nature from more recent developments which have led to the evolution of 'the classroom without walls', or the 'virtual classroom', as it has become known. Formal education has been profoundly affected by the 'information revolution' characterised by the spread of mass communications media, in particular the use of information and communications technology (ICT). Consequently, its enclosure and time-boundedness have been transcended. Education can now happen more or less anywhere there is access to a computer linked to the Internet, or a mobile phone, or some other means of 'wireless' communication. It can also happen at any time, since scattered communities of learners living in different places do not have to meet in physical space in order to engage in formal learning. This section briefly reviews what appear to be the main features of 'borderless learning' and their implications for managing these new learning environments.

Extending time and space in formal education

We have seen how forms of student activity such as 'homework' or 'project work' extend the classroom outside both its physical and temporal boundaries, its 'learning space'. There is also a well-established tradition of distance education in contexts such as Australia or Southern Africa, where communities are isolated and personal access to educational opportunity thus restricted. Until recently distance education has been reliant on services like the postal service, and more recently on communications technologies such as live radio and television, or video and audio recordings. The latter have been instrumental in enabling learners to manage study time for themselves. The more recent uptake of the educational opportunities suggested by the Internet has, however, extended learning spaces in ever more complex ways. The age of the 'virtual' classroom has arrived. It creates particular challenges for educators, and raises issues as follows:

- What are the effects on teaching and learning of working without a shared physical location or the collective time frames of conventional face-to-face classrooms?
- Do participants replicate common practices for managing conventional classrooms in extended learning space? For example, do borderless classrooms present more instances of disorder than institutionally-located classrooms?
- Do management practices in borderless learning imply new patterns and forms of participation and engagement? What are the specific discoursal, social, emotional and communication issues of the borderless classroom?

Spatial issues in the borderless classroom

In online learning, the physical space of the classroom has been replaced by 'virtual space' or 'cyberspace' – a computer-mediated context in which learning and teaching can take place (Quote 3.13). It is a very different world from the physical reality of classrooms primarily because when using it we cannot see or hear our classmates or teachers (unless some form of video linkage is provided). Despite the 'connectedness' of the Internet, we are isolated from each other in ways which affect how we experience teaching and learning.

Quote 3.13   Views of electronic space

The internet – 'a range of technologically-mediated spaces of communicative practice.' (Lankshear, Peters and Knobel (2000: 21)

... cyberspace, a place where people surf and navigate and browse through sites with rooms and bulletin boards.
(Bramall 2000: 85)

> One can approach a Web search as a process of locating a series of discrete 'sites' to be seen, with an emphasis on the visual 'product' of each path taken. On the other hand, one can focus on the process of navigation, a process that opens up *spaces* in which to act and interact.
> (McKie 2000: 130)

Only recently have educators started to come to terms with the effects of virtual space on teaching and learning. Kolb (2000: 136) points out that learners need a 'sense of place' online, and that without this it is difficult for learners to feel 'at home'. This has effects on a range of learning management issues such as interpersonal communication, a sense of community and individual engagement. Kolb (2000) argues for a sense of physicality in cyberspace that allows for exploration and also a degree of comfort (Quote 3.14).

Quote 3.14   Kolb on educational web sites

If an educational site is more than a series of pages I flip through, if it is a place where I am willing to linger, then I may have space and time to re-examine and reconstruct how I construe and evaluate information, and re-examine my values. . . . It would be the site or the location . . . that would be a place I could linger in. If I did, then I might be disposed to spend a lot of time on important screenfulls (of information), once I could tell which were the important ones.
(Kolb 2000:136–7)

Kolb also identifies our need to interact in digital space in addition to engaging with information individually. Even in the apparently empty reaches of cyberspace, there are still 'places' which have psychological significance to users, such as websites which we frequently visit and where we feel at home. Kolb further points out our requirement online for places to store things, a form of 'inbuilt memory' (2000: 142) in digital space. Thus, the physical metaphors of digital space – sites; rooms; navigation; connectedness; topologies; storage – are evidence of users' psychological need for dimensions and a sense of geography. It follows that any educational design using online space needs to be designed with the psychology of space in mind – people need to feel 'situated'. Where one is 'positioned' in online encounters – at the center or the periphery of a community – who one 'sits with' – or has relatively instant communication with – are as significant in the discourse of virtual classrooms as in face-to-face encounters. How this is managed in formal learning online is thus critical to the enjoyment and effectiveness of the learning experience.

Furthermore, virtual space for formal learning has boundaries which mark it off from other aspects of the virtual world in the same way that institutions attempt to segregate experience. Online classrooms are still sites for formal education, and they are subject to the same dilemmas and questions as physical classrooms. Sanger (2001) identifies a 'cultural airlock' separating the world of the formal classroom and the unregulated world of the Internet. He notes: 'for [students] a PC is a leisure window...in schools, the PC is a work tool' (2001: 10). In other words, extending learning outside the conventional classroom, using the Internet, could expose learners to different learning possibilities, including the adaptation of its entertainment or leisure uses; the Internet offers interesting possibilities of 'edutainment', whereby the best media practices and conventions are brought to bear on learning content, rendering it attractive and accessible in ways unimaginable in the conventional classroom (a teacher could also choose to bring the Internet into the classroom using a device such as the electronic whiteboard if it is available) (Quote 3.15). The question of boundaries between educational and non-educational worlds still exists in cyberspace, but the contrast may actually be even more stark online.

Quote 3.15   Lemke on technology and the future of schools

Schooling is just one, relatively recent educational arrangement. We all know that today many functions of classroom education are becoming technologically obsolete. Students will soon learn how to get information they need on any subject, including explanations and help in understanding them at their own level, from searching for sources on the internet, as they would in any good library. The teaching of many basic concepts and skills will soon be packaged attractively in combinations of videos, animations, simulations and interactive games that will be easily accessible. (2002a: 44–5)

Reconfiguring time in borderless education

ICT not only frees learners from the need to attend lessons at an institution or place for formal learning, but also enables students to work *when* they want. If they are working online, they may be relatively limited in physical space (if not cyberspace) by their computer's need for a power supply (although battery technology and wireless reception for the Internet enable those who are fortunate enough to overcome these restrictions). However, there is potentially no restriction on *when* a learner can participate in learning experiences online.

An interesting paradox of time-use online is that while the movement of information can be sent extremely rapid, people are not obliged to respond to or process it immediately. Users can take control, and, as Kolb (2000) notes, users like to linger on web sites they like, thus deliberately slowing down the experience. On the other hand they can browse through web pages at great speed in attempts to locate particular information sources or types. These are emergent skills for Internet use which experienced users are likely to transfer to online learning.

While classroom communication is typically synchronous, online communication can be either synchronous or asynchronous (Concept 3.13). Asynchronous participation in online activities, arguably the most common mode of participation, places the onus of managing learning onto the learner, who may not possess the skills or temperament to successfully overcome the apparent lack of pressure to perform that the virtual classroom can produce in events such as online discussion or conferencing (Concept 3.15). The 'any time' nature of learning on the Internet is not always seen by students as an advantage, and brings strong emotional reactions from some learners who may crave more structured uses of time to overcome the Internet's capacity to 'stretch' time in ways that classroom learning does not (Quote 3.16).

There is also the paradox that formal courses have time boundaries online, just as they do institutionally, although learning events themselves may last for several days rather than hours. The 'cultural airlock' which separates the timelessness of the web from the long-term time-boundedness of a course has the effect of insulating participants from the real world in ways as pervasive as those affecting time and space in the classroom. Long-term learning engagement is measured in just the same ways as face-to-face learning, and the effects of this on participants' responses to online work are likely to have similarities with face-to-face experiences. Time still pushes and pulls – deadlines still loom – and ultimately the institution in which the course is based has control over the pace of events through devices such as staging of learning events, requirements for assignments to be submitted and so on. If a group has worked closely together online they still 'leave' the course and the contacts which have become important for them for the duration of the course. They still 'mourn' the loss of their learning community.

Concept 3.14   Tasks and time online

Synchronous Communication – communication happens in real time (e.g. in an online 'chat' facility – written messages). All learners are online at the same time (even though they may be separated by time zones and geography) engaged in a common activity.

Asynchronous Communication – communication happens when learners are able or wish to communicate. Learners can log on to a system when it suits them. Participants in a programme can 'multi-task', accessing different sources of information when they wish, in one or several visits to a learning site.

Quote 3.16   Salmon on the problems of time online

In advising 'e-moderators':

You will find the concept of time is emotive and value-laden for both e-moderators and participants. The key issue is that the advantages of 'any time/any place' learning and

---

Quote 3.16   (Continued)

teaching mean that time is not bounded and contained as it is when attending a lecture of a face-to-face training session. Although a face-to-face tutorial may last two hours, it has a clear start and finish time and is rarely interrupted by anything else. The participants are either there or they are not, and if they are, they cannot be doing much else. Online is not like that. It has a reputation for 'eating time'.
(2004: 63)

Far from eliminating the problems of space and time-bound formal education, as many of its proponents claim, online learning has its own problems, many of them related to the nature of the medium itself, many of them replications of problems endemic to conventional education. Dropout rates from online and distance courses can be very high – as high as 80 per cent – suggesting an amplification of some of the difficulties of face-to-face learning. Written 'discussion threads' are unfamiliar learning modes for many learners; the technology can seem daunting, and the isolation and perceived lack of support and structure in many programmes can be demotivating. Rowntree (1992: 72) points out that 'learners without support are most liable to delay their completion of a programme or drop out altogether. They simply have noone to turn to when they run into problems.' Thus, while online learning environments have the potential for both autonomous and collaborative learner activity, they still have to be managed and nurtured, just as physical classrooms do.

Summary

Two of the most important consequences of formal education are its time-boundedness and its sense of spatial 'enclosure. Time and space have the effect of 'framing' education; teachers manage classrooms by being masters of many frames of activity at once. As we have seen in this chapter, the wider educational imperatives which initially led to the emergence of the spatial and temporal frames of classroom activity are ever-present and play an important role in the lives of teachers and learners. More recent technological developments promise to overcome some of the constraints and difficulties of conventional educational spatial and temporal frames, but create their own new set of issues as they mediate learning.

Further reading

Erickson and Shultz (1992) is a wide-ranging study of learners' experiences of the curriculum in action, in the classroom.
Goffman (1969 and 1974) provides a social theory of variation in human behaviour in different spheres of activity.

Hall's books (1966 and 1984) are readable and comprehensive studies of the influence of space and time in human life.

Hargreaves (1994) is a powerful study of teachers' lives with good material on how time affects teachers' and learners' lives.

Leask (2001) contains papers addressing online teaching and learning issues from a pedagogic viewpoint.

Murphy, Walker and Webb (2001) is a comprehensive collection of papers about the issues of teaching and learning online.

4
Classrooms as Multidimensional Contexts

4.1 Multidimensional classrooms

Classrooms are complex contexts for learning. This is an outcome of their designed and institutionalised character, and because of the minute-by-minute dynamics of classroom encounters. Complexity is their most definitive quality, reflected in well-known descriptions of classrooms (Quote 4.1).

Quote 4.1   Classrooms as complex

Classrooms are crowded and busy places in which groups of students who vary in interests and abilities must be organised and directed. Moreover these groups assemble regularly for long periods of time to accomplish a wide variety of tasks. Many events occur simultaneously, teachers must react often and immediately to circumstances, and the course of events is highly unpredictable.
(Doyle 1990, in Watkins et al. 1996)

Life in Classrooms
Stray thoughts, sudden insights, meandering digressions, irrelevant asides, and other minor disruptions constantly ruffle the smoothness of the instructional dialogue. Experienced teachers accept this state of affairs and come to look upon surprise and uncertainty as natural features in their environment. They know, or come to know that the path of educational progress more closely resembles the flight of a butterfly than the flight of a bullet.
(Jackson 1968: 167)

Classroom complexity results from the interaction of several variables, for which Doyle (1986: 394) claims a degree of universality, regardless of different educational ideologies or teaching methodologies (Concept 4.1). Doyle's conceptualisation captures the challenge of managing this complexity from the teacher's point of view, although it is worth reminding ourselves that learners, too, have to manage these conditions. They may also experience other variables and in different ways, from their individual and collective perspectives. Classrooms are multi-sensory contexts for both teachers and learners, in which interaction is worked out in time. This requires the emergence of relatively stable management practices to cope with the immediacy of action – as Doyle points out, 'a single event can have multiple consequences' (1986: 394). Unpredictability and simultaneity compound the complexity.

Concept 4.1   Features of the classroom context

Doyle describes classrooms as:

1. MULTIDIMENSIONAL: classrooms are home to many events and activities; classrooms are crowded; the students have different abilities and preferences and work with a limited range of resources to reach their goals. ' . . . a single event can have multiple consequences.'
2. SIMULTANEOUS: many things occur at the same time; different people are doing different things in parallel. Doyle notes that simultaneity increases when a whole class organisation is changed to small groups.
3. IMMEDIACY: events in classrooms happen quickly as well as simultaneously. People thus have little time to think before they act.
4. UNPREDICTABILITY: 'classroom events take unexpected turns'. Because there is so much interaction it is very difficult to predict how activities will happen on different days with different groups.
5. PUBLICNESS: classrooms are public arenas – almost everything is visible or audible to most people present. This can amplify the effect of particular events.
6. HISTORY: Classroom groups meet regularly over long periods and thus accumulate a common store of mutual experiences, routines, rituals and norms of behaviour. Doyle points out that the early meetings of classroom groups often shape future events.

(after Doyle 1986: 394–5)

A further issue raised by Doyle's description is the extent to which a classroom is both public – Erickson and Schultz (1992: 469) see the classroom as a place where interaction is 'audienced' – and also semi-private, in the sense that its shared history and the immediate outcome of learning emerges in a context physically cut off from the rest of the institution in which it resides. The accumulation of 'history' is a significant aspect of classroom life. It includes the outcomes of teachers' and learners' informal classroom learning and is evidence that there are always two sorts of learning going on in classrooms. Formal learning is the outcome of designed classroom activity. Informal learning also occurs as teachers and learners 'learn how to' manage their classrooms through experience and participation in educational discourse.

These local classroom issues are, as we have seen in Chapters 2 and 3, also influenced by the wider web of institutional, social and cultural contexts in which classrooms are located. Classrooms themselves are also social and cultural contexts in their own right, as well as being the crucible in which influences of external origin are locally mediated. There is enormous variation between classrooms (Concept 4.2) in terms of their underlying purposes, the stages of education and their geographical location. The notion of 'the classroom' in any generic sense is thus quite misleading, as universal characteristics of classrooms like time and space are always subject to local interpretation, and are culturally relative. From the viewpoint of different learners and teachers it is probably more appropriate to refer to 'my (*or* our) classroom'.

Concept 4.2   Variegated classrooms – key features

Classrooms vary in the following main ways:

- **Educational stages.** Typically mass education is divided into primary, secondary and further/higher stages. With the growth of adult education and other initiatives to promote 'lifelong learning' – in organisations, as well as in institutions – a further 'stage' has been created. Many classrooms of this type exist outside the framework of institutionalised educational opportunity and serve different purposes. The age (and possibly the gender) of learners is thus a significant variable, and possibly the gender of teachers, too. The terms of attendance – voluntary or compulsory – add a further dimension.
- **Learning purposes.** Classrooms are created to provide learning opportunities in different prescribed areas of knowledge and skill. The type of knowledge and/or skill and the ways in which classroom participants value it will influence many aspects of classroom life. Mathematics classrooms are different from language classrooms in part because of the respective conceptual nature of the two 'subjects'. They also differ in the ways in which modes of communication – verbal, visual and 'actional' are employed (Kress et al 2001) The holistic, 'subject-free' curricula of some primary classrooms differ from highly specialised higher education curricula in which knowledge tends to be broken down into ever-smaller components. These differences affect many aspects of classroom life, from the types of furniture and equipment in the classroom to the nature of learning tasks themselves.
- **Socio-cultural context.** There is enormous variation between classrooms globally. The societies and cultural contexts of which they are a part and emerge from influence virtually every aspect of classroom life, including both stage and learning purpose. Thus, for example, there are great differences between the character of primary classrooms in urban and rural areas in the UK, and also in different parts of the same urban area. Secondary English foreign language classrooms in Uganda and Malaysia differ – the English language also has a different significance to the peoples of these two countries. University Linguistics classrooms in India are not the same as those for the same discipline in Russia.

2 Classrooms As Social Gatherings (Communities and Cultures)

We have discussed the fundamental influence of space on classroom life, but despite its deep significance, it is not its most important characteristic. Classrooms are populated by teachers and learners. The social geography of who they are and what they do is the defining feature of classrooms. Classrooms are deeply and fundamentally social contexts (Quote 4.2). This has important implications. Managing classrooms is more than the organisation of instruction, or keeping order, or using classroom space and time. Rather it primarily concerns managing people, their relationships with each other, and the activities they jointly undertake.

Quote 4.2   Language classrooms as social worlds

The language classroom: . . . the gathering, for a given period of time, of two or more persons, (one of whom generally assumes the role of instructor) for the purpose of language learning.
(van Lier 1988: 47)

If we learn a language in the company of others in a classroom, then the nature of this social action is not merely a superficial frame for our work on language data. Social relationships in the classroom orchestrate what is made available for learning, how learning is done and what we achieve. The relationships and the purposeful social action of teaching and learning are directly realised through the discourse in which we participate during lessons.
(Breen 2001b: 309)

Recent debate and research about classrooms in Applied Linguistics and language education (Quote 4.3), has revolved around three main social 'facts':

1. Classrooms contain GROUPS of people, usually one teacher and any number of students from one (van Lier 1996) to even 300 or 400. Brumfit's (1984) notion of 'normality' of class size thus is clearly one that would only be recognised in a few contexts, not where large numbers in often cramped spaces are the norm, as described by West (1960) and more recently documented by Coleman (2002) and colleagues in international studies of large classes (Field Note 4.1).

Diary Extract 4.1   Working with large groups (Sudan – secondary school)

First afternoon session with the Form 1s. They are between 12 and 14 years old, all boys. 112 of them (that's what the register says) are crammed into a standard size classroom (designed for 40 students at most). Rather than two per desk, there are four and five

---

Diary Extract 4.1   (Continued)

(luckily that are not big and more or less fit in). There is a smallish area in front of the worn-out chalkboard for me to stand in. The desks are only a metre or so from the front wall. As I enter the room the class all stands and choruses 'Good afternoon, sir.' Lots of scraping of shoes on the floor, jostling and smiling. I respond to their greeting and ask them to sit down. Should I really take the register? It'll take half the lesson, surely. So where to begin?

The very existence a learning group implies social and social-psychological realities. As Littlewood (1981) points out, classrooms are 'real' social contexts in their own right. It follows that classrooms must share some of the features of any social context, and are not 'unreal' contexts, a further point against the in/out-of-school dichotomy discussed in Chapter 2. In fact, countless thousands of children spend most of their waking lives in classrooms, with profound effects on their patterns of learning and their socialisation. This is the essence of the point made by Claxton (1984). Schools and classrooms are places where children experience a range of social encounters.

2. Legutke and Thomas's (1991) notion of a *community* with specific goals – in their case reading and learning – emphasises the social nature of the classroom as well as its purpose – learning. How a learning group defines itself as a community and the extent to which it develops a collective identity is an important classroom management issue, and there is evidence that informal processes bring this about in the course of a group's history as a community, as Doyle (1986) has hinted, in addition to any attempts by teachers to 'form' their learning group.

Quote 4.3   Classrooms as social contexts

In a typical classroom, there is likely to be at least one teacher and somewhere in excess, in normal school systems, of 30 students.
(Brumfit 1984: 17)

... the classroom is a real social context in its own right, where learners and teachers enter into equally real social relationships with each other.
(Littlewood 1981: 44)

... for most children, school is an opportunity for *social* exploration. If school was not compulsory many children would still turn up to see their friends.
(Claxton 1984: 236)

... the nature of the classroom as a community of readers and learners.
(Legutke and Thomas 1991: 16)

Any classroom, in its social composition, is a microcosm of the wider society in which it is located. For it to function, a classroom community realises its own values and priorities through either implicitly or accepted procedures and routines.
(Breen and Littlejohn 2000: 20)

3. The notions of 'community' and 'learning purpose' define the social and learning activity of classroom groups. Both community and learning purpose also link the classroom to the wider worlds of the school, the family, the peer group and the community at large. Breen and Littlejohn (2000) remind us that students and teachers bring a 'slice' of society with them to classroom life, and that they therefore carry with them value systems, identities and priorities which they contribute to the community, and which the community can influence during classroom encounters. The fact that this is done publicly (Doyle 1986) further contributes to its problematical nature, due to the ever-present threat to participants' face and self-esteem.

Classrooms as cultures

The notion of 'classroom as culture' has been fairly widely adopted in Applied Linguistics literature (Allwright and Bailey 1991: 1) following Breen's (1985; 2001a) seminal paper in which he argues that classrooms are most profitably seen as 'cultures', although sometimes unproblematically (Quote 4.4). The 'culture' metaphor is a helpful and generative concept in discussion and analysis of classroom management. It integrates classroom socio-cultural and cognitive processes into one theoretical framework. However, 'culture' is an amorphous and 'tricky' construct requiring further explanation before we examine the cultural features of language classrooms identified by Breen (2001a).

Quote 4.4   Classrooms as cultures

. . . the individual classroom can be considered (and studied as) a cultural entity.
(Allwright and Bailey 1991: 1)

Just as gardens of coral were granted magical realities by Trobriand islanders, a language class – outwardly a gathering of people with an assumed common purpose – is an arena of subjective and intersubjective realities which are worked out, changed and maintained. *And these realities are not trivial background to the tasks of teaching and learning a language.* They locate and define the new language itself as if it never existed before, and they continually specify and mould the activities of teaching and learning. In essence, the metaphor of classroom as coral gardens insists that we perceive the language class as a genuine culture and worth investigating as such.
(Breen 2001a: 128, author's emphasis)

Defining 'culture'

In order to reach an adequate definition of the idea of 'culture', two common conceptualisations require attention. (The main arguments are summarised in Concept 4.3.)

Culture and ethnicity   We are familiar with constructs like 'Japanese culture' in everyday parlance. Roberts and Sarangi (1993) point out the narrowness and dangers of such nomenclature, commenting that in the context of contemporary Britain, 'culture' has come to be seen as 'fixed sets of practices and beliefs defined by (immigrant communities') differences with those of the (white) majority' (1993: 101). Such 'differences' (also noted by Scollon and Scollon 1995) are also used as an 'unproblematic explanation for difficulties in communication where participants are from different ethnic backgrounds' (1993: 101). Holliday (1999) also criticises the ethnolinguistic conception of 'culture' in everyday use as a construct which contains traces of 'culturalism', or ethnic stereotyping. Holliday consequently distinguishes between 'large cultures' ('Mexican culture') and a 'small culture', defined as 'any significant social grouping' (1999: 237).

Culture as a set of practices   In Chapter 2, we have seen that educationalists like Bruner regard the role of formal classroom learning is to provide a venue for 'culture learning', in the sense of learning the successful cultural practices of societies – for example, the 'scientific method' – in which we live. Bruner (1986) notes that culture is dynamic and open to change and development and likens it to a forum where meanings are negotiated between participants, and actions are explained. The word 'culture' has also moved into contemporary everyday speech in expressions such as 'the culture of blame' in society at large, or the 'culture of spin' of Tony Blair's New Labour government (from 1997) in the UK. These cultures are in the process of constant renegotiation since their relatively recent emergence, and signify that many people are now familiar with the idea of a culture being a *way in which we do things* rather than the 'large culture' ('national group's customs and habits') meaning, although the two are often used interchangeably. We have seen the notion of 'culture' being used with reference to teachers' working groups in Chapter 3, the key elements of Hargreaves' (1994) definition being beliefs, habits, values and assumed ways of doing things.

There appears to be a growing consensus that 'ways of doing things' is the nexus around which an understanding of culture can be developed. In social life, including educational practice, discourse is our primary means of establishing and maintaining social relations and 'getting things done', suggesting strong connections between culture and discourse. Discourse practices such as recontextualisation are thus the essence of classroom cultures (Chapter 2). As Roberts and Sarangi (1993: 101) emphasise, discoursal explanations of culture also entail consideration of aspects of both power relations between members (and non-members) and also ideological influences on beliefs, attitudes and values. Both power relations and ideology play a major part in classroom life, with ideology partly enshrined in curriculum design and teaching materials (Littlejohn 1998), and power a defining feature of teacher-student relations in all formal learning contexts (Keppler and Luckman 1991).

Scollon and Scollon (1995) and Sarangi (1994) see discourse as extending to both linguistic and non-linguistic behaviours and practices; Scollon and Scollon also at the level of non-verbal communication – important for understanding the multimodality of classrooms (Kress et al. 2001); Sarangi (after Fairclough 1991) at the level of social practice. From the point of view of understanding classroom cultures these are significant issues, which connect the internal classroom world with the external social and cultural world through discourse as a tool for making and negotiating culture. This conception also overcomes the limited notion of 'discourse as linguistic', which Holliday (1999) cites as a limitation of the discoursal perspective provided by Sarangi and others.

Concept 4.3   Culture – some definitions

1. Arising from issues in intercultural communication
Culture is viewed as in different ways:

- preference for different patterns of behaviour
- 'background' and 'resources' used by people: accumulated by groups
- behaviour or fixed values and beliefs

Problems

- 'celebration of miscommunication' and focus on interethnic differences
- seeing culture as fixed in terms of resources, patterns, behaviour, fixed values
- 'culture' as a necessary and sufficient explanation of intercultural difficulties
- reduction of linguistic differences to 'cultural' differences
- consequent stereotyping and 'culturalising'

Responses

- Culture is a way of understanding discourse systems (ideology, socialisation, forms of discourse – verbal and non-verbal, face systems) (Scollon and Scollon 1995:126)
- Culture as a process of doing rather than being. Therefore constantly in process of forming and reforming.
- Culture as ideology and lived practice (after Hall 1980 in Sarangi and Roberts 1993:99). A complex political and dynamic phenomenon.
- Social relations and interethnic relations are 'accomplished' in interaction as people create inferences about each other moment by moment in everyday encounters.

Concept 4.3   (Continued)

2. Arising from Applied Linguistics research on classrooms
The need to understand language classroom life presents problems because of its multi-faceted nature (see Doyle 1986) and highly complex.
'A particular culture ... entails particular relationships between social activities and psychological process and changes.'
'culture locates comprehension within the intersubjective construction of meaningfulness and the subjective reinterpretation of whatever may be rendered comprehensible.'
'The culture of the class *generates knowledges* ...'
'the classroom as culture extends across islands of intersubjective meaning and depths of subjective intentions which only rarely touch the surface of talk and which the discourse itself often deliberately hides. The discourse of lessons will mainly *symbolise* what participants contribute to those lessons and it will not signify what they actually invest in them or derive from them.' (Breen 1985 and 2001: 128, author's emphases)

3. Arising from the need to find an adequate definition of culture to account for classroom life
(Holliday 1999)
'... "large" (culture) signifies "ethnic", "national" or "international"; and "small" (culture) signifies any significant social grouping.' (1999: 237)
'Small culture is (thus) a dynamic, ongoing group process which operates in changing circumstances to enable group members to make sense of and operate meaningfully within those circumstances.' (1999: 248)
Emphasis on individuals' 'culture-making' capacities in formation, growth and maintenance.
'Small culture (a heuristic means of interpreting group behaviour) is ... more to do with activities taking place within a group ...' (1999: 250)

Features of classroom as culture

Breen's (2001a) cultural metaphor of 'classroom as coral gardens' derives from his advocacy of an anthropological approach to classroom research. Such an approach is more likely to lead to true understanding of the individual and collective social and psychological realities of classroom life than either normative or linguistic approaches (Quote 4.5).

Quote 4.5   Breen on classroom as culture

... a holistic and integrated framework which incorporates the experimental and discoursal attributes of the classroom, but which also locates these attributes within a richer cluster of typical characteristics' of classrooms.
... the classroom as culture and the features which represent its cultural nature are *universal* to language classrooms wherever they may be, a particular classroom will evolve both individual features and a synthesis of features in particular ways at particular times. And it is this synthesis of features which is the culture of a classroom group.
(2001: 135)

Breen has identified a series of features of classroom culture (Concept 4.4) which, taken both individually and in dynamic interaction with each other, provide a theoretical framework for investigating the complex classroom world. There is some overlap between these features and Doyle's (1986) categories – interactivity, immediacy, unpredictability. There is also a clear relationship between the norm-seeking nature of classroom culture and Doyle's notion of shared history. From the perspective of linguistic and non-linguistic, and social and political discoursal practices, a central element of the history of a group is the creation of its culture, including shared knowledge of its discoursal conventions. The inherent conservatism and tendency towards normed relationships is also intimately tied up with discoursal processes. A question remains as to whether or not norms can be challenged and whether or not change is possible, especially when new ideas about pedagogy or learning are introduced or find their way into existing classroom cultures. Breen is, however, like Doyle, mainly concerned with the *internal* dynamics of classroom life. This apparent limitation can nevertheless be overcome by using the notions of asymmetry in power relationships and differentiation between participants to establish connections with external social, economic, cultural and political forces.

Concept 4.4   Features of classrooms as culture

Interactive: participants are involved in verbal and non-verbal interaction, from ritualised to highly unpredictable; from easily to problematically interpreted.

Differentiated: the classroom is an amalgam and permutation of the different social realities of the participants.

Collective: the psychological reality of the classroom group results from the juxtaposition of personal learning experiences and communal teaching/learning activities and conventions.

Normative: Individual cultural membership is evaluated against certain norms and conventions – individuals need to show they belong in the culture.

Asymmetrical: teachers are expected to know what learners don't know, and this conveys different and rights and privileges to teachers. There are also asymmetrical relationships among students.

Conservative: classroom cultures seek social and emotional equilibrium and it is not easy to innovate in such contexts.

Jointly constructed: teacher and students construct and reconstruct knowledge in lessons. Lessons are rarely straightforward journeys.

Immediately significant: the day-to-day interpersonal rationalisation of what is to be done in classrooms, why and how gives the culture immediate significance to participants who invest in it as it unfolds.

(after Breen 2001a)

The classroom as culture is an outcome of both the social and psychological processes of cultural formation, and the continuity and extension of existing cultures. In formal education, this 'small culture' formation process is enacted many times over during formal education, as children and then adults form and reform groups with new teachers and peers during their lives in institutions. Emerging local rules for dealing with classroom management issues (as participants employ their emerging cultural toolkits which enable them to negotiate classroom cultures) and what participants bring with them to new encounters as cultural residues from previous encounters serve to create a rich discourse world. Using this framework, an analysis of classroom activities promises to reveal the bases of the cultures of classroom management and their associated discourses (Concept 4.5).

Concept 4.5   Cultures of classroom management – key features

- Active, dynamic and ongoing *processes* initiating and responding to internal and external realities. 'Lived and learned practice' ('Learning is the engine of practice, and practice is the history of that learning' – Wenger 1998: 96).
- Subjective and intersubjective meanings emerge, and are negotiated and explicated through the discourse systems of the culture.
- Bound up with ideology, power relations and socialisation.
- Accomplished through discourse systems.

Classrooms as communities of practice

The idea of 'communities of practice' extends and refines the 'cultural' characterisation of classrooms. Wenger's (1998) work, building on Lave and Wenger (1991), provides insights into the processes of daily informal learning in social, and especially organisational, contexts (Concept 4.6). The continued social encounters between members of a community of practice are the means by which they build and spread, and maintain and renew knowledge in an organisation; in short, the ways in which they learn.

Concept 4.6   Communities of practice

A community of practice is an intrinsic condition for the existence of knowledge, not least because it provides the interpretive support necessary for making sense of its heritage. (Lave and Wenger 1991: 98)

Being alive as human beings means that we are constantly engaged in the pursuit of enterprises of all kinds, from ensuring our physical survival to seeking the most lofty pleasures. As we define these enterprises and engage in their pursuit together, we interact with each other and with the world and we tune our relations with each other and with the world accordingly. In other words we learn.

Over time, this collective learning results in practices that reflect both the pursuit of our enterprises and the attendant social relations. These practices are thus the property of a kind of community created over time by the sustained pursuit of a shared enterprise. It makes sense, therefore, to call these kinds of communities *communities of practice*. (Wenger 1998: 45)

NB: Wenger prefers the term 'community of practice' to 'culture' (1998: 72) although there are many overlaps between the two concepts as actually used (Holliday 1999, for example).

(after Wenger 1998 and Lave/Wenger 1991)

Communities of practice are informally constituted, and any 'knower' can, if required, act as a 'helper' for other community members, especially newcomers to the community. Newcomers or novices have to learn about a community's practices in order to engage successfully in routine activity, and are normally assisted in doing so, or in less fortunate circumstances, are excluded. The processes of learning they experience are very similar to those described in other informal settings, relying on sustained interaction between members, with helpers fulfilling a variety of roles, and the collective achievement of the community's tasks. This happens through mutual engagement by members in the daily negotiation and renegotiation of the meaning of experiences. What is also significant about this type of learning, as with all human learning, is that it creates its own history. For a classroom 'community', therefore, their learning about how to perform becomes a collective resource and reference point for future learning, as expertise is built up and held in common by members.

All of us belong to many communities of practice at any one time, at home, in the workplace and in the informal social groups of which we are members. Swales (1988) refers to them as 'discourse communities – local groups with shared communicative genres. 'They are an integral part of our daily lives' (Wenger 1998: 7), but are rarely referred to directly, because their existence is tacit. In the context of our discussion of classroom management, a classroom group is a community of practice and also a collection of overlapping communities of practice to which the group members belong. Classroom groups are communities of practice because members are learning and participating in the practices of education and of teaching and learning. In classrooms, a great deal of 'learning to operate' occurs as a group establishes its routines and practices, drawing from collective prior experience and from the day-to-day negotiation of meaning, through informal participation and engagement with other members of the community. Lortie (1975) terms the process by which students learn about classrooms and teaching through participation in daily life 'an apprenticeship of observation'. Its particular significance for classroom management is dealt with in Chapter 9 where we examine how teachers learn about classroom management.

This experience of learning is 'natural' and informal, but, because a classroom is a task-specific environment, it is also goal-directed. As children learn through practice, they also by engaging in the set tasks learn how different 'adult' disciplines work. The process of legitimate peripheral participation – of gradually progressing from marginal to central participation in a community of practice (Lave and Wenger 1991) (Concept 4.7) is in itself a key process and goal of learning. Newcomers gradually acquire the knowledge and skills to become fuller members of both a classroom community, and the wider discourse community of the discipline they are studying. This involves participating in learning opportunities generated while interacting with experienced, established members of a community. It also entails learning to interact in the social world of the classroom. A teacher new to an established group often has to experience a process of legitimate peripheral participation as a newcomer to an established community of practice, despite tan apparent superiority in status, which has, in reality, to be established through participation.

Concept 4.7   'Legitimate peripheral participation'

Lave and Wenger have coined this phrase to describe the process by which newcomers learn to become members of a community of practice. They see the process of learning as one of 'changing participation and identity transformation' (Wenger 1998: 11) rather than a traditional master/apprentice or mentor/mentee relationship. They point out that 'required learning takes place not so much through the reification of a curriculum as through modified forms of participation that are structured to open the practice to non-members' (Wenger 1998: 100).

Wenger argues that 'educational processes based (like apprenticeship) on actual participation are effective in fostering learning not just because they are better pedagogical ideas, but more fundamentally because they are "epistemologically correct".... There is a match between knowing and learning, between the nature of competence and the process by which it is acquired, shared and extended.' (1998: 101–2)

In many ways the idea of communities of practice is a more appropriate analytical framework for classroom life than 'culture'. While both refer to the same issues and processes, 'practice' provides a more satisfactory explanation for what classroom groups do. The concept of practice covers both the social and the task-related or pedagogic aspects of classroom life, and legitimate peripheral participation accounts for the informal learning and socialisation of classroom members. What Wenger does not account for, however, is the precise nature of the discourse itself through which legitimate peripheral participation is achieved. This will be examined later in this chapter and in Chapter 7.

Classrooms as 'ecologies'

An ecological view of classrooms amalgamates cultural and community of practice perspectives. The classroom is at the centre of the formal educational context, as Gaises' 'crucible' metaphor aptly reminds us. At the same time, it is a complex and multi-dimensional system (Quote 4.6). The system emerges from the dynamic and interaction of learning goals, learning opportunities, learners and learning and teachers and teaching in classroom contexts. As van Dam (2002: 258) puts it, 'classroom cultures are emergent in everyday practices'. This arises partly as the outcome of the workings of the dynamic system for managing the relationships between the various elements and processes, and is also the essence of the system itself. The daily practices of a learning group, as they work together, accumulate into norms and histories, building the culture (or ecosystem) from the bottom up as they learn to cope with and create the unexpected and the regular. Classroom management cannot, therefore, in an ecological view, be described in cause and effect terms. Moreover, neither is the classroom 'nested' in a hierarchy of social and cultural worlds: rather, the various worlds *intersect* in the classroom, in an ecological relationship. The classroom is thus part of a much larger web of relations. The classroom system interconnects with social and cultural systems outside. The ecological metaphor also allows for a more holistic view of classrooms closer to the real experience of teachers and learners. For this reason it holds promise of research directions that teachers and learners which teachers and learners follow on their own terms. Learners, in an ecological view of learning, interact with whatever is available in the classroom, whether it is pedagogically intentional or accidental, linguistic or gestural. For learners, learning is naturally multi-channelled, and managing this requires a wide range of appropriate social and discourse skills.

Quote 4.6   Classrooms as central and complex

. . . the classroom is the crucible – the place where teachers and learners come together and language learning, we hope, happens. It happens, when it happens, as a result of the reactions among the elements that go into the crucible – the learners and the teachers. They do not however, go in 'empty-handed'. The learners bring with them their whole experience of learning and of life in classrooms, along with their

---

Quote 4.6   (Continued)

own reasons for being there, and their own particular needs that they hope to see satisfied. And the teacher brings experience too, of life and learning, and of teaching. The teacher also brings into the classroom the syllabus, often embodied in a textbook. But no matter what they all bring, everything still depends on how they react to each other (learner to learner as well as teacher to learner) when they all get together in the classroom.
(Gaises 1980, in Allwright and Bailey 1991: 18)

[A 'systems' view] At the classroom level, we have interaction between the presage factors, *students*, and their characteristics, individually or collectively, and *teaching context*, comprising the teacher and the school-determined constraints (curriculum, rules of interaction between teachers and students etc) which together focus on the central *process* issue of how students go about learning and what the *product* or outcome of learning is.
(Briggs and Moore 1993: 450)

Quote 4.7   van Lier on ecologies of learning

From an ecological perspective, the learner is immersed in an environment full of potential meanings. These meanings become available gradually as the learner acts and interacts within and with this environment. . . .

The context is not there to provide input . . . to a passive recipient. The environment provides a 'semiotic budget' (analogous to the energy budget of an ecosystem) within which the active learner engages in meaning-making activities with others, who may be more, equally, or less competent in linguistic terms.
(2000: 246, 252)

Van Lier (1996a, 2000) has described the complex reality of classrooms in ecological terms. Using ecological terminology, he claims that 'it is useful to regard the classroom as a complex adaptive system' (1996a: 38). The classroom system, in this view, has the capacity to self-organise and to change in response to external events (Quote 4.7). Self-regulating and self-organising classroom systems therefore by definition resist or accommodate external attempts to influence their workings. Exploring the classroom ecology may thus enable us to go beyond the multi-faceted surface described by so many researchers and see how social and cultural processes contribute to its complexity, and interconnectedness. The ecological view is thus a means of exploring the dynamic relationships between learners, and the contexts of learning which feature teachers, learning materials and the wider context beyond the immediate learning site (Concept 4.9).

Concept 4.9   An ecological view of language learning

1. A non-linear view of language learning – order emerges from disorder during learning. No direct cause and effect relationships. An ecological view posits many levels of relevance, from individual emotions to institutional life.
2. Interaction between, for example learners and language, is meaningful, rather than the learners and language themselves. Local interaction can emerge in broader patterns of social organisation.
3. Language systems are seen as constrained rather than rule-governed. Equilibrium is a temporary state. Learners learn to adapt themselves to the total learning environment – language learning is more than learning the system; it is also about learning how to relate to people who already use the system.
4. Language learning takes place on many timescales, and is influenced by memory of previous encounters. Timescales vary from minute-to-minute conversation to professional or social life in which various capacities to use language are integrated.
5. 'Teaching and learning . . . is an open process mediated by various semiotic tools in various activities' (2002: 21). In order to become a member of an institutional community, members have to learn how to use these tools to engage with the community successfully. This requires engagement with discourse processes. New or transformed entities can also emerge from the processes of mediation (e.g. unplanned classroom activities have the potential to generate new learning).

(after Kramsch 2002: 16–21)

The implications for classroom management of an ecological view of classrooms are significant – classroom management, rather than controlling or steering the classroom, is one process within the totality of the system, one of many activities. Classroom management is a form of systemic initiation and self-regulation of activity and naturally blends into the classroom ecology. The implications of this will be explored in Chapter 5.

Classrooms as 'discourse villages'

Wenger's theoretical work on communities of practice lacks a linguistic dimension – talk – and therefore does not adequately account for arguably the most prominent feature of classroom life. For Barnes (1976), the defining feature of classrooms is that they are 'talk-rich', a fact that informs Mercer's apt metaphor of classrooms as 'discourse villages' (Quote 4.8). Edwards and Mercer (1987) have pointed out that the process of education is 'essentially a process of cognitive socialization through language' (1987: 157). Talk itself is also a means of creating and defining the classroom context, and is a major resource for making sense of the context (Quote 4.9).

Quote 4.8   Classrooms and talk

Schools are places where people talk to one another. And where they write for one another. Nothing could be more obvious, but is it as straightforward as that?
(Barnes 1976: 11)

... [the] classroom is a discourse village – a small language outpost from which roads lead to larger communities of educated discourse.
(Mercer 1995: 83)

Schools are full of language, from the teacher's lecturing, the counsellor's good advice, the textbook's factual information, and the vice principal's voice blaring through the intercom, to the whispered wisecracks of a friend and the scribbled comments in the notebook. There can surely be no doubt that something so central to all human activity should be the centrepiece of all educational endeavours.
(van Lier 1996a: 95/6)

Communities use language to operate, but they do not simply take language 'off the peg' and use it as given. One of the marvellous and distinctive design features of language is what is usually called its 'openness'. That is language can be reshaped to suit new communicative demands as they emerge. New words and new ways of putting words together can be generated if people consider it necessary. If a group of people are striving to communicate about their special interests, they can adapt and extend language as a tool for doing so. The specialized language of a community can be called its *discourse*. Fluency in discourse is likely to be one of the obvious signs of membership.
(Mercer 2000: 106–7, author's emphasis)

Quote 4.9   Teachers and language

Wherever they are and whatever they are teaching, teachers in schools and other educational institutions are likely to face some similar practical tasks. They have to organize activities to occupy classes of disparate individuals, learners who may vary considerably in their aims, abilities and motivations. They have to control unruly behaviour. They are expected to teach a specific curriculum, a body of knowledge and skills which their students would not normally encounter in their out-of-school lives. And they have to monitor and assess the educational progress the students make. All these aspects of teachers' responsibilities are reflected in their use of language as the principal tool of their responsibilities.
(Mercer 2001: 243)

Even to an untrained observer, classrooms are places rich in talk. (One 'lay' view of teaching is that it mainly consists of talking, and that the worst misfortune to befall a teacher is to lose their voice. Sometimes, teachers find it difficult to shake classroom talk off, and our families may complain that we're still in 'teacher mode' when taking part in domestic conversation). We could characterise talk as the essential fuel of classroom management. Furthermore, the management of learning is closely bound up with classroom verbal interaction (Quote 4.10).

Quote 4.10 Allwright and Bailey on managing interaction and managing learning

If we think too much about the management of interaction in the classroom ... we may lose sight of the fact that what is much more important is the management of *learning*. We do not manage interaction purely for its own sake. We manage interaction in the language classroom for the sake of giving everyone the best possible opportunities for learning the language. In fact, everything we do in the classroom, any of us, can make a difference to what anyone else in the class could possibly learn from being there. In this way, managing interaction and managing learning come together. (1991: 21)

What is classroom talk like? What evidence does it provide of classroom management practices? Let us examine an example:

Extract 4.1 Classroom talk

```
     T   Mary stole my pen -- Mary stole my pen/yes
     S #3   my pen was / stolen by Mary
     T   one way - or - yes
     S #12   my pen was stolen
 5   T   my pen was stolen / good / now two people can try to do this dialogue one --
         you be the teacher - Patience / you will be Kathy -
     Ss  ⌈which page
         ⌊which number
     T   page 40 please
10   Ss  which one
     T   this one [holds up book and ponts] / how many pages are there
     Ss  two
     T   OK
     S #3   what happened
15   S #13   a window has been broken ma'am
     S #3   who broke it
     S #13   it was broken by a ball ma'am
     S #3   who kicked it
     S #13   nobody here ma'am -
20   T   good - Ozimba / teacher
     Ss  please ma'am please ma'am
     T   Nancy / Kathy
```

In this brief extract from the early stages of a lesson, we can see a number of instances of management in action.

1. Through the teacher's instructions. The teacher specifies which students are expected to 'do this dialogue' (lines 5–6). The teacher specifies the page number in the students' books (line 9).
2. Teacher clarifications. The precise location of the dialogue is identified (line 11) by pointing at the place in the book. The teacher checks that students know exactly where the material is (line 11).
3. Students are involved in managing the activity. Students ask about the page number of the book (lines 7–8). In line 21 they bid for turns to read the dialogue.
4. A pattern of activity. Students read from the course book, followed by teacher's comment – 'good' (line 20). These form short episodes in the text.

The overall pattern is of activity initiated by the teacher and then maintained through collective action. We might wonder why students participate so actively in the ongoing management of this activity; we might also wonder what the purpose of the activity is as well as where the classroom is, how old the children are, theirs and the teacher's gender, their mother tongues, and most importantly what came next. These questions create a framework for consideration of issues related to classroom talk, its management and the way in which participation in classroom activity is 'filtered' through talk in classrooms.

The role of talk in classroom life

It is clear that special uses of language are central to classroom life – in particular, for instruction and for establishing and maintaining social relations. Classroom discourse is the medium through which education is done, and constitutes a central element of the context of learning for learners. Mercer (1995, 2000, 2001) has built his theory of the educational uses of talk (Concept 4.10) around the concept of 'communities' who have access to 'resources for making meaning', as follows:

- **Language**: language itself is the primary resource for making meaning in educational settings. It is a pedagogic tool and a resource for dialogue.
- **History**: the accumulation of shared experience, which is the source of information and expertise, which existing members can draw on, and pass on to new members. This is the process underlying legitimate peripheral participation. Mercer (2000: 117) points out that this enables newcomers to use language as a cultural tool – to gain access to collective 'history'- and as a psychological tool – to review previous experience.

- **Collective identity**: the shared history of a group including what they have done together is a source of creating collective identity and meaning
- **Reciprocal obligations**: community members have responsibilities towards each other (Mercer 2000: 106). These rules enable access to each other's intellectual resources; there are also ground rules.

Concept 4.10   Issues in a socio-cultural view of learning

1. **Language is our most important pedagogic tool.** Language is a cognitive tool for gaining, processing, organising and evaluating knowledge. It is a cultural tool for sharing and storing knowledge for future generations. It is a pedagogic tool 'by which intellectual guidance is provided to children and other people' (2001: 254).
2. **Education is a dialogic, cultural process.** Development of learners' knowledge and understanding is shaped by their relationships with teachers and other students, and the culture in which these relationships are located – classroom and wider. Teachers facilitate students' learning through intellectual support and guidance, in particular, dialogue.
3. **Language carries the history of classroom activity into the future.** Assuming regularity of class contact, language is a means of students and teachers building a history, in that the meaningfulness of their current and future joint activities depend on their 'common knowledge', already established through dialogue.
4. **Classroom interaction follows implicit 'ground rules'.** Classroom participants draw upon previous shared knowledge of learning and educational encounters, encoded in hidden 'ground rules'. The ground rules are rarely made explicit, but may be in order to reduce difficulties.

(after Mercer 2001: 254–5)

Language is a major means by which classroom communities build and maintain themselves, enabling members to negotiate meanings in the present, access stored knowledge from the past and to imagine the future. Mercer (1995) also points out that in classrooms teachers have responsibilities very different from those of informal helpers (or 'guides to the construction of knowledge' (1995: 83), as he terms them) and these roles and responsibilities have a profound impact on the discourse of the community.

- Teachers are responsible for the education of large numbers of students simultaneously but they have 'no opportunity to build intense, individualised relationships' with students (1995: 83) as their parents do.
- The life of the classroom community whose goal (not necessarily sought by its members) is educated discourse (articulated knowledge of particular curriculum areas), is mediated through educational discourse – the *process* talk of classrooms.

Mercer emphasises the importance of teachers in the life of classroom communities as they try to make brief encounters part of the 'long conversation' of formal education. This is the means by which collective classroom activity is organised and continuously maintained and adjusted to meet changing circumstances, and is the basis for a learning group's collective history. Talk is central to the existence of classroom communities, the interpersonal relationships there and the way in which they go about teaching-and-learning. It is a cultural tool for thinking together and for learning, with a special capacity for assisting in the organisation of thinking (Quote 4.11).

Quote 4.11   Mercer on language as a tool for thinking and learning together

...for collectively making sense of experience and solving problems. We do this 'interthinking' in ways which most of us take for granted but which are at the heart of human achievement. Language is a tool for carrying out joint intellectual activity, a distinctive human inheritance designed to serve the practical and social needs of individuals and communities...
(2000: 1)

...the prime aim of education ought to be to help children learn how to use language effectively as a tool for thinking collectively.
(2002: 141)

Talk is part of the ongoing process of classroom life (educational talk) as well as the content or outcome of situated activity there (educated people). For the foreign language classroom this poses particular problems if the educational discourse is conducted in the target language. There are 'cultural' consequences for the choice of a medium of instruction. Breen (2001a), addressing this issue, points out that:

> The classroom may be a relatively inefficient environment for the methodical mastery of a language system, just as it is limited in providing opportunities for real world communication in a new language. But the classroom has its own communicative potential and metacommunicative purpose. It can be a particular social context for the intensification of the cultural experience of *learning*. (2001: 138, author's emphasis)

Language classrooms can thus be seen as venues for better understanding learning better if the latent communicative potential and possibility of talking about language and communication can be achieved. The choice of code with which to develop this conversation, as language is part target and part resource for reaching the target in the foreign language classroom, will be crucial.

Issues in classroom discourse

Characterisations of the classroom as 'culture', 'community' and 'discourse village' emphasise the central role of social practices in classroom life, and the discourses associated with them. Classroom discourse reflects classroom-specific social and psychological realities as well as external social and cultural influences, as we saw in Chapter 2. In a discussion of classroom language lessons as 'socially constructed events', Allwright (1984: 159) formulates two key concepts, later taken up by Breen (2001b) – 'navigation' and 'negotiation' (Quote 4.12). Allwright and Breen's work on language classrooms develops from the idea that 'input' (to use terminology from Second Language Acquisition Theory) is not to be equated with learners' 'uptake'. In short, what is taught is not necessarily what is learned, and discoursal processes in any lesson ensure that there is wide variation in the outcomes of learning. There are several interrelated reasons for this.

Quote 4.12 Navigation and negotiation

Negotiation
. . . any attempts to reach decisions by consensus rather than by unilateral decision-making.
(Allwright 1984: 160)

Navigation
. . . attempts to steer a course between, round, or over obstacles that the lesson represents for the participants (1984: 159) . . . a minor diversion from the lesson topic to something of more direct and immediate interest to at least one individual learner.' and 'many individual contributions . . . [by] learners individualizing the instruction they are receiving, making it relevant to their particular needs.'
(Allwright 1984: 160)

. . . one of the crucial things that learners learn in the classroom is how to navigate the opportunities and constraints provided by classroom discourse.
(Breen 2001b: 307)

Learners Learn Discourse Practices As Well As 'Subjects' Breen argues that learners are 'active practitioners within the discourse of the learning context in which they find themselves' (2001b: 309) and that classrooms, because of their special nature, contain opportunities for and constraints upon language learning. Breen also points out that learners learn how to navigate and negotiate their way through classroom discourse, or 'how to do formal education', in addition to any content (Concept 4.10). From the point of view of classroom learners, Wells (1999: 39) points out that 'children's ability to engage effectively in the different tasks that they may be expected to undertake in school depends on the extent to which they have internalised the socio-semantic functions of the specific modes of discourse that mediate these tasks'. In other words, children have to learn how to use language in order to maximise the learning potential of the classroom. For Mercer, as we have noted, mastery of language itself is the most important aim of education Learning how to participate in classroom discourse is itself a social activity, and part of the lived experience of every member of a classroom community. In the terminology of communities of practice, learning the discourses of classroom talk, and the discourses of different subject disciplines are indicators of the process of legitimate peripheral participation in two overlapping communities – the classroom community and the 'subject' community. The extent to which classroom discourse mirrors the discourses of various subject disciplines is thus an important issue. Much depends on the capacity of the teacher to embody the discourses and thinking patterns of their discipline through talk and other mediation tools such as realia and visuals. Kress et al. (2001) discuss this process in science classrooms, giving examples of how teachers model scientific discourse and enact scientific concepts kinesthetically. What language teachers do to recreate the world of the speaker of a foreign language and how they recontextualise their knowledge of the target language in the language classrooms remains an area requiring further investigation.

Concept 4.10   Navigating classroom discourse

Does a learner's success in learning language in a classroom depend upon 'the learner's successful navigation of the opportunities and constraints inherent in the discourse of lessons?' (Breen 2001b:309)

Breen argues that the texts of classroom life are reflective of discoursal and of social practices.

The following discoursal processes are at work:

1. because teachers shape the discourse of lessons in significant ways, learners are positioned in different ways which are manifested in the inter-textuality (interactive properties) of the discourse. Learners have to *navigate* the inter-textuality (trying to ascertain whether the discourse is real communication in the target language, metacommunication about the target language, and communication about the teaching-learning process) in order to keep track of teacher's direction of the discourse. We could also add Sarangi's (1998) idea of 'metacommunication', or guidance provided in trying to understand the pragmatic meaning of contributions in lessons.
2. learners participate selectively (although are also selected by teachers) according to their judgements which are derived from their definition of a particular teaching/ learning situation and from their experience in discourse realms beyond the classroom.

Thus: 'Learners... navigate the discourse in two constantly interweaving ways; for learning purposes and for social purposes' (Breen 2001b: 314).

Learners navigate the discourse in two ways: in a moment-by-moment interpretive manner – from both learning and strategic points of view – and anticipating that social practices construct knowledge and role identities and relationships between teachers and learners in very specific ways. Their work reflects their understanding of and contributions to the emerging culture of a particular learning group.

The analysis highlights two points regarding the management of classroom discourse.

1. Many believe the social world of formal education, the classroom, revolves around the pivotal position of the teacher (Quote 4.13). Indeed, Breen's rather gloomy conclusion that learners are actually encouraged to under-achieve by these discoursal positioning practices is grounded in a view that learners must 'adopt a responsive role in relation to the teacher's management of the discourse through his/her *control over the text of lessons*' (2001b: 316, my emphasis). There are also the other social pressures to underachieve. Chick (1996), for example, reports underachievement in secondary English classes in South Africa (pedagogic) and cites evidence from classroom talk to support the proposition that teachers and learners collude to underachieve in order to preserve face (social). A crucial issue in classroom management is thus the extent to which a pivotal teacher position is negotiated in ongoing discourse.

Quote 4.13   Breen on the teacher as pivotal

The teacher is a direct participant in this social event (a gathering of learners and a teacher) with the aim of influencing psychological development. The teacher is obliged continually to integrate the learning experiences of individuals with the collective and communal activities of a group which . . . he is not an outsider.
(2001a: 122–3)

---

2. Because learners are also active participants in the management of classroom discourse, through their practices of participation (and non-participation), they have the capacity to influence the direction and character of class-room discourse. This can result in collusion, collaboration or opposition to the dominant discourse. For example, Canagarajah (1993), in a study of tertiary-level English classes in the north of Sri Lanka, demonstrates how resistance to alternative pedagogies through non-participation is the way the learners struggle against new definitions of their identities as predicated by the teaching materials, which may be in conflict with pre-existing norms in the wider society, and challenge 'normal' social practices (Quote 4.14).

Quote 4.14   Canagarajah on pedagogies of resistance

...politically conscious approaches to learning/teaching which critically interrogate the oppressive tendencies behind the existing content and forms of knowledge and classroom relations to fashion a more liberating educational context that would lead to student empowerment and social transformation.
(1993: 603)

An emerging classroom management culture simultaneously creates and is created by prevailing social practices through which participants define the classroom learning situation and position themselves and each other within that situation. Practices such as navigation are binding elements across the three domains of text, discourse and social practice (Figure 4.1). Phenomena such as collusion, collaboration and opposition also permeate the three domains and are examples of how classroom management practice operates discoursally.

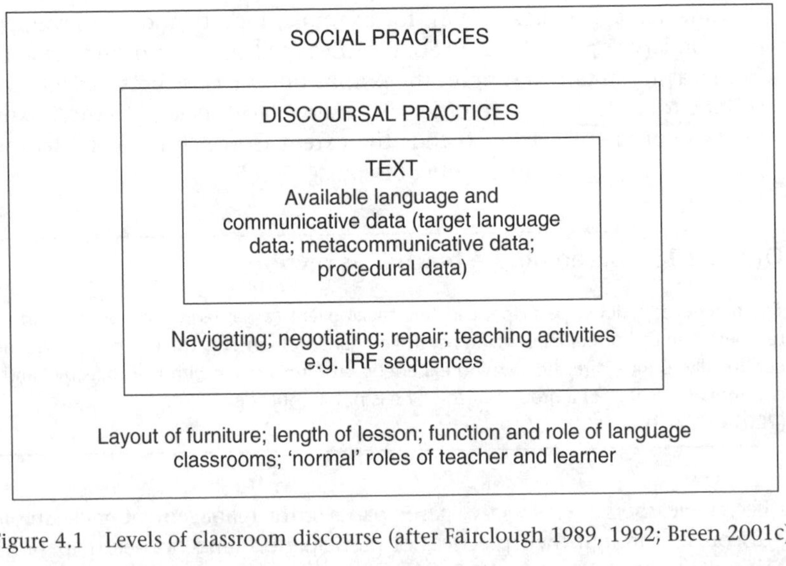

SOCIAL PRACTICES

DISCOURSAL PRACTICES

TEXT
Available language and
communicative data (target language
data; metacommunicative data;
procedural data)

Navigating; negotiating; repair; teaching activities
e.g. IRF sequences

Layout of furniture; length of lesson; function and role of language
classrooms; 'normal' roles of teacher and learner

Figure 4.1   Levels of classroom discourse (after Fairclough 1989, 1992; Breen 2001c)

Breen's analysis is not without its difficulties, however. By following the 'nesting' metaphor for linking internal and external features of context, Breen (after Fairclough) runs the risk of creating the impression that texts are *embedded* in discourse rather than being evidence of both discoursal processes and as well as their product. Similarly, nesting discoursal practices in social practices leads us to believe that we can always understand events and processes by referring the next higher level of generality. Classroom life generates and is maintained by discourses, and may more productively portrayed as 'woven', so that by examining the relationships between texts, discoursal practices and social practices, we can illuminate the relationships between pedagogic and social strands of classroom life. This model thus links higher order issues of culture learning with local lesson management practices and provides an important way of connecting broader educational processes with in-time management activities of teachers and learners.

Discourse, learning, experience and competence The central discourse in any domain of learning is the relationship between experience and emerging competence in any domain of learning. As Mercer (1995: 4) puts it: 'Language is a means for transforming experience into cultural knowledge and understanding.' In terms of the development of practice in any domain like a language classroom, however, 'the two-way interaction of experience and competence is crucial' (Wenger 1998: 139). Interaction itself, or the classroom discourse, contains within it the possibility for the transformation of both experience and competence, and therefore learning. Sometimes new classroom experience leads to a cognitive realignment which subsequently leads to new learning; sometimes new competence in a classroom community requires a realignment and further learning. This process is accomplished through the community's discourse, which evolves in turn as the community learns (Concept 4.11). Classroom learning is thus intimately bound up with classroom discourse.

Concept 4.11 Experience and competence in learning

'Knowledge is a matter of competence with respect to valued enterprise' (Wenger 1998: 4)
Practice (or 'the ways we accomplish things') evolves through the interaction between experience and competence.

EXPERIENCE of MEANING (what we do and what we experience)

Realignment made necessary by new knowledge/competence or new experience. Learning made possible by interaction in a community

COMPETENCE Engagement leads to participation; enables participation in a community's history (includes discoursal knowledge for negotiating meaning with community)

Summary

The nature of classrooms derives from their central role as the location for formal learning – they are at the heart of the educational process. They are cultural workshops and they are also cultures themselves, with unique practices for getting the business of education done. Their nature is inevitably multi-dimensional as individuals' and groups' agendas interweave with broader educational discourses. In this sense, they are truly 'discourse villages'. Classrooms are also social settings in which language is a key community resource for making meaning and regulating social life. They are communities of practice. Classroom management practice is thus reflective of and contributes to the discourses of classroom life generated by social and cultural activity.

Further reading

Breen (2001a) is a seminal paper on classroom as culture and also appears in Candlin and Mercer (2001). [Originally published 1985.]

Breen (2001b) is a key paper for understanding the social and pedagogic dynamics of the language classroom.

Cazden (1988) provides a very comprehensive overview of approaches to classroom discourse.

Lantolf (2000) features socio-culturally-oriented studies of second language classroom discourse.

Mercer (1995) is an excellent introduction to the analysis of talk in educational settings.

Mercer (2000) develops earlier ideas on discourse and extends these into other aspects of social life, providing the possibility for interesting comparisons with classroom life.

Tsui (1995) covers all the important linguistic aspects of classroom discourse.

van Lier (1988) is an in-depth study of language classroom discourse.

van Lier (1996a) is a comprehensive introduction to an 'ecological' view of classroom talk.

5
Concerns and Practices in Classroom Management

In Chapters 1–4, we have created a picture of classrooms, emphasising their formal and institutional characteristics and their social and cultural nature. Classrooms are, as we have seen, complex and multi-dimensional, open to many external influences as well as having a 'life' of their own, in real time. Classroom management is thus concerned with managing both internal and external events and influences. The characteristics and nature of classrooms suggest that there are fundamental concerns in classroom management, of establishing and maintaining order, of generating learning opportunities and how people feel and interact there. These concerns underlie an array of classroom management practices.

5.1 The concerns of classroom management: educational perspectives

Discussion of classroom management has traditionally, but not exclusively, encompassed teachers' practices to control or direct activity in their classrooms. Learners' participation in classroom discourse on the other hand indicates that for a more realistic view of classroom management, we need to account for classroom management practice as jointly constructed. Like all classroom phenomena, classroom management practices also draw from broader educational imperatives and at the same time are integral to the ongoing discourses of classroom activity. They are influenced by external sources and internal action in expressing their overriding goals.

There are three central concerns of classroom management, which express themselves in three management discourses (Figure 5.1):

- to establish and maintain *order*;
- to provide learning *opportunity*;
- to create a context of *care*.

In any classroom, these three concerns are present at all times, and classroom activity involves one or more of them at any particular moment. Teachers'

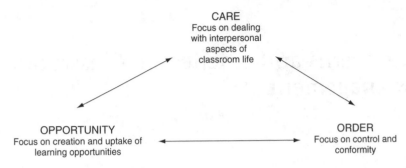

Figure 5.1   Concerns in classroom management

and learners' short-term and longer-term goals shift and change, and this is reflected in corresponding shifts in classroom management discourse. Occasionally, discourses conflict, when participants have differing classroom goals or concerns. At other times, one management concern may dominate proceedings at the expense of others.

Concept 5.1   Schools of thought in classroom management

- Authoritarian (control of knowledge and behaviour)
- Permissive (students given autonomy)
- Behaviour modification (rewards and punishments – reward good behaviour)
- Interpersonal relations ('healthy classroom climate' – caring and sharing)
- Scientific (based on systematic observation and analysis of successful teaching)
- Social systems (classrooms seen as representative of wider educational values)
- Folklore (management based on tricks of the trade and recipes)

(after Wragg 1993: 10–15)

Wragg (1993) provides a taxonomy of 'families' of classroom management which describes classroom management styles, but does not identify the underlying discourses of order, opportunity and care (Concept 5.1). The 'authoritarian' school, and its close relative, 'behaviour modification' both appear, however, to draw on discourses of order and control. The 'scientific' school, which has been successful in reducing classroom management to observable and measurable behaviour, has been recruited to reinforce the authority school. Doyle (1986) and Jones (1996) review research claiming the benefits of adopting 'scientific' solutions to the problem of classroom order. The 'permissive' school, on the other hand, contains the seeds of opportunity. The defining feature is student autonomy (Benson 2001), although what type of autonomy is unclear. However, 'permissiveness' can also be interpreted as 'less control' rather than the creation of conditions in which learning opportunity can flourish. The interpersonal and 'social systems' views of classroom management emphasise the establishment and maintenance of good social relations in the classroom, a position closer to the 'care' view. Finally, there is an acknowledgement in 'folklore' that a great deal of teachers' classroom management practice is grounded in the collective history of teachers in different contexts, the informal and 'unscientific' aspect of their practical theory, with its roots in intuition as well as experience. It is quite likely, though, that teachers intuitively and implicitly gravitate towards one or more of the main concerns in their day-to-day practices.

Order in classroom management

Classroom management practices have a strong tendency to converge on the establishment and maintenance of order in the classroom. Order is not a monolithic concept or a consistent set of practices, however (Concept 5.2). There is a continuum of views on order – from strong pressures from society and institutions for 'discipline' and adherence to strict codes of behaviour, enforced by a variety of sanctions against deviant behaviour of varying degrees of toughness at one end of the spectrum. At the other end is the idea of consensual calm and orderliness among the student group maintained by self-control. Management practices thus intend to preserve order either by means of imposition (force, if necessary, in some contexts) or by negotiation. The degree of imposition of 'rules' and codes of conduct, or other-regulation, is thus a significant aspect of order (Field Note 5.1).

Field Note 5.1   Order and discipline in the classroom

After two weeks visiting schools, overwhelming impression of teachers expecting quiet and order in class. Have witnessed the 'discipline master' at work beating a student – apparently he was rude to a teacher who sent him out of the class. Discipline master on patrol picked him up and took him off to his office to administer beating. But serious discipline problems – violence against teachers or fellow students, for example – non-existent. Younger, untrained teachers seem to spend more time trying to keep order, with frequent appeals for quiet. Three informal quotes from teachers:

Teachers are expected to teach to lead and the untrained teachers come unstuck because they merely discipline. They kick kids out of class for not understanding. – ANF

A good teacher acts as the pivot and controls everything. – ANF

There has to be some order. My students, even in the Upper Sixth, stand when I enter the class, and clear their desks of all previous lesson material when I enter the class.... Children are not as regimented these days. – SK

Disorder is an ever-present fact of life in classrooms, however. It can originate in more or less any event or process in the classroom – as students attempt to cope with the demands of pedagogic activity, or challenge the authority structure or the perceived rigidity of the teaching/learning process. There are therefore different types of classroom disorder in the same way that there are variations in order, depending on assumptions about the basis of order and origin of disorder.

Origins of disorder

Disorder is assumed to be deviance from strict rules and conventions for behaviour and conduct. Disorder also means disturbing or challenging the status quo. The response is to restore order by whatever means are available and permissible. Order is thus the basis for classroom activity in which learners obey and comply without question with what the teacher prescribes.

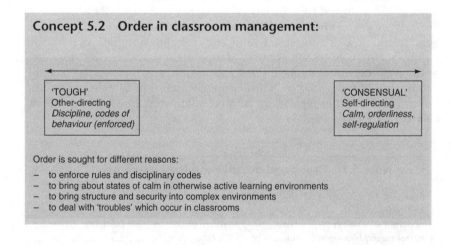

Concept 5.2   Order in classroom management:

'TOUGH'
Other-directing
*Discipline, codes of
behaviour (enforced)*

'CONSENSUAL'
Self-directing
*Calm, orderliness,
self-regulation*

Order is sought for different reasons:

- to enforce rules and disciplinary codes
- to bring about states of calm in otherwise active learning environments
- to bring structure and security into complex environments
- to deal with 'troubles' which occur in classrooms

There are other reasons for 'disorder' which do not derive from the tendency to control the classroom environment and behaviours of the students. Classrooms are complex environments, or ecologies, as we have seen in Chapter 4. Larsen-Freeman (1991) further reminds us of the inherent complexities of language teaching in particular, although much of what she says could be said of any curriculum area. Classrooms are complex because so much is happening at any one time, and because so much is interconnected. The potential for disorder is thus always present, even in the most simple or routine activity (Quote 5.1).

Quote 5.1   Managing classroom complexity

Managing in a Complex Ecology
The classroom must be understood as an ecology of language processes and cultural patterns. These include the spoken and written word; the use of personal and social space (proxemics) as part of the message exchange system; the body language of movement, posture and facial expression (kinesics); the changes of voice pitch, tempo and intensity – as well as intruding sounds and pauses.
(Bowers and Flinders 1991: 2)

Language Teachers Managing Complexity
... confronted with the complexity of language, learning and language learners every day of their working lives in a more direct fashion than any theorist does' teachers have developed 'the conviction that no single perspective on language, no single explanation for learning, and no unitary view of the contributions of language learners will account for what they must grapple with on a daily basis.
(Larsen-Freeman 1991: 269)

Teachers coping with complexity   Teachers have simultaneously to manage activities in the classroom itself, and also external forces and influences, expressing social backgrounds and cultural origins, in addition to curriculum specifications and teaching materials. Any pedagogic or social move that a teacher makes in the classroom can thus elicit a wide range of responses from students. Teachers typically acquire a repertoire for coping with this type of complexity and the unexpected, as any professional does through experience. As Schön (1983: 18) points out, professionals are constantly dealing with situations of complexity, uncertainty, instability, uniqueness and value conflict. He calls these 'indeterminate zones of practice' (1987: 6). From psychological and social viewpoints, the order problem is therefore one of relative certainty or uncertainty, rather than 'bad behaviour'. The more secure and certain a classroom is socially and psychologically, the more likely it is to be orderly. Teachers and learners 'need the security of shared expectations' (Prabhu 1992: 229). This illuminates the tendency in classroom life towards routine and ritual. Under these conditions both teachers and learners act to create and preserve order, and tend, Prabhu claims, to avoid the unpredictable and hence disorder.

Erickson and Shultz (1992: 470) regard the teacher's attention as central to the establishment of 'routine classroom social system and culture' which 'makes life predictable for... participants'. They point out that teachers' attention is focused on one of several objects:

- student deportment;
- students' feelings;

- student's informal identities and pecking orders (especially with younger children);
- student displays of knowledge and skill;
- development of students' reasoning capacities.

Order-oriented teachers are more likely to be watching for transgressions of deportment conventions and rules, or making sure that there is as little friction as possible between students' differing personalities and backgrounds.

Paradoxical forces Classrooms are also contradictory – they are places where teachers and learners seek security and routine, and yet these conditions are continually threatened by the very activities of teaching and learning. This is the pedagogic paradox. The teacher always risks social and emotional equilibrium in the classroom when new learning is proposed. Learning has the potential to disturb learners' emotional and psychological states. It challenges the known, and threatens certainty. Any activity leading to new learning is therefore potentially chaotic and risky. The resulting disorder may even stymie the goal of helping learners acquire specific knowledge and skills. Allwright (1996) has discussed this issue and has come to the conclusion that classroom behaviour is a 'tightrope walk...a continually reinvented compromise between competing social and pedagogic demands' (1996: 223). In order to help learners learn, a teacher necessarily creates 'troubles' of different types and degrees of seriousness, and at the same time is constantly ready to manage possible disorder (Concept 5.3).

Concept 5.3   Social and pedagogic forces in the classroom

[Lessons] are necessarily 'social', on the one hand, simply because they are events in which people come physically together and therefore become subject to the immediate influence of each other's behaviour, but they also need to be 'social' in the sense that they are collective events in the lives of the participants. Lessons also need to be 'pedagogic', on the other hand, simply because of the institutionalized purpose for which they take place. They are 'pedagogic' by intention...even if they by no means always realize this purpose effectively. (Allwright 1989: 4)

...there is an inherent conflict between the social and pedagogic pressures that obtain in the classroom [between needs to '*get on*' (succeed) and '*get along*' (work in harmony)] (Allwright 1996: 210)

Allwright also mentions '*getting by*' (survival), which lies more in the affective domain.

...pedagogic discourse must contain potential challenges to the topical, discoursal, linguistic and procedural competence of the participants....Such new material must...pose

challenges for learners . . . and . . . hold the risk of upsetting the social equilibrium in a classroom group, because any difficulty the teacher may have in helping such learners smoothly over such difficulties is potentially embarrassing for the teacher.' . . . teachers and learners cannot simply choose between the pedagogic and the social pressures.
(Allwright 1996: 210–11, 223)

Candlin (1998) adds the further dimension of '*getting even*' to account for students' deliberate attempts to subvert classroom activity.

Pedagogic activity therefore has the potential to threaten classroom order and create discoursal problems, even in the most apparently clear-cut of pedagogic situations. In Extract 5.1, students dispute the answer to a question from the teacher (line 2). The question is about the correct forms following transformation of direct to indirect speech, a closed question. The students call out contradictory answers throughout the sequence, and the teacher holds a straw poll (lines 12–22) in order to bring a sense of closure, a pedagogic 'side sequence' related to the topic (although the minority 'win'). The straw poll creates a degree of discord. A sense of order returns only when the teacher gives an explanation for the answer (lines 26–8). The teacher cues student collaboration in line 27 with a rising intonation on 'pronouns', followed by a minimal pause. The students immediately join in chorusing 'change', and in the process overlapping with the teacher. Order is restored as the 'rhythm' of the class is re-established (Data Extract 5.1). There is evidence in this extract that students, too, recognise the cues for order and are not necessarily pursuing a pattern of disruption or conflict. The classroom discourse has not 'degraded' as it might in such cases.

Data Extract 5.1   Order and rhythm in classroom activity

A Cameroonian English teacher is talking about the question of 'order' in classrooms. ANF reports an almost 'ideal' class in which there was '*give and take*'.

In a class where there is that rhythm which gives life, the students are excited in their lesson. They are being touched really, and they have a feeling they have participated and are learning. And if that sort of thing is absent in the class the students will always feel bored and they will always wish for the end of that class. Thus attempts to restore order are attempts to reestablish the rhythm of the class.

Extract 5.1   Order and disorder in classrooms

       T   yes she said that she would finish her homework today / that is if / I asked you/
            tomorrow / that is what you would say / bon / for example / if I asked you / two
            days later on -- what would you say -----
       Ss (inaudible)
   5   T   the answer two days afterwards / what would you say / yes
       S #19   she says she would finish her homework
       Sx yesterday
       S #19   yesterday
       T   is it correct
  10   Ss ⎡yes ⎡yes
            ⎣no   ⎣no
       T   those who say it is correct / hands up
       Sx (inaudible)
       T   those who say it is not correct / hands up
  15   Sx (inaudible)
       T   does the majority always carry the vote
       Ss ⎡no ⎡no ⎡no
            ⎣yes ⎣yes ⎣yes
       Sx he's a bit right
  20   Sx he's right all the same
                today yes
       T   the minority is right
       Ss yes
                no (*general noise*)
  25   T   the minority is right / okay / you people have to realise that you see / er when
            you change er / when you report a speech / eh / when you want to report a
            speech the / er / the tenses change / the adverb / the adverb of er / place
            changes / sometimes the pronouns do / the pronouns /⎡changes
       Ss   ⎣change

5.2   Opportunity in classroom management

An opportunity view of classroom management emphasises the creation of *learning* opportunity which is not necessarily pre-planned. Its realisation in classroom activity has discoursal consequences. Classrooms are, as we have seen, far from 'orderly' environments, and may actually have disorder 'built in' to them. Critics of the 'order' view of classroom management point out that an over-emphasis on order for its own sake is a barrier to learning, rather than a necessary precondition for its success because it stifles learning opportunity. For example, Bowers and Flinders argue that the 'order' or 'management' (1990: 3) paradigm in classroom management perpetuates a false process-product metaphor for classroom life (Quote 5.3) in which order is a feature of optimal learning conditions where students are 'on task' and gainfully occupied. Classroom management is thus a means of behaviour management in the service of learning. This is, in Bowers and Flinders' terms, a 'technicist' conception of teaching and learning, emphasising order and efficiency at the expense of learning opportunities which might otherwise emerge from the 'organic' classroom process.

Quote 5.3   Bowers and Flinders on order and the technicist (or management) paradigm

... research on classroom organization and management ... [emphasises] behavioural management [and] reflects the continuing dominance of the technicist approach to teacher professionalism. ... The explicit-observable of what is to be known makes it amenable to measurement and greater certainty. In turn, this fosters a greater emphasis on reducing classroom interactive patterns to their component parts for the purpose of reconstituting them in a manner that increases rational control and efficiency.
(1990: 8)

The order school of thought sees control and order as essential to successful classroom learning. In other words, learning does not emerge from classroom conditions – it happens only when conditions are controlled in such a way that teachers can instruct, and students do as they are instructed, and work in ways that are specified by teachers (Quote 5.4). This, somewhat simplistically, solves 'the problem of order' – order is unproblematically the outcome of regulatory behaviour. Teachers and students know intuitively that this is not true.

Quote 5.4   Doyle on classroom management: solving the problem of order

Classroom management is fundamentally a process of solving the problem of *order* in classrooms rather than the problems of misbehaviour or student engagement. These latter issues are not insignificant, but they are not primary targets of a teacher's management energies. Indeed, high engagement and low levels of inappropriate and disruptive behaviour are by-products of an effective programme of classroom organisation and management. At its foundation, then, the teacher's management task is primarily one of establishing and maintaining work systems for classroom groups rather than spotting and punishing misbehaviour, remediating behavioural disorders, or maximising the engagement of individual students.
(1986: 423)

Because teachers working from an opportunity perspective acknowledge the inherent ecological complexity of classrooms, they may actually seek to create uncertain conditions and exploit the potential of complexity to create learning opportunities. They push the boundaries. Such teachers are also opportunistic in the sense that they rejoice in the unexpected and unplanned, or uncontrolled eventuality (Data Extract 5.2). In opportunity-oriented classrooms, students are encouraged to take risks and make opportunities for learning. Control can still be, if necessary, maintained through, for example, close adherence to a sequence of learning activities if required (it may be desirable in certain contexts), with different activities allowing different levels of student – self-control or autonomy. Orderliness can also be invoked by other means, as in Extract 5.1, through contextual cues which enable the teacher to take control of the interaction. For example, eliciting 'change' from the class (lines 28/9).

Data Extract 5.2   Teachers talk about creating opportunities

The following is a selection from data where teachers are talking about enabling classroom learning:

You see, sometimes students need to 'fly', to create. There has to be a time in class for this.

I used to get quite worried if the lesson deviated from the plan. But now I see that the students are getting extra practice. Even if the topic isn't so relevant to the lesson.

I don't think we can predict in any way what is going to happen in a lesson. That's a bit frightening – I avoided this when I began teaching. But now it seems quite natural. I don't know if the head knows I teach like this and what she'd say if she knew.

Briggs and Moore (1993) (Concept 5.3) distinguish between high and low structure classrooms, structure being the strength of the teacher's definition of events and the relative amount of involvement of the teacher and learners in decision-making and control. A strong sense of order thus implies greater teacher involvement in decision-making and higher teacher definition of all learning elements of lessons. A tendency towards greater opportunity specifies more learner involvement in steering teaching-and-learning processes at all stages, including decisions about what and how to learn.

Concept 5.3   High and low structure in teaching

HIGH STRUCTURE – emphasis on teacher setting up the learning environment, few options allowed, and students mainly reactive.
LOW STRUCTURE – students are provided with several options and degrees of autonomy in the learning experience.

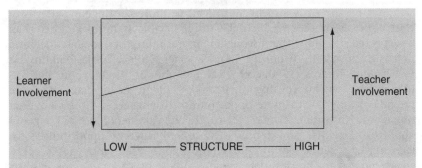

LOW ———— STRUCTURE ———— HIGH

This enables classroom management decisions to be analysed as follows:

Management Decisions	High Structure	Low Structure
PLANNING	Direct teaching	Grouping around activities
CLASSROOM PROCEDURES	Imposed routines	Participative decision-making and consultation
QUESTIONING	Limited range. Assertive	Authentic. Wide range
REWARD/PUNISHMENT	To modify behaviour	To encourage pupil self-discipline

(after Briggs and Moore 1993: 496–7)

The crucial difference between the order (high structure) and opportunity (low structure) views of classroom management is in the role of control. If teachers assume that control is a necessary precondition for learning, they will necessarily invest a great deal of energy and use classroom time initiating and maintaining it. In a classroom where management tends to order, control is typically imposed so that teaching can take place. New learning content is 'drip-fed', and under close teacher control throughout. An opportunity perspective, however, sees control as simply one aspect of a set of procedures designed to promote and encourage learning, including self-control. Opportunity-oriented classroom management favours, for instance, more open-ended questions, greater negotiation of all aspects of content and activity choice, and is likely to lead to less lockstep classroom activity, or direct teaching. A teacher, even if she is encouraging lower structure, still retains the authority to 'apply the brakes' if exploration degenerates into empty rambling, and to vary activities as required.

Opportunity and contingency

A more opportunity-oriented classroom management strategy is likely to prove more risky for teachers and learners, particularly if they are accustomed to an order regime. It is also likely to lead to more contingent patterns of classroom discourse, in which the unpredictable is normal rather than unexpected. In short, the discourse is more improvised, open-ended and rich with possibility (Concept 5.4). Van Lier (1996a, 2001), building on Bowers and Flinders' (1990) ecological metaphor of the classroom, believes that a move towards 'contingent classroom talk' in the language classroom provides learners with more opportunities to engage in more 'conversational' talk. Continuing the ecological theme, van Lier (2000: 253) equates opportunities with 'affordances' (Quote 5.5) whereby opportunities for learning are generated by the environment itself and the learners' engagement with the classroom context. Advocates of a more opportunity-oriented classroom regard this as a 'more emancipatory form of discourse' (Van Lier 2001: 97).

Concept 5.4   Contingent language classroom talk

The main features of contingent talk are as follows:

Interaction: (a) signalling of relations between current utterance and previous utterances (directly or through shared knowledge or shared contextualisation cues) and (b) raising of expectations and creation of deliberate ambiguities in utterances which move the discourse forward.
Linguistic: contingent talk unites structure and function; it encourages grammaticisation or the capacity of the learner to try to use more complex synatx (Rutherford 1987).
Conversational: utterances are constructed on the spot in an essentially symmetrical relationship; utterances look forward and backwards in both covert and overt ways, encouraging participation and attention of participants.

(after van Lier 2001: 98–9)

Quote 5.5   van Lier on affordances in language learning

In terms of language learning, the environment is full of language that provides opportunities for learning to the active, participating learner. The linguistic world to which the learner has access, and in which she becomes actively engaged, is 'full of demands and requirements, opportunities and limitations, rejections and invitations, enablements and constraints – in short, affordances' (Shotter and Newson 1982: 34). From the pedagogical perspective, the message may be to provide a rich 'semiotic budget'... and to structure the learner's activities and participation so that access is available and engagement encouraged.
(2000: 253)

Van Lier posits the existence of a continuum of classroom talk types from recitation to contingent, as shown in Figure 5.2. Under strict pedagogic control and order, talk is likely to be at the 'recitation' end of the continuum of classroom talk; as the teacher creates more opportunity through the use of more open-ended learning activity such as project work, so talk tends to become more contingent. Classroom discourse thus tends to become less asymmetrical, more open-ended and more dialogic (Wells 1999). Significant changes in the use of classroom space and time are suggested by more opportunity-oriented management practices in classrooms which are traditionally high-structure and order-oriented.

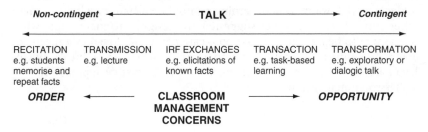

Figure 5.2   Contingency and classroom management (based on van Lier 1996a: 179)

The time taken by contingent talk is more difficult to predict and budget for. However, because contingent talk is less predictable, it allows for practice in situations closer to normal everyday conversation, where turns are not pre-allocated, but managed locally as talk proceeds, and where there is a high level of motivation to engage in talk because it is contributing to the maintenance and even enhancement of social relations in the classroom. On the other hand, students' expectations that the teacher will preserve asymmetrical order may conflict with the creation of opportunity. Quite simply learners may be reluctant to engage, having invested already in the prevailing order-oriented discourse, which has been acquired through participation. These rules are enforced – for example, students should stand when they wish to speak. Contingent talk challenges the dominant vertical classroom discourse, and although learners have already mastered the rules of participation in contingent talk in their mother tongue *outside the classroom*, the occurrence of these rules in the classroom may create difficulties for navigating a new set of discoursal relationships. Introducing new classroom management activities may thus generate new management problems.

5.3   Care in classroom management

Classroom management practices focused on the well-being of classroom participants highlight the emotional and interpersonal aspects of classroom life. These comprise the *care* dimension. Literary characterisations of classroom life often emphasise cruelty and ennui (Dickens, for example), and portray a largely uncaring and authoritarian classroom environment. The metaphor of 'student-as-sufferer' (Ellis 2001a) perhaps has its roots in these uncaring classrooms, defined by their preoccupation with imposed order.

Jones and Jones (1991) have identified a continuum of classroom management strategies which places interpersonal relations (or 'care') and the imposition of school discipline (or 'order') on opposite poles, a situation made possible by an appropriate combination of 'prevention' and 'correction' (Figure5.3). One difficulty with this conception, however, is that it does not allow the possibility of 'caring order' in classroom management, where teachers and students work towards a calm learning atmosphere based on self rather than other control. The strategies suggested are designed to manipulate what is assumed to be a difficult situation – care being employed as a means of preventing difficulty, and correction invoked when order breaks down. There are, however, views which constitute an alternative approach to care in classroom management.

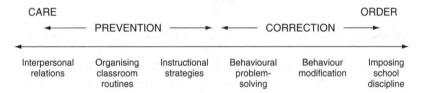

Figure 5.3   Continuum of classroom management practices (after Jones and Jones 1991: 21)

In accord with many authorities on classroom management (e.g. Prabhu 1990), Jones (1996: 509) identifies the creation of positive relations between all members of the classroom group as a necessary precondition for a well-managed classroom. Jones believes students should feel safe and secure and also empowered in classrooms (Quote 5.6). What is implied is a caring order. Less clear is the relationship between care and opportunity, although it is difficult to imagine an opportunity-oriented classroom in which relationships are poor, and order is strictly imposed.

Quote 5.6   Jones on the need for effective classroom management

. . . as more students enter the classroom feeling disempowered and confused, the decisions teachers make in selecting approaches to curriculum, instruction and classroom management become increasingly important in teaching caring, communicative skills and democratic principles.
(1996: 505)

Classroom control – or order – in the name of task completion can be, as we have seen, a barrier to effective learning and a problematic feature of a great deal of classroom management practice (Concept 5.5). In attempting to resolve this issue, McLaughlin reconceptualises classroom management as a 'metaphor for establishing relations of authority' (1994: 75), and criticises what he terms the obedience perspective to maintain control over young people. McLaughlin, concerned like so many educators in the United States that order is breaking down in secondary classrooms, suggests an alternative way of handling the changed relations between teacher and taught from the traditional practices of 'assertive discipline' and 'systems of technical control' (1991: 193) to a pattern based on *'legitimate* authority' (1991: 192, my emphasis). This arises from a transformed concept of control, based on 'ethical caring'. McLaughlin's work highlights the notions of:

- **Negotiated control**: achieved through encouragement of student participation in teaching-and-learning, in terms of decision-making and responsible self-discipline. Teachers therefore redefine their power and authority.
- **Development of caring relationships** in all aspects of teaching and learning, realised through communication channels – engaging in dialogue – and behaviours.

There are risks associated with any classroom management practices such as those proposed by McLaughlin which conflict with the status quo. Security and regularity are threatened. Institutional power structures and practices for establishing and maintaining power come under scrutiny and may resist attempts to 'control by caring'. More radical suggestions that negotiation and collaborative group work skills become part of the curriculum similarly have far-reaching consequences for formal educational practices, challenging the order-orientation of so many of these practices. Finally, McLaughlin notes that encouragement of student participation sets up tensions between control and caring strategies, and between individual responsibility and group solidarity. In pointing out some myths about control, McLaughlin emphasises that students confer real power on their teachers when their needs are met (1994: 76). Teachers may not be able to meet all their students' needs, however: they may have neither the necessary awareness nor skills.

There are also many contexts where a challenge to authority is seen as disrespectful and even dangerous. There is evidence that caring does work as part of a classroom management policy (Jones 1996) but there is inevitably a degree of conflict with existing practices of order if a more caring approach is introduced to classroom management. Caring classroom management again challenges the vertical and asymmetrical discourses embedded in the order view of classroom management, characterised by enforcement of rules and the invocation of sanctions if rules are broken. A discourse of care is also located in a particular teaching style – a concern for caring and nurturing classroom relationships provides models of behaviour and realises particular values of self-discipline, listening to students' voices and, if not making it the focus of learning per se, highlighting the positive aspects of caring as conducive to learning. There is therefore a greater congruence between care and opportunity (Data Extract 5.3).

Data Extract 5.3   Some students talk about their teachers

Some Namibian upper primary school students were invited to participate in a FOCUS GROUP discussion with the theme 'What our English teachers do and what we like or don't like in English lessons'. Here are some of the things they said:

'We like it when the teacher tells us a story and asks us what we think about the story.'

'It's good when the teacher tells some jokes. We laugh and that makes us at home.'

'Sometimes the teacher lets us choose what we want to do if there is extra time in a lesson.'

'It's not good when the teacher gives us work and then sits marking copy books.'

'It's boring when we just do exercises in the course book.'

Concept 5.5   Towards care in classroom management

McLaughlin's work starts from the issue of novice teachers' concerns with control, despite their professed ideals of caring.

Key Concepts
A. LEGITIMATE AUTHORITY – a means for transforming control through ethical caring (1991: 192)

- derives from interpersonal relationships with students that are founded on a balance of control and care. This occurs when teachers exercise 'the power to care';
- 'When ethical caring is enacted, the teacher is herself while engaging in dialogue, practicing caring, and confirming students' (1991: 193);
- is conferred [by students] and assumed [taken up by teachers]. Not reliant on directives from assumed positions of authority (1991: 193);
- is predicated on the power of caring to transform control and vice versa (Based on 'fidelity to students' [Noddings in Bowers and Flinders 1990: 15] Caring involves commitment, concern and good listening among other things. 'Control and caring are not opposing terms; but the form of control is transformed by the presence of care.'

[Bowers and Flinders 1990:15].)

B. REJECTION of the 'MANAGEMENT METAPHOR' – 'a preoccupation with scientific efficiency and bureaucratic political control at the school level' (1994: 75)
McLaughlin examines this from three perspectives:

1. Obedience – addresses 'myths' about control, e.g. that it is non-negotiable, there is consensus about the meaning of control, it is only a classroom matter, threats to control are individual and that classroom management is not part of instruction.
   'There is no sense in divorcing how one establishes and nurtures classroom relationships from how one teaches; the former is part-and-parcel of the latter' (1994: 78).
2. Responsibility – Classroom management is an issue of teaching students to take responsibility for their behaviour. (But there is always a tension between individual and group concerns).
3. Negotiation – of authority. There is a suggestion that group work skills and negotiation skills should be part of the curriculum.

A further issue is that most of the professional literature on classroom management has been written with school teaching in mind. Imposed order may not be appropriate for adult learners, but it may be what they may expect after years of control at school. The teacher of adults may thus be placed in a dilemma, working with a group on opportunity or even caring lines, or a combination of the two, but may confuse authoritative with authoritarian. Adult learners may not be able to cope with teaching that opens up a wide range of opportunity for learning, but without a single 'right answer' and react negatively. How care is manifested in adult education may be a sensitive issue – care for adults is a different matter from care for children for whom a teacher is *in loco parentis*. Care for adults is a question of respect above all.

The concern with care in classroom management opens up a relatively neglected area in classroom management practice – the affective domain. Chapters 6 and 11 will unpack care further by exploring the affective domain and management practices therein.

5.4   Teachers and classroom management tasks

The overriding concerns in classroom management of order, opportunity and care are at the basis of a teacher's teaching style. They combine with individual teachers' definitions of pedagogy (Chapter 8), individual personality factors, and how 'externals' such as institutional practices are managed, too (Quote 5.7). The influences on teachers' approaches to classroom management are summed up in Figure 5.4.

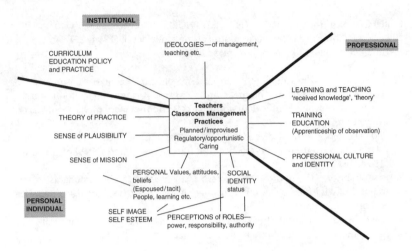

Figure 5.4   Influences on teachers' approaches to classroom management

---

Quote 5.7   Wright on teaching style

Teaching style is a complex amalgam of belief, attitude, strategy, technique, motivation, personality and control. It is usually worked out in response to the language teaching/learning situations in which teachers find themselves employed. There is more to classroom management than discipline and seating arrangements: teaching style lies at the heart of the interpersonal relationship between teacher and learner.
(1987a: 68)

In a teacher's style, there is a strong, although not always clear-cut relationship between how teachers manage and how they teach. Richards (2001) points out that effective teaching and learning is about dealing with the complexities of providing learning opportunities in small crowds. His view of classroom management is order-focused, although orientated more towards behaviour management than authoritarianism. It is in the 'order leads to good learning' mould, and, like Doyle, equates good teaching with 'control' (Quote 5.8).

Quote 5.8   Richards on the teacher's management task

Classroom management refers to the ways in which student behaviour, movement, and interaction during a lesson are organised and controlled by the teacher to enable teaching to take place most effectively. Good managerial skills on the part of the teacher are an essential component of good teaching. In a well-managed class, discipline problems are few, and learners are actively engaged in learning tasks and activities; this contributes to high motivation and expectations for success.
(2001: 170)

How teachers' styles are manifested in practice depends on how they handle the three broad levels of management task (Concept 5.7). Classroom management tasks are part of every teacher's professional activity both in and out of the classroom. The tasks that are conducted outside the classroom are generally larger scale or 'macro' and have an institutional and broader cultural element in them. 'Meso' level tasks enable teachers to plan ahead and use time most appropriately for particular classroom groups. The in-class or 'micro' tasks of classroom management are those most commonly associated with the activities and qualities of teachers, and their 'classroom management skills'.

Concept 5.7   Levels of management task in teaching

There are three interlocking levels of management task:

Macro – Defined by the occupation – enculturaltion of learners into subject disciplines and broad cultural practices (e.g. literacy and numeracy) and secondary socialization (especially of younger members)
Meso – Tasks which involve planning ahead – work plans/schemes of work, assessment and evaluation strategies; lesson planning; development of learning materials
Micro – Tasks in the day-to-day management of a classroom, principally managing time, space, engagement, participation, learning resources. Both planned and improvised, designed and emergent.

Pollard and Tann (1993: 206–10) identify the following micro-skills for management:

- 'withitness' (or capacity to be aware of a wide variety of simultaneous activities)
- 'overlapping' (or capacity to do more than one thing at a time)
- pacing (making judgements about timing and sequencing of activities in lessons)
- 'self-presentation' (ability to project personality, with skills in non-verbal behaviour, voice modulation and 'acting')

They also identify skills for managing classroom episodes:

- beginnings
- transitions
- crises (or 'troubles' (Allwright 1996))
- endings

A final area they note is 'coping strategies' – 'the strategies people adopt in response to their circumstances, as a means of sustaining their sense of self'. These manifest themselves in particular behaviours, such as dealing with conflict by enforcing rigid routines.

Macro level tasks   The macro task of enculturation is the dominant task of teachers, originating in broader society. Their duties, obligations, responsibilities and rights are defined by societies' definitions of teachers' primary roles (Wright 1987a). All teachers are expected to teach and enable learning, both of content and of ways of learning, or what Edwards and Mercer (1987: 157) call 'cognitive socialization'. They are also expected to fulfil what Bowers and Flinders (1990: 29) call their 'cultural gate-keeping' function with regard to learning the culture in which children grow up. Teachers provide the means for learners to enter the culture in which they live, or aspire to live, in many ways – from teaching basic numeracy and literacy to children, to apprenticeship in 'subject communities' like linguists, or vocational worlds like nursing, to enculturation of adults into professional worlds through training. In terms of language teaching, this is a vital area of action, involving identity and affiliation issues. The relevance of the issues for the language teacher is intensified if, for example, they are not mother tongue speakers of the target language. It is consequently very difficult for them to induct learners into the target language communities to which by rights they should belong.

Concept 5.8   Socialisation and the language teacher

Allwright (1996) delimits two main areas of socialisation in pedagogy:

1. Externally-oriented: relating to socialisation of learners into their own community, and the target language community (which may be local or distant).
2. Internally-oriented: relating to socialisation into the classroom group as a social group per se and as a learning group, with the task of learning the target language. (Bowers and Flinders refer to 'the processes of primary socialisation, framing, negotiating, maintaining the order of turn-taking, and the use of humour to strengthen solidarity in the classroom' (1990: 2).)

Allwright also identifies the possibilities of conflict between and among these types of socialisation, which may be the basis of classroom management contingencies.
(after Allwright 1996: 215–16)

A secondary macro task is, therefore, socialisation, a task most commonly associated with formal schooling, with teachers being assigned a broad socialisation (Concept 5.8) role in children's and adolescents' upbringing. This role varies across different cultural contexts and is accorded varying degrees of importance. It can also be argued that there is always a socialisation effect of an enterprise so fundamentally social as classroom teaching-and-learning, that such areas as 'ways of treating what other people say' are open to debate in adult as well as youth education. Decisions regarding rewards and particularly punishments and sanctions for errant behaviour are subject to wider social and institutional influence and may be areas of conflict which are worked out in the classroom. In both primary and secondary macro tasks, order and care dimensions of classroom management are directly involved, and teachers have an important role in modelling behaviours and attitudes, especially in schools, but also in adult and higher education, where teachers' attitudes to language and learning are no less influential.

Meso level tasks   Meso level tasks operate mainly at the planning and strategic level. They consist of creating plans for what is to be done and in what ways in classroom encounters. When teachers plan their work by the lesson and by the term or semester or 'academic year', they are making decisions about the order and intensity of learning experiences, their type, material resources required and available, and the timing and types of assessment as deemed appropriate. Some of these decisions are already made for teachers at institutional or administrative levels – there may be a set curriculum and public examinations, or a set course book which has to be followed in a particular manner – but the choice of actual lesson content and activity is typically in the hands of teachers. In addition, the extent to which the continuing experience of a teaching-and-learning group is used as the basis for ongoing decisions about the content and process of teaching, and how far this is bureaucratically constrained is also significant in influencing management decisions taken at the meso-level outside the classroom. One of a teacher's most important management tasks is to provide continuity to the learning experience over time, and its effect can be weakened by the use of rigid set curricula which specify timing (Chapter 3) and phasing of learning content. In other cases, where a course book acts as the curriculum, decisions taken by the writers of the book could covertly prevent the teacher providing continuity, and by so doing, demonstrate that she is in tune with her learners.

Micro level tasks   Micro tasks are what teachers do during lessons, and are at the heart of classroom management. Ways in which structure is given to learning encounters through managing time, space and activity will have been planned outside the classroom, but how this is executed in real time by teachers and learners will depend on what unfolds during the lesson, and how teachers manage participation, engagement, time and space during allotted time periods. This is realised by micro-management tasks such as initiating and terminating activity, maintaining order, providing continuity between phases of learning-and-teaching activity, monitoring activity, diagnosing and attending to difficulties and organising learners for different types of learning activity. A comprehensive list of these tasks is provided by Pollard and Tann (1993) (Concept 5.7). The performance of these tasks is also a major component of process competence (Legutke and Thomas 1991). Process competence covers the skills, knowledge and awareness teachers (and teacher educators) require to manage language classrooms and teaching/learning encounters (Concept 5.9).

Concept 5.9   Process competence

Legutke and Thomas (1991: 265), in their account of project-based language learning, identify a capacity of *Learners* which they term 'process competence' as a factor in successful project work. This incorporates:

Intrapersonal competence: self-knowledge, knowledge about personal growth, abilities to respond and be responsible
Interpersonal competence: knowledge of groups and their functioning, abilities to interact, cooperate and work on tasks with others.
'Project competence': knowledge about learning, learning process. Ability to manage learning, to learn and teach others.

For *Teachers*, Legutke and Thomas identify the following areas of process competence in moving towards a more 'facilitative' style concomitant with 'project teaching'.

Manager and organiser: identifies possible themes, topics and project ideas; builds on learners' ideas; develops a positive learning climate; chooses appropriate tasks; conducts feedback; conducts negotiations with learners
Instructor: provides language input; teaches learner autonomy; gives formal and informal assessment; provides technical and media guidance
Investigator/researcher: shares ideas and exchange experiences with other teachers; conducts peer observation;   functions as part of a team to experiment with new ideas; collaborates in team teaching

Reconceptualising process competence for *Teacher Educators*, Thomas and Wright (1999) identify three areas of knowledge, skill and awareness for facilitators:

Process management: including intra and interpersonal skills; procedural style in learning encounters; leadership and participation skills/knowledge
Group creation and organisation: group and team building; knowledge of roles; people management
Implementation of change: practical and theoretical knowledge of change processes; awareness and understanding of human response to change

(after Legutke and Thomas 1991 and Thomas and Wright 1999)

Process competence covers the micro tasks of classroom management such as group organisation, the meso tasks of planning, and the macro tasks concerned with implementing new ideas among others. It is a comprehensive view of teachers' management skills, knowledge and awareness. Legutke and Thomas also regard process competence as an important area of development for *learners* in their discussion of more opportunity – focused teaching strategies required by a 'project approach' to language learning. Learners too have micro management tasks to perform while working together, and also meso level strategic tasks as they take more responsibility for managing the course of their learning.

Relationships between management and instruction

By including the instructor role in their definition of process competence for teachers, Legutke and Thomas bring a central issue in classroom management into focus. An essentially order-oriented view of classroom management implies that instruction can only be successful when order has been established. In other words, instruction is built on a foundation of order (Quote 5.9). On the other hand, including instruction, the pedagogic side of teaching, in management activities, recognises its role in managing not only the learning activity sequence and process, but also issues such as group management. Like many contemporary language teaching practices, doing a writing task in a small group is integral to the task itself – the mode of work defines the nature of the task in communicative terms, and to separate instruction from management in describing this practice detracts from its naturally integrated nature.

Quote 5.9 Jones on the relationship between instruction and management

Teachers will be most effective in applying (management/instruction) principles if they realise their management system should be designed to support their instructional system. (1996: 511)

Doyle (1986: 393), despite his view that classroom management is founded on order, notes that it is 'difficult ... to separate managerial and instructional processes' and that research on teacher thinking, effective teaching and classroom discourse can all feed into an understanding of classroom management, acknowledging the interconnectedness of classroom activity. Jones (1996: 506–7, citing Brophy 1988) maintains that an effectively managed classroom encompasses teaching tasks of instruction, classroom management, socialisation and disciplinary intervention. However, both Doyle and Jones are concerned with the problem of order in school classrooms, in particular the issue of maintaining students' attention. Thus, instruction is a part of this system, as Jones notes: 'Clearly, when students are actively engaged in interesting work at which they can be successful, problems of student misbehaviour are minimized' (1996: 510). Instruction is a form of behaviour management – activities which are interesting and not too challenging help teachers minimise disruption.

Jones (1996) points out that when management is deliberately tailored to teaching methods in innovatory situations, it is more likely to be effective, especially 'as teachers move away from teacher-directed presentation and recitation, classroom management methods become more complex' (1996: 508). As pedagogy increasingly promotes opportunity, classroom management becomes more challenging, and disorder and even breakdown are potentially more likely. Consequently, the micro management tasks a teacher may need to perform in opportunity-oriented classrooms are likely to increase in range and difficulty as the levels of risk grow. Whether these are successful or not will to a large extent depend on the strategic and local management skills and capacities of the teacher, and the extent to which learners can handle complexity with less imposition of order. Much also depends on the capacities of the learners for handling change. There is a clear relationship between effective instructional strategies and the types of management activity they entail. But the major unresolved issue is whether the management practices favour containment or regulation at the micro level – a form of control – or extensions of opportunities to learn, needing subtle steering and negotiated order, a type of 'deregulation'. The former tends to stability at the possible cost of opportunity, while the latter hints at instability, but with the potential benefit of unexpected opportunities emerging.

Discoursal issues

The management/instruction question, and tendencies in classroom management to order or opportunity, raise discoursal issues. For example, language teaching practices which encourage experiential or more autonomous learning challenge long-established and deeply ingrained vertical discourses with their unique recontextualising and distributive rules (Bernstein 1996). Discoursal conventions have to be renegotiated in the local context of a classroom as new practices or activity types are introduced. Other examples might include open-ended exploratory discussion, particular types of language learning tasks and certain computer-mediated tasks under the control of learners. Such situations have the potential to impose great strain on participants' existing discoursal resources for managing classroom life. The focal point of any struggle is likely to be located in the relationship between two discourse types: regulatory and instructional (Bernstein 1996). Bernstein identifies two sets of rules which govern them:

- **Regulatory discourse** is in governed by distributive rules, which in turn govern social order, relating to the hierarchical and asymmetrical relations between teacher and student in the pedagogical relationship, including its conduct, character and manner. In classroom management terms they provide the tools for creating and maintaining order.
- **Instructional discourse** is governed by recontextualising rules which order the selection, sequencing, pacing and criteria for evaluation of knowledge in the classroom. In classroom management terms opportunity is either constrained by or created through the instructional discourse.

In Bernstein's terms, the regulatory discourse always 'contains' the instructional discourse (see Figure5.5).Thus in solving 'troubles' which arise from new pedagogic activity, there is always a tendency to attend to the social dimension of classroom life first. This could mean abandoning any attempt to create learning opportunity, so strong is the 'pull' of order and regulation. 'Smooth' classroom discourse would thus proceed under conditions of appropriate order, sufficient to allow the teacher to continue the instructional discourse successfully.

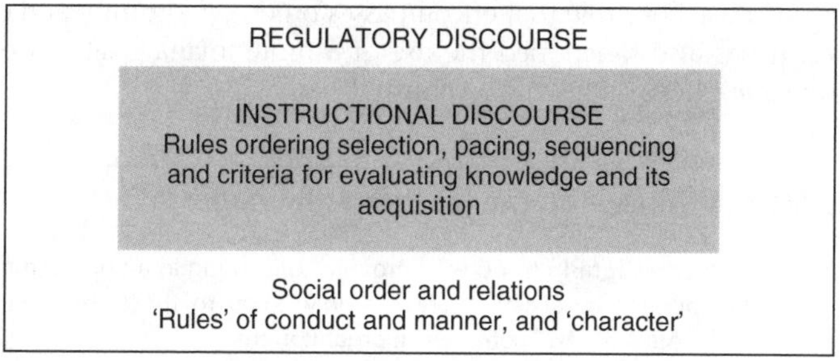

Figure 5.5   Relationships between instructional and regulatory classroom discourses

The model provides a theoretical framework for understanding what happens when more traditional practices of classroom management which focus on order and the transmission of recontextualised knowledge – for example, grammar-based teaching – are replaced by alternative models, such as task-based learning. In these more collaborative, socially pluralistic models of teaching-and-learning, the construction and definition of knowledge by both learners and teachers is accorded greater relevance than in more traditional models. The pedagogic device itself is therefore laid open for renegotiation at the classroom level, requiring the improvisation of new ways of framing the classroom relationship, and the role and status of knowledge.

The implications of the relationship between regulatory and instructional discourses are thus significant in terms of classroom management tasks in all three dimensions. In addition to the power of the regulatory discourse in 'traditional' vertical relationships between learners and teachers, there are implications for more 'responsive' or 'ecologically-sensitive' classrooms, where the regulatory discourse is weaker or there is less need for strong regulatory discourse. The opportunity to address asymmetries in such a classroom is enhanced, but not without risk to the existing social order outside the classroom. New meso and micro level classroom management tasks are implied, in particular to deal with 'troubles'. New types of instructional strategy typically suggest new discoursal relationships between teachers and learners – but the invitation to challenge hierarchies in the classroom may not be supported by social conditions outside the classroom, and the opportunities might be rejected or avoided by learners and teachers.

5.5   The teacher-as-manager

A major outcome of recent debate about teachers' roles in changing approaches to teaching and learning has been the emergence of the idea of 'teacher-as-manager' (Whitaker 1995) (Quote 5.10) On the one hand, this has the advantage of allowing a more holistic view of the teacher's work, permitting a definition of a teacher's role that encompasses order, opportunity and care; on the other, it has also sanctioned the use of a more 'managerial' discourse in delineating a teacher's duties and responsibilities.

Quote 5.10   Whitaker on the teacher-as-manager

Teachers are charged with tasks to do with organizing learning in a pupil community. The complexities of this responsibility are certainly equal to those experienced by senior managers in industrial and commercial organisations.
(1995: 26)

Briggs and Moore (1993) share Whitaker's view of the 'teacher-as-manager'. They observe that 'teaching is a matter of establishing a manageable relationship with the entire class, the context being mutually rewarding engagement in worthwhile tasks' (1993: 494). Problems of order are addressed by careful meso level planning, to prevent them occurring in the first place, and local micro strategies, such as regular routines and activities, provide a platform for effective teaching and learning. Teaching has become a more complicated task (at the macro level) as society has become more complex and traditional authoritarian models of teaching (order-focused) are no longer either appropriate or tenable (Briggs and Moore 1996: 493). They further point out that teachers' personal resources such as enthusiasm, empathy, high self-esteem (in the 'care' dimension) are as important in maintaining order and control in the classroom as the imposition of discipline (Concept 5.10).

The emerging metaphor of 'teacher-as-manager' also has its roots in a shift in emphasis in many educational systems from a focus on *teaching* (or instruction) to a concern with *learning* (and learning about learning) as a prerequisite for successful adaptation to conditions in the 'information age' (Concept 5.10). This view reconstructs learners as individuals responsible for their own learning and its management, diagnosing their own needs and setting their own goals. A management view of teaching also includes areas of professional practice and personal qualities more generally associated with management in the broader occupational sense. For example, contemporary views of management emphasise the behaviours and qualities of 'leadership' (Concept 5.11). Broadly, leadership models tend to emphasise a focus on either people management or task management. In the former, tasks are completed efficiently when people feel well-treated and engaged in the task.

In the latter, the task is successfully completed, regardless of how people feel – efficiency is more important than personal fulfilment. Leadership styles tend to cluster around these two poles. 'Good leaders' have access to the full range of behaviours associated with the two poles and employ them mindfully in the pursuit of goals.

Concept 5.10 Skills and qualities for effective classroom management

1. Teaching as Management (Whitaker)
'The essence of management in schools is the transaction of classroom learning' (1995: 26).

Elements of management
A. Skills and qualities: Occupational (subject matter knowledge, curriculum knowledge, teaching methods and techniques); Personal (listening skills, assertiveness, responding to others needs, clear and appropriate speaking); Managerial (creating – by anticipating and providing solutions, planning, communicating, motivating, organising, evaluating)
B. Personality/experience: experience, awareness, skill, intelligence, intention. Turns capability into action.
C. Operational modes: capacity to operate between fixed and flexible modes.

2. 'Teacher-as-Manager' (Briggs and Moore)
The teacher-as-manager 'has the know how to control a complex and essentially difficult situation.' (1993: 488). This metaphor has grown, they claim, to accommodate social changes (in Australia) which influence the way in which a teacher's authority can be exercised.

Among the tasks and qualities of the teacher-as-manager (drawing on Coulby 1988) are:

- Negotiating acceptable levels of dominance
- Setting up classroom operating procedures
- 'Withitness'
- Reducing and controlling disruption where it does occur
- Maintaining smoothness and momentum
- Effective planning, instruction and evaluation
- Establishing and maintaining effective teacher/student and other interpersonal relations

---

In a management view, a teacher has leadership responsibilities in her classroom context – how she discharges these responsibilities shapes her classroom management practices. There are differing views on how this is achieved however. For example, Whitaker's (1995) definition of leadership in teaching (Concept 5.11) emphasises the human side of management – helping people to learn and a concern with effectiveness and quality of experience.

He notes that 'good leadership is the delicate process of anticipating...needs in others and striving to satisfy them' (1995: 32). Whitaker highlights the importance of personal qualities and concomitant responses teachers can make to learners' stated or emerging needs. This contrasts with a more instrumental and efficiency-based (or technicist) view of management, which advances the view that 'effective classroom management is about the skill of decision-making' (McGuinness 1993: 2). The basis of a successful management approach is, in McGuinness' view, in the clarification of educational objectives, the assembly of resources to use in pursuit of objectives and understanding in detail the environmental influences in which we work.

Concept 5.11   Leadership styles/qualities

1. Sayer (1988): Different demands on teachers call for different modes of management, metaphorically:

- train driving (predictability, clarity of task, following rules)
- medicine (emergency, promotion of healthy lifestyle)
- farming (getting maximum yield from different types of land, equipment, in different weathers)
- rod-fishing (speculation, instinct)

2. Tannenbaum and Schmidt (1958): Styles of decision-making – telling/selling/consulting/sharing

A 'telling' style has teacher ordering the student; when 'selling'; teacher appeals to student's reason or emotions; in a consultative mode, the teacher overtly negotiates and elicits suggestions before agreeing a decision; a 'sharing' mode has a strong and weak version – in the former, the teacher defines the limits and asks students to work within them. In the latter, students are allowed to follow their own path.

3. Whitaker (1995): Leadership in Teaching
'...helping people to tackle the prescribed tasks to the optimum of their ability' (1995: 32) requires:

- genuine interpersonal behaviour
- warmth, care and respect for colleagues
- empathy
- strong belief in others' potential to grow, develop and change

This translates into:

- teachers' ability to understand the classroom experience from each student's perspective
- respect for each individual student
- ability to relate 1-to-1 with each student

4. Tayeb (1996): Decision-making model, based on level of trust and confidence of manager in subordinates.

    a. The Autocrat – low trust/confidence. Makes all decisions and passes them on. Makes threats to ensure compliance. (Tells)

    b. The Benevolent Autocrat – father figure. Convinces subordinates t follow decisions. Some delegation of responsibility. Motivation by reward and punishment. (Sells)

    c. The Consultative Democrat – communicates and consults widely before making decisions. Has final say. (Consults)

    d. The Participatory Democrat – has complete confidence and trust. All decisions are collaborative (Shares)

Sayer's (1988) metaphors imply that leadership means responsibility, power and authority, whatever the general orientation – 'sharing' or 'telling'; 'farming' or 'medicine' (Concept 5.11). Authority is part of the inbuilt asymmetry of a teacher's work – the institutional authority that confers the capacity to control, as well as the professional authority conferred by experience, expertise and knowledge. As Briggs and Moore have pointed out, social forces that question a teacher's positional authority are already in motion. Furthermore, teachers work in an era when the likelihood of having full access to all the knowledge bases of their disciplines is practically impossible. And this is in addition to their inevitable separation from the fields of practice of their chosen specialisations – languages, sciences and so on. Thus where there is open access to information and the means to process it and convert it into working knowledge, through the Internet, for example, the knowledge-based authority of teachers, and hence the professional asymmetry, is being further eroded in the learner's favour. A teacher's work in these circumstances is more likely to be focused on assisting learners in becoming skilful at locating and processing information than in presenting it to them. Much of the presentational work is already taken care of by the designers of web pages and computer software, in the same way that materials writers and textbook writers have traditionally complemented and on occasions dictated the teachers' role as a source of information. However, textbooks are finite and the resources of the worldwide web and ways of accessing them are potentially infinite. Teachers thus face the difficult prospect of adapting to changed circumstances, and even rebuilding professional self-esteem under these conditions. In response, Whitaker (1995) attempts to achieve a melding of practices of caring with those of effectiveness in promoting learning in his view of 'teaching-as-management'. He contends that 'the ways that people in organizations interact and relate to each other and the behaviours they display towards each other in the working environment' constitute 'process', 'the most vital aspect of organizational life' (1995: 40).

'Managerialism' in education

The 'teacher-as-manager' conceptualisation also raises the issue of the influence of management theory and practice on educational practices. It has an influence on teachers, in particular on the relationship between school and teacher cultures. The experience of British education is a case study of the effects of the incorporation of management ideas from the business world into education, a trend which seems to be spreading across national boundaries, and is thus worthy of attention, as it impinges on occupational and practice-based constructions of teaching, and what is possible or desirable in classroom management practice.

Hoyle and Wallace (2003) analyse the rise of 'managerialism' in education. They contrast this idea with definitions of 'management' based on the types of task/person orientations already discussed. 'Managerialism' aims to transform institutions like schools by integrating their work to the service of a mission and vision, a set of beliefs and ideologies rather than a set of practices. The traditional separation of 'management' and teachers in schools is challenged by the requirement that teachers and students agree to the premises of the mission. Managerialism this aims to integrate different sub-cultures – teachers, learners and support staff – under its leadership and develop common institutional cultures, with shared values and missions (Quote 5.11). It is believed that this leads to more focused and efficient schooling. Practices in teaching which are not efficient or in some way measurable are discouraged in this conception of schooling.

Quote 5.11   Hoyle and Wallace on common cultures in schools

The reforms in schools [in Britain] are underpinned by an assumption that school leaders can create a common culture for their school. The culture of management will incorporate the culture of teachers, via the new professionalism, and the pupil culture through its acceptance of the value of individual academic achievement as symbolised by academic credentials.
(2003: 99)

New themes in professional life, such as the spread of documented standards or 'quality', 'efficiency' (being 'professional' in the detached, no-nonsense sense), collaboration (directly confronting the autonomy of teachers in their 'private' classroom domains) and a focus on teaching skills which can be assessed, have been a central feature of the 'new professionalism' aimed at integrating school functions towards the achievement of a common mission. These ideas are also directly and indirectly becoming a part of the learners' classroom and school lives too, as the integration of schools under 'transformational' leadership, which aims to enable schools to achieve their goals and missions, takes place.

In discoursal terms, the 'teacher-as-manager' metaphor echoes Sarangi and Roberts' (1999) conception of professional expertise based on the co-management of three competing discourses in any professional's work. Professionals have to exist in three 'talk and action modes' – professional, institutional and personal. An example of professional discourse in teaching is when a teacher is engaged in the activity routine of error correction, focusing on a student's written work, for example. The institutional mode of this professional activity would entail giving and recording marks. In more personal mode the teacher might remark informally to a student in a moment after a lesson that their work was improving. Successful professional communication demands a seamless blending of these three modes, which invoke the discourses of evaluation and of gate-keeping (students cannot progress without teachers' approval). However, the management metaphor tends to advance institutional interests to the cost of the professional and often the personal. A discourse of 'care', with its emphasis on the personal and professional modes of talk, does not sit easily with the imperative to orderliness and efficiency that characterises institutional discourses. 'Accountability' conflicts with 'availability to help' in professional life, because accountability means doing a job in time-saving ways. Attention to learners' needs and the rhythms of learning does not flow easily into specific time frames.

No doubt teachers are now sensing a tension between their allegiance to values such as 'child or learner-centredness' or 'progressive' education and the establishment of inventories of skills which characterise 'effective classroom management'. Hoyle and Wallace report that in Britain, the move towards integration in schools has given rise to greater ambiguity – professionals still work in zones of uncertainty and have to make judgements, and classroom management is a key area in which this occurs. This runs counter to the technicist discourse of targets and 'quality standards'. It will take time for managerialism to work through the British education system, and while it does, teachers will find their values and practices challenged and held accountable.

Care and opportunity will have to be justified as relevant ideologies in the face of the ideology of control that managerialism has brought to education. The opportunity discourse in classroom management may generate too many risks both for learners and teachers – in particular failing to meet targets, or lack of success in public examinations. Time has become ever more important resource to manage, and the risks of 'wastage' in concerns for opportunity or care may be seen as too great. The preference for a tightly-controlled curriculum over learning may seem preferable, but this does not prevent the classroom from ever becoming anything less than a zone of uncertainty.

Summary

Classroom management activity requires teachers and students to blend three discourses – order, opportunity and care. Sometimes in practice they merge, at others they diverge, and there is discord. Classrooms are unpredictable and can change state very rapidly from order to anarchy or from chaos to calm. Classroom management, rather than attempting to control these movements, is a form of piloting through all sorts of conditions. It is as likely to trigger the events which lead to different conditions as it is to bring them under any form of control. Because instructional and managerial discourses are intertwined in anything other than a functional sense, any move in the classroom is likely to affect either what is learnt or the conditions under which learning is taking place.

Further reading

Allwright (1996) discusses the interaction between social and pedagogic goals in classroom activity.

Bowers and Flinders (1990) articulate the argument against 'technicist' views of classroom management with great force.

Briggs and Moore (1993) Chapters 16 and 17 are a readable practical analyses of classroom management issues from an Australasian perspective.

Doyle (1986) and Jones (1996) review research on classroom management conducted mainly in the United States.

Holliday (1994) provides rich ethnographic descriptions of classroom management practices from Middle Eastern contexts.

Jones and Jones (1991) provides a comprehensive overview to all aspects of classroom management.

Legutke and Thomas (1991) discuss 'process competence ' for teachers and students.

McLaughlin (1991, 1994) articulates the arguments for a concern with care.

Whitaker (1995) is an accessible view of management theory applied to educational contexts.

Wragg (1993) contains a useful overview of 'families' of classroom management.

6
Managing Engagement: The Affective Dimension of Classroom Life

This chapter explores the affective dimension of classroom management, developing issues raised by the core concern of 'care' (Chapter 5). As well as focusing on the care dimension of classroom management in which affect is intentionally foregrounded, we also discuss the emotional consequences of order and opportunity orientations to management in, for example, classroom participation patterns, as revealed in the discourses of learning encounters. In Chapter 1, I referred to this as *engagement*. Engagement, or a lack of it, is integral to classroom management practice.

6.1 Emotions in learning – a contemporary trend

Educators who have been championing 'humanistic approaches', inspired particularly by Carl Rogers (1969, 1983) (Concept 6.1), have long insisted on the pre-eminence of the affective dimension in learning. However, apart from a strong influence in certain parts of the English language teaching profession, the affective dimension has been marginalised in much of mainstream education until recently. Difficulties in motivating schoolchildren (particularly adolescents) have, however, led to a reappraisal of the relationship between order and care domains in classroom life. As McLaughlin (1994) has argued, the 'management metaphor' is associated with discipline and control of the individual. He argues that responsibility is superior to obedience and, as we saw in Chapter 5, advocates negotiation between students and teachers to create solidarity, the basis for responsibility. McLaughlin applauds 'the emphasis on engendering students' self-discipline through teachers' caring acts' (1994: 79)

Since the publication of Goleman's (1995) *Emotional Intelligence* (Concept 6.2), there has been a wider revival of interest in the role of the emotional domain in many aspects of institutional and public life as well as in formal teaching and learning. The recognition that success in life and learning may not simply a matter of being 'smart' has provided the timely impetus to what for teachers and learners have known for generations: teaching-and-learning is an emotional business (Quote 6.1).

Concept 6.1   'Education from the neck down as well as the neck up'

The humanistic psychology of Carl Rogers (1969, 1983) led him to see education as an extension of his practices in non-directive counselling seeking to 'develop and integrate the emotional and intellectual aspects of personality' (Joyce et al. 1997: 31). For Rogers (1983: 19) learning exists on a 'continuum of meaning'. His goal was to shift learning from the 'nonsense', 'meaningless' end of the continuum to 'significant, meaningful, experiential learning'. Thus the emotional immediacy of learning is central to the learning experience. 'Significant learning', contends Rogers (1983: 20), 'combines the logical and the intuitive, the intellect and the feelings, the concept and the experience, the idea and the meaning.' Rogers terms this 'whole-person learning'.

'Significant or Experiential Learning'
It has a quality of personal involvement – the whole person in both feeling and cognitive aspects being in the learning event. *It is self-initiated.* Even when the impetus or stimulus comes from the outside, the sense of discovery, of reaching out, of grasping and comprehending, comes from within. *It is pervasive.* It makes a difference in the behaviour, the attitudes, perhaps the personality of the learner. *It is evaluated by the learner.* She knows whether it is meeting her need, whether it leads toward what she wants to know, whether it illuminates the dark area of ignorance she is experiencing. the locus of evaluation, we might say, resides definitely in the learner. *Its essence is meaning.* When such learning takes place, the element of meaning to the learner is built in to the whole experience' (Rogers 1983: 20, author's emphases)

Concept 6.2   Emotional intelligence

1. **Knowing One's Emotions** – self-awareness, monitoring of emotions
2. **Managing Emotions** – handling feelings, in particular the effects of negative emotions
3. **Motivating Oneself:** – goal-setting; emotional self-control; use of 'flow' states
4. **Recognising Emotions in Others**: empathy or attuning one's self to others' emotional states
5. **Handling Relationships**: managing others' emotions, or 'social competence'

(after Goleman 1995)

The emotional classroom

Classrooms are, as teachers and learners know, emotionally charged contexts. Several factors contribute the emotional character of classrooms:

- Actually being present in a classroom as a student is either voluntary or compulsory. This will have a profound effect on the emotional tone of a learning context, and, in formal contexts, is a primary factor in conflict and disturbance.
- The relative 'distance' of teacher/student relationships. The quality of the relationships between people in classrooms is different from those in more informal or intimate (parent-child) learning contexts (Mercer 1995). This has discoursal ramifications (Chapter 2). Hence the concern for caring relationships.
- Members of the classroom community also *invest* emotionally, socially and psychologically in the situation (Wenger 1998: 56; Norton 2000; Breen 2001a and b).
- The relative 'difficulty' of the learning task itself. As we have seen, classroom learning is often made more difficult by being psychologically and physically distant from contexts of use of new learning.

The affective domain is central to learning and its management a central concern in teaching-and-learning. Managing affect poses specific challenges to teachers and students – it is difficult and delicate. Teachers have addressed the challenges directly in two main ways, a 'weak' and 'strong' version of affect in educational practice:

1. Through the creation of optimum emotional conditions for teaching-and-learning (a 'weak' version), and
2. By adopting the more wide-ranging and problematic construct of the growth of human potential into their beliefs and practices (a 'strong' version) (Quote 6.1).

Quote 6.1   Arnold on why focus on affect in language teaching?

... attention to affective aspects (of language learning) can lead to more effective language learning.

... attention to affect in the language classroom reaches beyond language teaching and even beyond what has traditionally been considered the academic realm.

(1999: 2–3)

An understanding of classroom management practices is legitimately concerned with the first, but perhaps less so with the second goal, which does more than generate a response to affective aspects of classroom life.

Teachers' ideological commitment to the belief system of 'humanism' (see Concept 6.1) may lead to practices with more wide-ranging goals. Askew and Carnell (Quote 6. 2) regard this as the development of 'emotional literacy', while Arnold (1999) (Quote 6.1) sees common ground in values among 'humanistic educators' to contribute to the growth of human potential. More modestly, Underhill (1989), discussing the contributions to English language teaching of Abraham Maslow and Carl Rogers, notes: 'The job of the facilitator is not to decide what students should learn, but to identify and create the crucial elements of the psychological climate that helps to free the learners to grow' (1989: 251). Underhill regards these elements as the ingredients of 'process'. They encompass several areas of concern in that part of classroom management devoted to creating optimum leaning conditions.

However, Legutke and Thomas (1991), in a wide-ranging critique of 'humanistic methods' in language teaching, point out the dangers inherent in a teacher 'forcing' a 'caring classroom climate' on their learners, unknowingly using their position as teacher to engineer particular conditions without the consent of learners. They see this as 'consistent with [a] primarily interventionist and teacher-centred view of learning, that the creation and maintenance of the learning climate is not seen to result from cooperative effort and discussion' (1991: 66). In other words, caring can easily become a form of control if it is imposed.

Quote 6.2   The affective domain – more than marginal

Affective language learning fits within what appears to be an emerging paradigm that stretches far beyond language teaching. There is evidence from a wide variety of fields which indicates that attention to affect-related concepts is playing a very important role in the solution to many types of problems and in the attainment of a more fulfilling way of life.
(Arnold 1999: xii)

In very diverse areas of experience there is a growing concern for humanistic approaches and for the affective side of life. Perhaps the common ground upon which all rest – both in language learning and the greater whole of society – is a desire to contribute to the growth of human potential.
(Arnold 1999: xiii)

. . . CHAT [cultural historical activity theory] is not concerned only with *cognitive* development. All action, whether practical or theoretical, involves the whole person – body, mind and spirit.
(Wells and Claxton 2002: 5)

. . . emotional literacy . . . includes challenging our emotional reactions. Emotions affect learning and are themselves shaped by cultural ideas, practices and institutions.
(Askew and Carnell 1998: 28)

Classroom climate

Concept 6.3 Classroom atmosphere, tone and climate

...most teachers have a good idea of the sort of 'atmosphere' they would like to have in their classrooms, and do their best to plan to set up such an atmosphere (whether they want it to be relaxed and friendly, or brisk and business-like, or whatever). (Allwright and Bailey 1991: 22)

To create a climate for moulding their students into a cohesive and supportive learning community, teachers need to display personal attributes that will make them effective as models and socializers: a cheerful disposition, friendliness, emotional maturity, sincerity, and caring about students as individuals as well as learners. The teacher displays concern and affection for students, is attentive to their needs and emotions, and socializes them to display these same characteristics in their interactions with one another. (Brophy 2001: 8)

Classroom climate could cover some or all of the following: (after Williams and Burden 1997: 195–9)

- Quality of relationships.
- Goal orientation (including competitiveness).
- System maintenance and change (including order, rule clarity).
- Satisfaction/friction/competitiveness/difficulty and cohesiveness (aspects of classroom environment after Fraser 1988, in Williams and Burden).

The focus of these factors is on the participants' experience of classroom life. Pollard and Tann (1994) also refer to Fraser's model. Pollard and Tann emphasise the role of good teacher-student and student–student relationships in the creation of a good classroom climate.

Rogers (1996: 165) identifies four main constituents of classroom climate:

1. Warmth – strength of emotions and identification between the teacher and learners. Welcoming? Dismissive? Exclusive? Encouraging to the learner?
2. Directness – direct or indirect interactions between teacher and student. 'openness' of communication – honesty/directness. Direct or less direct contact between teachers and learners e.g. whole class teaching or independent group work?
3. Enthusiasm – teacher's attitude towards subject, students and their learning. Commitment of both teacher and learner to the learning task.
4. Organisation – teacher's competence in managing – its strength and efficiency. Sense of being 'on-task'

The atmosphere of the learning group may be relaxed, warm and friendly, or it may be tense, cold and hostile. The responses of the student participants could be on the one hand apathetic, obstructive, uncertain and dependent, or on the other alert, responsible, confident and initiating. (Rogers 1996: 165)

Teachers and learners working in classrooms together are acutely aware of the psychological and emotional conditions in which they interact and the effects on the quality of their relationships and of the productivity of what they are doing. Underhill (1989: 252) points out the importance of affective phenomena in successful learning as a 'management' issue. Like Underhill, we typically describe the 'tone' of classroom activities, or its 'atmosphere' or the 'climate' (Concept 6.2). Classroom management is thus quintessentially concerned with creating good conditions for teaching-and-learning, and the emotional domain is the zone of action in this respect. Teachers' and students' metaphors can give us useful indications of their emotional constructions of the classroom. The five below show how a metaphor can contain a great deal of emotional resonance. Several explicitly mention the atmosphere – 'positive' or 'good'. Notions of balance, rest and comfort, and descriptions of supportive and warm behaviour all feature. We can perhaps begin to gauge the climate of these teachers' classrooms from their metaphors.

Data Extract 6.1   Some classroom metaphors

These metaphors for the classroom were created as part of an introductory session on classroom research. Some of the descriptive language the teachers used is quoted. (See Part 3 for the use of metaphor in research on classroom management.)

Puppet Show – 'the teacher should be a giant, not in size, but in his knowledge, understanding, love, sympathy, manners, behaviour and humanity.'
'Karesanui' (Japanese raked garden in Buddhist temple grounds) – 'waves might be a tough time'; 'straight lines might be "working steadily" '. 'Natural/balanced/dynamic.'
An oasis – 'a traveller in the desert seeks this place to revitalise and move on'; 'travellers enjoy the water and dates'.
A family and neighbours chatting outside their house – 'positive atmosphere. No domination by one individual. They are beside a stream which flows silently and gently. People there are free to flow with the stream, not tied by 4 walls.'
Clown's performance – 'must create a good atmosphere'; 'classroom is fluid – changes from day to day'; 'clowns love their audience of children'.

However, the reality may not match the image, which more often than not describes an ideal. A fuller description of the fabric of classroom life may offer more clues regarding the affective domain (Field Note 6.1).

Field Note 6.1   Looking for Affect in Classrooms (Secondary English – Malawi)

It is the first class of the day. The teacher walks into the classroom, smiling. She brings along her record book, the class register, a textbook and some posters. She greets the students. The students stand up and greet her back. She then takes the register. She walks to the chalkboard and writes the word 'Deforestation'. She asks the students what they understand from the word. She elicits the answers from the students and gets three different responses. She writes the responses on the board. Next, she asks the students to take out their dictionary and check the meaning. She then asks for a volunteer to write the meaning on the board. She asks the students to compare what they understand of the word with the meaning provided in the dictionary. Afterwards she takes out some posters and tapes them to the board. The teacher asks if the students have seen it happening around them. A few students put up their hands. The teacher asks the students where they see it and the reasons for cutting down the trees. There are some murmurs from the students. The teacher writes the question on the board. She asks the students to call out from number one to seven, and then sit according to their numbers. The students move to sit in their respective groups. The teacher moves to the front of the class and gives the students instruction on what they are supposed to do. She clearly states that the students have to discuss the question on the board. They are given 15 minutes to do so. They have to select a 'secretary' for their own groups and decide who will present afterwards. The teacher reminds them to use English as much as possible through out the discussion.

What may immediately strike readers is the relative lack of emotional content or tone in Field Note 6.1, which is a largely 'methodological' account. We learn that the teacher enters the classroom room smiling. The 'busy-ness' and continuity of the activities indicate the classroom group's engagement in the activities, as does their response to the teacher's question on tree cutting. The students may have been smiling. They may have been working noisily and energetically, with a lot of gesture and kinesthetic involvement in the group work stages. Without these 'indicators', though, we lose a sense of the emotional climate of any lesson. In 'process' terms, we see teaching-and-learning activity, but we do not gain access to the subjective realities of the participants (Concept 6.4) which are the basis of their emotional response. In order to account more fully for classroom climate, we need access to subjective experiences as well as surface features of activity.

Concept 6.4   Process and atmosphere

Process concerns 'anything that contributes to the ambient atmosphere of the classroom, including the values, attitudes and beliefs of teachers and learners (Underhill 1989: 251):

- The way the content is taught and its relevance to the lives of learners.
- The immediate subjective reality of the learning group and how they see themselves and relate to others.

Issues in process are concerned with:

- Authority and self-determination.
- Expectation and motivation.

Concept 6.4   (Continued)

- The individual and the group.
- Security and risk.
- Self-esteem (and its absence).
- Personal meaning.
- How participants think, feel and relate to each other.

(after Underhill 1989)

In describing the classroom climate we are summing up the multitude of actual and possible emotional states of participants, individually and collectively experienced. These include:

- Learners' emotional states while experiencing and navigating classroom activity.
- Teachers' emotional states during classroom activity.
- The interpersonal responses of teachers and learners to the emotional conditions of the classroom at any given time in a lesson, and to each other.

The classroom climate thus describes the conditions under which teaching and learning are experienced, and also the conditions that are created during the course of a classroom encounter. Emotional states can and often do continue after a lesson, in the same way that they can be 'brought' to a lesson. Many of these indicators are, as we have seen, 'intangibles' – how a lesson or classroom 'feels' to the observer or participants is impossible to measure, but, if we believe that individuals' subjective accounts are trustworthy and valid, we can learn more about the emotional domain in classrooms and how it is managed by participants.

6.2   The emotions of learning

Learning fuses cognitive and affective processes, involving phenomena such as the capacity to persist in learning regardless of setbacks and short and long-term motivation to engage with the learning task (Claxton 1999). Learning languages also presents a unique set of affective issues related to the 'foreignness' of new identities implied by speaking another language. The traditional division of cognitive and affective in learning is challenged by these phenomena which connect them. Recent work in neurology and in human learning has provided further evidence in support of a more holistic view of the role of affect in learning (Quote 6.3). Notions of 'whole-brain' learning are now well-established in foreign language teaching and general education. Socio-cultural views of learning (after Vygotsky 1978) emphasise the close relationship between thought and feeling. This is further evidence to support the close connections between management and instruction in formal learning. New learning, for example, is likely to create both affective and cognitive difficulty. Response to difficulty takes many forms, which are themselves ways in which learners manage the experience – positively and negatively – and also has to be 'managed', by both learners and teacher.

Quote 6.3   Learning as both cognitive and affective

... learning in the ZPD [zone of proximal development] involves all aspects of the learner – acting, thinking and feeling.
(Wells 1999: 331)

... the affective and volitional tendency stands behind thought.
(Vygotsky 1987: 282, in Mahn and John-Steiner 2002: 47)

... purely cognitive theories of learning will be rejected unless a role is assigned to affectivity.
(Hilgard 1963: 267, in Arnold 1999: 7)

Self and other-management of emotions on a minute-by-minute basis and on a longer-term basis is a basic classroom activity. It is rare to be immediately successful in learning or teaching, or necessarily even to enjoy the experience, particularly when one has not chosen to learn, or perhaps dislike one's fellow learners or the teacher. The short-term management of 'difficult' emotional states and the long-term management of students' commitment to the learning task are very much part of the fabric of classroom life and are encapsulated by the notion of engagement (Concept 6.5).

Concept 6.5   Engagement

Engagement links immediate classroom responses to experience ('local motivation') with long term motivation, commitment and self-esteem, among other factors.

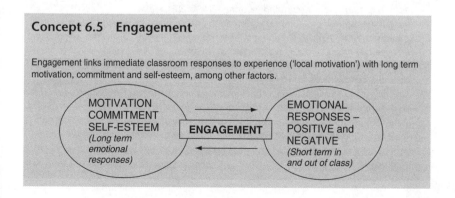

Learning, affect and change

Learning involves change in a number of different ways – changes in pre-existing ideas and concepts (or 'unlearning'), perhaps of deeply held beliefs and attitudes, even values, of skills, of ways of responding to events. All learning thus carries some degree of threat to the individual's current state. Learning also contains elements of discomfort and risk, as the status quo is challenged. As Brookfield (1990: 46) remarks, 'learning is rarely experienced in an emotionally denuded, anodyne way'. Learning anything new involves a range of emotional responses which signal the affective quality of the learner's engagement with the task – from anger and frustration on the negative end of the scale, to extreme exhilaration and excitement, even euphoria, on the other (Concept 6.6). In a single lesson, a learning group could experience all of these emotions as they deal with a difficult concept and are at first unable to understand it, then experiencing the excitement of insight and the pleasure of success in mastering the new concept, especially as it has involved effort and sacrifice. It is also the case that an experience will be differentiated in terms of its intensity and also the onsets of various states. At all stages, the teacher and learners are involved in the management of these immediate and fluctuating emotional responses. Strong negative emotions can 'block' progress; whereas overexcitement can prevent consolidation. Managing this is a delicate task for teachers and learners, all the more difficult because it entails responding on the spot, and without a 'rulebook'.

Concept 6.6   Learner's experiences of the emotionality of learning

Brookfield has collected adult learners' responses to learning events through a 'critical incident recall' procedure (see Research Techniques). Some of the emotions recalled were as follows:

1. Physiological effects (or metaphors) 'stumbling across insights'; chills, knots of anxiety in the stomach, hot with embarrassment, flushed with anger (teaching experienced as 'exhaustingly, mind-numbingly boring' (1990: 46).
2. Negative responses: 'profound embarrassment at inability to feel as assured or confident as desired' to 'deep angry resentment' of teachers' dismissive arrogance.
3. Positive responses: 'aroused and excited at breaking out of conventionally accepted ways of thinking and behaving' and exhilarated' when they can do difficult things or understand difficult concepts.
4. Grieving for lost certainties. Questioning assumptions or seeing the taken-for-granted as distorted is distressing and disturbing.
5. A sense of risk and exposure (can add to the significance of learning episodes) which turns into satisfaction and a feeling of liberation and empowerment when challenge is met.

(after Brookfield 1990: 46–7)

Emotional Factors and Difficulties for Learners

Anxiety – some physical symptoms (sweating, shaking) but mainly internal. Also hesitation and uncertainty. Typical reaction to stressful situations. Withdrawal from situation is common.

Fear of failure – individual may refuse to take risks. Feelings held back.

Reluctance to join in learning activity – wish to avoid pain, uncertainty, possible ridicule.

Reluctance to 'play' – teaching and learning is a serious 'academic' business.

Low self-esteem – people can't see resources available in the context or themselves and thus have a narrow 'learning horizon'.

Fear of ambiguity – avoiding situations where there might not be a correct answer or instant 'black and white' outcome.

Fear of disorder – dislike of confusion and complexity. Need for 'neat' boundaries to concepts.

Fear of being assertive – people not wanting to appear too assertive or aggressive, and may be hesitant to identify with new ideas or points of view

(after Rogers 1996: 211–18)

Summary key aspects of emotions in learning

1. *Physiological Responses* – positive and negative: from anxiety to excitement.
2. *Behaviours*: positive: engagement with activity; purposeful and enjoyable activity; 'play' negative: withdrawal, avoidance, provoking conflict, lack of assertiveness.
3. *Psychological Explanations*: like/dislike of ambiguity; desire for closure/openness; grief at loss; threats to identity; self-esteem; fear of risks.

Brookfield's (1990) account of the emotions of adult learning draws on learners' actual experiences of learning and examines learners' emotions exhaustively, detailing physiological effects, positive and negative feelings in-time responses, and longer term emotional responses such as feelings of loss and risk. Rogers (1996) has produced a similar, although slightly more negative, list (Concept 6.7). These conceptualisations indicate that learners respond in three main ways while learning.

- Physiological – changes in physical state, e.g. increased or slowed heart rate.
- Behavioural – immediate manifestations of emotional response in classroom situations, e.g. withdrawal from activity.
- Psychological – grounded in longer-term affective processes, e.g. increased self-esteem.

In order to examine these systematically, it helps to distinguish between the physiological, the behavioural and the psychological, moving from more to less concrete accounts of emotionality (Concept 6.8).

Concept 6.8   Emotional/affective states in learning

Many emotional states are associated with learning. Learning is never neutral emotionally. Some common emotions experienced while learning include:

Positive – euphoria, 'flow', excitement, feelings of achievement and empowerment, heightened sense of meaning.
Negative – fear, frustration, 'loss of control', infantilisation, boredom, anger, embarrassment.

Goleman (1998) notes the importance and difficulty of self-management and the need for sensitivity in management of such emotions in others.

Signs of all three aspects may be present as learners react to a classroom situation as they experience it, differentially as well as collectively – short-term engagement patterns, infused with fluctuating positive and negative feelings, are the outcome (Concept 6.6). These emotional responses may also reflect longer-term engagement patterns. For example, many learners appear to have low self-esteem, which is also an explanation of why they don't grasp challenges or withdraw, often claiming inability. Their longer-term engagement in learning is disabled by this state, which may in turn be amplified or mollified by further difficult classroom experiences. Trying to understand one's self as a learner means 'unpacking' this complex array of feelings. For a teacher, this poses possibly the major management challenge – how to gauge the emotional states of a group of people in order to help manage their immediate and longer term engagement in learning and also to help learners manage their own levels of engagement.

Managing change

As we have seen, learning is potentially destabilising for learners. It is also subject to 'blocks'. Rogers (1996) observes that these 'range from what may be called emotional variables at one extreme to conceptual difficulties at the other extreme' (1996: 205). The blocks are related to three factors:

1. Emotional investment in previously-learned knowledge – any challenge to the authority of this knowledge is seen as a challenge to 'significant others' like former teachers, parents and our own judgement. Learners may resist attempts to introduce them to new ideas (Quote 6.4).

Quote 6.4   Rogers on resisting learning

. . . many student participants put a great deal of investment into defending their existing patterns of knowledge, attitudes and behaviour. Attempts to build up new patterns, to introduce learning changes, may result in strong emotional reactions. The teacher must tread carefully.
(1996: 219)

2. Existing prejudices – Rogers terms these phenomena usefully as 'over-certainties' (1996: 208). It appears difficult for adults to reveal their prejudices to critical scrutiny, and exposure of these may result in extreme emotional responses of anger or sadness.
3. Habits – many are habit-bound through a need for security and also a reverence for the past. People are also conformist and cling to widely-held views. Again, there is emotional investment in these habits. It is reasonable to speculate on the extent to which these tendencies are established during childhood and adolescence.

Unwilling learners and potential disturbances to calm, and the accompanying negative feelings they entail are ever-present realities for teachers and learners. On the other hand, failure to address difficulties or frustrating aspects of learning can result in a cumulative 'learned helplessness' or dependence on the teacher to keep the level of challenge down. Teachers may also wish to introduce change into their classroom routines on the basis of new ideas gained from either reflection on practice or external sources. They are thus positioned both as change agents and as change managers, a problem further alluded to in Prabhu's (1992) analysis of the potential disruption that might follow from the introduction of discovery learning (Quote 6.5).

Quote 6.5   Prabhu on problems in timing of a teacher's input

A recommended teaching procedure may incorporate the principle that learners' efforts should precede the teacher's input, such that much of the learning takes place as a form of discovery by the learner, and the teacher's input is responsive to the learner's effort, rather than be preemptive of it. But the classroom lesson as a social genre includes the notion that it is part of the teacher's role to provide the necessary inputs and that it is therefore unfair or incompetent of the teacher to demand effort by learners in the absence of such inputs.
(1992: 230–1)

Changes in pedagogy threaten the social status quo as well as the climate. The types of response to change (Concept 6.8) that have been recorded have many similarities to the emotional responses of students to learning.

Concept 6.8   Responses to change

- Low self-esteem, feeling hopeless and inadequate in the face of new knowledge.
- Fear of the unknown.
- Desire to return to the past after initial acceptance of new ideas.
- Helplessness in the face of perceived ambiguity, or uncertainty about new meanings.
- Active dislike of the teacher for making the challenge too great.
- Open challenges to teachers' competence and expertise.

Concept 6.8   (Continued)

- Fear of looking inadequate or foolish in class.
- Fear of loss of control over situations.
- Anger at 'having been wrong all these years', of losing face.
- Fear of being 'different' from peers.
- Anxiety about being able to do the same outside class, 'in the real world'.
- Annoyance about having to do extra work.

(after Whitaker 1993 and Brookfield 1990)

Research and practice in education (Whitaker 1993), business (Stewart 1996) and medical counselling (Kubler-Ross 1997) indicates that individuals appear to go through a process of adapting to changed circumstances (Concept 6.9). Emotions of anger, grief, helplessness, anxiety, loss, hopelessness are all present at different stages. We can speculate that learners experience similar if not such extreme or deep emotions when they encounter new knowledge that disturbs their worldview. A recurrent example from recent experience in English language teaching is the challenge posed by new conceptualisations of grammar and new descriptions of language made possible by analysis of corpus data (for example, Carter and McCarthy 1995) to language teachers' and learners' knowledge, and their self-esteem which comes from previous mastery, and their sense of plausibility for pedagogic success.

Concept 6.9   Responses to change

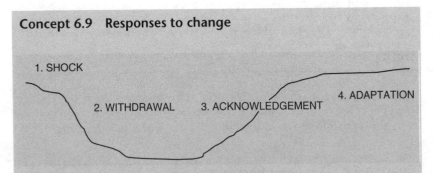

People experiencing changes in personal or professional life have been observed going through a series of stages as they deal with the change. The length of time and intensity of each stage vary enormously partly in response to the gravity of the change: moving to a new class can be as emotionally demanding as moving house, for example.
(after Whitaker 1993)

Learning and emotion – neurological bases

The physiological manifestations of emotion and learning are grounded in the complex workings of the brain's limbic system. Recent and ongoing discoveries of the biological bases of emotion have been very influential in the teaching profession's (and others') reappraisal of the role of emotion (Concept 6.10). Neurological work has demonstrated that people have only marginal and not always reliable control over their emotional states.

Concept 6.10   Neurological bases of emotions

Goleman (1995: 289) proposes eight basic 'families' of emotions: anger; sadness; fear; enjoyment; love; surprise; disgust; shame. He notes physiological manifestations of all these – from blood running out of the face in fear, through relaxation induced by laughter, to the curl of the upper lip and wrinkled nose in disgust.

Research reported by Goleman (1995) Carter (1999) and Greenfield (2000) indicates that the limbic system or midbrain is the seat of the emotions. The amygdala is the main organ for processing incoming sensory information, and giving it emotional 'tone'. It is connected to the hippocampus, seat of long-term memory, and the two organs work together to provide a simple but powerful way of classifying experiences. The cortex, the seat of reasoning, receives incoming information very slightly later than the limbic system. This is just enough time for the emotional colouring of information to set in motion physiological changes. Goleman calls this 'emotional hi-jacking' (1995: 13). However, because the bulk of incoming information is processed by the thalamus (also part of the limbic system) and then the neocortex, the brain has a means of dampening the effects of strong emotions.

Learning and the underlying message of change pose a threat to the learner – the brain is predisposed to fight or flee when faced with a threat. The powerful physiological responses to threat or challenge cannot be prevented – the brain is 'wired' in such a way that emotion is triggered and experienced before more rational thought. People therefore tend to respond emotionally before they can 'think things through'. If learners are 'on the back foot', and ready to 'run' from difficulty, teachers need to be able to recognise this and respond, perhaps by reducing the level of difficulty of the challenge, or otherwise assisting the learners in overcoming difficulty.

To some extent, therefore, we are at the mercy of the electrochemistry of our brains, but this, as Goleman (1995:7) points out, 'is shaped further by our life experience and our culture.' A further issue raised by Goleman is the extent to which teachers are responsible for the 'emotional education' of children, an issue raised by the 'humanists'. This is important not only because teachers spend such large proportions of childrens' lives as their carers and guardians. Caring and socialisation coalesce in the affective domain.

How teachers manage the negative and positive emotions of formal learning in terms of the way they model behaviours, attitudes and values may be crucial to the emotional development of children.

Language learning activities – challenges, anxieties and responses

Allwright and Bailey (1991) claim that learning a foreign language is more difficult than any other 'subject' because of the combination of risks and difficulties the enterprise poses, problems which are amplified by being in a public setting like the classroom (Quote 6.6). Language learning potentially risks loss of face and feelings of foolishness or inadequacy, which are all direct threats to one's sense of self and one's confidence in oneself. These are powerful negative feelings and, as Allwright and Bailey point out, require a certain 'strength' or robustness of character to withstand. Submission to these feelings may, on the other hand, lead to withdrawal or 'hiding'.

Quote 6.6   Allwright and Bailey on the problem of classroom language learning

. . . performing in a foreign language class is in itself potentially somehow more stressful than performing in other subject classes. In mathematics, for example, you may get the answer wrong, but at least you can be reasonably sure of saying the numbers correctly. In language work, by contrast, even if in a sense you get the answer right (you find the correct form of the verb, say, in a blank-filling item) you may still make an almost infinite number of mistakes in what you say – for example, with imperfect pronunciation of individual sounds, wrong word stress, wrong sentence stress, and so on. . . . In short, the risk of making a fool of yourself in a language class is very high, and you need to be a singularly robust character to avoid being affected adversely by feelings of anxiety in such a setting.
(1991: 174)

Overcoming low levels of self-confidence is an important aspect of attending to the emotional domain in classroom language learning. A common explanation is that learners often lack confidence. Williams and Burden refer to 'individuals who lack confidence in themselves as language learners, who have negative self-image as regards speaking other languages, and who are afraid to express themselves in the foreign language' (1997: 72). On the other hand, Brookfield (1990: 53–4) notes that learners, in their self reports on significant breakthroughs in learning, reported that these were often unexpected and gave rise to surges of self-confidence, coupled with feelings of excitement and liberation because, Brookfield feels, the learners felt that they had made the breakthroughs of their own accord, and felt what he calls a 'sense of agency'.

Data Extract 6.1   Some emotional responses to learning

Selected extracts from adult learners' reviews of learning experience:

'When I was travelling to the course, I was wondering 'will I be up to the challenge?'

'What happens if I can't understand or manage an assignment?'

'On the very first day of our classes the fears disappeared. We students talked about our doubts. It felt better.'

'Being observed by colleagues was a stressful experience because we feel threatened and are worried about saving face.'

As well as providing students with a sense of being in command of their own learning, resilience needs to be nurtured. Claxton (1999) (Quote 6.7) identifies resilience as a basic foundation for learning. Without a measure of resilience, a learner will not have the emotional strength to try again after failure or mistakes, or even to make the first move in a learning event. Many people arrive on new courses with little resilience and a fragile sense of their own worth as learners (Data Extract 6.1). Nurturing their resilience must therefore be an urgent requirement in the early stages of a new programme or course, as a major 'macro-strategy' in the management of engagement.

Quote 6.7   Claxton on learner resilience

... learning itself is an intrinsically emotional business. That is why resilience, the ability to tolerate these emotions is so important. Even when learning is going smoothly, there is always the possibility of surprise, confusion, frustration, disappointment or apprehension – as well, of course, as fascination, absorption, exhilaration, awe or relief. If the first whiff of frustration makes you want to withdraw, your learning is going to be shallow and unadventurous.
(1999: 15)

There is thus little doubt that language learning is an anxiety-ridden activity. Allwright and Bailey (1991: 173) note that learners may not present themselves in a positive light if they are trying to use the target language. By preventing learners from using their mother tongue, language lessons may be depriving them of a significant aspect of their self-worth. This type of anxiety is unlikely to be salient outside the classroom. However, learning a foreign language may provoke deeper anxieties which are tied up in the identity of the learners. This point will be dealt with below, as it suggests a broader explanation for a particular emotional response to its role in feelings of 'foreignness' when experiencing novelty in learning (Kaikkonen 2001: 74).

Deciding to engage: costs and benefits

One of the problems teachers face in the management of the emotional domain is the 'unengaged' learner. There is considerable pressure on the teacher to draw all learners into the teaching-and-learning experience, but it is not always possible. Learners may decide not to engage for entirely rational and also intuitive reasons. The thinking process they go through may conceivably be re-enacted every time they encounter a new learning opportunity, a process of continuous appraisal and monitoring of the learning context. They are engaged in a 'cost/benefit' analysis, undertaken before deciding on whether or not to engage in new learning (Claxton 1996). Claxton's work is focused on the adult learner whose participation is voluntary, and there is a degree of choice in whether or not to participate, and may not be applicable to younger learners. (Concept 6.7)

Concept 6.7   To engage or not

'Integrated learning theory' (Claxton 1996)
1. Learning reflects ongoing decision-making about whether to engage with the challenges presented, and if so how (this includes consideration of goals, current priorities, perceived support and emotional costs and risks).
2. The decision-making process is a sort of 'intuitive cost-benefit analysis', which attempts to work out the most desirable course of action based on perceived opportunities, demands, costs, rewards and risks inherent in the situation and learners' self-images.
3. Learning is not a homogeneous activity, and learners have a repertoire of strategies and processes to deploy.
4. Learners, as well as having ways of engaging their competence, also have defensive strategies which enable them to make choices about whether or not to engage.
5. Learners' views of risks and rewards are based on 'views-of-the-world' which are the residue of past experiences of life and learning.

However, Claxton singles out the importance to learners of support (of all sorts, including emotional) and emotional risks, such as looking foolish, fear of dropping out, and predicted challenges to individuals' self-image.

Breen (2001b) adds a discoursal dimension to the significance of learners' decisions to participate, and the strategic nature of learners' decision-making. Because learners navigate the classroom discourse according to their expectations of particular social practices (e.g. asymmetry), and because they are 'sifting' the discourse to discover 'what counts' – as a valid interpretation of the situation, valid knowledge and appropriate strategic behaviour, 'they (learners) are obliged to work in order to maximise the learning and social benefits they may gain from the discourse while minimising its potential psychological and social costs' (2001: 314–15) Learners, in Breen's terms 'navigate' between the social and psychological costs and benefits of classroom action, and, in particular, learning activity.

Affective difficulties – adults and adolescents

Data Extract 6.2   Behaving badly

These are extracts from interviews with teachers from different contexts.

Sometimes I wish I was able to disappear. Some of the students' behaviour is dreadful, and they seem to wait for group work to behave badly. That's when they start pinching and pushing each other, throwing books at other groups, and hiding each other's property like pens and so on. It's just so wearing.

When students talk behind my back, while I'm writing on the board, I feel myself getting mad. Sometimes I throw the chalk at them. I know I shouldn't but I have to release my frustration somehow.

I know they're testing me, seeing what my limits are. It doesn't take long to find them unfortunately. How can I get a thicker skin?

I've tried to get them to talk about their behaviour, but it's no use. They don't seem to want to know. The longer it goes on this mayhem. The more learning time we're losing.

The extreme emotions (often very negative) experienced in many adolescents' classrooms are more likely to be 'challenges to authority' or negative reactions to what is felt to be 'boring activity' than personal discomfort in the face of cognitive difficulty (Data Extract 6.2). The extensive research done on behavioural problems in classrooms both in North America and Europe (Doyle 1986; Jones 1996) suggests that there are emotional aspects of the problem, and 'bad behaviour' is one of the most important problems for teachers today (Quote 6.9). Disruptive behaviour is time-consuming for all members of the learning community, and can make teaching impossible, and the occurrence of learning opportunity remote.

Quote 6.9   Kyriacou on some causes of bad behaviour

Most people will find, from time to time, that being trapped in a situation that is unpleasant and from which they cannot escape extremely frustrating. If coercion to participate is also exerted, the sense of frustration can become unbearable. The most serious incidents of pupil misbehaviour are likely to occur when such a tension has built up, and when the pupil feels your attention is aggressive coercion rather than sympathetic and supportive. (1992: 84)

Jones (1996: 509) believes that the goals of classroom management should aim for 'classrooms in which students have the sense of safety, security, empowerment, and support that facilitate learning positive social and academic skills'. He is concerned that a balance between care and order is preserved 'as teachers face (in the United States) increasing numbers of students who desperately need models of caring adults who can simultaneously provide a sense of order and safety in their lives' (1996: 505). This resonates with Bowers and Flinders' (1990) call for 'responsive teaching' in which 'the form of control is transformed by the presence of caring', and McLaughlin's (1991) call for a teacher's authority to be legitimised through care. Classrooms are always going to be contexts in which negative emotions surface because learning is never easy and it is not always possible to 'get on' and make progress. In schools, where the student group is 'captive', the problem may be exacerbated. Classrooms are also venues for the difficult struggles of adolescence, where 'getting even' may be the motive, and where alienation can fuel opposition to authority as represented by teachers. How teachers handle these difficulties in their classroom work is dealt with in Part 2.

Positive emotions

Much of the discussion on the emotional aspects of classroom life has tended to focus on overcoming negative states where learners for one reason or another are not engaging in classroom activity. The impetus for this is pedagogic – engaging students in classroom activity is the most challenging of all tasks facing the teacher. After all, the dice are loaded against the teacher in so many situations – 'captive' and probably uncooperative students, learning something with apparently little intrinsic value, like a foreign language. Although English, because of its pre-eminent international position, has greater currency than most other foreign languages at the beginning of the twenty-first century, this may not be enough to counteract negative responses, as Canagarajah (1993) has pointed out.

However, despite the emotional difficulties created by the learning process, there are moments in classroom learning when positive emotions predominate. In this context, van Lier (1996a: 105–6) describes the importance of 'flow' (Csikszentmihalyi (1990) (Quote 6.10)) in *motivation in the present*. If learners are fully absorbed in learning tasks, and enjoying the experience, they are in a 'flow' state. People in a flow state experience a range of positive feelings from calm to curiosity, deep interest and even euphoria.

Quote 6.10   Flow

. . . optimal experience . . . the state in which people are so involved in an activity that nothing else seems to matter; the experience itself is so enjoyable that people will do it even at great cost, for the sheer sake of doing it.
(Csikszentmihalyi 1990: 4)

> ... an experience in work or play, when time seems to be suspended, everything happens just the right way, and one is totally absorbed in the activity. Preconditions for this state of flow are a perfect balance between available skills and challenges. Anxiety results from insufficient skills and challenges, and learning means that skills and challenges are increased in order to promote opportunities for 'hitting the flow channel'.
>
> (van Lier 1996a: 106)

Cynics point out the unreality and impossibility of achieving this state in a classroom. However, without a measure of positive affective response to learning it is unlikely that learners will persevere. Teachers work hard to minimise negative emotions, knowing the importance of a positive and warm climate for learning. Avoiding worry and boredom among learners is an important element of this. Achieving positive states is seen as a task of the teacher, working with the learner to produce a positive emotional state termed 'receptivity', a state which might be a precursor to flow (Stevick 1976). Allwright and Bailey identify a number of factors which influence 'receptivity', or 'openness' (1991: 158) (Concept 6.12).

Concept 6.12 Receptivity

* To teacher as person
* To fellow learners
* To teacher's way of teaching
* To course content
* To teaching materials
* To being a successful language learner
* To the idea of communicating with others
* To target language and culture

Stevick regards 'receptive' learning as 'what happens to seed that has been sown in good soil' (1976: 111) Among a number of factors he identifies as being important for receptive learning, he emphasises that 'we need to bring to our work an understanding of the ego-defences which both teacher and instructor use, and of the reasons why they use them' (1976: 112).

(after Stevick 1976, and Allwright and Bailey 1991)

Receptivity includes some of the learners' predispositions towards engaging in the learning task, and they are also part of the longer-term 'background' affective issues noted earlier. Together with resilience, self-esteem, strength of self-image and other predispositions, these make up what the individual learner brings to the learning event and thus what may, in turn, be reinforced and challenged. These specify, for individual learners, the minimum conditions which must prevail if the learner is to engage in learning activity, let alone succeed.

Engagement and motivation – long-term

The longer-term affective dimensions of learning are closely related to motivation. Schumann (1999) discusses how a learner's perception of the relative 'unpleasantness' of an immediate experience may be traded off against longer term learner goals (Quote 6.11). Citing the example of Eva Hoffman, a Polish immigrant to Canada, he argues that a learner may be willing to reclassify negative experience as positive if, in hindsight, it seemed to lead to valuable learning. In other words, strategic motivational forces come into play. These can be strong enough to overcome the risks and perhaps sense of loss involved in learning a foreign language. Learning a foreign language can also provide learners with the means to express things which they are unable or unwilling to articulate in their mother tongues.

Quote 6.11   Schumann on the long-term goals and emotional responses

Eva (Hoffman 1989) seemed capable of dissociating local appraisals of the pleasantness of agents, events and objects from the value she placed on the goals she wanted to achieve. We might surmise that certain experiences that she found unpleasant may have been appraised positively because of the contribution they made to her long-term goal to speak excellent English and to achieve the status associated with that skill. Therefore she seems to have been willing to endure events that she appraised as unpleasant because they were desirable as steps to the achievement of a long-term goal. (1999: 36)

NB: The role of self-reports and life-histories is central to the investigation of the emotional dimensions of classroom management, teaching and learning.

Practices of classroom management affect, and are in turn influenced by, motivational forces. The strength of Hoffman's long-term goals was such that she was able to overcome temporary emotional difficulties in order to satisfy these. However, only a part of her learning was done in a classroom setting. She was fully immersed in the culture and life of her adoptive country, an experience the great majority of foreign language learners worldwide are unlikely to experience. For them, the role of motivation (Concept 6.12) in keeping them engaged and committed in the task of learning a foreign language is of far greater importance because of its potential effect on their classroom responses. Dornyei puts it as follows: 'smoothly running and efficient classroom procedures enhance the learners' general well-being and sense of achievement and thus promote student motivation' (2001: 36). There is thus a tendency for responsibility for motivation to shift towards the teacher in formal contexts of learning.

Concept 6.12 Motivation

In a general sense, motivation can be defined as the dynamically changing cumulative arousal in a person that initiates, directs, coordinates, amplifies, terminates and evaluates the cognitive and motor processes whereby initial wishes and desires are selected, prioritised, operationalised and (successfully or unsuccessfully) acted out.
(Dornyei and Otto 1998: 65, in Dornyei 2001: 9)

The emotional dimension is captured by the notion of 'dynamically-changing, cumulative arousal'. From the classroom management point of view, the dynamism, changefulness and cumulative nature of arousal are central in both immediate and longer-term engagement.
(after Dornyei 2000: 9)

It is likely too, that Hoffman has made a strong *investment* (Concept 6.13) in learning. Norton (2000, 2001) has elaborated on the notion of investment in learning, to encompass a learner's relationship with the target language (socially and historically constructed) and their desire to learn and practice the language. A learner's levels of investment are also likely to fluctuate. Norton (2001) problematises this phenomenon in terms of the 'imagined communities' of her research subjects. She develops an understanding of why her subjects stop participating in language lessons by demonstrating that they are learning 'not from a position of peripherality (in terms of a community of practice) but as an act of resistance from a position of marginality' (2001: 165). Engagement is the connection between everyday experience in the classroom and more global long-term forces such as motivation and investment in learning.

Quote 6.13 Norton on investment in second language learning

. . . if learners invest in a second language, they do so with the understanding that they will acquire a wider range of symbolic and material resources, which will increase their value in the social world. Learners will expect or hope to have a good return on their investment in the target language – a return that will give them access to the privileges of target language speakers. Thus an investment in the target language is also an investment in a learner's own identity, an identity which is constantly changing across space and time.
(2001: 166)

6.3   The emotions of teaching

Quote 6.14   The emotions of teaching

Teaching is the educational equivalent of white-water rafting. Periods of apparent calm are interspersed with sudden frenetic turbulence. Boredom alternates with excitement, reflection with action. As we successfully negotiate rapids fraught with danger we feel a sense of self-confident exhilaration. As we start downstream after capsizing our self-confidence is shaken and we are awash with self-doubt. All teachers sooner or later capsize and all teachers worth their salt regularly ask themselves whether or not they are doing the right thing. Experiencing regular episodes of hesitation, disappointment and ego-deflation is quite normal.
(Brookfield 1990: 2)

Emotions are at the heart of teaching. They comprise its most dynamic qualities, literally, for emotions are fundamentally about movement.... When people are emotional they are moved by their feelings.... Emotions are dynamic parts of ourselves, and whether they are positive or negative, all organizations, including schools, are full of them.
(Hargreaves 1998: 835)

...a teacher must be willing to become vulnerable, taking risks with the clear knowledge that 'risk' by definition means occasional painful losses.
(Stevick 1980: 294)

Learning contains both cognitive and emotional dimensions, closely bound. Teaching, a 'caring profession', is also an emotional activity, but for different reasons. Recent discussion has stressed that teaching is an 'emotional profession' to the point that it is so stressful that it becomes unmanageable (Claxton 1989). A contemporary view of teaching acknowledges the importance of intuition in teaching and a caring disposition as part of teachers' personal and practical knowledge. This includes a teacher's capacity to read inner states of learners, and to know when to engage with them and when to keep a distance (Hargreaves 1998: 836). Furthermore, teachers are also engaged to various degrees in their work and empathically in the struggles of their learners. Their own levels of engagement may model to learners' attitudes towards learning (Quote 6.14).

Data Extract 6.3   Teachers' emotional responses to teaching

Here are some teachers from different countries talking about emotions in teaching.

Part of the stress of the job is that you go up and down like a yoyo even in one class. But the main feeling is satisfaction that they (the learners) have made some progress.

> *I feel an enormous emotional force to tell students the answers – when I put them in groups to do a task, I see them sometimes not fully committed, and almost waiting for me to say okay and this is what you should be saying.*
>
> *When the new activity I tried today went well I was so happy. I'd spent weeks wondering how to bring an end to the topic, and by accident I stumbled on this. The students seemed happy too.*

In a seminal paper Hargreaves (1998) (Concept 6.14) examines the emotions of teaching in the context of educational reform. He is uncompromising in his criticism of the school of thought that acknowledges emotions 'only insofar as they help administrators and reformers "manage" and offset resistance to change, or help them set the climate in which the "really important" business of cognitive learning or strategic planning can take place' (1998: 837). Hargreaves is interested in the significance of the emotions in teaching and in the relationships teachers create with their learners. For Hargreaves, 'emotions are embedded and expressed in the human relationships of schooling' (1998: 838). Feelings of pride in student success, emotional risk, guilt and despair are thus all prevalent in teaching (Data Extract 6.3).

Concept 6.14   Dimensions of emotion in teaching

1. Teaching is an emotional practice (after Denzin 1984: 89, in Hargreaves 1998) which affects both teachers' and learners' experience of classroom learning.
2. Teaching and learning involve emotional understanding – where feelings are shared, or, as is so frequent in educational encounters, misunderstood. Obstacles to emotional understanding include the power relationships between teachers and taught, class size, assessment practices and curriculum overload.
3. Teaching calls for 'emotional labour' – teachers 'give' to a greater or lesser extent of their selves to teaching in order to make it work.
4. The emotions of teaching are shaped by moral purpose, a sense of mission and therefore of values in action.

Hargreaves reports his empirical study which demonstrated that teachers 'valued the emotional bonds and understandings they established with students and valued the purposes of educating their students as emotional and social beings as well as intellectual ones' (1998: 850). Teachers' emotional connections and commitments energised and articulated everything they did, including how they taught, how they planned and how they preferred to structure teaching.

Hargreaves adds further support to the idea that 'sociological, political and institutional forces shape and reshape the emotional landscapes of teaching' (1998: 836) and that to see 'emotional intelligence' (Goleman 1995) as essentially an individual matter is to ignore the social contexts in which the emotional practices of teaching are realised. In other words, classroom management practices are primarily social and coloured by emotional responses at every juncture. These responses are part of both the discoursal practices of learning groups and also reflective of the wider social practices of the communities in which they are embedded.

Teachers' contributions to the emotional domain

The essence of a teacher's management of engagement is in contributing to creating a climate conducive to learning and by managing the ongoing teaching–learning process. Teachers also influence the emotional tone of a classroom through their own levels of engagement in quite unconscious ways – even the most peripherally-engaged teacher will influence the emotional climate of the classroom through the ways in which learning activities are managed mechanically and the distant manner in which learners are treated. In Chapter 5 we have seen how some micro and meso management strategies, such as pressurising students to complete work quickly, are related to classroom climate. To some extent the way a teacher manages engagement in the classroom will reflect their more general 'management style'. For example, a teacher who adheres to the type of management qualities favoured by Whitaker (1995) would regard the establishment of good classroom climate as central to their work and responding to students' needs as a key task (Concept 6.15).

Concept 6.15   Responding to students' needs

Students need to:

- be trusted;
- be listened to;
- be noticed;
- be encouraged;
- develop;
- be challenged intellectually;
- be valued;
- be informed;
- be supported.

(after Whitaker 1995)

Teachers who are responsive to learners' needs and affective states believe that good emotional conditions are the basis of good learning. However, the extent to which teachers are able to base their practice on these qualities may be limited by a number of factors in the real school environment.

Pollard and Tann (1993), in the context of a discussion of primary practice in British schools, note three difficulties in establishing an emotional tone of unconditional regard (Quote 6.15). Perhaps an overemphasis on 'good' emotional conditions removes some of the 'edge' from learning situations, an issue to be taken up later in this chapter.

Quote 6.15   Difficulties in establishing 'unconditional regard'

1. Children need to learn adequately and appropriately. There is a curriculum to cover.
2. Teachers are generally dealing with large groups, and issues of order and control are inevitably likely to condition their actions.
3. Teachers have emotional needs themselves, and need to feel accepted. However, the establishment of mutual positive regard is unlikely without the teacher having won the respect of her children, which may entail establishing a framework for order and discipline. Otherwise, she may be seen as 'weak'.

(after Pollard and Tann 1993: 88)

Support and challenge

The relationship between classroom activity and students' affective response is partly a question of 'face'. Activities which are difficult or risky can at any time threaten students' face (or self-image) by challenging their intellectual and social resources. Breen (2001b) observes that learners 'navigate through classroom discourse in ways that will enable them to avoid individual trouble for themselves, in particular avoiding to appear foolish in public' (2001b: 315). On the other hand, activities may not be challenging enough: a teacher may be providing so much support, overtly or covertly, that students contribute nothing. A teacher also wishes to preserve face and may collude with learners to do this by not stretching them intellectually, for a host of reasons. For example, the need to avoid embarrassment is so great that participants covertly reach a *joint* consensus to manage the situation so that no one is hurt emotionally. A helpful way of looking at this interplay of emotional, interpersonal and pedagogic forces at work in classrooms is to consider the levels of support and challenge at work at any particular time in a lesson or a programme of learning (Concept 6.16).

Concept 6.16   Support and challenge in learning and teaching

Support refers to the emotional and intellectual ways in which teachers (or 'experts' or coaches) acknowledge the learner's struggle, and provide the learner with ways of strengthening resilience and improving confidence and self-esteem, as well as scaffolding them through ZPDs. (See Chapter 7.)

Concept 6.16   (Continued)

Challenge refers mainly to the level of difficulty of the learning task set by a teacher and the pressure it places the learner under, both cognitively and emotionally. Prabhu (1987) refers to teachers 'regulating the challenge' of new learning in comparison with 'providing reasonable challenge' to learners in the learning process.

Prabhu (1987: 55–7) discusses the effects of teachers' varying the level of 'reasonable challenge' in order to respond to students' perceived difficulty in responding to tasks (Quote 6.16). His discussion is infused with references to positive and negative emotional states induced by various levels of challenge in tasks. It is all too easy for teachers to respond inappropriately, because they respond emotionally to student difficulty, and there is no way of predicting accurately such responses in advance. Managing these rapidly changing states in real classroom time poses considerable challenges for teachers and learners alike. Classrooms need to be managed sensitively enough to respond to changes and to handle contingencies.

Quote 6.16   Prabhu on reasonable challenge

Although what is important for language learning is learners' engagement in a task rather than their success in it, some measure of success is essential for maintaining learners' desire to make the effort, as repeated failure can lead to a sense of frustration or a negative self-image. It is therefore important for the teacher to regulate the challenge offered by tasks and operate generally with some notion of what represents reasonable challenge for a given class. The concept of reasonable challenge implies that the learners should not be able to meet the challenge too easily but *should* be able to meet it with some effort.
(1987: 56)

A helpful way of conceptualising the elements of challenge and support in learning comes from a model devised by Daloz (1986) in the context of professional learning for social workers. Daloz sees challenge and support as two dimensions in any 'helping' situation, interacting to produce four broad possibilities (Figure 6.1). Both support and challenge are undoubtedly significant for learners and teachers too, and there is evidence to suggest (Legutke and Thomas 1991; van Lier 1996a) that they appreciate being challenged but also require support.

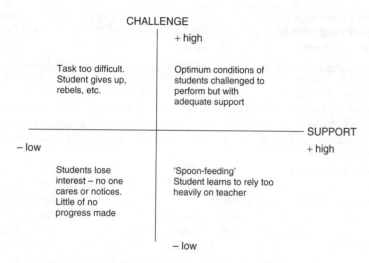

Figure 6.1   Support and challenge in teaching and learning (after Daloz 1986)

The ideal situation is one in which challenge and support are both high, so that learners feel supported as they attempt new challenges. In such circumstances the emotional and cognitive are in sufficient balance for learners to feel able to attempt new learning.

Security and the affective domain

Prabhu (1990, 1992, 1995) has consistently argued for the need for security in the classroom for both students and teachers. He argues that classrooms are contexts which are inherently insecure and that the response to insecurity and threat is to opt for routine and regularity, a sense of 'expectations met'. Prabhu (1992) identifies four ways in which a lesson can be viewed, all of which are potentially in conflict (Concept 6.17). For example, a cooperative task introduced by the teacher could conflict with learners' perception of the competitive nature of the classroom. There would be variation in how such conflicts are resolved depending in part on teachers' teaching styles. However, as conflicts are resolved, all participants prioritise those options which protect their self-esteem and allow them relative security. The emotional dilemmas for teachers are compounded if teachers' 'sense of plausibility' (a sense that their work is worth doing because of its positive effects in terms of learning, similar to Brookfield's idea of 'credibility') is compromised by a need to attend to disturbances in the emotional state of a group created by the use of particular teaching methods. Teachers and learners are thus driven by the need to protect their self images which are threatened by problematic learning events and their unpredictable emotional outcomes.

One of the ways in which classroom communities do this is by establishing routines, not only to sustain teaching-and-learning, but also to make classroom time 'endurable' (Prabhu 1990: 173). Classrooms consequently need to be secure environments, to minimise the threat to face that new learning inevitably brings (Prabhu 1992). New learning, as Allwright (2001, 2002, 2003) points out, creates 'discoursal troubles' if it is to be effective. The need for security thus drives the need for consensual order, and also underlies the natural conservatism of classrooms. There is a strong emotional dimension in regularity in classroom life and a certain emotional investment in 'normality'.

There is a danger, however, that too much security can lead to 'cosiness' and a lack of challenge, and therefore avoidance of learning opportunity. This is an issue which teachers address by deciding to adopt teaching procedures which they believe are necessary to encourage a range of positive emotional responses. This does, of course, place a heavy burden of responsibility on the teacher for setting the emotional tone of lessons. Schumann (1999: 38) points out the 'formidable challenge because the teacher has fifteen to thirty, or possibly many more, different appraisal systems to deal with in one classroom'. He concludes that teachers should negotiate their judgements with those of the students. 'The negotiation space may frequently be very narrow, but it would appear that negotiation is the only alternative, and I suspect that teachers cease to be motivating when they stop negotiating' (Schumann 1999: 38).

Concept 6.17   Security and routine in language lessons

Prabhu identifies four ways in which a lesson can be seen:

- Unit of curriculum.
- Implementation of method.
- Social event.
- Arena of human interaction.

He regards the social and human aspects as the most potentially threatening to teachers' self images and 'sense of plausibility' (1990).

Teachers need to operate with some personal conceptualisation of how their teaching leads to desired learning – with a notion of causation that has a measure of credibility for them.... The ... concept of how learning takes place and how teaching causes or supports it is what may be called a teacher's *sense of plausibility*.... When a teacher's sense of plausibility is engaged in the teaching operation ... the teacher can be said to be involved ...
(1990: 172)

> The classroom lesson is a recurrent encounter between people and, like all recurrent encounters, needs a sense of security arising from shared expectations. Human encounters which are entirely unpredictable, with no foreknowledge or even an expectation of what is to happen, are inherently threatening and would be intolerable as regularly recurrent events in any social group or institution, including the family.
> (1992: 228)
>
> The more recurrent the encounter, and the more numerous its participants, the greater the need for shared routine and a shared set of expectations. It is only with some notion of where one belongs and where the others belong that one can engage in a repeated encounter with no sense of threat.
> (1992: 229)
>
> Conducting a lesson is, first and foremost, handling a collection of friendly and unfriendly people in a way that maximally protects or projects, and minimally hurts or diminishes, one's own self-image as a teacher. The learners in their turn perceive the teacher as being friendly and unfriendly, helpful or hostile, tolerant or vindictive, and so on, both to themselves and their fellow learners, and try to act in a way that protects or enhances their own self images.
> (1992: 229)

Managing engagement: harmony, conflict or cosiness?

Management of engagement is more likely oriented towards the achievement of harmony rather than challenge, conditions tacitly agreed upon by a classroom group, thus allowing for differing interpretations of harmony. When there is harmony, participants' emotional needs are met and their emotional states are positive. As we have seen, though, emotional states are momentary and harmony can easily tip into disagreement, or into a form of agreement or collusion which prevents anything from being achieved in terms of learning and teaching. The classroom becomes a social club or similar – this may be a desirable state from time to time – for example, when socially and emotionally significant events like birthdays are acknowledged. The possibilities are illustrated in Figure 6.2. Harmony is that point at which tendencies towards conflict and solidarity are in balance.

Another way of looking at the overall tone and atmosphere of a classroom is to think in terms of its 'health' or 'quality of life'. Allwright, in discussions of Exploratory Practice (EP) (2001, 2002, 2003), has singled out the attainment of a good 'quality of life' in classrooms as a major priority for teachers (Quote 6.18). Beginning with the problem of workplace dissatisfaction, which he believes is created by a belief that an improved quality of work can improve difficult situations, he argues that because classroom life is fundamentally social, accomplished on a lesson-by-lesson basis, paying attention to understanding the quality of social life is a way to increase the quality of life generally in the classroom.

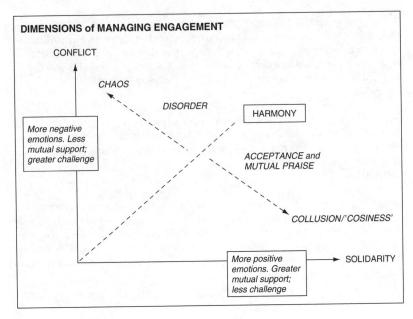

Figure 6.2   Dimensions of emotional engagement in the classroom

---

Quote 6.18   Allwright on towards quality of life in language classrooms

Experience with Exploratory Practice, however, suggests that *the first priority, and ultimate aim, is be concerned for the quality of life* in the language classroom, not the *quality of work* there, even if issues do present themselves initially as problems to be solved, or as new pedagogic practices to be implemented. This is because if *the quality of classroom life* is properly addressed, then problems in the quality of work can be expected, at best, to look after themselves or at the very worst you can expect to find yourself in a stronger position to deal with them than before, simply because you will feel better able to understand what is going on. But unless and until the quality of life is successfully addressed, then there is little point in trying to address issues in the quality of work.
(2001: 1)

Paying close attention to the quality of classroom life through Exploratory Practice is a way for teachers to find a better work/life balance, and to see work as a necessary aspect of life, but not the priority. Greater understanding of classroom life, Allwright argues, enables us to feel more in tune with our environment and less likely to struggle to attain unrealistic work goals. In the light of this idea, classroom climate may better be seen as a matter of attaining a degree of harmony in classroom life, and in teachers' work lives, informed by an understanding of how the social and affective aspects of classroom life contribute to a reasonable quality of life in and out of the classroom. Daily attention to the problem of attaining harmony in classroom engagement seems to be a reasonable point from which to begin. Indeed, the very act of conceptualising classrooms in terms of 'health' and 'harmony' may assist everyone concerned in benefiting from the perspective it offers. However, too much harmony may not be conducive to good learning, because teachers and learners may not be able to 'distance' themselves sufficiently from events to make sense of them.

6.4   Managing engagement – discourse and affect

So far in this chapter we have seen how a wide range of affective factors influences classroom engagement; for example, the predispositions of the learner towards the task, and the emotional tenor of actual engagement. This section examines how emotional engagement in classroom activity intertwines with the discourses of classroom management – of order, opportunity and care. Discoursal practices reveal both social and affective processes at work, where participants seek and express personal and collective meanings and interpretations of activity. This is the nexus of managing engagement.

Affective markers in discourse

Affective markers are ways in which a speaker can 'manifest his attempts at self-regulation' and are 'linguistic manifestations of private speech' (Frawley and Lantolf 1985: 39). They also indicate of the learners' level of control over the task they are attempting, and are evidence of self-regulatory activity. They result from the recognition of new information in the course of learning activity and can be construed as externalised evidence of the process of inner speech proceeding, perhaps as a means of releasing tension during an activity, or signaling to others that understanding has been reached, and object regulating, as opposed to other-regulating (social) functions of speech in the classroom (Concept 6.18).

Concept 6.18   Affective markers

The assumption behind the idea of affective markers is that they are evidence of *internal* conversation, and not intended to communicate directly with others.

- Laughter in the middle of an utterance.
- Exclamations like 'Oh!' followed by laughter.
- 'Thinking noises' like 'hmm'.
- Expressions of frustration – 'Oh boy'.
- Sighs.
- Expressions of breakthrough or insight – 'Oh ho!'
- Expressions of 'astonishment.'

(Frawley and Lantolf 1985: 40)

The list could be extended to include all indications of emotional expression from sniggering through to raised voices or even shouting. Evidence from self-talk may be helpful in exploring further the connections between cognition and affect in learning, as Frawley and Lantolf indicate. The affective aspects of classroom talk have not received much attention from researchers, and it is interesting that these markers are often recorded in transcripts, but not included in accounts of episodes. Analysis of the discoursal indicators of emotional involvement or 'local engagement' which occur in teachers' and students' attempts at other-regulation in lessons would also be a productive route for investigation (Quote 6.18).

Quote 6.18   Breen on analysing engagement

... the omission of the socio-affective dimension of language learning, particularly in the analysis of talk that occurs in the public space of the classroom or the interpersonal space of task work, remains as a hindrance to both hypotheses in fully explaining *how* language may be acquired specifically through classroom interaction in context. (2001c: 118)

Extract 6.2 shows how affective markers are woven into classroom discourse. This is an extract from a debate on coeducation in a mixed class of adolescents. Students' contributions elicit various spontaneous reactions – laughter and outbreaks of 'noise' – many students talking at one, in some cases shouting at each other. The teacher demands silence (line 8). In line 9, a student 'steals' a turn to disagree, without having been nominated by the teacher, and again in line 11. This extract shows a group engaged and passionate about the topic, and thus more likely to be 'carried away' and participate in non-standard ways. These instances may be indicative of lower levels of teacher control, and consequently compromised order – a context in which students make their own opportunities.

Extract 6.2   Classroom talk

```
    T   any other points (B/B: 18 secs) people who say no – why do you say we should
        not mix the boys/and the girls/yes – give as many points as you have –
    S #3   we should not / separate the boys / from girls because the boys (laughter;
        noise) we should separate the boys from girls / if the boys / if the / if the boy
 5      and the girl sit together/they disturb each other
    Ss   yes   yes
         no   (noise)
    T   silence/silence/silence
    Sx   it's wrong –
10  S #3   and the girl / the girls will take to fancy very much in front of the teacher
    Sx   yes
```

As Extract 6.2 demonstrates, the ways in which a classroom group handle discipline and class control are also candidates for discoursal inquiry. The order/care discourses are highlighted on these occasions. At these times in classroom life emotions are overt, and what people utter is less important than the ways in which it is uttered. A second reason for focusing on these junctures is that breakdowns of order may prevent students from participating. Opportunity is denied or lost. How these instances are dealt with may provide evidence of how the floor is regulated in order to provide opportunities for participation. For example, such markers as a loud sigh from a student during a silent phase of a lesson could be construed as an attempt to disturb calm, and a challenge to a teacher's authority (Field Note 6.2).

Field Note 6.2   A classroom emotional incident

The class is silently working at their desks. They are doing a piece of writing individually. The teacher is walking up and down the rows of desks. One student towards the back of the class looks up and lets out a long sigh, loud enough for all to hear easily. This elicits a murmuring from the rest of the group. The teacher moves quickly to the front and tells the class to continue working in silence. It takes about 15 seconds for silence to return. Outside there are grasshoppers making a din. They are easily audible. 'Five minutes more,' says the teacher.

How such incidents are handled is clearly of interest in understanding engagement. Prosodic analysis of descriptive categories such as 'astonishment' would further add to the richness of understanding in the affective domain. In this connection, the issue of whether or not an utterance like a whisper has been noticed and acknowledged publicly is important in understanding how engagement is managed. Extract 6.3 shows that a group of secondary students whispering among themselves while their teacher writes on the board. In line 5 she admonishes them. It is interesting to speculate what the effect of ignoring such utterances might be.

Extract 6.3   Classroom talk

T   good/now I'm going to write some sentences on the board/and we're going to correct them/we shall do it orally first/now when I'm writing/just read them silently to yourselves (*noise; T cleans board*) excuse me please/while reading/just look at the board and read silently (*Ss talking/whispering; birdsong; T. writing on B/B: 2 mins 10 secs*) when you're reading silently/your lips/you're not supposed to say anything/I'm not supposed to hear your voice

Play and enjoyment

Recent work (Quote 6.19) stresses the importance of play in language use and learning. Play is a means of enjoying an activity and contributes to both the process and the conditions of learning. Much of the so-called humanistic trend in teaching and learning stresses 'fun' as a social lubricant which enhances the conditions of learning, although 'fun' typically describes outcomes rather than processes.

Quote 6.19   Play and language

Everyone plays with language or responds to language play. Some people take mild pleasure from it; others are obsessed by it; but no one can avoid it. We play with language when we manipulate it as a source of enjoyment, either for ourselves or for the benefit of others. . . . We take some linguistic feature – such as a word, a phrase, a sentence, a part of a word, a group of sounds, a series of letters – and make it do things it does not normally do. We are, in effect, bending and breaking the rules of the language. And if someone were to ask why we do it, the answer is simply: for fun.
(Crystal 1998: 1)

Recognition of a ludic function has the potential to guide language teaching out of its apparent dilemma. In language teaching, structural and communicative syllabuses shared the error that a focus upon form is non-functional. In the structural syllabus, which used manipulation of form as its starting point, its potential to mean was ignored. In the functionalist syllabus it was assumed that interest in formal patterns and relations could only emerge as a result of needs to communicate. The lesson of play is that this dichotomy is unnecessary. If formal patterning is approached as an end in itself, meanings and interactions will emerge from it, if they are allowed to do so.
(Cook 2000: 193)

We could assume that play and fun are managed out of many classrooms where 'serious work' is the focus, despite numerous claims for laughter and humour as being vital to successful classroom pedagogy and learning. Play and 'fun' are also interwoven into classroom activity and an important indicator of the emotional climate of the classroom. Sullivan (2000: 119) in a study of Vietnamese University classrooms provides a telling example of how the notion of 'work' permeates pedagogic thinking by inviting us to consider the effect of changing 'group work' to 'group play'. Cook too argues for the 'ludic function' to be given greater credence in classroom learning.

How the 'playful' aspects of classroom life are managed – that is, initiated and responded to, is a vital part of classroom life. (See Extract 6.4) In this case it is a student's *sotto voce* joke – a word play on the name of a classmate during a question/answer sequence (line 7). Jokes in themselves must be regarded as affective markers. Their occurrence and acceptance is an indicator of the quality of the affective domain in any classroom, and of the availability of opportunity for self-expression in the management discourse.

Extract 6.4   A classroom joke

```
    S #19   I would park at the car park
    T       at the car park – what's your name?
    S #19   Ngwa Thomas
    T       eh
5   S #19   Ngwa Thomas
    Sx      Ngwa
    Sx      Ngwa Tomato (laughter) –
```

The enjoyment of classroom activity may also raise ideological issues related to the 'seriousness' of education and the importance of 'getting on with work' in classrooms. For example, the amount of 'social talk' or 'chit-chat' that is conventionally permissible in lessons may be a broad indicator of the overall emotional climate of a classroom. For instance, it is fairly normal in many classrooms for the first few minutes of a lesson to be given over to some form of 'warm-up' or social chat.

Extract 6.5   Beginning lessons

Example A

```
    T   put away all your books please/put away everything – just get out your readers
        (much class noise) – give me the past tense / of / these sentences I'm going to
        give you/I will eat groundnuts today – I will eat groundnuts today – Asungwan
    S1  I ate groundnuts yesterday
```

Example B

```
    T:  someone tell me where he or she spent erm – his or her primary school days –
        where did you attend/this (points to student) –
    S1: in St. Martin's School / Wum
    T:  in St Martin's School / Wum / with whom did you stay / with your father your
5   uncle / or any other relative
    S1: I stayed with my family
```

Both examples A and B in Extract 6.5 are at the beginning of lessons. In A. the teacher goes straight to 'business'. In B, the teacher does the same, but with a personal question. The difference is noticeable in setting the classroom climate. Often, the abruptness with which personal talk is terminated is an indicator of its relative significance to the teacher. For learners, these occasions may be the only opportunities to participate in genuine communication about their lives. However, the invasion of the classroom domain by the 'technicised' discourses (Fairclough 1992; Holliday 1994) of methodology, as Sullivan (2000: 128), in her study of the Vietnamese classroom, observes, is tied to Western notions of 'work and technology'. She further remarks,

'I think it more appropriate to give emphasis to the notion of play as a mediator of classroom language learning' (2000: 128). The need for play may thus also be a focus for ideological as well as cultural struggles in the classroom, and how teachers manage classroom events to provide for play and their attitude towards it are important discoursal factors. Far from being simply a 'relaxant' in classroom life, play appears also to be important in learning. Thus playful engagement may be sought by learners as well as promoted by teachers, both informally, through 'social talk', and more formally, through activities designed to enable learners to 'play' with the target language.

Van Lier (2000) observes that a more 'ecological' approach to classroom life tries to overcome the limitations of the widespread input-output metaphor of language learning. The classroom is a context from which learning opportunity emerges, and that its qualities for creative language use 'from banter and puns to poetry and songs' (2000: 258) can be given greater prominence in an ecological approach. This view builds upon socio-cultural research into children's language development which demonstrates learning is wrapped up in play and enjoyment, and a realisation that much of our everyday language use is playful, some uses being semi-formalised in punning games and improvised performance. Van Lier (1998), discussing the role of conscious linguistic knowledge in learning, does, however, note that although play (among other activities) is important in children's first language learning, they are also engaged in 'countless acts of conscious learning, with a keenly perceptive stance, the application of deliberate effort and the investment of their growing personal and social identities' (1998: 142).

Distance: effects on engagement and the emotional domain

Teaching and learning encounters are rarely likely to feature the emotional intimacy of parental or peer encounters, despite the emotional intensity of classroom activity, or the fact that teaching is regarded in many contexts as a 'caring profession'. Classroom discourse positions learners in particular ways, as we have seen in Chapter 2. The 'magisterial' type of discourse that Bourdieu (1977) describes also features *physical* positioning, with the teacher seated above the level of the students, metaphorically as well as physically talking down to students. Even though such situations may be less common than in the past, they have a powerful effect on the climate as well as the pedagogic possibilities (Field Note 6.3).

Field Note 6.3   University classroom: Romania

I have to try to run a workshop with teachers in a lecture room which has a low platform by the chalkboard. A large desk is fixed to this. I face six semi-circular rows of fixed benches. I am some 4 metres from the front of these. The separation is exaggerated by the participants occupying the back four rows. I feel unable to work as I normally do – I feel forced to lecture. But this is an interactive session.

Concept 6.19   Institutional and discoursal positioning

One of the effects of institutional talk may be to distance 'clients' from 'professionals'. The effect may be to create a relatively neutral communicative context emotionally.

1. Institutional talk is goal-oriented and thus 'business-like' in nature.
2. Institutional talk is constrained – the nature of the 'business' being transacted precludes certain types of contribution. 'certain actions, which may be inhibited in a conversational context, might be promoted in institutional contexts.' Breaking of these constraints is likely to lead to difficulty.
3. Because institutional talk departs from the conversational, certain contributions are possible in professional discourse which would be seen as unfriendly or distant in social contexts. For example, professionals may withhold emotional responses such as surprise, sympathy, agreement or affiliation in order to preserve their distance.

(after Drew and Heritage 1992)

The institutional positioning of students as 'clients' or 'people-in-need-of-treatment/help' contributes to the social distance between teachers and learners. Classroom talk is, as we have seen, a form of institutional talk, and thus characterised by the features of all institutional discourses (Seedhouse 1997). Teachers are thus invariably goal-driven, and contributions to the discourse are constrained, for example, by external 'rules' of academic conduct in writing. The positioning of participants in institutional discourse may also be reinforced by particular ways in which departures from norms are interpreted. For example, for a teacher to engage conspiratorially with learners in an overt manner to subvert the authorities would probably be regarded as unacceptable, in the same way that, in some contexts, a teacher sharing confidences with a class might be seen as disrespectful (Concept 6.19).

Summary

This chapter has examined the affective dimension of classroom language learning, and how teachers and learners manage their engagement in classroom discourse. There is always an emotional tenor or climate when people interact – in the classroom the climate is influenced by many factors, individually and collectively. Learners' and teachers' engagement in classroom activity at any given moment is the outcome of the complex interplay between local emotional responses to events and interactions, an ever-shifting and changing tapestry of feelings on the one hand, and long-term attitudes, attributes, personality factors, and motivations on the other. In classrooms, institutional and educational discourses meet; personal and collective goals merge. Pedagogic and social goals intertwine and conflict – woven into these threads are the emotional dimensions. Whether participants' orientations are towards order or opportunity, regularity or unpredictability, there are emotional consequences which relate to the care dimension of classroom life.

Further reading

Arnold (1999) contains a number of valuable papers on the affective domain.

Brookfield (1990) contains a powerful account of a teacher's perceptions of the affective domain.

Claxton (1999) has a strong account of the emotional dimensions of learning.

Cook (2000) is a full discussion of the role of play in language learning.

Dornyei (2000) provides a comprehensive account of motivation.

Goleman (1995) is a comprehensive and readable introduction to the role of emotions in all aspects of human life.

Legutke and Thomas (1991) has a critique of 'humanistic' approaches to language teaching in action, and is singular in its treatment of the emotional domain in language teaching.

Rogers, A. (1996) is a wide-ranging text on adult learning with a good section on affect.

Rogers, C. (1983) is a classic argument for a 'humanistic' alternative to formal education.

Stevick (1976) is a teacher's view of the affective domain on language teaching in the 'humanistic' mould.

Whitaker (1995) examines the affective dimensions of management in education.

7
Pedagogy, Models of Teaching and Classroom Management

Pedagogies are different ways of conceptualising teaching, and entail both instructional and management activity. We have already seen the close relationships between the managerial and instructional aspects of teaching, and thus an analysis of pedagogies provides further insights into classroom management. Pedagogies view learning and the role of teaching in various ways, which in classroom management terms implies different degrees of concern with instructional and managerial classroom discourses, in the same way that views of formal education, such as transformation or 'lifelong learning', are realised by specific practices. Pedagogies also imply different management concerns in terms of order, opportunity and care.

7.1 Pedagogies and teachers' theories of practice

Data Extract 7.1 A teacher remembers

After attending a course on Communicative Language Teaching, this teacher decides to try out some of the new activities. Here is her story:

I was particularly thrilled by the possibilities of role play and group work. I had used these before, but I am afraid they weren't really communicative. I had never used group work, though.

The first time I used group work, the students enjoyed it so much that I found it difficult to end the lesson. It was a debate about choosing a candidate from a list. The students were unable to reach a majority decision in their groups, and were all very busy trying to convince the others that their choice was best and all of this in English. They had become so involved that they even forgot about break and the next class.

After the class, the students were very enthusiastic and asked me to do activities like this on a regular basis. This gave them the chance to really speak English. I think they were very thrilled by the realisation that they could really communicate in a foreign language.

Data Extract 7.1 is from a written account of a 'Key Moment' in a teacher's career. For this individual, trying new pedagogy was the issue. A new activity makes it difficult in a *positive way* for the teacher to manage her class. This type of data allows us a window onto teachers' classroom management decisions and how they manage their classrooms in the way they do. They also allow us to speculate on the extent to which tradition, training and experience help to shape thinking and action in teaching. Here a teacher is enthusiastically embracing the new; other accounts of failure and difficulty would build up a rich picture of teachers' management practices and pedagogic choices, from the outside and the inside, too. A 'teacher thinking' view of pedagogy, which inspires this type of research, sees teachers' practices emanating primarily from cognitive activity, particularly decision-making', which in turn draws on different types of teacher knowledge. (Concept 7.1) What teachers do in practice is thus intimately connected with cognition. These connections are explored by Prabhu (1995) in a conceptualisation of language pedagogy (Concept 7.2) which declares that teaching has two sides – an individual, practice-oriented face, and an institutional, value-laden face.

Concept 7.1   Research on teacher thinking

Research on teacher thinking (or teacher cognitions) is an essentially 'cognitive' information-processing view of teacher activity and its origins in different types of thought, primarily rational, although not always conscious once routines for teaching are well-established. Inquiry aims to identify the cognitive processes and the relative levels of awareness teachers have of the processes. Topics include teacher planning, interactive decision-making, judgement, tacit or implicit theories held by teachers.

'Research on teacher thinking asks teachers to 'think aloud' describe their thoughts and decision processes, and to make the invisible aspects of teaching visible.'
(Clark 1992: 75)

At the conceptual level of teachers' thinking, Prabhu distinguishes between teachers' ideological (institutional) and ideational (individual) knowledge, and how they inform action. (Quote 7.1). Ideational aspects of teaching include individual teachers' ideas about both learning and language. The ideational also includes idealised 'approaches' or methodologies, for example, which are often portrayed as 'the answers' to problems in teaching and learning. These are key aspects of teachers' thinking, a set of 'ideas' or concepts, on which practices in teaching are grounded. Conceptual material such as this is frequently the content of formal teacher education (Chapter 9). Ideologies, on the other hand, encompass the purposes of education (Chapter 2) and overlap conceptually with Fullan's (1993, 1999) idea of moral purpose in education. The ideological element captures both society's

Concept 7.2 Components of language pedagogy

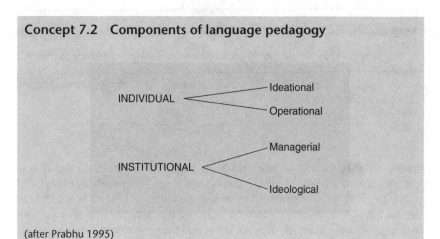

(after Prabhu 1995)

meta-purposes for educational activity and the individual teacher's sense of mission for teaching. On the other hand it also includes opposition to prevailing ideologies (Quote 7.2).

The ideational aspects of teaching are closely related to what Prabhu terms the 'operational' component, or how teachers actually carry out teaching activity on a minute-by-minute basis. This is similar to Schön's (1983) notion of 'knowing-in-action' (Quote 7.3). It encompasses what we have called 'micro-management' activities (Chapter 5). The managerial component of Prabhu's model is linked to the ideological component, and accounts for the institutionally-driven aspects of classroom management such as meso-level lesson planning, and translating an official syllabuses into teaching plans.

Quote 7.1 Prabhu on language pedagogy

Ideational: 'ideas or concepts about what constitutes knowledge of a language and what the process of learning a language consists of.'
(1995: 57)

Ideological: 'centrally involves the pursuit of an ideal – a desire to change, maintain, or resist the order of the world, in some way, through the practice of pedagogy'.
(1995: 65)

Managerial: 'the making of practical decisions of various kinds in the planning and conduct of teaching, both at the individual teacher's level and at the institutional level.'
(1995: 67)

Operational: 'has to do with pedagogic action or practice.' Operationally, 'teaching is ... a matter of translating learning theory into teaching action [and] ... using teaching action as a source with which to confirm, disconfirm, or help develop learning theory.'
(1995: 61)

Quote 7.2 Fullan on moral purpose in education

At the micro level, moral purpose in education means making a difference in the life chances of all students – more of a difference for the disadvantaged because they have further to go. At the macro level moral purpose is education's contribution to societal development and democracy.
(1999: 1)

Prabhu's conceptualisation of pedagogy thus encompasses all the major individual and institutional influences on a teacher's daily activity. We could infer from observation that teachers are following a particular 'methodology' or 'teaching model' by noting the different types of activity they use, the order in which they use them and the ways in which participation in classroom talk is managed. The teacher's on-the-spot actions could be linked to their operational knowledge and their managerial knowledge in action. However, there is no guarantee that what they are doing is anything other than using a set of learning activities 'which work' – drawing on what Prabhu (1987: 103) refers to as their 'sense of plausibility', and their 'practical theory'.

Quote 7.3 Schön on knowing-in-action

. . . intelligent practice as an *application* of knowledge to instrumental decisions.
(1983: 50)

. . . the sorts of knowledge we reveal in our intelligent action. . . . The knowing is *in* the action. We reveal it by our spontaneous, skilful execution of the performance; and we are characteristically unable to make it verbally explicit.
(1987: 25, author's emphasis)

What teachers actually do in classroom management terms is grounded in a 'theory of practice' (Handal and Lauvas 1987), or 'practical knowledge' (Quote 7.4). Teachers' management practices thus emerge from an array of influences, including the ways they make decisions, received knowledge, and above all their experience, the filter and forge of practical theory. In the enriched view of pedagogy that emerges from these views classroom management and pedagogy are both aspects of the individual teacher's knowledge and expertise.

Quote 7.4 Elbaz on practical knowledge of teachers

... encompasses first hand experience of students' learning styles, interests, needs, strengths and difficulties, and a repertoire of instructional techniques and classroom management strategies. The teacher knows the social structure of the school and what it requires, of teacher and student, for survival and success; she knows the community of which the school is a part and has a sense of what it will and will not accept. This experiential knowledge is informed by the teacher's theoretical knowledge of subject matter, and of areas such as child development, learning and social theory. All of these kinds of knowledge, as integrated by the individual teacher in terms of personal values and beliefs and as oriented to her practical situation . . .
(1983: 5)

Recent research by Breen et al. (2001) appears to support the notion of 'strands' of practical theory or 'principle', interwoven in practice (Quote 7.5). Breen et al. note that 'principles significantly influence how the teacher orchestrates the interaction between learner, teacher and subject matter in a particular classroom context with particular resources' (2001: 472–3). These principles appear to be sensitive in situational terms and both shape what a teacher does and how a teacher responds to specific incidents and behaviours in lessons.

Quote 7.5 Breen et al. on teachers' principles and classroom practices

The individual teacher appears to have a personal configuration of pedagogic principles that is realised, in selective ways, through a set of favoured practices. On the basis of background knowledge and experience and during further classroom experience, the influence of one upon the other is likely to be very interactive.

A single principle held by the individual teacher may be realised in action through several distinct practices. Conversely, a single practice may be an expression of one or more than one principle.
(2001: 495)

7.2 'Models' of teaching

Discussions of pedagogy typically focus on 'models of teaching'. In Prabhu's terms, these models cover only the ideational and operational components of language pedagogy, consisting of a view of content and the learning process – typically tacit – and the means of operationalising it at classroom level through the combination of classroom management practice and instructional strategy. There are also overtones of ideological, institutionally related aspects of pedagogy in models of teaching – the purpose of education is encapsulated by a model of teaching and inevitably, 'political' versions of the educational process are involved. All models of teaching touch upon the basic concerns of classroom management – order, opportunity and care. A view of models of teaching as pedagogies rather than simply ideologies thus enables us to take a wide-angle view of classroom management.

Before examining some of the most influential pedagogies and their implications for classroom management, we should note that one pedagogy is rarely if ever followed by teachers to the exclusion of others. In fact, as a great deal of classroom research has shown, teachers use a fairly wide variety of teaching activities. However, teachers seem to gravitate towards a set of shared beliefs and assumptions about what constitutes 'good practice', from which a common pedagogy emerges. As Edwards and Mercer (1987: 35) put it, 'every teacher relies at some level of self-justification on a set of beliefs about how teaching should be done'. They call this a 'common philosophy', and it is the basis of pedagogy.

Teaching as transmission

Field Note 7.1   Junior Secondary English – Malawi

There are about 45 students, aged about 12, mainly boys. The teacher stands in front of them. They sit in fixed desks, three or four to a bench. The teacher has a table – books on here. Teacher writes ten items of vocabulary on b/board in a column on left hand side. Points to first one – 'operation'. Asks class its meaning. One or two hands go up, some clicking of thumbs and fingers. Teacher nominates one boy to answer. He stands and speaks. Teacher asks him to speak up. Teacher nominates another boy, who answers. The teacher repeats the answer and says it's correct. He then writes this beside the item. 'My brother went to hospital for an operation. Afterwards he was better.' Teacher tells class to copy this neatly in their notebooks. And so on for the next 30 minutes. Class is instructed to learn the sentences for homework, and test tomorrow morning.

The scenario described in Field Note 7.1 is probably very familiar to many readers. It has attracted many names – 'didactic', 'transmission', 'recitation', 'traditional' or 'teacher-centred' (Concept 7.3). It is the norm in many contexts and is probably the most widespread pedagogy currently practised around the world with many local variations. It dominates the lives of millions of learners in every continent, young and old. Its driving force is authority – the authority of special knowledge and its bearer, the teacher.

In some cultures, the sense of authority is even inherent in the meaning of the vernacular for teacher, for example *guru* in Bahasa Malaysia.

Concept 7.3   Transmission teaching

Main Features
The teachers' role is to present new information. Teacher controls all aspects of the learning context. Whole class teaching. Students usually seated facing the teacher. Time is 'lesson-bound', with strong influence from syllabus and testing. Essentially behaviourist learning assumptions (memorisation, rote learning, practice, drills, question-and-answer).

... the 'traditional' position in which the tutor has the responsibility of defining the students' needs and providing an appropriate stimulus or instruction for them to act or reflect upon. The students' responsibilities are then to respond appropriately; the tutor's are to evaluate the appropriateness of this response and provide further instruction accordingly.
(Rowland 1993: 19)

The seating in a transmission classroom is arranged to ensure that all students face the teacher in the optimum position to 'receive' the message. The teacher is often standing, sometimes on a platform above the students. From this position, the teacher 'teaches' or 'instructs'. The predominant discourse is 'I Tell You', capturing the directionality of the process and the close association of teaching and telling. Both the content and teaching-and-learning are under the direction and control of the teacher. In classroom management terms this is known as 'whole-class teaching', with the emphasis on each individual member of the group receiving the same undifferentiated message.

The transmission model is also inevitably order-focused to ensure silence while the message is delivered. It is also high structure (Briggs and Moore 1993: 496) – all the crucial management decisions about use of time and space, and learning content are made by the teacher, with apparently minimal involvement from the students. However, it would be wrong to see transmission as monolithic. Rather there is a range of activity. An extreme form of transmission is perhaps the moral lecture without immediate audience response, where behaviour and attitude are prescribed, usually under threat from some superior authority. Weaker forms would include rule-focused grammar lessons, which feature the teacher explaining a point, often at length and uninterrupted, and then checking 'comprehension' with their learners, either during or immediately after the talk through question and answer. This activity is followed up later (often the following day after homework to memorise the content) with some sort of test.

In language teaching, the commonly-used 'presentation/practice/production' (or PPP) model is grounded in the homogeneity of the message of the presentation phase and its gradual acquisition through the other two phases of a lesson. The teacher's work is to manage the various phases and the transitions between them. It is a weak form of transmission, where the main content is specified by the teacher. 'Freer' practice is allowable in the third phase, but generally this is an extension of the 'learning point' contained in the presentation phase, and still effectively under the direction of the teacher through the specification of task and choice of activity type, and most importantly the means of assessing whether or not the point has been learned. More inductive ways of presenting new information or content, such as language awareness activity, feature activities which encourage students to observe and notice linguistic features and then consciously explore them may feature teacher explanations *after* these phases. These explanations may be transmissive and tell students what 'the right answers' were. Or alternatively, a teacher may sum up what the students report they have discovered, with or without correction, and add one or two further points. The boundary between transmission and non-transmission is a fine one in this case. It may indeed be the case that teachers switch to transmission mode for particular purposes, as part of their wider repertoire of teaching techniques. There is no one dominating body of learning theory behind transmission. Broadly speaking, transmission is grounded in the following beliefs:

1. Memorisation and practice are key means of learning. The Behaviourism of the 1950s, and its realisation in the Audio-Lingual method in language teaching, a method that entailed strict teacher management and control over lessons, is one body of learning theory that has been influential in defining objectives and specific learning outcomes. Such a set of practices requires close control over the learning group's activity. Tharp and Gallimore (1988) have also criticised the recitation type of teaching which is grounded in this view of learning.
2. Teacher talk (or transmission of information) can modify learners' knowledge and behaviour. The natural asymmetry of the classroom is further exaggerated by the unequal distribution of knowledge.
3. Reinforcement and repetition are essential components of effective learning. A system of rewards, punishment and tight discipline is designed to ensure that students stay 'on-task', in this case, primarily listening to the teacher.
4. Knowledge is finite and well-defined, and the teacher has a mastery of it. The best way to learn this body of knowledge is by gradual accumulation.

For and against transmission

Although transmission is widely practised, it has its critics both from ideational and ideological perspectives (Concept 7.4). More historically recent challenges to transmission in the Anglo-Saxon world derive mainly from a loose coalition of educational and political interests. From a political perspective they challenge authority and unequal power relationships throughout society, as well as in the classroom. Advocates of 'critical' pedagogy (Paolo Freire, for example) argue that education should aim to 'empower' students rather than forcing them to 'bank' unnecessary knowledge on unequal terms, without choice. Educationalists, on the other hand, maintain that transmission takes little account of learners' previous knowledge and experience, puts them into a relatively passive role, and leads to a culture of assessment rather than learning. Furthermore, because transmission tends to happen in large groups of learners of varying abilities, it is also a problem for teachers to pitch their lessons at the right level of difficulty. Transmission has strong associations with 'subjects', or bodies of knowledge, and learning under such a system tends to be fragmented, making it difficult for students to build a deeper understanding of concepts and their relationships within and across disciplines.

Concept 7.4 Criticisms of transmission

1. Barnes (1976) contrasts Transmission teaching with Interpretation teaching, on the basis of (a) how teachers view knowledge, (b) what teachers value in their students, (c) teachers' views of their own roles, and (d) how teachers assess students' potential to participate. He criticises the reliance of transmission on established knowledge, limited communication patterns and close control of students' participation, the emphasis on fact-based instruction and testing.

2. The Brazilian educationalist Paulo Freire criticises this pedagogy as 'banking' in which learners are handed over 'narrated content':

A careful analysis of the teach–student relationship at any level, inside or outside the school, reveals its fundamental *narrative* character. This relationship involves a narrating Subject (the teacher) and patient, listening objects (the students)'. (The teacher's task 'is to 'fill' the students with the contents of his narration. . . . Education becomes an act of depositing, in which the students are the depositories and the teacher is the depositor. Instead of communicating, the teacher issues communiqués and 'makes deposits' which the students patiently receive, memorize and repeat. This is the 'banking' concept of education . . .
(1972: 45–6)

3. Rowland (1993, citing Cantor 1953) challenges the following assumptions:

- Teachers are responsible for specifying what is to be learnt; students' responsibility is to learn it.
- Knowledge is education.
- Education can happen through disconnected 'subjects'.

Concept 7.4   (Continued)

- The subject matter means the same to the student as it does the teacher.
- At times students need to be coerced to learn.
- Knowledge is more important than the process of learning.
- Education is mainly intellectual.

Rowland also warns that many 'new methods' are just as didactic as 'traditional teaching:

If the lecture is a typically didactic process, a package of programmed learning can often be seen to be even more didactic with its regular sequence of instruction and checks. (1993: 20)

4. Transmission is very limited in terms of its interaction types:
'Typical genres of traditional education constitute only a fraction of the interactive forms available to the contemporary teacher.'
(Kozulin 1998: 158)

There are some advantages of transmission, though. Because of the high degree of control by the teacher (textbook writer or curriculum designer) over the linear organisation and sequencing of learning experiences, and the choice of content, it is relatively easy to provide continuity to the educational experience over long periods of time, if required. In this way, large groups of learners can benefit from the expertise of the teacher, who has a platform from which to engage the learners (in effect, an audience) in an exposition of their subject, in a logical and cumulative way. Learning is thus a progressive assemblage of 'building blocks' of knowledge. This is reinforced by 'question and answer', a key teaching strategy for checking previous knowledge and learning, a discourse which is replicated and reinforced in assessment procedures.

Because transmission is so often associated with the 'Gradgrindism' of Dickensian England and its boring and callous teachers, it tends to be seen as at best 'cold' and at worst, uncaring. However, there is evidence emerging from many transmission classrooms of close teacher-student bonds, and a warm, friendly atmosphere (Field Note 7.2). Care in classroom management seems to exist independently of instruction, and is closely bound up with the emotional responses of teachers and students to each other. Not all transmission teachers are as distant as Friére's caricature of the 'banker' pedagogue, or as violent as Wackford Squeers in *Nicholas Nickleby*.

Field Note 7.2   Rapport between teachers and students (secondary language class)

Teacher is opening up lesson based on reading passage. She asks class (65 mixed) whether any stay away from their families in order to attend school. Some hands raised.

She asks if any are mistreated. One student volunteers that he's given very little money for food at school. Another says he has a very uncomfortable sleeping place whereas the family's children have a comfortable one. Another student (boy) volunteers. Starts as Q/A with teacher and ends with student monologue about how he's treated by his aunt. Teacher does not interrupt. Listens. Rest of class listen avidly for about half a minute. Boy and teacher have not shifted eye contact during all this time. Teacher makes a light joke about the boy's love of a particular food, and then looking at rest of class thanks the boy for his contribution. Then – let's look at page 45. Our passage is about a cruel aunt.

Alternatives to transmission

The search for viable alternatives to transmission is not new. There is a long history of 'progressivism' in education, countering the underlying 'I Tell You' discourse of transmission.

Concept 7.5   Some alternative views of education

1. Dewey's 'Articles of Faith' (1916)

- All education proceeds by participation of individuals in social consciousness which begins at birth and constantly shapes an individual thereafter.
- School is a form of community life and education is a process of living, not a preparation for the future.
- The true centre of education is a child's social activity.
- Children should be active in schools.

2. Rabindranath Tagore

Tagore was a Bengali poet and educationalist, who founded a unique 'village school' project in Bengal in the 1930s. Reporting a conversation with him on the philosophy behind the school, his long-time collaborator, L. K. Elmhirst wrote:

Education is sometimes called a tool and is thought of as a factory process. Much of it is perhaps so, and the raw material, the child, is caught and moulded into the desired product as with a machine. But education implies growth and therefore life, and school-time should be a phase of life where the child begins to achieve freedom through experience.
(1961: 83)

For example, in the United States and further afield in the early part of the twentieth century, the ideas of John Dewey were (and still are) highly influential. In rural areas of Bengal, in British colonial India, Tagore experimented with educational practice which aimed to provide people with the means to make a living and also spiritual and intellectual enlightenment. Both these educators opposed transmission from an ideological perspective

(Concept 7.5). However, the most influential challenges to transmission of the last half century have emerged from the psychology of learning and its appropriation for educational purposes.

The contributions of constructivist psychology

More recently in the West, the development of constructivist views of learning in psychology has provided educationalists with a new basis for more contemporary alternatives to transmission, based on empirical work in child development, and learning in all age groups. Constructivist views are based on a cognitive view of human learning, in contrast to the behavioural leanings of the transmission model. Constructivist views of learning have also been used to justify and inform more 'progressive' pedagogies which acknowledge the central contribution of a learner to create their own knowledge and understandings, to make their own connections and generate their own meanings (Concept 7.6).

Concept 7.6   Constructivism – main tenets

A. Piaget – people learn through the interaction of thought and experience, and go through a sequential series of developmental stages of increasing cognitive complexity.

B. Humans are goal-directed and seek information. New knowledge is built upon previously existing knowledge, skills and understandings. All knowledge is constructed from existing knowledge, regardless of any teaching.

- Active Learners: People actively construct knowledge for themselves through exploration.
- People determine their own knowledge and decide what is important for them.

C. Vygotsky – Knowledge is based on categories derived from **social** interaction rather than observation, and the way we look at things is as important as what we look at.
There are two main forms of constructivism which influence teaching:

1. 'Individualist or Pure' Constructivism, inspired by Piaget and his followers, which combines A. and B.
2. Social Constructivism, inspired by Vygotsky and his followers, which combines A, B and C, with an emphasis on C.

There are two broad 'families' (see Figure 7.1) of constructivist approaches to teaching-and-learning – those emphasising individual exploration and discovery, inspired by Piaget, and those which are socially-based, or social constructivist, associated with the work of Vygotsky (1978). Historically, however, the ideas of Piaget were the first to be drawn upon by educationalists, in particular during the 1950s and 1960s. Vygotskyan ideas have had a relatively recent, but profound influence on educational thought worldwide. The crucial difference between these two models of learning and the types of classroom teaching-and-learning is that a social constructivist view of learning emphasises the role of the social context of learning in the learning process. The discoursal message is 'We engage in talk', whereas in a discovery model such as Piaget's the discourse is 'You find out for yourself'. A shift to either of these models from a predominantly transmission model has huge consequences for classroom management practices as well as challenging well-rooted understandings of learning and the role of teaching from both teachers' and learners' points of view.

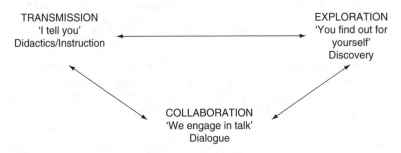

Figure 7.1   Three models of teaching (based on Rowland 1993, and Pollard and Tann 1996)

The remainder of this section will focus on the following four constructivist pedagogies and examine the implications for classroom management of each of them:

1. Exploratory teaching or discovery learning (e.g. Bruner 1966)
2. Assisted performance (Tharp and Gallimore 1988)
3. Responsive teaching (Bowers and Flinders 1991)
4. Dialogic inquiry (Wells 1999)

Discovery or exploratory teaching

Field Notes 7.3   Exploratory teaching

(*University Environmental Design Freshmen: Service English – Saudi Arabia*)

The students – 22 young men – are scattered around the desert *wadi* in small groups. Some group members are taking photographs of the sides of the *wadi*. Others are making sketches and notes of the vegetation. One is busy picking up rock samples of different sorts. The tutor moves from group to group, asking what they have found, and whether they have any questions. They exchange jokes and smiles. After 30 minutes, the tutor calls the students back to where their vehicles are parked and suggests a drinks break. At the same time, they start comparing notes in their groups

---

Field Notes 7.3   (Continued)

and making sure they have completed all the survey and data-gathering tasks they had previously agreed upon. This is done in Arabic. After they have finished their cold drinks, the students decide they need 10 more minutes to finalise the tasks. It's getting hot – it's 8 am. . . .

   Back in class at 9.30 and it's busy – students are creating displays of their material, and have assigned tasks of writing captions and notes in the groups. Sketches are being tidied up and neatly annotated. After 30 minutes, each group gives a short oral presentation of their findings and materials. The tutor listens and asks questions, as do the other students. The group arranges to have their photographs developed and to begin to write up their accounts of the fieldwork in rough overnight. It's now 11:00.

The activity described in Field Note 7.3 features types of exploratory teaching, where the learners are relatively free to engage with subject matter – environmental and linguistic – and to record, classify and discriminate. The class group is less guided than a more standard university language lesson, as they are collecting material for further work back in the classroom.

Exploratory teaching draws heavily on Piaget's constructivist psychology (1929 *passim*). In some circles it is known as 'progressive' teaching. Piaget's work focused on children's learning in terms of how they accommodate and assimilate new knowledge through direct experience (Concept 7.7), and a set of principles as to how teachers might best help learners learn in formal contexts. In the UK, for example, a constructivist theory of learning became the basis of reform in primary education in the 1960s and 1970s. The classroom management implications for teachers were enormous – for example, 'rich learning environments' had to be created so that children could have a wide range of stimulating experiences. The traditional subject-centred curriculum was also broken down in favour of 'integrated' activity, and to provide individual children with learning experiences tailored to their personal requirements. This all had to be managed and executed by teachers with groups of children of differing ability (Concept 7.8).

Concept 7.7   Assimilation and accommodation

Assimilation: the fitting in of new stimuli/information to existing mental structures (schemata).
Accommodation: the creation of new mental structures from old, or the modification of older schemata.

Concept 7.8 Some principles of 'progressive' pedagogy

1. Creating conditions which allow children to discover things for themselves.
2. Creating opportunities to enable children to have direct, concrete experience, and which involve action as well as listening, speaking and writing.
3. Referring to children's out-of-school experience in lessons.
4. Use of activities and techniques like 'guessing game' question and answer sessions to elicit ideas from children, rather than tell them directly.
5. Not strictly defining the plan for the lesson in advance.
6. Not defining the criteria for successful learning.

(based on Edwards and Mercer 1987: 33–4)

In exploratory teaching and learning the learner is at the centre. The teacher's main responsibility is in assisting learners in designing for themselves the selection, pace and evaluation of appropriate learning experiences. This is 'negotiated' with the learners, an assumed motivational factor, as learners tends to engage with learning experiences and material they have chosen. The emphasis is on the individual learner's direct experience through which they 'discover' new knowledge and formulate their own ideas and meanings, as 'active scientists'. In primary classrooms managed to facilitate this type of learning, a concern with 'constructive play', the exploration of materials, stimulation of the imagination and creative arts all feature prominently (Pollard and Tann 1997). The closeness of these experiences to what children 'do naturally' out of school is central to a constructivist view of learning and teaching. There are many parallels between this approach and with the type of 'informal' learning described in Chapter 2 (Quote 7.7).

Despite its advantages, this approach has been criticised from a number of perspectives. First, it can place an immense strain on a teacher to manage the individual activities of 30 or more learners each engaged in individual activity. Teachers need to rely on learners' judgements about the success of their learning in determining whether they are 'ready' to move to more conceptually demanding tasks, and they may not be particularly good judges of the quality or depth of their own learning. Learning may often be superficial, and the learners may learn incidentally a great deal that is not actually in the curriculum.

The most significant criticisms are concerned with the asocial nature of Piaget's learning model. Learning, as we saw in Chapter 2, always takes place in a social context. Even if individual children are engaged in personal individual exploration, they are still operating on the basis of cultural blueprints absorbed from countless interactions with parents, siblings and peers, as well as teachers in classrooms. There are further cross-cultural issues, in that the stages of development which Piaget identified may not be experienced universally across different cultures, for a range of reasons. The readiness of learners to move on is also linked to a somewhat discredited model of child development. For example, in many cultures, children are required to work at an age which in other contexts would be illegal. The experience of working will have an influence on how a young person sees the world which may cut across Piaget's idealised stages.

Quote 7.7   Mercer on the cultural experience of learning

The way in which children (learn how to use language in their communities) is rather similar to the way in which they learn to use other tools – by a combination of watching experts at work, receiving some guidance from them and trying out the tools for themselves. Learning to use the functional artefacts of our society is not a matter of 'discovery learning, but rather a course of informal apprenticeship. We do not learn what tin-openers, hammers and screwdrivers are good for by finding one lying around as a strange and unknown object, experimenting with this object in isolation and eventually discovering it is good for something like knocking in nails. We learn about hammers at the same time as we learn about the human *action of hammering*, by observing the tool being used by other people, by being shown how to hold and wield it, and by trying to use it ourselves to perform similar kinds of actions. Our first encounters with tools happen in a social context . . . and so our understanding of the nature and function of these tools will be shaped by that social context.
(2000: 14, author's emphasis)

There are three further features of exploratory learning which have disturbed teachers and created uncertainty and ambiguity in practice:

1. There is the myth that teachers should never *tell* learners anything directly (Bransford et al. 2000: 11) in case it 'interferes' in their learning processes. Bransford et al. point out that this confuses a theory of pedagogy with a theory of learning, and that learners often need and appreciate some explanation for what they discover, or to clarify misunderstandings.
2. The myth of 'freedom' offered by 'exploration'. Rowland (1993), in a discussion of exploratory learning in adult education, observes that adults have many constraints in their lives and also the tutor is not the only person imposing on them. Thus, a non-interventionist tutor may, by not helping participants critically question their assumptions sufficiently, simply serve to perpetuate the conditions from which they wish to escape through education.

3. In children's education, without supportive and critical feedback on their efforts, learners will never be able to develop their own values and standards. In other words, they still need an element of 'verticality' in their educational experience. Exploration, by denying children direct access to the criteria for assessment, adds to the learning load, and to uncertainty.

Exploratory teaching poses particular challenges for teachers working with large groups, and where material resources for learning are limited. Teachers have to modify more directive approaches to order and to rely on learners adopting a measure of self-control, or teach them to do this. While exploratory learning generates a multitude of learning opportunities, these can be haphazard and unpredictable, adding to the emotional load and risk of teaching and learning in such fluid conditions. Teachers may be tempted to resort to closer control of the learning group and context as a consequence, thus further increasing the ambiguity of the situation. A final problematic issue for teachers is the type of care they can offer in exploratory teaching. Equal care for all students is impossible to achieve, despite the best of intentions, because of the difficulty of allocating time equally and at the same time meeting students' individual emotional and learning needs. Thus at both micro and meso levels of action and planning, a higher order management knowledge and skill is required than in high structure transmission contexts.

The strong version of exploratory pedagogy has had relatively little influence in mainstream language education, apart from individualised forms of autonomous learning (Benson 2001), some types of project work (Fried-Booth 2002) and in guided discovery learning (e.g. language awareness; Bolitho and Tomlinson 1995; Arndt et al. 2000). The growth of language learning for young children has, however, tended to draw on the values of child-centredness prevalent in the UK in the middle part of the twentieth century (Vale and Fuenteun 1995). The role of direct experience in learning is, however, now acknowledged as a key feature of foreign language learning at all ages (Quote 7.8) but managing language classroom teaching-and-learning for individual learning and discovery under these circumstances remains an organisational challenge, as order, opportunity and care compete.

Quote 7.8   Kohonen on experiential foreign language learning

Experiential learning techniques include various interactive practices where the participants have opportunities to learn from others' experiences, being actively and personally engaged in the process:

[examples: personal stories and case studies; role plays, drama activities, games and simulations]

Quote 7.8   (Continued)

All of these [experiential learning techniques] contain a common element of learning from immediate experience and engaging the learners in the process as whole persons, both intellectually and emotionally.
(2001: 23)

Social constructivist pedagogies

Exploratory teaching or 'discovery learning' has been heavily criticised from a number of perspectives, some ideological, some conceptual. However, from a pedagogic point of view, perhaps the most trenchant criticisms are levelled at the apparent lack of structure on the one hand – and therefore the threat to classroom order – and on the other, its failure to incorporate or acknowledge the social and cultural nature of learning. Bruner, a keen advocate of discovery pedagogy and its central value of 'child-centredness' in the 1960s, has more recently shifted his allegiance to social constructivism because of its focus on the social dimension in learning (Quote 7.9). Many educationalists have also commented that social constructivist approaches have liberated them from the endless debate between 'traditionalists' and 'progressives' which has dominated debate for the last 50 years or more (Quote 7.10).

Quote 7.9   Bruner on changing from discovery to dialogue

Some years ago [during the 1960s] I wrote very insistent articles about the importance of discovery learning – learning on one's own. . . . What I am proposing . . . is an extension of that idea, or better, a completion. My model of the child in those days was very much in the tradition of the solo child mastering the world by representing it to himself in his own terms. In the intervening years I have come increasingly to recognise that most learning in most settings is a communal activity, a sharing of the culture. It is not just that the child must make his knowledge his own, but that he must make it his own in a community of those who share his sense of belonging to a culture. It is this that leads me to emphasise not only discovery and invention but the importance of negotiating and sharing – in a word, of joint culture creating as an object of schooling and as an appropriate step en route to becoming a member of the adult society in which one lives out one's life.
(1986: 127)

Quote 7.10   Wells on social constructivism as a way forward

For more than a quarter of a century, educational reform efforts have been locked in a sterile argument between those who advocate a 'progressive', child-centred form

of education and those who argue for a return to a more structured, teacher-directed curriculum that emphasises basic knowledge and skills. However the recognition that cultural continuity and individual creativity are complementary and interdependent facets of all activity, and hence of the developmental learning trajectories of those who participate in them, Vygotsky's social constructivist theory offers a way out of this impasse. In place of traditional transmissional teaching on the one hand and unstructured discovery on the other, his theory places the emphasis on the co-construction of knowledge by more mature and less mature participants engaging in activity together.
(1999: xii)

For social constructivists, learning is a social, psychological and above all a cultural process – it has history. Several social-constructivist pedagogies draw extensively on Vygotsky's (1978) theories of learning (Concept 7.9). These were developed over several years' observation and experimental work with young children learning in their normal social surroundings. They are essentially theories of informal learning (Chapter 2) and child development subsequently appropriated by educationalists who believe that learners can co-construct their own understandings while learning in formal settings with the assistance of a mediator-teacher.

Concept 7.10   Social constructivist views of learning and implications for pedagogy

Key concepts in a social constructivist or socio-cultural view:

A. Vygotsky's ideas about language
Language has two functions in learning:

1. 'as a communicative or *cultural tool* we use it for sharing and jointly developing the knowledge – the 'culture' – which enables organised human social life to exist and continue.'
2. 'as a *psychological tool* for organising our individual thoughts, for reasoning, planning and reviewing our actions.' (Mercer 2000: 10)

B. Zone of Proximal Development (ZPD)
The ZPD is a 'psychological space' between a particular activity a learner can manage to do with assistance, and what they can manage to do without assistance. Crossing a ZPD can best be done in the company of a helper who is more competent than the learner. Mercer (1994: 102) points out that 'assistance or instruction is a normal, common and important feature of human mental development' and that 'the limits of a person's learning or problem-solving ability can be expanded by providing the right kind of cognitive support.'

Concept 7.10   (Continued)

C. Scaffolding

Originating in the work of Wood, Bruner and Ross (1976), scaffolding represents the type of cognitive support which a helper can provide a learner in the process of learning. Scaffolding is most typically linguistic and consists of moves on the part of the helper to move the learner through increasingly difficult stages of the learning task. It is a contested and problematic notion (see Section 2 of this volume), and may best be attributed to very specific forms of teacher intervention to assist learners in doing tasks they cannot do on their own. The teacher must have the goal of specific new learning at a higher level than currently available. Scaffolding is clearly more specific than the types of assistance that are often given informally.

D. Appropriation

A socio-cultural view of learning regards internalisation of new learning as achieved by the appropriation of the ways in which significant others – helpers, teachers – mediate an individual's learning. The main medium for creating meaning is **language**, and its use as a means of mediating learning activity in the social encounter with a helper is central. During the learning activity a lot of language used by learners is self-referential or *private speech*, addressed only to oneself. Socio-cultural theory posits that private speech becomes *inner speech*, and is the primary means by which 'higher' learning is facilitated.

As we have seen in Chapter 2, helpers (mediators) play a significant role in both informal and formal classroom learning. A Vygotskyan view of the learning process has led to the refinement of the central teacher–learner relationship in the classroom as mediation (Concept 7.11), a position empha-sising the collaborative nature of teaching-and-learning between teacher and student. From the pedagogic point of view another key element of Vygotskyan theory is the 'zone of proximal development' – ZPD. Learning something new is about successfully 'crossing' a ZPD, from a state of incom-petence to a state of competence, during the process of which a more experienced or knowledgeable member of the community mediates by guiding or 'scaffolding' the learner in gradually appropriating new know-ledge and skill to the point where they have mastered it and internalised it. For social constructivists like Newman et al. (1989) the classroom is a 'construction zone', an 'interpsychological' location which 'mediates between the thoughts of two people' (1989: xi) (Quote 7.12). In classroom manage-ment terms, one of the teacher's primary tasks is to organise classroom activity to create occasions for collaborative work between students and teachers. In the 'construction zone', where many ZPDs are simultaneously being attended to, the teacher is an active and often the focal helping figure in the classroom.

Quote 7.12   The 'construction zone' and ZPD

ZPD is the locus of social negotiations about meanings and it is, in the context of schools, a place where teachers and students may appropriate one another's understandings.
(Newman et al. 1989: xii)

. . . learning [happens] in the 'collaborative space' between student and teacher.
(Kozulin 1998: 161)

A further component of social constructivist pedagogy is language itself, the primary tool for constructing joint and personal meanings in learning (Chapter 4). Language also has a primary role in the storage of new learning, and its organisation cognitively. As children grow up, they interact with their families and communities. They experience various aspects of their culture which are mediated through language: skills and strategies of thinking are developed through language use (or 'interthinking' – Mercer 2000) in order to reach mutual understanding. Language and concepts shape, challenge, amplify or limit thinking processes. The process mirrors the process of learning as legitimate peripheral participation (LPP) (Wenger 1998) in communities of practice and affiliation. Language is the means through which much of LPP takes place. The learning journey from periphery to centre in a community can be compared to the crossing of a succession of ZPDs in collaboration and interaction with a community's members. The teacher's role in managing language use is thus crucial to the classroom process, not only in social constructivist pedagogies, where it is regarded as central; it is also central to transmission and exploratory teaching, although for different reasons. (Chapter 8)

Concept 7.11   Learning as a socio-cultural process – mediation

Learning is mediated by a 'knower', typically an adult for children.

The three major components of mediation are held to be (a) intentionality and reciprocity (b) meaning and (c) transcendence, i.e the mediator must be clear about her intentions in setting tasks and must also determine that the learner(s) are willing and able to respond appropriately to these stated intentions. The personal and cultural meaning of the task should be explained and its relevance beyond the present time must be emphasised. Effective mediators will also encourage learners to develop a sense of competence and confidence in their own abilities, to take control over their own behaviour, and to seek for and respond to new challenges in life.

> ## Concept 7.11   (Continued)
>
> Mediators will also provoke the desire to seek, set and achieve appropriate goals. Cooperative sharing behaviour should be fostered, whilst at the same time emphasising the unique contribution that each individual can make. Allied to cooperation will also be a developing sense of belonging to a group, a family, a community and a culture. Finally, the teacher should instil in the learners an understanding that humans are both capable of change and are constantly changing. The effective lifelong learner is one who has the ability to recognise, assess and contribute to this change.
> (Burden 1994: 312)

Social constructivist pedagogies require a wide range of management knowledge and skills, in particular the capacity to engage learners in dialogue. The dialogue takes place in ZPDs, or 'intermental development zones' (IDZ) Mercer (2000: 141) (Quote 7.13). This emphasises the quality of *joint* achievement in which the classroom management task is to maintain the IDZ so that teachers can assist learners in operating at levels slightly beyond current levels of knowledge and understanding so that the learning experience can be both 'consolidated' and extended into new domains.

> ## Quote 7.13   Mercer on the Intermental Development Zone (IDZ)
>
> For a teacher to teach and a learner to learn, they must use talk and joint activity to create a shared communicative space, an 'intermental development zone'on the contextual foundations of their common knowledge and aims. In this intermental zone, which is reconstituted constantly as the dialogue continues, the teacher and learner negotiate their way through the activity in which they are involved. If the quality of the zone is successfully maintained, the teacher can enable a learner to become able to operate just beyond their established capabilities, and to consolidate this experience as new ability and understanding.
> (2000: 141)

In examining social-constructivist pedagogies, the key aspects are therefore:

- the role of language in classroom teaching-and-learning;
- the types of learning activity which teachers organise, and the ways teachers mediate learning through these activities;
- the nature of the relationships between teachers and learners in the co-construction of knowledge.

These are illustrated in the classroom described in Extract 7.1.

Extract 7.1   Co-construction of knowledge

Secondary Level Language Lesson

    T: OK / now (*B/B: 14 secs*) I want somebody to complete that/you've said she is always absent-minded in class

    Ss: class

    T: for example / last Monday / keep in mind / we are / using now / the what

5   Ss: past tense

    T: the past tense / OK / let somebody who will volunteer before I / appoint him / to complete / complete that sentence – yes – Bame Irene – for example last Monday / you now have to / give an example / to support the – fact / she is / always absent-minded in class – make a statement/to support that thing – quick

10 S #7:   last Monday

    T: for example

    S7:   for example / last Monday she was in class / and she wanted to say something and

    Ss: (*laughter*)

    T: that you see is going to be a very long sentence – for example /make it

15   shorter than / than that

    S #7:   last Monday the teacher asked her – the teacher asked her if a question / she wake up and asked (*inaud.*)

    T: she

    Ss: woke up

20 S #7:   if she woke up /and asking her neighbours that what has the teacher asked (*laughter*)

    T: wonderful / it's a whole paragraph – make it shorter / OK / Irene sit down / for example

---

In this lesson extract, we observe collaborative work between teachers and students. For example, in lines 17–19, teacher and students jointly construct the correction of another student's utterance. The students are clearly enjoying the class and the rapport with the teacher. There are several instances of laughter at student-constructed contributions which the teacher does not comment on, and allows as part of the texture of the lesson. The teacher provides quiet guidance regarding the task without 'feeding' the students with language (lines 14/15 and 18). The learning activity itself invites students to construct sentences based on the theme of 'absent-mindedness', introduced earlier in which they are referring to themselves and previous shared classroom experiences.

Assisted performance

Tharp and Gallimore (1991) propose a version of this pedagogy which they call 'assisted performance' (Concept 7.12). They draw analogies from 'natural teaching' of the type described by Vygotsky in which children are assisted in doing things which they cannot do alone. Teaching is a means of assisting learners' performance across ZPDs, and thus only occurs when learners perform with assistance. Many types of classroom activity provide assistance to learners ('lectures, demonstrations, cooperative learning exercises/activities, textbook reading...even recitation and assessment' (1991: 2)). Like many pedagogies, it has an element of eclecticism – a wide range of activities is necessary to create the opportunities for assisting performance. However, the main concerns are the development of speech and writing as means of developing thinking skills. For this to occur, dialogue, or the questioning and sharing of ideas in conversation, is necessary. They term this 'instructional conversation'. In order to solve the potential paradox of a combination of instructional authority and conversational equality, they point out that 'parents and teachers who engage in instructional conversation are assuming that the child may have something to say beyond the known answers in the head of the adult' (1991: 3).

Concept 7.12   Assisted performance (Tharp and Gallimore 1988, 1991)

Teaching consists of assisting performance through a child's zone of proximal development (ZPD). *Teaching must be redefined as assisted performance; teaching occurs when performance is achieved with assistance.*
(1991: 2)

Seven means of assistance

1. Modelling – offering behaviour for imitation (learner receives information and a remembered image that can serve as a performance standard).
2. Feeding Back – providing information for learners to compare their behaviour with a standard and allows for self correction.
3. Contingency management – applying the principles of reinforcement and punishment.
4. Directing – requesting specific action; specifying correct response, providing clarity and information and promoting decision-making.
5. Questioning – inviting learners to perform when they cannot or will not produce unelicited.
6. Explaining – providing explanatory and belief structure which assists learners in organising and justifying new learning and perceptions.
7. Task structuring – chunking, segregating, sequencing or otherwise structuring a task into or from components. This helps the task fit better in the ZPD.

...the critical form of assisting learners is *dialogue* – the questioning and sharing of ideas and knowledge that happen in conversation.
(1991: 3)

Some Experimental Evidence for the value of assistance
Newman, Griffin and Cole (1984) compared children's behaviour in two settings – one a standard 'laboratory' task and the other a 'loosely supervised' science activity. They discovered that when the researcher spelt out the task demands, and provided training in doing the task, the children were able to carry it out according to the structure laid down by the researcher. The other children in the classroom worked out their own routines once they had found a relevance for the task. They demonstrate the impact of their 'teaching' in preventing independent learning.

Assisted performance has many implications for classroom management.

1. In order to build 'communities of learners', conditions must be created in the classroom to enable dialogue and instructional conversation to take place. The care dimension of classroom management will thus feature strongly – people must feel secure and listened to.
2. Classrooms also need to be arranged physically in order to allow for dialogue, to allow full exploration to take place, and so that participation patterns reflect dialogue, so that engagement of both teachers and learners in ZPDs is achieved.
3. Time needs to be allocated to allow for conversation to follow its natural course – there is no way of predicting how long this process can take.
4. Activities must be directed towards learning goals, and resources appropriate to the task, including language itself, as well as what learners and teachers already know, made available for learning, either materially or through the instructional conversation itself.

Responsive teaching

Bowers and Flinders' (1990) 'ecological' (Quote 7.14) approach to classroom management advocates 'responsive teaching'. Rejecting 'order' conceptions of classroom management (Chapter 5), they argue for an approach to teaching which draws from and contributes to the cultural complexity of the classroom.

Quote 7.14   Bowers and Flinders on responsive teaching

Understanding the deep cultural foundations of the language dynamics of the classroom, which we see as including the thought process, behaviour patterns and patterns of communication, is an essential part of the teacher's professional knowledge.

Quote 7.14   (Continued)

We think that as an understanding of the formative influences of culture and language is deepened, there will be corresponding changes in thinking about the structure of knowledge that makes up the content area of the curriculum and in thinking about the processes of learning – from an individualistic to a more culturally centred view of learning.

(1991: 3, 22)

Responsive teaching is embedded in a deep understanding of classroom processes, an acknowledgement of the centrality of language and other non-verbal forms of behaviour in learning and an acceptance of the value of teachers' judgements in classroom management. Students and teachers are 'cultural beings' who have internalised everyday culturally shared views of how to think and behave. The modelling influence of teachers in classroom life is a strong element in responsive teaching. Above all, responsive teaching is sensitive to the unfolding classroom context and the learning needs of the students which emerge from learning activity and dialogue. The need to maintain the quality and potential of the classroom environment in turn facilitates educationally significant communication. Bowers and Flinders' view of professional knowledge emphasises the role of talk in classrooms as the key to learning and development, together with a teacher's knowledge of curriculum. The notion of the 'ecology' of the classroom (Chapter 4) predicates a pedagogy of responsiveness to ongoing events, similar to the idea of micro classroom management activity. What they describe is the 'culture' of the classroom at work, and the necessity for an opportunity approach to managing it – responsive teaching.

Dialogic Inquiry

Wells proposes 'Dialogic Inquiry' as an alternative to didactic and exploratory teaching, a pedagogy which he claims allows teachers and students equal access to the cultural tools of talk (Concept 7.13). Dialogic Inquiry draws on some of the key tenets of discovery – for instance, the goal of developing learners' capacities for creative thought. This is realised through activities which engage students in often open-ended inquiry, based on situations devised or 'engineered' by the teacher. He adds to this the more ambitious aims of encouraging students to develop reflective and responsible dispositions as aids to both learning and living.

Concept 7.13   Dialogic inquiry

Wells appropriates Vygotsky's ideas as a way out of the impasse of current educational debate. He claims it can replace competitive individualism with 'a collaborative community in which, with the teacher as leader, all participants learn with and from each other as they engage together in dialogic inquiry' (1999: xii).

Classrooms based on dialogic inquiry would feature:

1. A community which shares a commitment to caring, collaboration, and a dialogic mode of making meanings.
2. A curriculum organised in terms of broad themes for inquiry that encourage a willingness to wonder, to ask questions and to collaborate with others in building knowledge, both practical and theoretical, in order to answer them.
3. Negotiated goals that:
   • challenge students to develop interests and abilities
   • are open-ended enough to allow for alternatives
   • are focused on the whole person
   • provide opportunities to master the culture's tools and technologies through purposeful use
   • encourage collaborative group work and individual effort
   • value equally process and products
4. Ensuring there are occasions for learners to:
   • use a variety of modes of representation
   • present their work to each other for critical, constructive feedback
   • reflect on what they have learned, individually and as a community
   • receive assistance and guidance through ZPDs

(Wells 1999: 335–6)

Wells emphasises the negotiation of learning goals within a classroom community. Collaborative learning and teaching activity is the rule in this pedagogy. Learner activities such as sharing products of activity and offering each other feedback are emphasised. There is a strong affective element to Dialogic Inquiry – Wells recognises that the type of classroom community he advocates requires a strong commitment to caring relationships. As with responsive teaching, classroom management tends towards care and opportunity (especially when learners are invited to ask questions, 'to wonder') in dialogic inquiry. The dynamic and creative learning environment envisaged thus presents teachers with the challenge of practising according to the main management challenges implied by such a potentially open-ended context. These are summarised in Concept 7.14.

Concept 7.14 Classroom management and social constructivism

Pedagogy based on social constructivism has the following main implications for managing language classrooms:

1. The teacher has an important role, not only as source of information, but also as guide and helper across ZPDs. The element of care is thus important in order to create trust between the guide and the learner.

Concept 7.14 (Continued)

2. Although talk is important in any pedagogy, in a social constructivist classroom it is overtly a tool for learning, and a range of different talk types is possible – from monologue through to open group conversation.
3. Learning is likely to arise from activities created by management practices which create opportunities for learning. In this sense the classroom is more risky, ambiguous and unstable than either a transmission or an exploratory classroom, and demands more from teachers and students in the way of managing skills.
4. The order dimension of managing is concerned with design and structure rather than discipline and control. The creation of a community (in itself a major management task) is the bedrock for success in this dimension.

7.4 Other perspectives on pedagogy

The three broad 'teaching models' we have so far examined are grounded in views of learning and the nature of knowledge. This section examines three alternative perspectives on pedagogy.

Repertoires of teaching

Hopkins et al. (1997: 60) claim all teachers have a repertoire of learning activities and modes of teaching (Concept 7.15). The repertoire consists of more than a set pedagogy and its associated activities. It also contains generic teaching skills such as explaining or eliciting, and encompasses styles and 'models'. 'Quality teaching', it is argued, consists of three main areas – skills, models and 'artistry'. Quality teaching mainly refers to the meso level of classroom management skills, involving planning and strategy. At the micro level, the in-time management of activities also draws upon a wide repertoire of generic teaching skills and artistry.

Concept 7.15 Repertoires of teaching

In practice, more effective practitioners have a wide range of teaching skills, styles, models and approaches which comprise a teaching repertoire.
(Hopkins et al. 1997: 60)

Powerful learning does not occur by accident but is usually the result of an effective learning situation created by a skilful teacher.
(Hopkins et al. 1997: 60)

Aspects of 'quality teaching':

• Skills (dimensions of content knowledge, curriculum knowledge, influences of 'other factors', knowledge of own teaching. Skills are goal-directed, contextually sensitive, require 'fine tuning', performed smoothly, acquired through training and practice).

- Models ('distinct approaches designed to bring about particular kinds of learning and to help pupils become more effective learners') (1997: 62).
- Artistry ('highly creative and highly personal activity' of teaching, which matches teaching and learning).

According to Joyce et al. (1997) there are four main 'families of teaching' (or 'models') (Concept 7.16) which inform pedagogic activity. During their careers, teachers accumulate a repertoire of successful strategies from these models on which they draw in the planning and execution of learning activity. One important implication of this is that teachers are likely to use different pedagogic approaches for various purposes. It is rare for a teacher to be limited only to one pedagogic mode, despite strong tendencies in one direction or another. Teachers vary activities for different purposes, and these call upon different skills and attitudes. For example, using activities from the personal 'family' would involve a degree of sympathy with the activities themselves and the interpersonal skills with which to manage classroom activity requiring disclosure and feedback by students, and therefore management of the emotional risks.

Prabhu (1995: 67) notes that the practical decisions in teaching operate at both individual and institutional levels. These include the capacity to signal clearly to students a change in mode of activity. A single lesson can quite conceivably feature a teacher using whole class didactic, individual discovery and collaborative learning modes. Classroom groups quickly learn to acculturate to different modes of activity when an eclectic pattern becomes routine, provided that the process of adding new elements to the repertoire is in itself managed effectively. This managing skill is in itself part of a teacher's repertoire.

The thrust of the work of Hopkins et al. and Joyce et al. is to generate a research-based understanding of 'quality teaching'. The drawback of this approach to conceptualising pedagogy is that it makes teaching vulnerable to assessment in terms of 'skills demonstrated' or 'models employed correctly', the language of managerialism. It also equates 'artistry', or the creative side of teaching, to being able to 'match' teaching and learning closely, presumably as a way of rendering classroom mysteries measurable. By reducing a vital aspect of classroom management to the creation of cooperative classroom relationships in this way, Hopkins and Joyce manage perhaps inadvertently to 'technicise' micro-management skills.

Concept 7.16   Joyce et al.'s families of 'models' of teaching

1. *Information processing* – 'emphasise ways of enhancing the human being's drive to make sense of the world by acquiring and organising data, sensing problems and generating solutions to them, and developing concepts and language for conveying them.' (1997: 26)

Concept 7.16   (Continued)

2. *Social* – 'When we work together, we generate collective energy that we call 'synergy'. The social models of teaching are constructed to take advantage of this phenomenon by building learning communities. Essentially 'classroom management' is a matter of developing cooperative relationships in the classroom.' (1997: 28)
3. *Personal* – 'Personal models of learning begin from the perspective of the selfhood of the individual. They attempt to shape education so that we come to understand ourselves better, take responsibility for our education and learn to reach beyond our current development to become stronger, more sensitive and more creative in our search for high quality lives.' (1997: 30–1)
4. *Behavioural systems* – ' . . . human beings are self-correcting communication systems that modify behaviour in response to information about how successfully tasks are navigated.' (1997: 31)

Artistry and tact in pedagogy

Artistry is defined by Hopkins et al. (1997: 61) in the following terms: 'teaching is . . . a highly creative activity involving the use of sophisticated repertoires of responses and the ability to reflect upon teaching'. They claim high degrees of classroom effectiveness when effective teaching influences effective learning – in other words, the learning context is managed for optimum effect to provide a rich context for learning (1997: 62). In this scenario, engagement, participation and resources interrelate and feed each other. They point out that the best match is possible when artistry is involved.

Stenhouse (1984) takes a less pragmatic view of 'artistry' (Quote 7.15), but at the same time links the art of teaching with reflection. The artistic character of pedagogy, in his view, comprises the ways in which teachers give meaning to their subjects. It carries with it the sense of 'enthusiasm' and passion for one's subject, as 'lived knowledge'. It is thus not open to quantification. However, Hopkins et al might argue that we can see artistry at work and therefore collect evidence for its existence.

Quote 7.15   Stenhouse on artistry and teaching

[Teaching is an art], an exercise of skill expressive of meaning.

Teaching is an art which expresses in a form accessible to learners an understanding of the nature of that which is to be learned.

[Example]: Teaching French expresses an understanding of the nature of language and culture and of that particular language and culture. [Views on nature of knowledge]

The art of education expresses a view of knowledge as people live it. The medium is schooling. It is at its highest when the learner is brought to reflect consciously on the message he or she receives. This fulfilment depends not only upon the quality of the curriculum but also the art of the teacher.

All good art is an inquiry and an experiment. It is by virtue of being an artist that a teacher is a researcher.

(1984: 70)

On the other hand, Stenhouse's vision of artistry is closer to the notion of intuition in teaching (Atkinson and Claxton 2000) (Quote 7.16).

Quote 7.16   Atkinson and Claxton on intuition in teaching

Intuition can provide a holistic way of knowing – it appears to be unconscious insight but it is not, therefore, without basis. Rather, its basis is the whole of what has been known but which cannot, by nature of its size and complexity, be held in consciousness.... (p. 5)

... Intuition in teaching draws on: routine procedures which are second nature to the practitioner, and pattern recognition which allows them to read the context at a glance and to adapt the preconceived plan in the light of the changing context. (p. 6)

(Atkinson and Claxton 2000)

Another view of the artistic or intuitive aspects of teaching is expressed by van Manen (1991) who articulates a 'pedagogy of thoughtfulness' (Quote 7.17). The main component of a pedagogy of thoughtfulness is 'pedagogical tact'. Tact describes the 'feel' that teachers demonstrate as they work closely with learners, staying sensitive to their moods and emerging learning and emotional needs. Local micro management decisions are taken effectively by working tactfully, attuned to the pedagogic moment. This intuitive, artistic aspect of classroom management is at the heart of any teacher's practice. It is free of ideology, and, as van Manen (1991: 128) indicates, it is a manifestation of teachers' moral responsibilities for protecting, educating and helping children grow. It is the most delicate realisation of a teacher's engagement with learners, a teacher's presence given emotional and intellectual authority, rather than mere physical proximity.

Quote 7.17   van Manen on the 'tact' of teaching

It is possible to learn all the techniques of instruction but to remain pedagogically unfit as a teacher. The preparation of educators obviously includes much more than the teaching of knowledge and skills, more even than a professional ethical code or moral

---

Quote 7.17   (Continued)

craft. To become a teacher includes something that cannot be taught formally: the most personal embodiment of a pedagogical thoughtfulness. (p. 6)

Someone who shows tact seems to have the ability to act quickly, surely, confidently and appropriately in complex or delicate circumstances. (p. 125)

Tact is a kind of practical normative intelligence that is governed by insight while relying on feelings. Tact is possible because human beings are capable of exercising the complex faculty composed of perceptiveness, sensitivity, insight and being attuned to each other's experience. (p. 146)

(van Manen 1991)

Tact is mediated through speech above all, but also through non-verbals such as use of the eyes, gesture, silence, creation of atmosphere, and through example, by modelling behaviours. Engagement, as well as participation, has a verbal aspect – talk is a means of connecting the two processes and providing continuity and immediate relevance for events in the classroom. It is a fundamental set of classroom management practices, bridging emotional, cognitive and social domains.

Critical pedagogy

Another pedagogy which has implications for classroom management is critical pedagogy (Concept 7.17). Critical pedagogy has the aim of transforming education in order to empower students, develop critical thinking and democratic values and practices. It is also, as Fréire (1972) famously claimed, is anti-didactic, a pedagogy of liberation, no less, in which learners would be able to gain the skills and the capacities to improve their lot in life and to meaningfully engage with the political process in their context. Its basis is in dialogue between teachers and students and teachers and teachers, and as van Lier (1996a:159) points out, changing pedagogy so that the rules of participation and interaction are changed (management decisions) 'would change the rules of the pedagogical game in fundamental ways'.

Concept 7.17   Critical pedagogy

Critical pedagogy has its roots in 'liberationist pedagogies' (Fréire 1972) and critical theory.

1. Teachers, through research and inquiry into their own practices, aim to transform their own practices.
2. Through dialogue with students, teachers challenge them to attempt personal action for change.
3. Inquiry is motivated by commitment to ideologies and values (e.g. justice, personal empowerment).

Recent work in the TESOL field (e.g. Canagarajah 1999) has alerted us to the potential domination of externally imposed models of teaching and learning which may be culturally alienating and provoke forms of 'resistance' in daily classroom activity. Pedagogies which oppose the forces of domination – in this case definitions of language as content, and the types of classroom relationship implied by transmission – are increasingly advocated by educators conscious of the ways in which education reproduces oppression.

A pedagogy which also positions teaching-and-learning as the source of problem-posing activity inevitably will demand different ways of managing classrooms to equalise power relations, to create conditions in which problems can be addressed safely. It will call upon all the management skills and resources of a teacher as well as their moral and political engagement. It may ultimately be the case that any change from a transmission pedagogy entails a new political reality at the classroom level, even if the aim is not social and political transformation, and management of the transition from order to opportunity, and order to care. Thus the mission and skills of a pedagogy of resistance are brought to the service of change.

Summary

The pedagogies outlined in this chapter are all grounded in particular views of education and learning. They suggest approaches to the classroom management process in terms of relationships between order, opportunity and care, through the relationships between teachers and learners and how they manage classroom space and time. One drawback of ideas in pedagogy is that they can easily become prescriptions for action – as we have seen, classrooms are open to ideological influences on a number of levels, and ideas about teaching and learning are among the most influential on teachers' thinking. Rather than see these ideas as exclusive choices, however, it may be more helpful to see them as possibilities. In teaching and learning, there is inevitably a gap between planning and action, and pragmatic decision-making is often more appropriate for classroom management. For example, Tharp and Gallimore point out that instructional conversation is one of several ways of teaching, and include other means in their discussion. Some of the protagonists of 'learner-centred' views are less pragmatic, however, and more likely to be swayed by ideology as well as ideas in their choice of pedagogy and management procedures. The guiding principle in pedagogy, as in classroom management is fitness for purpose – students' learning is the primary goal, and teachers search for the most appropriate and productive means meeting the students' goals, managing the context through their chosen and improvised pedagogies. As Prabhu reminds us one of the main problems facing teachers in the managerial aspect of their role is 'deciding an action despite ideational and operational uncertainties, and conflicting over-certainties of ideologies' (1995: 68).

Further reading

Bransford et al. (2000) has a wealth of material on learning and teaching.

Brumfit (2001) has a wide-ranging discussion on the nature of language teaching.

Bruner (1986) is a revealing account of on how he was 'converted' to a more social view of learning.

Canagarajah (1999) expands on his ideas about pedagogies of resistance.

Jarvis et al. (2004) contains a clear discussion of learning theories and their implications for teaching.

Pollard and Tann (1997) examines the three main pedagogies from the primary education perspective.

Prabhu (1995) is a clearly-written article on language pedagogy.

Rowland (1993) has a comprehensive exposition of the three main pedagogies.

Stenhouse (1975) is a 'classic' discussion of alternatives to transmission views of the curriculum.

Tharp and Gallimore (1988) is a passionate plea for constructivist principles to be adopted in teaching and learning.

Wells (1999) makes the case for 'dialogic inquiry'.

8
Patterns of Participation: Managing Classroom Talk

The various aspects of classroom management – institutional, social, pedagogic, affective – and their connections with the primary concerns of classroom management – order, opportunity and care – have strong discoursal characteristics. The patterns of participation revealed by analysis of how the main activities of teaching are realised in classroom talk provide insights into classroom management practice. By examining what learners and teachers actually do when participating in classroom activity, the relatively abstract entities of pedagogies (Chapter 7) are brought to life. Chapter 4 has already established the metaphor of classroom as 'discourse village', and this chapter explores further what this means. Mercer's (1994, 1995, 2000, 2001; Edwards and Mercer 1987) work sees classroom talk contributing to and as an outcome of the formation of unique social contexts, created for the purposes of learning. Classroom talk is thus a form of social action managed with the aim of enhancing learning and a window on classroom participation.

Concept 8.1 Teaching techniques

Teaching techniques are 'intentional, goal-directed ways of talking . . . which reflect the constraints of the institutional setting in which schoolteachers work.
(Mercer 1995: 25)

Eliciting knowledge from learners: direct (questions) and cued (Socratic dialogue) elicitations.
Responding to what learners say: confirming, rejecting, repeating, reformulating, elaborating on what learners say.
Describing significant aspects of shared experience: amplifying (instructions for clarity), explaining (often instructions for activities), using 'we' statements (referring to previous shared classroom experience), recapping (emphasising points covered in learning activity).

(after Mercer 1995: 25–6; 2001: 246)

The essence of classroom talk is captured in what Mercer (1995: 25) calls 'teaching techniques' (Concept 8.1). Mercer's classification, based on detailed analysis of classroom talk data, captures a teacher managing classroom talk, and shaping it 'into a set of tools for pursuing their professional goals' (2001: 246). Talk also reflects the requirements of a curriculum as teachers guide their learners towards common knowledge. Teachers are thus 'discourse guides' (Mercer 1995: 83), a role tied to their pedagogic obligations, with classroom talk the means of negotiating the curriculum. Talk is thus employed as a tool for managing participation in learning activities.

Teachers typically open classroom exchanges – in Extract 8.1, for example, the teacher opens an exchange in line 7 and then invites contributions from all or one member of the classroom group, to initiate particular types of social and cognitive activity. The use of 'we' statements to establish common learning history is an interesting example of management activity and a strong indicator of how regulatory and instructional management functions coalesce. On the one hand a 'we statement' is a means of drawing attention to the communal nature of the learning task (lines 7 and 14 in Extract 8.1). (The 'echoed' overlap by the students (line 16) is further evidence of shared knowledge and activity.) A 'we statement' is also a means of signalling connections between present and previous learning activity.

Extract 8.1   Classroom talk

```
     T:   good morning
     Ss:  good morning sir –
     T:   you people have used / twenty minutes of our time
     Ss:  yes sir
5    T:   you don't want to tell me that the sports master -- kept you there --
          indefinitely – you were supposed to have left the sports field ten minutes --
          before -- the end of these -- sports period and come to class / OK erm / do you
          remember we have been stressing on/the use of two tenses / since the beginning
          of this week / who can tell me what these tenses are --- yeah/Christine
10   S #1:  present tense and simple
     Sx:                         past
     S #1:  past tense and present
     T:   have you heard what she said
     T:   you remember the statement we made – shop assistants / always / make / one
15   feel / ignorant
     Ss:         ignorant
```

8.1   Patterns of participation in classroom discourse

An understanding of how interaction is structured and accomplished by teachers and learners in the classroom provides valuable insights into how the classroom is managed on a moment-by-moment basis. This occurs at the level of specific episodes or series of exchanges to whole lessons and beyond, at the course or programme level (the long conversation of teaching we examined in Chapter 2). This section will look at several interconnected ways of analysing classroom talk: teacher–learner dialogues, teachers' questions and turn-taking, teacher monologue and other types of talk that pedagogic activity can promote, such as collaborative talk. The insights gained from the different types of analysis provide a framework with which to understand the linguistic dimensions of order and opportunity modes of classroom management.

The techniques for analysing classroom talk include combing through the actual texts (or transcripts) of classroom activity to locate patterns and consistencies to reveal facts about the teaching/learning process in action. However, we need to remind ourselves that despite the elegance of many of the analytical schemes, they are simply tools to extract evidence of cultural, social, psychological or educational processes – the discourses of classroom management – at work. Talk data provide evidence of real socio-cultural practices in action at the local classroom level, rather than simply as 'interactions' or residual texts from these encounters.

The IRF

Sinclair and Coulthard's (1975) work on classroom discourse established a hierarchical set of interlocking categories (act, move, exchange, transaction and lesson) based on a *linguistic* analysis of the discourse of pupils and teachers. This early work was primarily concerned with the problem of analysing language above the level of sentence, not educational processes. Indeed, Sinclair and Coulthard regarded classrooms as ideal sites for the linguistic analysis of spoken discourse because they believed participants' roles were fixed. They thus treated as unproblematic the social and psychological dimensions of classroom activity. However, their analysis did reveal strong evidence for a basic mechanism for the management of classroom activity, what has come to be known as the IRF: initiation-response-feedback. (Concept 8.2) Wells (1993: 2) has termed the IRF a 'default mode' which seems to be adopted by teachers unless there is good reason to behave otherwise.

Mehan's (1979) analysis of classroom talk drew heavily on Sinclair and Coulthard's analytical scheme, and identified the high frequency of the IRF sequence in the primary school classrooms he investigated. As much as 60 percent of classroom talk conformed to the IRF pattern. Investigators like Wells (1993: 2) have claimed that as much as 70 per cent of classroom talk is of the IRF category. This is cited as evidence of the pedagogy of recitation and transmission. It is also regarded as inimical to the creation of learning opportunity, and primarily concerned with preserving order and routine.

Concept 8.2 The IRF

Originally called 'the teaching cycle' (Bellack et al. 1966), Sinclair and Coulthard (1975) termed it the 'exchange', the 'basic unit of interaction', based on the frequency of its occurrence in lessons they recorded and analysed. Van Lier (1996: 149) notes, 'There is probably nothing that symbolizes classroom discourse quite as much as this structure, the much-noted IRF exchange.' It consists of three parts:

INITIATION (or question, or elicitation) *TEACHER*
RESPONSE (or answer) *STUDENT*
FEEDBACK (or follow-up, evaluation) *TEACHER*

Examples of IRFs

```
    T    put away all your books please/put away everything --- just get out your readers
         (much class noise) -- give me the past tense / of / these sentences I'm going to
         give you / I will eat groundnuts today -- I will eat groundnuts today -- Asungwan
005 S1   I ate groundnuts yesterday
    T    good / Mary / Mary has come late today / Mary has come late today / yes
    S2   Mary came late yesterday
    T    good / class 2B is not noisy today --
    S3   class 2B was noisy yesterday
```

IRF 1 – Lines 2–6
IRF 2 – lines 6–8
IRF 1 takes slightly longer to initiate than IRF 2, probably because the teacher is talking over the top of students who are taking their course books out. The teacher uses the turn in line 6 to also open another sequence, completed in line 8, and so on.

(after van Lier 1996a: 149)

However, as work on classroom discourse has developed, the notion of the IRF as a single monolithic exchange type has been superseded. Van Lier (2001: 94–5), drawing on Wells (1993), summarises this work, noting the capacity of the IRF to perform a number of pedagogic functions (Quote 8.1).

Quote 8.1 van Lier on the versatile IRF

In the IRF format a number of things can be accomplished. At the most mechanical, rote-learning end of IRF, the teacher's questions require the students merely to recite previously learned items. IRF may also be used by the teacher to see if students know a certain word or linguistic item. IRF can demand more, challenging students to think, reason and make connections. At the most demanding end of IRF, students must be articulate and precise: they are pushed by successive probing questions, to clarify, substantiate, or illustrate some point made previously.
(2001: 94, after Wells 1993)

Van Lier identifies a continuum of IRF types from simple recitation and recall to more complex thinking and articulation (Concept 8.3). These entail progressively deeper levels of cognitive processing and response by learners. In this respect the further along the continuum one progresses from recitation – or essentially closed I-moves – the more likely that responses will be open-ended.

Regardless of the pedagogic purpose of a particular exchange, the IRF provides striking evidence of teacher control over the classroom process. Van Lier (2001: 95–6) argues that, because 'the teacher is unequivocally in charge' (2001: 95), the IRF exchange pattern severely restricts students' opportunities to exercise initiative or develop a sense of control and self-regulation – a sense of ownership of the discourse, a sense of being empowered, however, only with reference to the linguistic text, not learners' accounts. At the very 'controlled' end of the spectrum, IRFs almost certainly do restrict student initiative and are evidence of teacher control. This is a major feature of transmission teaching. Mercer's description of teaching techniques on the other hand appears to regard more open-ended IRFs which require a greater depth of processing on the part of students as part of learning particular forms of reasoning, and thus necessary to their eventually becoming independent thinkers. In other words, IRFs are a necessary part of teaching and learning, if learners are to be gradually assisted to perform higher level activities, and are also means of managing this long-term process.

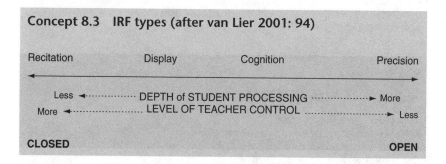

Concept 8.3   IRF types (after van Lier 2001: 94)

Recitation	Display	Cognition	Precision

Less ◄·············· DEPTH of STUDENT PROCESSING ··············► More
More ◄················ LEVEL OF TEACHER CONTROL ···················► Less

CLOSED   **OPEN**

Initiating and responding: question and answer

Van Lier's (2001) analysis suggests that the I-move of the sequence performs different functions. As the initiating move becomes more open and 'inviting', demanding more processing on the part of the learner, the opportunities for more extended student talk are increased. Asking students to reason and to be more precise are ways of extending their participation opportunities. There is potential in these moves for students to take the initiative in different ways. For example, students could ask for clarification of a teacher's question, or when asked to be more precise, the detail they provide could amount to a fairly lengthy monologue. However, the central point remains that it is the teacher who typically initiates exchanges and therefore retains ultimate control of the directions classroom talk can take.

The IRF structure also suggests that teachers exert control on classroom talk through their questions. Because questions are so pivotal in the management of classroom discourse, it is not surprising that they have attracted attention from educationalists. However, analyses have tended to focus on the pedagogic rather than the discoursal functions of questions, and have consequently failed to identify some of the more subtle aspects of I-moves. For example, an I-move does not need to be an interrogative form. Bloom's taxonomy of questions (Concept 8.4) is a standard point of reference for this aspect of classroom life. Bloom (1956) (see also Morgan and Saxton 1989; Fisher 1990) identified a six-level categorisation of questions, working from closed to open-ended, divided into two groups, each leading to the development of lower and higher order thinking skills.

Concept 8.4   Teachers' questions: pedagogic initiators in classroom discourse

Classroom exchanges dominated by IRF structures invariably begin with teachers' questions. Bloom's classification (below) is according to pedagogic function:

KNOWLEDGE
COMPREHENSION } Lower Order Thinking Skills (More Closed)
APPLICATION

ANALYSIS
SYNTHESIS } Higher Order Thinking Skills (More Open-ended)
EVALUATION

Examples from language classrooms might be:

Example A – Language focus
KNOWLEDGE: *What is the past tense form of 'take'?*
COMPREHENSION: *Where could you find out information about verbs with irregular past forms?*
APPLICATION: *When are past forms used?*
ANALYSIS: (with a sample text) *Can you reconstruct the story beginning with the first event, going up to the last event?*
SYNTHESIS: *What is the effect of transforming past tense forms into the present perfect?*
EVALUATION: *What have you learnt about past tense verbs from this session?*

Example B (based on a story told by the teacher)
KNOWLEDGE: *Who were the main characters in the story?*
COMPREHENSION: *Why did it happen like it did?*
APPLICATION: *What would you have done if you'd been character Y in the story?*
ANALYSIS: *Which part did you like best? Which parts couldn't be true?*
SYNTHESIS: *Can you think of a different ending to the story?*
EVALUATION: *What did you think of the story? Who do you sympathise with in the story?*

> ## Concept 8.5   Contextualisation cues
>
> These devices call up background knowledge about language and social relations, and cultural knowledge, about understandings of political realities and routines in speech. For example, 'okay' uttered at the end of an extended interactive sequence in the classroom with a falling intonation, signals the end of the sequence.
>
> ... surface features of a message form ... the means by which speakers signal and listeners interpret what the activity is, how semantic content is to be understood and how each sentence relates to what precedes and what follows.
> (Gumperz 1982: 131)

There is a degree of match between van Lier's analysis of IRFs (classified according to the type of I-move) and the categorisations produced by Bloom et al. As van Lier (2001: 95) points out, 'knowing the purpose of a particular IRF exercise ... is crucial in determining its pedagogical value.' However, ascertaining the purpose of an IRF exchange in real class time is a matter of students reading the contextualisation cues (Concept 8.5) successfully. A post-hoc analysis may provide a neat description of what happens, but cannot reveal a teacher's precise intention.

> ## Extract 8.2   Classroom talk
>
> ```
>     T:  OK / erm / you notice again / you said something / concerning the simple
>         present -- when do we use the priz / present simple / come on now / these exercises /
>         we've been doing which you told me yesterday please sir I don't understand
>         (Ss laughter: scattered) ahha / Ambo / when do we really use the/simple present
>   5     tense/just what we've been doing this week
>     S #3:  to tell a thing that is happening
>     T:  uh
>     S #3:  to tell a thing that is happening
>     T:  is that right
>  10  Ss:  no-oh
>     T:  to tell a thing that is happening (inaud.) ..... yes
>     Ss:                                          (general noise)
>     S #4:  to tell an action that is (inaud) habitual
>     T:  to establish or to express/a habitual action/something that you have always
>  15  been / doing
>     Ss:       ⌊doing
>     T:  something that is very true of / you
>     Ss:                                    ⌊you
> ```

The Bloomian type of question-based analysis is thus flawed in a critical respect, and is only helpful in understanding classroom talk up to a point.

It is of more assistance in the construction of teaching materials where design is realised. It is a pedagogic categorisation predicated on the intention rather than the outcome of questions. Teachers may not have planned particular questions or I-moves, many of which are means of repair after a failure to respond appropriately, as in example. In Extract 8.2, the teacher opens an exchange in lines 1–4. The first I-move is in line 2 'when do we use the present simple'. After reconnecting the group with the previous day's work, the teacher reiterates the I-move in line 4. The R in line 6 elicits a request from the teacher. The teacher then initiates a further sequence in line 9, which also functions as an F-move. The teacher initiates the exchange again in line 11, and in line 13, following a brief period of inter-student discussion, another R-move is made. The teacher confirms its accuracy in line 14/15. Wright (1987b) terms this type of overlapping IRF sequence 'running repairs'.

A teacher's questions must always be considered in context, 'as one element of her whole interaction, *(so) that we can see how she uses language to guide her students' endeavours.* The same kind of question, or even the same words, can be used by teachers to very different effect on different occasions' (Mercer 1995: 31, my emphasis). The pedagogic point relates to the range of elicitation techniques the teacher uses. As an I-move demands greater levels of processing from students, so control is subtly handed over to the student. If, in management terms, the teacher is order-driven, there is a greater likelihood that the teacher will favour a higher number of recitation and display moves; a more opportunity-focused teaching strategy will tend towards a greater use of open-ended questions inviting deeper levels of processing. A final point is that a teacher always retains the right to regain control of a teaching episode if it is failing to achieve its objectives, or is leading to disorder. One way in which they can do this is to resort to closely-focused I moves, as in Extract 8.2, lines 14–18.

The more 'high order' the questions, the more likely it is that the R-move, and possibly the F-move, of an IRF will be extended and complex, as the thinking task invites more complex cognitions. Higher order questions are, to use Barnes' (1969) categorisation more 'open-ended' (rather than closed). By this, Barnes means that open-ended questions invite a range of possible answers, that there is less and less likely to be a single correct answer, and that more talk is invited. There are restrictions, however. For example, the teacher may invite a solitary response to a question or no response at all may be forthcoming from the student group. Nothing can be predicted in advance. While this may be true in many instances, there are innumerable times in classrooms when closed questions elicit much more than a simple RF completion, as Extract 8.3 demonstrates.

Extract 8.3   Classroom talk

```
    T   OK / sit down -- what was Therese doing when -- Clifford came in / Ambo
    S #2   Therese was knitting
    T   when
    S #2   Clifford came in
 5  T   so the two actions are there -- Clifford came in / when / Therese was / knitting –
        then what happened to / Therese --- you -- what happened to Therese ---
    S #1   she stood up and said oh
    T   what happened to Theresa – yes / stand up
10  S #11   Clifford said hello and she / Clifford said the second time hello / and she
        stand up and said
    Sx1   stood
    Sx2   stood stood
    T   and she
15  S #11   she stand
    T   stood
    Ss   stood
    S #11   she stood up and said aaah
    T   and said aar / OK / Clifford came in when Therese was knitting
20  Ss:                                                    knitting
```

The teacher's first I-move takes two attempts, including a follow-up I-move in line 3 to ensure its completion. The next I-move (lines 6–7) elicits a first response in line 8. Either the teacher does not hear this, or she ignores it and asks another student to respond. The response (lines 10–11) elicits student-led responses (lines 11–12). These fail to remedy the error which the teacher elicits again (line 14). The response elicits a correction from both teacher and students (lines 16–17). The teacher responds to the student's response in line 19, and confirms it ('OK'). IRFs rarely proceed smoothly and, as Wright (1987b, 1992a) has observed, there are a number of ways in which simple closed questions lead to multiple answers, guesses, attempts or other 'critical moments' which require repair, an issue to be discussed later.

While this is not the type of 'exploratory talk' discussed by Barnes (1976), it is unpredictable talk. In a strict IRF framework, or a Bloomian taxonomical approach, a large amount of such classroom talk might be regarded as deviant, regardless of whether learners might genuinely be guessing, or in some way challenging or subverting the pedagogic event. It is at precisely these times that teachers feel impelled to reimpose order if they conclude it has broken down. In classroom management terms these are critical moments, and reveal active learner intervention into the management of learning.

Responses and feedback

Learners' contributions at the R-move in teacher-initiated classroom talk are restricted because they are contingent on the I-move. As we have seen in Extract 8.3, it is learners offer dispreferred responses (e.g. line 12) which lead to repair sequences. Goffman (1981) identifies a 'reference-response' system in talk (Concept 8.6) containing the 'rules' for operating the turn-taking system. It also indicates what deviance from the rules is possible, but not necessarily acceptable. The rules govern issues such as the imposition of obligations on others, the exercise of individual rights in so doing, and the dereliction of duties (elaborate excuses can follow reasonable requests for example). In A-B exchanges in everyday conversation, speakers in a B move have greater degrees of freedom to choose from a range of different responses depending on their intentions and social goals. The impositions and constraints of the classroom IRF are thus not present. In many classrooms, a teacher's speaker rights may not be challenged, and only some speakers can 'play' with the system for effect. In others, where more contingent talk is allowable, these conventions can be overturned.

Concept 8.6   The reference-response system in talk

Goffman points out that there are many ways of responding to a simple request such as 'Do you have the time?' Responses can be as follows:

1. Consensual: 'Yes I do. It's 3 o'clock.' 'Six.' 'Sorry I don't have a watch.'
2. Procedural problems delay response: 'I didn't get that.' 'I'm busy.'
3. Delayed response – responder initiates side-sequence: 'What lovely English. Where did you learn to speak so clearly?' 'Haven't I seen you before somewhere?'
4. Assumption that A is 'up to something': 'Are you trying to pick me up?'
5. Use of turn-taking rules for fun or derision: 'Yes I do.' 'And what would you like it for?'

Talk as a system of response-reference moves on the part of participants: 'such that each choice of reference must be awaited before participants can know what that choice will be.' Thus responses are always constrained by initiating moves, and subsequent responses. The IRF 'smooths out' such uncertainties in classroom discourse by constraining response moves.

(after Goffman 1981: 68–74)

In transmission classrooms, feedback has typically been understood as 'evaluation', and some accounts discuss the IRE exchange pattern. However, as Tsui (1998: 186) notes, 'with advances in theories of cognitive learning and second language acquisition, teacher feedback is now understood as providing information for learners to confirm or disconfirm the hypotheses that learners are formulating about the language that they are trying to master'. Contributions at the F position thus appear to have two main functions – to evaluate or pass some sort of judgement on what the learner has said at the R position and close a sequence, or to provide help to learners in reformulating their response, as we have seen in various examples (Extract 8.1, line 13; Extract 8.3, line 14).

Learners soon come to know that their R-move contributions can just as easily be dismissed as they can be accepted and praised. Learners also know that this position conveys a certain power to them by offering feedback on their classmates' contributions, either solicited or otherwise. There is a shared understanding of the meaning of these moments which acknowledges the controlling and judging functions of F-moves. It is an instance of asymmetry being enacted – the less didactic a classroom is, or the lower the priority at any given moment on order, the weaker the F-move. Because of this, teachers may be reluctant to become less didactic. In many ways, the weakening of the power of F-move in these circumstances also subtly weakens the ties between teacher and institution, and teacher and broader educational goals.

The F move also has a prospective function when it sets up another IRF. Continuous 'strings' of IRFs (as in Extracts 8.2 and 8.3) are further evidence of tight teacher control of the management of talk (a form of scripting – either planned or improvised), and the strength of the feedback move as a talk management device, and, on occasions, simultaneously as an initiating move. This use of 'feedback' – either positive or negative evaluation – contrasts strongly with other notions of feedback as 'information about behaviour' (Egan 1998, for example) or cues to self rather than other correction. Control of this aspect of performance modification is a fundamental mechanism in classroom management; it constrains learning opportunity, it regulates the flow of talk and maintains the authority of the teacher by 'having the last word' as well as the opening move. In more contingent classrooms or learning situations, the lessening of judgmental force in feedback is a feature of classroom talk, but not without its risks or difficulties. To learners from a background of didacticism and control, it may appear as nothing more than disguised criticism, and might even be regarded as 'insincere' by learners. This type of difficulty might well be a further factor in the problems of changing from one pedagogic style to another, either as teacher or learner, or both.

Turn-taking and the local management of classroom talk

The basic mechanism of talk in or out of class is the turn-taking system, the means by which teachers and learners claim rights to participation and to influence the conditions for participation. We have seen some of the intricacies of the IRF, in particular the R-move, and how this turn is used. The IRF is a series of turns constructed for various purposes in the classroom. It is a pervasive way in which participants use the 'floor' (Schegloff et al. 2002) during their encounters in language lessons. Participants differentially value occupation of the floor and the opportunities it provides for self-presentation. The turn-taking system itself operates according to local ground-rules. The IRF structure mobilises some of these rules, which also underlie the mode of classroom management and its tendency towards order or opportunity. Van Lier (1988: 98) terms the turn-taking system a 'distributive device' for learning opportunity and access to knowledge (Concept 8.7).

Concept 8.7　Turn-taking in language classrooms: a distributive device

1. Main features of turn-taking in classrooms:

   - One person speaks at any one time.
   - Teachers usually arrive with some idea of what is to be said and done during an encounter.
   - The ideal sequence of events is usually determined in advance, and is 'framed' or 'prefaced' for participants by teachers, typically entailing 'instructions to the learners about permissible ways to participate' (van Lier 1988: 98).
   - Because the purpose of the encounter in a language classroom is language learning, the normal social lubricants are downplayed and emphasis is given to turns which move learning forward in linguistic terms.

2. The ground rules which emerge for students as a consequence of these features are:

   - speak only when teacher nominates you.
   - talk about what the teacher asks you to talk about or directs you towards.
   - keep to the point/topic of the lesson.
   - don't waste time on social niceties.

(after van Lier 1988: 98–9)

The IRF structure by its very nature restricts learner turns, in a ratio of 2:1 in favour of the initiator. Thus, an $IR_1R_2R_3F$ exchange structure with two additional responses may be regarded as a disturbance to the order of the classroom and invite sanction or negative comment from the teacher. Extract 8.4 contains some instances of this: A student's uninvited response in line 2 is admonished and the teacher re-elicits, with three responses, all incorrect, as it turns out. The IRF is also in this example a means of systematically maintaining order in the classroom, as well as managing the teaching/learning dialogue. Because of the teacher's almost total control of the I-move, the teacher usually begins sequences; and because the F-move is almost always a teacher move, teachers close pedagogic sequences. In a control-centred classroom, this is a major way in which order is established and maintained. I- and F-moves have a dual function – they are key elements of the instructional conversation, and they are also 'levers' with which to manage the flow of specifying who speakers are and what types of contribution they can make. I and F moves are akin to opening and closing a valve, regulating the flow. The more open-ended the I-move, the greater the flow. The turn-taking system is thus a key tool for managing participation and therefore the overall direction and outcomes of teaching-and-learning encounters.

Extract 8.4   Classroom talk

  T   correct/why is has/why was the question wrong/why's that question was
        wrong
  Sx   (*inaud.*)
  T   and don't speak – because
  S #9   because he/he has
5 Sx   she / she
  S #4   because she has / she has used the singular / the singular in the past tense
  T   is there not/explain it/what was she supposed to use
  Sx   (*inaud.*)
  T   the sentence is (*B / B: 6 secs*) were looking then she said / was looking / so I said
        she was wrong / because (*B / B: 3 secs*)

This pedagogic mechanism allocates turns and is a characteristic of transmission classrooms which feature a great deal of recitation and 'question/answer'. When the IRF device is working undisturbed, there is a sense of 'rhythm' to the talk. There is plenty of evidence, however, that various student asides, private side sequences among students, or appropriations of the teacher's R- or F-move occur regularly during IRF led talk, for example in Extract 8.5, lines 2–6. There is thus potentially room for subversion or overt flouting of these ground rules. In classroom management terms, these instances are significant and worthy of greater attention than they appear to have so far gained.

Classroom discourse is rarely 'smooth', no matter how close a teacher's control on proceedings, as our examples have demonstrated. This raises the issue of allocation or self-selection in classroom turn-taking, an issue at the heart of classroom management. Questions include the following:

- How do turns constrain what is to follow? For example, are turns constrained in terms of length (IRF is an obvious example) or allocation of the floor to speakers? Is the allocation of speakers unspecific or specific, or is the floor 'grabbed'? Allocating without nominating can lead to learners transgressing other 'rules' – for example, all talking at once.
- How do turns act retrospectively in lessons? For example, do they predict who the next speaker will be on the basis of what has already transpired? (Are turns pre-allocated by the IRF, or is self-selection allowable?)
- Is there much 'concurrent' turn-taking? For example, back-channelling while someone is speaking?

Field Note 8.1   Allocation of turns

Teacher asks class the meaning of 'descend': 'What is the meaning of descend?' Lots of hands go up. Some flicking of fingers to grab attention. Teacher nominates S to her left, in front row. Student stands, leans on desk, speaks – 'go down'. 'Yes' says teacher. 'OK sit down'. S sits down. Teacher repeats S's answer while she is sitting.

A further issue is the extent to which turns are taken non-verbally. For example, (Field Note 8.1) a student's raised hand following a teacher question for information could be construed as a turn. Failure to raise a hand before taking one's turn in some classroom settings could lead to sanctions. The 'nomination' of a student speaker is a social move within the pedagogic exchange; this example demonstrates further how closely instructional and regulatory talk are interconnected. Extract 8.5 illustrates this phenomenon.

Extract 8.5   Classroom talk

T   the sentence is (*B/B: 6 secs*) were looking then she said / was looking / so I said she was wrong / because (*B/B: 3 secs*) the next is / she was talking or shouting loudly – Anna
S #10   was he shouting an/and talking loudly

Teacher monologues

Teachers make substantial contributions to classroom talk with 'lectures', stories, explanations, instructions, impromptu summaries and more. In theory such contributions could account for all the lesson time available – we might imagine lessons with no teacher–student verbal interactions, although in practice this is very rare, except perhaps in mass lectures in higher education institutions where the learner audience is so large and so physically distant from the speaker that interaction is unlikely. If we view 'lectures' as 'pure transmission', they are rather like extended I-moves. Learners' recall of the content of lectures is typically 'tested' later: the R-move. The grade awarded for the test is the F (*sic*) element of the sequence.

This is only one rather restricted view of teacher monologue, however. Lectures are only very rarely lacking in interactional features. A teacher's use of gesture, aids such as realia and diagrams, and references to these in talk are designed to involve the learner audience in the content of the lecture. In the talk itself there are many features which are evidence of attempts by the lecturer to engage students. Goffman (1981) presents an account of 'lecturing' which portrays a lecture as being partly memorised text, partly reading aloud and partly 'fresh talk' (1981: 171) where the 'text is formulated by the animator from moment to moment, or at least from clause to clause'. Goffman emphasises the performance and responsive nature of lectures, with the audience taking part through non-verbal back-channelling behaviour, applause and other signals of a covert dialogue. What is central to this is a synchrony between speaker and listeners which the speaker adjusts through a set of practices which Goffman (1981) calls 'footing' (Concept 8.8). Montgomery (1981) describes 'planes of discourse' where lecturing is always a mix of transactional (delivery of information) and interactional (establishing and maintaining the social relations between lecturer and audience). He notes that 'extended monologues are designed interactively' (1981: 39). We might add that they are also executed to best effect when maximum audience rapport is achieved through footing and its means such as keying, or the use of asides, jokes and other 'parenthetical' remarks.

Concept 8.8   Footing

Footing – Ways in which the 'textual self' (or speaker) can manage their talk to INTERACT with listeners, as follows:

Keyings – ways of signalling attitude towards text.

Text Brackets – ways of opening and closing, which set the tone of the talk, its direction and the speaker's intentions.

Text-parenthetical remarks – asides, digressions, etc. for 'greater interactional interest.

Management of performance contingencies – 'dealing with the unexpected', e.g. faulty equipment, coughing (and choice of whether or not to acknowledge this to listeners e.g. apologizing for inaudibility).

(after Goffman 1981: 173–86)

This is also the case with spontaneous explanations, purposive instruction or random narrative asides in normal lessons, where teachers 'depart from the script' to attend to difficulties, add detail, illustrate points, sum points up, admonish a group of students for misbehaviour, give a long set of instructions for doing an activity, or engage in what Rowland (1993: 30) terms the 'provision phase' of a learning event after students have explored a topic or issue (Field Note 8.2). It is wrong therefore to see teacher monologue as only a display of knowledge or authority (moral or otherwise). Extract 8.6 is an example of an improvised piece of teacher monologue with chorused completions of teacher's contributions from students, cued with a rise in pitch in the teacher's voice immediately before the students chorus the completion – line 7 on 'you' and line 12 in 'in'. The whole stretch of talk is personalised with the address form 'you', and 'I'. It is clearly not an example of cold, distant, magisterial talk. The teacher also amplifies her talk with improvised blackboard notes during her explanation. Pedagogic and social strands of classroom activity are intertwined quite overtly in this sequence.

Field Note 8.2   Storytelling (Primary English – Cameroon)

The teacher – youngish 30? – tells the children to put away their books, sit up and listen. He's going to tell a story. For the next 15 minutes, a local legend is recounted, with different voices, actions, rises and falls in volume. The children visibly move with the cadences of the story, one minute frightened, the next minute giggling. The teacher fixes the class with his gaze, which doesn't falter. He is standing for much of the time, but sits for quieter moments of the story. When he finishes, he leaves a silent pause, which the children begin to fill within 5 seconds or so with murmurs.

Extract 8.6   Classroom talk

```
    T   OK / today / we are going to have a look at / the use of the when clause (B/B:
        5 secs) when you want to use the when clause / two actions / must / be related /
        in time / for example / if I say when I meet Mary / I kiss her / that is in the
        present / when you meet Mary / you kiss her --- when you meet Mary / you kiss
 5      her / these are two actions which are / related / in time / you can use the when
        clause / therefore / in the present / like in the sentence / when I meet Mary /
        I kiss her / you kiss Mary / whenever you meet her
    Ss                                                    meet her
    T   you can also use / it / when you want to / use the future (B/B: 7 secs) when
10      he comes / we shall go to / Douala / when he comes (B/B: 5secs) we shall / go to
        Douala – when he comes / that's one action / we shall go / is another action / that
        is / two actions / which are related / in time
    Sx                                                 time
```

Teachers choose to construct their talk as monologue for a variety of reasons. Mercer (1995: 21–5) offers examples of narrative and collaborative narrative from a diverse range of cultures to illustrate the universality (and possibly, fundamental human character) of narrative and monologue in talk: monologue as narrative is a fundamental human activity and would not be proscribed in any society. Pontecorvo and Sterponi (2002), for example, provide an analysis of collaborative narrative between parents and children, a discourse form often found in classrooms, and one which can provide learners opportunities for co-construction, an opportunity-oriented practice.

They observe that 'it is important that the teacher promotes co-narration and multi-voicedness, orchestrates the participants' contributions and scaffolds the co-constructing of meaning' (2002: 139). A test to gauge the extent of collaboration and opportunity in collaborative narrative is to isolate the teacher's contributions in a transcript and to see if they form a coherent narrative on their own, or whether they do not make sense without the learner's contributions. Teacher monologue thus has considerably more interactive potential than at first glance. Because a group of learners does not make any audible utterance during a monologue it does not mean that they are not responding to the speaker and the message. There are clear non-verbal signs that the monologue is reaching its audience and is perceived as relevant – for example, rapt attention, alert body posture, sympathetic murmurs, laughter (Field Note 8.2). In Goffman's (1974) terms, these responses are indicators of how participants are framing the event (Concept 3.3) and how the speaker's footing adjusts the frame from moment to moment. In discoursal terms these are also indications that learners are recognising and responding to contextualisation cues. There is a fine line between didacticism and interactionality in the case of monologues – and this is a case where participants' views of the event are absolutely necessary as part of any research to establish whether a monologue is (a) intended, (b) perceived to be didactic and (c) whether or not participants are actually concerned about 'being lectured to'. In a monologue, the speaker initiates but is not solely responsible for managing the situation which can become interactive when learners join in, by, for example, nodding, and other back-channelling behaviour. Subtle use of footing can also invite a group of learners to participate in co-narration and exploratory narrative, thus signalling more significant frame shifts.

8.3   Repair

A great deal of classroom time is spent on repair, a major pedagogical activity type, because there are frequent 'cognitive and interactional *troubles*' in teaching and learning (Erickson 1982). Several questions are raised by the issue of repair management.

Why do things 'go wrong' in the first place? Who initiates repair? Who signals that repair has been successful? Does repair always occur success-fully? Is successful repair 'maintained' so that 'mistakes' do not recur? Who manages repair? What is the relationship between repair and learning? Is repair only related to learners' errors in language use, or are there other types of repair practice in the classroom?

IRF sequences are not always realised 'smoothly', as we have seen, and very often in a display or recitation sequence on R-move is incorrect. The IRF device has the discoursal effect of leading the talk towards a 'correct answer' in these cases. This can take time and a great deal of discoursal work, as Extract 8.7 demonstrates. The teacher initiates an IRF to identify alternatives to 'deliberately' (line 5) on four separate occasions, eventually in line 23 giving the response she was looking for.

Repair is also necessary on other occasions. Teachers' instructions or explanations may be misunderstood, for example. The resulting repair-oriented talk between teachers and learners aims to ensure that activities are performed according to instructions or that new items of content knowledge are correctly interpreted. The former is a particularly common occurrence when teachers are trying out new activities with students. These occasions often present management challenges as students' activity frames are confounded; discoursally, the familiar contextualisation cues are absent. Teachers have to call upon all their contingency resources to work towards an adjustment of the footing. These passages of classroom talk, or repair sequences, are very frequent and are indicators of various management practices for adjusting and moderating the classroom dialogue.

The ways in which repair is dealt with indicate tendencies towards either order or opportunity. In educational terms the ways in which teachers manage learners' attempts to master new domains of knowledge or skill in the classroom also derive from basic models of the teaching/learning process and thus views of the learning process (whether tacitly or overtly professed). In the most basic terms, a pedagogic stance is activated by the response to this question: Is a 'mistake' an opportunity for learning or a symptom of failure which must be rectified? In a rigid transmission classroom culture, the correctness imperative (Concept 8.8) has a great deal of influence on the discourse, as Extract 8.7 shows. Teacher and students are prepared to invest their energy in locating the right answer.

Concept 8.8   The correctness imperative

The correctness imperative insists that:

- There are absolute standards of correct and accurate language use in the L2 classroom.
- There are clear rules for appropriate behaviour in the L2 classroom.
- There are correct ways of performing in T/L activities in the L2 classroom.

In transmission cultures, there are always 'right answers', and the presence of an examination system to ensure that teachers teach a certain body of knowledge and students prepare to be tested on this knowledge.

(Wright 1992a)

Extract 8.7   Classroom talk

    T   willingly (*B/B: 4 secs*) yes another word / in place of deliberately / Munji / can you give us one ---
    S #9   willingly –
    T   Naomi -- can you think of another word/you can use in the place
5   of / deliberately
    S #10   offered
    T   uhm
    S #10   offered
    T   offered / offered / yes / but not in the real sense of it / just remember / the /
10   sentence in the passage / Moremi deliberately allowed herself / to be captured / by the raiders / now if you were to rewrite that sentence / which word would you have used / in the place of deliberately / Mbungwa Selvis – yes

```
     S #11   intentionally
     T   intentionally (B/B: 8 secs) intentionally / Moremi intentionally allowed
15   herself to be captured by the raiders / who can give words opposite of the word /
     intentionally / the opposite of the word intentionally / yes
     S #12   mistakenly
     T   not really / not really – not really / intentionally / you do something intentionally /
     you do something deliberately / if you don't do something
20   intentionally / which other word can you use / yes
     S #13   innocently
     T   innocently / what does that mean / you can put a prefix here / and you get the
     word unintentionally (B/B: 9 secs) unintentionally
```

Repair is also a means of bringing discoursal closure to a difficulty. In a more opportunity-oriented classroom management culture, repair may be initiated to ensure that interpersonal misunderstandings or conflicts are resolved, and are managed by participants themselves under the teacher's guidance. Here, repair is socially rather than pedagogically motivated, and also an indication of a care orientation.

The need for repair is inevitable in all learning contexts as learners and teachers are forever regulating and adjusting their contributions, as Frawley and Lantolf (1985) point out in the context of adult language learning:

> An individual never actually becomes an adult to remain an adult. He must continuously adjust his cognition to the circumstances at hand, since he is fundamentally a social being. (1985: 40)

The process of learning creates such troubles because learners are incompetent before being competent. Frawley and Lantolf (1985: 41) also speculate that error may be an indicator of a 'speaker's attempt to gain control of a task' in interactive classroom work. The learner may try any response in the R-position in order to elicit feedback from the teacher, in effect changing the R-move to an I-move (Extract 8.8, lines 3, 6, 13). The teacher's next contribution acts as another R. For learners it may thus be more important to be in control of the direction of the discourse itself in order to elicit feedback than to make code errors. In essentially monologic classrooms, however, where the teacher controls the floor for long stretches of activity, learners are prevented from gaining control (often actively so), and may be forever consigned to 'cognitive childhood' both in learning and discoursal terms.

8.4   Other collaborative ways of managing classroom talk

In section 8.3, we examined different types of classroom talk which feature a degree of teacher control over the discourse, and thus some of the ways in which teachers overtly manage participation. These demonstrate tendencies either towards order or opportunity views of management. The IRF is a device which can lead to both closed and open-ended talk, but that still retains the potential to seize control through the F-move. In Chapter 7, we encountered the 'traditionalist/progressivist' issue in teaching. Progressivists have long argued that patterns of participation in transmission teaching limit learners' opportunities for learning and also socialisation. Beginning with education-alists like Barnes (1969, 1976) this argument has therefore centred on the role of talk in teaching and learning, and in particular the deficiencies of recitation (Tharp and Gallimore 1988), the constricting nature of teacher control (Bowers and Flinders 1990) and the limitations of IRF structures in teaching.

Teachers' close control of turn-taking through IRF structures in language learning is criticised by van Lier (1996a, 2001) among others because (a) it prevents learners from exploring how turn-taking works in the target language and (b) it is not 'conversational', preventing opportunities for learning how to converse in the target language. In other words, there is no intrinsic need in such a classroom management regime for participants to participate in the target language as they would in normal conversation, nor to develop their listening skills in any more than an opportunistic 'being on their toes' sense. It does not assist them in becoming more skilled and aware as commu-nicators. Moving towards a more open pattern of turn-taking, it is argued, less under teachers' control, leads towards a more exploratory and dialogic classroom culture, where rights and obligations of speakers are more evenly distributed and where the teacher is positioned as a co-explorer in talk. In these circumstances, classroom discourse could be under the control and dir-ection of the children themselves, when they are working collaboratively on tasks (Quote 8.2).

Quote 8.2   Talking and working together: for and against

...the reasonable explanation for the traditional discouragement of pupil-pupil talk is that, as an incidental accompaniment to whole-class, chalk-and-talk teaching, it is disruptive and subversive. Even in less formal regimes, teachers have an understandable concern with limiting the amount of 'off-task' talk that goes on. So, while the experience of everyday life supports the value of collaborative learning, educational practice has implicitly argued against it.
(Mercer 1995: 89–90)

Wells (1999: 119–20) advocates 'the creation of the kind of classroom community in which the search for understanding, and the dialogue through which this is accomplished, pervades all areas of the curriculum and is inclusive of all students'. This is achieved by the creation of 'communities of inquiry' in which 'exploratory talk' ('when small groups of students worked at interpretive tasks that they found interesting and challenging' (1999: 125)) between teachers and students, and students and students (Barnes 1976) is the primary discourse mode for seeking knowledge and understanding.
(after Mercer 1995; Wells 1999)

Responsibility for the management of more collaborative types of talk follows different rules. Exploratory talk, initiated, maintained and evaluated by learners, or appropriated by learners after an initial question from either a student or a teacher, is subject to both teacher *and* learner management when it takes place among students working together. This type of talk enables learners to take fuller control of the management of their learning than under conditions when the teacher is initiating exchanges. This teaching style is, in Barnes' (1976: 144–15) terms, 'interpretive' rather than transmissive (or didactic style), a more discoursally open style that actively encourages learners to initiate and develop their own learning dialogues. There is a tendency however among adherents of an 'interpretive' position to ascribe more 'traditional' forms of learning less value simply because they are didactic. On the other hand, a socio-cultural vieiw of classroom talk, which is less ideologically bound, has the advantagge of acknowledging the central role of talk in creating meaning and identity both inside and outside the classroom. A socio-cultural view, while acknowledging the influence of ideology, is more concerned with understanding how talk contributes to learning.

Concept 8.9   Collaborative talk types

1. **Disputational talk** – characterised by disagreement and individualised decision-making. Features short exchanges of assertions and challenges or counter-assertions.
2. **Cumulative talk** – speakers build positively and uncritically on what each other says. Common understanding is 'accumulated'. The discourse is characterised by repetitions, confirmations and elaborations.
3. **Exploratory talk** – participants engage constructively and critically with each others' ideas. Statements and suggestions are offered for joint consideration, which may be challenged and counter-challenged. Knowledge is made public and reasoning is explicit in participants' contributions.

(Mercer 1999: 104)

Accordingly, collaborative talk is a form of 'transformation' (Van Lier 1998: 134). Talk is best seen 'as a medium for sharing knowledge and potentially transforming understanding' (Mercer 1994: 95). Mercer identifies three talk types – disputational, cumulative and exploratory (Concept 8.9). The ground rules of these types of talk are self-allocation of turns, the interactive work of building on others' contributions to move dialogue forward, self-repair, a low incidence of correction and frequent movement to new topics. In other words, they are inherently more 'conversational'. In learning management terms, the primary resources for 'dialogue' – transformative or exploratory talk are participants' existing knowledge and experience, and their knowledge and skills for operating the ground rules in this activity frame. Outcomes are unpredictable and open-ended. There is no guarantee, either, that learners will be able to participate in this type of activity without some form of guidance, especially if it is a form new to them in a classroom where right answers have hitherto been provided by the teacher, or a course book. Many claims are made for the value and efficacy of this type of talk although they are, to an extent, ideologically bound (Askew and Carnell 1998; Wells 1999). However, more empirical work is required before these claims can be fully substantiated, in particular in contexts other than the Anglo-Saxon world.

Scaffolding: towards joint constructions of meaning

Scaffolding is a form of transactional talk in the classroom which operates between recitation and exploration (Concept 8.10). The construct of scaffolding provides a way in which to interpret a great deal of classroom behaviour between teachers and students, and students and students. In its classic form, scaffolding describes an expert/novice learning relationship. It is the principal discoursal means of helping learners through ZPDs or IDZs and is a central concept in socio-cultural accounts of teaching-and-learning. How scaffolding is managed and how crossing ZPDs is managed is of crucial importance in understanding classroom language learning. Mercer's consistently argued position is that a socio-cultural analysis is helpful in coming to an understanding of teaching-and-learning in all its discoursal forms. It is not a prescription for action in the classroom and in this respect his position is more moderate than Wells (1999) who argues that a socio-culturally influenced approach to teaching-and-learning overcomes most of the disadvantages of other competing models.

Concept 8.10   Scaffolding

Originating in the work of Wood, Bruner and Ross (1976), scaffolding represents the type of cognitive support which a helper can provide a learner in the process of learning. Scaffolding is most typically linguistic and consists of moves on the part of the helper to move the learner through increasingly difficult stages of the learning task. It is a contested and problematic notion (see Part 2 of this volume), and may best be attributed to very specific forms of teacher intervention to assist learners in doing tasks they cannot do on their own. The teacher must have the goal of specific new learning at a higher level than currently available. Scaffolding is clearly more specific than the types of assistance that is often given informally.

Claims are made for its effectiveness in expert-novice relations (van Lier 2001: 103). Through scaffolding, 'an effective teacher provides the kind of intellectual support which enables learners to make intellectual accomplishments they would never accomplish alone; and one way they do so is by using dialogue to guide and support the development of understanding' (Mercer 2001: 254).

Wells (1999: 221), drawing on Mercer and Fisher (1993: 343), identifies three qualities for a learning event to qualify as an example of scaffolding:

- learners should be enabled to do something they could not do before the event;
- learners should be brought to a state of competence which enables them to complete the task on their own;
- Be followed by evidence of learners having achieved a greater level of independent competence as a result of the scaffolding experience.

Scaffolding is realised and managed through asymmetrical talk, in which the 'adult knower' or teacher guides the initiate or novice through a ZPD to the point at which the learner can 'take over' (Bruner 1983: 60, in van Lier 1996) – this crucial juncture in learning is also known as 'handover'. Van Lier (1996: 152) discusses handover and whether or not IRF sequences can be conducive to creating conditions for handover. He concludes that they do not, because they are not sufficiently open-ended, and students do not 'grow out of IRF into true dialogue' (1996: 152). IRF structures are indicators of strong teacher regulation and control over the discourse; for handover to be realised, there has to be opportunity for the development of learner-self-regulated talk so that learners spontaneously contribute to the management of learning. In classroom management terms, there are two levels at work: the local management of talk (micro) and the strategic planning of instruction (meso). The problem for the teacher attempting to scaffold learning is to link these two levels in classroom activity. Successful initiation of a learner into new levels of competence is only achieved when and if handover occurs. We would expect, therefore, to be able to trace such junctures in classroom talk. In van Lier's terms, talk would be more contingent, IRFs would make way for a more conversational style, in which topic shift was jointly constructed and that rights, duties and obligations in talk were more evenly shared. This, however, is an idealisation of the practice of scaffolding and handover, and achieving this state is not without difficulties or problems.

Mercer (1994) points out that the bulk of insights from analyses of classroom talk based on neo-Vygotskyan theory see the 'supportive intervention of adults in the learning of *individual* children' (1994: 108) as essential. Mercer remarks on the irony of sociocultural models of teaching and learning not leading to research on classroom groups which feature peer mediation as well as teacher-led activity. In the same paper, Mercer also points out that *group* scaffolding within the context of the classroom culture has not been investigated. Van Lier (1998: 140) later discusses data from group discussion in a language classroom. He notes that joint construction of meaning has occurred despite there being no 'experts' available to assist.

Constructs like scaffolding have been embraced by language learning and teaching theory and practice informed by a socio-cultural view, grounded in activity theory – 'a unified account of Vygotsky's original proposals on the nature and development of human behaviour. Specifically...the implications of his claim that human behaviour results from the integration of socially and culturally constructed forms of mediation into human activity' (Lantolf 2000: 8). Constructs like the ZPD, mediation and cognitive apprenticeship have also been appropriated in accounts of second language learning (Concept 8.11). The emphasis on emerging mastery of target languages by learners assumes a self-directed learner, and the importance of the development of inner speech is a means of developing understanding in addition to the role of mediation. One of the most significant claims made is that the 'acquisition' metaphor for second language learning can be augmented by a 'participation' metaphor. In other words, individual learning is influenced by social or collective learning. These ideas have important implications for the management of second language learning in the classroom, and indicate that a variety of patterns of participation in classroom talk, each appropriate to the task at hand, is more realistic than a particular model. However, practices are well-established in different contexts, and to expect rapid change in the ways in which classroom talk is used to manage classroom life is naïve in the extreme.

Concept 8.11   Recent socio-cultural research on second language learning

1. **Mediation by others**: experts and novices (teachers and students); peer mediation; mediation through L1
2. **Self-mediation**: studies of peer mediation encounters in which self-directed speech occurs.
3. **Artifact mediation**: portfolios (for self-assessment); tasks; technology – video and computer-mediated learning

Some significant outcomes
1. The contribution of learner agency to learning, rather than language acquisition.
2. Influence of classroom culture on learners' perspectives on tasks.
3. The difficulties of investigating private speech, and yet a hunch that it is important in learning (as predicted by the theory).
4. The different effects of monologic and dialogic teaching.
5. The effects of strong teacher control of classroom talk on learners.
6. The role of play in learning.

(after Lantolf 2000)

Towards emotional scaffolding

A pedagogic sequence of IRFs working from recitation to exploration, if successful, also acts as a form of emotional scaffolding for students, as it can build confidence prior to moving into new territory. There is also the option to retreat to more secure recitations and question/answers if the moves fail to achieve their effect. The ZPD is thus navigated emotionally as well as socially and cognitively. How each aspect of the IRF structure is used will have consequences for the quality of emotional scaffolding. The F-move is arguably the most emotionally loaded of the three moves in an IRF exchange. It is the point in any teaching-led exchange where the normative nature of the class-room culture (Breen 2001a) surfaces. It is the epitome of the reward and punishment system prevalent in any classroom, and is markedly so in strongly transmissive or high-structure classrooms. Learners risk self-image and face when contributing R-moves. For example, not knowing a 'right answer' to a closed question may be an indication that they have not performed a prescribed task in advance. Resultant put-downs can do more than deflate the less resilient – long-term motivation can also be adversely affected by prolonged ridicule or a sense that one is being nominated to provide a foil for a teacher's jokes. Classes often willingly collude in this behaviour, further exacerbating its effects. Extract 8.8, lines 1–4 show teacher and students 'ganging up' on a student who has made an incorrect response. There is thus a sense of anxiety attached to the F-move. In some contexts, negative feedback can even be combined with punishment or humiliation (Field Note 8.3).

Field Note 8.3 'Stand up'

Teacher asks student at front (a young girl, 11 years old?) to stand up and answer a question. 'What is the past tense of see?' She struggles to her feet. Leans on desk, eyes averted and mutters inaudibly. 'Again,' barks teacher. The same result. 'You stay standing. You...,' he says, and directs the question to another student. Fifteen minutes later he asks the standing student to sit.

Extract 8.8 Classroom talk

```
    T   what is wrong with that
    Ss ⎡ it is wrong yes
       ⎣ it is wrong
    T   if /it is wrong /you stand up and say why /yes
5   S # 20  be / because / if you say / to see how the flower is growing / is / it means that /
            he was standing and the flower was growing / and at the particular
    T   yes / and that is why I've marked this wrong / this / these are the ones which are
        correct / the ones I press out / sentence number two – yes
```

The quantity and quality of positive feedback provided by teachers is an important indicator of the emotional climate, and its absence indicative of 'frosty' conditions. As we have seen, feedback is often used to judge learners' performance, and may be destructive. In pronounced asymmetrical situations this is often the case, in marked contrast to the sort of informal conversational 'inter-thinking' described by Mercer (2000) where peers collaborate to solve problems or help each other understand, or in mother-child interactions (Rogoff and Lave 1984). Feedback is potentially more beneficial to the learning process if the following conditions prevail, similar to the types of interaction suggested by counseling experts like Egan (1998) who believe that constructive feedback from others is a valuable part of the learning process.

- Constructive feedback can be challenging and can lead to consideration of alternatives.
- Constructive feedback can be positive (praise, encouragement etc.).
- Constructive feedback includes giving information to others on how their behaviour affects others.

These suggestions for a more facilitative teaching style also have relevance for more transmissive classroom management styles. Example: withholding praise could be used as an emotional 'weapon' – a primary factor in student demotivation is a sense that 'you can never win' (Dornyei 2001: 147). In a more positive vein, consistent use of the F-move to invite a group to consider alternatives to a response is an indication of a more accommodating and opportunity-oriented classroom atmosphere.

Extract 8.9   F-moves

Example 1

    T   I want all of you to read the sentences/the second section -- read it

    Ss Mr Acha got a lot of money for his house / he was selling

    Ss   he sold   was sold

5 T   read the sentence/please read what you see -- this one means you should not read it – 'cos it's wrong

Example 2

    T   correct / next sentence

    Ss it was sold while my father was wondering whether or not to buy it himself

    T   next

In Extract 8.9, Example 1, the teacher's I-move elicits a mass response from the class. Her F-move indicates that all who have answered have read the sentence aloud wrongly. It is direct and unequivocal. In Example 2, the teacher does not directly provide feedback to the student and at the same time uses the F turn to initiate further activity in the teaching sequence. The teacher does not offer direct feedback, but appears to assume the group is engaged and is ready and able to continue contributing. Different types of IRF thus have an affective 'participation orientation' (van Lier 1996: 154) as well as a pedagogic purpose. If teachers work through sequences of IRFs that gradually increase in cognitive complexity there is a shift from support to challenge, and from the external motivation that support might provide, to more intrinsically-motivated engagement. This is a difficult balancing act, however, and pursuing this strategy with IRFs may have precisely the opposite effect from the one intended (Quote 8.3).

Quote 8.3   van Lier on possible effects of IRFs on engagement

. . . if IRF discourse is perceived by the students as *controlling* (as seems inevitable, at least in the display/assessment orientation), then it will not foster motivation and autonomy.
(1996: 156)

Since the IRF is other-controlled (from the learner's perspective) and since the rewards (in the form of teacher appraisal or praise in the third turn) are extrinsic, prolonged use of the IRF format may have a negative effect on intrinsic motivation and cause a decrease in levels of attention and involvement.
(2001: 97)

Managing participation online

Managing online teaching and learning raises many of same issues facing pedagogy in conventional classrooms, most significantly in the view of learning underlying any specific pedagogy, and the ways in which participation is managed. In the early period of developing online learning, the capacity of the internet to 'deliver' vast amounts of information combined with ever-increasing sophistication of graphic and audio support led, in many cases, to the development of online learning systems which simply transmitted information and required learners to process it in their own time by particular deadlines. In such environments, there is very little interactivity and little of the human contact that characterises classroom management practices even in the most transmissive face-to-face classrooms. The combination of a transmissive model of teaching and learning with the tendency of the Internet towards individualism has thus led to the emergence of individualised educational experiences online (Sanger 2001). In classroom management terms, the tutor's task is simply to monitor the programme web sites and sources of information, adding and subtracting information as required, and to 'collect' assignments or tests.

In response to these limitations, many of the developments in pedagogy online have concentrated on the potential of the medium for interactivity. These trends are leading the development of new means of learning in higher education, 'especially adults studying at a distance, and particularly at postgraduate or professional development level' (Mason 1998: 8). There is a strong push to create 'online communities' to overcome the potential alienation of the medium, and those online programmes which exploit the Internet's potential for interactivity do appear to have had more success in terms of completion rates, but are not without either controversy or difficulty. As Loveless et al. (2001: 79) have observed, new ways of knowing and new technologies require teachers to establish new classroom routines and procedures that reflect evolving epistemologies. This applies equally to students engaged in new educational experiences. In Breen's (2001a) terms, classroom cultures emerge in cyberspace, and it is more than likely that new types of task and modes of social participation in online learning environments will also influence the experience of teachers and learners. How they manage the virtual classroom raises intriguing questions about the nature of engagement and of participation online.

Managing online 'conferences'

Online discussion groups have become one of the Internet's most common features both for educational and other purposes. 'Online conferencing' (Concept 8.12) is the education world's way of harnessing the interactive possibilities suggested by these informal groups. It exploits the inherent interactivity of the Internet, in particular for asynchronous communication (Extract 8.10 is asynchronous). The creation of online conferences in effect formalises the online discussion group, and introduces an online tutor/ moderator into the interactions. This creates particular challenges which illustrate well the ambiguities of 'borderless' education.

Concept 8.12   Conferencing (computer-mediated conferencing or CMC)

A widely used form of online learning which features discussion between participants, using the internet to gain access to a website.

Main features:

1. A conference is a web area in which discussion **threads** (or continuing topics) are created and developed through discussion by tutors or students.
2. **Posts** are made in written form, of any length, but generally fairly short.
3. Participants post messages to a thread for example, in answer to other participants' contributions, or to change the direction of a discussion.
4. A tutor can participate by posting direct contributions to a thread, adding summaries of participants' contributions or by closing a thread down if it seems to be unproductive.
5. Conferencing (unlike online 'chat' which is synchronous) is asynchronous, and participants can contribute to a conference at any time and from any place in the world, provided there is computer access.

Salmon (2004) has created a five-stage model for setting up or 'moderating' a CMC-based programme based on research at the UK's Open University which addresses many of the classroom management issues implicit in online education (Concept 8.13). Her work is initially focused on addressing the emotional problems of online learning – isolation and the need for community, and fear of the technology. She has found that the early stages of an online course require attention to the basics of participation with the technology, in particular using the software and hardware. Many students have difficulty in making the systems work and require a great deal of help. She recommends a process of induction so that when a participant posts their first message in a conference, they can do it without making errors – the potential for error, and consequent embarrassment is high. Many students are nervous and unsure of themselves, and they may require support via personal e-mails and possibly phone calls. The situation in the early stages is complicated by the fact that there may be some students who are confident users of IT and who become impatient with the slowness of the proceedings. She suggests using their skills to help the less experienced. This may prevent them from becoming disruptive.

Quote 8.4   Salmon on the problems with online time and space

The virtues of a sense of time and place are those of finding 'roots' – provided by continuity, connectedness with place and others who share it and our own internalised set of instructions for how to behave, how to make judgements, feeling comfortable and 'at home in one's world' and the reassurance of the familiar. When CMC fragments and expands this sense of time and place, the usual pillars of well-being may be less available. There is evidence at stage two (of Salmon's model) that individuals struggle to find their sense of time and place in the online environment. Hence the importance of enabling induction into CMC to take place with support and in an explicitly targeted way. When opportunities for induction into the online world are taken, participants report benefits to their later online learning.
(2004: 34)

Once students are familiar with the system, a second stage of 'online socialisation' can begin. In this stage, Salmon begins to build an 'online community' which tries to overcome some of the difficulties of the displacement of the medium (Quote 8.4). There are many barriers to overcome in this process – Salmon points out how some participants find it difficult to adjust to communication without paralinguistic and other visual cues. Others feel liberated by the lack of face-to-face communication, and can concentrate on the content of messages. They are able to disagree relatively unemotionally, and shyer students can take part in discussions without having to 'wait their turn', or interrupting. Participants also find it easier to ask for help online than face to face.

Online conferencing additionally overcomes many of the management problems in the emotional domain – the online classroom culture is less immediate, is not simultaneous, and thus less threatening than a conventional classroom where asking for help openly could be regarded as weakness. However, the tutor still has to manage students who post multiple messages, who start arguments deliberately, who criticise the tutor or the system in different ways if they feel that the experience is too slow, or that some students are holding proceedings up with their slowness and tentativeness.

Concept 8.13   Teaching and learning online

STAGE 1: Setting up the system and enabling students to gain access. *Tutor provides encouragement, a welcoming environment and personal support to participants who are having difficulty.* HELPING STUDENTS OVERCOME FEARS and WORRIES.

STAGE 2: Sending and receiving messages. *Tutor provides activities to enable students to send personal messages to each other, to enable the learning group to bond and for each individual to establish their presence online.* HELPING STUDENTS SOCIALISE AND ENGAGE WITH BOTH THE MEDIUM and EACH OTHER.

STAGE 3: Searching for information and personalising the software. *Tutor facilitates search tasks and supports the use of the learning materials.* HELPING STUDENTS FAMILIARISE THEMSELVES WITH THE SOFTWARE and the WEB.

STAGE 4: Conferencing (Knowledge Construction) *Tutor facilitates conferencing with appropriate tasks or discussion threads, or invites students to set up threads.* STUDENTS FORM LEARNING COMMUNITY; TUTOR MEDIATES. MAXIMUM PARTICIPATION PERIOD.

STAGE 5: Providing links outside closed conferences. *Tutor supports and responds to students, although at this stage, students have developed enough independence and familiarity with the written message format to challenge the tutor and each other constructively.* STUDENTS EVALUATE CONFERENCING AS A MODE OF DISCUSSION and LEARNING.

(after Salmon 2004: 29)

Extract 8.10   Classroom talk

THE COURSE TUTOR SETS A QUESTION TO PARTICPANTS, AFTER A SHORT TEXT ON ORGANSIATIONAL CHANGE
THE MOVE FROM EVANGELIST TO ORGANISATIONAL CHANGE MODELS

CONTRIBUTION 1
Managing_Change (*The Conference Topic*)
From: GM (*Course Moderator*)
Subject: Re: Why do we need to manage change?
To: Managing_Change (*The Name of the Complete Conference*)

JEC writes:
THE MOVE FROM EVANGELIST TO ORGANISATIONAL CHANGE MODELS
Can we have a straw poll from you as to whether your organisation is working in the 'evangelist' mode, or in the 'strategic organisational change' mode? (**The Tutor's Contribution**)

(**Student Response**)
Dear J,
First of all, I'd like to thank you for this most excellent initiative. The kind of input that you have provided is what we needed.

As to our own university, hardly anything has been going on at the policy level, so we must fit under the 'evangelist' mode. I have tried to convince the university that they cannot ignore e-learning, but so far the response has been lukewarm. Many 'established' professors are very critical of e-learning, probably because they don't know much about it, but it is those 'established' professors or the computer scientists who are asked for advice when it comes to innovations like e-learning.

We are an old and respected university, but I have the feeling that the inertia (and arrogance) that it creates is beginning to be a disadvantage. On the other hand, it is the newer HE institutions who are taking the lead.

In our university, a committee is set up with 'experts' and nothing comes of it (so far). It is very frustrating.

CONTRIBUTION *2 (Student Response)*
Managing_Change
From: GJ
Subject: Re: Why do we need to manage change?
To: Managing_Change
We're evangelist although we have a new rector now so things may change.
G

CONTRIBUTION 3
Managing_Change
From: GJ
Subject: Re(2): Why do we need to manage change?
To: Managing Change FK

GM writes: (*The Conference is organised so students responds to particular contributions or make start new 'threads' of discussion. This contribution is responding to Contribution 1*)
We are an old and respected university, but I have the feeling that the inertia (and arrogance) that it creates is beginning to be a disadvantage. *On the other hand, it is the newer HE institutions who are taking the lead.*

(**QUOTE FROM CONTRIBUTION 1**)
Hi GM
Yes, this sounds very familiar. I think newer HE institutions are often better at tackling new initiatives in general, not just on-line learning, perhaps because they are more commercially-minded than the traditional organisations. And academics can be very stubborn when faced with perceived threats to their ways of doing things.
G

Extract 8.10   (Continued)

The extract is the beginning of a lengthy discussion lasting some 37 turns, of varying length – contributions 1 and 2 represent the approximate maximum and minimum parameters of this discussion. An interesting feature is that the IRF pattern is modified to IR1, R2, R3 etc. Once the tutor has initiated the discussion, she does not contribute again until considerably later. Meanwhile the students interact – the quoting of each others' contributions is an aspect of this.

Additional participation problems are likely to occur in the 'socialisation' stage. Because some students feel reluctant to participate fully in the early stages, Salmon suggests encouraging them to look at others' contributions first before posting messages themselves. Non-participatory online behaviour is known commonly as 'lurking' and can cause difficulties more severe than those created in face-to-face group work when certain students do not participate and rely on colleagues in their group to do most of the work. 'Problem' students and behaviours online are as common as they are in a conventional classroom – the 'virtuoso' whose posts mainly consist of display; 'freeloaders' and 'sponges' who appropriate others' contributions. These behaviours appear to cause more offence online than in conventional classrooms. In transmission-dominated face-to-face classrooms, with students in the 'action zone' answering all the questions, students on the periphery obviously gain from their colleagues' efforts, but similar circumstances online seem to lead to more difficulties which need managing.

The moderator has a major task in the early stages of enabling mutual trust and respect to develop between participants, and this requires setting up the community's virtual work space so that informal socialisation can take place. Discussions on, for example, preferences online are examples of ways in which this process can begin. Meanwhile the tutor can try to assist those who feel left out or who have been offended by messages, usually via e-mail or synchronous chat facility, if it is available. Opinions are often expressed very forcibly and there may be clashes. 'Flaming', as this behaviour is known, is the online equivalent of the noisy or argumentative student in a face-to-face classroom.

Furthermore, online student participation is remarkably similar to face-to-face classrooms, with students naturally seeking to interact in the 'shadows' or 'off-stage' as well as being in the spotlight (Erickson and Shultz 1992). In fact, Kolb (2000) observes that the success of conferencing often depends on the availability of means to engage in side conversations, and social trivia. He imagines the impossibility of 'a virtual classroom where the students were in effect chained to their desks and where they could not be distracted by what was happening outside the windows during the discussion' (2000: 142). The difference is that with the written medium, there is a permanent record, and the tutor may *encourage* such activity as a way of enhancing engagement and participation.

Issues in managing written online participation

In order to participate effectively in online learning, students must, as we have seen, overcome a number of difficulties. Working online in a conference may, on the other hand, have the advantages of participation in a 'neutral' communicative environment as Salmon (2004: 18) indicates; in cyberspace we do not know the age or ethnic background of our interlocuters. Online participation thus empowers some learners and, because it distorts normal conventions of turn-taking and address forms, has the potential to legitimate non-authoritative contributions and forms. It may thus be perceived as more democratic than face-to-face classroom communication.

Commentators like Goodfellow (2003, 2004) dispute the apparent neutrality of computer conferencing. (Quote 8.5) Because online education is still conducted in institutional frameworks, it inherits the trappings of institutionality. It may also have the effect of deconstructing the institution. Ultimately, however, the role of institutions in their power to award status, apply sanctions and decide the standards for evaluating the quality of contributions is a powerful factor.

Quote 8.5 Goodfellow on institutional and virtual settings for education

...the breaking of the physical connection between learning communities and the social institutions which have previously been their setting, may not have the effect only of liberating the communities. Separating community from its institutional embodiment could have the effect of deconstructing both.
(2003: 3–4)

Discussing written contributions to conferences, Goodfellow identifies a number of issues which appear to affect the management discourse of online education. Asynchronous communication in conferences is very close in form and process to academic writing (unlike synchronous 'chat' which works on a reduced code and is closer to speaking, and is being refined into a new hybrid code altogether, somewhat like phone 'texting'). How participants represent themselves in the written medium is obviously crucial to the character and nature of the discussion, and raises the issue of literacy, which is only partially implicated in face-to-face classroom encounters (although some – e.g. Bernstein 1996 – would argue that the hyper-correct 'final draft' mode of spoken classroom discourse raises similar issues).

Because writing is also the main medium of work in academic institutions – for assessment especially – there are inevitable pressures to produce writing online which conforms to academic norms and standards, even without overt direction to do so. Goodfellow (2003) (Quote 8.6) discusses the critical aspects of literacy, pointing out that, despite the growth of 'multiple literacies' of the type which enable people to take part in 'edutainment' activities, in formal online courses, the written mode predominates. He argues that students struggle with the written form and may also resist the written culture of online education. Such students may not have the 'repertoire' with which to negotiate meaning or signify our membership of communities. This may adversely affect the experience of, for example, students from communities in which writing is not a particularly widely-used form of communication in both academic as well as everyday social life.

Quote 8.6   Goodfellow on problematising online participation

Online learning literature has tended to emphasise the possibilities for democratisation of the teacher-student relationship, or to celebrate the affordances of peer collaborative learning, rather than to problematise the literacy practices they give rise to. This is because research and practice in online teaching and learning are fixated on the operational and pedagogical dimensions of online interaction, and tend not to take account of the struggles of individual learners (and sometimes teachers too) to construct the virtual social environment in a way that makes most sense to them.
(2003: 4)

There is the possibility that students feel excluded by the written form, and do not participate. Perhaps these are the same students who are marginalised in face-to-face education. Whether or not conferencing is seen as genuinely interactive, and how 'personalised' it can become is also an issue. For example, the extent to which participants can tailor the appearance of their contributions through the choice of fonts and visuals in their postings to conferences may help to alleviate a feeling of exclusion. Such issues raise the overarching issue of learning as 'engagement-in-practice', and the need to learn how to use the potential of conferencing for personal advancement. The key research areas emerging from this discussion are as follows:

1. Students' and teachers' emotional responses to online learning. The effect of different time frames (synchronous or asynchronous) and activities (collaborative or individual) would be important domains to investigate.
2. The discourses of online communication. The influence of institutions and the development of different practices and 'cultures' on online discourses are central areas of investigation. This is particularly urgent in view of the current preponderance of social constructivist pedagogies

in online learning, and the issues of equality of opportunity and care raised by such apparently democratic practices.
3. The differences between fully online and 'blended' (mixed online and face-to-face) experiences in the context of 1 and 2 above are also of interest, particularly because of their growth as alternatives to pure online engagement.

Summary

In this chapter we have seen how practices for managing classroom participation are intimately interwoven with discoursal practices which operate at local, classroom level. Classroom talk is the most obvious indicator of classroom management in action at local level and by examining the texts of classroom talk, we can discern patterns of participation which exemplify different classroom management practices. Through the use of talk in classrooms, teachers and learners provide their interpretations of the stream of activities that comprise classroom life. Using contextualisation cues in talk, they initiate and navigate classroom discourse; their contributions indicate 'readings' of situations. An increased understanding of classroom talk indicates that simplistic matching of talk types and pedagogic models, for example, is misleading. While talk use indicates adherence to particular ways of conceptualising the educational process, the connections are subtle and deep. Order or opportunity in classroom life represent not a simple choice but rather a range of different discoursal possibilities, and perhaps it is helpful therefore to see classroom management as either encouraging or reducing uncertainty as well as providing contexts for teaching and learning. Part 2 presents a selection of research studies which explore these themes.

Further reading

Dillon (1990) illustrates the value of exploratory talk in classroom activity.
Erickson (1982) introduces the idea of pedagogic 'troubles', an important classroom management concept.
Mercer (1995) is an excellent introduction to a complex field.
Salmon (2002, 2004) offers helpful practical ideas and theoretical support for online learning moderators.
van Lier (1988) is a comprehensive study of turn-taking and other discoursal phenomena in the language classroom.

9
Teachers' Knowledge and Classroom Management

A central issue raised in earlier chapters concerns how a teacher's knowledge enables her to manage classroom engagement and participation. Because classrooms are complex contexts for learning, the sheer range of expertise that a teacher requires in order to do this work adequately is enormous. This is complicated by the fact that managing classrooms is also a social activity, and learners too are involved in managing the context. One of the most difficult issues raised by the recent shift of emphasis in education from a focus on teaching to a focus on learning is that many of the responsibilities that have been hitherto discharged by teachers are being handed over to learners, a process requiring the acquisition of new skills and knowledge both for learners and teachers.

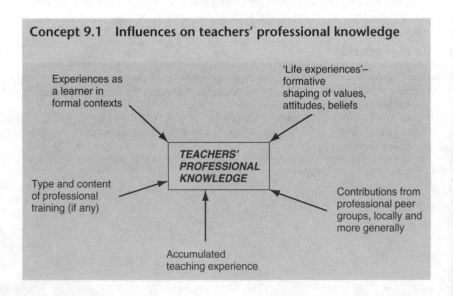

Concept 9.1 Influences on teachers' professional knowledge

Experiences as a learner in formal contexts

'Life experiences'– formative shaping of values, attitudes, beliefs

TEACHERS' PROFESSIONAL KNOWLEDGE

Type and content of professional training (if any)

Contributions from professional peer groups, locally and more generally

Accumulated teaching experience

9.1   Teachers' professional knowledge

In this section, we examine the origins of the notion of professional knowledge (Hoyle and John 1995) and explore different research paradigms which have endeavoured to reveal its nature. Several factors contribute to this knowledge base: 'apprenticeship' knowledge, teaching experience, formal opportunities for further learning and different institutional contexts (Concept 9.1). Personal life histories also contribute to a teacher's underlying value system and knowledge of how to work with people, and are therefore important when considering, for example, a teacher's attitudes towards certain types of classroom behaviour.

Theory and practice in teaching

There are a number of representations of professional knowledge in teaching, centred primarily on different conceptualisations of the role of 'theory' (or propositional knowledge) in professional knowledge. Schön (1983, 1987) contends that professional practice is not guided by normative rules derived from abstract knowledge – or what he refers to as 'technical rationalism' – 'applying theory and technique derived from systematic, preferably scientific, knowledge (1987: 3–4). Furlong (2000) believes this has led to a deepening crisis of confidence among education professionals, and increasingly contested definitions of professional knowledge generally. We broadly agree that teachers, like all professionals, work in transitory classroom situations characterised by uncertainty, the unexpected and ill-defined events (Quote 9.1). This has meant a concomitant questioning of the more traditional forms of knowledge upon which the teaching profession has been founded (psychology, sociology and history of education, for example, or in the case of language teaching, linguistics). Traditional 'expert objective knowledge' has at the same time been called into question. This has, in turn, led to the growth of the research-based 'teacher thinking' movement, which aims to generate knowledge of how teachers use their knowledge to make sense of and act in (Chapter 8) the complex and often unstructured classroom context. We have characterised classroom management as complexity management (Chapter 1) and, if it is to be effective, it is presumably sensitive to the ongoing and unfolding nature of classroom life. Not only has research focused on what teachers do, but also on how and why. The emerging consensus is that professional knowledge is ultimately personal, and forged through experience of professional action. This also poses a problem, because knowledge in teaching is at the same time personal and private; the real crisis may be located in the 'theory/practice' debate. The 'theory/practice "gap"' is 'a mismatch between an observer's and practitioner's theory' (Griffiths and Tann 1992: 70). They propose paying more attention to uncovering teachers' personal theories in order to find a closer fit between 'public' (or propositional) theory and personal theory, between the large-scale and universal and the small-scale and particular. It is thus likely that in searching for understanding of teachers' management practices, we need to explore personal theories, and their basis in professional knowledge.

Quote 9.1   Schön on the crisis in professional knowledge

The Contemporary Context
... we have come to see ... over the last twenty or so years, the problems of real-world practice do not present themselves to practitioners as well-formed structures. Indeed they do not present themselves as problems at all but as messy, indeterminate situations. (1987: 4)

The Nature of Professional Work
Depending on our disciplinary backgrounds, organizational roles, past histories, interests and political perspectives, we frame problematic situations in different ways. (1987: 4)
Often a problematic situation presents itself as a unique case. (1987: 5)
Some problematic situations are situations of conflict among values (1987: 5)
Often, situations are problematic in several ways at once. (1987: 6)

Professional Practice
These indeterminate zones of practice – uncertainty, uniqueness and value conflict – escape the canons of technical rationality. ... It is just these indeterminate zones of practice that practitioners and critical observers of the professions have come to see with increasing clarity over the past two decades as central to professional practice. (1987: 6–7)

Defining and researching teachers' professional knowledge

All definitions of teachers' professional knowledge are ultimately rooted in notions of professionalism and appropriate action at the classroom level. The challenge to technical rationalism and the consequent questioning of its theoretical bases, has meant that the claim to professional status shared with professions such as medicine – grounded in science and research – has to some extent been lost. Similar doubts are expressed by language teaching practitioners such as Richards and Nunan (1990) who are concerned that language teacher education and thus language teaching rests on a firm theoretical footing (Quote 9.2). Many now believe, like Griffiths and Tann, that this foundation is best developed from the study of teachers' actual practices (Concept 9.3).

Quote 9.2   Richards and Nunan on research in language teaching

While there has been an expansion of the theoretical concepts, research issues, and subject-matter content which constitute much of the field (of language teaching), few who are engaged in developing this knowledge base or research agenda would claim any direct relation between their work and the preparation of language teachers. Research or theory

that deals with the *nature* (my emphasis) of second language teaching per se is scant in the professional literature. While there is a body of practice in second language teacher education – based almost exclusively on intuition and common sense – until recently there has been little systematic study of second language teaching processes that could provide a theoretical basis for deriving practices in second language teacher education.
(1990: 3–4)

Professionals are licensed because of their special nature of their knowledge (Schön 1987). The growth of research in search of the roots of an 'epistemology of practice' (Claxton and Atkinson 2000) and the subsequent characterisations of teachers' professional knowledge – their special knowledge – is an attempt to connect a practitioner's knowledge and thinking patterns to their actions in the classroom – where they enact the essence of their professionalism. 'The knowledge and thought of a practitioner is evident most fully in the actions of the practitioner' (Claxton and Atkinson 2000: 1). In a similar vein, Eraut (1988) reconfigures professional knowledge to account for the fact that a professional's knowledge is enacted through practice, in conditions of some uncertainty through the application of case knowledge. Eraut categorises knowledge according to the ways in which it is used in practice (Concept 9.2). The typology accounts for knowledge of the routines of classroom life and rhythms of practice, the transformation of declarative knowledge into classroom action, the use of case knowledge and 'experience' in formulating judgements, and the use of intuition in acting in uncertain situations.

Concept 9.2   Professional knowledge

Replicative – the routines of professional life
Applicatory – how professionals translate technical knowledge into prescriptions for action
Interpretive – the use of wisdom and judgement in situations
Associative – indeterminate, intuitive modes of knowledge

(Eraut 1988)

Professional knowledge consists of these accumulated ways of doing things and their associated thinking patterns in the repertoire of any practitioner, including classroom management. One of the major problems with the professional knowledge base of teaching though is that it began to develop only once the profession had become established and has thus emerged to solve ongoing problems in education (Hoyle and John 1995). The nature of the knowledge base itself is also contested – a positivist view is that the knowledge of teachers can be formulated into 'rules' and standards, by which teaching effectiveness can be measured and appraised. An interpretive view, on the other hand, holds that professional knowledge is intuitive, creative, practical and highly personalised because practice is ambiguous, and 'messy' (Schön 1987) (Quote 9.1). Classroom management is the epitome of living with 'messiness' – defining its knowledge base thus poses considerable challenges.

Concept 9.3   Teachers' professional knowledge

- Teachers' practical knowledge (Claxton and Atkinson 2000)
- Practical know-how (Marland 1997)
- Professional common-sense knowledge (Hargreaves 1993, in John 2000)
- Practical professional knowledge (Furlong and Maynard 1995)
- Working knowledge (Yinger et al. 1991)
- Craft knowledge (Brown and McIntyre 1993)
- Tacit knowledge (Schön 1983)
- Practical knowledge (Elbaz 1983)
- Practical theory (Handal and Lauvas (1987)

Early conceptions of teachers as lacking in technical expertise or professional knowledge (Jackson 1968; Lortie 1975) and reliant on custom or tradition ('dismal' characterisations – Hoyle and John 1995: 45, in the 'folklore' school of classroom management thinking identified by Wragg 1993) have, as we have seen, largely been replaced by different ways of viewing professional knowledge. Hoyle and John (1995) and John (2000) have classified these according to the research traditions which have generated the knowledge. They form a framework for understanding teachers' classroom practices and behaviours and the cognitions that inform these. They also draw attention to ways in which professional knowledge comes into being and accumulates (Concept 9.4).

Concept 9.4   Teachers' professional knowledge

1. **Cognitive** Teachers' information-processing skills, including decision-making models and expert-novice studies. Focuses on the contents of teachers' thoughts and their cognitive processes, especially decision-making.
2. **Practical** Teachers' practical knowledge, including practical and personal knowledge. Aims to understand the complexities of interactive teaching and thinking-in-action within teachers' lives and personal experience (Includes BIOGRAPHICAL and CONTEXTUAL knowledge).
3. **Pedagogic** Pedagogical content knowledge. Aims at uncovering what teachers know and understand about their subject, how this knowledge is translated into classroom activity and how it influences children's learning.

(after Hoyle and John 1995; John 2000: 86)

Cognitive views (teacher thinking)

There are three broad schools of practice in the teacher thinking area:

- Cognitive or 'teacher thinking' (or teacher cognition) studies focus on planning and decision-making in classrooms and thus inform understanding of the meso and micro levels of classroom management (Chapter 5).
- Information-processing approaches attempt to clarify the complexity of teachers' tacit professional knowledge of learning and classroom management. This knowledge is 'event-structured knowledge, rich in patterns and images, highly specialized and domain specific, organized in the form of scenes and procedures' (after Carter 1990).
- Expert/novice studies show that experienced teachers' knowledge is based on a series of 'typifications' which define classroom events: '...pupils' behaviour, modes, cognitions – how teachers use their knowledge to make sense of the complex, ill-structured classroom world of competing goals and actions' (Carter 1990: 302, in John 2000: 86). Teacher thinking of this type informs the highly elaborate system of activity in the classroom, and 'in consequence, improvised behaviour is controlled and used within a highly-structured system of routines' (Hoyle and John 1995: 58).

Practical views of teacher knowledge

Practically-oriented research aims to explore teachers' personal practical knowledge and implicit theories. For example, Elbaz (1983) identifies five domains of personal knowledge: self, milieu of teaching, subject, curriculum, and instruction, which is organised at three levels of generality: (a) rules of practice, (b) practical principles and (c) values, beliefs, needs, feelings. Connelly and Clandinin (1988), on the other hand, note that teachers' images of teaching are bound up with their experiences in personal realms of knowledge. For example, exploration of teachers' metaphors provides a 'way in' to this knowledge. Professional knowledge of classroom management is thus produced by the interaction of teachers' personal practical knowledge with classroom events. Teachers' practical theories are to a great extent bound up with their use of language: 'The images and allusions that surround key words of a practice are essential to the thinking and understanding which will inform future actions' (Griffiths and Tann 1992: 75), and are part of the bases of 'intelligent action' by teachers (Quote 9.3).

Quote 9.3   Griffiths and Tann on personal theory and professional practice

To recognise the crucial way one's personal theory affects one's practice is a critical prerequisite for any attempt one might make to change one's practice. For, to examine the consistency of one's theories with one's own practice, the coherence and adequacy of that theory are vital and essential parts of reflective practice if it is to lead to refining, reframing

---

Quote 9.3   (Continued)

and change. Such an examination can fruitfully be stimulated and extended by comparing and critically analysing one's personal theory against a range of public theories, which challenge and encourage retheorising.'
(1992: 80)

Biographical studies

Studies of teachers' lives and personal histories (Concept 9.6) which focus on the way teachers develop expertise and build knowledge through their careers are also within the 'practical' tradition. Biographical knowledge can facilitate professional understanding and thus influence future professional development. A key aim is to understand the power and prominence of teacher cultures (Feiman and Nemser 1986) (Quote 9.4) and school cultures in teachers' lives and how they influence practice. To some extent, therefore, there are overlaps with more contextually-oriented studies.

Concept 9.6   Teachers' life histories – biographical studies

...these stories [about teaching and teacher education] capture...the richness and indeterminacy of our experiences as teachers and the complexity of our understandings of what teaching is and how others can be prepared to Engage in this profession.
(Carter 1933: 5, in Goodson 2003: 24)

Conceptual Foci in Studies of Teachers' Lives and Work
1. Life experiences and background
2. Teacher's lifestyle
3. Life cycle (Huberman's 1993 study of Swiss teachers is a classic example)
4. Career stages and decisions
5. Critical incidents (Tripp 1994 has many examples of critical incidents)

(Goodson 2003: 59–62)

Quote 9.4   Feiman and Nemser on cultures of teaching

Teaching cultures are embodied in the work-related beliefs and knowledge teachers share – beliefs about appropriate ways of acting on the job and rewarding aspects of teaching, and knowledge that enables teachers to do their work.'
(1986: 508)

Main Focus Points
- Teachers' beliefs about norms for social interaction
- Teachers' views on rewards in teaching
- Teachers' 0personal practical knowledge
- Genesis and growth of teachers' cultures and shared beliefs/knowledge

Contextual studies

These studies present an ecological view of how teachers' understandings are influenced by classroom events, which lead to their learning. Classroom management knowledge is thus organised around specific events, and case knowledge is referred to for problem-solving. Doyle (1986) and Jones (1996) report studies of classroom management practices in this vein (Concept 9.7).

Concept 9.7   Classroom studies of teachers' classroom management activity

Key Themes in Research on Classroom Management (Doyle 1986)
1. Order in classroom management practice
2. Complexity of classroom life
3. Importance of rules of social participation and demands of academic work
4. Need for teachers to balance forces and processes
5. Teachers' management success depends on their understanding of events and skills for guiding and monitoring

Key Skills for Effective Classroom Management (Jones 1996)
1. Creating positive social relationships
2. Influence of instructional strategies
3. Organisational aspects of classroom management
4. Effects of disciplinary intervention

Teachers appear to judge their actions in terms of their ability to create a stable environment in which student activity can flourish (Brown and McIntye 1993: 39) and have multiple classroom goals and improvised tactics to achieve a 'normally desirable state'.

Pedagogical content knowledge

Professional knowledge is connected to subject knowledge (Concept 9.8). Teachers' knowledge is a combination of subject matter knowledge, pedagogical (knowledge management) and curricular knowledge (Shulman 1986). Teachers' knowledge is also prepositional, consisting of tacit maxims and principles, and strategic aspects. Teachers draw on strategic knowledge in classroom management activity. It tends to develop in contradictory pedagogic situations, where knowledge which has sufficed in one situation is contradicted in another. Shulman makes a further distinction between pedagogic content knowledge and 'pedagogical knowledge of teaching' – 'knowledge of generic principles of classroom organization and management' (1986: 14).

Concept 9.8   Pedagogical content knowledge (after Shulman)

1. **Propositional knowledge:** When we examine the research on teaching and learning and explore its implications for practice, we are typically exploring propositions. When we ask about the wisdom of practice, we tend to find such knowledge stored in the form of propositions as well. (1986: 10)
2. **Case knowledge:** ... knowledge of specific, well-documented, and richly-described events. ... The cases may be examples of specific instances of practice (or they may be) 'exemplars of principles. (1986:11)
3. **Strategic knowledge:** ... comes into play as the teacher confronts particular situations or problems, whether theoretical, practical or moral, where principles collide and no simple solution is possible. (1986: 13)

Practical theory and practical knowledge in action

The notion of teachers' professional knowledge argues that education is essentially 'non-technical' because it resists the application of standard recipes to all contexts. According to Marland, it is 'knowledge which is used to get things done in practical situations' (1997: 5). Practical knowledge is consequently developed through experience and trial and error. There are several explanations of this process of learning from experience which provide evidence of how teachers' practical theory is developed, and the ways they manage classrooms.

Practical theory is accumulated through experience and reflection and also experiment, where new ideas are tried out in practical situations. Practical theory is thus tested in and derived from action, and provides capacities for prediction, identification of significant elements of the teaching-learning enterprise and the relationships between them. This is congruent with notions of expertise which identify capacities for fine-grained recognition of events and instances in the classroom by experienced practitioners, and the capacity to act on these.

Concept 9.9   Teachers' practical theories

1. **Personal** – cannot be employed meaningfully or effectively by other practitioners
2. **Situation-specific** – generally bound to classroom contexts where it is created
3. **Implicit** – seldom articulated or set down (an issue raised by Argyris and Schon (1974) in a discussion of professionals' 'thinking-in-action')
4. **Practical** – experienced as successful in action: 'it works'

(after Marland 1997)

Teachers' practical theories provide:
'an understanding of the contexts they are operating in and some notion of the purposes to be served by their work. ... Their practical theories shape their decisions and actions.' (Marland 1997: 8)

Through experience teachers acquire 'practical wisdom', building up a repository of deep professional knowledge. Professionals also gain new knowledge through 'reflection-in-action' (Schön 1983) (Concept 9.10). Teachers may develop their knowledge in this way, although Schön (after Glazer) does remark that teaching is not regarded as a profession in the same way as the law or medicine (1983: 26). Because it lacks a research base or accepted theoretical base does not mean that it is lacking in the capacity for self-reflective activity however. Furthermore, teaching has acquired a research base since (and before) 1983, and, while educational institutions may still be inimical to professional learning because of the relatively slow speed at which events unfold there (Schön 1983: 324), there is still reason to speculate that teachers do reflect in action, as Tsui (2003: 17) among others does.

Concept 9.10   Reflection-in-action as professional learning

1. Professionals build up a store of routinised responses to professional situations. These become readily normalised and are dealt with through 'knowing-in-action' – tacit, unconscious routines of practice.
2. Routine activities produce outcomes which are unexpected. We notice.
3. The unexpected leads us to question our tacit responses.
4. The unexpected event is 'reframed' or a new problem is framed in order to develop an understanding.
5. We experiment on the basis of the new understanding. This may produce the intended outcome or unexpected results which lead to further reframing and experimentation.

(after Schön 1987: 28)

Learning from Reflection-in-Action

When the practitioner reflects-in-action in a case he perceives as unique, paying attention to phenomena and surfacing his intuitive understanding of them, his experimenting is at once exploratory, move-testing and hypothesis testing. The three functions are fulfilled by the very same actions. And from this fact follows the distinctive character of experimenting in practice. (Schön 1983: 147)

The learning derived from a 'reflective' mode of thinking differs from modes of learning reliant on external sources of expertise. 'Reflecting-in-action' is an unconscious process, hence the difficulty of articulating reasons for specific actions. The routines themselves are peculiar to the 'professional artistry' of the practitioner, and are a part of the process by which the professional adjusts their routine responses to situations and tacit knowledge. In the process of reflection-in-action, pattern recognition and spontaneous performance are in a working relationship, each feeding the other, and creating new meanings. Because the processes are private they are particularly 'deep' and personal, and thus likely to be difficult for the practitioner to articulate, and therefore tend to be resistant to change. Professional development requires reflection on one's personal theories, but it is difficult to make them explicit (Griffiths and Tann 1992: 70). Through these processes, teachers continue to build up a knowledge base and understanding of students, contexts of learning, learning curricula and teaching/learning procedures and procedures/routines for solving problems in these contexts. Their professional awareness and capacity for 'reading' classroom situations is thus enhanced.

Teachers' beliefs

The role of teachers' beliefs in their thinking and practice is a recurrent theme in studies of teachers' professional knowledge. Pajares (1992), reviewing the research, regards the idea of 'beliefs' as a problematical and 'messy' construct and in a study of ESL teachers' expertise, Tsui also comments on the plethora of concepts in the area of teachers' professional knowledge, including beliefs, and uses 'teachers' conceptions of teaching and learning' (2003: 61) as a way of summing up the various approaches (Quote 9.5).

Quote 9.5   Teachers' beliefs

...teachers have their own personal conceptions of teaching and learning, which are influenced by their personal life experience, beliefs and values, their disciplinary training ['subjects'], their teaching and learning experiences, and their professional training, if they have any.
(Tsui 2003: 63)

Few would argue that the beliefs teachers hold influence their perceptions and judgements, which, in turn, affect their behaviour in the classroom, or that understanding the belief structures of teachers and teacher candidates is essential to improving their professional preparation and teaching practices.
(Pajares 1992: 307)

Many researchers regard an understanding of teachers' beliefs as the basis of understanding their behaviour. Burns (1996) questions the extent to which 'underlying thinking and beliefs the teacher brings to the classroom shape the processes and interactions that occur' (1996: 154) (Quote 9.6). An exploration of teachers' beliefs about, for example, how people behave, how misbehaviour should be treated, and most centrally how learning occurs, has the potential to reveal what underlies classroom management practice. However, it is not always easy for teachers to articulate their beliefs – again language is both a barrier and a means of engagement with informants. In research it is common to elicit statements about beliefs directly or more indirectly through exploration of practices in interview or similar situations (for example, critical incident recall), and the research is dependent on teachers' articulatory capacities and our interpretation of what they say.

Data Extract 9.1   Teachers talk about teaching

Three teachers disclose some of their beliefs about teaching:

'The goal of education is to produce human beings who can influence others for the better.' – SK

'Teaching is to direct students, to cause learning – to think for themselves, to solve problems for themselves.' – AN

'A teacher should be respected because he helps to build society. Whatever you are depends on the teacher.' – ANF

'Students enjoy what the teacher directs them to do. They enjoy it in class if you motivate and lead.' – AN

'Some teachers command a lot of respect from their students, and the more so the students are very sensitive to know a teacher who knows what he is doing and one who is merely wasting their time. They also know a teacher who respects them as students and leads them in a way to enable them (to) benefit, and the teacher who merely fulfils a role. And so the one who concentrates and spends his time to help the students is highly respected.' – ANF

Quote 9.6   Burns on exploring teachers' beliefs

. . . the thinking and beliefs teachers hold are fundamental in motivating classroom interactions. They determine what is represented for learning and how the representation of content takes place.
(1996: 154)

Burns' research was conducted with 6 teachers and their classes. A combination of audio recording and transcription of classes, semi-structured interviews, and verbal response to transcriptions and recordings of the lessons. One teacher's work is used a case. The outcome of the analysis:

. . . suggests that interconnecting networks of belief appear to be foundational to classroom operations, constituting the theories, prior texts or schemata which are manifested in institutional practice.
(1996: 174)

Burns speculates that the complexity encountered in the classroom, and the teachers' typically improvised responses leads her to reconsider teacher education practices.

Teacher decision-making

The study of teachers' decision-making processes 'focuses research on the teacher and recognises the central importance of his or her cognitive world.' (Freeman 1996:362) For example, what teachers do when students' behaviour goes beyond their 'tolerance limit is a point of interest (Tsui 2003: 32). A course is the outcome of a large number of management decisions made by both teachers and learners as they negotiate through classroom activity – a 'course is the trail that the decision-making process leaves behind' (Woods 1996: 13) and is the outcome of a 'structuring' process engaged in by teachers and students *during* lessons, on a moment-by-moment basis. Because teachers have been 'invited' into the students' learning process, Woods further argues that an understanding of the role their decisions have in influencing the course of classroom events is vital.

Woods characterises teacher cognition as a cycle of activity working from action/event, through understanding/interpretation to planning/expectation (Concept 9.11). There are two cycles which teachers experience: an 'active' or intentional cycle, and a more passive one, where 'things happen' to them (Woods 1996: 81). From the active point of view, teaching activity – experience – is the 'raw material' of learning. Teachers actively interpret the outcomes of activity in order to shape the outcomes. These interpretations are the basis of further 'planning' – both for immediate new action (on the spur of the moment in a lesson) or more long-term planning for subsequent teaching activity. By working actively through the cycle, teachers are also able to continually monitor and develop their practice. By contrast, the more 'passive' cycle of event-understanding-expectation characterises a more fortuitous (or 'geological') path for the development of teacher thinking and beliefs. The iterative recursive feedback loops modelled by Woods are strongly reminiscent of other cyclical views of the professional learning process (action learning: Revans 1988; McGill and Beaty 2001); experiential learning (Kolb 1984) which highlight the role of reflection as a means of coming to understand and learn from experience. Woods also regards teaching as a cyclical process. The combination of Woods' and the other views of professional learning promises to contribute to the continuing professional education of teachers by mirroring their natural learning processes in any new learning activity in formal teacher education.

Concept 9.11   A model for teacher thinking (after Woods 1996: 82)

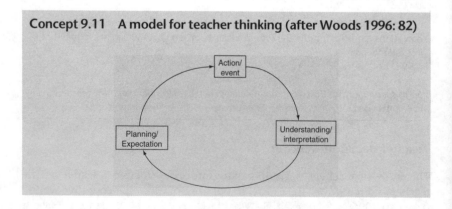

Intuition

Partly in response to a preoccupation with conscious reflection ('reflection-on-action' – Schön 1983) in teacher education, and the rationalism of teacher thinking and decision-making models of what teachers do in their classrooms, there has been a revival of interest in the role of intuition in teachers' thinking and practice (Claxton and Atkinson 2000). Intuition is regarded as the basis of professional awareness, a capacity for focusing on the here and now ('presence' – Underhill 1999). Intuition is important because it appears to be engaged at key classroom moments or crisis, confusion or perplexity. John (2000), in a discussion of how intuition might contribute to teachers' practical knowledge (Concept 9.11), proposes that 'the more effective teacher is one with a more highly tuned and highly differentiated intuition for understanding and interpreting classroom life, and with a wide repertoire of appropriate models of reacting to different situations' (2000: 101).

Concept 9.11   The role of intuition in teachers' practical knowledge

Intuition:

1. Facilitates problem avoidance
2. Guides teachers' interpretation of classroom cues, behaviours etc.
3. Helps teachers create opportunities for learning
4. Is the basis for improvisation
5. Guides the assessment of mood or climate

(after John 2000)

The essentially reactive nature of intuitive performance contrasts with the less-often encountered proactive intentions of teachers that Woods highlights in 'planning' activities. Intuition is viewed here as an aspect of cognitive activity enabling teachers to hold 'reflective conversations' (Schön 1991) and to frame and reframe problems in action. However, John's (2000) study indicates that intuition may be grounded on, and complement the more consciously 'grooved' or routine type of knowledge or internalised recipes for action (Concept 9.12).

Concept 9.12   Classroom routines

1. Management – to maintain discipline and control
2. Support – to define and specify learning and classroom behaviours
3. Exchange – to specify interactive behaviours

(after Leinhardt et al. 1987, in John 2000)

Intuition draws on internalised practical theory at critical moments or in creative improvisation. Deep routine knowledge enables a teacher to identify problematic moments. This type of on-the-spot thinking is significantly absent in many novice teachers.

Research into teachers' professional knowledge has identified both content and process features of this knowledge. Combined with knowledge of the discourses of classroom life, and the affective characteristics of the classroom context, a more comprehensive picture of what is entailed by classroom management emerges. Classroom management is grounded in cognitive processes of different types, proactive and reactive thinking and behaviour, all to enable skilled action in the semi-public, group-centred classroom world. There is good reason to suppose that this knowledge assists teachers in investigating the 'hunches, instincts and tacit knowledge that shape...practice' suggesting 'different possibilities for practice, as well as helping us understand better what we already do and think' (Brookfield 1995: 185).

9.2 Learning about teaching and learning

Classroom management is featured in most initial training courses for language teachers, and some teacher development programmes. The major difficulty in attempting to 'teach' classroom management in formal teacher education programmes is to find ways of enabling student teachers and experienced teachers to integrate the accumulating body of research-based professional knowledge about teaching, learning, students and classrooms into their unique personal and contextual understandings. Learning is relevant at all stages of a teacher's career, although precisely how it occurs is subject to the same types of controversy that accompany any discussions of human learning. Views on teacher learning are summarised by Roberts (1998) (Concept 9.14) Teachers learn informally – what we could term a 'natural' route through 'situated learning' – and a more structured and planned route via periods of professional training. In both cases, teachers come into contact with the cultures of schools and teaching, as well as their 'subject' disciplines or even learning stage peer groups (primary, secondary and so on). However, there are clear differences in how teachers learn initially and later in their careers.

Concept 9.14 Views of teacher learning and teacher education

Roberts' conceptualisation of teacher learning and teacher education is based on broad models of human learning, each with consequences for teacher education.

1. **Person as input/output system:** human behaviour and development determined by external conditions. Behaviouristic learning theory. Model-based teacher education (e.g. micro teaching).

2. **Person with self-agency**: people are autonomous and self-determining. Humanistic learning theory. Action is motivated by individual experience, unlike behaviouristic views which see action as externally-motivated. Person-centred teacher education (e.g. counselling model of supervision).
3. **Person as constructivist**: an individual is an intelligent system developing increasingly sophisticated models and representations of the world to frame perceptions and actions. Cognitive learning theory. Learning is a constant process of construction and reconstruction. Reflective (self-awareness) and experiential (integrated task-based) teacher education).
4. **Person as a social being**: behaviour and norms determined by social interaction in groups. Socio-cultural learning theory. Free choice of group membership and potential for individual influences on groups. Social constructivist teacher education (e.g. action cycles featuring opportunities for talk).

(after Roberts 1998)

A key issue in Roberts' work is the extent to which teacher learning is seen as an individual or a collective process. For example, a 'humanistic approach' is very individualistic, whereas a social-constructivist perspective is broadly collective.

The 'natural route': the apprenticeship of observation

In Chapter 2, the major differences between informal and formal learning in classrooms were outlined, and the case for a socio-cultural view of learning, both inside and outside the classroom, was presented. Teacher learning also has its roots in these processes. In the ways we initially learn about it, teaching is quite unlike professions like medicine and law. Situated learning in formal education ensures that participants have already experienced a great deal of teaching, as learners. A large proportion of people who have been educated in a formal school setting would even claim knowledge of how to teach, or at least how it should be done, on the basis of this experience. Experience of the operating theatre as patient or court as a defendant or witness would not similarly appear to qualify people for the surgeon or legal practitioner roles in quite the same way as classroom experience as a learner apparently does. However, the skilful management of a group of 30 teenagers is almost certainly beyond the scope of all but perhaps the most naturally gifted (or lucky!) of 'lay' practitioners. Any student teacher confronted with the reality of such circumstances would readily admit the gap between their current state of knowledge and skill and what is actually required for successful performance. Lortie (1975) termed our experience of teaching and learning in school the 'apprenticeship of observation'. Following his argument, the basis of our practices as classroom teachers is in our experience – as much as 13 years' formal school education in many countries (Quote 9.7). This goes some way towards enabling us to understand the **processes** of the 'apprenticeship of observation' which every classroom learner undergoes, in which they learn about:

- Classroom discourses.
- Behaviour patterns of teachers (including particular procedures of management and instruction) and other learners.
- Classroom climate.

Quote 9.7   Lortie on the apprenticeship of observation

What students learn about teaching ... is intuitive and imitative rather than explicit and pedagogical; it is based on individual personalities (of teachers) rather than pedagogic principles. (1975: 62)

Lacking a sense of the problematics and a sure concept of technical performance, they (students) are not likely to make useful linkages between teaching objectives and teacher actions; they will not perceive the teacher as someone making choices among teaching strategies. . . . (1975: 63)

The student's learning about teaching, gained from a limited vantage point and relying heavily on imagination, is not like that of an apprentice and does not represent acquisition of the occupation's technical knowledge. It is more a matter of imitation, which, being generalized across individuals, becomes tradition. It is a potentially powerful influence which transcends generations, but the conditions of transfer do not favour informed criticism, attention to specifics, or explicit rules of assessment. (1975: 63)

As we learn to teach, we build up a stock of implicit theories about teaching and learning and we also internalise the discourses of formal teaching and learning. A socio-cultural view emphasises the interactive and typically dyadic nature of early learning encounters. In Vygotskyan terms, 'the very processes or relationships that are involved in social interaction are eventually taken over and internalised by the child to form individual cognitive processes' (Wertsch et al. 1984: 157). In this way a new, educational, discourse is learned relatively quickly.

Mercer (1994), notes that this is a 'crucial field of investigation, because 'it is only through that discourse (spoken and written) that concepts are shared and differing interpretations of them can be revealed and resolved' (1994: 105). One major concept will be the nature of the learning process itself, and it is learnt together with other classroom participants. A further factor in the accumulation of knowledge of classroom life is that during the learning process, children appropriate the ideas, opinions and 'voices' of teachers, parents and other influential people in their lives by 'ventrilocating' (Maybin 1993, in Mercer 1994: 105) these voices in their conversations and language games.

Beginning teachers and learners therefore approach classroom activity with implicit theories of how activity should proceed and speculate how to make the new teaching-learning situation manageable. Through the creation of a stable environment, they create a culture (Quote 9.8). Breen's (1991) contribution provides a link to Mercer's (1994) goal of discovering the means by which teachers create a 'learning culture in the classroom' (1994:104) in the face of a multiplicity of student ZPDs.

Quote 9.8 Breen on reaching cultural equilibrium

When teacher and learner work together in order to make the (classroom) situation manageable, they seek an equilibrium between what may be quite diverse implicit theories of the teaching-learning process. Although at least the teacher's set of justifications for what is done in the class might be explicitly shared, the learners will make sense of classroom activity through their own theories. What all parties undertake, however, is the gradual establishment of a structure within which co-operative endeavour can take place. Their diverse theories become *routinised* through overt classroom discourse and procedures. And the structure teachers and learners seek is consolidated by these routines. In essence, what is jointly created is a culture where overt routines *have* to exist in order that the multiplicity of meanings and values which participants give to their own actions and those of others can be contained and naturalized.
(1991: 216, author's emphasis)

In other words, beginning teachers already possess a personally constructed version of classroom management practices from their experience in classroom communities of practice. Like all formative life experiences, the influence of formal classroom learning in childhood and adolescence on beliefs, values, attitudes and behaviours is profound – there is also evidence that teachers and learners cooperate and even collude in establishing and maintaining classroom cultures (Chapter 12). Furthermore, the knowledge acquired through the apprenticeship of observation is almost always tacit and hidden, learnt unconsciously in context. In Denscombe's (1982) terms, novice teachers have already absorbed the 'hidden pedagogy' – 'an implicit view of teaching' (1982: 250) – from their own experience (Quote 9.9). Denscombe's argument is that beginning teachers have seen their own teachers struggling to control classroom groups, and this experience has led to newcomers suffering 'control anxiety'. This feeling is further reinforced by established teachers they meet during practicum periods at school, and has a significant influence on classroom management practices.

Quote 9.9 Denscombe on the 'hidden pedagogy'

The hidden pedagogy permeates the understanding teachers (including newcomers) have about the essentials of the job. It is an implicit theory of teaching and is based on the assumption that without first establishing classroom control and being able to establish it without help from colleagues, there is no chance of being able to put across the subject matter of the lesson and, consequently, little chance of being regarded as a competent member of the teaching profession. (1982: 230)

Quote 9.9   (Continued)

... recognising the need for pupil control does not pose too many problems for the vast majority of new teachers. They already know that control is a crucial part of the real demands of teaching because their own experience as pupils has taught them that any weakness on the part of a teacher is unacceptable and can be ruthlessly exploited by the pupils ...
(1982: 252)

At the same time, the apprenticeship of observation provides only a partial understanding of teaching as an occupation or profession – rarely, if ever, are students party to the backstage regions of teachers' lives in staff rooms (Richards 1997), engaged in the cultures of the school and their profession. In the same way, children are not fully conversant with the 'off camera' discourses of parenting, and patients are (hopefully) unaware of the activities of their surgeons when they are under anaesthetic.

9.3   Formal professional learning

Periods of formal training also have an impact on teachers' classroom management practices. Tsui (2003: 63), for example, reports the influence of various types of initial and continuing teacher education on teachers' practical principles and beliefs (e.g. Borg 1998). It is in these formal contexts that teachers are *taught* to teach.

The beginning teacher

There are four major issues involving classroom management in the early stages of professional development, which all relate to the apprenticeship of observation:

1. The powerful and all-pervading influence of previous learning experience on classroom management strategies and knowledge. Trainees have internalised a model of classroom management from their own schooling which is difficult to influence in training.
2. The necessity of learning classroom management skills and procedures early on in order to 'control' the context and minimise the inevitable threat to face that classroom activity poses for the novice.
3. The need for the novice to clarify their self-image and personal style as a teacher at the outset before any further development can be made (Kagan 1992). This can enhance protection of face.
4. The relatively rapid automatisation of routines as a novice attains degrees of expertise – the confidence factor in the emerging teacher who discovers 'what works'.

There is, therefore, a tension in formal teacher education between what might seem natural and or 'common sense' to the novice teacher who, from their learner perspective knows 'what works' in classrooms on the one hand, and the formal learning experiences which a trainee encounters during training, which may conflict with what the trainee already knows, or, paradoxically, may reinforce the pre-existing model derived from experience. There is also the issue of how student teachers encounter the professional knowledge base identified in sections 9.1 and 9.2.

Quote 9.10   Pajares on the influence of pre-service teachers' beliefs

... preservice teachers are insiders. They need not redefine their situation. The classrooms of colleges of education, and the people and practices within them, differ little from classrooms and people they have known for years. Thus the reality of their everyday lives may continue largely unaffected by higher education, as may their beliefs. For insiders, changing conceptions is taxing and potentially threatening. These students have commitments to prior beliefs, and efforts to accommodate new information and adjust existing beliefs can be nearly impossible.
(1992: 323)

Beginning teachers' belief systems are already quite well formed (Quote 9.10). John's (1996) description of the beginning teacher emphasises their previous knowledge and experience as learners, and accepts this as a normal condition for new entrants to the profession (Quote 9.11).

Quote 9.11   John on beginning student teachers

It is now widely accepted that when student teachers enter courses of professional training, they are not *tabula rasa* but have imprinted on their minds numerous images of teachers, teaching styles and learning processes which have been shaped by what they witnessed as pupils.
(1996: 91)

Many teacher educators regard the development of 'professional thinking' and beliefs as a central problem to be tackled in teacher education. Diamond (1991) puts the case in terms of 'transformation':

> The transformation entailed in learning to teach starts with the exploration and articulation of the personal understandings that constitute a beginning teacher's perspective. (1991: 45)

Shulman (1986) frames the issue less extremely as follows: 'Our central question concerns the transition from expert student to novice teacher' (1986: 8).

Student teachers have been successful learners at school, successful enough to be considered eligible for higher education and so learning to teach in formal settings is a matter of *transition*. A teacher is constantly in the process of evolving during their career, and expertise is as much a state of becoming as a definitive end-point in development. (Expertise is also a quality bestowed by peers and clients, rather than any definable quality.)

John's (1996) study of initial trainees establishes that their beliefs about teaching and learning can be traced to their school experience. (Concept 9.14) In common with many professionals grappling with the issues of pre-service teacher preparation, John argues that student teachers' implicit theories and 'the concern network that supports them' (1996: 101) need to be challenged in training or they are likely to be reinforced in the school situation. Concerns include:

- Not knowing enough to teach, connected with a view of expertise in which teachers know all the answers and can think on their feet.
- Inability to manage classrooms (see also Denscombe 1982) leading to a reliance on 'practical tips' from expert practitioners.

Concept 9.14   Student teachers' implicit theories of teaching and learning

Aim: To examine the extent to which student teachers' (STs) experiences as pupils influence their developing conceptions of teaching and learning.

Main Findings

1. STs' experiences provide them with many positive and negative images of teachers. These give rise to assumption that 'good teaching is closely linked to a positive set of personal and affective characteristics' (99). Warmth, enthusiasm, commitment, humour and patience are key positive qualities. 'Making pupils feel good and being liked in return are seen as essential to successful practice.' (99)
2. STs' strong feeling of having 'lost out' at school, and expressed need to set things right in their own classrooms. However, this is balanced by an 'ingrained belief' that transmission teaching is the only way of putting content knowledge across. (100)
3. STs' understandings of learning developed from their experience – 'learning=knowledge extension' (100) and a strong belief in practice at data handling. Possibly 'subject enculturation'. (100)
4. STs may well see their beliefs as generalisable across a range of school situations.
5. Oversimplified images of teaching and learning abound because of a dominance of a pupil-centred view which limits their capacity to examine their own and others' teaching.

A number of issues regarding novice teachers' views of teaching emerge from the study.

1. A view of the 'natural born teacher' predominates among the trainees – teaching is seen as 'stand-and-deliver' (1996: 100).
2. Teaching is mainly an extension of one's character, and teaching style does not therefore develop.
3. Teachers are experts and that expertise resides in subject knowledge. Good teachers are seen as knowing their material backwards. Expertise also defined by the teacher's control of the flow of information to the pupil.
4. Student teachers are anxious for instant solutions to the problems of classroom management. 'As a result of their anxieties the students often displayed a need for recipes to deal with classroom control and management because they were already familiar with the teacher being seen as a controller' (1996: 101).

Processes and stages of beginning to teach

Learning to manage classrooms is a major challenge for the beginning teacher, and incorporates emotional/affective, cognitive and social demands. It may also involve a struggle between the notions of classroom management accumulated through experience and those advanced by a teacher education programme. How teachers learn the complex behaviours of class control and learning management and absorb their attendant belief and value systems is thus a fundamental concern of teacher education programmes, both initial and continuing.

Kagan (1992) in a major review of 'learning-to-teach' studies, has identified a narrative of early professional development (Concept 9.15). What is clear from this narrative is that there are a number of key influences on the emergent teacher, all of which are significant in the acquisition of classroom management expertise.

1. Previous experience of classroom life
2. Student teachers' self images as both learners and teachers
3. Views of teaching presented on the pre-service programme
4. Interactions over time with students in school settings
5. Interactions with established teachers in school settings
6. Degree of autonomy afforded by head teachers

It is clear from Kagan's and other studies that the process of acquiring classroom management expertise is bound up with the development and establishment of a professional self-image and the development of new skills which become gradually second nature or 'automated'. From the very outset of learning to teach, issues of classroom management are viewed as vital to the novice teacher and are integral to their eventual development of expertise.

Concept 9.15   A narrative of early professional development

1. STs arrive on training programmes with well-established personal beliefs about classrooms, teachers and learners. These tend to remain fairly inflexible and STs seek to confirm them.
2. STs are presented with often contradictory and inconsistent views of teaching and learning on programmes.
3. STS usually approach teaching experience with an inadequate knowledge of students and classroom procedures, and are unprepared for problems of classroom control and discipline. STs become obsessed with control and design instruction to maintain control.
4. Prolonged interaction with students and a cooperating teacher who can challenge a novice's beliefs can help begin the process of restructuring beliefs.
5. An image of the self as teacher is built up. 'An initial focus on self appears to be a necessary and crucial element in the first stage of teacher development' (1992: 155).
6. Early classroom practice is spent accumulating procedural knowledge – developing standardised routines for handling class management and discipline. Then novices turn to issues of instruction.

(after Kagan 1992)

Kagan (1992) also sees professional growth during the initial training period marked by increasing expertise, as follows:

1. An increase in meta-cognition – novice teachers become aware that their knowledge and beliefs about classrooms are changing.
2. Reconstruction of knowledge about students – used to reconstruct self-image as teacher.
3. Shifts in attention – from self to instruction.
4. Development of standardised procedures to integrate management and instruction.
5. Growth in problem-solving skills and their use across different contexts.

Studies by Berliner (1988) and Maynard and Furlong (1993) (Concept 5.16) have also identified broad stages (without specific time limits) in the development of novice teachers' expertise.

Despite the clear differences in approach, Berliner and Maynard and Furlong both regard the acquisition of classroom management skills and knowledge as essential ingredients of early teacher learning. Kagan (1992) in addition points out that all 'learning-to-teach' studies show the novice developing:

- unconscious ability in recognising classroom events;
- fluid, flexible and automated routines;
- strong influence of personal experience and predictive power of events;
- increased focus by the teacher on the students and their work.

These developments show the student teacher acquiring aspects of 'expert' teachers' professional knowledge, thinking and intuition.

Concept 9.16   Stage theories of teacher learning

From Novice to Expert (Berliner 1988)
Stage 1 (NOVICE) Teacher labels and learns each element of the classroom task. Set of context-free rules of performance acquired. Performance is rational, inflexible and needs purposeful concentration
Stage 2 (ADVANCED BEGINNER) Similarities across contexts are recognised and episodic knowledge acquired. Strategic knowledge gained; knows when to ignore or break 'rules'. Prior classroom experiences begin to guide behaviour.
Stage 3 (COMPETENT) Teacher able to make conscious choices about actions, to set priorities and plan. Teacher knows, from experience, what is important and not important. Teacher now knows about dealing with errors.
Stage 4 (PROFICIENT) Intuition and knowledge begin to guide performance. Recognition of similarities across contexts acquired. Teacher picks up information from classroom and can predict events with some precision.
Stage 5 (EXPERT) Has an intuitive grasp of situations and non-analytic sense of appropriate behaviour. Teaching apparently effortless and fluid. Automatic, standardised routines for management and instruction now operate. Teacher is likely to have difficulty in describing their thinking. (NB Not all teachers reach this stage.)

From Novice to Expert – Stages in Trainee Development (Maynard and Furlong 1993)
Stage 1 (Early Idealism) *Strong identification with students; often hostile to class teacher; clear image of themselves as teachers*
Stage 2 (Survival) *Focus on class control and management, 'fitting in' and establishing self as teacher in school; trainee 'can't see' – tendency to go for 'tips'*
Stage 3 (Recognising Difficulties) *Becoming sensitive to multiple demands, keen for assessment – 'How am I doing?' Focus on methods and materials, often referring to lack of materials and resources*
Stage 4 (Hitting the Plateau) *Novice has found a way of teaching that works. Difficulty in focusing away from self to others or from materials to students*
Stage 5 (Moving On) *Experimenting, looking at Ss needs (needs continued intervention for further professional growth)*

Issues in initial teacher education and training

Many studies of initial teacher education report student teachers' dissatisfaction with these programmes. Kagan (1993) reports a strong indication that university courses of training 'fail to provide novices with adequate procedural knowledge of classrooms, adequate knowledge of pupils or the extended periods of teaching practice needed to acquire that knowledge, or a realistic view of teaching in its full classroom/school context.' (1992: 162) Bransford et al. (2000) echo these sentiments, citing a national survey in the United States reporting the following problems regarding preservice programmes:

- Not enough time for practice and the acquisition of skills – too short a time to learn subject matter and teaching (This is borne out by the novice-expert studies referred to earlier.)
- Fragmented and disjointed programmes – too many separate courses.
- Uninspired teaching – usually lectures and recitation.
- A superficial curriculum – depth in neither educational nor subject studies.

They report the complaints of pre-service teachers that their courses are 'disjointed and irrelevant to practice, or are "too theoretical" and have no bearing on what "real" teachers do in "real" classrooms with "real" students' (Bransford et al. 2000: 202). It is clear that initial training needs to acknowledge:

- the personal beliefs of the trainees;
- the influence of experience in shaping practical action;
- the role of the professional context (training institute or school) in reinforcing or resisting current practices;
- the practical imperatives of the routine management of classrooms.

These criticisms are contextualised in schools facing issues such as (a) lack of resources, (b) class size and (c) time constraints. The picture is complicated by the need for a novice teacher to establish a personal style and sense of plausibility which is congruent with the situation, in which he/she feels able to operate from moment to moment in zones of uncertainty. Hence there is a need for 'direct practical experience' in the learning to teach process (Maynard and Furlong 1993). The primary focus should be 'practical classroom knowledge – of students, the situation (classroom, school culture), subject matter and strategies (to facilitate learning)'. Contemporary practice in initial teacher education indicates that such experience should be guided in a principled manner by school mentors, who are themselves experienced teachers. In this way, a principled apprenticeship to the craft knowledge of teaching can be undertaken, with opportunities for 'reflective conversations' between novice and mentor, aimed at developing professional knowledge. This approach addresses some of the shortcomings of pre-service teacher education – notably a tendency in many contexts to focus too much on propositional and subject knowledge at the expense of practical experience. On the other hand, there is also a drawback of focusing initial teacher education in schools, without the opportunity for learning other sorts of knowledge or the disciplined intellectual capacities of inquiry and introspection also necessary for teacher learning (Dunne and Harvard 1993). Furthermore, school cultures and cultures of teaching exert a powerful influence on novice teachers, and tend to exacerbate any anxieties novices have.

9.4 Continuing professional learning

Initial training occupies a very small proportion of the vast majority of teachers' professional lives – three or four years is the normal upper limit. Most of teachers' learning about professional practice actually occurs during their subsequent working lives. During this period the classroom management practices of experienced teachers become, as all expert's routines do, internalised, automatic and second nature. This happens in the contexts of school and teacher cultures, as well as in the classroom, in the course of many encounters. Practices for classroom management are thus learned and refined 'on the job'. Teachers are also very likely to experience continuing professional learning during their careers, typically 'in-service', although there are other types of experience. Further formal professional learning may be undertaken voluntarily or be compulsory. As we shall see, this distinction is critical in understanding what transpires during in-service teacher education programmes.

Developing routines

A teacher's classroom management practices are established, as we have seen, early in their career, as a response to 'control anxiety'. As they gain more experience, teachers develop a sense of what Brown and McIntyre (1993) call a 'natural desirable state of pupil activity' and 'progress' (Concept 9.17), and thus act to ensure that pupils behave accordingly.

Concept 9.17 Factors influencing teachers' classroom routines

Natural Desirable States (NDS) of Pupils: lessons are viewed by teachers as 'satisfactory' as long as students behave in ways which teachers see as routinely desirable (1993: 54).
Examples: students' responses to highly structured tasks and activities; students following established routines for using equipment; students thinking for themselves.
Progress: development of students' knowledge, skills, confidence; generating a product; accomplishment of a sequence of activity. Contrasted with NDS (steady state routine) as developmental (1993: 61).
Teachers' actions either maintain NDS or promote 'progress'.
Conditions Influencing Teaching: teacher action varies according to states of students, teachers, content, material conditions and time (1993: 69–70).

(after Brown and McIntyre 1993)

Unlike experienced teachers, student teachers frequently express concern that their plans do not work out and that they have to improvise. By way of explanation, Brown and McIntyre emphasise that because of the 'immediacy' of the teaching situation, teachers have to act quickly and spontaneously, and that experienced teachers have a variety of routines to choose from in the event of 'troubles'. For instance, teachers' and students' emotional states also vary from moment to moment, and classroom conditions constrain what teachers are able to achieve. Even the type of content they teach can also constrain teaching, and routines are learnt in order to cope with these contingencies. These routines are wider in scope than the types of 'control routines' discussed by, for example, Doyle (1986), and are significant ways in which managerial and instructional aspects of teaching are connected, extending beyond the structuring of activities like handing in homework to choice of particular teaching-and-learning activities such as group work.

Teachers' routines also provide evidence of what they value in terms of learner activity, what they themselves have learned about teaching and are a 'window' into teacher know-how (Quote 9.12).

Quote 9.12   Olson on teachers' routines

The routines of teaching show us what teachers value. They show us what has been learned by teachers. In the routines of teaching, the know-how of teaching is expressed.
(1992: 23)

Through classroom routines, teachers express themselves. To understand what is being said in classrooms it is important to know what the routines are because such routines are rituals – performances involving significant symbols.
(1992: 25)

Teachers have well-established practices for conducting life in their classrooms which allow for the business of the class to be done, which says something about who the teacher is and about the significance of what is done.
(1993: 26)

Routines reflect judgements teachers make about how to structure daily life in their classroom. They are routine only in that they recur, but they are not thoughtless and dull.
(1992: 27)

Practising teachers learn routines which enable them to bring about normal states of activity among students, and which lead to some form of progress. They are, as Olson and Brown and McIntyre have discovered, tacit and to a great extent intuitive. The 'folkways of teaching' are typically seen as negative and barriers to change (Olson 1992: 27). Routines are important because they are closely connected with a teacher's beliefs, and express a teacher's value system; thus, accusations of teacher negativity are somewhat unfair, and not based on a proper understanding of the roots of resistance to innovation.

Professional learning occurs not just within the confines of classrooms, but also in the wider contexts of school cultures and the communities in which schools are situated (Quote 9.13). Hargreaves (1994) also observes that 'what goes on inside the teacher's classroom cannot be divorced from the relations that are forged outside it' (1994: 165). Teacher cultures are instrumental in the formation and development of teachers' beliefs. Hargreaves distinguishes between the content and form of teacher cultures (Concept 5.18), and argues that the form, or pattern, of teachers' relationships with each other is a major influence on teacher learning and change.

Quote 9.13   Olson on teachers' values

Teaching takes place in a communal world with shared meanings. This world is held together by commitments to certain values which neophytes (or novices) have to learn. It is through belonging to the world of teaching that teachers are able to do what they do – to know how to express themselves as teachers through the routines of the classroom which have evolved over time.
(1992: 22)

Concept 9.18   Content and form in teacher cultures

Content: attitudes, values, beliefs habits, assumptions and ways of doing things *shared* by teacher groups. Various cultures: subject, pastoral, level (e.g. primary or secondary).
Form: 'patterns of relationship and forms of association between members'.
Contents are realised, reproduced and redefined through different forms of teacher culture. Any changes in, for example, beliefs, are contingent on changes in form.

(after Hargreaves 1994: 165–6)

Experienced teachers' expertise is congruent with the cultural beliefs of their peers. In the case of language teachers, this is also likely to extend internationally. The influence of experienced colleagues and superiors in modelling and informally discussing their expertise is acknowledged and taken into account in building a picture of how beginning teachers develop. Studies of teachers' experience of school cultures have shown 'the ways in which teachers use their colleagues as models, as "professional parents", to provide ideas, information and practical help, for emotional support and for friendship' (Nias 1989: 135) and that the quality and intensity of professional relationships have a strong influence on early teacher learning (Quote 9.14). A form of legitimate peripheral participation takes place. Classroom management practices are the bedrock of teachers' expertise and thus emerge through a complex process of situated learning, in the company of other teachers, administrators and students, in institutional settings.

Quote 9.14   Nias on beginning teachers and learning

Nias is discussing her interviews of teachers in the primary school in UK:

Few of the teachers felt fully competent when they began and many recalled wanting to know more about other teachers' routines, habits and ways of behaving. Not surprisingly, it was therefore to their colleagues that they most often looked in their first appointments, for examples of craft skill and knowledge in action.
(1989: 136)

Head teachers helped by, for example:
- efficient administration;
- provision of resources;
- classroom planning done in an atmosphere of shared understandings and sound communication;
- creating a supportive climate for individual control and discipline.

One of the limitations of studies of teacher cognitions and decision-making is the asocial nature of much of the research. The work on teachers' learning in working contexts offers compelling evidence of the process of legitimate peripheral participation in learning to teach, and the social nature of the development of expertise.

Changing practices

As a professional group, teachers are continuously open to alternative educational ideas and practices developed outside their immediate contexts of practice. As social, political and economic conditions change through a teacher's career, educational practices may have to change in order to meet the challenges these new conditions pose. This may require innovation and change within a system, or even more fundamentally a reconsideration of the teacher's role and purpose (Fullan 1993). Bringing about new teacher learning in these circumstances is an interventionist activity with specific goals which may, however, bear little relation to what teachers actually experience on a daily basis. More pertinent questions might be: How can teachers be assisted in learning *during* their working lives? How do they continue learning? What opportunities are available to them?

As in pre-service teacher education programmes, teachers enter continuing education and training with deeply-felt understandings of the nature of teaching and learning, by now reinforced and tuned to particular working contexts. Freeman (1992) comments:

> teacher education is a weak form of intervention. In the greater scheme of their professional lives, formal education in teaching probably has only a minimal impact on what teachers do in the classroom. (1992: 4)

We cannot expect continuing education programmes to have any more impact than the other means of teacher learning, and there is good reason to believe that the impact they make will be patchy at best unless they acknowledge the following:

- Teachers' knowledge and experience: experienced teachers have already worked out successful routines for preventing disruption to their classes, for example (Tsui 2003: 138). New teaching ideas threaten the investment that has been made in these routines, and the equilibrium of classroom communities. Olson (1992: 26) has noted that 'we can see what routines mean to teachers most clearly when those routines are threatened'.
- Innovation's threat to teachers' self-esteem, control of anxiety and presentation of self (Olson 1992: 71). Innovation implies risk and threats to teachers' sense of plausibility, as well as to the security of classroom groups (Prabhu 1992).
- The professional communities within which teachers work, and the extent to which their traditions (Olson 1992) have been built up, and are protected. Teachers' identities and how they construct themselves are also at the heart of this concern. Hargreaves (1994) is adamant that an understanding of teacher cultures is a means of 'understanding the limits and possibilities of teacher development and educational change'.
- The impact of innovations on teachers' personal and professional lives. Goodson (2003: 54) proposes that 'life history studies of the teacher's life and work provide a valuable lens for observing contemporary moves to restructure and reform schooling'. This implies the importance of hearing the teacher's voice and therefore insiders' perspectives on classroom life, in ways similar to those employed by researchers like Brown and McIntyre (1993), Breen et al. (2001) and Tsui (2003).

These views resonate with Markee's (2001) notion of a 'diffusion-of-innovations' approach to innovation in language teaching. As he points out, 'teachers are key players in any attempt to promote innovations in syllabus design' (2001: 119). An understanding of how teachers learn and the influence of the social and cultural contexts in which they live and work on their learning and their practices is essential in external shaping of any efforts at stimulating new teacher learning. It also provides a helpful framework for considering why and how well-established practices and beliefs make it hard to change teaching. Because classroom management practice is at the very heart of teachers' daily practice, it has to be a focal point of any programme of continuing teacher development.

Summary

The ways in which teachers learn how to teach, and the specific practices of classroom management, are complex and multi-faceted. A transmission model of learning and teaching is inadequate for describing what happens to people as they learn to handle groups of learners and manage learning contexts. Teachers are pivotal in classroom life, and they learn to take on the responsibilities and duties that this work entails within specific socio-cultural contexts. Learning to teach is a social as well as a psychological process. It is also tied up with professional practice, communities of professionals and the constraints of institutional life. To view this in any way other than holistically is to miss the essence of teacher learning. Being a teacher means constructing an identity which is also partly constructed by of those with whom we work. Classroom management practices are thus contextually sensitive and collectively created. Formal attempts to 'teach' these practices on teacher education programmes are constrained in the same ways as innovations at the classroom level, and presents dilemmas to the individual practitioner.

Further reading

Biott and Nias (1992) present a good selection of papers on teacher learning and culture in the UK.
Brown and McIntyre (1993) is a study of teaching, and how professional knowledge is put into action.
Eraut (1994) is a helpful account of professional knowledge.
Freeman and Richards (1996) is a collection of papers on ESL teachers' thinking.
Goodson (1992) has a valuable selection of papers on teachers' life histories.
Hargreaves (1994) is excellent on the issue of professional cultures in teaching.
Hoyle and John (1995) is a comprehensive review of research on professional knowledge.
Kagan (1992) is a valuable review of 'learning-to-teach' studies.
Lortie (1975) is still fresh in its argument for changing our perspective away from curriculum towards teachers' practices and social contexts as a way of understanding teaching.
Olson (1992) argues for a teacher's voice in understanding teacher learning and is helpful on pinpointing issues in change and development.
Roberts (1998) is a comprehensive overview of issues in language teacher education, and Chapters 1 and 2 cover issues in teacher learning and research on teaching.
Schön (1983, 1987) argues passionately for a redefinition of professional learning.
Tsui (2003) is an excellent addition to the literature on teacher learning and expertise and has the value of being set in Hong Kong.

Part 2
Classroom Management Practices

Introduction

Part 1 has outlined the main theoretical and conceptual issues in developing an understanding of classroom management. Building on the framework of classroom management as the management of educational time, space, engagement and participation, we have taken a broadly discoursal view of classroom management and traced the main influences on practice as well as conceptualising practice itself. In Part 2, we shall examine a selection of research studies which illuminate our understanding of classroom management practices, particularly at the micro and meso levels of activity, and illustrate ways of going about researching language (and other) classrooms. The material is arranged in four interconnected chapters. The first discusses accounts of how classroom time and space are managed. It also provides examples of the burgeoning area of research into the management of 'classrooms without walls'. The second chapter highlights studies which inform our understanding of the affective domain of classroom management – engagement. Participation is the focus of the third chapter, which examines studies that coalesce around the analysis of classroom talk. The final chapter features other studies of classroom life which provide a more holistic view or different or unusual perspectives on classroom management. Studies that focus on the specific topic of classroom management are few and far between. However, there are numerous studies focusing on aspects of classroom management as I have delineated it in this book. I provide a representative sample of the available work; the material presented is not an exhaustive listing of available sources, but offers ways into researching what appears to be a central aspect of educational life, which I have termed elsewhere 'complexity management'.

10
Practices for Managing Time and Space

Chapter 3 identified the following issues arising from a discussion of the management of classroom time and space:

- the extent to which the chronological boundaries of education conflict with 'natural learning rhythms';
- the influence of spatial arrangements on classroom life, and individual and collective responses to the arrangement of classroom space;
- the effects of continuing with formal learning activity outside the classroom – at home, online and in the community.

The discussion of practices and the case studies which I present in this chapter illuminate these and other classroom management themes in three main sections: time, space and 'classrooms without walls'.

10.1 Managing time

Teachers manage classroom time in two broad ways – through course and pre-lesson planning, and through their practices at the micro level of the minute-by-minute encounter. As we saw in Chapter 3, planning (or strategic) and 'local' (or classroom) practices are likely to be influenced by the particular requirements and broader rhythms of educational time, for example, completion of curricular objectives and semester dates. Teachers also try to exert a measure of control over their immediate temporal conditions. Hargreaves (1994) makes a distinction, which is relevant to an understanding of time management in the classroom, between:

- 'going with the flow' time which is 'flexible, multi-dimensional, people-oriented', over which teachers and learners have a sense of control and ownership; and

- 'getting done' time which is controlled by others – segmented, essentially task-oriented and linear, over which teachers and learners have less ownership (Woods and Jeffrey 1996: 44).

Lessons and lesson planning

As we have seen, like many other activities, formal education is defined by time periods. The division of education into time units is also a way in which it is managed. For a doctor, the consultation may be the defining unit of time, for the athlete, a game or race may be the natural unit; for teachers and students it is the lesson (or period, or session). Units of classroom time are typically referred to as 'lessons', a usage reinforced by the practice in initial teacher training of teaching student teachers 'lesson-planning'. Lessons are thus interpreted as the units into which content is divided, so that pupils 'learn their lessons'. This is further reinforced by the use of learning materials divided into 'lessons'. Significantly, Doyle (1986) does not regard a 'lesson' as the primary time unit. Rather, he refers to the 'class session' and the possibility that a class session may contain more than one lesson. The other possibility is that a lesson may extend over several class sessions.

Classroom management practice for most teachers is thus grounded in planning and preparation of activity in lessons or sequences of lessons. The planning process also inevitably 'tangles' conceptual and chronological aspects of the process. The interweaving of temporal and conceptual dimensions in this way originates in the practice of planning initially at the course level and then at the lesson level (Quote 10.1). This has consequences for the in-time management of classroom events, and requires signalling from the teacher during lessons.

Quote 10.1   Woods on 'tangles' in planning

...because the teacher maps conceptual structures (course content) onto chronological (calendar and clock) structures, two different hierarchies are operating at once, and...the teacher needs to signal different aspects of each. This leads to the case where a number of elements (of a lesson) have a double function – a function with regard to each of the two structures.... For example, in her introduction to the brainstorming activity, C (a teacher) states that it is also 'a warm-up for what we are going to do today', i.e. an introduction to the day's (chronological unit) activities, as well as the conceptual units of activities.
(1996: 110)

Lesson planning is thus the art of arranging conceptual material in appropriate chronological sequences, which 'lead' to a 'punch line', or outcome, or resolution. For many teachers, planning is fairly limited, as the writers of their set texts are likely to have made most of the decisions already as to what to teach and when. This is a practice cemented by the writers of teachers' guides to teaching materials, often suggesting timings and sequences of activity to teachers. There is unlikely to be a great deal of choice regarding the planning of time use under such circumstances. Regarding the teaching/learning process, there may also be 'methodological pressure' in a lesson plan. The PPP (presentation-practice-production) model is an example in which classroom time is allocated according to a predetermined stage of activity. Prabhu (1992) observes that 'A method is what lies behind a lesson plan – what guides the teacher in deciding what activities are to be undertaken, and *in what order*, in the course of the lesson' (1992: 227, my emphasis). In the PPP lesson, these decisions are, in effect, imposed on the teacher and greatly constrain activity. For other teachers, however, planning entails fitting lessons to particular student groups and their perceived needs within time constraints (Freeman 1996: 97). Woods (1996: 129) lists the following as the influences in lesson planning on one of the teachers in his study, none of them directly referring to time:

- Number of students attending the class.
- Availability of photocopying.
- Knowledge about students' prior course experience.
- Recent conversation with a colleague.
- Estimation of the complexity of the task.
- Estimation of how well the students and individuals in the group are progressing.
- Estimation of what the students can manage.
- Class and individual dynamics

So, lesson planning activity normally entails making decisions about teacher's, students' and, in many cases, a course book's potential contributions in the classroom (Figure 10.1). These will be called into play at different junctures in the session and for different periods of time.

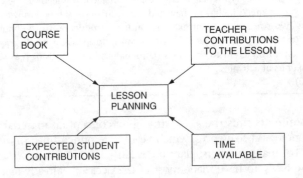

Figure 10.1   Contributions to lesson plans

A lesson plan is thus the amalgam of conceptual, or content, material in a chronological sequence. Other factors need to be considered in planning, however, as the first case study demonstrates.

Case Study 1: 'Pressures to plan' – Cadorath and Harris (1998)

Cadorath and Harris ran in-service training programmes for English teachers in Mexico. They observe (1998: 191–2) that the teachers faced administrative, training and pedagogic 'pressures to plan', in addition to the particular problems they experienced in coming to terms with a new 'communicative' methodology, and allocating class time for novel activities with which they themselves were not familiar. A key issue was whether or not to allocate more time than normal for new activities, within the existing constraints of time available. While the authors acknowledged the necessity for the teachers to have a script to work from while trying out the new methodology, they also saw during classroom observation and after examining the transcripts of recordings that both teachers and students wanted to 'play' with the language. Cadorath and Harris thus encouraged the inclusion of 'chatting' interludes of 5–10 minutes at the beginning or end of lessons, partly to allow for 'real' language use, but also to try to widen the range of types of activity teachers could include in lessons.

Using classroom time

One of the main research traditions uses essentially quantitative techniques to analyse how time is used in lessons. There are two sets of temporal characteristics of classrooms (Doyle 1986: 394–5). Most research focuses on the short term:

- *Short-term*: multidimensionality ('waiting a few extra moments for a student to answer a question can affect that student's motivation to learn as well as the pace of the lesson' (1986: 394)); simultaneity – many things happening at once; immediacy ('the rapid pace of events' (1986: 394)).
- *Long-term*: 'history'. Doyle points out the importance of early encounters in a group's history, and also notes the effects of seasons, absences and the 'broad cycle of the year' (1986: 395). He observes 'planning for a single event must take into account the broader context of the class's history' (1986: 395).

Doyle cites a number of studies of 'segments' (Concept 10.1) of classroom activity, and identifies the following issues:

- Any change in, for example, students' seating position, type of behaviour allowed and so on, 'represent a potential change in the nature of the situation in which students and the teacher work' (1986: 397).
- Changes in activity (e.g. seatwork, presentation) signal different uses of time. Citing work on the 'occupancy time' (after Gump 1967) of classrooms,

he quotes the following figures: '65% of classroom time is spent in seatwork, 35% in whole class presentation or recitation, and 15% in transitions and other housekeeping events' and that 'students generally spend their time in schools working alone (seatwork) or in whole-class presentations' (1986: 398).

This research also illustrates the close relationships between time and space use.

Concept 10.1   Research on segments of classroom activity

'...a classroom is a behaviour setting...composed of segments that *surround* and *regulate* behaviour.'

Research
- Begins with accumulation of narrative records ('chronicles').
- Narratives are divided into segments – 'natural units of organised action' (Doyle 1986:397) – typically, changes in seating patterns; changes in support resources; change of interaction or working types; changes in activity (e.g. from silence during individual book work to talk during break times).
- Segments are coded for time, pacing, number of participants, involvement etc.
- While occupying a group for a 55-minute class period, a teacher typically arranges activities through time to try to match the length of activity to the length of session, 'bound together by a common focal content' (Doyle 1986: 398).

Summarising the research, Doyle concludes that there are different levels of 'structure' in classroom lessons (Concept 10.2). Research has tended to focus on the involvement of students in on-task behaviour, and also how time is used in other teacher-led activities, primarily to change activity and for routines such as opening segments of classroom sessions.

Concept 10.2   Main structural units of lessons

1. The **class session** (or unit of time defined by the signal for students to assemble in the classroom, and for them to leave, or the lesson to end).
2. The **lesson**, or set of activities bound by common focal content.
3. The **activity**, or the distinctive pattern of organising students for working for a unit of time within a lesson.
4. The **routine**, or supplementary programme of action for handling housekeeping matters in classrooms.

(after Doyle 1986: 399)

Research on time use in lessons is still a major means of understanding of the relationship between classroom teaching and learning, and their management, as Case Study 2 demonstrates. Much of this qualitative research appears to be driven by the need to see that students' time is being used productively in lessons, and as such, has evaluative overtones. It also has a potentially powerful influence on policy-making, as the case study illustrates.

Case Study 2: Practices and interactions in the primary classroom – McPake et al. 1999

The studies

1. The main aim was to 'investigate how teachers and pupils spend their days in the classroom'. There was observation in detail of one class in each of 12 Scottish primary schools. Two researchers spent a week in each of three classes (Primary 1, 4 and 7). They observed the class teacher and six 'target pupils' who had been identified as representative of different ability levels. Teachers and students were interviewed to gain access to their views of classroom activity.
2. Observation of how teachers employed 'setting' (grouping students of roughly equal abilities) in 4 selected schools, using the same techniques as already used in the earlier study.

The findings (relevant to time use)   The target pupils were engaged on task for about 66 per cent of the time they were in class. Pupils were most likely to be 'on task' working together with other pupils or working one to one with teachers and least likely to be engaged when working without direct teacher supervision. For the research team, the time spent by pupils on task was considered a 'proxy measure for learning'. It is when pupils are engaged on task that they are – overtly – in a position to learn.

Teachers spent about 80 per cent of their classroom time on teaching and activities relating to teaching. The rest was spent on non-curricular activities such as administration (taking the register, collecting money, clearing up, etc.). In the 'setting' study, they found that just under 50 per cent of pupils' class time was spent in whole class teaching compared with around a third in non-setting classes.

The studies also found that the way the time was used in class diverged quite markedly from the curriculum guidelines for the relevant age group.

Questions raised   The research team raise interesting questions about time use and classroom management and learning:

- Is being on task two thirds of the time reasonable? How would adults fare on this measurement?
- Is it appropriate to increase the amount of time which pupils spend working together on collaborative tasks and to reduce the amount of

time pupils spend working in situations where they can socialise with other pupils?

- How can schools reduce the time devoted to administration in class time?

The findings of the Scottish primary study seem broadly in line with the types of finding reported by Doyle, and contribute further to the prevailing view that 'on task' behaviour of students is the most desirable form of participatory behaviour. Other studies discussed by Doyle (1986) point out that disruption occurs most frequently during periods of seatwork (supervised individual study or work with reading groups in pre-school classrooms) and individual 'pleasure reading'. A further motivation for the research is the need to discover best ways of maintaining order in classrooms (Doyle 1986; Jones 1996). The weight of evidence seems to support the idea that students are most likely to be engaged actively during whole-class teaching and closely supervised collaborative work in small groups. The proportions of time devoted to these activities are thus significant measures of on-task behaviour. In detailed studies of seatwork, researchers have also found significant variations in activity during different phases of this type of activity, with the lowest involvement levels observed in the early phases, or the first 4 minutes.

An across time examination of lessons has thus enabled researchers to see how teachers' management practices facilitate student involvement, which in itself is a predictor of achievement. This has to some extent reflected the desire to focus on positive aspects of students' classroom performance rather than simply on misbehaviour and its management. The main focus of these studies has thus tended to be student involvement or on task behaviour or 'active engagement in working' (Doyle 1986: 400).

The basic pedagogic shape of a lesson is governed by its activity structure and the relative proportions of time usage also give it a sense of movement or 'flow'. Nunan (1996) notes that the images and metaphors used by the teachers in his study 'are shot through with references to pace, flow, tempo and movement. One teacher noted, 'time was running out. I had to keep the pace moving along' (1996: 49) (Thornbury 1999), exploring metaphors for lessons, includes 'theme', 'plot' and 'sense of ending' in his list.) By examining these features of classroom sessions, we can build a picture of how students and teachers pass the time. However, the fact that a student is involved or not involved in activity does not in itself indicate whether or not learning is taking place. As the Scottish primary study team point out, this is a 'by proxy' indication, and far from definitive.

The research reviewed has also tended to focus primarily on what *teachers* do to manage time in lessons. Fenwick (1998: 622) observes that teachers create 'temporal structures to regulate pace and student attention to task'. Regular shifts in learning activity are part of these management practices. In the context of examining how teachers managed the balance between work and play, quiet and talk, Fenwick further observed that students seemed 'vigilant to carve out any possible spaces (or *times*) in the highly structured classroom life for improvisation and surprise'. And that 'when unchecked, these diversions can produce a directionless and fragmented pandemonium that even adolescents will admit is "not fun"' (1998: 623, my emphasis). Fenwick's finding reminds us that students also look for ways in which to manage their time in the classroom, perhaps unconsciously in the early stages of education, but more knowingly as they progress to adolescence. Clearly, more research is required which focuses on how students look for and use opportunities to use classroom time for their own purposes, whether legitimate or not.

Practices for managing classroom time

The raw percentages of class time use are a starting point for understanding the management of time in the classroom, but they reveal little about what teachers and learners actually do interactively by way of time management. Field Note 10.1 gives us a glimpse of some specific practices for managing classroom time. Observations such as these are useful starting points in researching complex issues such as time use in classroom management. They also require minimal use of resources and techniques.

Field Note 10.1 Namibia – Primary – Rural

The teacher comes into the classroom (30 or more children (8–10 years old) sitting in a semi-circle on the earth floor facing the worn blackboard), greets the children, who chorus a reply. 'Right,' says the teacher. 'Who can remember yesterday's lesson?' Many hands raised, fingers clicking. 'Me sir, me sir.' 'Yes – you'. Teacher points to child who stands and says 'Spellings.' 'Yes, good. Sit down.'

We see here the Namibian primary teacher creating a link back in time between a previous lesson and the current one. This is achieved through question and answer, and is an example of a teacher creating a sense of continuity (Quote 10.2) between different sequential parts of the students' learning experience. This is a process which continues throughout an encounter between learners and a teacher, and is evidence of the way in which the 'long conversation' of education is managed cumulatively across time boundaries. It is also evidence of strategic management in time by the teacher, and unlikely to have been explicitly written down in a lesson plan. It is a routine – not a 'housekeeping' one – that features in the practice of teachers worldwide, and reflects a view implicit in the practice of the Namibian primary school teacher and many like him who see lessons as 'building blocks', with what has been covered in a previous lesson seen as central to new learning in the next lesson, closer to the idea of 'sessions' (Doyle,

Concept 10.2). There is thus a segment at the beginning of each lesson in which there is a reference back to the previous lesson. In many settings, education revolves around 'lessons' (or 'packets' of content) which fit into the specific time frames provided for work with student groups. This has the effect of magnifying recitation and transmissive practices (Chapter 7), and also amplifying the effect of the 'completion imperative' (Chapter 3) in the individual classroom sessions. This is very similar to the practice of 'lessons' in the Christian church service – readings from the Bible. Each contains a message or 'lesson' to think about or learn from. It is possible that the emergence in the West of schools from church education has provided us with this historical legacy.

The example also provides some support for Nunan's (1996: 44) assertion that 'lessons are not discrete entities that come neatly packaged', reflecting the reality for many classroom participants that the chronological boundaries of lessons (35, 40 or more minutes) are (a) unlikely to be significant in learning, and (b) are extremely limited as tools for managing learning experience. They are ways of 'bracketing' the educational experience, and are typically signalled by a bell or similar in schools. These essentially administrative boundaries ensure that all aspects of the curriculum are covered, that teachers have a fair workload, and so on. In reality, teachers see lessons in clusters and sequences rather than as discrete units with specific objectives (Freeman 1996: 97).

Quote 10.2   Mercer on providing continuity

An important task for a teacher is to help learners see how the various activities they do over time contribute to the development of their understanding. Education cannot merely be the experience of a series of consecutive events, in which earlier experiences provide the foundations for making sense of later ones. For those involved in teaching and learning, continuous shared experience is one of the most precious resources available.
(2001: 248)

Another way of understanding how classroom time is managed is to refer again to the notion of 'framing' (Goffman 1974) (Chapter 3, Concept 3.3). The 'lesson' or any period of classroom time is a setting for social interaction. A frame is a set of expectations held by participants as to how a social interaction should proceed. Framing practices for lessons appear to operate at two levels: strategic and local. They establish the procedural framework of lessons, providing overall structure and direction to a lesson through a sequence of activities, referring to use of time and space and creating the climate. Figure 10.2 shows how the segments of a lesson are linked by local framing, and arranged in an overall structure by strategic framing. The strategic frame of a lesson, or its 'shape', gives it an overall 'direction' in time.

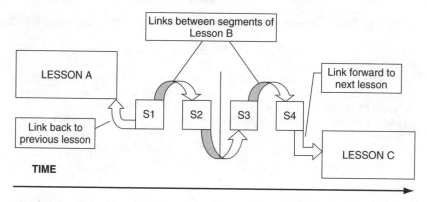

Figure 10.2   Strategic and local framing in lessons

Strategic framing not only works for individual lessons. It also provides curricular continuity through programmes of learning, and socio-emotional continuity for a learning group through time. By providing links between lessons strategic framing practices are an important means of giving a learning group continuity of experience, and are one way in which a group's history is written. This form of framing exhibits itself both in lesson plans and in the ongoing management of classroom encounters.

The dynamic nature of classroom time management practices is further conceptualised by Erickson (1982). By treating a lesson as an example of social interaction or an encounter (after Goffman 1961), Erickson sees teachers and students as 'doing a lesson together' (1982: 153) and drawing on two sets of knowledge at the same time – academic task structure and social participation structure (Concept 10.3).

Concept 10.3   Procedural knowledge in classroom management

1. ACADEMIC TASK STRUCTURE (ATS) 'a patterned set of constraints provided by the logic of sequencing of the subject matter content of the lesson' (1982:154)

In terms of time management, there are two main aspects of ATS which are significant – logic of the sequencing of subject matter, and the information content of the various sequential steps. Both of these are signalled by teachers during the course of lessons.

2. SOCIAL PARTICIPATION STRUCTURE (SPS) 'governs the sequencing and articulation of interaction' (1982: 154)

There are two main aspects of the SPS which are significant social aspects of the task environment are the sequencing and timing of various 'slots' in an interaction and the simultaneous actions of all involved in interactions during a lesson.

Concept 10.3   (Continued)

ATS and SPS are intertwined in locally constructed classroom discourses.

Erickson (1982: 156) sees face-to-face interaction as a 'radically cooperative enterprise'. Participants have access to patterns of timing and sequencing in verbal and non-verbal behaviour in classroom interaction. These function as a signal system which contains **explicit** (with direct reference to time or proximity) and **implicit** signals for timing – past, present and future.

(after Erickson 1982)

In terms of lesson management, the academic task structure is initially framed in the teacher's lesson plan, and signals for the sequencing of steps in any instructional activity will be conveyed with reference to this structure. The teacher will also plan in the social participation structure (for example, statements about group work), which, as we have seen, may well be 'entangled' in the ATS. Routines creating continuity with previous lessons are specific examples. Students are able to participate in the improvisation of lessons because of their procedural knowledge of these patterns and to 'read' the contextualisation cues (Chapter 8, Concept 8.5) implicit in any utterance with reference to the ATS and SPS. These practices enable all student participants to follow instruction. We can, through examination of these time management practices, also understand why new classroom activities have to be 'learned'. They create new ATS and/or SPS and thus new contextualisation cues.

Extract 10.1   ATS and SPS in action

```
 1  T    put away all your books (class noise) you remember last time we were
          doing/the past continuous tense / I want us to make a sentence in the past
          continuous tense --- yes
     S #1   when I was coming to school / I saw a boy carrying a basket of fruit...
 5  T    when I was coming to school I saw a boy / somebody should name/point out
          the tense/the past continuous tense in that sentence --
     S #2   was
     T    please speak aloud
     Sx   was
10  pS #2   was
     T    was
     S #3   coming
     T    good
     Sx   was
15  S #4   was coming
     T    correct – I want another sentence/yes
```

Examining samples of classroom talk is a productive means of seeing framing in action. In Extract 10.1 we can see the ATS at work in line 1, referring to the previous class session, establishing continuity with previous activity. In line 3, the teacher's use of 'yes' (an explicit SPS signal) cues a student response, following a period of silence in which the teacher surveys the class for a potential respondent. The SPS is also explicitly referred to in line 8 'please speak loud'. Line 9 contains an unsolicited student response, which passes without admonishment, and is presumably permissible as part of an implicit SPS. The student might also have been correcting or encouraging his classmate to negotiate the ATS. The teacher repeats the response in line 11, again an implicit reference to the ATS. The collective completion in lines 12–15, with teacher signalling correctness, brings the sequence to a close before the teacher refers explicitly to the ATS again in line16. Such an analysis enables us to 'map' the progress of a lesson through the framing devices of ATS and SPS.

Improvisation – escaping from time's constraints

Lesson plans are frequently abandoned or departed from during lessons, and classroom encounters improvised. This may partially explain why, as Breen (1987) has asserted, there is often a considerable difference between 'task-as-work plan' and 'task-as-process', or the difference between teachers' agendas as expressed in lesson plans and students' agendas of what they want to get out of a lesson (Holliday 1994: 143). What actually happens in lessons frequently fails to 'follow the script'. A number of studies of teachers' decision-making (Nunan 1996; Woods 1996; Borg 1998) have pointed out that teachers frequently depart from the script and use time in unpredictable and unplanned ways. We can therefore also approach the question of managing classroom time in terms of planning rather than improvisation. This provides useful insights into the reasons for teachers' decision-making, as seen in Case Study 3.

Case Study 3: Departing from the script – Bailey 1996

The study   Bailey worked with six experienced teachers. Her main goal was to try to uncover and document factors which guided teachers while they were in the process of decision-making during lessons and what they were guided by when deciding to depart from their plans. She observed classes, and tape-recorded them as well as making field notes while watching. These were subsequently made into prose descriptions of the classes. The teachers were then interviewed about the lessons and their plans. She was interested in how the lesson 'fitted' the plan, and whether the teacher was aware on any departures from the script. Unexpected events, when noticed, were reconstructed. Teachers were then asked to talk about principles which may have informed their decisions.

Findings   The study identifies six main reasons teachers divert from their plans:

1. Serving the common good – change focus to a problem many experienced in the class.
2. Teach to the moment – react to immediate opportunities in lessons. Bailey (1996: 28) refers to this type of decision as 'timeliness'.
3. Furthering the lesson – move the lesson on when possibilities are exhausted.
4. Accommodating different individual learning styles – improvising with different teaching strategies.
5. Promoting student involvement – allowing space for students to participate. 'To promote the students' involvement, teachers create the time to do so by eliminating some portions of their own lesson plans' (1996: 33). Bailey cites Politzer's (1970: 41) 'Principle of Economics' while discussing this issue: 'since classroom time is limited, the value of any activity is partially determined by the offsetting value of the activities the teacher could choose to do instead' (1996: 33).
6. 'Distribute the wealth' – allocating turns or longer turns to some students (stopping the more voluble learners dominating and encouraging the quieter ones to participate).

The research highlights the delicacy of teachers' management practices, and the fact that skilful teaching is more than good lesson planning, and refers to 'those myriad points in our daily lives as professionals when we must make an on-line judgement as to what is best for our students, whether to stay with the lesson plan, safely on firm ground, or to head out into the uncharted waters of spontaneous discourse' (1996:15). This demonstrates teachers' and learners' inclination to 'go with the flow' and how learning opportunities are created by overriding the constraints of time. As she points out 'teaching and learning transcend time boundaries' (1996: 28).

Quote 10.4   van Lier on planning and improvisation

On the one side of the coin, planned, recurring activities lend a certain reassuring predictability to lessons, an element of ritual which is an essential part of any culture. A teacher who, for the sake of spontaneity and variation, looks for new things to do all the time, and just lets things happen, may be forgetting that most students also need points of stability in lessons, and these are achieved by recycling tasks, planning certain sequences of activities in predictable ways, ritual beginnings, endings and transitions, and so on.

For this reason it might be a good idea to design syllabuses and lessons as if they formed a small organic culture (or an ecosystem) in themselves, where participants strive to combine the expected and unexpected, the known and the new, the planned and the improvised, in harmonious ways.

(1996b: 200)

We can thus make a distinction between planned and improvised elements in lessons. These can be identified in transcripts, and teachers' perspectives then sought. One issue not dealt with is the *effect* on classroom discourse and learning opportunity of these departures from the script. Student perspectives might illuminate us further. Planning for improvisation raises further questions (Quote 10.4). Van Lier favours an 'ecological' approach to planning in which stability and improvisation link. Budgeting time for improvisation might for many teachers be a new concept, and the thought of departing from tried and tested planned sequences in order to do this is quite daunting. The discoursal consequences may be deeper as, for example, students may not recognise new contextualisation cues. We need to learn more about the significance of 'seizing the moment', and its role in normal classroom discourse.

Other studies

Marina, one of the teachers in Tsui's (2003: 149–50) study of expertise, is very aware of time as a resource, but in a quite different way from the teachers in Bailey's study. First of all she is extremely punctual and, from experience, has learned that laying down a punctuality rule at the beginning of a school year is necessary. This practice is similar to others described by Emmer and Stough (2001: 105) for identifying and teaching desirable behaviours, particularly in the first few weeks of a school year. Marina also takes an alarm clock to class to time activities, to keep herself and her students on task – without a time limit, she feels students might be tempted to drift off-task. She also sets up permanent groups at the beginning of a school year in order to speed up group formation on those occasions when she used group work. As Tsui comments 'this results in a brisk pace in her teaching' (2003: 150).

Pacing

Another way in which time is experienced and managed is in the 'pace' of activity. This includes completion of syllabus items or course book units in specific time frames, which can have the effect of telescoping or compressing classroom activity. In language teaching, there appears to be an underlying ideal of a relatively high pace of activity, perhaps a hangover from Audio-lingualism, or perhaps dictated by a need to 'keep learners on their toes', and keep them on-task, as well as to pack as much teaching as possible into a limited time period. Teachers' and learners' perceptions of pace have not been extensively researched, and are a promising area of inquiry.

Early studies reviewed by Doyle (1986: 407) focus on three interconnected issues, all of which rely on 'signal systems' (after Gump and Kounin 1974 in Doyle) to change and initiate activities. These are verbal and non-verbal.

- Involvement of students proved to be higher when students' work was externally paced (i.e. by the teacher – and probably materials). Studies cited note the phenomenon of students being 'pulled along' by teaching which features an active input of stimuli compared with self-paced work. The studies note how pacing of learning appears to be dependent upon students' understanding of the sequence of activity.

- Levels of continuity in lessons proved to be high when the teacher was present, leading all activities. There were lower levels of continuity with group work, which featured low involvement and high levels of off-task behaviour.
- Scheduling – teachers tended to schedule and pace different classroom segments to fit the available lesson time, and used standard opening routines such as copying the date or work plan from the board at the beginning of a lesson to involve students immediately.

Studies referring to pace

As we have seen with some of the decisions that teachers take when managing time in the classroom, there is a degree of tension between 'getting things done' (or completing the plan as stated) and 'doing things which emerge' in the course of lessons. Marina in Tsui's study appears to prefer the former, whereas the teachers in Bailey's study preferred the latter. The teachers in Nunan's study had a tendency towards completing plans, explained as a characteristic of their inexperience (1996: 48–9). Alternatively, setting up group work or more elaborate sequences of self-managed work for students can take valuable time, a point made by Guthrie (1990) in favour of persisting with traditional teacher-fronted activities in contexts where resources are sparse and class time is the only real opportunity for educational time that children have. Collaborative modes can also slow the pace of activity and conflict with the completion imperative.

Lament for reflective periods   Brookfield (1990: 62) provides an interesting counterpoint to the idea of classes being action-packed and 'brisk'. He notes that his students 'lament the absence of reflective interludes'. He discusses how he creates reflective interludes in his classes, in effect punctuating a period of activity with a deliberate attempt to slow it down and provide time for contemplation, rumination or simply rest from the intensity of intellectual activity, and the associated interaction. Brookfield also observes that periods of silence are often embarrassing for students, so expectant are they of activity and noise, and suggests alternatives like taking a walk or playing 'unobtrusive music' to mask the effects of silence. This may well be a phenomenon in certain 'action-centred' teaching contexts, unlike, for example, the Athabaskan Indians whose preference for silence and non-engagement is reported by Scollon and Scollon (1981). In language teaching, more meditative activities are proposed by a number of practitioners as an antidote to the perspective that classrooms must be seen to be busy. Useful examples of using silence can be found in, among other sources,

Davis and Rinvolucri (1990). This type of activity challenges the prevailing view that students should be engaged in actual performance, and if they are not, then time is not being used 'efficiently'. It is a powerful, often all-pervading belief that is at the root of a lot of educational practice. Moon (1999: 97) notes that it may not be easy to enable students to reflect as a means to learning, and that there is no guarantee that they will. From a pedagogic point of view, however, the idea of creating 'quiet time' for students to do something other than actively engage with subject matter, classmates and ideas may well create a new frame and require time to establish as a routine. To allocate a substantial part of valuable class time to silence, especially in a language classroom, is at odds with a model of efficient time use – i.e. a great deal of 'doing'. On the other hand, this might be more appealing to some of the types of learner described by studies cited in Erickson and Shultz (1992: 475–6) whose culture favours long periods of contemplation in silence, or who need time to discuss topics informally with classmates.

The current interest in more 'reflective' forms of classroom activity, and the increasing importance of recognising the particular nature of adult learning, indicate that the issue of pacing needs revisiting. Suggested lines of inquiry are to examine students' preference for particular levels of pace during activity, and to focus on teachers' reasons for the provision of periods of 'slower' activity. The on/off task issue also needs re-examining in the light of recent developments of theories of learning and the relationship between teaching and learning. An opportunity view of classroom management (as opposed to the 'order' views reviewed by Doyle et al.) indicates that pacing will vary according to the perceived potential for learning at any given moment, and that slow 'side sequences' are as valuable as quick-fire question-and-answer sessions. This accords with Claxton's (1999) notion of 'slow thinking'.

Summary

Because of time's properties and its capacity to structure people's lives, teachers and learners invariably find themselves managing time and simultaneously being managed in time in their daily activities. There is inevitably conflict between the two forces, and these are exacerbated by the character of time in the classroom – its immediacy, fragmentedness and pressing nature – which teachers, despite rigorous planning and pre-lesson preparation, find themselves managing minute-by-minute, while trying to attend to longer-term learning goals. However, time management in the language classroom and its immediate environs is an under-researched area and one that holds promise in coming to understandings of the influence of time in formal education, particularly in an era when the traditional constraints of classroom time are being questioned, and at the same time, greater intrusions are being made by educational practices into people's private time.

10.2   Managing classroom space

This section will focus on whole-class teaching, the international norm and variations in spatial arrangements in whole class teaching, including different ways of grouping students in classrooms to enable more collaborative pedagogies to be used. Figure 10.3 (also reproduced in Chapter 3, as Figure 3.1) shows various classroom layouts, and Field Notes 10.2 and 10.3 refer to specific examples.

Researching whole-class teaching

Whole-class teaching is conceivably the 'international norm' and has become so because it is so common across a range of different cultural, economic, social and political contexts. Because of the methodological move towards more 'communicative' language teaching, and its associated seating patterns, research on the more traditional management of classroom space has tended to be somewhat negative in its findings. However, the research evidence for the superiority of alternatives is ambiguous in its findings. Lambert (1994) reports various studies which show little significant difference in instructional effects of changing to more collaborative modes, and some which demonstrate a slight decline, reinforcing the criticisms of educationalists like Guthrie, who point out that classroom facilities in many contexts may not be appropriate for some teaching styles such as 'liberal student-centred classroom methods' (1990: 223). Recent research in language classrooms has not attempted to make causal links between use of space and achievement. Instead it has tended to attempt to understand the dynamics of classrooms without any agenda for change or desire to demonstrate the advantages of one pedagogy over another.

The best way in which we can gather information about the influence of classroom space on classroom management in any form of classroom teaching is to watch and record life in classrooms, with a focus on the following issues:

- Organisation of furniture and seating arrangements.
- Movement patterns of teachers and students during lessons.
- Particular conventions such as students' standing to answer teachers' questions.
- Use of resources if any, including any 'board', and use of wall space.
- Other physical features of the classroom – colour, lighting, entrances and their position.

The studies cited in this section all draw on the tradition of detailed ethnographic description. Arguing for an alternative to the 'traditional' teacher role, Salimbene (1981) (Quote 10.5) describes what she sees as the archetypal classroom in a European school. Drawing on her experience, she refers to the various territories, especially the teacher's, and the use of furniture as 'protection'. Particularly significant is the observation that the teacher's desk affords

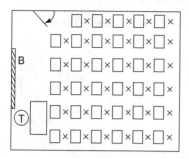

1. 'Traditional': Individual desks in rows.

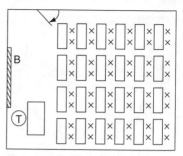

2. 'Traditional': Benches for 2 or more students. Often fixed to the floor.

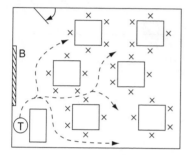

3. 'Restaurant': Random clusters, often permanent or semi-permanent.

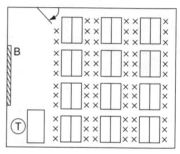

4. 'Islands': Regular groupings. Can be created by modifying 'benches' so that students on odd-numbered benches can turn to face those behind them.

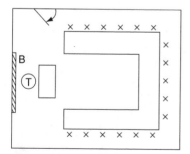

5. 'Horseshoe': Popular in Higher Education.

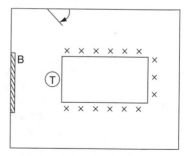

6. 'Seminar': A variant is when the teacher sits on the long side of the table, or 'cabinet meeting'.

Figure 10.3   Classroom layouts – a selection

NOTE: The figure depicts layouts I have seen in classrooms around the world, and is based on my field notes. It is, however, by no means definitive, and there are sure to be other layouts. The 'board' position is marked 'B', and the typical 'teacher base' is marked 'T'.

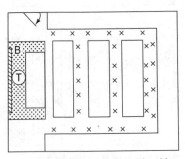

7. 'Laboratory': Layout determined by fixed installations of equipment.

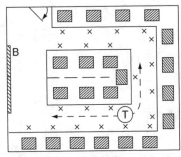

8. 'Looking Out': Typically a configuration in computer rooms, where access to power sources dictates layout.

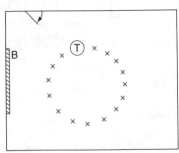

9. 'Circle': Typically chairs only or standing.

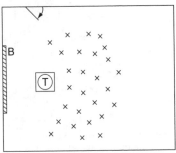

10. 'Story': Semi-circles of listeners surround the story teller, who is typically seated.

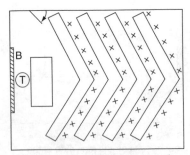

11. 'Chevrons': Occasionally seen in lecture theatres or laboratories.

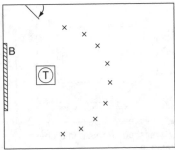

12. 'Semi-circle': Normally found in small classes. Individuals gather round the teacher.

Figure 10.3   (Continued)

a degree of elevation over the students. The description is a collage, however, and not based upon the sort of detailed ethnographic description that characterises more recent work on classrooms. Space management is, however, not typically a research focus in its own right, and is often interwoven with discussion of verbal interaction patterns. The field notes 10.2 and 10.3 which follow allow a richer picture of classroom space to emerge.

Field Note 10.2   Bangladesh – Secondary School, Urban

The classroom is nearly square in shape. By the door, the only entrance, is the teacher's area, a raised platform (6 inches or so) with a heavy old desk and metal-framed chair on it, behind the desk. The desk and chair face the students; behind the desk is a chalkboard, roughly 2 by 1.5 metres. The students, about 90 of them, are in 4 rows seated on benches, 3 or 4 to a bench, facing the teacher. Girls sit in the half of the classroom by the inner wall, and boys on the outside wall. The students are packed in closely to one another, although there is quite a wide gangway between the boys and girls' 'areas'. There is only subdued natural light in the room, from smallish windows on the right hand side of the class. The left hand side of the class is in semi-darkness. Many of the students have a textbook in front of them; many don't. The teacher begins her class, standing in front of the desk on the platform. 'Good morning'.

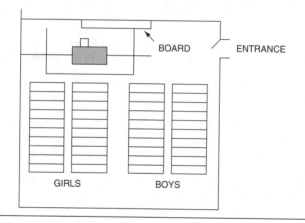

Quote 10.5   Salimbene The 'traditional' classroom space

The physical arrangement of the classroom sets the stage for the teacher-dominated lesson by dividing the room into 'teacher space' and 'student space'. Traditionally, the space between the students' desks and the chalkboard is the teacher's domain. The teacher's desk can either be used as a shield to protect the 'ruler' from the 'masses', or can be used as a platform upon which he sits, further elevating him above his pupils. The students also use their desks as protection and rarely leave them to cross the no-man's land to the teacher's desk.
(1981: 93)

In 'traditional' or teacher-fronted classrooms, the following features are fairly universal:

- Students' furniture is likely to be organised in rows, with individual desks or shared benches for students occupying the bulk of the classroom space. In some classrooms these are fixed to the floor permanently.
- All the student seats face towards the teacher's space, or 'front'.
- The teacher's space is occupied by a teacher's desk or table, with or without a chair, close to the main entrance to the room. Sometimes this area contains a raised platform on which the teacher's desk is positioned.
- The space typically has a blackboard (or whiteboard) behind the teacher if she is facing her students. (Very frequently this is the only 'resource'. There may also be other resources, such as a 'class library' or cupboard for books, or even an overhead projector.)
- In some cases there is a large floor space between the teacher's and students' areas. (See Salimbene's description.) The larger the teacher's space, and quality of furniture, and presence of teaching aids there may contribute significantly to how students and teachers perceive the relative status and prestige of the teacher's zone.

Field Note 10.3   (Malaysia – Secondary School, semi-urban)

The classroom is large, rectangular, well-lit and spacious. It has entrances at both ends of the room. Both sides of the room have louvre glass windows which are open to allow a breeze through. It is over 30 degrees. There are large gangways between the three rows of benches and also around the perimeter of the room. Each bench is occupied by three students; there are 45 in total. In a corner by the board is the teacher's table and chair. The walls at the back of the room and the front, on either side of the blackboard (which covers most of one wall), have 'subject' notice boards. The English board has cuttings from the local newspapers of various stories, and some student composition work.

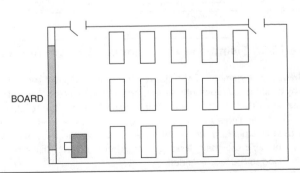

BOARD

Quote 10.6   Two classrooms

Primary English in Botswana
In the Standard Six lessons which I observed the main mode of interaction was between the teacher and the class as a whole. It was customary for pupils to stand before answering a teacher question, whereas, in the Setswana cultural tradition, respect is shown by remaining seated.
(Arthur 1994:68)

Elementary bilingual (Spanish/Quechua) class in rural Peru
The classroom is fairly spacious, with barely adequate light from two rows of small windows in opposite walls. About half the window-panes are broken. There is no electricity (or running water or other amenities) in the school or in Tiyaña as a whole, for that matter, and the room is quite cold early in the morning. The sixth grade students (ten children) sit at one end of the room, facing the back wall, the first grade students (seventeen children) at the other facing the front. (p. 369)
    . . . The first graders have the 'good' blackboard, whereas the sixth graders have a makeshift one made of a piece of sheet metal. The students sit at tables about three to four feet long, on low benches without backs or boards placed on concrete blocks. Girls and boys always sit at separate tables. One student is standing by the wall because there is no convenient place for him to sit. All the children in the first grade have pencils, but in some cases they are down to the last inch. Two children have their pencil tied around their neck with a string (indicating how valuable pencils are here). Unfortunately the string is so short that they practically strangle themselves when putting pencil to paper. All children have lined notebooks, in some cases inherited from siblings who were in first grade before them, with some blank pages left. (pp. 371–2)
(van Lier 1996b)

Organising furniture

How classroom furniture is organised is a 'significant practice' (Breen 2001a: 132). As we saw in Chapter 3, the spatial organisation of classrooms is, at a deep tacit level, a strong indicator of underlying beliefs about teaching and learning. For example, the practice which has produced the 'directionality' of the classic teacher-fronted classroom positions teachers and learners ideologically as well as spatially. As well as being potentially adversarial it also signals the nature of the teaching/learning process – transmission, with authority invested in the teacher. It is a strong symbolic statement about the respective roles teachers and learners play. As Arthur (1994) (Quote 10.6) has observed in Botswana primary classrooms, there are classroom management conventions regarding whether students should be seated or standing when responding to a teacher. It is interesting that Arthur does not describe the seating layout, but we assume that it is traditional, as described in Field Notes 10.2 and 10.3, and van Lier's (1996b) vivid description of deprived classrooms in rural Peru (Quote 10.6). Significantly, van Lier does not attribute the poor performance of students to the conditions under which they work, but rather to the pedagogic practices which they experience, although the two are clearly connected, as space management is a key part of pedagogy. Lessons do, however, revolve around the use of the chalk board – vertical space – on which the teacher writes and from which the students copy. The teacher augments the copying work, which appears to occupy most of the lesson time, by calling students to the front of the class to 'read' the sentences on the board (van Lier reckons they have memorised them). We can speculate that the pedagogic practices had evolved in response to the basic physical conditions of the classroom and the resources available to both teachers and students. There was, for example, a shortage of course books for both students and teachers. From the perspectives of research and innovation, van Lier's and Arthur's studies are significant, in that suggestions for change and development of pedagogic practices in those contexts were made on the basis of the physical and educational realities they found. The critical difference between them is that van Lier's classroom description is grounded in the wider social realities in which he works, whereas Arthur's focuses on curriculum and discoursal issues.

Case Study 4: Secondary English classrooms in Pakistan – Shamim 1996b

Shamim's study was undertaken as part of a wider study of the effects of large class sizes on classroom learning and innovation in methodology, and in particular, the perceptions of teachers and learners in these classrooms. Her main findings were as follows:

Classroom space   'Twenty dual desks to accommodate 40 students. Often three students have to share a desk meant for two. Most of the classrooms have four rows of five or six dual desks. There are narrow pathways between the first and second rows and between the third and fourth rows' (1996b: 124–5). Classes contained anything between 40 and 100 students.

Conducting classes   'Teachers usually conduct their classes from the centre of the front of the room. From this position they have easy access to the blackboard. . . . Thus teachers directly face the middle two rows, but they can also "keep and eye on" students sitting in the two wings on the left- and right-hand side in the front two or three rows. It is not always possible, however, for teachers to "see" the students at the back of the classroom' (1996b: 125).

Effects   The front of the class in the SURVEILLANCE ZONE of the teacher and the back is outside the teacher's ATTENTION ZONE. The front is the VALUED zone 'the choice location' (1996b: 134) – there are more attention and speaking turns from teacher in this 'ACTION ZONE' – 'as the two major sources of input (i.e. the teacher and the blackboard) are situated up front, the front becomes the place where the action takes place' (128).

More difficult and challenging tasks are set for students at the front. They are asked more questions. At the back, students are either ignored or asked simple questions, often as mild disciplinary means of bringing them back into lessons.

'Students who sit in the front of the classroom are generally perceived to be better than the students who sit in the back' (1996b: 133). The students who sit at the back of the class are perceived as being lazy, dull, lacking in motivation, weak personalities, who don't study. Those students who study at home press to sit at the front because there they can display their knowledge. There are big risks for students at the back trying to participate. They have low status and there is peer pressure not to participate at the back.

Shamim notes that 'classrooms in Pakistan are mainly teacher-fronted' (199b6: 124) because:

- Teachers are seen as authority figures in the culture, and are respected for age and superior knowledge.
- The society's view that teaching/learning is transmission of knowledge.
- Teachers lack awareness or are insecure in organising classrooms differently.

These 'givens' of cultural and social conventions for classroom management may well have an influence on teachers' attitudes and feelings about attempting to use alternative pedagogies. In attempting to bring about change in teachers' practices for the management of space with a view to creating more learning opportunities for more students, Shamim favours a gradualist approach of helping teachers to extend the 'action zone' without damaging either authority or status in the classroom.

Case Study 5: University English classrooms in Vietnam – Sullivan 2000

Sullivan (2000) conducted a study on the ways in which CLT has been adapted to Vietnamese classrooms at tertiary level in a way which retains the essence of the Vietnamese cultural view of the teacher–student and the student–student relationship. She notes the importance of the relative locations of teachers and students in an analysis of discourse patterns: 'In analyzing classroom discourse it is crucial to consider the physical set up of the classroom' (2000: 124). Seating positions provide both opportunities for and constraints on communication and learning opportunity.

Classroom space

...the teacher generally sits in front of his students. The students sit closely together on shared benches, so closely that their arms rub and their books and papers overlap. Even if they wanted to do 'independent' work, it would not be possible. Nor is it physically possible for the teacher to hover over an individual's desk, speaking to that student alone. There is barely room to walk between rows of benches, and any speaking to one person would, by necessity, be speaking to all those around the same bench. The physical set-up is most conducive to a teacher-fronted class, with the teacher guiding and leading all students as a whole class. (1996: 125)

No information is provided regarding numbers, although the photograph of the class shows 17 students and the teacher, and there are probably at least five more students in the class.

Classroom practices   Sullivan describes the students in this classroom checking each other's written answers, calling out answers together – working collaboratively but not in ways which would be recognisable to British or American observers as 'communicative language teaching' (CLT). The Vietnamese teacher has 'adapted CLT to a whole-class, teacher-fronted format, one that does not emanate from the values of choice, work, or information exchange, but instead emanates from a value of group harmony' (2000: 125). Sullivan further argues that the closely packed seating actually serves an 'underlying value that the good of the group outweighs the good of the individual' (2000: 125). In her view, CLT has been successfully adapted to a whole-class, teacher-fronted scenario, because local sociocultural conventions have been respected, allowing teachers to maintain their position of authority and leadership.

Case Study 6: Tertiary education, Indonesia – Coleman 1996

Further evidence that whole-class organisations do not adhere to the rigid, orderly and regimented stereotype is provided by Coleman's study of practices in Indonesian tertiary classrooms. Coleman's study highlights the fluidity of the use of space in Indonesian classrooms.

Classroom space management   Coleman observes a range of space-related behaviours and practices:

> ... there seemed to be at least 80 [students] present and dribs and drabs continued to join the group during the time I was present
> ... Throughout the lesson, there was a tremendous amount of coming and going, of people changing places, of late comers arriving and searching for seats
> ... other students from other classes came in and noisily removed chairs from the room during the lesson
> ... a lot of moving around ... one girl wandered around ... then went outside for a couple of minutes, and finally came back into the room. (1996: 56–68)

The examples show how the students are free to move around in classes and even how they can 'invade' a neighbouring class and take furniture. The 'learning festival', as Coleman terms it, takes place in a classroom culture which is managed ritually as follows:

> The teacher normally (stood) on a raised platform or behind a lectern, whilst the students sat in a closely packed crowd facing the teacher, usually as near to the front of the lecture hall as possible. (Coleman 1996: 65)

Thus, while the basic directionality is adhered to (teacher-fronted), the conventions with regard to the seating positions, movement and inter-student talk are significantly different. There is no restriction on students' movement. Students can sit where they choose, and choose to be close to each other. In many ways this is reminiscent of the classrooms van Lier (1996b) describes, where there are regular interruptions from outsiders, which he explains by reference to the fact that local people regard the school as a public space. Both Coleman's and Sullivan's studies emphasise the influence of socio-cultural realities on practices for managing classroom space, and the ways in which the 'traditional' teacher-fronted class layout has been adapted to different cultural conditions in widely differing environments. The three case studies reveal:

- a wide range of practices for managing space in whole-class teaching, from almost 'laissez-faire' in Indonesia to more structured in Vietnam;
- different interpretations of 'space' from the literal physical sense of space to Sullivan's more metaphorical interpretation, which also includes the sense of psychological and emotional learning space. The more holistic interpretation is attractive as it enables us to trace connections between the physical and the psycho-social;
- the effects of space management on classroom discourse. For example, it is sometimes constrained by a 'traditional' layout, and given greater freedom by the removal of barriers and creation of physical opportunities for inter-student communication. The Vietnamese study shows that regardless of spatial organisation, the group do not feel constrained to participate.

The practices that are described have emerged as a result of complex social and cultural forces. In some contexts, classroom communities have created what appear to be 'restricted' practices, which ensure that only a minority of the learners receive direct instruction, or engage in communication with the teacher. In other words, whole class teaching is a better description that whole class learning, because it is clear that in these classrooms, many do not participate, either because of learners' relative physical position or distance from the teacher or because of the discoursal practices that have evolved in response to the physical realities.

Alternative organisations of space for whole-class teaching

Whole-class teaching and learning is not managed only on the 'rows and desks' model. There are other common arrangements of space and furniture which position teachers and students in different ways (Quote 10.7 has examples). The adoption of these practices for managing classroom space, particularly the reconfiguration of furniture positions, for pedagogic or social reasons, has implications for the physical positioning of the teacher relative to students, 'zoning' of classroom activity and basic classroom proxemics. These may challenge local conventions and cultural views of teacher status and role if transferred to other contexts.

Quote 10.7   Richardson and Fallona on some alternative classroom layouts

1. Darlene's lessons

. . . students were sitting in 'prides' of four in clearly demarcated squares consisting of four desks. A curved reading desk is located at the side of the room . . .

. . . two rows of desks, pushed together, are placed around thee sides of the classroom, and the curved desk is in the middle of the classroom. Students are in groups of four (no longer called prides), but the groups are physically quite close to each other. (708)

2. Kia's lessons

. . . the tables built for two students were lined in horizontal rows facing the front of the room . . .

. . . one row of tables faced the front and two groups of six tables were located in the centre of the room.

(. . . along one wall of the classroom was a large fireplace in front of which was a large, brightly coloured carpet and some teaching equipment, including a large easel displaying several picture books'). (705)

(Richardson and Fallona 2001)

Appel (1995) notes in his diary the impact of such shifts in his English lessons at a German secondary school, although he at first underestimates their importance (Quote 10.8) and their effect on his students. Appel is keen

---

Quote 10.8   Appel on changing the shape of the class

Tina [a student] comes to me at the end of the lesson saying my classes are all about shifting furniture. This is what she is going to remember. I don't know what to say. Thinking about it later, Tina's statement sounds more positive than it had in class. Yes, moving tables takes time and persuasion. At the same time it is a powerful symbol, at least to me, of the fact that something can be changed in the classroom, even if it is just the way the tables are arranged.

(1995: 67)

to introduce more 'humanistic' classroom spatial organisations to facilitate language practice among his students, and to move away from more traditional patterns of behaviour. The changes are motivated by social as well as pedagogic reasons.

Appel later notes that the climate of the classroom has changed for the better and his role has also shifted, as 'the "frontal" part of the lesson is taken away from me for part of the lesson' (1995: 67). The change is perhaps more profound in the way it affects the atmosphere and discourse of his classroom, demonstrating that behind the symbolism of space are important messages about learning and social relations.

There are two main reasons for changing the classroom layout and seating arrangements. They are either **pedagogic** – to encourage student-student interaction for the purposes of *language* practice, for example; or **social** – to help foster better relationships between students, as seen in various forms of 'social learning' (Joyce et al. 1997). In language teaching, changes to classroom layouts as proposed by various versions of communicative language teaching (CLT) ranging from 'weak' to 'strong' (Howatt 1984) 1have been a source of controversy and difficulty for teachers and learners in many contexts. It is one of the canons of CLT that pair and small group work provide the settings for interactive communicative *spoken* practice of the target language among students (Quote 10.9). This practice has emerged organically in CLT (Knight 2001: 155). Successful communicative language teaching is grounded in the requirement for teachers to create the conditions in which learners will practice using the target language 'communicatively'. Many teachers regard the arrangement of students into pairs and small groups for this purpose as the central management task of CLT. From a classroom management perspective these alternatives have created both practical problems and ideological conflicts for teachers and learners more used to the 'rows and desks' model.

Quote 10.9   'Weak' versions of communicative language teaching

Pair Work

Students must [also] learn to relate language to the social meanings that it carries and to use it as a vehicle for social interaction. To this end, it is necessary to increase their sense of performing in a meaningful social context, rather than simply responding to prompts (from the teacher or in materials).

An initial step in this direction is to free the activity from dependence on teacher or tape, so that learners begin to interact as equal partners in an exchange, rather than reacting to stimuli. For example, after an initial period when they learn to make and reject suggestions under the teacher's control, they may be asked to interact in pairs.

(Littlewood 1981: 12)

Quote 10.9   (Continued)

Group Work
1. Increases student talking time
2. Provides opportunities for students to 'really use language to communicate with each other'.
3. Students are increasingly self-reliant and both learn and teach.
4. Can be better than pair work because

   – more people to interact with
   – greater chances that someone can find answers and solve problems
   – more relaxing: students not continuously active.

(Harmer 1991: 245–6)

For many language teachers working in 'large classes' these issues have become entangled with the fundamental physical difficulties of managing large numbers of students in confined spaces. Furthermore, such deviations from the traditional teacher-fronted classroom management pattern are typically associated with alternative pedagogic strategies, most notably those involving a degree of collaboration or inter-student communication. The 'traditional' classroom arrangement is fundamentally a context for transmission, led and directed by the teacher. These practices are the root of difficulties for teachers, students and school administrators (for example, Difeng Li 2001, Case Study 7). Changing classroom furniture may be prohibitively expensive, but such a move is predicated on whether or not the decision has been made to break up the traditional classroom layout. The question remains as to whether or not it is possible to innovate under such constraints, or even whether it is worth innovating. Some of the alternative classroom arrangements which are proposed by CLT are not in fact as controversial as many believe, as Thompson has argued, paving the way for more constructive dialogue on these issues (Quote 10.10).

Quote 10.10   Thompson on an alternative view of pair work

Instead of just seeing pair work as a useful follow-up, a way of getting *pair work* everyone practising at the same time after a new language point has been introduced, we can see it as a potential preliminary stage to any contribution from the learners. They can work together to do a grammatical exercise, solve a problem, analyse the new language structures in a text, prepare a questionnaire for other members of the class, or agree on the opinion they want to present to the class. Once pair work is seen as a preparation as well as (or more than) an end-point, the range of possibilities increases dramatically. It is less a question of: 'When in my lesson do I get to the freer practice stage so that I can fit in a role play in pairs?' and more a question of 'Is there any reason why I can't use pair work as part of whatever I'm planning to do now?' (Of course, one reason for not using it may be simply variety – even the best techniques can be overused.)

(1996: 13)

Case Study 7: Problems with grouping students (Difeng Li 2001)

This research was designed to understand South Korean secondary English teachers' responses to CLT and the difficulties they faced when trying to implement it in their classrooms. Li used a combination of questionnaires and semi-structured interviews with English teachers.

Main findings

- The teachers cited the students' resistance to class participation as a primary constraint in trying out CLT. Students had, after six years of schooling, become used to a more 'traditional' classroom pattern of activity, 'in which they sit motionless, take notes while the teacher lectures, and speak only when spoken to. After so many years in schooling in traditional settings, students rely on the teacher to give them information directly, making it very difficult to get the students to participate in class activities.' (2001: 157) Li, like other researchers, notices the connection between the physical layout of the classroom and pedagogy, and cites it as a cause of resistance.
- Large classes (48–50 students) were regarded as a major constraint on their attempts to use CLT. 'The teachers found it very difficult, if not entirely impossible, to use CLT with so many students in one class because they believed that oral English and close monitoring of class activities were essential in CLT' (2001: 158). Class size is seen to be a major constraint to implementing CLT, because teachers felt constrained to follow practices such as 'close monitoring' as part of the methodology.

One of Difeng Li's teacher respondents comments as follows: 'with so many students in one regular classroom, there is not even enough space for the students and the teacher to move around to carry out the communicative activities. Especially when the desks and stools are fixed to the floor, you cannot even move them' (2001: 158). Difeng Li's research provides further evidence for the connections between classroom layout and pedagogy, and also of the difficulties of changing to alternative methodologies because of previous acculturation to one spatial layout.

Case Study 8: Views of Southeast Asian second language teachers on groupwork – Jacobs and Ratmanida 1996

Jacobs and Ratmanida collected data from 31 teachers from six countries in Southeast Asia with the aim of eliciting their ideas about the appropriateness for their classroom contexts of placing students in small groups.

Seeking an understanding of the data, they examined 'cultural' factors, drawing on Hofstede's four dimensions of cross-cultural difference. Bearing in mind the issues raised regarding 'culture' in Chapter 4, some of these results may not be entirely helpful however. They also cite a study which identifies four arguments against group activities (Rodgers 1988, in Jacobs and Ratmanida) as existing evidence of attitudes in the region.

Findings
- Every informant reported using groups for at least 20 percent of class time, and all but one reported that the mode was 'generally successful in aiding learning' (1996: 111).
- Many of the teachers felt that 'lack of motivation to learn the target language' (1996: 111) was a major factor. However, this is not necessarily a problem of the group mode. But non-participation can prevent the activity from taking place at all, and the authors note a tendency by students to put pressure on the teacher to transmit, even when students are *positioned* in groups. This issue was also related to task difficulty and proficiency.
- Large numbers of students led to supervision problems. Breaking a class of 60 into groups of four created 'many groups to supervise'. The teachers felt that 'large classes exacerbate the management problems involved in group activities, such as getting students into and out of groups' (1996: 113).
- Many teachers regarded the physical conditions in which they were working as significant. Teachers made connections between wall thickness and noise levels as factors which inhibited group work. Where there were no walls or extreme crowding, again teachers reported difficulty in organising students into groups. Occasionally fixed furniture was reported as a cause of difficulty.
- The influence of the school administrators or inspectors was important – if they were in favour, teachers reported that there were more incentives to place students in groups.
- Some teachers noted a tension between communicative syllabus and activity design and the pressure to finish textbooks (the completion imperative again). Significantly, several noted that 'more material can be covered in a teacher-fronted mode' (1996: 114).
- Many felt that group work was 'culturally appropriate' as they felt their cultures to be cooperative. They also felt that teachers needed to endorse group activity and reduce uncertainty by circulating among the groups while students were working together.

The authors concluded that group work is indeed widely used in the Southeast Asian region, but that more needs to be known about what group work contributes to student learning. Questionnaires and interviews are valuable ways of gathering data on issues and for including teachers' and learners' voices in research on classroom management. However, there are limitations, mainly due to there being no way of assessing the veracity of what the teachers said in this study by observing them in action over an extended period of time to see if their actual practices corresponded with their espoused practices.

The evidence from the two case studies quoted is somewhat contradictory. One further issue to emerge from Jacobs and Ratmanida is that the influence of the school and educational authorities is an important influence on classroom practice in Southeast Asia, and further research on the use of groupwork might incorporate this dimension into its design to search for influences on practice from *outside* the immediate classroom.

Case Study 9: Classrooms in different contexts – Holliday 1997

Holliday, discussing innovation in traditional classroom settings, observes:

> Cultural continuity between communicative language teaching and more traditional forms is necessary if innovation is to succeed. This may be achieved in a variety of ways; but the maintenance of lecturer authority and status may be the key in university settings. (1997: 236)

The implication of 'cultural continuity' for managing classroom space is significant, and Holliday's study of six tertiary level English language classrooms in China and India highlights not only the variety of layouts that are possible for whole class teaching but also the flexibility of activity within the more conventional (rows/benches) layouts. Two of the classrooms he observed and recorded had variations on the 'horseshoe' arrangement (see Figure 10.3) but three had the typical rows-and-desks arrangement. What is more significant is that Holliday noticed more interaction between students in the rows/desks classrooms than in the horseshoes. The lecturers tended to remain at the front in all the lessons he observed, and they only ventured into the room 'occasionally' in these classrooms. He demonstrates the control and authority of the lecturers discoursally – 'in all the six lessons the teacher maintains a very strong position'; 'however, they manage their authority in different ways' (1997: 228). What is significant is that even in the less traditional classes, teachers still maintain discoursal control, indeed even in one lesson where students are grouped, where the teacher stands in the middle of the floor. He notes how lecturers move about to maintain their control of the discourse by positioning themselves physically so that the discourse is channelled through them. These 'communicative networks' (1997: 229) are an essential part of the fabric of these lessons, and 'control is therefore central to the fulfilment of communicative principles' (1997: 229). One classroom was laid out in small groups, with the lecturer positioned standing in the middle of the groups of students, directing the talk and channelling it as in the other classes. What is most significant is that Holliday does not see classroom seating arrangements as necessarily constraining the types of classroom discourse. Rather it is the way in which the teacher exploits his or her central role – thus meaningful interaction *is* possible in classrooms with rows. He concludes that 'the size or layout of the class... does not necessarily inhibit communicative involvement. The layout may indeed facilitate cultural continuity' (1997: 236), as Jacobs and Ratmanida's study hints.

Other research studies – exploring alternative seating plans

Holliday's and Jacobs and Ratmaninda's findings corroborate earlier conclusions drawn by Naidu et al. (1992) in the Indian setting. From a management perspective the key issue is for teachers operating in what they call 'interactive' mode, using the frontal position to stimulate and facilitate a range of interactions between students. This is what Sarwar (2001) did when introducing her large class of 100 + students to individualised learning. One technique she used was the creation of permanent small 'friendship' groups of four students who always sat together in a permanent seating arrangement. This proved an effective means of managing the continuation of activities out of class. It is not clear what the configuration of Sarwar's classroom space was – again it can be inferred that it was traditional. By making certain adjustments to this arrangement in the form of permanent small groups, in addition to other means of providing a greater sense of individuality, responsibility and choice, she felt that she had been able to change the role configuration in her class from traditional, in which 'the student is a passive learner as the teacher 'talks' without any interaction or break for the whole teaching period' (2001: 128), to gradually greater levels of independence.

Tsui (2003: 158) cites the case of Eva, a teacher who used group work in oral lessons, when she had extra physical space. The extra space was created by halving the class numbers, and thus providing more opportunities for oral English practice. Eva organised her students into five groups which she moved around her classroom to ensure that some groups did not sit at the back of the class all the time. She also asked students to form a horseshoe to enable them to see each other practising difficult aspects of pronunciation. Tsui (2003: 248) discusses the issue of teachers' use of group work and points out that the teachers use it for very different purposes (Quote 10.11). She claims that teachers' understanding of group work is an indicator of the extent of integration between classroom management and instructional objectives. There is also a degree of confusion in some of her case study teachers regarding the physical and pedagogic connotations of group work. This she believes is because the teachers in question still see learning as an individual matter rather than a collective activity.

Quote 10.11   Meanings and uses of group work

Marina – group work as a means of achieving instructional objectives. Tasks designed for group interaction. Outputs from group tasks shared in the whole group. Groups of 4–5. Grouping by turning chairs around.

Eva – group work as a means of realising personal conceptions of teaching and learning, but not always successfully Group's monitoring of use of English designed to increase responsibility for learning. Groups of six.

Genie – group work to give mutual support and provide a safe learning environment. Groups for double but single lessons because of time-consuming movement of desks. Large group numbers – seven – prevent proper student-student interaction. Students often doing individual work. Group seating rather than group work.

Ching – infrequent use of group work. Groups of 6 when used. Group work not seen as entirely beneficial. Realises differences between grouping and group work, but sees learning as primarily individual, as the educational culture of Hong Kong typically indicates.

(after Tsui 2003)

The central classroom management issues raised by the option of group work or pair work are practical – moving furniture and disruption and waste of time and extra noise and disturbance that this leads to, for example – and also, more fundamentally, located in individual teachers' beliefs about learning, and whether or not they subscribe to transmission or social-constructivist views of learning. The type of belief shift as described by Sarwar (2001) is necessary for change to occur. Otherwise, group work is simply a means of students sitting together in a different configuration to do individual work.

The conventional norm of classroom organisation, with its strong socio-cultural messages about issues such as teacher's status or classroom group solidarity (Sullivan 2000), is directly challenged by these alternative student groupings. These pose questions for:

- views of teaching and learning;
- the authority of teachers;
- school cultures, routines and organisation.

Classroom climate and discourse can be altered significantly when seating arrangements are changed. However, as well as a new pedagogic dynamic, a new social dynamic is created, despite teachers' preference for stability and 'normality' – or 'routine' (Prabhu 1992) – in most contexts. In this vein, arguing for a more 'appropriate' methodology in language teaching, Kramsch and Sullivan (1996) focus on the 'symbolic value' of language teaching. They argue that 'terms like 'communicative approach', 'learner-centredness' and 'group work' have long become for many non-native teachers and learners synonymous with progress, modernization and access to wealth' (1996: 200). However, the symbols have not always proved strong enough to entice teachers to depart from tried and trusted norms and rhythms of teaching.

For many language teachers worldwide, pair and group work (termed 'collective work' in this discussion) are seen as synonymous with 'communicative approaches' to language teaching. In CLT, teachers can elect to organise their student group in various ways which enable particular types of learning activity and communication pattern to occur. The possibilities include the following:

- Teachers may teach the whole class for part of a lesson, varying this with different groupings (e.g. students working individually, in pairs or small groups) within the whole class, typically in students' normal seating positions, or by moving furniture into configurations to enable pair and group work. Nolasco and Arthur (1988: 42–5) show how pair work can be introduced in classrooms by setting up exchanges across the classroom without disturbing seating arrangements. (Field Note 10.4 describes how a teacher in a large class successfully uses different layouts for different purposes in his classroom.) Asking students to face each other rather than the front, moving furniture around and reorganising seating arrangements are familiar landmarks in the territory of communicative language teaching. Nolasco and Arthur (1988: 81–3) regard pair and group work in promoting the types of interaction as essential to students, and present a number of alternative classroom arrangements which 'arrange the seating so that opportunities for student to student communication can be maximised' (1988: 82).
- The furniture may be rearranged so that the whole class is broken down into smaller groups on a permanent or semi-permanent basis or 'islands' – as described by Holliday (1997). Some classrooms are furnished with rearrangement in mind – light, easily transportable chairs and tables which fit together. In others, teachers are forced to improvise if they wish groups to work together.

Field Note 10.4   Using different classroom layouts (Secondary English, Cameroon)

The usual 80–90 kids packed into rows of benches and desks. Four or five to a bench. Last period of the day. Quite hot and humid. Kids are late from the sports field. The first 20 minutes of the class are question-and-answer with a lot of board work showing examples of the use of the present simple. T's already taught it this week. Now he's following up:

T moves the lesson forward to today's topic. They spend a lot of time in question and answer. T cajoles and badgers the students into answering. But there's a good atmosphere. They are eating out of the palm of his hand. The topic is set up, and then group work starts.

> T: we have already/exhausted twenty minutes of our time before we've really begun/ and we have very little time left/but I want you/just on your desks/right
>
> Ss: yes
>
> T: get your grammar exercise books/take note of what we've been doing in the simple present and the past tense – uh
>
> Ss: yes
>
> T: then discuss among yourselves/choose a friend/it may be in this class or somewhere/ say what he always and give examples of what/give examples to/support/your general statement about the friend/right/uh/okay/just bring out your exercise books (*class noise: 5 secs*) I don't want you to break into your groups/it will take a lot of time (*class noise: 10 secs*) you see you have got some words expressions there/you may have a friend who is – being lazy/careless/generous/quarrelsome/great
>
> The kids swing into action facing each other bench by bench to form groups of 6–8. They soon get started on the task. Teacher squeezes down the rows to monitor and prompt. One or two children ask procedural and vocabulary questions.

Second language acquisition research (e.g. 'pushed output' Long (1996), the 'interaction hypothesis' (e.g. Pica 1994) and the role of comprehensible input in student group interaction) has further tended to favour small group work as the most appropriate way of teaching and learning languages. However, Breen (2001), in an extensive review of the SLA research, points out that a focus solely on interaction without a broader socio-affective focus is likely to be misleading. The SLA research tends to support purely *pedagogic* reasons for changing classroom layouts. Approaches to language teaching which, on the other hand, draw from traditions of cooperative and collaborative learning (e.g. Kohonen 1999 – experiential language learning) have fused the pedagogic and social aspects of teaching and learning by identifying the small group as the central classroom learning unit. The types of negotiated curriculum suggested by contributors to Breen and Littlejohn (2000) raise space management-related issues in the implementation of these ideas in terms of 'ways of working': 'Who will work with whom? (the teacher with the class, a group or an individual? the students in groups, in pairs or alone?)' (2000: 31).

As these practices are adopted by increasing numbers of teachers in different contexts, there is a clear need for further research on the ways in which teachers and learners manage classroom space in these configurations.

Using vertical space

Apart from whether or not classroom participants stand or are seated, most of our concerns about the use of classroom space are concerned with the use of the floor space, or horizontal aspects. The vertical dimension is, however, potentially significant. The use of vertical space for display and, more significantly, the 'board' space in a classroom are both aspects of the management of classroom space.

Field Note 10.5   A professional development course in Swaziland

It is the first time we ask the group, now broken into smaller groups despite the crowdedness of the Domestic Science room with its kitchen equipment and surfaces, to do posters. The task is to collect together an initial list of constraints to change in Swazi Primary Schools. After 30 minutes, the posters are displayed on the wall, covering the posters on food hygiene and nutrition. There is a sense of excitement as the participants now circulate and look at the other groups' efforts, noting differences and similarities with their own. In the plenary session, again seated, there is frequent reference to the posters which are at the sides and back of the room, even to the extent of participants getting up and identifying issues on the posters. Participants also make asides about size of lettering and layout. Instead of being focused on the tutors, the session now focuses on the posters.

After two weeks the classroom is prepared for the coming term's work at the College. The posters are taken down over the weekend. Participants are aghast on the Monday morning when they see their posters have gone. They are rescued from the untidy heap they have been left in and re-erected. At the end of the course, some participants ask if they can take the posters home with them as study aids, even though the contents of many have been recycled in the form of study notes and task sheets. This causes some difficulty of ownership, but a compromise is reached, and the posters taken away.

Field Note 10.5 shows how use of the wall space as a display area quickly enables participants to feel a sense of ownership over their classroom space. Classrooms are typically impersonal or even dull places in which to work, but the use of walls and notice boards for display adds a further dimension to learning opportunity and also, enables the sort of sharing of resources which is otherwise impossible. Establishing a sense of ownership over the classroom through use of the wall spaces with student work, no matter how untidy or graphically limited, is an important psychological step. Putting up posters on the classroom walls can also brighten the environment in small but significant ways.

Classroom wall spaces can be used for several purposes, for example:

- Permanent displays of information (for example, the 'Spanish Room' – if this is institutional practice – can be decorated with artefacts and texts from Spanish and Latin American sources both for colour and information). These provide alternative points of focus and can also provide useful information.
- Temporary displays – e.g. posters, photographs – of on-going work by a group. These are useful as a record of work done, and a point of reference in learning sequences.

All uses of wall space have the potential to provide colour and decoration in even the dullest and most miserable classroom. This can positively influence well-being, and if produced by students, certainly add to a sense of achievement and investment in the space.

The 'board' – blackboard, chalkboard or whiteboard – is a central feature in classrooms all over the world. It is often the only vertical pedagogic area in a classroom. Its position in the 'front' zone of the class, and its semi-exclusive use by the teacher serve to emphasise its role as an extension of the teacher's position. Because of its centrality, and because teachers use it to amplify and exemplify their messages, it is a potentially very influential vertical space. The quality of its use varies enormously, however, from hasty semi-legible scrawls to well-organised and clear writing and diagrammatic use of the space. In contexts where the board is often a substitute for a book because of shortages, what the teacher puts on the board for students to copy is of paramount importance. If it is illegible or unhelpfully organised, it may serve to 'teach' errors or reinforce already existing ones (van Lier's description in Quote 10.6). The fixed position of the typical board does, however, emphasise the frontal origin of information and expertise, and, when considering alternatives to frontal use of the classroom, its influence needs to be remembered. Work on the multi-modality of pedagogy (Kress et al. 2001) emphasises the importance of non-verbal and non-talk-related aspects of classroom life. Studies of how, for example, the board is integrated into language teachers' pedagogic routines, and the influence of wall space on students' learning, promise helpful insights into a relatively neglected area of classroom management.

Summary

The management of classroom space influences:

- Interaction patterns;
- Teacher/student relationships and student/student relationships;
- Classroom atmosphere;
- Learning opportunity;

and is influenced by:

- Social and cultural conventions;
- Views of 'good practice';
- Institutional/systemic constraints';
- Contingencies of classroom life.

The management of classroom space is, in general, an under-researched area. More recent incorporation of ethnographic and social representations of classroom life into the research (for example, Holliday 1994; Coleman et al. 1996; van Lier 1996; Canagarajah 1999; Norton 2000) have of necessity included rich descriptions of the spatial aspects of classroom contexts featuring analyses of how the ways in which classroom space is managed are related to pedagogy. For example, the survival of the IRF exchange pattern in alternative seating arrangements such as 'islands' reported by Holliday (1997) provides an interesting insight into the routinisation of the exchange pattern, and its deep cultural roots in the use of classroom space. Further research which began from the study of the management of classroom space and its effects on participants' learning and teaching would be a valuable addition to the growing body of knowledge on learning and teaching in formal settings. It would also provide the basis for appraisal of propositions that less formal and extramural contexts are more effective locations for learning and teaching.

10.3   Extending classroom time and space: classrooms without walls

---

Field Note 10.6   Zocalo, Mexico City – project work

I am in the Zocalo [central square] when I'm approached by three teenage girls. 'Excuse me can we ask you some questions?' I agree. One reads from her notebook 'Which country are you from?' 'I'm from England.' 'England! Not the United States?' 'No, England.' The questions develop into a dialogue when they discover I'm an English teacher. They tell me they're doing a project from English lessons at school to try to interview a foreigner or two.

Classroom time is routinely extended into time which is managed by the students themselves. Activities like 'homework', 'study time' and 'project work' all imply a certain degree of time management by learners. As Field Note 10.6 illustrates, an extension of classroom time can also entail going outside classroom space to continue or complete work begun in the classroom. Recent technological developments have further enabled people to enter formal learning programmes which are completely outside conventional educational time and space.

Homework

Traditionally, homework has been the main means of extending class time, and into non-classroom space. Studies of homework are few and far between, although in many contexts, the bureaucratisation of homework through its inclusion on school timetables, and thus its potential intrusion into students' backstage time, has made the need for studies all the more urgent. Homework tasks are typically set in the classroom and completed by students in their own time. While the teacher might be able to influence the pace and on task behaviour if the students were present, when they are not in class this is more or less impossible, and standardisation of the task is thus likely to be unattainable. Case Study 10, a socio-cultural study of the experience of homework conducted in a small number of primary and secondary schools in the West of England, illustrates the value of investigating such a common-place but little understood practice.

Case Study 10: Homework – Hughes and Greenhough 2003

Aims of research   The researchers were interested in exploring the contribution that homework makes to student learning. In theoretical terms they were interested in the 'boundaries' between home and school; and homework is a practice that crosses boundaries, which students cross routinely, but parents do not.

Main findings
- A range of homework tasks was set by teachers, from practice of material covered or demonstrated in class, to more creative writing and language-based activity, to work with 'real world' materials.
- Most homework tasks were done alone, with occasional collaboration from parents or siblings.
- Many parents were positive about homework and saw it as a useful extension of school and also an opportunity for students to work independently. Parents were often unable to help. The authors also note that 'homework could founder in the gulf between the everyday understandings of the home and the more technical language of the classroom' (2003: 187).
- Teachers had mixed feelings about homework: they saw it as building on class work, providing practice opportunities, consolidation periods and was essential for completing the curriculum. On the other hand they disliked the way it was imposed and how they were locked into schools' homework timetables, against the 'natural need' to set homework.
- Students had various views ranging from positive, helping them learn and providing something to do at home. Some however were unsure of its purpose and saw it as an encroachment of their private time.

Broad conclusions
1. Homework tasks are too similar to formal school learning and do not take advantage of the more informal learning environment provided by the home.
2. Homework is too much of an individual chore, and might be more productive done collectively.

'... homework has obtained some kind of symbolic value, in which layers of meaning and expectation have been placed upon what is essentially a straightforward, if rather mundane practice.' (2003: 191). However, our knowledge of how this extension of classroom time is experienced by learners, and the values it is ascribed by teachers and students is limited. North and Pillay (2002) also analyse the use and value of homework in the Malaysian context, and provide insights into the 'management' aspects of the practice.

Project work

The growth of approaches to learning and teaching such as 'project work' (Concept 10.4), 'portfolio work' and 'experiential learning' approaches such as work-based learning (Weil and McGill 1989) has been another way in which the time and space of the classroom has been transcended with technologies which pre-date ICT.

Concept 10.4　Some alternatives to classroom learning

1. **Independent learning** – learners are offered control of the learning process, typically with a learning contract. Topics and situations are of learners' choosing. Often uses 'problem-solving' and project-based methods.
2. **Work and community placement** – includes apprenticeship, shadowing activity, mentoring and work in a relevant environment.
3. **Project-based learning** – a structured learning experience in which students select topics, perform tasks like data-gathering, design or research. Activity-based learning is another type of experiential learning, including classroom-based activity such as practicals and simulations under teacher supervision.

Problem-based learning is broadly similar to project-based learning, except that it is designed to solve real-world problems.

(after Weil and McGill 1989)

The project work conducted by Carter and Thomas (1986), for example, is a classic example of extending the classroom into another environment for the purposes of engagement of the students in different types of learning experience, closer to the 'real world' of interpersonal communication. In these pedagogies, tasks set in the classroom require students, either individually or collectively, to 'gather data' outside the classroom. Data are processed both outside and inside the classroom, as described by Legutke (1995), necessitating in his view new metaphors for the classroom.

Quote 10.12　Legutke on new metaphors for the classroom

The Classroom as an Observatory

... classrooms can be seen as an observatory from which both teacher and student look out into the world in many different ways using different media in order to gather data which are brought back to the classroom. Data are derived from direct and mediated encounters.

(1995: 15)

The 'observatory' (drawing on Breen and Candlin 1980, Quote 10.12) is arguably the most apposite when considering how classroom time and space can be both extended and inner and outer interwoven during learning activity. Project work done outside the classroom is always processed and managed from the classroom as a 'base' (Quote 10.13). Work completed outside is often presented in class in a subsequent session – either orally, in written form, or as a display or presentation of some type. The opportunities for learning created by breaking time barriers are, in theory, greatly increased; the type and quality of learning depend on the nature and quality of the activity itself and how students themselves manage it. Most students require periods of learner training (Ellis and Sinclair 1996), and Legutke and Thomas (1991) observe that an important component of learners' process competence similarly enables them to manage their own time successfully. Teachers need to learn how to manage 'extra-mural' student work and how to support their students who are engaged in work outside classroom walls in self-managed time.

The virtual classroom – beyond time and space?

Online learning environments challenge the links between the physical embodiment of an institution and its educational practices and the learners. New configurations of learners in 'virtual space' are emerging. Learners now work at home or where there is access to the Internet, often thousands of miles from the institution which provides the educational experience. New learning and management practices are also emerging. Research into this new educational world is also new, but growing rapidly. Areas of focus include:

- the effect cognitively and affectively of asynchronous learning, often across time zones (Chapters 11 and 12);
- the effect on learning of there being no physical manifestation of the classroom space;
- the benefits of working in online learning communities.

The technology enables new uses of time, and communication can be both synchronous (in real time) or asynchronous. A large proportion of web-based learning is asynchronous. Only deadlines and start/finish dates appear to be significant. Otherwise the learners are fairly free to organise their own study time. The technology also transcends space. With no physical classroom, learners are, in theory, isolated from one another. However, the phenomenon of the online learning community is now being recognised as a key aspect of virtual learning. Even though they have no physical setting, learners tend to 'cluster' through their regular communication patterns. Online learning environments are also full of spatial metaphors – 'discussion forum', 'café area', 'chat room' – and so on, presumably to compensate for the lack of physical space, and to acknowledge learners' need for togetherness.

Procedures for investigating these and other phenomena in the world of online learning differ from those used in face-to-face settings only in the way that the medium generates data. For example, online learning is currently dominated by written language, and much of the data is gathered in written form, or by survey at distance.

Case Study 11: Teachers' and learners' perspectives on online courses – Lindh and Soames 1994

The authors were interested in finding out how teachers and learners experienced online learning and whether they perceived similar advantages and disadvantages in online learning.

Procedures   It was important for the researchers to work with a student insider (who was also gathering research data) who administered questionnaires pre- and post-course. 19 students started the course; ten finished.

Significant findings

- The researchers established that many left the programme because they preferred to work alone, whereas the course contained a fairly large number of group activities, often with difficult instructions. Despite geographical independence being a major advantage of working online, many students left because the type of learning experience afforded by the medium did not suit them.
- A learning community did not form because there had been no face-to-face meetings prior to the course. Many students would not take the initiative to work collaboratively online.
- It was difficult for the teacher to provide feedback to all learners at the same time, and he found it very stressful and time-consuming keeping track of the learners. Learners complained that they had to wait for feedback which they would normally have received instantly in a classroom.
- Some students found the freedom and privacy of online learning to their liking. Whereas in classrooms the 'noisy' ones might have been judged as greedy in their use of time, online they were free to indulge, and found they had more human contact than on other courses.

The primary conclusion is that 'it is important to establish a virtual place where students can meet together on group assignments in privacy, and that they need a reason to come back to the web page – the content must be "sticky"'. (Ways of achieving this are by constantly updating the content of a website, and providing new tasks on a regular basis.)

From teachers' perspectives the major issue is the amount of time they must spend monitoring and participating in activity in online courses. From the learners' perspective, occupying virtual space in the company of others appears to be a divisive issue. Interestingly, differences between learners which are apparent in face-to-face classroom sessions where learners may occupy particular spaces to gain advantage or to hide are replicated and even amplified online, where the pressure to work collectively may be very strong, as course designers try to compensate for the lack of physicality by insisting on collaborative work.

Summary

There is a relative dearth of research into the ways in which time and space are managed in and out of the classroom, as extensions of classroom activity, or 'virtual' classroom activity. While online learning has generated a large number of studies in recent years, prompted largely by its novelty and the need to evaluate its effectiveness, research on time and space use in conventional classrooms is urgently required. The effects of time and space on patterns of participation and engagement are apparent from existing studies, greater depth and range are needed. One suspects that the 'raw' experience of cramped classrooms, or hurried classroom sessions, and the ways in which classroom management discourses are woven into these practices are highly significant in coming to an understanding of the nature of this experience and its effects on the quality of classroom life.

11
Managing Engagement

The concern for 'care' in the classroom discussed in Chapter 6 gives rise to a variety of management practices and activities. Some of these operate at the macro level of classroom management – for example, conscious decisions to implement particular 'humanistic' values or a 'philosophy' of care. Others relate to the planning of activity in long-term schemes of work or more immediately in lessons. Most, however, are improvised spontaneously during real time classroom activity. Research and practice in the affective domain naturally begins at the classroom level and will be enhanced by the incorporation of data from the meso and macro levels to understand practices.

Research on the management of engagement in classroom life is relatively sparse in comparison with the amount of discussion of affective issues, or the availability of learning materials which explicitly focus on this domain. This may be because of the 'softness' of the data, or the perceived lack of linguistic indices of affective involvement. Chapter 6 identified areas where there is promise of further work (e.g. 'affective markers') however. There is a vast terrain to explore, and the tools are available. The case studies reported in this chapter show the directions in which we can journey.

11.1 Creating and managing classroom climate

Concept 11.1 Creating and managing classroom climate

... the social-affective climate' is 'a result of the individual behaviour of all those participants in the learning process, and is an expression of their relationships.
(Legutke and Thomas 1991: 68)

- CREATING TRUST – seen as fundamental to successful learning
- DEALING WITH POWER – basic part of teacher's managerial role

(see Underhill 1989 on four types of power in the classroom) (Concept 11.5)
- FACILITATING the LEARNING PROCESS – part of teachers' process competence. Involves setting tasks, conducting feedback etc.

(after Legutke and Thomas (1991: 291–4)

The spread of 'humanistic' practices in English language teaching during the 1970s and 1980s focused attention on the affective domain, and classroom practitioners opened debate on many salient issues regarding its management. There has been a subsequent growth of consensus that the 'climate' constitutes the foundation of classroom learning activity. Areas such as trust and power, and changed teachers' roles have been highlighted by these developments. (Concept 11.1) Research directions are suggested by the following:

1. The definitively social and emotional nature of classroom encounters – the 'group experience' – is at the core of many classroom management practices.
2. It is widely recognised that positive emotional states are conducive to learning, so close are the connections between cognition and affect.
3. The emotional-affective states of participants contribute to and are an outcome of the social life of a classroom group and constitute a further element of the complex social-psychological world that is created.

We have seen that classrooms are highly complex settings. A major contributory factor is that so much of what happens there is internal to the individual. Behaviour is not always a reliable guide to internal states, and for all classroom participants 'reading the signs' is a continuous process. The 'climate' (atmosphere or 'tone': Allwright and Bailey 1991: 19) of a classroom cannot therefore easily be described or analysed with any degree of objective certainty because it is *'felt'* and experienced by participants and visitors subjectively, and quite unconsciously and instinctively. For example, Allwright and Bailey (1991: 21) describe a visitor to a classroom group as having 'an opportunity to get a feeling for the *general classroom atmosphere*' (author's emphasis), which they acknowledge is fairly enigmatic. This poses problems for research into the affective domain in the classroom. Despite the limitations imposed by the domain, classroom observation and description is the basis for research, but investigation will also have to 'go below the surface' and gain access to teachers' and learners' feelings, thoughts, memories and values, attitudes and beliefs (VABs) in order to build a complete picture.

Field Note 11.1   Young adults, mixed. UK Private language school

The students (12) are asked to put their desks to the side of the room and to form a circle with their chairs. The teacher puts his chair in the circle. 'Can we close up the circle a bit?' Students shuffle forward. 'OK. So how did you like doing that activity?' (A role play with one person apologising to another for inadvertently offending them has just finished.) There is a long pause – 30 seconds or more. A student looks up and catches the teacher's eye. 'Yes Marcus.' 'I was getting angry at one time.' The teacher asks the student to say more. 'Yes, I felt like he [*gestures to his neighbour*] was really insulting me, and was, like, myself.' 'I felt a bit like that too,' says another student. 'I wonder how many others felt like that,' asks the teacher. More than half the group raise their hands. 'Is that a bad thing then?' asks the teacher. 'Not really. Perhaps I was more, how can you say, myself?'

In Field Note 11.1, we see a teacher and his class focusing directly on the affective domain, by responding publicly and collectively to a role play activity which has an affective element. The teacher encourages the students to disclose their emotional responses to the activity. (As a by-product of this work students are also engaging in genuine language practice, exploring feelings and reactions in the target language.) The classroom layout has been changed to a circle for this phase of the lesson, and the teacher has joined the students in the circle. Knowing why the teacher adopted this configuration would be valuable data. The fragments of talk that have been recorded reveal an open-ended pattern of contributions. Students self-nominate and signal their willingness to participate by catching the teacher's eye. The teacher prompts students to give personal responses, and encourages contingency by asking them to develop their contributions. The discussion shows no signs of being pre-planned, and the teacher's response to a declaration of anger is spontaneous – he could not have known in advance that this contribution would be forthcoming. Readers might infer a 'warm' climate from this description, despite there being relatively little specific data about factors like the posture, tones of voice, facial expressions and so on of the participants. We are perhaps justified in assuming that the climate must be good for the teacher to have attempted such a risky and potentially 'difficult' activity. But we cannot rely too heavily on inference if we are to fully understand this 'slippery' dimension of classroom life.

In order to develop our understanding of this and other classroom events in the affective domain, we can record classroom activities and explore the transcripts for 'affective markers' (Chapter 6, section 6.4). Photographs or video footage would provide data of physical responses to activities, and also be interesting to share with students and teachers to elicit information about their states during the encounter, as well as to inform 'outsider' perspectives.

In order to go further, though, we need to gain access to the participants' inner selves. We could interview the teacher to test Allwright and Bailey's proposition that 'most teachers have a good idea of the sort of 'atmosphere' they would like to have in their classrooms, and do their best to plan to set up such an atmosphere (whether they want it relaxed and friendly, or brisk and business-like, or whatever)' (1991: 22). We can also solicit learners' views on the emotional climate of their classroom and their engagement in activity in similar ways.

The affectively-oriented classroom management practices we might explore in these ways are summarised in Concept 11.2. These practices are simultaneously enabling – creating the climate – and *facilitating*, a combination of responding and channelling behaviours (Quote 11.1) – the type of behaviour exhibited by the teacher in Field Note 11.1. A facilitator 'actively pays attention to the psychological learning atmosphere and the inner processes of learning on a moment by moment basis, with the aim of enabling learners to take as much responsibility for their own learning as they can' (Underhill 1999: 126). The way in which a teacher manages participation and engagement through talk is therefore a central, if unexplored area of classroom management. Pedagogy and engagement are always interwoven, a feature that is made explicit in classroom encounters when attention is given to the affective domain. This concerns the types of activity chosen by teachers, the ways in which they are managed, and whether or not the emotional dimension of an activity is the content ('strong' affect) or built into procedures such as seeking feedback from students on their feelings about an activity.

Concept 11.2   Managing classroom climate

Managing classroom climate involves the following interrelated areas, aimed at establishing and maintaining a POSITIVE emotional climate and diminishing NEGATIVE emotions:

Control: Keeping order and calm when required; disciplining: dealing with disruptive individuals, conflicts etc. Prohibiting or preventing students from interacting with each other. Maintaining order so that students can interact with each other in ways that can create learning opportunity.

Social relations in the class: Establishing and maintaining social relations individually and collectively – greetings/leave-taking, naming, finding out about individuals, socialising (revealing material about self) This also includes –

   Groupings: Using different social groupings (creating potential arenas for communication and learning) (See also Chapter 7) and

   Interaction: Helping students interact with each other; group-forming, building etc.

Concept 11.2   (Continued)

Creating and developing continuity: Maintaining and encouraging 'the long conversation' (developing a sense of continuity to the experience and belonging through the history of a group's work together).

Support for learners: Providing support for learners through various means – encouragement, praise, challenge, feedback, a sense of achievement and progress, listening, helping students build resilience and confidence (emotional feedback and support: use of authority to proscribe negative behaviours such as laughing at mistakes).

Learner motivation: Helping students build motivation, sense of identity, self-awareness.

Quote 11.1   Underhill on facilitation

[Facilitation is] a triple area of expertise, consisting of my knowledge of the subject matter, my skilful use of teaching methods, and my developing capacity to generate a psychological climate conducive to high-quality learning. My enlarged equation connecting people and learning embraces the psychological learning atmosphere itself, which in turn contains all the work we do on language and all the learning techniques we use. This new equation includes the relationships in and between people in the group, the degree of security felt by individuals, the sensitivity of the trainer to undercurrents, the quality of listening and acceptance, the possibility of non-judgmental interaction, the way the needs for self-esteem are met, and so on. It also includes the issue of power, that is who makes the decisions, how, and about what and who carries them out.
(1999: 130)

Managing the group

The creation of a cohesive and supportive group is regarded as a central management task in creating a warm classroom climate, and also, for some practitioners, a way of forestalling any problems of discipline and control. The recent developments in language teaching away from a preoccupation with teacher-led teacher-student interaction, prompted by the growth of CLT and the necessity for student-student interaction and cooperation, has prompted a corresponding interest in practices focused directly on the management of classroom climate. In this context, there has been widespread discussion on how different types of interaction in groups can benefit learning. However, this is unlikely to be a consensus view. Holliday (1994: 53) identifies the 'learning group ideal' which he argues 'sets the conditions for a process-oriented, task-based, inductive, collaborative, communicative English language teaching methodology' (1994: 54). Creating a warm and 'caring and sharing' classroom climate is thus a primary management goal for a teacher in this type of classroom, where such conditions foster particular types of interaction. The 'learning group ideal' may, however, be a peculiarly Western notion, and practices which have evolved and which work in Western educational contexts like private language schools with small, multilingual classroom groups may not be 'appropriate' in other contexts, in particular where traditions of transmission thrive, or where teachers are supposed to 'keep their distance' from students.

One difference between 'weak' and 'strong' versions of CLT (Howatt 1984) is that weak versions (Littlewood et al. 1981) recommend small group work to practice language without teachers' direct involvement, whereas strong versions (Breen et al. 1987) see learning groups and their processes as the *central focus* of language learning. Despite these evident differences, adoption of even a weak version of CLT in various contexts has not always been successful. Chapter 10 has cited studies from South Korea (Li 2001) and Southeast Asia (Jacobs and Ratmaninda 1996) which offer evidence of teachers' difficulties in introducing group modes of work in their lessons. Various rationales are offered for this, but none in the affective domain, where the real difficulties might lie.

Creating 'good groups'

Even if teachers are not intending to invite students to participate in pair and small group work in the classroom, the establishment of a good climate is still regarded as vital, and the process of 'group formation' central to good climate. A useful way of looking at learning groups is through an intrinsic/extrinsic division of the aims and purposes of group activity (Jacques 1991). This division is mapped in Concept 11.3, and provides a way of examining language teaching practices. Intrinsic group tasks are those in which the means and the ends are congruent – students do the task for social and emotional as well as the cognitive benefits. The *process* of classroom activity is the focus. Extrinsic group aims are essentially product-focused and internally linked to the tasks themselves, although Jacques argues that even externally-oriented tasks can also support deeper affective aims. For example, following up a lecture with a group discussion of feelings during and after a lecture as a prelude to processing the content.

Jacques' practices emerge from the context of higher education teaching in the UK, but have implications for language teaching practice anywhere. The central issue regarding groups and groupings in language teaching depends on whether a grouping of students is simply a mechanism for locating and 'forcing' language practice or whether it is intended to fulfil wider social and emotional aims in the classroom, such as providing mutual emotional support for students, helping to build self-confidence and the wider aims of 'emotional literacy' (Goleman 1995).

Concept 11.3   Aims and purposes of group work

INTRINSIC (process-directed)

Affective Aims	*Task Aims/Types*
Greater sensitivity to others	Expressing selves in subject
Judging self in relation to others	Judging ideas in relation to others
Encouraging self-confidence	Examining assumptions
Personal development	Listening attentively
Tolerating ambiguity	Tolerating ambiguity
Awareness of others' strengths/weaknesses	Learning about groups

EXTRINSIC (product-directed)

Affective Aims	*Task Aims/Types*
Giving support to learning	Follow up to lecture
Stimulating to further work	Understanding text
Evaluating student feelings about course	Improving teacher/student relations
Giving students identifiable groups	Gauging progress of students

---

Case Study 1: Building and managing classroom groups – Senior 1999, 2002

Senior's research in Australia provides valuable insights into management of the affective domain. In the earlier study, she aimed to find out the perceptions of 28 experienced English teachers (predominantly female) regarding the nature of 'good' English classes, using open-ended questionnaires and extensive interviews.

The 'bonded' class   Senior uses the metaphor of 'bonding' to account for the teachers' emotional attachment to their classes, the underlying notion of friendship, and also to capture the idea of the teacher as an integral part of the class – as a 'friendly and accessible helper' (1999: 4) but also slightly distanced because of their position of authority.

Her research establishes that the teachers believe that a 'good' class depends on the level of cooperation and cohesion between members, and that the 'single, unified classroom group' is the ideal (confirming Holliday's speculations). The teachers also saw this a necessary precondition for the development of proficiency through oral practice. She reports preliminary confirming evidence from students of their liking for a 'relaxed' and emotionally 'safe' classroom climate, where they feel free to practice without fear of ridicule. Senior also explores eight facets of the group bonding process:

1. *Breaking down barriers* – sharing individual students' personal information in ice-breakers: disclosure and recall, especially in the initial classroom encounters.
2. *Creating the climate* – teachers make deliberate mistakes: to develop an atmosphere of relaxation and safety in the classroom, modelling a relaxed and safe environment.
3. *Convincing the customers* – self-disclosure of professional competence and experience: e.g. invite personal questions from a group at the beginning of a course. Initial challenges to teachers' competence were reported in the data.
4. *Defining directions* – developing common course goals with a group, even if they are relatively unmotivated. Teachers reported that this contributed to bonding.
5. *Harnessing the headstrong* – dealing with difficult students: giving specific roles for group-building ends, such as good students supporting weaker students.
6. *Establishing expectations* – teacher discloses expectations about classroom behaviour as part of building group internal discipline of self and other-regulation. The data reports some dilemmas for students unused to a liberal atmosphere.
7. *Recognising roles*– teachers acknowledge that each group member has a unique role in the group and that their contributions or behaviour are learning opportunities. Over time, shyer students are drawn into the group in different ways.
8. *Maintaining momentum* – the data indicate that groups do not always remain bonded or productive, and that teachers pay attention to this by, for example, renegotiating goals.

In a subsequent paper (Senior 2002) she explores eight intensive English classes for adult learners from various cultural backgrounds. Her aim was to follow the social development of each class from the first to last sessions of their courses. The data were gathered in weekly observations, weekly interviews with the teachers and questionnaires. Senior also interviewed all the students. Her main findings were:

- Teachers were very concerned with the general atmosphere of their classes.
- Teachers often made spontaneous classroom management decisions 'according to what seemed to be right for their class at a particular time' (2002: 398). Such practices including allowing students a few minutes to relax and reinvigorate, or to pay special attention to individuals in agitated emotional states.

- Teachers set up learning tasks to accommodate both social and pedagogic priorities. These included brainstorms, group listening, collaborative checking of answers to exercises, quiet independent classroom work, oral presentations and whole-class information-gathering tasks.

She concludes that the teachers in her study based much of their classroom management and pedagogic behaviour on an 'intuitive understanding' of group development processes and principles.

A further significant aspect of Senior's work is that the teachers in her study were working with multinational and multilingual groups, comprising members who were not familiar with the 'liberal' climate in which they were learning English. The cross-cultural and gender issues are hinted at in her work, and might be the basis of important further research, which examines 'cultural' aspects of engagement, and also contributes to understanding the process of affective enculturation. Ways of building on Senior's work following a group and creating its 'history' from the different perspectives of teacher and learners could entail examination of classroom transcripts to search, for example, for evidence of how teachers worked to help groups bond, and students' positive and negative responses. Other documentary sources could include a teaching log and student learning logs or diary entries.

Dealing with 'troubles': from control to care

The various dimensions of an understanding of care and control in the classroom are summarised in Figure 11.1. Management practice is somewhere on a continuum of control and care. Control involves coercion and the discourse of 'commanding'. In this position, teachers exercise power, and students are not required to take responsibility. Care reverses these tendencies.

CONTROL		CARE
Coercion		Cooperation
−	Learner Responsibility	+
+	Teacher Exercise of Power	−
COMMANDING		NEGOTIATING

Figure 11.1   Dimensions of power and control in the classroom

Senior's (1999) work on the affective domain identifies issues of classroom order and control, particularly at the initial stages of a group's life. Managing these incidents provides teachers with some of their greatest challenges, which are further amplified if new pedagogic practices are being introduced. Because various interpretations of the 'opportunity' school of classroom management invite a degree of surrender of teacher's control over students' behaviour, coercion has to give way to persuasion and to negotiation, a move towards care in McLaughlin's (1991) sense. A 'cooperative imperative' infuses the management discourse implying that the main outcome of any lesson is the mutual benefit of all members of the learning group, and that behaviour which prevents this cannot be sanctioned. For example, setting up interactive work between students requires calm and order, and when teachers give instructions for activities they exercise their right to impose order if necessary so that the instructions can be heard. To hear a teacher in a transmission class, the students must be silent 'to gain the knowledge'; in an activity-centred lesson, students must be silent in order for the teacher to explain what they have to do when they work together. Problems occur if, for example, a teacher tries to impose order when self-control might be more appropriate or if students challenge or dispute a teacher's right to impose order. In these instances, the climate can lurch into conflict, and a negative emotional ambience.

On other occasions, students want to 'test' a teacher's resolve or their professional competence. 'Discipline' problems result, as the example from Appel's (1995) valuable study of a language teacher's life shows.

Case Study 2: a 'discipline' problem – Appel 1995

Appel is describing the early years of his teaching career in a large secondary school in Germany. His study is based on a diary he kept during this period, from which he quotes extracts or constructs incidents. As many novice teachers would testify, establishing order in a class is often the main preoccupation at the outset of a career.

> It had taken a long time to establish any order and I had just about succeeded in getting them to do an exercise when a boy from the second row of seats got up to open the window. The windows are, admittedly, difficult to open. The boy was pulling it very hard but did not manage to open it. Meanwhile the class's interest had switched to him. They started to laugh. The more he struggled with the window, the more hysterical their laughter became. At that point I lost my nerve. I could not face another round of calming them down. Something drastic had to be done. I wrote the name of the boy who had gone to the window in the register (which means there will be some disciplinary consequence) and sent him out of the classroom. (Appel 1995: 8)

Appel remarks that in his early days as a language teacher, most of the unpredictability and stresses of teaching arose from discipline problems, where the children under his tutelage misbehaved, provoked conflict and tried by many means to sabotage lessons. Appel comments on the fundamental difficulty facing teachers in this area of practice:

> The task facing a teacher is to resolve the dilemma between making a class work within the rules of the institution and, at the same time, taking

care of the emotional climate in the classroom. Teachers are supposed to direct a class towards and through a task and at the same time base their work with a class on a relationship with pupils that is both personal and motivating. (1995: 13)

The teachers in Senior's studies appeared to have solved this problem, although there is always a fine line between authority and friendliness in managing classroom climate. How teachers learn to find the appropriate balance and to 'think on their feet' as they negotiate the line is an issue requiring more detailed investigation, possibly other long-term studies of teachers' pedagogic histories, like Appel's. Appel discovers that he is gradually able to establish order and control, and that one of the reasons appears to be that he learns to talk to his students 'as people' rather than talking down to them from a position of assumed authority, the very authority that the students dispute in their early encounters.

Studies of how teachers establish and maintain order are not often based on the personal testimony and reflections of teachers, and Appel's study is a reminder of how such research can appeal directly to teachers. Students' perspectives on the same incidents would provide a richer picture of what happens, but would almost certainly need to be collected by an outsider not involved in the issues. Observation and recording (video, photographic and audio) of classroom events which were 'troubled' would add a further layer of data.

Case Study 3: Introducing 'active learning' to adults – Rowland 1993

Rowland's case study focuses on negotiation – of adult learners' responsibility for their learning, and how much control they can exercise over what and how they learn. Rowland reports his own perspectives on the process of working on a course with the specific aim of introducing 'active learning' to students and also his students' perspectives on the process, gleaned from their writing.

The tutor's view

1. At the outset, Rowland discloses many doubts and dilemmas – for example, the contradiction between handing over responsibility to a learning group, and the fact that, as tutor, he would be expected to be directing matters. He is also acutely aware that his 'non-directive' approach might seem manipulative. He resolves to (a) disclose his anxieties to the group and (b) limit the extent to which he hands over responsibility to the group.
2. In the initial session, a discussion on the shape of the course led to a sharp division in the group between those who were content to go along with an open agenda, and those who were hostile to the uncertainties that the lack of a course plan gave them. Some of the participants were

also concerned that what he was proposing might be painful, and that support would be necessary. Rowland responds with a long open letter to the group by way of explaining his motives and rationale.

3. In the next session, Rowland notes a much less threatening atmosphere as the group engaged in joint planning for a residential weekend away. They also leave the formal classroom to discuss the arrangements.

4. The residential weekend (two days away from the university) highlights the following problems:

   • The need to 'break the ice' to begin the group bonding process. In the event, this did not really happen.
   • The need for specific tasks to focus individual and group energies.
   • There were wide variations in the group's understanding of the learning agenda.
   • It took a whole day of intensive talk for participants to begin to talk about their feelings, which were what appeared to be 'blocking' the process.
   • As the group began to talk more freely and to listen to each other more closely, some participants experienced intense emotions as old memories surfaced.
   • The sessions ended with a group product, the content of which was nearly all in the affective domain, and its intersection with the pedagogic.

5. Following the intense residential weekend, the issues of transfer of new learning to professional lives, and of assessment arose. Rowland reports that during the discussion of assessment, he feels that he has been forced back into a bureaucratic and controlling role.

Participants' views   In written reviews, the students (extensively quoted in the study) reported:

• their worries and doubts in the initial session, especially about what the tasks were and expectations that the process should be defined by an 'external' voice;
• the dynamics of the negotiating process – of alliances, arguments, strong negative emotions;
• the emerging dynamics of group support;
• the sense of struggle, difficulty, pain in the process;
• issues of group leadership, and Rowland's role;
• the value of listening, providing more time for self-reflection.

Rowland's case study demonstrates what a teacher can do by way of exploring their own practices, and also the immense value of counterbalancing this with the voices of the other participants in the classroom experience. What emerges is a sense of collaborative endeavour, intensely emotional and 'difficult', full of risks, but also high-gain in the long run. While not suggesting that all practitioners should engage in such emotionally demanding experiences, there is clearly much to learn about the affective domain by close attention to the group process and its effects on the classroom experience.

Other approaches to order and control

Gower, Phillips and Walters (1995) identify a number of practices for teachers to establish and maintain order and discipline, and to repair breakdowns (Quote 11.2). There is an underlying assumption of a link between three aspects of climate management, as follows. 'Good rapport' is related to 'good working relationships', which in turn are related to 'maintaining discipline'. As they also point out 'the balance to be achieved between exercising control and encouraging a relaxed, friendly atmosphere in which the students can interact with each other' is a challenge for the teacher (1995: 60). The essential pedagogic assumption of this position is that good conditions for inter-student interaction must be created. However, it is precisely the creation of these conditions which leads to the dilemma that Appel analyses, as he tries to be 'firm'.

Quote 11.2   Gower, Phillips and Walters on working atmosphere

. . . it is generally the teacher who creates the working atmosphere of a class. If you [teacher] over-dominate, the students tend to invest little of themselves in the class and you may even have discipline problems. On the other hand, if you fail to direct the students when necessary, and give firm guidance, they are likely to make an ineffective working group and suffer feelings of frustration and insecurity.
(1995: 59)

There appear to be three main causes of classroom discipline problems: the teacher's attitude and behaviour, the students and variables affecting them, and the attitude of the institution to 'bad behaviour' (Harmer (1991) (Concept 11.4). Teachers are recommended a 'code of conduct' for dealing with disruptions to order and control in the classroom (1991: 252). In the event of a breakdown he recommends six courses of action:

1. **Acting immediately** – 'the longer a discipline problem is left unchecked, the more difficult it is to take action' (1991: 252).
2. **Stopping the class** – waiting until order is re-established before continuing.
3. **Reseating** – moving a student to a different position, often at the front, can deal with the problems (another example of the influence of space on behaviour).
4. **Changing the activity** – e.g. switching to a writing task if there is too much noise.

5. **After the class** – allows for more discussion of the problem (another example of time frames being stretched).
6. **Using the institution** – referring cases to the higher authority of the institution. Harmer points out that teachers should not suffer discipline problems alone and recommends a team approach (1991: 253).

These and other similar practices endorse the underlying importance of order and control in the classroom to create the basic foundation to enable classroom activity. They are, however, prescriptions for action. For the novice teacher, they may provide a degree of direction, and fulfil a valuable role. However, no empirical evidence is presented to support the claims; in fact, the variables as set out provide an excellent agenda for research into this area of classroom management. Research examining the relationships between the variables in Concept 11.4 would provide a deeper understanding of classroom order and discipline, perhaps undertaken by student teachers as part of their induction into institutional life, as well as practising teachers and educationalists.

Concept 11.4 Variables influencing control and discipline in classrooms

1. **Gower, Phillips and Walters (1995)**
   - Age of students
   - Students' reasons for learning – voluntary or coerced
   - Class size
   - Institutional ethos
   - Respect of students for teachers

2. **Harmer (1991: 249–53)**
   Teachers' behaviour preparedness, consistency of action, calm (no raised voice), no threats of punishment, fairness to all students, positive attitude to learning, leading by good example – e.g. punctuality.
   Influences on students time of day (can also influence teachers!); students' attitudes to learning languages or classrooms; desire to be noticed – particularly among adolescents, but not confined to this group; students stirring each other up.
   Institutional systems for dealing with problems, policies, rules.

Other influences on classroom climate

Managing groups and order are the bases of managing classroom climate. However, the multi-variant nature of classrooms means that we need also to look into issues such as the use of time and space, and how they interrelate to issues in the affective domain in the same way as pedagogy relates to affect. Students often challenge how teachers arrange space or use time, and these aspects can also influence the mood of a group. Signs include responses to the use of space and the constraints of working to an imposed time frame. Simply observing the involuntary movements of teachers and students in class – are they still or fidgeting? Is the teacher pacing briskly up and down in the class or sitting still? What is the effect of the pace of the lesson on the climate? (Quote 11.4).

In a classroom in which the teacher is in a controlling position, the teacher contributes in a multitude of ways to the climate. Pedagogy also has an influence, in that transmission teaching positions the teacher as controller and thus creates a potentially adversarial relationship. Lehtovaara (2001), discussing the practice of 'controlling reality', comments:

> A good example (of this stance – *calculative and technological thinking*) is the rigid and stern discipline in school, not so unfamiliar to us old-timers at least. For a teacher favouring strict discipline it is only rational and self-evident that she alone defines the educational situation – students are in school to be educated and to serve the purposes of the society that provides the education. There is no need to allow them to participate in defining the situation. Let the experts do it. (2001: 149)

Lehtovaara is describing an extreme form of affect management in which institutional and societal power is central. Emotionally, it is 'rigid and stern', a far cry from more recent liberal and 'warm' portrayals of teachers' practices, which are less imposing; and less likely to require the use of sanctions to modify behaviour.

Quote 11.4   Vale on the pace of learning

Children do not all learn at the same pace or in the same manner. Pace within a lesson is a matter of experience, and sensitivity to individual needs. The temptation is often to work too fast through materials, rather than to exploit the ability and the interest of the children. It is not necessary, for example, for all the children to complete all the activities that a book suggests. Moreover, when children have successfully mastered an activity, it may well be more useful to build on this success than to move on to the next unit. It is also important to incorporate many changes of activity within one lesson. This means that the children should be introduced to language and content through a variety of steps and activities. Some may involve movement, others may be more passive. Since the attention span of young learners can be extremely short, change of pace (and approach) within a teaching sequence is vital.
(1995: 35)

Empowering the learner – towards a warmer climate?

Legutke and Thomas claim that 'a fundamental part of the teacher's managerial role is the empowerment of the learner' (1991: 292). By this they mean in particular the capacity of learners to enjoy being in a secure and non-judgemental atmosphere. They draw extensively on Underhill's (1989) analysis of four types of classroom power.

Concept 11.5 Classroom power (after Underhill 1989)

Classroom power is seen as having four possible manifestations on the dimensions of being in the learners' interests, and teacher imposition/control.

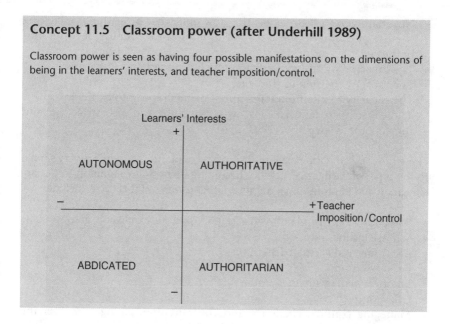

When learners' interests are the main focus of action, the teacher can opt for a pedagogic stance of either autonomy for the learners. Alternatively a teacher can take an authoritative position by providing learners relevant new knowledge or enforcing control so that students can work in appropriate conditions. In contrast, abdication of responsibility is likely to lead to chaos and a poor climate, as teachers would be perceived as not caring. In the authoritarian position teachers would impose control on learners against their interests.

Case Study 4: Towards a humane classroom – Legutke and Thomas 1991

Legutke and Thomas (1991) is an extended and theorised study of the experiences of introducing and using over a long period a 'strong' version of communicative language teaching with young people in state and private schools. They identify and describe many classroom management practices in the context of building a description of a teacher's process competence. They include:

- The ability to build trust (they see participation in activities as a primary means of doing this) (1991: 75).
- The use of awareness-raising tasks to enable students to develop an understanding of some of the emotional and intellectual processes their methodology initiated (1991: 85).
- Setting tasks and allowing learners to proceed without interference.
- Intervening when appropriate.

- Negotiating with learners on the how and what of learning, including the use of evaluation as a way of tapping into students' feelings and opinions.
- The capacity to conduct feedback which is honest and supportive.
- The capacity to listen to students.
- The capacity to assert oneself without being drawn into conflict.
- The capacity to tender one's own viewpoint and also to accept and respect other viewpoints (1991: 294).

These capacities and their realisation as practices in the classroom are very similar to the types of 'facilitative' practice becoming increasingly common in tertiary education and in professional training. Other features of this 'style' include:

- 'Presence' – verbal and non-verbal signals (posture, expression, gesture, etc.).
- Self-disclosure.
- Attending and accurate listening.
- Basic assertion.
- Emotion management.
- Questioning.
- Managing conflict, challenge and confrontation, giving and receiving feedback. (after Brockbank and McGill 1998)

To these lists we can add the capacity to attend to a group's emerging history and an awareness of a learning group's investment in their group process. A 'good group' may well build an intense emotional bond as it grows together. By facilitating communication in the group, the teacher is both the instigator of and participant in this process, although a very cohesive group is likely to assert its own needs and direction as it achieves a degree of autonomy.

Legutke and Thomas (1991: 65) assert that two premises underlie criteria (they identify seven) for the selection of communicative activities: clarity and a 'learning climate of trust' (1991: 64). For the authors they are 'indispensable goals' (1991: 65). Legutke and Thomas make important points about the locus of classroom control in creating a warm and supportive classroom climate. For example, in discussing the use of activities requiring self-disclosure and the consequent risks involved, they argue that students should make a contribution to the creation of classroom climate in order for them to trust the situation fully.

> The security which is supposed to arise from a positive social-affective climate ... will remain questionable unless this security has come out of collective negotiation and co-determination. (1991: 67)

They point out the potential dangers of teachers not clarifying the inherent problems of asymmetry of roles (and power/control) for students and the potential for mixed messages about 'freedom' conflicting with the requirements to give marks to students for performance – very similar point made by Rowland. In a multitude of teaching/learning contexts, the mixed messages could lead to disorder, conflict and demotivation, among other negative effects.

Activities for managing classroom climate

Teachers have at their disposal a variety of activities to use in their lessons as ways of establishing and maintaining a good classroom climate. The activities have two main focal points:

- Trust-building.
- Group-building.

Building trust

Trust between teachers and learners is at the heart of classroom climate, and, as we have seen, its creation is a primary management job for the teacher. The foundations of trust are located in what Carl Rogers refers to as the teacher's 'unconditional positive regard' for the student, essential for the necessary empathy and respect for trust to develop. Trust is thus central to 'partnership' in the classroom (Williams and Burden 1997: 59) and it is the fulcrum of negotiation and collaboration in learner-centred or collaborative classrooms. Returning to Briggs and Moore's (1993) concept of high and low structure management, the essential feature of high structure is a low trust 'Theory X' belief system (after McGregor 1960). Low structure classrooms are on the other hand tend to be 'Theory Y' focused, and low trust.

Quote 11.5   Briggs and Moore on the influences on classroom climatic conditions

High-structure decisions may tend to elicit a cold climate, because they frequently assume Theory X; students are basically not to be trusted, so I shall have to make all the major decisions for them and ensure that they are properly enacted. Low-structure decisions tend to assume Theory Y; students can be trusted to make good decisions. Nevertheless, it is perfectly possible to set up a formal, high-structure classroom in an atmosphere of caring and goodwill. Equally a low-structure classroom can be cold and uncaring as it would be a in a completely *laissez-faire* classroom; a teacher leaving students to live with poor decisions, or no decisions at all, is definitely uncaring.
(1993: 498)

Trust is also a vital element of successful group learning and in order for any learning from experience to occur, a 'group must operate in a climate where there is a degree of mutual trust and tolerance and where participants feel free to take risks in admitting failings and anxieties and in experimenting with newly learned behaviours' (Jacques 1991: 185). Trust is a two-way street – it is mutual.

Jacques suggests that the development of self-awareness using the Johari Window (Concept 11.6) contributes to the growth of trust. Wright (1999) (Figure 11.2) has developed a developmental model for this process, and argues that self-awareness enhances honesty and confidence, both of which are necessary preconditions for the type of collaborative work – sharing, negotiating – which builds trust and shared concepts – or a 'common language' – in a group. The latter enable the development of new knowledge and skill as more learning opportunities are afforded by an improved climate.

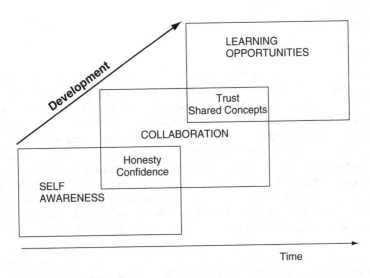

Figure 11.2   Group development

Group-building

Teachers who wish to exploit the potential of groups in language learning draw on a special range of classroom management skills, knowledge, awareness and personal qualities. Dealing with the spectrum of activities from organising working teams and monitoring their interactions to coping with learners in deep conflict over working methods, or emotionally disturbed by classroom activities which probe the personal requires quite specific management activities. Group dynamics are above all a matter of the personality and style of the teacher, the personalities of the people in the group, and it is up to the individual teacher to establish a relationship with the students in his or her own distinctive way (Hadfield 1992: 14).

Concept 11.6   The Johari Window

The Johari Window was devised by Joseph Luft (1984) in collaboration with Harrington Ingram. It is described as an awareness-raising model. The window consists of four domains – public or shared, private (or personal/secret), hidden and unknown. Its main 'engines' are the practices of DISCLOSURE and FEEDBACK, both leading to increased self-awareness. A comprehensive account appears in McGill and Beaty (2001).

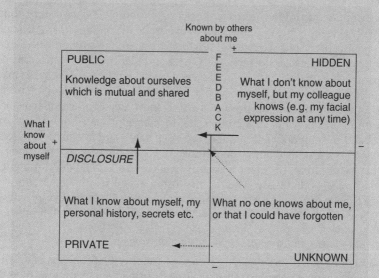

Under conditions of *disclosure*, private knowledge becomes public, in the same way as when a colleague gives me *feedback* about something I was unaware of. These processes can trigger memory and loosen material in the 'unknown' area which has been forgotten.

During their working lives, teachers develop a practical knowledge base for working with groups. In enabling a group to achieve a degree of cohesion, the teacher is also tapping into frequently observed stages of group formation – forming, storming, norming, performing, adjourning ('mourning' – added by Hadfield 1992) (after Tuckman and Jensen 1977, in Jacques 1991). The fluctuating history of a learning group is written through these stages. The stage of group formation is a powerful influence on classroom climate. For example, at the forming stage, there may either be uneasiness or a great deal of warmth; the 'storming' stage can match the metaphor in terms of conflict and unhappiness.

Teachers also build their knowledge and skill in the following areas:

- Participation patterns (see Chapters 8 and 12).
- Quality of interpersonal communication (including listening).

- Group norms or 'rules' and preferred procedures.
- Tendency for large groups to form sub-groupings.
- Structuring behaviour – emergence of leaders, for example.

Not only do teachers gather detailed knowledge of how groups function, they also learn to 'read' situations and to make appropriate management decisions in real time. There is more to managing groups than simply setting up activities designed to engender a good social climate. The climate itself may have to be conducive to interventions of this sort. For example, Legutke and Thomas (1991: 171) identify the creation of a positive group dynamic as a central goal of the opening phase of a sequence of teaching activities, in common with Senior. Many practitioners would agree with them and identify the creation of good group cohesion at the outset as fundamental to the learning process. What many of these practitioners fail to point out, however, is the need to maintain the level of attention to group process. There is inevitably conflict, disagreement and unproductive work in a group's life. In managing classroom groups, the social and the emotional dimensions are inseparable, and it is likely that social cohesion is the basis of emotional health in classroom groups; the character of the classroom mangement task thus tends towards social development as a basis for a good climate. The teacher also makes a strong contribution to group climate in the 'leader' role, as model and guide. The activities in Hadfield (1992) are a valuable example of how these factors can be treated in practice.

Activities for personalising and 'humanising' classrooms

A number of practitioners have focused on the specific problems of creating a classroom climate conducive to learning, focusing directly on the issues discussed so far. Griffiths and Keohane, for example, claim that their activities 'help in (among other things) creating trust between class and teacher, and facilitating positive group dynamics in your class' (2000: 2). They envision teachers participating actively in the activities, disclosing at levels which they expect their students to disclose (Quote 11.6).

Quote 11.6   **Griffiths and Keohane on personalisation**

Personal involvement is one very effective way of enhancing motivation. By this we mean making language learning content personally meaningful. If learners feel that what they are asked to do is relevant to their own lives, and that their feelings, thoughts, opinions and knowledge are valued, and crucial to the success of the activities, then they will be fully engaged in the tasks and more likely to be motivated to learn the target language. (2000: 1)

Rinvolucri (1999) argues that there should be coherence between the choice of activity and the process stage which the group has reached. By this he means that a group is not 'ready' for 'strong' humanistic activities at an early stage after its formation, and needs to have reached a degree of ease with each other, and the creation of a caring enough climate to proceed. Hence there is a need for the teacher to work on building group trust and cohesion to facilitate the use of more deeply humanistic activities. He says 'the humanistic exercise is likely to be used in a classroom where the teacher has a strong awareness of group process and how this affects learning' (1999: 197) (Quote 11.7).

Quote 11.7   Rinvolucri on the reasons for humanistic exercises

The heart of the humanistic exercise is a personal experience and a group experience in the here and now, which is where the learner comes from. The students speak to the teacher because they have something to express, something that has welled up from their emotions.
(1999: 199)

Collaborative learning activities are also regarded as important ways of improving classroom climate (Quote 11.8). Proponents argue that in addition to more language practice opportunities, there are positive benefits in the affective domain, such as increased self-awareness. It is a slight concern, however, that collaboration is seen as a way of enhancing *individual* capacities rather than the group per se. More research on the connections between collaborative experience and individual learning are suggested by this anomaly.

Quote 11.8   Crandall on cooperative learning

Cooperative learning has been shown to encourage and support most of the affective factors which correlate positively with language learning; for example, decreased anxiety, increased motivation, the development of positive attitudes to learning and language learning, promoting self-esteem, as well as supporting different learning styles and encouraging perseverance in the difficult and confusing process of learning another language.
(1999: 227)

Various activity types and sources of teaching materials designed to assist in creating classroom climate are listed in Concept 11.7. They contain a range of tasks and activities which focus both on the processes of group-building, a group's history and the learners themselves. All of these activities feature a varying level of focus on language as content and the learners themselves as content, but all aim to work with groups in particular ways to draw on the collective energies of the participants, and also to enhance classroom climate.

> ## Concept 11.7 Classroom learning activities – focus on the group process and history
>
> - Ice-breakers, 'warmers' (Dornyei and Malderez 1999)
> - 'Starting the course' (Griffiths and Keohane 2000), e.g. 'Initiating and maintaining conversations'
> - 'Thinking about groups' (Hadfield 1992), e.g. contributing
> - Warming up (Griffiths and Keohane), e.g. Finding out what you have in common
> - Empathy activities; establishing trust, a sense of belonging (maintaining the group)
> - Learning to listen; coping with crisis (all Hadfield)
> - Ending the group experience (Hadfield)
> - Closing the course (Griffiths and Keohane)

Managing the emotions of learning

Chapter 6 outlined a number of issues related to the management of emotions in learning. For example, in exploring the roots of failure or slow progress in classroom language learning, the roles of negative emotions such as fear and anxiety have been highlighted as major contributors to individuals' and possibly groups' emotional states 'blocking' learning. Again, it is an area which has not received a great deal of attention in the research literature.

Learner anxiety

In Chapter 6 we saw that learners were likely to be anxious about learning a foreign language, especially when there was a perceived oral performance aspect to it. This is borne out by Case Study 5.

Case Study 5: Learner anxiety – Tsui 1996 and Hilleson 1996

Tsui (1996), in her study of Hong Kong learners' reticence in English language classes, which was based on the classroom action research projects of 38 trainee teachers, identifies the notion of 'performance fear' – a sense that 'when communicating in a language in which they are not fully fluent, learners cannot but feel that they are not fully representing their personality and their intelligence' (1996: 156). In these circumstances, Tsui points out that learners feel vulnerable to criticism and negative evaluation of their errors. These lead to embarrassment, nervousness, fear of mistakes, and poor self-image as users of English. She also points out that very competent students are anxious about speaking in class because they don't want to stand out from the crowd.

Tsui's study locates anxiety within wider classroom cultural norms – the 'rules' (1996: 157) – and speculates that students deal with a hostile situation, i.e. teachers' questioning, by either avoiding or withdrawing from classroom talk. Much of this 'climate of fear' she attributes to teachers' intolerance of silence and resorting to uneven allocation of turns at speaking in order to keep the lesson moving, based on a belief that responsible teachers should be eliciting material from students and filling any silent spaces with their own talk.

Hilleson (1996) in a study of a multicultural and multilingual group of learners aged 17 and 18 in Singapore, also identified anxiety regarding classroom performance, and linked it to an anxiety about performing tasks in an unfamiliar language, with the added pressure of being correct, especially in writing. The correctness imperative (Wright 1992) has an all-pervasive influence on the climate of many classrooms, and this is a further manifestation of its power, producing the sort of debilitating anxiety that inhibits practice and prevents learning.

Both Hilleson and Tsui present 'anxiety management' strategies (Hilleson 1996: 269) as ways of coping with the negative effects of anxiety induced by classroom performance (Concept 11.8).

Concept 11.8   Anxiety management strategies

Teachers can try the following strategies:

- Increasing wait time after asking questions, and accepting the 'right to silence'.
- Moving to increased numbers of referential and open-ended questions with written answers.
- Acceptance of a variety of answers.
- Increase peer support and group work (assists facilitative anxiety).
- Focus on content, not form.
- Establishment of good relationships with learners – involving students in discussions of learning, group counselling to examine students' self-perceptions.
- Use of low-stress, positive classroom activities – role play, drama, oral interpretation of texts.
- More opportunities for student self-management of activities plus learner training.
- Focus on potential anxiety in all skills areas as well as speaking – change the balance of perception.

(after Tsui 1996 and Hilleson 1996)

All of these strategies entail altering interaction patterns, in the types of I-move selected (more referential questions release the pressure of 'right answer-ism', for example) and the management of talk to allow more time for students to respond. The practice of accepting a range of answers to a question also signals that the pressure to be 'correct' is not the main focus. These practices can help lower stress levels. Other practices contribute to improved trust and interpersonal relations in the group, aimed at creating a more supportive atmosphere. Finally, the choice of activity types such as role play which are not form-focused contribute to a better atmosphere, and lowered anxiety levels. One 'hidden' dimension of the suggested strategies is a greater level of 'privacy' for the student – more individual work, less performance in front of the class. In effect, a change of classroom culture is suggested.

Helping learners achieve 'flow' – the role of support

In Chapter 6, we examined the work of Czsikszentmihalyi (1990) which identifyied the 'flow' state, a metaphor for ideal learning conditions which can be created by effective classroom management in the affective domain. Under 'flow' conditions, the level of challenge of the task, and the learners' available skills for mediating it are in balance. So the learner is completely absorbed in the task at hand, apparently unaware of time and even place, and the task proceeds effortlessly (Figure 11.3). The state of flow is also analogous to the state known as 'eustress' where a person is performing optimally, neither over-stressed nor under-stressed.

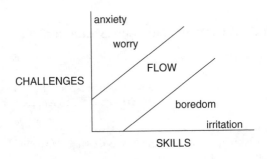

Figure 11.3   Flow States (after van Lier 1996a: 106)

If the challenge is too great, a learner will be worried and anxious; if the challenge is not high enough, a learner will be unstimulated and most probably irritated and frustrated, or some other negative emotional state. A third dimension can be added to the model to show how, under conditions of maximal support and challenge from teacher and tasks, and even fellow learners, a learner can perform most effectively. The teacher's management work is therefore to balance challenges to learners' current abilities and to support them in learning tasks. One issue that emerges is that flow and eustress are seen as enhancing the learner's feelings of empowerment and control, whereas Daloz's analysis highlights the role of teacher support. Evidence from anxiety studies and 'good group' studies suggest that emotional support from a teacher is an important enabling and sustaining factor in the achievement of optimal learner states.

Case Study 6: 'The gift of confidence – Mahn and John-Steiner 2002

In a study of ESL learners developing writing skills, Mahn and John-Steiner (2002) single out the role of 'caring support in facilitating risk-taking in both the learning and creative processes' (2002: 47). Working within a socio-cultural view of learning, they identify 'the power of caring support in instilling the confidence with which to meet new challenges, sustain creative endeavours and attempt something new' (2002: 58). They term these: 'Joint activities in which both (teacher/student and artist/artist) are enhanced when the interactions are supported by 'the gift of confidence' (appropriated from Jean-Paul Sartre).

The authors identify the following as central to success in learning in the zone of proximal development (ZPD, Chapter 7):

1. Connection and emotional rapport between teacher and student. (Normal between parent and child, but less so between teacher and student. Perhaps students always feel short-changed emotionally?)
2. Careful listening, intense dialogue and emotional support sustain the cooperative construction of understanding, of scientific discovery and of artistic forms.
3. Teachers are able to collaborate with students in creating environments conducive to transformative teaching/learning if they attempt to understand the students' lived experiences, knowledge and feelings (2002: 53).

Using student diaries as their main data source, the authors established that:

- Use of a diary freed students from anxiety, and fixation on form and mistakes.
- The students started to use writing without teacher direction as a means of self-discovery.
- Responses from the teacher were important in motivating them and giving them confidence to take risks.
- The diaries were a good way to gain an understanding of how the students experienced classroom life and thus enabled teacher to provide appropriate support when required.
- Students expressed themselves in a rich range of metaphors and vivid descriptions.

Diary-keeping is also an example of 'real' language practice, and the inspiration for dialogue about the learning experience which acknowledges emotional difficulty. Attention to the emotional aspects of what students write is the basis of assisting them in achieving optimum states, where learning appears to proceed with less affective baggage to block its progress.

A 'playful' learning climate

Another interesting aspect of the emotional domain in the classroom is the incidence, function and value placed upon 'play' in the language classroom. For example, Rampton's studies of children learning languages in Inner London contain descriptions of playful behaviour, although outside the classroom in the main. Where the foreign language is used in class, it is, perhaps surprisingly, used to subvert the conventions for silence (Quote 11.8). Foreign language learning is evidently intrinsically enjoyable, although not necessarily in ways which teachers would necessarily have intended. Studying classroom transcripts for instances of playful behaviour and careful observation of students' behaviour outside as well as inside the classroom promises to provide rich insights into this relatively unknown, but significant area.

Quote 11.8   Rampton on learning German in Inner London

... we have been surprised by the extent to which adolescents used German *outside* their German classes, in break time, in corridors, in English, Maths or Humanities lessons. (1999: 484)

Foreign language lessons are the main source of German used by the youngsters. Outside class, German is used in impromptu call-and-response sequences; for game-playing; as a means of subverting conventions such as being quiet while entering classrooms:

the use of German in these episodes can be ... related to ritual, music and performance. (1999: 496)

Case Study 5: Play in the Language Classroom – Sullivan 2000

Sullivan's account of 'play' in a Vietnamese classroom marks a significant advance in our understanding of how, in apparently 'traditional' classrooms, there is considerable emotional investment by teacher and students in the activities of lessons, in the Vietnamese case, playfulness being a vital ingredient. After analysing the discoursal patterns of a tertiary level language lesson, and focusing on specific incidents, Sullivan writes:

> The playful exchanges (described in the study) are a socially mediated activity that stand between the individuals (teacher and students) and the language being learned. The students are not demonstrating passive responses to the teacher's playfulness, but are jointly engaged in it themselves. These playful exchanges serve as tools that result in awareness of language meaning and form. (2000: 123)

As well as recording and transcribing 22 different classes, Sullivan also interviewed teachers and students, as well as a number of administrators, and curriculum designers in order to check the accuracy of her observations and interpretations. Documentary sources as well as her own field notes completed a rich data base.

Sullivan emphasises the broader cultural implications of her study, placing special emphasis on researchers' potentially value-laden preferences for verbal over non-verbal play. She also theorises her study by contrasting the behaviour she observes with more 'technicist' (Fairclough 1992) descriptions of classrooms which are 'tied either to the notion of work or technology' (2000: 128). This work, and other work in the Vietnamese context by Kramsch and Sullivan

(1996), is an important sociocultural contribution to our understanding of the emotional domain of classrooms. Enjoyment and participation are intertwined in Sullivan's data, and further studies in this direction suggest a stronger role for playful behaviour in the creation of classroom climate.

In another study of mediated classroom language learning, Lantolf (2000: 82) cites a study by Broner and Tarone (1999) on language play among children in a Spanish immersion class. He distinguishes between ludic play – between children – and private play – where the children are manipulating the language for 'fun', as part of the learning process, for their own apparent benefit. The latter form of play is an aspect of self-mediation (Lantolf 2000: 88). Lantolf also cites classroom studies which capture individuals' 'mumblings or asides...for which there was no response or reaction from a peer' in learning situations (Villamil and deGuerro 1996: 63, in Lantolf 2000: 88). Although Lantolf argues that these instances are evidence of self-mediation, they are also affective markers of engagement in the classroom activity, and affective markers of the frustrations and joys of learning.

The role of feedback

The affective markers in classroom talk were identified in Chapter 6. In Chapter 8, we have seen how the IRF exchange pattern can dominate classroom talk. With such a high frequency it is very likely that there will be affective consequences. The F-move is an important marker in affective terms, because it carries the weight and force of judgement on a learner's R-move. At the F-move the learner is potentially most vulnerable to harsh criticism or rejection – the F-move is therefore a vital indicator of affective conditions.

Case Study 8: Supportive Teacher Talk – Cullen 2002

Cullen's study is based on the analysis of transcripts of language classroom activity at secondary level from Tanzania. While much of the analysis is pedagogically-oriented (see Chapter 12), Cullen does identify, within what he terms 'dicoursal' moves (compared with 'evaluative' F-moves), uses of humour and cognitive support which encourage learners to say more in exchanges. Cullen argues that F-moves featuring comment and elaboration often contain humorous asides or references. F-moves like this, which are responsive to students' R-moves, demonstrate that a teacher has listened carefully to the students' R-contributions. These F-moves are 'authentic' rather than ritualised, and indirectly contribute to the affective domain and its management, as students intuitively feel more secure and acknowledged by teachers who listen to them. Similarly, rising intonation effectively signals to students that teachers are engaged in the learning dialogue, and interested in what is being said.

Evaluative F-moves, when accompanied by praise presumably have a strong positive impact on learners, and allow us to speculate that the use of praise may be a means of managing the affective domain. Thus, as Frawley and

Lantolf (1985) have speculated, affective markers inhabit classroom discourse, but in often surprising ways, as Cullen's study reveals. One shortcoming of this valuable study, which demonstrates the importance of examining even the most apparently humdrum material from classroom life, is that the teachers and students in Cullen's study have no voice, and are unable therefore to contribute to our understandings. For example, it would be interesting to hear what the teachers believe the uses of humour are, and whether or not they believe praise to be an 'affective lubricant'.

11.3 Teachers' emotions

Understanding how teachers' emotional states influence the ways in which they manage classroom activity is a significant way of understanding classroom management. Because a teacher leads the classroom group, they have a major role in setting the emotional tone of a lesson, or a longer period of activity like a course. There are several areas in which teachers can manage their own and others' emotions (Concept 11.10).

Concept 11.10   Managing emotions – self and others

- Awareness and knowledge of one's own emotions.
- Managing emotions – frustration tolerance and anger management; stress management; enhancement of positive feelings about self and others.
- Self-motivation – being more responsible; concentrating better; improved self-control.
- Awareness and knowledge of others' emotions – standing in others' shoes.
- Handling relationships – conflict resolution; understanding relationships; assertive communication; cooperation.

(after Askew and Carnell 1998 and Goleman 1995)

A teacher sets the tone both consciously and unconsciously, verbally and non-verbally. The types of 'bonding' behaviour noted by Senior (1999) where teachers overtly aim to influence the emotional climate are examples of conscious verbal and non-verbal strategies. Teachers also unconsciously influence the climate – a nervous teacher makes students nervous in the same way that a smiling teacher elicits smiles, for example. These are examples of what Goleman (1995) refers to as 'collective' emotional states.

Case Study 9: Classroom management as method and manner – Richardson and Fallona 2001

Richardson and Fallona's study takes a holistic view. Classroom management practice is related closely to other aspects of classroom activity, such as instruction. They focus on 'manner' in teaching – 'a teacher's virtuous conduct or traits of character as played out or revealed within a classroom context' (2001: 706) – as the way in which a teacher's virtuous traits of character relates to their conscious attempts to develop virtuous conduct in students. The concern shows by teachers is an indication of a care orientation.

Their study is of two experienced teachers' classroom management practice with primary-aged children, following their stated theoretical interest in who a teacher is, what she believes and how these beliefs manifest themselves in a teacher's conduct. Multiple data sources were analysed – video tapes of two days in the life of each one, and interviews.

Findings 'Darlene' exhibits the virtues of friendliness – a positive caring disposition – wit and humour, truthfulness, mildness and temperance (her classroom was described as a 'peaceful kingdom'), justice and practical wisdom. The authors point out that she consciously models these virtues in her everyday management work in the classroom.

Kai is magnanimous – exhibiting pride in herself, her students and her profession, friendly, truthful, honourable, and just. She models and also directly refers to these characteristics in her classroom management.

The authors note interesting similarities and differences between the two teachers, most notably in their beliefs about the role of education, and how this manifests itself in the classroom, and in the way they practice caring. Kai exhibits what is known as 'tough love' for the group, whereas Darlene is more individual-oriented. Both teachers' classroom management is characterised by what the authors term 'seamlessness', or coherence, which they speculate is implicit in the authenticity of teaching. The authors conclude that classroom management is 'interwoven with the goals and beliefs of the teacher, and with his or her manner' (2001: 724). They also found management and instruction interwoven in the person, conduct and practice of the teacher and her students. They also remind us of the cultural relativities of these features and their contextual character.

Other significant studies of the emotional dimensions of teaching

In Chapter 6, we encountered the concept of emotionality in teaching. Hargreaves (2001) has subsequently extended his research in this area of teaching to an understanding of 'emotional geographies'. In a study of 53 teachers' interactions with parents, Hargreaves establishes five socio-cultural 'geographies' through a process of in-depth interviewing on a wide range of topics which relate to emotional aspects of teaching (Concept 11.11). The implications of this research for classroom management are immense, as it is highly likely that teachers' classroom management practices, particularly in the affective domain, are infused with their emotional geographies. As Hargreaves has consistently argued, teaching is an emotional as well as a technical and intellectual pursuit. Emotions are a 'window on the fundamental nature of teaching'. Research on the emotional geographies of teachers and their students promises to unpack some of the difficult affective territory of classroom management, and how teachers both manage affect and contribute to it during classroom activity. Hargreaves' (2001) study provides some pointers in this direction. From the research perspective it is clear from this and similar studies that capturing the teacher's voice and sympathetically analysing what is said with reference to the contextual conditions in which teachers work is an generative and necessary procedure.

Concept 11.11   Emotional geographies of teaching

Emotional geographies: describe the relative distance and closeness between humans, expressed through their interactions. Hargreaves' (2001) study focused on the distance between parents and teachers:

1. Sociocultural – where teachers cannot understand parents from different cultures from themselves.
2. Moral – where teachers' and parents' purposes are at odds.
3. Professional – teachers are distanced from parents because of self-perceived superiority derived from expertise and knowledge.
4. Political – where power is asymmetrical or ambivalent, the relationship is distorted.
5. Physical – simply the conditions for developing sustained relationships and the time available for interaction.

Zemblyas (2004) continues to explore the emotional terrain of teaching. Her case study of one teacher over three years explores the theoretical areas of the socio-cultural construction of emotion, the reason/emotion split and emotion as a discursive practice. This broadly social and public view of the private world of emotion provides useful counterpoint to the types of study done by Hargreaves which have an avowedly political purpose of generalising teachers' lives in order to influence policy-makers. Zemblyas' study more modestly focuses on the role of emotion in the everyday life of the informant, and of most interest regarding classroom management practices is how the teacher's emotional states affected her teaching.

Several key data gathering methods were employed – observations, field notes, recordings, interviews, document searches, and an 'emotion diary' in which the teacher recorded how she felt about people and events in her classroom. The main findings were as follows:

Evaluative: The teacher's emotions and actions constitute evaluations of her teaching world – classroom, students, teaching, learning.
Interpersonal: The teacher's emotions are about relationships – social actions in her classroom.
Political: The teacher's emotions are involved with self-evaluations based on emotional rules and partly account for her self-image as a teacher.

The study raises important issues regarding management and caring, as well as prompting speculation about similar research being carried out on foreign language teachers, and the extent to which the uniqueness of this type of teaching has emotional expression. The techniques could also be used for personal self-reflective studies or for studies of groups of teachers in institutions to see what they share in common and whether this affects classroom management practices, as indicated by so much of the literature.

Managing affect in online learning

Learning in a virtual learning environment (VLE) is as emotional an experience as face-to-face learning. The same human emotions occur in cyberspace as they do in a bricks and mortar classroom, but with subtle differences that research is only just beginning to establish. A significant difference between research online and research in face-to-face learning contexts is that research has accompanied in the innovation, with the consequence that we are learning about the effects of the medium on the affective domain as the medium develops in real time. An interesting paradox is that the outcomes of research may be influencing new developments before earlier models of online learning have fully run their course.

From the beginning, using ICT is an emotional experience as learners struggle not only with the demands of the content of their courses, but also the software and the keyboard or mouse. The research reveals that many online learners feel alienated, distanced and cut off from their colleagues, resulting in massive dropout rates on courses which are entirely online. Without paralinguistic cues, the essentially textual medium is colder and less immediate for many learners than in-person talk. It is therefore more difficult to 'listen' to fellow students or the tutor online. Sometimes the written medium allows for extreme emotions – 'flaming' (anger) or 'glooming' (despondency) are more likely online where there are no visual cues to 'speakers' to stop because what they are saying is embarrassing. It is easier to 'offload' negative emotions online. The strange effect is that they remain encoded in discussion threads for months after their passing. On the other hand written disclosures can provide invisible and uncertain participants with the necessary courage to confront people from whom they might run if they met them face-to-face. As a result, there is considerable debate and experimentation in forming 'online communities' where social interaction is as highly valued as task-oriented interaction.

Many students complain about 'absent' tutors, who might only visit threads rarely, and report increased motivation when the tutor is an active participant. Feedback at distance seems to be on important issue – simply knowing that someone else has read one of your posts to a discussion thread can raise the spirits.

In short, the online medium confounds many of our expectations about emotional response. Research has begun to demonstrate that these responses are, however, crucial to the success of online courses.

Case Study 10: Exploring social presence in discussion threads – Na Ubon and Kimble 2003

The authors conducted a longitudinal study on an online course for health professionals at the University of York, UK. They examined the transcripts from the conferencing threads for up to 6 modules over two years. The conferencing study pattern was 'blended' with occasional face-to-face meetings for short periods. There were between 13 and 18 students in each module and an average of four tutors per module. Over 1200 messages were posted in this period.

A 'content analysis' was carried out, requiring coding and compilation using computer software to identify the main items in the postings.

Affective responses, most frequent in the first module, declined over the period of the course, once participants had got to know each other. The expression of personal values was the most frequent affective response in postings, compared with expression of emotion, humour or self-disclosure. The researchers contrasted the affective response with the length of time it took to establish social cohesion, which similarly fell away towards the end of the module period. However, they concluded that the affective involvement facilitated social cohesion. The authors also found that the tutors tried hard to establish rapport with students, and their messages contained a high proportion of affective markers and expressions. This was a consistent pattern with different tutors who maintained the high affective engagement throughout, expressing emotion very frequently.

This type of study is the basis for discovering the cultural practices of learners working in online groups, and, although modest in its findings, demonstrates that affective markers have an important role in the management of online learning.

Case Study 11: Emotion and e-learning – O'Regan 2003

Like Case Study 10, this study uses a social constructivist framework to explore the connections between cognition and affect online. In fact, the author emphasises the ways in which online learning highlights the connections between cognition and affect. Her study is set in an Australian university and aims to investigate the following:

- The emotions associated with learning online.
- The specific teaching/learning contexts of these emotions.
- The relationship of the emotions with student learning.
- The practical implications for learning and teaching online.

As the author states her aim was 'to explore in qualitative terms the lived experience of students learning online ... in relation to its emotional dimensions' (2003: 82). A group of 11 students took part in the study, providing data in long (1 hour) interviews which enabled O'Regan to explore each in depth and to establish common themes as well. The analytical method was different from Case Study 7; O'Regan transcribed the interviews and analysed them according to emotions expressed in which contexts of learning and teaching. The data are rich and multilayered, and enable her to identify and verify five key emotions:

1. **Frustration** – the most 'pervasive emotion experienced online'. Typical instances were linked to the failure of technology, the difficulty of locating information or sites, the structure or nature of the online material, the often 'rambling or superficial nature of un-moderated online discussion' (2003: 85). Isolation and administrative processes also created frustration.
2. **Fear, anxiety and apprehension**– this was due to delays, or lack of information. For some, the lack of a visible audience was a key issue; failure to operate programmes only served to increase these feelings. Some also felt less anxiety as there was less time pressure.
3. **Shame/embarrassment** – feelings of incompetence were quite frequent when students confronted tasks they could not do, or when they had not been participating fully.
4. **Enthusiasm/excitement** – for some, online learning was exciting, particularly when the content related to professional issues or the learners' lives in some way.
5. **Pride** – if a participant presented an assignment that drew praise from the tutor, received positive feedback from a colleague or simply succeeding in using the online environment.

O'Regan draws a number of conclusions from the research which have implications for practice:

- Technological or website-related – maintenance, ease of use, up-to-date.
- Guidance – provision of guidance in using the websites.
- Humanised – efforts to be made to communicate with real people.
- Encouragement of risk-taking.

Case studies 10 and 11 explore the rich and complex emotional landscape of online learning, and both confirm that emotion and affect are central to the management of the learning process in formal settings online.

Summary

Research on the affective domain of formal learning is relatively restricted compared with more cognitively oriented work. Only in recent years with the gradual acceptance of the primary role emotion plays in learning has the management of positive and negative emotion attracted attention. Studies of the role of classroom climate in learning have revealed its importance in learning. More directly, studies of emotion management have illustrated the importance of this aspect of a teacher's role. The growth of online learning has provided fresh impetus to research in the affective domain because of the specific affective issues raised by the online medium for learning. Cross-fertilisation of research between the face-to-face and online learning environments has the potential to extend our understanding and our practices in both contexts.

12
Managing Classroom Participation

In Chapter 8 and elsewhere I have argued that a holistic and integrated view of classroom management includes an account of the central role of talk in classroom management activity. Studies of classroom talk have rarely concerned themselves directly with classroom management practices. Rather they have highlighted and accounted for processes which are integral to classroom management, such as turn-taking. The lack of studies of the role of talk in classroom management is as reflective of the instruction/management dichotomy as a lack of interest in classroom management. The concern with the 'effectiveness' of various teaching methods in the language teaching world may have diverted attention away from what is arguably more fundamental to classroom life. The studies examined in this chapter are therefore 'edited' to isolate those aspects which have a bearing on classroom management. They also suggest new studies focusing on the discourses of opportunity, order and care.

12.1 Teacher talk

Studies of teacher monologue in the language classroom are quite rare perhaps because of research interest in the 'interactivity' of classrooms in the 'communicative' era of language teaching. However, there is ample evidence that there is more teacher talk in classrooms than many authorities would recommend or sanction. Despite the introduction of 'communicative methodologies', language teachers still talk a great deal, and studies reveal that this plays a significant role in teaching and learning. Teachers talking in the target language is an important source of learning input in contexts where the target language is not heard frequently outside the classroom, and where there is a shortage of resources (e.g. audio and video tape). (See Section 12.4 on the implications for bilingual classrooms.)

Case Study 1: Teaching style – Katz 1996
Katz' (1996) study of four university language teachers in the US identifies the 'dominant structure of talk' and 'use of narratives' as two main modes

of discourse in their lessons. Three of the subjects employed 'lectures' as a dominant part of the interactional routine of the lessons observed. These are seen as one end of a continuum from 'traditional' lecture-style teacher talk to teacher-student interaction of various types. All used stories about themselves or others to:

- provoke laughter;
- establish camaraderie;
- illustrate teaching points, and exemplify points;
- provide context for teaching points.

Katz views teacher monologue as a form of interaction; narratives are ways of creating a good classroom climate, and also a form of lesson content. Using narrative to provoke laughter and build camaraderie are both significant uses of this form of teacher-managed talk – not for the imposition of control or message on students, but as part of a more innocent but necessary playfulness on the part of teachers. Students' responses in laughter and smiles are enough to demonstrate the interactional quality of these narratives.

Students' responses do not need to be verbal – a limitation of many interactional studies that they restrict their data to verbal responses.

Example: 'Karen' explaining 'loop writing' to her class (1996: 83)   Karen likes to focus on content – the ideas represented in a text. Classroom interaction in her class thus consists primarily of formal lectures plus rhetorical questions. (1996: 85).

> T: All right, uh, today's work is going to concern a reading which I'm going to give you. I'll give you a copy but I don't want you to read it yet. It's from a book that was written for Chinese who are going to come and study in the United States. And it's not an ESL book or anything. But it has just a couple of pages that I thought were worth working on because paragraphs are not simple paragraphs and I want you to look closely at them. In fact, we're going to go backwards from what you usually do. If you write a complex essay, and after you brainstorm and after you loop write, or after you do anything to get your ideas out and get this group of ideas, and then you do something with them. You have to organize them, right? How do you organize your ideas? Or do you just skip that part? You just get your idea and write it down in the order that it comes?

The example demonstrates how teacher talk incorporates explanation, instruction, and personalisation of content for the students through a series of rhetorical questions. It is complex and many-levelled.

Other studies of teacher talk

Tsui's (1996) study of teachers' practices in Hong Kong secondary-level language classrooms identifies low levels of 'wait time' as a distinctive characteristic of their practice. The teachers, she reports, prefer to continue 'keep a lesson moving' rather than allow for students to become bored and possibly disruptive while waiting for responses to questions. Tsui regards the practice as a 'misconception' (presumably from an opportunity perspective) – reporting the views of an informant 'that a responsible teacher should be talking all the time' (1996: 153). Harrison (1996) examined the practices of two teachers in secondary classrooms in Oman. Again, very high proportions of class time (up to 42 per cent – this accords well with the 'two thirds rule', whereby someone is talking for two thirds of classroom time, and the teacher is talking for two thirds of that time) were occupied by teacher 'lecturing, describing, explaining, narrating and directing' (1996: 292) before the introduction of new curriculum materials which emphasised more student–student interaction and allowed for more open responses from students.

The study documents changes in one teacher's behaviour, but not the other's, when new methodology is introduced. Studies of the effect of changes in methodology are a growing sub-genre in classroom discourse studies, and provide a valuable point of entry into classroom management practices. Like all classroom talk, these practices are dialectical and are influenced by and extend into both the social-emotional and the pedagogic domains. In many instances they are bridges between the domains – a story told by the teacher may simultaneously create a calm and relaxed atmosphere and also provide the basis of the linguistic work of a language lesson. Explanations of difficult points or provision of rationale for answers further may provide temporal links between different parts of a course in which previous teaching is recycled as part of an explanation, or have the effect of calming agitated students.

Extract 12.1   Explaining a point

  T we are protected at night by the/night watchman (*WRITES ON B/B: 7 secs*)
      prevent/protect/we are dealing with those two words/and what did we say
      about prevent -- who can tell us what we said about the word prevent -- yes
  S#7 you said we should use from
5 T we use/from not to/prevent is followed by the word⌈from
  Ss   ⌊from
  T not to/and/prevent is used in the sentence/when we hinder somebody/from
      doing something/or we hinder something from taking a second action (*B/B:*
      10 secs)hinder / hinder means the same as prevent/when we hinder (*B/B: 24*
      secs) please take out your exercise books/and you copy the words/and their
      meanings/then protect/the word protect/carries the note of (*WRITE ON black-*
      board: 22 secs)

In Extract 12.1, we see the teacher, with a little help from the students (line 6 – echoing, in chorus, the correct form), establishing and reinforcing a grammatical point. Using the blackboard to write examples and 'rules' adds further force to the explanation. Frequently, a teacher uses the board to illustrate an explanation, or a visual is a necessary artefact to help structure talk, the resulting narrative or explanation referring directly and indirectly to its content or meaning.

Other instances of teachers using long turns in talk include:

- Explanations of instructions may provide the social stability and emotional reassurance that learners require in order to do particular activities.
- Demonstrations which typically contain a great deal of talk which refers to the shared context of the learning group, and jokes, asides and other means of 'personalising' talk.

Case Study 2: Common knowledge – Edwards and Mercer 1987

Edwards and Mercer (1987) conducted a study of the discoursal practices of teachers and learners as they 'constructed' what they term 'common knowledge' (social, cultural and intellectual) in science lessons in British primary schools. After a close analysis of the transcripts of many lessons, and extensive interviews with teachers among their conclusions was that:

> The negotiation (between teacher and learners) is a rather one-sided affair in which the teacher's role as authoritative bearer of ready-made knowledge simply finds alternative, more subtle means of realizing itself than the crudities of brute 'transmission'. (1987: 163)

Teachers were overtly following new curriculum materials which were based on an ideology of 'child-centredness', which in pedagogic terms prescribed 'exploration' and 'discovery' of knowledge. Among teachers' discoursal practices they identified were:

- Teachers did not signpost their lessons or allow students access to the goals of their lessons (which the learners have to *discover*) or the direction in which they were heading.
- Teachers did not provide students with knowledge about their progress.
- Learners had to discover the 'rules' of the 'exploratory' discourse for themselves.

This evidence contributes to a realisation of the tension in teachers' beliefs and practices between the ideology of individualistic 'child-centredness' and their 'socializing role as the society's agents of cultural transmission in the context of a system of compulsory education' (1987: 168). As Edwards and

Mercer observe, 'the experiences and activities of the classroom are made meaningful by the sense made of those things by classroom talk' (1987: 169). Their conclusion was that there was not enough of a '*shared* conceptual sense of the meaning and significance of experience and activity' (1987:169). The reality was that the teachers, although professing a child-centred approach to education, actually did not practice it consistently. Scaffolded learning was the exception rather than the rule in the classrooms they studied. It appears then that transmissive practices of teaching do not simply disappear when a new educational ideology is introduced. Analysis of the classroom talk established that teachers and students were still following the familiar routines of 'guess what I'm thinking' and 'what am I going to do next'. This finding is additional evidence for the problematical relationship between what they term ritual knowledge and principled knowledge (Concept 12.1).

Concept 12.1   Ritual and principled knowledge

Ritual – knowledge that is essentially procedural, routinised, expedient.
Principled – explanatory and reflective knowledge, not tied to specific courses of action.

In Edwards and Mercer's terms, 'ritual' knowledge is the core of classroom management practice. They maintain the instructional/managerial dichotomy in classroom discourse. An alternative perspective is that principled knowledge is difficult to separate from ritual knowledge in practice and that they are, in effect, interwoven *strands* of educational discourse.

(after Edwards and Mercer 1987: 162)

A very important aspect of Edwards and Mercer's study is that they use the analysis of classroom talk to build theory about the nature of educational discourse, and remind us that when we examine classroom discourse and participation patterns, we are not only looking at the minutiae of classroom talk, but also the underlying ideologies and ideas that inform and drive it (see Chapter 7).

12.2   Studies of exchange patterns in classroom discourse

Mainstream classroom discourse studies have drawn on traditions well-established in applied linguistics for text analysis. The IRF exchange (Chapter 8) is the central analytical unit in this type of study and is also the 'default' type of classroom discourse for many other classroom studies. The allocation and use of turns in talk is also integral to classroom management micro-practices, and provides important evidence about pedagogy as well as social relations in the classroom.

Case Study 3: IRFs, triadic dialogue – Nassaji and Wells 2000

Nassaji and Wells' quantitative analysis of a large corpus of classroom data collected over six years in nine teachers' elementary and middle school classrooms in and around Toronto, Canada offers a further glimpse into the complexities of the triadic (three-part) IRF exchange pattern. Using a coding scheme which takes account of the variety of IRF types and moves (based on Wells 1993), they have analysed numerous exchanges or 'sequences' (the basic unit of analysis in their scheme). Their main findings were as follows:

- The triadic pattern was the dominant discourse genre, but this enabled the use of a variety of teaching strategies because of the prospective nature of 'questions' in the I-move.
- The choice of initiating question has important implications for the type of exchange that is possible (whether closed or open). However, they maintain that it is the F-move that is more significant. For example, a relatively closed question can lead to exploratory dialogue if the F-move is non-evaluative.
- IRFs allow the teacher to monitor students' understanding and retention of material.

They present the beginnings of a taxonomy of triadic exchanges, working from the three possible roles a teacher takes. These are highly significant for an understanding of classroom management.

1. **'Primary knower'** – teacher, student or no pre-selected knower (all participants can contribute to knowledge construction).
2. **'Manager'** of discussion – responsible for selecting speakers, and pacing or direction of the talk.
3. **'Initiator'** – in the managerial role, the teacher has the option of self-selecting or selecting a student to initiate activity.

While Nassaji and Wells' study would be extremely difficult to replicate, given the length of time it took, and the funding it required, the basic idea of using their coding system or a modified form of it (Concept 12.2 is a codified system for examining scaffolded classroom talk within the IRF framework) which might focus on the activity of scaffolding is an opportunity to explore further the management of participation. Figure 12.1 (p. 390) shows the continuum of talk types in lessons from pure teacher monologue to student-student interaction. Scaffolded interaction can begin at any moment when the teacher engages students in progression from the known to the new. It is therefore feasible to conceive of teacher monologues which explain or correct learners as a 'weak' form of scaffolding.

Concept 12.2 Scaffolded teacher/learner interaction

There is a scale of scaffolding routines, from closed IRFs strictly under the control of teachers to student-student interaction with minimal teacher interference. Teachers often retain the right to delayed intervention during student-student interaction: pair work or group work, when they 'patrol' and note linguistic or other problems that emerge from student-student talk. If a teacher does raise issues retrospectively, these routines may also be classed as scaffolding towards successful performance. (Refer also to TL Process – publisher document)

TYPE	Initiation	Purpose	Preferred R	Purpose of F
IRF Closed	Closed Qs	recall	correct item	evaluation
IRF Elicit	Closed Qs	recall or 'guess'	correct item	evaluation
IRF Open	Closed Qs	recall as prelude to open Q explore	correct item	evaluation
	Open Qs	explore	topically relevant	refinement
IRF Expand	Open Qs	explore	topically relevant Multiple Rs Extended (side sequences)	summarise Rs suggest Is or Rs Explain, extend evaluation

Participation and engagement

How classroom talk constrains or liberates participation, and hence potential opportunity for engagement and learning is central to an understanding of the role of pedagogy in classroom management. In Chapters 6 and 11, we have seen that the discourse of language classrooms contains a multitude of indicators of emotional states and engagement. For example, a teacher may praise all contributions a great deal in order to encourage students to speak, despite any factual or grammatical inaccuracy in what is said. Or teachers may allow mistakes in the R-move to go untreated or unspotted. Students familiar with a more authoritarian regime may be tempted to think that such a teacher is insincere or 'not a real teacher'. They may, as a consequence, self-select F-moves to provide corrections, or find other ways of revealing the teacher's true intentions, or subverting the teacher. Changing teaching styles or deliberately manipulating and changing interactional structures thus has emotional consequences for classroom discourse (van Lier 1996a: 159).

There are other ways in which teachers can subtly influence the emotional tone of classroom discourse, for example, through the use of 'concurrent' signals. Teachers give overt signals that 'they are listening' – back-channelling (van Lier 2001: 101) synchronised with eye contact, for example. A great deal of the emotional dimension of classroom discourse is thus non-verbal, and hence the salience of the affective markers that Frawley and Lantolf have identified. These are also part of classroom management practice as they are also incorporated into longer stretches of talk.

Teachers can moderate the effect of the I-move by 'softening' it, or in van Lier's (1996a) terms, making it less threatening. (Extract 12.2 is an example of a teacher softening the I-move by eliciting the topic from the learners – lines 1–2.) This demands particular skills of the teacher (the pedagogical tact or 'mindfulness' discussed by van Manen 1991, Chapter 7) and also requires learners to interpret what is said in novel ways. Such a change from a direct questioning style associated with a 'tough' form of IRF to a more 'invitational' style may create difficulties if learners question its sincerity. Deep-seated patterns of emotional response and associated action may be disturbed by the introduction of this type of pattern, and is further evidence for the connectedness of emotional and cognitive strands of classroom management.

Transcript Sample 12.1   Classroom talk

T: any other words
S5: dimples
T: dimples -- OK you said dimples / stand up Florence / smile / let me see / watch
     her / smile (*Ss laughter*) do you / have you seen any m / mark there spots here /
5   when she smiles / any holes / we can call them holes / depressions / have you
     seen it
Ss: yes maam
T: those are dimples

Case Study 4: F-moves – Cullen 2002

Cullen's micro study of the F-move (also discussed in Chapter 11), based on transcripts made in Tanzanian classrooms, adds further detail to our growing knowledge of how IRF exchanges function. He distinguishes between (a) evaluative and (b) discoursal F-moves, both of which are characterised as supporting learners. Evaluative moves are primarily pedagogic and perform functions like error treatment, or filling in gaps in knowledge. Discoursal F-moves provide 'a rich source of message-oriented target language input' (2002: 122) and are focused on the content rather than the form of the students' F-moves. There are four strategies which the teacher uses discoursally at the F-position – reformulation, elaboration, comment, repetition (a fifth quality, responsiveness, is dealt with in Chapter 11). In effect, these strategies are the fine texture of more open follow-up activities, in which the teacher extemporises on students' contributions. Unlike evaluative F-moves, which tend to close down possibilities for further exploration of a topic, discoursal moves hint at further possibilities in dialogue. Tantalisingly, we do not learn what happens after the F-move, a clear limitation of IRF-focused analysis. However, these are significant ways in which teachers manage learners' participation in classroom activity, opening or closing down opportunities, or creating opportunities for participation in a more conversational dialogue. Transmissive teaching does not necessarily restrict learning opportunity – indeed it can make certain new types of linguistic data available to students as teachers react to what they say in R-moves. In management terms, this is opportunity-focused and a prospective practice that is prospective.

More open-ended IRFs

The spread of overtly interactive language teaching methodologies has instigated research on classroom discourse which aims to establish whether or not the new methodologies are having an effect. An early example is Nunan (1987), who examines lessons for evidence of 'communicative activity'. He finds, however, that they are mainly constrained by closed IRFs. He sets up an experimental lesson encouraging students to bring their background knowledge to the class ready for classroom activity. The teacher employs referential questions as opposed to display questions in the lesson, using pictures as points of reference, and a topic of interest to students. The 'genuineness' of the resultant interaction reported by Nunan is disputed by Seedhouse (1996), who notes that because it is in a classroom, it is still a form of institutionally-mediated talk. The extent to which classroom talk becomes conversational enough to be regarded as 'non-institutional' is a productive direction for talk-based studies. Research can explore the relative 'informality' of classroom discourse and the ways in which the teacher fills the mediating role as they participate in classroom management.

An example of pedagogically-oriented research on IRFs is Seedhouse (1997), who reports on the dilemma of accuracy or fluency posed by combining form and meaning in activities. He contrasts data from closed IRFs and more open IRFs. He expresses a concern about a tendency towards 'pidginisation' in the more open-ended sequences, in which learners generate language from their existing stock of linguistic resources and knowledge. Overt and covert correction strategies for combining formal and fluency-focused classroom work are contrasted for their respective outcomes.

Case Study 5: Insiders' perspectives on classroom interaction – Nunan 1996

Nunan's study is concerned with closing the 'gap' between teachers and researchers by providing the informants with a voice to help explain the patterns of talk in their lessons. The study is based on data gathered in the lessons of 9 Australian teacher informants undertaking a professional in-service qualification. It consists of lesson observation notes and transcripts, interviews and lesson plans. The data describe the following key aspects of the lessons:

1. **'Getting going'** – the first few minutes of a lesson are when the tone and atmosphere is created, often persisting until the end of the lesson. Teachers provide continuity between lessons, and introduce the topic or route of the lesson.
2. **'Controlling the flow of events'** – Nunan recounts ways in which teachers control the direction and pace of activities, work within shared teacher/ learner histories, and modify lessons on the basis of the feedback they receive from the students as the lessons proceed.
3. **'Instruction'** – There is relatively little 'direct instruction' in the lessons, rather a series of extended exchanges in which learners are dynamically engaged. '... both teachers and learners are actively involved in the con- struction and interpretation of their worlds' (1996: 52). The openness of the IRF exchanges he cites as evidence are not directly referred to in the study, but are the essence of the free-flowing and participative interactions that take place, where students' guesses are employed to initiate further discussion.

In research terms, Nunan argues forcefully for an appreciation of the class- room world *for what it is*, and the outsider researcher's position as 'a shadowy figure inhabiting a world which is neither connected to the ongoing drama, nor entirely divorced from it. It is a voice which needs to be complemented by the other, often hidden voices of the classroom, if anything like a three-dimensional picture of what drives the learning process is to emerge' (1996: 53). Simply examining transcripts is not sufficient for a real understanding of what teachers and learners do.

12.3   Culturally-oriented studies

We have seen in Part 1 that classrooms are cultural and social contexts, and that they also vary in character geographically. Studies of classrooms which highlight either the effects of broad cultural practices or influences from outside the class- room contribute to understanding of how classroom management practices have roots and connections outside as well as inside the classroom. This is reflected to a greater or lesser extent in the discoursal patterns of classroom talk.

Case Study 6: Embarrassment and hygiene – MacKay 1993

Mackay's (1993) study of practices in a cross-cultural teaching-learning situation identifies teachers' 'hygiene resources' with which they attend to moments in lessons when students are 'embarrassed'. He demonstrates how, by a series of strategies, teachers make tasks cognitively less demanding and also more context-embedded. He cites the example of a failure to prompt students' written composition work despite careful prior preparation. The teacher abandons group work and, through a tightly-constructed series of IRFs eliciting previous knowledge from the students, she constructs the outline of the composition on the blackboard. The students' task is considerably simplified and all they eventually have to do is copy the story from the board. The use of the board is also significant in this example. The process of writing material on the board structures the trouble-shooting sequence and also provides a written record of the students' Rs, thus confirming their correctness.

Because students in the study area (northwest Canada) often found both subject matter and classroom activity too complex, teachers employed 'reduction' strategies to help students in order to 'maintain the appearance of normal functioning' (1993: 38).

'Embarrassment' (students' behaviour signals in moments of difficulty):

- silence in response to teacher question;
- delay in response to teacher question;
- incomprehensible response;
- inarticulate response;
- delays in producing constructed written response;
- incomplete written work.

'Hygiene resources' (devices to reduce embarrassment and allow students to participate, and to save face by maintaining *appearance* of appropriate grade standards):

- expansion of minimal responses;
- reduction in question complexity – to 'yes/no';
- rapid reading of textbook by teacher;
- use of fill-in-blank worksheets;
- verbatim copying of blackboard notes;
- dictation of notes orally;
- reading aloud from textbook by students of correct answers;
- oral composition with whole class at the board;
- reading aloud for students;
- vicarious dialogue conducted by teacher who takes both parts – students listen;
- academic palliatives (use of non-technical language to reinforce what students say in simple everyday language);
- substitution of simple task for difficult task.

Mackay confirmed all these behaviours with the teachers concerned. The study highlights the ways in which teachers modify their use of talk in concert with their teaching strategies in order to create learning opportunities.

These adjustments in discourse style are responsive to learners' cultural practices and are also integral to the classroom culture. In cross-cultural classroom situations, such micro management practices are worthy of further inquiry as indicators of acculturation, and of the development of a classroom group's history, as well as a student group's way of handling different pedagogies.

Case Study 7: Safe talk – Chick 1996

Chick's study is a valuable exemplar of how a researcher can seek understanding of classroom management practices by examining the influence of wider context realities on classroom activity. Chick worked as an in-service training adviser in the former KwaZulu region of South Africa, trying to implement communicative approaches to English teaching. There was considerable resistance to or lack of uptake of the new methodology, which Chick surmised might be due to the interactive styles favoured by Zulu speakers. These feature status markers and practices quite different from the European communication practices which inform CLT. As he puts it, 'teachers and students in KwaZulu schools resisted the adoption of 'egalitarian, decentralised ways of interacting' (1996: 22). Chick decided to investigate by:

- collecting classroom data (recorded and observational);
- discussions and interviews with teachers (the students' perceptions might have given his study even more impact).

The key features of a Mathematics lesson he analysed were as follows:

- high teacher volubility, high student taciturnity (a deference strategy in Zulu culture, but common worldwide) – teachers talk a lot, students are mainly silent;
- high incidence of chorusing from the students, prompted by two types of cue: yes/no questions and rising intonation (the latter is significant in Zulu, which is a tonal language and relies on more paralinguistic and other non-verbal cues than English, which was the medium of instruction.) On closer inspection, Chick realised that the restricted responses actually provided students with an 'escape route' by seeking only confirmatory responses. The cultural practices ensure that there is marked asymmetry between teacher and student;
- the exchanges are extremely rhythmic, which provided synchrony and therefore the sense that something important was happening.

Chick speculates that these practices are social rather than academic. They enable both students and teachers to save face by (a) not being wrong, or (b) not being seen as incompetent. They are thus low-risk, a set of practices he terms 'safe-talk'.

An important feature of this study is that Chick is not satisfied with the outcomes of his micro-ethnographic analysis. He goes further by linking the classroom events to forces emanating from outside the classroom. The outcome is a discussion of the roots of practices in the practices of apartheid. The practices Chick observes and analyses are in fact ways of teachers and students coping with the difficulties of education in poorly funded schools which the ideologies of apartheid had created. Rather than adopt the new mode of discourse, students and teachers had invested so much in safe-talk that change was next to impossible. Despite the dismantling of apartheid some years earlier, the practices had persisted.

Case Study 8: English in Botswanan Classrooms – Arthur 1994

Botswana is a country where English is used as a medium of instruction in education. English has a limited functional role in wider society, however, as the vast majority of people share a common mother tongue, Setswana. Arthur's ethnographic study highlights how the limited range of English use outside the classroom appears to be transferred into the classroom, with the consequence that a transmission mode is perpetuated. This has consequences for the ways in which participation is managed. Drawing on talk data from two Primary level classrooms, Arthur points out that:

- Teachers used Setswana for complex classroom instructions, but English for more simple ones, or more serious matters of indiscipline.
- Students only very rarely asked teachers questions.
- A great deal of time is spent going over learning material through sequences of repetition and recitation. English in these instances is used to display already codified information, what the children already know, in grammatically correct 'final draft' form (Barnes 1976) Students, rather than struggling to give correct information, struggle to encode these correctly.

Like Chick, Arthur explores the social and cultural context of language use as a way of coming to a more informed understanding of what she encounters at classroom level. She notes that despite the adoption of 'new', more communicative methodologies, closed IRF patterns of talk persisted and prevented the establishment of the more open discourses implied by the new methodology, suggesting that these patterns are deeply etched in the classroom cultures of Botswana, and other contexts like the UK, as Edwards and Mercer (Case Study 2) point out.

Prophet (1995) finds similar phenomena in his study of the impact of a more 'communicative' methodology on Botswanan classrooms. Following the development of a new curriculum and materials, twelve 'trial schools' were set up in a government initiative to 'field test' the new approach. Prophet's observations, recordings and interviews with teachers and students were conducted at two of these schools. His conclusions were that:

- teacher-centred whole-class teaching persisted;
- students continued to listen passively and participate minimally;
- teachers spent little or no time working with individuals or small groups;
- teachers generally continued to ignore incorrect student responses and not to offer remediation.

Students, Prophet discovered, 'preferred the security of silent and individual written desk work' (1995: 136). Teachers, in their efforts to maintain the management status quo, deliberately distorted the materials to 'normal' classroom routines (recitation, closed IRFs, strict discipline and enforcement). Interestingly, Prophet explores the reasons for this and locates these within:

- the teacher culture and low affective quality of the schools;
- teachers' negative attitudes about students' capacities to speak and learn; and
- students' resistance to new teaching methodologies, for example a need to stay quiet or risk corporal punishment.

Both Arthur's and Prophet's studies demonstrate the powerful influence of school and local cultures on classroom discourses in one context and help us understand some of the roots of resistance to change pertaining to classroom management practices.

Case Study 9: Code-switching in Sri Lankan secondary lessons – Canagarajah 1995

Canagarajah's study of 24 secondary school teachers in Jaffna (Sri Lanka) reveals different uses of Tamil, the teachers' mother tongue, and English for different functions in lessons. He argues that this 'natural' or unintended use of code-switching in lessons prepares students for the sociolinguistic world they face outside the school. Classroom practices therefore serve a valid function for learners. 'The evolving patterns of bilingualism in the larger society can help explain the basis of code choice in the English classrooms' (1995: 173). Canagarajah studies the transcripts of a number of lessons and identifies what he terms management and instructional uses of Tamil.

Uses of Tamil for classroom management
- Opening the class – for example, to organise the room.
- Negotiating directions – pre-instructions are in Tamil (but there is no choice about the use of English for the activity itself).
- Requesting help – students request help to perform an activity in Tamil.
- Managing discipline – students used Tamil to complain about their classmates.

- Providing encouragement – teachers encouraged students to perform.
- Providing compliments – teachers' compliments were given in Tamil.
- Motivating students – by using Tamil markers of solidarity and relative closeness, teachers are motivating students to participate.
- Pleading – Tamil is used by students for excuses and asking for favours.
- Gossip, etc. – students used Tamil for 'unofficial interactions'.

Content transmission   Explicit instruction should have been in English, but code switches were made:

- For review sessions.
- To provide definitions.
- To explain – teachers used many means such as reformulations, qualifications, providing examples and anecdotes.
- Negotiating cultural relevance – for discussing culturally relevant anecdotes.
- Parallel transitions – Tamil and English are used sequentially to describe drawings on the board, for example.
- Student collaboration – Canagarajah noted that all 'backstage' conversation between students was in Tamil.

He concludes that while English is used for interactions demanded by textbook and lesson, Tamil was used for all other functions. The management/ instruction dichotomy serves to separate two broader functions, but the data cited in the study shows instruction and management flowing into and out of one another. The instructional uses of Tamil are perhaps more usefully construed in management terms as part of a discourse of lesson management designed to enable penetration of the alien code, English.

Case Study 10: Classroom culture – Kramsch and Sulivan 1996

Drawing on data collected in Vietnamese university classrooms, Kramsch and Sullivan demonstrate what happens when a Vietnamese teacher uses teaching materials written in the UK with a group of 20–30 students. The discourse is analysed with reference to various aspects of the Vietnamese university classroom culture, as follows:

- The student group stay together throughout a day and for periods of years rather than terms.
- Highly differentiated teacher and learner classroom roles, reflecting Confucian values.
- A 'national culture' with a rich oral literacy tradition.

The encounter with the foreign culture is through the teacher training system, run in the main by mother tongue English-speaking experts who adhere to a broadly 'communicative' view of language teaching.

They identify three broad aspects of classroom culture and participation patterns:

1. Class responses are frequently chorused. The talk is collaborative and accretional. Teachers and learners 'build' sequences, and the emphasis is on verbal creativity and even poetic licence. They identify students and teachers who 'enjoy playing with the ideas and using new words' (1996: 205).
2. The teacher is a mentor who guides students in moral behaviour. They cite examples of this running through exchanges where teacher offers admonitions for behaviour and attitudes. They point out that this persists despite the apparently informal teacher-student relationship.
3. Playing with language – quick responses, puns, repartee are all part of the classroom discourse and valued as such.

The outcome is that 'Vietnamese teachers and students... transform British authenticity (in the course book) into Vietnamese authenticity' (1996: 210). This results in a more collective approach to managing participation, and greater tolerance of apparently 'random' contributions to classroom talk than might be permissible in a European setting. In this case, opportunity is created jointly, not in a contrived manner, but in a manner drawing directly from the social and cultural traditions in which the classrooms are located. There is no issue regarding order *per se*. Rather, the talk is both self and collectively managed in an atmosphere of calm and enjoyment. The affective domain and the discoursal domains intersect in ways which less collaborative classroom cultures do not and possibly cannot replicate, despite the efforts of teachers to engineer collaboration. The conclusions they draw are that collaboration has to emerge organically from the culture, and that working within the established routines of a classroom culture may be more successful in bringing about this confluence than any amount of new teaching material, even in apparently 'friendly' contexts of origin. The management discourse appears either to be dominant and enabling in classrooms, or correspondingly discoursally disabling, thus overriding or 'localising' instructional strategies intended by course book writers.

Case Study 11: Resisting methodology – Cangarajah 1993

In a groundbreaking ethnographic study of a university classroom in northern Sri Lanka, Canagarajah traces the history of a classroom group's encounter with teaching materials written in the United States. It is a study of the experience of perceived domination by externally-imposed values and of opposition to this domination. Unlike many studies of classroom life, Canagarajah's overtly takes the learners' point of view as the starting point for discussion. It is also more than a descriptive study of how classroom participants mange their context. It is an interpretive and ultimately *critical* study, ideologically sensitive and culturally oriented, questioning asymmetries implicit in the teaching materials. Working as a participant observer in his class for one year, the author also used initial questionnaires, free recall procedures where students were asked to write down their impressions of English, and oral interviews towards the end of the year. Student notebooks were also a useful source of data and comment. The rich data built up through these means provides him with a basis for interrogating the classroom culture.

He traced three distinct periods in the life of the group:

1. **Pre-course determination**. Students were keen to learn English and had positive attitudes towards it. However, the author suspects some inhibitions at this stage.
2. **Mid-course resistance**. The inhibitions surface. Attendance fell from 94 per cent to 50 per cent after two months. Many excuses were made. At the same time, students deface their course books – an active under-life, or backstage life, emerges where students initiate another discourse in the twilight zone. This mediates the course book content on the one hand and on the other challenges the textual language, values and ideology. (1993:613/4) The participation in the underlife consists for example, of ways of making fun of the book, 'localising' drawings by adding local features. The author notes that the students are able to produce language of far greater complexity and range in their underlife than in the grammar drills which they frequently get wrong.

   The book also proposed dispreferred ways of learning such as pair and group work. The students rearranged the furniture to fit a teacher-led lecture-based mode despite the teacher's requests. They also forced the lessons to become product rather than process-focused; they resisted English as a medium of instruction. Canagarajah explains this as the result of the challenge to their identity posed by English. The author sees what he terms as a dual-oppositional trend' – on the one hand opposing the alien discourses represented in the book and on the other desiring a product-oriented pedagogy (1993: 616). Essentially, because students could see no relevance for the course in their socio-cultural background, they saw little meaning for it other than satisfying institutional demands.
3. **Post-course contradiction**. Canagarajah discovers that students are taking private English lessons outside the university. The tutors used Indian or Sri Lankan texts, with a strong grammatical orientation. Surprisingly, the students showed no open antipathy towards American culture, but seemed to have learnt it as content. This was in direct contrast to the lived classroom culture Canagarajah had witnessed.

In conclusion, Canagarajah observes that he believes his own identity contributed to the classroom culture in significant ways. It leads one to speculate on the extent to which students may have hoped to recruit his ethnic solidarity in their own struggles. He concludes that the students did not display resistance to the course book and pedagogy, rather it was a more unfocused, non-ideological *opposition*. The study demonstrates that observation and other procedures can uncover important patterns of participation, and interpret them in juxtaposition to the local context. Canagarajah sees this type of study as the basis for a more critical pedagogy which is both ideologically liberating as well as educationally meaningful, presumably entailing new discourses of care and opportunity, and challenging the existing order.

12.4   Studies of lesson management

Pedagogically-oriented studies of classroom discourse provide useful insights into micro-level classroom management practices at work. These studies are deepened by interpretation which refers to 'external' and 'psychological insights.

Case Study 12: Managed Improvisation – 2002

Van Dam studies the English first lesson of a group of Dutch secondary school children. His aim is to trace the emergence and roots of a classroom culture. He does this by analysing the transcript of the lesson on a 'moment-by-moment' basis, working within the 'ecological' tradition to produce a highly detailed and fine-grained account. The key events van Dam identifies are, he posits, the basis of an emerging classroom culture. Three significant ones are:

1. **Starting out** – pre-lesson business. The first part of the lesson is organisational, getting the children to sit in pre-assigned places and to introduce the course book, and the routines to be followed in the course. The students are encouraged to speak up right from the start, as well. All of these events are important in the context of first lessons as 'gate-keeping' events (after Erickson and Shultz 1992). The teacher also introduces an element of play into the class, as well as digressing frequently, in one instance about differences in target language proficiency and their lack of social or intellectual significance.
2. **The 'first class question'** – this opens the discussion of common ground. At this stage, a turn-taking system is negotiated. Prosodic features of speech and timing are central to this process. The rhythms of participation and the contextualisation cues are laid down and tried out, under the teacher's control.
3. **'Wasp hunt'** – a wasp is disturbing the teacher. She makes this into a dramatic incident, with a student appointed to dispatch the insect. Solidarity and equal status is established in a matter of two minutes – the message is 'this is one of the ways we can work together'.

The author returns to the class three weeks later and sees that the culture has evolved from a whole-class, teacher led participation system to a more student-led and collaborative system, with different individuals in the class taking specialised roles. Whole-class participation is reserved for repair and rehearsal. Communication is now more direct, and less overtly polite. The interplay between play and serious work has become established as a norm.

Van Dam's argument that the classroom culture is grounded in its participation system is significant. Employing such delicate and detailed analysis opens up the possibility of similar longitudinal studies of how teachers and students create and learn their culture together. In a similar vein, Bannink (2002) further demonstrates how an analysis of 'spontaneous talk' in the classroom reveals evidence of improvised talk management within a framework of 'rules' and contextualisation cues.

Case Study 13: Learner initiative – Garton 2002

Garton's small-scale study explores what happens to the discourse when learners take the initiative. She defines learner initiative as 'an attempt to direct the interaction in a way that corresponds more closely to the interests and needs of the learners' (2002: 48). This happens when:

- a learner's turn is not a direct response to teacher elicitation (it is self-selected); and
- the learner's turn gains control of the floor (there is subsequent uptake from teacher or other learners).

Using extracts from classroom transcripts gathered in 5 different teachers' adult general English classrooms at an Italian University, Garton demonstrates the effects of learner initiative. In some of her examples, learner initiative elicits direct teaching – overt correction, provision of explanations on the teacher's part, for example. She also shows that the teacher-student exchanges which follow an instance of learner initiative can lead to students being more accurate, as the exchange 'shapes' their contributions by forcing them to be clear.

Garton concludes that learner initiative is a healthy aspect of classroom interaction. Teachers are not creating learning opportunities – learners are. The research demonstrates that given time and space (in the 'psychological' sense) to think and formulate utterances, teachers can provide learners with opportunities for joint management of the discourse, and thus, indirectly, of their own learning. Garton's research also explores the notion that classroom discourse is a form of institutional discourse (see also Seedhouse 1997) which positions teachers and learners. Her understanding of initiative draws on an analysis of how learner initiative challenges the prevailing institutional discourse, grounded in a deeply transmissive view of education.

A number of other classroom management strategies have been discovered in which teachers overtly assist learners either to understand a task (clarifying instructions) or to arrive at correct answers to closed questions. These are particularly striking in the studies of bilingual classrooms (e.g. Addendorf 1996; Lin 2001) and also as reviewed by Martin-Jones (2000) (Concept 12.3). The primary strategy in these classrooms is to use the students' L1 either as an amplifier to ongoing pedagogic activity, or as a problem-solving device. (See also Case Study 9 in this chapter.)

Concept 12.3   Talk management strategies in bilingual classrooms

Code-Switching between L2 and L1 (using L1)
- Paraphrasing in L1 to reinforce or reiterate messages by listing or summarising, reformulations and clarifications – particularly noticeable in I and F positions of IRFs.
- To encourage students to share enthusiasm.
- To emphasise social distance or solidarity between students and teachers.
- To clarify e.g. instructions by distinguishing between classroom management and lesson content.
- Signal transitions between phases of lessons.
- Signal difference between doing a lesson and 'talking about it'.
- Making a personalised aside (change of footing).
- Distinguish quotes from a written text from talk about the quotes.
- Bring out voices from a narrative.
- Explanations of difficult points, e.g. vocabulary.
- Create links with cultural content and outside world.
- Raise interest in a topic.

(after Addendorf 1996; Lin 2001; Martin-Jones 2000)

Other examples of teachers working together with students in the management of their learning include teacher-guided reporting (Gibbons 2001) joint storytelling (Kramsch and Sullivan 1996) and language play (Kramsch and Sullivan 1996; Sullivan 2000). In all of these instances there is joint construction of discourse between teachers and students. IRF patterns are broken down and there are more sequential turns by students. Teachers' turns tend to be relatively non-directive and prompt rather than 'push' students' contributions. In a small-scale study Gibbons (2001) studied the transcripts of an ESL science lesson in a primary bilingual classroom in Australia. He establishes that the teacher assists the learners through a discoursal routine termed 'teacher-guided reporting' (2001: 262) following experimental 'hands-on' work aimed at 'stretching' learners' language. The teacher's contributions to student talk are amplifying and affirming through repetitions, and by offering positive feedback and praise to student speakers.

Case Study 14: Exploratory talk with children – Haynes 2001

Haynes has spent several years practicing and researching the techniques of 'philosophy with children' or 'philosophical inquiry' in the UK (2001: 119–24). Looking at the process very much from the teacher's perspective, she has identified a series of skills and qualities required in order to facilitate this type of exploratory activity. Discoursally, this type of work is likely to feature learner initiative, collaboratively 'built' talk among children and teacher, and a non-evaluative teacher managing with care and opportunity foremost in her mind.

Teacher qualities and skills required for facilitating philosophical enquiry:

1. **Presence** (cognitive, affective, psychic understanding of learners. Developed with frequency of teaching a group. Recognising unique and original aspects of teaching encounters):

   - 'In the classroom of a teacher with presence, children are volunteers rather than captives' (120).
   - Body language, voice, attention to detail, hope and expectation are communicated to learners.
   - 'Holding a class' intellectually and emotionally, firmly, strongly, lightly to allow personal freedom, choice, intellectual independence, growth.
   - Attention (focused and unfocused) to the immediate fabric of classroom events, to respond to children's contributions, to maintain dialogue, allow intuition to guide. It 'belongs to the *potential space* that the teacher establishes with the children's consent and within which the teacher and the children explore the possibilities that each lesson offers' (121)

2. **Preparation** (of physical and material surroundings, materials, etc. – children can assist – and personally)

   - Rehearsal – a 'mental run through the unfolding of a lesson' (122).
   - Dwelling – 'staying with the detail of rich episodes of classroom interaction and trying to hold on to nuances and fragments' (122).
   - Staying with the unexpected, critical moments in teaching/learning.
   - Readiness – awareness and use of strategies that assist in 'deploying energy, creativity and energy' – physical and emotional.
   - Freewheeling – allowing the mind to 'freewheel' and for solutions to problems to emerge.
   - Hooks and Bridges – 'original ways of starting lessons, or pushing children's thinking a bit further on' – bridges in lessons (123)

- Ways in which meaning and engagement can be brought to the fore.
- Active Listening – encourages all participants to suspend their own answers and opinions to hear and understand each other properly.

Learner-managed talk – handover

More recently, studies in the socio-cultural tradition have explored aspects of the management of classroom discourse using concepts like scaffolding. One aspect that interests researchers is the notion of learner management of talk. In scaffolding terms, once learners begin control a sequence of talk (or appropriate it Lantolf 2000), contributing from their own resources in the target language, 'handover' may have begun. (See Figure 12.1). Handover is not a definitive and undifferentiated notion however. It does not, as the metaphor suggests, imply immediate transfer, like a relay baton. As in a relay race, there is a zone for handover, in which teachers retain the right to intervene for a range of reasons. This occurs in the early stages of handover when learners are engaged in producing their own talk or writing, when they are assumed still not to have fully appropriated and internalised the knowledge or skill. Teachers retain a degree of control over the activity through the task itself, which may have built-in restrictions regarding goals and anticipated outcomes. Van Lier (1998) cites an example of learner-learner instruction in producing a group essay in which two students teach a colleague the pronunciation of a word in a 'brief side sequence within a larger interaction ... jointly initiated, jointly constructed and jointly concluded' (1998: 140). What is interesting is that in this student-mediated episode initiation is collective, marking the interaction as fundamentally different in quality to the teacher-initiated interactions which can lead to the handover zone.

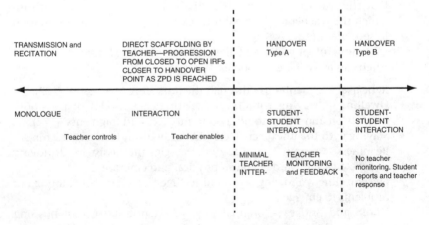

Figure 12.1   Scaffolding and handover

When students embark on tasks they have helped to design themselves, and work without direct supervision (teacher in a 'consultancy' position, or not even physically present – 'project work' outside the classroom), they are simulating real-world language use and manipulation, under their own direction (production activities). Classrooms remain part of the handover zone when students report on work they have done in either public (orally or 'presentation mode) or private (written) domains.

Concept 12.4   Teaching/learning management in the handover zone

Teachers – camouflage correction, entering flow of S-S talk as co-participants
        confirm learner accuracy or success in communicating
        lower social distance in entering group talk
        'patrolling', monitoring, answering requests for assistance
Learners – scaffold each other (often in closed IRF – expert/novice – mode)
        co-construct talk and writing within the parameters set by tasks
        practice 'private speech'
        negotiate meaning
        self-correct and initiate correction

Studies of students working across the handover zone have identified both teacher and learner management of interaction (Concept 12.4). Pedagogic tasks still drive the interactions, but what learners actually do under these conditions is rather different from what they do under teachers' control. The evidence suggests that learners are more skilled at managing talk than they are often given credit for. Lynch's (1997: 321) comment that 'when teachers intervene to avoid a problem [in student task work], they may also remove the need to negotiate meaning, and so, perhaps, the opportunity for learning' illustrates the paradox of learning management in the classroom – that it is only when teachers intervene that they realise that students are often able to solve problems on their own. The nature of the task (open or closed; student or teacher-generated; form or meaning focused) influences the types of difficulty that students may encounter and it may therefore be possible for teachers to gauge their interventions accordingly. One strategy that may prove fruitful in these circumstances is for a covert ground rule to be established which enables learners to initiate teacher intervention (Case Study 13), rather than as Lynch suggests in raising students' awareness of 'negotiating strategies', which the evidence demonstrates are already well-developed, regardless of code. There is clear evidence from the Donato (1994) Seedhouse (1999) and de Almeida Mattos (2000) studies that learners are more than able to scaffold themselves within a task framework provided by the teacher.

Learner-managed talk – summary of selected studies

Donato (1994)

In this study of university students learning French in the USA, Donato analysed classroom transcripts. The main findings confirmed that there was a great deal of mutual student support and assistance:

- During non-structured tasks, students 'create a context of shared understanding in which the negotiation of language form and meaning co-occur' (1994: 43).
- During social interaction in class: Donato found 'a rich fabric of inter-individual help . . . in social interactions'. He found students 'quite capable and skilful at providing the type of scaffolded help that is associated in the development literature with only the most noticeable forms of expert-novice interaction, such as parent-child (1994: 52).

Lynch (1997)

A study of teacher's interventions in student group work (in EAP classes in a university setting) in a pre-writing task. It shows teachers' interventions into learner talk (a) entering students' talk, (b) using their role to 'nudge' students towards understanding. This is evidence of 'supportive rather than pro-active' interventions (1997:321) 'not to initiate the process of negotiation but to support the learners in a process which is already under way' (1997: 322).

Seedhouse (1999)

This is a study of the effect of tasks on student–student interaction. 'Task-based interaction as a variety has certain striking and distinctive characteristics' (1999: 150). Teacher withdraws after allocating tasks to learners to allow them to manage the tasks themselves. Students can ask for assistance. Main findings: (a) students create a turn-taking system appropriate to the task itself, (b) interaction is very 'life-like' due to minimalisation of linguistic forms and indexicality – context-bound (1999: 152), (c) tasks generate many 'scaffolding' activities – requests for clarification, confirmation checks, etc.

De Almeida Mattos (2000)

In a study of students preparing collaboratively (pair-work) for an oral test, de Almeida Mattos reveals students engaged in expert-novice dialogue, drawing on their respective strengths to solve problems. She demonstrates that this can 'go wrong' where students' contributions can lead to wrong conclusions. This is negative evidence for the power of scaffolding. She shows how material appropriated from pair work is reproduced in individual interviews. De Almeida Mattos also cites evidence of differential work on tasks and also students engaging in private speech in moments of difficulty.

12.5   Online classroom discourse

In Chapter 8, we examined the issue of the emergence of new discourses online. Managing the online classroom, as we saw, presents special challenges for the moderator and the learner, most notably in the area of interacting in a textual medium. The online classroom culture shares features of the face-to-face classroom culture. The same educational issues are replicated, and even amplified in online courses, most particularly in the ways in which participants manage communication and the work of a course through the written medium.

Case Study 15: Relationships between online discussion and writing for assessment – Goodfellow et al. 2004

Goodfellow and his colleagues are concerned with establishing the ways in which literacy practices are being 'reconfigured' online. A critical area is in the relationship between the use of writing for more informal discussion and for formal assessment. In the study the authors look at how students in an online university course used written language for the various tasks during the course, and how the discussion stage of the course contributed to the written assessment.

The research methodology entailed a participant observer in two parallel online communities observing online conferences (10–15 students) and engaging in e-mail dialogue with the four students who agreed to participate. The participant observer also managed to obtain copies of four completed assignments.

Some of the significant findings were:

- There was tension between students' desires to come to a collective and socially constructed understanding of tasks – by, for example, discussing the bases of tasks, and offering criticism – and the way in which they gave value to the 'correct procedure' given by the tutor and implicit in the written assignment.
- Students found it difficult to reconcile different audiences for their work: coursework for professionally real audiences and assessment for the tutor's eyes.
- The course forced students to switch between dialogic discussion modes of learning to the monologue of a written assignment.
- Citation of online discussion sources in written assignments. The authors identify this as a newly-emergent practice resulting from the reflective orientation of the courses.

The authors note in conclusion that the tensions and practices revealed by the research indicate a need for further research into collective modes on learning online. Their goal is the establishment of online learning *communities* and they are concerned, ultimately, that the practices of face-to-face education are being replicated online, making it difficult to establish more collaborative modes of learning to exploit the opportunities the medium presents.

Summary

The selection of research studies cited in this chapter offers a rich tapestry of means of examining classroom discourse for evidence of classroom management practices. These studies appear to be particularly valuable for examining the effects of new curriculum practices on existing practices, and locate opposition to change in a number of talk-related and local cultural practices.

13
New Directions in Research on Classroom Management Case Studies

Chapters 10–12 contain discussion of classroom management practices and selected illustrative case studies on the themes of time and space, engagement and participation in classroom management. This chapter examines a series of studies in and out of the classroom which, either through their methodological stance, or through their direct relevance for classroom management, point us in new directions in researching the area.

13.1   Research on teacher cognitions and practices

Case Study 1: Teachers' classroom practices and teachers' thinking – Lee 1999

Purposes   To investigate the problematical relationship between teachers' thinking and their classroom practices; and to investigate the impact of participation in research on teachers' practices.

Participants   Two experienced secondary school English language teachers in Kuala Lumpur, Malaysia. Both volunteered to take part in the research. A third volunteer withdrew from the project at an early stage.

Research procedures   Intensive one-to-one interviews (39) with the teachers and observations of their classroom practice (18 lessons) over four months. Lee was attached to the school as a teacher-researcher and took part in the life of the school in and out of the class. Interviews were held at times suitable for the teachers, and were unstructured, but with a conversational 'gambit'.

Examples of gambits:

- Roles of teachers and learners.
- The nature of language learning.
- Class management.
- Teaching resources.
- Teaching metaphors.

Classroom observation and recording was conducted whenever possible. Ethnographic data about the school context were also collected to enrich the interpretation of the interview and classroom data – school context and culture have an influence on teachers' views of teaching.

Data analysis
Lessons were transcribed and analysed in a four-step process:

- Analysis of individual lessons to identify key features of structure and activity.
- Comparison across individual teacher's lessons to look for recurring features.
- Re-examination of individual lessons to verify and confirm features.
- Comparison of features of both teachers' lessons.

The interviews were transcribed and analysed thematically, and systematically coded. Emergent themes and incidents in the interviews were used as a source of material to explore the thinking behind practice. Example themes were control, teacher role, and discipline. Incidents and patterns in classroom activity were matched against themes in the interviews in a search for consistency of thinking and action.

Outcomes
1. The two teachers' dominant metaphors for teaching revealed a rich inner world of cognitions about classroom teaching and learning, not always neatly packaged, however.
2. The teachers' classroom practices were consistent across a range of lessons in terms of their management strategies – a consistent lesson structure emerged:

Stage 1 'HOUSEKEEPING' – up to seven minutes' classroom time. Teacher–student activity to reduce the uncertainty of new situation (e.g. the presence of a researcher in class), settle class after previous lesson, or do administrative tasks. Teacher A initiated all housekeeping; Teacher B allowed her students to initiate housekeeping activity.

Stage 2 TEACHING and LEARNING ACTIVITIES – the bulk of every lesson. Based on syllabus topics which were activated by 'discoursal topics' (what teacher and students talked about). Teacher A maintains control over topic initiation, and topics follow a teacher presentation-student engagement – teacher feedback sequence. Lessons appear very episodic. Teacher B allows some student initiation of topics. Activities are punctuated by 'side topics'; more side topics in Teacher B's lessons, often student-initiated. Teacher B links activities and begins new activities with a 'warm-up', followed by a sequence similar to Teacher A, but when there is written composition, returns to a more open-ended management of the activity, assisting students in 'building' new language.

Stage 3 CLOSURE – leave taking. Students stand to thank teacher, and vice versa. Closure is ritually observed, even if activity has not been finished.

Both teachers attest to the benefits of talking about their teaching – as a safety valve and an aid to improving what they do. Lee speculates that the types of dialogue he initiated with the teachers could be an effective teacher development format and that metaphor is a useful bridge between theory and practice.

Issues raised by the research
1. Research on teaching is itself a socially constructed enterprise and has effects on researchers and informants. The process itself is a learning activity for both informants and researchers. There is a potential need for an 'outsider' to enable teachers or learners to express themselves, and to assist them in this articulation. (See Nunan, Case Study 6 in Chapter 12.)
2. Representations of teachers' inner lives and thinking as elicited through talk. Informants may become more adept at articulating what they think and believe as a result of a long-term process of dialogue. Data drawn from one-off interviews should be treated with circumspection. Representing informants' voices is problematic.
3. Problems of participant observation and ethnographic field relations, including access to research sites and informants.
4. Management as a guiding and linking element in classroom life. All activities and stages are linked through teachers' management of time and discourse. Teaching and learning also need to be understood in relation to the school contexts in which they occur. Teachers' constructions of themselves and their teaching are bound up with views of the role and nature of work in individuals' lives.
5. Difficulties of establishing congruity between thinking and practice. Causal links are rejected, but indirect connections are established and realised through management practices.
6. Relativism – small-scale, in-depth research may not reveal broad 'truths, but can be replicated across different contexts. Comparative studies are necessary.

Case Study 2: Teachers' principles and classroom practices – Breen et al. 2001

Purpose To understand experienced teachers' classroom practices in relation to underlying pedagogic principles (see also Breen 1991).

Participants Eighteen Australian ESL teachers (14 female, 4 male), of whom ten were teachers of adults and eight primary school teachers. ESL experience ranged between three and 26 years (average eleven years). Most had done further studies and all had participated in in-service training. They taught classes for students with a very wide range of L1s. All participating teachers were volunteers. The data collection took approximately five weeks and all five members of the research team were involved.

Research procedures
1. Initial meeting with volunteer in their work place to explain the purpose of the study, and the planned sequence of observation and discussion.
2. Classes were observed and interviews conducted immediately afterwards for approximately one hour. The teachers were asked to describe what they and the students did in the lesson. As the teacher spoke, each practice mentioned was written on a card. The researcher then asked how typical the practices were and if there were any other practices they used but had not featured in the lesson. The researcher was able to identify some 8–10 practices. The researcher then asked the teacher the reasons for each practice in turn on separate cards. A bio-data questionnaire was given to the teacher after the interview.
3. Before the second interview, a grid for each teacher was drawn up by each researcher, as follows:

REASONS FOR ACTIONS	1	2	3	4 etc
ACTIONS	1	2	3 etc	

In the interview, the teacher is asked to look at the relationship between each action and each reason in turn and to rate their relationship on a strong-weak scale (1–3). These were recorded onto the grid. At the end of the interview the researcher asked the teacher to nominate any aspect of classroom practice to focus on in the next observation. The teacher was also asked to write a short account of a critical incident in their teaching that had been significant to them.
4. Second observed lesson: researcher observed and took field notes on specified practice. Immediately after the lesson the teacher was shown the grid analysing the pattern of relationships between actions and rationale. Researcher points out the particular practices with strong rationales clustered around them. The teacher is asked to give a phrase of sentence which expresses or thematises the relationship between the practice and its reasons. A new set of cards containing the themes was thus created. When this process was complete, the teacher was asked to read through the new set of cards and then to arrange them in order of priorities as a teacher. The researcher then discussed the lesson and explored the observed practice in depth – its significance and typicality. The teacher

was asked which of the new principles it most directly expressed. The critical incident is then explored with relation to the cards. The teacher is thus able to confirm, adapt and elaborate on the emergent principles. Agreement then made for the teacher to video record and preview the recording before the next interview.

Researcher writes a 3–5 page description of the teacher in the third person, based on practices and principles. A draft model of the teacher's pedagogy is drawn up. Teacher is asked to read the description before the next interview.

5. Teacher and researcher watch video-recorded lesson and teacher indicates key features/incidents. Researcher explores the notion of typicality with reference to the lesson. The description and model are discussed, and a final, agreed model is drawn up.
6. The description is agreed at a fifth and final interview, as well as the model.

Data analysis Researchers exchange expressed and prioritised lists of principles and models of pedagogy. Decisions to group the principles under 5 headings based on conceptualisations of teachers' knowledge and concerns in the professional literature, which they describe as concerns:

- how learners undertook the learning process;
- particular learner characteristics;
- how to optimise learning with classroom resources – human and material;
- subject matter;
- contribution teachers can make in role.

There was independent analysis by the research team of all the teachers' principles to check reliability of the categories. This resulted in a grouping of what appeared to be related principles across categories. Some re-categorisation of the data was undertaken.

Profiles of individual teachers were drawn up on the basis of descriptions of practice and interviews. Profiles then analysed to trace practices across the sample. This was done in reverse to confirm the relationships. Practices and principles across the samples were traced for the entire sample, and relationships identified.

Outcomes
1. The teachers differed in the way they selected and relied upon different practices. Considerable variation in principle/practice relationships across the sample.
2. Some twelve principles were common across the group – for example: being aware of and acting upon individual differences between students. Considerable variation in how this principle was put into practice according to age of students and individual teacher.

3. A compilation of the data across all the sample revealed that there was not much overlap between practices the teachers related to one particular principle compared with those they related to another. This demonstrated that a different shared principle is expressed through a different set of practices. The reverse principle to practice procedure revealed that there was a consistent relationship between classroom practices and 'clusters of principles'.
4. The overall conclusion derived from the analysis is that consistent and widely-held principles underlie diverse practices.

Issues raised by the research
1. The authors challenge research which infers thought from behaviour (e.g. questioning, feedback, etc.) or which impute action from expressions of cognitions. They point towards research which attempts to connect thought and action.
2. There are indications of a common 'ideology' of practice among the sample (expressed through shared principles). Research in different contexts or with teachers of different age ranges or stages of learners might extend this notion.
3. The research was, as the authors point out, 'a snapshot'. Longitudinal studies might either confirm or disconfirm teachers' practice-principle thinking and action, and deepen what might prove to be a relatively preliminary set of findings.
4. The researchers tried as far as possible to use the teachers' own ways of describing principle and practice. This poses questions for researchers working cross-culturally and through second/foreign languages, and may lead us to question some of the findings of research where teachers and learners have expressed themselves in L2s, or where researchers and informants do not share a common culture (in the broadest sense). However, sharing a pedagogic and occupational culture may compensate for this.
5. The insider/outsider problem emerges in the research, in that the elicitation procedures were seen to work from outside to inside. There could still be a sense in which the teachers felt they were being 'probed', despite the fact that they had volunteered.
6. Classroom practices were viewed through the lens of teacher and observer. The learner's voice is missing from this picture. As a way of confirming the outcomes, a learner perspective might have been useful. Learners, not surprisingly, have valid and articulate perspectives on what their teachers do.

The research was conducted by a small team, which enabled them to obtain a larger sample in a shorter time than the individual researcher. It also enabled them to conduct elaborate cross-sample analyses of complex and voluminous data.

Case Study 3: Life histories of teacher educators – Choong 2001

Purpose   To investigate the impact of a 'development project' on participating teacher educators' thinking and training practices.

Participants   Six Malaysian teacher educators from different parts of the country, two male, four female, chosen from a group of 31 teacher educators engaged in the project. Participants were approached personally and invited to take part in the project.

Research procedures   Extended fieldwork in Malaysia – four months. Life history interviews (unstructured) and personal construct interviews were conducted with informants. Training sessions involving participants were observed, and feedback comments from trainers and students sought. Documentary material such as session plans and handouts were collected. Feedback on research interviews was sought by email. Transcripts of interviews were verified with informants. Informants were invited to comment on accounts of training sessions. All written portraits of informants, and analyses of interviews were shared with informants. Final accounts were verified with informants.

Research diary provided material for reflexive analysis. Choong also wrote memos while in the field to record her initial impressions of events. These enabled her to 'reconstruct' events surrounding interviews and training sessions, and were valuable aids during analysis.

Data analysis   Both life history and personal construct interviews were transcribed in full. The transcripts were analysed and emergent themes recorded. The themes were classified and verified with field memos and informant feedback, and case histories constructed which outlined inform- ants' personal histories and their professional lives. A further stage of analysis of the case histories identified stages of development and influences, among other factors, in the informants' biographies.

Observed training session recordings were transcribed and the transcriptions examined for session structures and interactional patterns. Incidents were extracted from the transcripts as illustrations of the trainers' practices. The post-session discussions with trainers were analysed to establish possible rationale for practices, and to search for evidence of transfer of practices or thinking from their project training. Again, field memos and the research diary were invaluable aids in reconstruction and in analysis.

The progressive writing and refinement of the case histories was in itself a means of analysis and led to the refinement of Choong's thinking.

Outcomes

1. The analysis revealed a number of major themes in the trainers' biographies:

   • personal identity;
   • schooling experience;

- professional self-definition;
- extension of professional identities.

The third theme consisted of sub-themes of professional development – decisions to be a teacher, emerging as a teacher, decisions to go into teacher education, emerging as a teacher educator – and response to innovation – emerging as a trainer of trainers and transfer of training. The category of 'emerging as a teacher' revealed the informants' views of formal learning, the influence of models on teaching style and the influence of professional and social 'push' factors in development (to conform).

2. There was little evidence of transfer of training from the project to trainers' practices, although all were able to articulate in detail the rationale behind new training approaches. Most of the training observed was structured like classroom teaching activity and fronted by the trainers; the project training emphasised 'process' and active learning by students. There was little evidence of this. The process of training on the project had raised awareness and opened the minds of participants to alternatives in experientially based learning and teaching, but the uptake was generally low. The concept and practices of reflection was not clearly understood, despite being the central ingredient of the training process. The new educational ideas had not been internalised and 'owned'. The informants' professional life histories and experience had not been fully engaged in attempting to introduce the new ideas. Classroom management practices are deeply rooted in experience and personal history. Short-term training schemes are not particularly successful at bringing about changes in practice.

Issues raised by the research

1. The value of sharing analysis with informants is illustrated by this research. Analytical depth is an outcome of the sharing, and greater veracity is derived.
2. The reflexive stance of the researcher generated valuable data and insights. A research diary and memo-writing while in the field and during data analysis are significant aids in this type of research.
3. The use of multiple methods of data collection yields possibilities for multiple interpretations and different interpretations of similar phenomena. The research process is enriched by these multiple sources, and is more likely to lead to insights and understanding of complex activities like classroom management.
4. The informant's articulations of beliefs and experiences is valuable to the informant as a way of understanding practice and resolving dilemmas presented by practice and by innovation. Choong regards this type of work as an important ingredient in teacher and trainer development on the

grounds that articulation can help develop the teacher's capacity for theorising. Professional development as a consequence has a strong element of self-awareness. There are potential connections between teaching and research which are best expressed through a 'stance' of dialogue and inquiry in both activities.

13.2   Studies of management practices

Case Study 4: Managing classroom space, energy and self – Fenwick 1998

Purposes   To discover the nature of teachers' management practices – to find out what they manage and how they see themselves as managing – within a 'successful' school context.

Participants   Thirty-seven teachers of all curriculum subjects in a junior high school (300 adolescents aged 13–16) in Edmonton, Canada. Team of three researchers worked in the school over three years.

Research procedures   Case study methods of classroom observation, recorded interviews immediately post-observation, and documentary study. 'Thick', verbatim descriptions of classrooms were written during observation (20 classes observed in the study, some more than once). Interviews designed to explore classroom reasoning and meanings ascribed to goings-on. Prompts referring to specific classroom events were used for the interviews. Ethnographic details of the school context also collected as evidence of the well-orderedness of the school.

Data analysis   Observation notes were correlated with the interviews, and themes developed from the data. The author describes the process as 'sorting through' the data, from which teacher-managed elements emerged. The methodology is adapted from Carter (1994).

Outcomes   Three elements are identified in 'management':

1. **Space** – teachers manage the classroom space in order to ensure it is safe, to balance work and play, quiet and talk, and balance student responsibility and external control. They do this by such acts as arranging objects and routines, and moment-to-moment gestures.
2. **Energy** – teachers manage the unpredictable energy in the student group, helping students to remain focused, being flexible enough to respond to individual needs, energising when necessary. They do this by, for example, telling students to remove potentially distracting objects from their view before beginning to address the group.
3. **Self** – teachers were very conscious of the need for self-management and consistency in behaviour, and a strong sense of identity (elicited from

teachers as 'general principles of practice'), feeling comfortable balancing control and caring, looking to the future with a focus on the present, comfortable in the knowledge that they are developing and learning, and, significantly, that they were unable to express exactly what it was that they did.

The overall finding is that teachers' management practices are more about 'floating and rolling' than control and fixity.

Issues raised by the research

1. The lack of a language among the informants for describing what they did and why in managing space and energy, compared with descriptions of lesson plans and pedagogic structures. The author refers to the 'moment-to-moment improvised drama of classroom life.' Much of this is implicit, intuitive and often very physical (p. 629).
2. The need for contextual reference in order to deepen understandings of classroom events and behaviours. While the study makes reference to the school context it does not explicitly make connections between teachers' management practices and the school's context. Was there, for example, a school ethos or culture of classroom management, consistently adhered to, which all the teachers bought into?
3. The relevance of highlighting learners' characteristics in attempting to understand practices. The teachers' management practices reported in the study were evolved to handle potentially troublesome adolescents, and were sensitive to the energy and spatial demands of this learning group. Would the same tensions between caring and control exist for the teacher of infants or adults?
4. The value of detailed descriptions of classroom activity rather than recordings in attempting to understand management practices. Because so much management practice appeared in the study to operate non-verbally and contingently, rich descriptions of classroom activity are necessary, capturing the physical realities of movement, gaze and interaction.

Case Study 5: Three teachers' practices – Carter 1992

Purposes   To describe the different ways teachers understand their task of managing classrooms – to represent the cognitions of teaching and to describe teachers' comprehension of classroom events; to suggest that teachers' different interpretations of classroom events influence their own actions, students' actions and reactions and classroom histories.

Participants   Three (of an original 17) teachers in junior high schools in Texas. The research team (university faculty) worked over one year, with a focus on the first three weeks of school.

Research procedures Observations of classrooms – detailed narrative observations for two lessons. The entire sample of teachers were then rated on
various indicators of success in management (e.g. student success, amount
of disruptive behaviour etc) in order to formulate case descriptions of
'successful' and 'less successful' managers.

Data analysis Cases are constructed as follows:

1. Description of daily life of teacher – typical activities, routines etc. drawn
   from detailed lesson observation records to establish what instructional
   routines, activities and procedures the teacher has chosen in order to
   manage the classroom in a particular school.
2. Description of how teachers react to contingencies in the classroom in
   order to establish how individual teachers see classroom management and
   reacts to unforeseen situations.
3. Metaphors are developed to capture the ways in which teachers understand
   the task of managing the classroom context, and contain the potential to
   explore the value of different ways of thinking about classroom management.

Outcomes The main features of one case are presented:

1. The teacher had well-established routines and 'rules' – e.g. silence for roll
   call, punctuality, being in charge of class closing sessions. The teacher
   liked to keep students focused on the curriculum during lessons and
   tended to play down disruptive incidents. Reprimands were group-centred
   and designed to highlight the fact that student behaviour was slowing
   the class down.
2. Work was mainly organised into three types of activity:

   - Content development (oral) – content presentation mixed with
     question/answer about the content.
   - Seatwork activity – to practice skills or apply content learned from
     oral work.
   - Oral review – teacher gauges students' understandings and provides
     extra practice or explanation.

3. The teacher reacted to slow work (off-task behaviour) and rates of
   completion of work or 'production'. The teacher also reacted to students
   who persistently digressed from the lesson.
4. The teacher metaphor is 'pathfinder and pacesetter' (p. 124) a sense of
   'directed group movement, regulation and tempo'. The teacher plans for,
   attends to and reacts to signals that that students were not proceeding either
   in directions or at a pace that she had prescribed. Five general principles
   relating to reconciling competing classroom agendas, selection of pathways

through the curriculum, daily attendance to order and tensions between order and academic progress.

Issues raised by this research

1. The time-consuming nature of case production. In order for a case to be authentic and of sufficient depth it requires a great deal of observation and analysis. The incorporation of classroom transcript data might assist researchers in producing cases in a less laborious way.
2. The value of cases in both research and teacher education. This is a significant point at which research and education agendas intersect. However, the two agendas may be in conflict – the needs of teacher education programmes are somewhat different from those of 'pure' researchers.
3. The need to verify descriptions and cases with informing teachers. There are ethical as well as intellectual issues at stake – is the teacher aware of how she is being portrayed in a case? Does the case coincide with the teacher's self-image and self-concept as a teacher?
4. The need for alternative perspectives. Do the teachers' students and their colleagues agree with the metaphor, for example? It seems a relatively simple procedure to undertake this sort of triangulation.

Case Study 6: Facilitating discussion – Szesztay 2001

Purposes   The research had two broad aims:

1. **Managing group discussions in teacher education** – to understand the processes involved in group discussions and the factors that affect the course of a discussion, the potential learning outcomes of group discussions, the characteristics of a discussion leader – knowledge base, skills, qualities, and how discussion leaders can develop themselves.
2. **Research on practitioner development** – to understand whether practitioners can develop through long-term research, and whether there are any design principles for this type of research that can inform the long term development of teacher trainers.

Participants   The author herself, working reflexively on her own practice, and three different groups of trainee teachers in a Hungarian university.

Research procedures   Apart from close observation of her teaching and the groups with whom she works, critical incident analysis, her own diaries and those of the participants, Szesztay identifies three further intriguing means of data generation, congruent with practitioner research.

- **Feedback dialogue:** a procedure in which research is embedded in the educational process. The exploration of students' feedback when engaged in dialogue with students enables her to (a) fine-tune her teaching and

(b) generate and analyse data on group discussions. She notes, 'in the process of the dialogue we already moved into an initial analysis stage' (2001: 99).

- **Being interviewed**, a second data-generating method, enables her to gain insights into her own values and thinking.
- **Imaginary interviews** are a way of writing which helps her clarify her own thinking about being a practitioner researcher, and provide further insightful material.

Data analysis and outcomes – group discussions This section identifies the main outcomes of Szesztay's research in terms of the management or facilitation of group discussions. The analysis of group discussion sessions enables Szesztay, among other findings, to identify key aspects of discussions.

HIGH QUALITY DISCUSSION She first identifies features of 'high quality discussions' (pp. 153–4) – this is an amalgam of liberating and structuring forces, and processes, as follows:

> **Liberating forces**: Participants feel free to express opinions, and display open-mindedness towards subject matter.
> **Structuring forces**: generalisations are challenged; no jumping to conclusions; contributions 'intimately rather than superficially related' (p. 153); assertions substantiated and opinions supported by reasoning; critical but constructive engagement with ideas; participants listen and respond to perspectives expressed thoughtfully and sensitively.
> **Processes**: key, underlying themes in a discussion might recur in a cyclical manner; new ideas are sparked off in the flow of interaction; connections are made between ideas.

INDIVIDUALS and GROUPS The study investigates the contributions of individuals and groups to discussions. The author lists participants' individual characteristics likely to lead to effective contributions to discussion as follows:

- willing to take responsibility for own learning;
- sees discussion of ideas as a way of learning;
- openness to new ideas and perspectives;
- tolerance of complexity and ambiguity;
- believes good teaching involves understanding of what goes on in classrooms;
- trust in and respect for facilitator;
- self-confidence, and clear and coherent expression of ideas;
- concern to learn about oneself and the effect on others in the group.

She distinguishes between 'on-the-spot' group features and long-term group characteristics. The former are experienced in real time – level of group energy, for example – whereas the latter are, in effect, the realisation of the group's history. Both areas are important contributions to our understanding of classroom life, and are part of a facilitator's awareness and knowledge of classroom process.

She identifies five long-term characteristics of groups as follows:

- trust (among members and between group and teacher);
- openness (open in the sense of feeling free to speak and also towards others' contributions);
- cohesion (in-tune-ness of a group with, for example, the pace of a session)
- awareness (combined self and group awareness);
- self-direction (able to take the initiative and pursue its own agenda or direction of inquiry).

LEADING DISCUSSIONS The study provides an account of the characteristics and qualities required for leading discussions. Szesztay regards it as axiomatic that teachers *lead* discussions, and that it is always the teacher who takes the ultimate decision as to whether or not discussion will take place. The facilitator or teacher is always making leadership decisions before, during and after discussion sessions. The teacher therefore needs a range of knowledge and understanding in order to come to 'informed decisions about how to lead a discussion, or indeed, to decide whether a group is ready to have exploratory discussions in the first place' (p. 216).

Again using a selection of critical incidents, diary entries and interviews as well as analyses of observed sessions, the account identifies first of all, the 'invisible side of leading discussions – core qualities and knowledge base' (p. 217). This includes the following:

- Empathy, genuineness and respect (after Rogers 1969).
- Deep knowledge of the subject area under discussion (to enable the facilitator to see and make connections).
- Social and emotional maturity (to deal with conflict, for example).
- Intellectual maturity (e.g. openness to alternative solutions and contributions).
- Self-awareness and sensitivity to others (core qualities).
- Democratic values (exploratory discussion 'can only work if the trainer holds liberal educational views': p. 221).

Szesztay describes an interacting set of capacities, attributes and knowledges which are activated during discussion. These inform discussion management practices, the 'visible side' of facilitation. Strong beliefs in the value of dialogue as an educational process and discussion as a tool are implicit in this profile. A further feature she identifies is the capacity for learning in any of these aspects, and therefore for change.

The visible side of facilitation is a set of what Szesztay terms 'roles and functions activated in a learning context'. She adds two new leadership roles in her own practice to categories already identified by Bridges (1988):

1. Directing attention means directing the students' attention to a particular aspect of an issue which might help in deepening the discussion.
2. Managing group energies means continuously assessing group energy levels, and adjusting pace and depth to group energy levels. It includes activity such as listening attentively, supporting and giving encouragement. Using her analysis of her own emerging understanding of facilitation, she identifies 16 visible functions of a facilitator.

Concept 13.1 Functions of a discussion leader

INITIATING (e.g. focusing on main questions)
MANAGING CONTRIBUTIONS (e.g. ensuring no views are cut off or ignored)
LINKING (e.g. linking a contribution to a previous one)
STRUCTURING (e.g. sequencing, sorting out information)
MOVING TOWARDS CLARITY (e.g. asking participants for clarification)
PERSONALISING (e.g. telling personal anecdotes)
KEEPING DISCUSSION ON TRACK (e.g. giving/asking for summary of points)
PROVIDING/IDENTIFYING DIRECTION (e.g. redirecting attention to main questions)
MOVING LEVELS (e.g. providing/asking for specific examples)
CHANGING THINKING MODES (e.g. inviting creative thinking)
PROBING CONTRIBUTIONS (e.g. asking for specific examples)
MANAGING GROUP ENERGIES (e.g. taking a break when appropriate – low levels)
DEALING WITH CONFLICT (e.g. identifying differences of opinion)
COMMENTING ON PROCESS (e.g. stop and draw attention to distracting factors)
CONTRIBUTING IDEAS

(in Szesztay 2001: 227)

She demonstrates how her thinking and practice developed in depth in six of these functions. Relevant examples include:

- Managing contributions. This includes encouraging contributions through actively listening to all contributions and bringing reticent group members into the discussions.
- Managing group energies. How to generate energy when it has reached a low point, or 'inject' energy are both ways of achieving this. The sensitivity and awareness of the facilitator to the fluctuations of group energy are important in formulating responses to social and emotional problems

related to too slow or too rapid a pace. Subtle acts such as avoiding eye contact, or seeking eye contact with group members are identified as ways in which a teacher might manage the expression of emotion.

EVOLUTION OF PRACTICE A final contribution which the research makes to our understanding of classroom management is Szesztay's description of how her practice in structuring discussion has evolved four stages. The discussion draws on categories from the professional literature.

1. Preparation – preparing participants by 'seeding' them with themes, for example. A preparation task can also act as a link to the second stage – 'opening up' – by suggestion the first moves of the next stage. For example, responding to the first task can be a prelude to 'opening up'.
2. Opening up – problematising issues and questions from experience or preparation activities can be a useful way of opening up a discussion.
3. Exploration – clarification of the topic and exploration of participants' various views on it. Szesztay points out that it is impossible to say how long this part of a discussion will take, and therefore to plan the time. Rather than look at the clock, her experience tells her to monitor group energies.
4. Stock-taking – this stage is intended to help participants see what they have learned from the discussion. This is a stage at which summaries of main points made can act as a way of highlighting learning points or principles, a concrete outcome from what might have been an hour of intensive talk.

Issues raised by the research
1. From the classroom management point of view, the 'elasticity' of time in discussion management will be a concern for many practitioners working within strict time constraints. For the full value of exploratory discussion to be experienced, time is of the essence, and its adoption as a procedure in curricula and by institutions and individual practitioners will depend in part on a rethinking of time constraints and lesson/session boundaries. That will depend, however, on authorities embracing the educational values that discussion represents.
2. The relationship between 'visible' and invisible' processes invites further exploration in any classroom setting. The combination of emotional and social factors identified by Szesztay, and their interaction, are influences on classroom management in deep and often implicit ways.
3. Szesztay's work exemplifies well the practices of practitioner research. It highlights the issues and dilemmas of this stance in addition to its positive findings, and accepts the open-ended and provisional nature of its findings, in keeping with the evolutionary nature of professional development defined by its author.
4. The study emphasises the potential of classroom participants' contributions to classroom activity, and the development of students' capacities of

self-expression as central to the educational process. The management of this alternative discourse demands new knowledge, skills and awareness on the part of practitioners as well as redeployment of existing pedagogic management practices

5. Data in the study are constantly re-analysed retrospectively in order to move forward in understanding. This provides an insight into the ways in which teachers construct themselves and their teaching; for Szestay, teaching is not simply a series of lessons conducted in linear fashion, and knowledge about teaching is never permanent. This knowledge is being excavated and refreshed at the same time as it is being extended, implicitly in practice, explicitly in inquiry. Szesztay also reveals the immensely ambivalent nature of practitioner research, the conflicts between thought and action, feeling and conceptualisation. Practitioner research personifies a stance and an approach to teaching and research which requires courage and tenacity to sustain. The development of a research procedure like 'being interviewed' as a way of clarifying and making explicit values and beliefs is a necessary task in practitioner research is an example of the disciplined subjectivity (Erickson 1986) that the author establishes.

6. Establishing a 'high quality discussion culture' is likely to take time and effort, especially in contexts where the values underpinning such a view are not present. Szesztay locates the study in the wider context of post-1989 Hungary, arguing that, although the general educational culture has been largely unaffected by the changes since 1989, there are indications of the appearance of 'islands' of change towards a more 'liberal' approach to the educational process in individuals and institutions. She also frames her understanding in the broader values that 'discussion' exemplifies a socio-cultural view of learning and, a commitment to democratic values.

7. The study does not contain extensive classroom transcripts. One may speculate that closer analysis of the texts of lessons and training sessions, supervisory encounters and coaching sessions can yield new understandings of the qualities of 'effective facilitation', and a more detailed account of the ways in which facilitators communicate, including ways their body language and other paralinguistic features contribute to interactions.

13.4   Studies of classroom and teacher research

Case Study 7: Learners as observers in the classroom – Eken 1999

Purposes   Eken's research aims to answer one question: whether learner observations of teaching and learning work in practice, and become a central part of exploratory teaching, or whether the notion is simply theoretical.

The research sought to describe and account for the process of using learners' observations to give 'direction' to a teacher's practice. In management terms, Eken was also taking the opportunity to adopt a more collective process for making decisions about classroom process and content. Her initial decision to do this is the starting point for the work.

Participants The author in her role as teacher, and her group of 13 university students in Turkey. She describes the students as 'weak as a group', and in need of plenty of encouragement.

Research procedures This is an example of Exploratory Practice, a process developed by Allwright (2003) to assist teachers in addressing 'puzzles' (not problems) in their classroom practice. Data gathered were immediately acted upon in classroom practice, and were used as the basis of decision-making about subsequent practice. Analysis was therefore continuous and immediate, feeding into subsequent practice.

The project lasted four weeks. Data were gathered using five different learner observations, using five different observation tasks. The individual learner observers provided informal feedback on each observation. Five student questionnaires given to the whole class (of 13 tertiary level 'upper intermediate' – but weak – repeating students), audio recordings of three lessons and Eken's own self-evaluation and reflection on lessons and data completed the data sources. In her report of the project, Eken focused mainly on learner observations.

The research followed an 'exploratory framework' created by the author. She describes the following steps:

STEP 1 – Introduce idea of learner observation to class. Statement of aim ('improving the quality of teaching and learning in the class by collaboratively exploring what goes on in our lessons', 1999: 241) and discussion of the need for teacher-student collaboration and possible learning from the activity.

STEP 2 – Decide on the focus of the learner observation. Eken decided on the first observation focus herself – a general one: 'learning and teaching in general'. A general observation instrument was designed for the student observer to use (see below).

Time	What is the teacher doing?	What are the students doing?	Ideas, comments and suggestions

(Eken 1999: 247)

A less active student was approached and asked to do the observation in the next lesson. The observer was briefed before the lesson. In subsequent lessons, the observation focus is one which has been derived from the previous lesson, going deeper into issues raised. For example:

Lesson 1 – learning and teaching in general
Lesson 2 – teacher nomination of speakers and student participation
Lesson 3 – teacher talk and student talk
Lesson 4 – individual, pair and group work activities
Lesson 5 – the use of L1 (Turkish) in the classroom

STEP 3 – teacher's decisions on recording and self-evaluation instruments and procedures. Eken decided to audio record lessons where possible. Her examination of her lessons involved interrogation of what she noticed in the transcripts, using agreed lesson focus points to guide her.

STEP 4 – Sharing the learner observer's findings with the class. After the observed lesson, Eken briefed her observer to tell the class about what sort of notes they had taken and observations considered important or unimportant. The reporting of the observations leads to a discussion in the class. The accumulating impact of the observations leads to (a) voluntary observation (b) greater subsequent discussion of learning issues in lessons, of increasing depth and sophistication

STEP 5 – Brief discussion ('mini-chat') of the observation experience with the learner observer after the class. Recorded for analysis.

STEP 6 – Teacher privately listens to tapes for review and conducts self-evaluation. Results of questionnaires are triangulated with points raised by learner observers in completed observation sheets. Implications for future practice considered.

STEP 7 – the results are presented to the students – main issues raised by all the data are shared with students, as well as Eken's own reflections. These are used to promote discussion and to provoke more suggestions from students. They are also used as the basis for decisions on new action. The case of L1 use is reported and how Eken agrees a procedure and its monitoring by students for regulating use of L1 in the class.

Outcomes   There were several outcomes of this work for Deniz Eken:

1. She found learners have as much to contribute to the teaching-learning process as peer teachers. Most significantly, they contribute to the 'directions' of future exploratory practice. They also have abilities as observers.
2. The 'insider' views of learners provide insights into the working of a class in ways which 'outsider' observers cannot.

3. The process is beneficial for learners, raising awareness of teaching and learning, and possibly their own learning (meta-cognitively). The process of learner observation can help teachers involve less able and less motivated students. Eken speculates about the possibility of learners ultimately being able to decide on lesson foci and even developing their own observation instruments together with the teacher. (A further stage might be where learners conduct analysis of data.)

4. Teachers can incorporate findings into their decision-making about future lessons and their own practice. For example, Eken discovered that her learners appreciated teacher talk, especially explanations. A potential development point for Eken might conceivably be improving the quality of her explanations in different ways. Her students' observations would inform her whether she was successful.

5. Exploratory procedures should not be a permanent feature of classroom life – when the teacher thinks it is relevant and necessary – when there is a need created by a puzzle. Variations in data-gathering are recommended too. Eken also points out that learner observations should be conducted when there is less 'input' of material on language and skills so that learners do not feel that they are missing important teaching points. (The management of classes which feature 'new input' may be a research focus more suited to peer or outsider observation, although the benefits of students' perspectives cannot be minimised. Deniz Eken's work demonstrates the importance and power of students' perceptions of teaching.)

Issues raised by the research

1. Eken records classroom talk but does not provide detailed analyses. She learns enough by listening and noting key passages. There is enormous 'academic' pressure to be rigorous and detailed in the presentation of data. While Eken is certainly systematic and thorough in her presentation, there remains a doubt that what she has done would be taken seriously by the academic community, rather than the pedagogic community, despite its obvious value to both.

2. Exploratory practice is a unique means for teachers to manage their classrooms, opening up the possibilities of new modes of participation of both teachers and students. Teachers doing this work would find themselves engaged in a different discourse– a transmission discourse is replaced by a shared 'let's talk' discourse. Clearly there are implications for both initial teacher preparation and continuing professional development for such a shift – teachers need to prepare themselves for this change and its potential outcomes. Students also need to be prepared, particularly if they are invited to take a larger role in the research process as Eken suggests they might.

3. Exploratory practice has to be systematic and has to be managed, and Eken demonstrates how this can be done. By creating new roles for students,

Eken opens up new participation possibilities and new learning opportunities. The classroom becomes a learning community, but without necessarily changing anything fundamental about a teacher's overall style.

4. The project must have affected classroom relationships positively – trust is central to the whole thrust of the project. Exploratory teaching accounts need an affective dimension.

5. There is a dearth of studies which report on how classroom action research and Exploratory Practice affect classroom life and management as practices *in their own right*. If a teacher adopts a research stance in their teaching, it changes the nature of the underlying classroom discourse. A metacognitive awareness is present in classroom activity in ways which it is not during regular teaching and learning – does this improve the quality of the classroom experience? Does the different management style which the teacher adopts when in 'inquiry mode' differ from 'teaching mode'? If so, in what significant ways? Are there significant differences between classroom action research and exploratory teaching in practice?

Case Study 8: Action research and teacher development (a transnational project) – Gierlinger 1999

Purposes The project 'Sharing the European Classroom: Classroom Action Research Across Europe' was set up to widen familiarity across Europe with Classroom Action Research (CAR) as applied to the language classroom and to develop a framework that could be used by others to encourage the initiation of CAR projects. It ran from 1996–1999. The project also wanted to explore whether or not CAR was an effective teacher development strategy.

Participants Five countries (Austria, Finland, Portugal, Germany and Belgium) participated. In each country, the project was centred on a teacher education institution. Groups of up to six serving teachers volunteered for the project in each centre. The case study reports the experience of the Belgian group, reported by Andre Mottart.

Procedures

1. Introductory sessions on action research, principles and practice, initiated by the local facilitator. Aim: to introduce participants to 'philosophy' and practices of CAR. Participants agreed research projects, individually or in collaboration.

2. Participants worked in their classrooms with assistance from the facilitator (mainly logistical, although some professional – classroom observation)

CAR TOPICS

- use of the target language in group work
- use of the target language in lessons

- exploration of 'communicative grammar teaching'
- dealing with heterogeneity in a group (L1, ability, origins)
- students' motivation and collaboration between subject teachers
- Projects written up and presented at a course for participants from all countries in a sixth country (UK). Cross-border projects established on common themes.

Data analysis   The Belgian projects generated data of two types:

1. On classroom activities and processes: Classroom projects generated written data (from students' work), audio and video recordings of classroom activity (usually 'experimental'), questionnaires, documents – lesson plans and learning materials. Example – the teacher faced with a hetero- geneous learning group video-taped her own classes, and analysed the tapes with the facilitator and research group members. From the outcomes she devised a differentiated lessons of a task-based and multi-level nature. These lessons were video-taped and discussed in the same ways.
2. On the process of learning to do CAR: Mottart traced the development of the group's attitudes through observation, and discussion with the group, and with the use of a standard questionnaire to measure levels of concern people experience when adopting an innovation (CAR).

Outcomes
From the teachers' action research projects:

- learning about self as a teacher;
- learning about students and their motivation, attitudes and capacities;
- learning about similarities and differences of beliefs between teachers;
- learning about the effectiveness and impact of new teaching procedures;
- learning about the use of action research and how a changed stance to teaching influences classroom management.

From the process of doing CAR

- increased confidence in selves as teachers (more critical, self-aware);
- changed perspectives on teaching;
- the value of articulating plans to colleagues;
- support and interest in CAR from students in class, leading to increased awareness of pupils and sensitivity in their teaching (CAR helped to break down teacher/learner barriers);
- sense of autonomy and empowerment ;
- enjoyment of networking and sharing of ideas, and mutual support in the research group;
- value of having teacher peers introduce action research.

From the process of introducing CAR

- raised awareness of the importance of time and its management (not to 'push' or over-structure);
- importance of support and guidance during CAR (especially form outsiders);
- need to spend more time preparing teachers for an alien concept such as CAR before they undertook projects (increased systematicity, and clearer focus the likely outcomes).

Issues Raised by Research   Many of these issues are also raised by Gierlinger in his evaluation of the project.

1. Sharing concepts of action research across a range of contexts in which it was often quite unfamiliar to teachers was very problematical. The literature assumes a more or less uniform 'desire to improve' among teachers. This is evidently not the case. Action research, like any other innovation or practice, does not always travel well. The importance of developing a common frame of reference and professional language is a key issue transcending the CAR project – language teaching is an international business, but locally interpreted and often contested.
2. The interest shown by students in the teachers' research is evidence that doing research changes discourses of management. Teachers showing interest in their students and trying new ways of helping them learn engaged students across contexts. The more consultative management style promoted by action research may have been more instrumental in bringing about improvements in quality than the actual experiments in teaching in some contexts.
3. Although the project featured informal and locally-motivated attempts to introduce action research, there was wide variation in the rigour and clarity of focus of the projects. For some of the facilitators in different countries this was a problem which hindered the teachers and detracted from the value of their work. The cultures of academia and the school appear to be at odds over this issue: if the types of intervention that the teachers attempted led to improvements in the quality of the educational experience, then the interventions could be said to have been successful. The inherent theory-practice divide between teachers and academics was not entirely overcome by this project.
4. CAR had strong effects on many of the participating teachers. The CAR work initiated a process of change in many that was seen as threatening; it highlighted shortcomings and difficulties in some teachers' current contexts. Many of the teachers also found that collaborating across national boundaries liberating, and felt freer to discuss issues with colleagues from abroad than peers from their own contexts.

Wider influences on teachers' lives and practices

Case Study 9: A wider cultural framework – Ou Yang Huhua 2000

Purpose   To understand the changes in discoursal and socialisation systems experienced in change from one 'teaching methodology' to another through ethnographic investigation of individuals' experiences in teacher training programmes.

Participants   One practising English teacher in China. The informant was known to the researcher, who had been closely involved in her training.

Research procedures   Construction of a case from personal communication, interview and observation with one (of twelve) informants. Interviews with twelve informants who had experienced the reform programme were analysed for themes and patterns. The individual invited was seen as 'typical' of these patterns. Other field notes taken during interviews with the main group were also referred to for confirmation of findings.

Data analysis   Construction of informant's 'story' – a professional life history – from data sources, interpreted using a discoursal framework (Scollon and Scollon 1995 – 'discourse system': history/ideology, socialisation, form of discourse, power/face relationships). Critical incidents isolated to illustrate key processes and points of crisis or difficulty in which values and ideologies are revealed.

Outcomes

1. In-depth account of how 'traditional' teachers were 'converted' to CLT in a two-year long institutionally-based training course. The author concludes that the teachers were under great pressure from institutional practices to accept the enforced change (which involved a complete turnabout in their thinking and practice). The new rules and practices of the CLT discourse system (fully accepted by the staff of the training institution) were imposed on the teachers, accentuating their 'difference' further. The teachers were from rural areas and also older than most of the other undergraduates.

2. An account of the cultural alienation experienced as a result of committing to new teaching procedures and embracing the discourse system of CLT. Educational institutions, including training institutes, all subscribe to the traditional discourse. The innovators are excluded and, despite the consequences, many leave teaching. The informant 'goes private' and opens a successful tutorial school where she is able to teach in ways she has chosen. The rural-urban gap is shown to be vast and a further factor in cultural alienation – CLT is viewed as 'foreign', i.e. 'urban'. CLT practitioners naturally feel more at home there and also have access to greater

wealth. Methodological change is seen as part of a wider social change, with all the consequences of such change for values and social cohesion.

3. The disruption created by the transition and practice of CLT leads individuals to make decisions about their career and their preferred workplace. Many found compromises where, in the newly emerging economy, they could enjoy higher salaries as well as regain self-respect as teachers in a hybrid system of traditional and CLT. This entailed migration to coastal cities, often far from their homes, in order to establish professional respect and closer interpersonal relationships in schools. Acceptance of change has its roots in personal value systems and conflicts. CLT becomes 'nativised'.

4. The change to CLT is seen as contributing significantly to changes in society and the emergence of a more liberal and open society of individualism. Educational reforms are not simply pedagogic – they are always to be seen in the context of the wider society.

Issues raised by the research

1. The value of seeking understanding of teachers' pedagogic experience through an understanding of the social, economic and political forces which influence their work. Understanding classroom management practices is always partial unless these forces are acknowledged and used as interpretative lenses. Classroom ethnography requires a 'macro' dimension, which can be provided by the depth that ethnographic studies provide.

2. The need to search for signs in classroom life of anxiety, confusion and uncertainty as teachers and students come to terms with new classroom management practices. An ethnographic and critical perspective will enable a deeper understanding of the value conflicts that change engenders, an approach that situates classrooms in a matrix of complex and ambivalent forces.

The importance of 'extended conversations' in research on classroom life. Ouyang's work was the outcome of many years' contact with the informants, not a one-off or short-term encounter. Engagement with informants in different contexts, through different media and longitudinally, will contribute to deepened understanding of practices and change in practice at both micro and macro levels.

Summary

The case studies presented in this chapter indicate a number of important directions in which research on classroom management can develop, at the classroom level, and also inquiring into 'external' processes and phenomena which have a bearing on classroom management practices. Most significantly, the direct participation of researchers in the daily lives of classroom participants appears to demonstrate the capacity of the research process itself to influence teachers and learners in positive ways, leading to raised awareness of their practical theories and specific practices. The reflexive nature of research, as demonstrated by Szesztay, also has potential for self-development among teachers, while learners' participation provides rich new perspectives and provides a voice for the oft-neglected majority in classroom life.

Part 3

Researching Classroom Management

Introduction

In Part 1, I examined the theoretical bases of and understanding of classroom management as 'complexity management'. Part 2 detailed specific classroom management practices and reported a range of research conducted on classrooms under the headings of time and space, engagement and participation. It demonstrated the broad as well as more narrow concerns of researchers in the field.

The aim of Part 3 is to provide readers with a brief discussion of the issues I believe to be central to the investigation of classroom management. This includes, in the first chapter, an account of some of the main purposes and approaches to research in and on classrooms (Wright 1992). It continues to examine specific procedures and techniques for inquiry into classroom management in the next chapter which also includes a selection of ideas for getting started on inquiry. The material in this part of the book is intended to assist teacher practitioners in particular in developing an approach to their practice which enables them to question what they do without burdening themselves with more additional work than they can manage within their daily duties. It is also designed to stimulate debate in the Applied Linguistics community of ways in which the classroom, a pivotal research 'site', can be meaningfully understood through research.

14
Issues and Practice in Research on Classroom Management

Research in language teaching and Applied Linguistics focusing explicitly on issues of language classroom management is comparatively rare. This is, in part, due to the relatively narrow definition accorded classroom management, and also the preoccupation of many language teaching professionals with matters such as instructional techniques. In general education, however, particularly in the United States, interest in issues of classroom control and discipline is strong, and major research publications reflect this interest. In language teaching, research which implicates or touches upon classroom management issues is generally (and probably rightly) enmeshed in discussions of other aspects of classroom life, especially spoken interaction.

Applied Linguistics research on classroom management needs to account for the complex nature of classrooms in attempting to reveal the essence of classroom management practices. This has two key implications:

1. research should account for both observables and unobservables in classroom management;
2. research needs to be multi-dimensional and multi-disciplinary, to include understandings of the social, cultural and psychological realities of the classroom.

Research of this type is likely to add to our knowledge of classroom management, and also to enhance the quality of classroom life.

14.1 Issues in research

Purposes of research

Brumfit (2001) distinguishes between three types of research (Concept 14.1). All are necessary for a deeper understanding of educational processes in action, for professional learning, and for generating knowledge about classroom life.

Concept 14.1   Types of research

1. **'Pure'** – aims 'to increase our understanding of the most important unclear areas of current study'. Increased clarity and reduced uncertainty are potential outcomes. Knowledge generated enables the construction of a map of the workings of a particular field.
2. **'Action'** – aims to enable teachers to develop understanding of their situations and to act pedagogically upon new understanding.
3. **Policy-oriented** – aims to monitor and evaluate the effects of policy in action. Produces information for planners and policy-makers and facilitates adjustments to implementation strategies and action.

(Brumfit 2001: 147–8)

'Pure' research – goals and limitations

'Pure research' enables us to understand classroom management as culturally-situated educational practice. At present, our knowledge of classroom management, both in theory and of practice, is relatively limited. Much is anecdotal at best, or has been generated as a by-product of other research on aspects of classroom life. I have attempted to map our current knowledge in this book, and in so doing I have also identified (a) the lack of a shared understanding of classroom management and (b) large unmapped areas of practice. Pure research would enable mapping to proceed, bearing in mind that pure research in classroom contexts is unlikely to prove conclusive – research into complexity usually raises more questions than it answers. There are also potential pitfalls in this venture:

- Analytical research on classroom management practices runs the risk of reductionism (although it could be argued that a 'naming of parts' is a necessary part of atlas construction – the index is normally between one third and one half of an atlas). Analysing complexity requires holistic thinking to counteract this tendency.
- 'Thick descriptions' (Geertz 1973) may give good accounts of the territory, but may fall into the relativistic trap, and be too local to be of value to practitioners in other contexts unless they are effectively theorised.

Neither reductive identification of parts nor global descriptions of the 'whole' classroom are useful on their own, and a knowledge of one or the other does not lead to an understanding of how it either came to be (in the case of the whole) or contributes to the whole (in the case of the parts). The most important questions in classroom management will connect the parts and the whole and lead into what Stewart and Cohen (1997: 63) call 'Ant Country' – where parts and the whole blend in the generation of activity: classroom life. Description and understanding are thus both essential in research on classroom management. The differing perspectives of researchers and participants must also be accounted for. (Concept 14.2) Description must contain the seeds of action and an understanding of the educational process if it is to be of use to either planners or practitioners. Similarly, analysis must be grounded in an understanding of how elements interact. However, in education, understanding and action are necessary outcomes of research. As Brumfit (2001: 146) points out 'research must be useful'.

Concept 14.2   'Emic' and 'etic' in research

An 'emic' perspective in research aims to capture the viewpoints of the participants. These are the ways in which members of classrooms interpret and assign meaning to their experiences.

An 'etic' perspective is the point of view brought to a situation by a researcher, and may include his or her theoretical position or particular cultural relativities. These frameworks are external to the situation, unless the researchers are also participants in the ongoing activity under investigation.

Issues in action research

Action research – the activities of teachers exploring their own practices in their own classrooms – has become part of the professional world of the English language teacher since the mid 1980s, albeit relatively late in comparison with other curriculum areas. Much is claimed for its potential in enabling teachers to innovate, solve problems and develop as professionals (Quote 14.1), and there is no doubt that its adoption has led to interesting and valuable insights and action. The action research approach is also ideally suited to exploration of classroom management practices and issues, as it is classroom-centred.

Quote 14.1   Burns on action research

Action research is:

1. contextual, small-scale and localised – it identifies and investigates problems within a specific situation.
2. ... evaluative and reflective as it aims to bring about change and improvement in practice.
3. ... participatory as it provides for collaborative investigation by teams of colleagues, practitioners and researchers.
   Changes in practice are based on the collection of information or data which provides impetus for change.

(1999:30)

Purposes and the personal in teacher research   Despite its impact, there is no broad agreement about the purposes of action research, apart from the notions of 'improvement' or development. However, without a sense of social action, there is always a danger of localised self-interest on the part of the practitioner. 'Reflective practice', often combined with action research, may also be over-particularistic (Quote 14.2).

Quote 14.2   Lampert on the personal in teacher research

How we regard the personal in teacher research is both a practical and a deeply episte-mological question, forcing us back to the enduring puzzles educational researchers deal with about how to relate what is learned from a single 'case' in all its complexity to other situations in which similar problems arise. What does it mean for problems that arise for a particular people in particular contexts to be similar across settings? What additional skill or knowledge does a practitioner, or for that matter a scholar, need to have to take knowledge from one case to another?

(2000: 93)

Systematic inquiry and action   Action research (or teacher inquiry) is often criticised as being undisciplined and unsystematic, and may not count as 'research' because of this. Teacher inquiry can however, get closer to the day-to-day thinking and practical reasoning undertaken by teachers as they review events. It may therefore be best to distinguish 'daily review and ruminative activity' (a valuable activity in its own right – Quote 14.3) from action research. Action research is 'systematic' as Wallace (1998: 1) points out. It must also be open to public scrutiny. Otherwise, any understanding generated through the work remains unchallenged and relativistic. A further related issue is the extent to which action research can contribute to a propositional basis for professional knowledge – or 'evidence-based profes-sionalism', and whether or not teachers need to learn the skills and practices of action research (Quote 14.4).

Quote 14.3   Atkinson and Claxton on research on intuition

. . . we believe that the importance of the deliberate, conscious articulation of knowledge, whether others' or one's own, may . . . be overestimated., while intuitive forms of knowledge and ways of knowing have tended to be ignored or under-theorised. The assumption that professional competence is best acquired when you 'know – are able to explain and justify – what it is you know, needs questioning.

. . . to explore the functions of intuition in professional learning and practice, and to uncover the ways in which explicit knowledge and 'know how', reason and intuition are braided together in professional contexts.

(2000: 2–3)

Quote 14.4 Roles of research in education and training

Would it be better to let many trainees acquire their basic professional common-sense knowledge... before expecting them to research, discuss and deliberate in a highly sophisticated way? Would this not allow trainees to build confidence to progress to the outer segments (of professional knowledge), where reflection and research are more likely to pay dividends since they are no longer in competition with the trainees' deep desire to acquire basic competence?
(Hargreaves 1993: 91)

... classroom and school-focused action-research approaches... highlight the role of teachers as researchers in effecting improvements in practical situations construed as complex, ambiguous and unpredictable.
(Elliott 1993: 17)

Puzzles or problems? Action research tends to be problem-focused, setting up a professional discourse of problem-solving. This has the danger of limiting the practitioner to the status of 'trouble-shooter'. Allwright (2001) proposes an alternative – 'exploratory practice' (EP) (Quote 14.5) – which regards research and practice as indistinguishable. A danger of this approach is again over-localisation. However, this might only be the case if teachers' pedagogic knowledge is limited only to what is learnt from practice. Exploratory practice holds promise for a more healthy relationship between different types of professional knowledge than the traditional 'theory-practice' dichotomy that so dominates professional discourse. EP is 'practitioner research' in its broadest sense and is vital to an understanding of processes which are implicit and intuitive. Practitioner research of this kind *may* identify problems which are local or more widespread. Only dissemination of findings and questions will ensure the latter.

Quote 14.5 Allwright on exploratory practice

Principles for Exploratory Practice

A. Practitioners (preferably teachers *and* learners together) working to understand:

    a. what *they* want to understand
    b. not necessarily *in order to* bring about change
    c. Not primarily *by* changing
    d. But by *using* normal pedagogic practices as investigative tools, so that working for understanding is *part of* the teaching and learning, not extra to it
    e. In a way that does not lead to 'burn-out' but that is *indefinitely sustainable*

B. In order to contribute to:

    f. *teaching and learning* themselves
    g. *professional development*, both individual and collective

(2001, author's emphases)

Policy-oriented research – issues

Most educational innovations driven by policy initiatives disturb the status quo of classroom management practices – for example, in how time and space are used. Innovations may even be devised explicitly to challenge existing practices. Policy-oriented research needs to serve the interests of teachers and learners in contributing to an understanding of the status quo prior to taking decisions about whether or not to innovate. Unless 'pure' research can provide a strong and testable knowledge base upon which to base decisions, policy is always going to be decided on the basis of ideological predisposition or strictly pragmatic issues – 'doing what works' or what is most cost-effective. It is imperative, therefore, for policy-oriented research to (a) aim to generate new knowledge of educational realities in classrooms, where innovations ultimately have an effect and (b) be conducted by researchers operating independently of the policy makers (although no researcher is ever completely neutral). As policy is implemented, there may be a need for classroom action research in the form of formative and possibly illuminative evaluation (Weir 2004), but with an awareness of the danger that formative evaluation can be reduced to 'performance indicators', 'targets' and other quantifiable outcomes rather than a description and analysis of what is actually happening.

Types of research

The types of research available for investigating classroom management derive in part from their purposes. There is a palette of research types and data-gathering procedures to work with, depending on the focus and the field of inquiry that the research aims to investigate. An issue for the would-be researcher on classroom management is the level of integration between research and routine classroom activity. This will vary according to the research stance adopted.

Prescriptionist

Prescriptively-driven research dominated early efforts to understand educational practice, but its central aims were to enable policy-makers and academics to justify theoretical positions and to prescribe classroom action. This type of research all too frequently serves the discourse of 'handing down' ideas. In Applied Linguistics, theoretical knowledge has tended to precede classroom action – the emergence of Communicative Language Teaching is a case in point – and there are adherents to the ***experimental*** tradition of finding out if a new idea is being used as prescribed (Quote 14.6). The prescriptive tradition also supports ***interventionist*** studies in which new ideas are tried out in specific contexts, and is employed in support of the transfer of knowledge developed in one context to another. The 'pilot study' is a typical procedure, often carried out with reference to 'control groups'.

Quote 14.6   Ellis on the relevance of second language acquisition research

[SLA] can contribute to the appraisal of pedagogic issues. To this end the applied SLA worker can assist by making research accessible to teachers, by developing theories of instructed L2 instruction and by advancing pedagogical proposals based on these theories. SLA also has a role in application. The applied SLA researcher can seek to illuminate pedagogical problems and their possible solutions through conducting experimental and interpretive studies in and, particularly on L2 classrooms.
(2001b: 68)

Any teacher trialling a new idea suggested by the professional literature, or they have encountered at a conference or in-service workshop, is informally engaged in such a set of practices; any student teacher who tries out a teaching idea acquired during their training course for the first time in teaching practice is also engaged in a similar procedure. The discourse of 'handing down' is further reinforced by a discourse of 'it works/doesn't work'. It is thus a form of action research driven by a need for improvement and 'development'. It is a natural part of professional work, and the discourses should be acknowledged rather than ignored as they tend to encompass empty 'theory-practice' debates. All such interventions and experiments risk disturbing well-established cultures (Quote 14.7). Because of this, such work needs knowledgeable and empathic support, training in research procedures, and an understanding of the dynamics of classrooms. It is a means of improving quality in educational experience; better management of the process and more open-minded debate among practitioners will enhance its usefulness.

Quote 14.7   Breen on new teaching ideas and established cultures

Perhaps one of the best ways of revealing the established culture of the classroom group is to try to introduce an innovation which the majority neither expects nor defines as appropriate. Most teachers have direct experience of the effort to be radical in their approach with a class (be it through different material, tasks, or procedure, etc) and have suffered the experience of at least initial rejection.
(2001a: 132)

Descriptive

Descriptions of classroom life are an effective basis for both interventionist and developmentally orientated research. Professional researchers working in the ethnographic tradition (Concept 14.3) have long provided this type of descriptive material. They provide detailed information from real working contexts. One issue is the extent to which intervention is based on description. Interventionist initiatives often fail because they are not grounded in an adequate understanding of the contexts in which they are being applied (Quote 14.8).

Concept 14.3   Ethnography

... seeks to describe and understand the behaviour of a particular social or cultural group. In order to do this, researchers try to see things from the perspective of members of the group and this requires extended exposure in the field.
(Richards 2003:14)

Quote 14.8   Holliday on research for appropriate methodology

In order to arrive at appropriate methodologies, practitioners need to take time to investigate what happens in the classroom. They need to incorporate into their approach the capacity to look in depth at the wider social forces which influence behaviour between teachers and students, and to take a broad view of how these are in turn influenced by social forces from outside the classroom.
(1994: 17)

Descriptive studies do not result in improvements on their own, however. They generate information about contexts, and contribute to a more 'ecological' approach to research and innovation. Classroom language teaching and learning is deeply embedded in its contexts of practice, and innovation can only take place within the limits of tolerance inherent in the context (Quote 14.9). Similarly, description can illuminate the ecology of the classroom.

Quote 14.9   van Lier on teacher research and classroom contexts

Traditionally, teacher research is envisaged primarily as action research on classroom issues, since the classroom is the domain in which the teacher is professionally active. It is appropriate that classroom pedagogy will remain the central focus for the theory of practice, but the critical stance and the contextual analysis that are part and parcel of this work will inevitably mean that the teacher researcher will broaden the focus of enquiry to include the multitude of forces that impinge on classroom processes from the outside: the social context, the institutional structures, the political climate and so on. This broadening of focus means that the knowledge base of the teacher researcher is correspondingly widened, even though relevant knowledge will necessarily be refracted via the lens of the classroom. Indeed . . . the classroom itself is turned from a field of activity into a subject of inquiry.
(1996a: 30–1, after Kozulin 1990)

Some practitioners might argue that they already know their contexts well enough not to need to have them described. But this may be a defensive routine aimed at preserving a comfortable and hard-won status quo in the face of perceived threat from outsider research, or, more positively, it might emanate from the teacher research discourse that puts the professional at the heart of innovation and change in the classroom. A teacher may believe that they know their classroom like the back of their hand, but important events and processes go unnoticed, and a practitioner's description is in fact a mental model, a map of the territory.

Classrooms are not like tidy laboratories in which to experiment. They are dynamic environments which can lurch suddenly from stability to chaos and just as suddenly back again. Teachers are inured to this. It is their natural habitat. The question is whether they see the need to positively influence the quality of the learning experience (cognitively, affectively, socially, or ecologically) in order to change conditions and increase opportunities for learning.

This presumes that teaching does not necessarily cause or directly lead to learning, but that the more learning opportunities are created, the more possibilities there are for learning to take place. This may entail making classrooms less like the ones we know, and while not necessarily radically 'redesigning' them (Legutke 1995), at least shift them in small ways in new directions. A shift from the mode of action in the classroom to a more contemplative mode after classes have finished is normal enough for teachers. A descriptive stance, grounded in observation and recording of daily events, significant and apparently trivial, adds discipline and structure to these otherwise transitory modes of thought and action. By engaging in inquiry, practitioners can adopt this stance to the mutual benefit of themselves and their students.

Understanding and interpretation

In order to understand why things happen in the ways they do in classrooms, research needs to go beyond description to develop deeper understanding. In such a way we can add to theoretical knowledge. Similarly, by assisting teachers in more structured contemplation, professional researchers may be able to them to innovate in ways more in tune with the culture of their classrooms. Research that leads to understanding attempts to 'get below the surface' of events and descriptions and to document the influences and forces that have given rise to them. Socio-cultural research of the type reported in Parts 1 and 2 has this aim, as does any research seeking to understand the discoursal action that is the basis of socio-cultural and psychological reality. Descriptive work can thus be brought into a closer relationship with research which aims at understanding. It can also illuminate the processes and outcomes of intervention. In this way, research on classroom management can escape from the twin traps of inappropriate prescriptivism and parochial relativism, and aim for the type of critical action that on the one hand satisfies a need for accountability in the public domain and on the other creates a dialogue between intuitive and rationalistic modes of thinking and knowledge. This position on the research process – to engage in critical discourse on personal knowledge and values – lies at the heart of professionalism (Furlong 2000: 27). It is through such a discourse that interpretations of 'quality' in classroom life can be seen. An understanding of classroom management practice is likely to be central to this endeavour.

The co-existence of three research traditions embodied in the types and purposes of research provides the researcher a rich range of theoretical bases for action. The researcher's choice of research aims and tools will to a great extent depend on the stance taken within the three apparently conflicting stances. A clear articulation of research purpose will help the researcher decide on an appropriate mode of research activity, which itself will assist in refining purposes in the process of research.

Who does research on classroom management?

Research into classroom management can be conducted by the following groups:

- 'outsiders' – professional researchers typically from the tertiary sector;
- 'insiders' – teachers and other education professionals;
- collaborative groups – combinations of outsiders, insiders, other education system stakeholders, including students.

Traditionally, educational research has been conducted by professional researchers, typically from higher education institutions. Typically, too, these researchers are pursuing their own carefully-defined 'pure research' agendas and fulfilling the requirements as a knowledge-generating institution. Professional researchers are often employed in policy-orientated research as well, to fulfil requirements of objectivity and 'distancing'. They are thus likely to be associated both with generating new theory and also with informing policy. In language teaching, the picture is further complicated by the tradition of Applied Linguistics research which generates ideas and 'solutions' for teachers, often based on non-educational academic disciplines such as theoretical Linguistics. This has tended to build up a sense of suspicion among teachers regarding the role of the professional researcher and the extent to which what they have to say can be trusted and treated as 'relevant'. The lack of a shared agenda between academic researchers and practitioners may be a serious obstacle to resolution of this communication gap (Wright 1992b). Ellis (2001b) (Quote 14.6) argues for the relevance and value of SLA research and attempts to build bridges between insiders and outsiders, for example 'the SLA worker can act as a facilitator of teachers' own research by helping them formulate research questions and choosing appropriate research methods' (2001: 68). Disputes between education practitioners and researchers are, though, debilitating and ultimately self-defeating. The generation of knowledge and theory, provided it is useful (and the practitioner will always be in the best position to decide on this), is central to the development of an understanding of classroom management. In contexts such as the UK, Austria, Australia and China where the teacher researcher position has become well-established it is common to see collaboration between academics and practitioners in the investigation of issues. (Quote 14.11) The dissolution of boundaries between professional groups like academics and teachers can only be of benefit to both groups, especially if educational research is seen to contribute to an understanding of classroom life that at the same time leads to the solution of problems and the improvement of quality for all concerned.

Inclusion of students in research is a further type of collaboration which can mutually benefit all parties (Eken 1999, Chapter 12). In an educational ideology of learner-centredness, there is probably no better way to develop understanding of classroom processes and to improve the quality of experience than by involving learners in the research process.

Quote 14.11   Mercer on research partnership

... the kind of applied action research which has most potential, in a whole range of fields as well as education, is socio-cultural research in which practitioners and external researchers work in research partnership, each contributing their expertise and experience. The gathering and analysis of data must take account of the different and potentially conflicting perspectives and agendas of each partner. For this to happen there has to be some negotiation of what aims and agendas are being pursued, and of course the relationship has to be one of mutual trust.
(1995: 120)

Future research on classroom management might inevitably be multi-disciplinary and collaborative because of the nature of classroom management. It will involve different research types for different purposes and focuses. Its success will ultimately be assessed in terms of its capacity to affect the quality of teaching and learning in the classroom.

Research into classroom management also has a major role to play in teacher education, as a means for novice teachers to investigate the classroom world both experientially and through understanding of others' research, and also to investigate teacher education practices themselves and the cultures of teacher education. Research into classroom management under these conditions is a *learning tool* for student teachers, teachers, teacher educators, managers (Concept 14.4).

Concept 14.4   Research as a learning tool

- *For the novice teacher* – a means of investigating real classrooms and educational contexts and their actors as a means of working on pre-existing models of teaching and learning and school contexts, and induction into school and classroom cultures. 'Insider', collaborative and 'outsider' perspectives.
- *For the serving teacher* – a means of understanding current practice before deciding on new learning; a means of monitoring the effect of new teaching ideas in practice; a means of identifying issues and problems with a view to taking action; alone or in collaboration with other teachers and/or learners.
- *For the teaching team* – a means of understanding professional action in context through mutual research and collaborative action; a form of personal and team development.
- *For the teacher educator* – a means of investigating teacher education practices – in collaboration with peers and/or students.

Research generates dialogue among practitioners and between practitioners and students, practitioners and leaders. The dialogues themselves can be analysed in order to understand how professional knowledge is jointly constructed. Interests can be acknowledged and incorporated into outcomes. Outcomes can be used to generate new practices grounded in knowledge about the present.

(after Burns 1999, Mercer 1995, Wright 1992b)

14.2   Procedures for research on classroom management

Research in classroom management has tended to fall into two broad groups – research on discipline and control on the one hand, drawing from the 'control' school of classroom management, and a catholic collection of research on many aspects of classroom life and activity, which collectively can be referred to as 'classroom research'. Classroom management is sometimes the focus of this research (Senior's work – Chapter 11 – is a case in point), and sometimes identified as part of the context or as a factor which influences classroom activity. It is thus not a clear-cut field, which is both an advantage and a disadvantage for the would-be researcher. Parts 1 and 2 have hinted at three broad areas for research on classroom management:

- Exploring the terrain of classroom management, along all its main dimensions of time, space, engagement and participation. Classroom management is not about what students learn or teachers teach, but the conditions under which teaching-and-learning are conducted and experienced.
- Examining the nature of classroom management practices in different educational contexts. A sociocultural view of classroom language learning enables investigation along a number of paths, aiming to illuminate our

understanding of how in practice teachers and learners establish and maintain conditions in classrooms and deal with the unexpected.

- Establishing how different classroom management practices contribute to the quality of life in classrooms. It is far from clear whether or not one classroom management practice is necessarily more effective than another in influencing the quality of learning experience. However, the extent to which different practices create learning opportunity provides a way of understanding how quality can be improved and how classroom participants experience it. The social and affective elements of quality demand attention in this framework.

Inner and outer

The notion of observables and unobservables was introduced in Chapter 1 as a way of problematising classroom activity. As we have seen in Parts 1 and 2, a great deal of classroom management activity takes place 'below the surface', either psychologically, in the heads of the individual participants, or through the collective use of implicitly understood and learned routines and rituals, at a discoursal level. Researching any of the three broad areas of concern which we have identified entails working in psychological and social-psychological domains as well as in physical classroom contexts. Simply to restrict research to the 'visible' or audible without reference to the implicit and the hidden has the potential to limit research to description. As a consequence, the search for understandings is likely to draw inferences from data about real time action that are psychologically groundless. Research on classroom management, like any classroom research, needs to account for both the 'inner' and 'outer'. (Concept Box 14.5)

Concept 14.5   'Inner' and 'outer' in classroom management research

INNER – consists of psychological states; previously-acquired knowledge and stored experiences (situational and prepositional knowledge e.g. shared discourse conventions); values/attitudes/beliefs; mental models or self, others and contexts (constructs); decision-making routines and processes; theories of various types.
Characterised by 'invisibility', tacitness

OUTER – consists of all features of the classroom situation: physical (including all classroom artifacts – desks to teaching materials and writing implements), temporal, social and interactional.
Characterised by observability, recordability, concreteness.

*Behaviours in the 'outer' world are interpreted in the 'inner' world according to individuals' psychology and vice versa. Adequate understandings can be reached through attempting to forge connections between inner and outer.

CLASSROOMS IN CONTEXT

Another area of concern to the researcher is the location of the classroom in overlapping and interwoven contexts of the school or institution and community. A fuller understanding of classroom life is obtained through (a) positioning the classroom 'inside' other contexts and (b) regarding the context of, say, the school, as the product of both 'inner' and 'outer' action.

For example, quality may emanate from the enhanced emotional health of participants. In classrooms, as in other domains of social life, how behaviour is interpreted by participants is central to how contexts emerge, and their subsequent cultural continuity – teachers interpret classroom behaviour (e.g. students yawning) through a filter of 'inner' knowledge and thinking processes. The response to behaviour is typically almost instant, but also the product of complex cognitions. Research into classroom management thus needs to establish how inner and outer interact and influence each other.

Researching discourse, a central underlying process of classroom management, is problematic. Classroom discourses emerge from participants' interpretations of the unfolding context – they are invisible, but implicitly understood. For example, the discourse of didacticism – 'I tell you' – is implicit in the activities of teachers and students. It is routinised, and may only become apparent in moments of crisis – for example, when it is challenged. In many senses, processes like discourse connect the inner and outer in classroom life, and investigation of these relationships is a major goal of research into classroom management practices.

Exploration of classroom management practices can lead to understanding: action can be taken on the basis of understanding. Action research procedures should aim to make these connections explicit. A way of doing this is to acknowledge and account for the essentially *reflexive* nature of the research process (Quote 14.12) (Concept 14.6). The researcher's interpretive process is a central factor in generating new knowledge and understanding; making this transparent can lead to new learning and enhanced meta-cognitive processes in the researcher and other participants, in particular students. Introducing research into classrooms alters the discourse in subtle ways, and guarantees that, at least in the short term, the research discourse dominates, as participants try to establish new ground rules. Teacher researchers pursue at least two interlocking agendas (teaching *and* research) when they undertake research on their own classrooms – their understandings of how their action affects their personal and the learning group's world is a central part of the research process.

Quote 14.12   Reflexivity

Subjectivity is a resource, not a problem, for a theoretically and pragmatically sufficient explanation.... Research is always carried out from a particular standpoint, and the pretence to neutrality ... is disingenuous. It is always worth considering the position of the researcher, both with regard to the definition of the problem to be studied and with regard to the way the researcher interacts with the material to produce a particular type of sense. In many cases it will be helpful to explore this position in a reflexive analysis. A reflexive analysis which respects the different meanings brought to the exercise by researcher and volunteer is an ethical exercise, and characteristics, whether of the situation or the person, are treated as valued resources rather than factors that must be screened out.
(Parker 1994:13)

Reflexivity is perhaps *the* most distinctive feature of qualitative research. It is an attempt to make explicit the process by which the material and analysis are produced.... The research topic, design and process, together with the personal experience of doing the research, are reflected on and critically evaluated throughout.
(Tindall 1994: 149–50)

Research on classroom management thus has two essential dimensions and a further optional, but highly generative, dimension.

1. *Inner Dimensions*. Researching inner dimensions involves the use of various procedures aimed at establishing the nature of individual psychological processes, people's VABs (values, attitudes and beliefs) and (previously-acquired knowledge and experience – PAKE – for example. The research procedures are different ways of 'asking' (van Lier 1988: 57) and they are both introspectively and psychologically-oriented (Concept 14.6). Metaphors, for example, are a 'gateway' to individuals' thinking and their emotional responses to classroom life (Quote 14.13).

Quote 14.13   Altrichter et al. on metaphors in research

... a metaphor ... becomes interesting through the ramifications of its meaning, including its emotive connotations, all of which are transferred to the new object. By this means, a metaphor provides the opportunity to do something freshly, offering a new perspective on the concept, object or event to which it describes.
(1993: 128)

---

2. *Action Contexts* ('Outer Dimensions'). Researching the action context requires the use of various procedures to describe and account for classroom management activity and contexts in which the classroom is situated – the

school and the community. The procedures consist of different ways of 'watching' (van Lier 1988: 57) and asking, and are ethnographically-oriented in order to capture the richness of the classroom context. An enriched ethnography also attempts to account for the relationships between classrooms and their contexts, and seeks understanding through watching and asking in the contexts of the school and community (Concept 14.7).

3. *Reflexive Work.* Research accounts are enriched by researchers' understandings of their reflexive processes. How teacher researchers *learn* from doing research, particularly action-oriented research, is a significant further dimension of the research process. By sharing their reflexive accounts of the research process with research participants researchers can add a further learning dimension to the process (Concept 14.8).

Concept 14.6   Research procedures – inner

*These can be self-administered and/or done together with research participants. Data are generated both in the form of products (e.g. representations of metaphors) and through talk between researchers and informants (e.g. 'interviews').

Introspective Techniques

- Exploration of metaphors/images (e.g. for classroom, learners, etc.).
- Personal construct work (to establish how informants construe the classroom and learning worlds, for example, after Kelly 1955).
- Critical incident analysis (accounts of key moments from personal/professional histories; elicitation of narratives and analysis re. values, beliefs, 'influences') This can include the study of 'cases' (exploring 'cases' generated by teachers from their practice. A requirement is that the cases should be rich in contextual data, c.f. narratives).
- 'Making Strange' (Garfinkel 1967) (examining the everyday and commonplace from the point of view of a 'stranger' or 'innocent' to reveal values, meanings, constructs e.g. through detailed interrogation on a teacher informant's written description of a classroom).
- 'Mapwork' (construction of mental 'maps' of phenomena to explore constructs, VABs, etc.).
- 'Histories' (accounts of 'learning' or 'teaching' or life/career histories to identify key events, processes, influences).
- Diary studies (e.g. to identify 'filters' of experience – what is included/excluded in accounts of practice).
- 'Model-building' (informants construct models of e.g. classrooms, as a poster of the 'classroom world' for example) (after Schratz 1993).

Interviews (one-to-one) there is a continuum from pre-planned questions to open-ended dialogue, depending on the purpose of an interview, and relative familiarity of researcher and informant. An interview can be used as an exploratory (following up hunches and puzzles from either observed practice; or in-depth on, for example, metaphors) or a discovery tool (to establish themes for further exploration in a teacher's practice,

Concept 14.6 (Continued)

for example). In a focus group, small groups of informants form discussion groups around issues or questions decided by the researchers. These may be incidents or initial findings from research.

Questionnaires – devised for particular purposes (e.g. values clarification) or to examine a specified area of practice, or to gather basic contextual information.

Concept 14.7   Research procedures – outer

Data are generated by observation and recording in the classroom and other contexts. Recorded data is typically transcribed (in various ways – see Swann 2001 for an account). Field notes can be written up into accounts and cases/critical incidents. Such material – transcripts, cases etc – can be the focus for interviews and discussion groups as a means of exploring the thinking inside action. (see for example, Bourne 1999 on use of spoken transcripts in language learning classes to explore learning with her students)

- *Observation (and field notes)* – standard ethnographic practice. Can be highly selective or global, depending on research goals, stages etc. Can include mapping (Hitchcock and Hughes 1995) of classroom space, and details of use of time. Details depend on purposes and goals. Burns (1999: 90) recommends the creation of proformas to guide observation and note-taking.
- *Recording of classroom talk – audio recording and transcription* to create texts of classroom encounters for exploration either by researcher alone or in collaboration with other researchers and/or informants, especially students.
- *Recording of classroom activity – video recording* and analysis can provide rich data on classroom life. Again, cases and incidents can be isolated. Transcription in conjunction with video images can provide interesting insights into the emotional domain (body language etc) Selectivity is a key issue with this medium. Students can act as 'cameramen' as a source of data about what they believe is relevant in the classroom world. The modern generation of light digital camcorders has brought this type of work within reach of many more.
- *Recording of classroom activity – still photography*. Both a record and a source of talk about classroom incidents, atmospheres and behaviours. (See Walker and Adelman 1975 and Burns 1999:101/5). The range has been extended by the development of digital cameras which are portable, relatively cheap and easy to use. Digital pictures can be viewed more or less instantly if downloaded onto a laptop computer. Many possibilities for constructing accounts and montages using software. Students can be 'official photographers'.
- *Learner Texts*. Students' writing (diaries, reflections, etc) is a valuable reference point for discussion. Analysis can reveal themes, inclusion/exclusion.
- *Verbal Recall*. (also referred to as protocols) Recording or asking informant to record activity as they are performing a task, or immediately after completion. Can give insights into, for example, decision-making processes. (see Wallace 1998: 76–91).

Concept 14.8   Research procedures – reflexive

Reflexive procedures are designed to enable the researcher (and informants if required) to collect data which enables them to scrutinise their own processes as they conduct research or are engaged as informants in research activity. The aim is to derive accounts of the research process, the learning process and other effects of the research process on participants.

Research Diary – A personal record of the research process, to include responses to working in the 'field'. Summarised and thematised, these accounts can form the basis of research memos, and may be the basis of theorising. They can also be used to explicate the process of data analysis.

Audio/Video Diary – A personal record of responses to the research process, to capture emerging ideas, learning and particularly the emotional effects of research.

Analytical/Observational – arranging transcripts, field notes or other data so that notes can be included at the same time as the researcher or informant examines the material. This material can be a valuable aide memoir to the development of theories and deepening of meaning. (Useful examples of different observational formats are provided by Burns 1999: 91–4.)

2.2   The research process

The research process is difficult to describe in its true 'messiness' (but in this sense it reflects the ground it maps). However, there are ways of managing the process which can bring it under some degree of control and Figure 14.1 is a schematic representation of one particular pattern. The starting point of research on classroom management is classroom experience – either a practitioner's or a colleague's, or their students'. The experience of managing classrooms creates dilemmas, poses questions and reveals puzzles. Awareness of these is the point at which there is potential for inquiry. Inquiry begins at the point of framing a question or identifying an issue, no matter how informally. Research actually commences when a commitment to systematic collection of data and its analysis is made. At every stage of the research process outlined, the researcher can engage in reflexive action which will feed back to prior stages and feed forward into subsequent stages of the process.

The process described shows how learning is initiated, pursued and brought to fruition, at each stage moving to a deeper level. Following Moon (1999 and 2001: 70) there are five different types of learning. Potentially, these could occur at different stages in the research process as shown in both Figures 14.1 and 14.2. However, it is plausible that different types of learning might predominate at different stages of the research

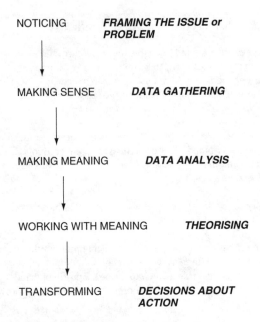

Figure 14.1   Stages and processes in research and learning

process. Hence, doing classroom research entails personal learning management as well as management of research activity. The ways in which learning can occur during research are described with reference to a sequence of research activity in Figure 14.2. The 'lower-order processes' (noticing, making sense, and making meaning) are very likely to occur at any time in the research process, during data collection, as data is analysed and re-analysed in the search for meaning, and as more abstract descriptions and understandings are formulated. Research does not advance on a linear path; it proceeds in fits and starts and retreats as well as advances. Of all the activities involved in research, analysis is the pivotal process which connects the abstract and the real world, and involves both lower and higher order learning. 'Higher order' learning begins as the researcher moves away from the data and refines categories and understandings developed from the data. It is at this stage that the practitioner is in a position to consider new classroom action.

In an action research scenario, the outcomes of research inform new pedagogic action, and an iterative cyclical process emerges. Each new cycle of action and research activity generates increments of new understanding and deep learning about classroom life and processes, as outlined in Figure 14.3.

LEARNING PROCESS	RESEARCH ACTIVITY
Noticing – another way of expressing 'immediate perception'. It is a form of surface cognition and likely to be partial as details are readily forgotten, or distorted by memory and distance from the experience.	A problem or issue enters awareness. For example – '*The class don't seem to be doing very much in group work*' A decision is made to find out what is happening and to address any problems. Question formation or issue framing links noticing and sense-making. '*What can I do as a teacher to help students maximise the opportunities for learning provided by group work?*'
Making Sense – finding patterns and coherence in data. Sense-making can occur as data is being collected as it is at this stage that pattern making begins, usually below the level of consciousness, as sensory data is 'processed'.	Researcher decides to watch the class closely during group work and note some of the behaviours. A preliminary form of data analysis is likely to occur as the researcher observes.
Making Meaning – at this stage, the learner actively looks for meaning with reference to existing knowledge and understanding. Making connections between new and existing knowledge and awareness. An 'exploratory' stage.	Data collected is reviewed with reference to (a) patterns and islands in the data itself and (b) knowledge of group behaviour (experiential and received). Classification and grouping/organising of ideas, and 'naming' begins. Descriptive accounts created of what the learning group does. '*One or two people seem to dominate most groups' work*'
Working With Meaning – There is a 'distancing' from the original data and situations, and they may be seen afresh from the developing new perspective. Characterised by a growing clarity of understanding.	Analysis moves beyond the descriptive towards a stage of 'understanding'. The outcomes of data analysis are drawn together into more abstract categories, judgements are made; critical analysis with reference to context. '*Tendency for 'slower students' to defer to the more able.*' '*Better at exam passing?*' '*Convergent tasks seem to lead to more of this behaviour than more open-ended ones.*'
Transformative – Movement towards a summing up and restructuring of understanding and perception. The learner has 'risen above' the situation and has developed sufficient understanding to view the situation afresh.	The drawing of conclusions and formal theorising takes place as appropriate. More questions may emerge, hinting at the need for either action to test hypotheses or further research and data-gathering. The initial situation may be seen in more clarity and preliminary thoughts about action may emerge. '*Group tasks need to be organised so that everyone has a specific role*'

Figure 14.2   Relationships between learning processes and research activities (after Moon 1999)

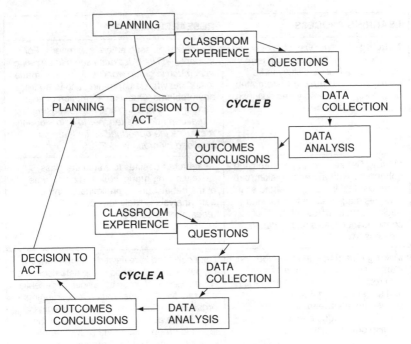

Figure 14.3   Cycles of classroom action research activity

In Cycle A, the researcher derives questions from experience – either past or present. These guide data collection. Analysis leads to outcomes, and on the basis of these a decision to act is taken. This leads to new activity and experience in the classroom, starting the cycle again. Elliott (1993: 71) describes a similar process. The action research process aims not only at understanding classroom management issues, but also attempting to influence them through research-based intervention. Pure research draws conclusions and overtly aims to add to theoretical understanding – whether these become the basis of voluntary classroom action depends on the plausibility of the conclusions for practitioners.

Summary

Researching classroom management raises many questions and issues. However, the essentially dynamic nature of classroom management processes precludes a clear-cut approach to the research. To explore the 'universals' of time, space, participation and engagement in classroom management requires both looking inwards into ourselves and also in classrooms themselves. Whether we wish to explore practice, or understand more deeply the dynamics of classroom life, or to influence policy, the essential starting point is classroom life itself.

Further reading

Allwright (2003) is the best available statement of the principles underpinning Exploratory Practice.

Brookfield (1995) is a very helpful guide for teachers interested in a more critically reflective stance to their work, and is the basis for inquiry and action research.

Burns (1998) offers guidance and theory for practitioners wishing to work together on action research projects

Elliott (1993) raises important issues regarding the purposes and value of educational research.

Holliday (2002) contains stimulating discussion of qualitative research methodology as well as clear examples of research on language education.

Pollard (2002) blends professional development and inquiry issues.

Richards (2003) is a comprehensive and accessible guide to all aspects of qualitative research in TESOL.

Stenhouse (1975) is a 'classic' account and rationalisation of the teacher-researcher.

Wallace (1998) is a useful first-time action researcher's guide, containing good practical advice and helpful case studies.

15
Doing Research on Classroom Management

15.1 Areas of interest for researchers

Parts 1 and 2 have hinted at various areas of interest and concern for both classroom participants and professional researchers alike. As I argued in Chapter 14, outcomes of research on classroom management may also have an influence on policy at institutional level, teacher education and broader educational initiatives.

Investigating classroom management in action

Investigation of classroom management practices as they occur 'live' in everyday classroom contexts is of supreme importance. The studies discussed in Parts 1 and 2 draw on the rich traditions in language classroom research of classroom ethnography, text and discourse analysis and socio-cultural analysis. There is clearly a basis for development of our knowledge of classroom management in these studies. However, the studies themselves have tended to treat management issues as peripheral or even trivial ('obvious'). What is required is for the procedures of classroom ethnography, discourse analysis and socio-cultural analysis to be brought to bear specifically on issues in classroom management.

There is a choice facing researchers in action contexts – to focus on understanding contexts themselves in all their richness, along all the dimensions of classroom management, and to develop a holistic understanding of a context – for example, primary English classrooms in rural Guatemala – or to begin with specific issues in the different dimensions of classroom management, such as participation. A further area to investigate is the effect of curriculum change on classroom management.

Time management

Time is a key dimension of classroom life, but very under-researched. Some important areas of concern include the following:

- whether teachers' planned uses of time (e.g. in lesson plans) are realised in lessons;
- who controls time use in classrooms and how they do it;
- how the pace of lessons is experienced by learners and teachers, and the extent to which it influences student learning opportunities and their uptake;
- how time is used in the short and longer term – how curriculum pressures interact with in time contingencies in the classroom, for example;
- the relationship between time use and lesson stage, and whether or not there are clear boundaries between stages;
- the relevance of time periods like 'lesson' in understanding classroom management practices;
- how participants in classrooms signal to each other their awareness of temporal issues;
- the relationship between emotional state and time use – for example, participants' experience of 'impatience';
- interaction between temporal and spatial dimensions of classroom management (e.g. homework, project work;
- the effect of online learning on time management.

Space management

In the spatial dimension, there is a need for studies of the type that Burns (1999: 106–10, drawing on Hitchcock and Hughes 1989) recommends:

- how space use affects learners and teachers emotional responses in different sizes of class;
- whether space use and classroom layout affects participation – in terms of quality and proportion;
- in particular, the influence of patterns of student grouping on all other aspects of classroom life;
- the relative importance to teachers and students of 'home territory' in providing a secure basis for learning and teaching;
- the use of 'vertical space' – 'boards', wall displays – and its influence on other aspects of classroom life;
- the effect of extending classroom space outside the physical confines of the classroom;
- the influence of new media's effects on learning and teaching 'without walls' – psychologically and socially, including the issue of 'control' of space.

Recent work by Di Giovanni and Nagaswami (2001) is illustrative of the type of direction which this research can take.

The affective domain

The affective domain is an area which is attracting more interest than hitherto, but still has great potential for classroom management studies, especially with the increased respect granted to introspective and other interpretative studies. Promising topics might include:

- classroom climate and its contribution to classroom culture – whether it is 'cool' or 'warm', or fluctuates;
- the influence of classroom climate on participation and learning opportunities;
- the 'riskiness' of classrooms, and how risk is managed by teachers and learners;
- how participants manage troubles such as conflict;
- the nature of the relationship between the maintenance of order and the emotional states of teachers and students;
- how teachers provide emotional scaffolding for learners during new learning;
- whether there is a relationship between levels of formality and affective response, and whether this influences learning;
- the relationships between 'care', 'order' and 'opportunity;
- how changes in classroom management practices influence the 'emotional health' of classroom groups.

Participation

There has been a great deal of research on classroom talk, but relatively little of this work has focused on the relationship between talk and classroom management, or as I have termed it 'participation'. Issues might include the following:

- how the management of participation patterns positions learners relative to learning opportunities;
- how learners manage their contributions to classroom activity;
- how learning opportunity is created or suppressed by the management of the relationship between talk and other classroom artefacts;
- how talk signifies and manages power and status relations in the classroom;
- how learning materials contribute to the management of participation patterns;
- whether talk regulates or liberates learners' participation;
- how participants use talk to create and maintain the classroom culture;
- whether online classrooms bring about the development of new participation patterns and uses of talk;
- the relationships between participation and time, space and affect respectively.

Cross-cutting issues in classroom management research

Research on classroom management, either from the practitioner or the Applied Linguistics perspectives, has the potential to illuminate understanding of complex 'ecological' issues in educational practice, and also to allow for the development of new dimensions in classroom research. The issues discussed below apply to any 'pure' research on classroom management, and may also trigger new directions and approaches in classroom action research. Practitioners are naturally concerned about teaching and learning material, and may benefit from a concern with learners' voices (Eken 1999; Razianna 2003) and may want to include them in their thinking and their accounts.

Learner perspectives The voice of learners is missing from much of classroom research, although this is changing, influenced by theoretical perspectives such as Breen (2001c), which focuses on learner action in context, and a growing realisation that progressive educational practices emphasise learners' contributions. A great deal of the research conducted on classroom management is focused on what *teachers* do. The reticence with which learners are treated in research may well be because of the prevailing discourses of control and transmission, and the perceived powerlessness of learners to influence their learning experience. A socio-cultural view of classroom management as a co-construction of teachers and learners requires a corresponding interest in learners' experiences, as well as teachers'. Specific areas highlighted (after Breen 2001c: 180) are:

- a focus on how *learners* manage their direct participation in classroom activity (interaction, discourse and activities);
- learners' strategies – for managing learning and classroom discourse;
- learners' self-management processes and strategies: towards the exercise of agency, autonomy (see also Benson 2001) and self-regulation.

Further research into the contribution of classroom management practices to the shaping of learners' identities *as learners* may also prove helpful in building our understanding of how being a learner affects a person.

The influence and contribution of teaching materials The 'methodological scripts' contained by teaching and learning materials are important influences on classroom management. If a teacher chooses to follow a course book or other prescribed material, the teacher is in effect a 'ghost manager', activating the classroom management constructs of the materials writer as well as their views of the educational process (Littlejohn 1998). There is thus a third voice in classroom life. How the management of space, time, the affective domain and participation are affected by this third voice is significant. Research along these lines will also provide further understanding of the complex interaction between subject knowledge and participants' sociocultural knowledge, or instructional and management practices.

The contribution of the social context of formal learning   The influence of the wider social context on both individual participants' activity and the classroom context is of paramount importance in classroom management practice. More work of the type pioneered by Canagarajah (1993) Chick (1996), Shamim (1996) and Holliday (1994) is required to uncover the complex interactions of the social contexts (e.g. school cultures, professional cultures) of education, classroom contexts and individual participants' understandings and contributions. This requires that the perspectives of people outside immediate classroom contexts should be sought, as well as those within, as a means of building interpretations grounded in a wider reality. Questions might include the following:

- Does a school ethos on classroom management, and a shared discourse among teachers, exist in different contexts?
- In the professional culture, is there a shared set of conventions for classroom management?
- How does the 'back stage' life of teachers influence their classroom management practices? Do EFL teachers, for example, recognise each other by their adherence to such constructs as 'pair and group work' and erect cultural barriers against other subject groups on this basis?

The effects of classroom research on classroom activity   Classroom action research and exploratory teaching involves new socio-cultural action. The extent to which 'doing research' influences classroom management is unknown – research has implications for time management. It may influence classroom climate. Is classroom research itself a set of management practices derived from a broader discourse of inclusion and participation, and thus based on assumptions which treat transmissive practices pejoratively? This research direction revives the Stenhouse (1975) notion of an organically-evolving curriculum, with classroom research as type of regulatory tool generating evaluations of classroom practices and opening up possibilities for new action. Classroom research (and its variants) appear to have been adopted somewhat uncritically in second language education however. A reflexive approach demands that classroom research practice is included in accounts of research on classroom management because classroom research goals entail a revised management agenda, driven by research itself.

The effects of formal teacher education on classroom management practice   As we saw in Chapter 9, teachers learn about classroom management practices both in formal training and in the classroom. Research into teacher education practices and their impact on teaching and learning management is, however, relatively limited (although see Gimenez 1994, Hagos 2000, for example). There is clearly a need to see whether teacher education influences classroom management practices. For example, are teacher educators influential as models of practice in their formal institution-based training sessions? Or are they peripheral figures in how the cultural processes of classroom management is acquired and internalised? The relative impact of teacher education on teachers' practices is a significant matter for policy makers as well as practitioners and teacher educators, particularly in view of the pressure to innovate English language teachers have lived with during the 'communicative' era.

15.2   Understanding classroom management – research projects

In this section I shall outline a selection of research projects to guide readers in formulating their own research into language classroom management practices. Both 'pure' and action research variations will be featured.

Researching time management
Research focus

> *Pace of lessons.* The issue of lesson pace is a central part of learners' experience. Both teachers and students control pace, and this project aims to find out what they do and under what circumstances. From a teacher's point of view, lesson pace is an important part of daily management practice and may be worth an action research focus.
>
> *Action research questions* (to adapt as necessary): What is the pace of my lessons like? What can I do as a teacher to maximise students' thinking and processing time? How can I assist students in making the best use of time in small group work?

Data generation and analysis (establishing current practices)

Tape-record teacher-led activities or lessons. Four will provide a reasonably large sample for analysis, and for the establishment of patterns of behaviour:

1. Examine stretches of interaction in which the teacher is leading question/answer. Note (a) overlaps between speakers, especially following initiation moves (b) pauses after initiation moves. Transcribe significant extracts if required although whole lesson transcripts may be needed to support significant theory-building activity.
2. Share extracts with students on tape and written transcripts either in one-to-one interview or focus group, and elicit their responses to the incidents, in particular how they feel about the amount of time they have to formulate responses.

Tape-record small group work from setting up to termination of activity. (N.B. It is quite difficult to obtain clear recordings of group work in a crowded classroom, but still worth trying to do.) Also, if possible, make a visual record – either video recording or a series of photographs.

1. Analyse how students manage their time – for example, how long they need to organise the group's work before starting the task.
2. Analyse the effect of teacher's instructions to complete the work and the impact of signals indicating the amount of time remaining for activity.
3. Convene a focus group with the students involved. Use the focus topic 'Making best use of time in group work'. Ask the students to prepare a poster listing ways in which they believe they can make best use of time, and what they do when they waste time.

Towards understanding

1. Identify typical patterns of teacher and student behaviour, with examples.
2. Decide whether you need to seek further understanding from sources outside the classroom, or if you are a teacher working collaboratively with a colleague, invite them to watch you teaching and to focus on the pace of your lessons. Provide your colleague with examples of behaviour you have analysed.

Potential action (if teachers use the project for action research)

1. More sensitive pacing of activities. For example, allowing students thinking time in question/answer phases of lessons.
2. Provision of 'thinking questions' to assist students in consolidating any learning or insights. For example: What for you were the main learning points of the last activity? What questions do you have now?
3. Negotiation with students to provide more control over the pacing of group activities.

Researching the management of classroom space

Research focus

Use of the black (white/chalk) board. Use of the writing surface is a significant aspect of space management, and is a prime source of information on the relationship between management and instruction.

For the great majority of teachers, the chalkboard is the main display surface in their classroom, and a central point of focus for their students. Their use of this medium is thus of the greatest importance in the management of their lessons.

Action research questions (to be adapted as necessary)

- What do I use the chalkboard for?
- In what ways can I make better use of the chalkboard space to assist students in their learning?

Data generation and analysis (establishing current practices)

Recording of lessons (minimum of four, but this could be a long-term project and result in the recording of a number of lessons). This could be done collaboratively with a colleague, or students could be appointed as 'observers' to record. Recording and analysis might use simple tabulations (on a page of A4) as laid out below. These also enable association between different activities during analysis – for example, the board may be an important supporting device during explanations, or it may be used to bring order to material elicited from a group.

Teaching Activity	Use of Board	Other Significant Activity; Comments

Photographic or video records of board work are very valuable data sources. These can be analysed to establish 'permanent' and 'transitory' areas of the board, unused areas, for example.

Invite students to complete a questionnaire to obtain a snapshot of their responses to board use and its relative importance in their learning experience.

BLACKBOARD USE

Students' Questionnaire.
Please take some time to answer the questions below, by ticking the alternative that is closest to what you think. Please write some comments in the spaces provided.

1. How often does the teacher use the blackboard in lessons?
Every lesson   More than half of all lessons   A few times   Very rarely   Never
COMMENTS (Please write your comments):

2. What does the teacher use the board for?
Writing new vocabulary   Writing notes for you to copy   Drawing diagrams
Summarising what the class says   Writing the lesson outline
Others (please specify)
COMMENTS:

3. Do you think your teacher organises their board work? YES/NO/DON'T KNOW
COMMENTS

4. Would you like your teacher to do any of the following on the board:
write more clearly   write larger   write less   write more for you to copy
COMMENTS

BLACKBOARD USE   (Continued)

5. How much time in a lesson does your teacher spend at the board?
Too much   too little   about right
COMMENTS

6. Are students allowed to use the board during lessons? After lessons?
COMMENTS

An interview (or focus group) with students can assist in going deeper into the students' responses. This is best done after the results of the questionnaire are collated, and the main trends have been identified.

Towards understanding

1. Assemble a complete picture of the use of the board from all the different data sources. Identify positive points and practices which can be developed or improved.
2. Observe a colleague and compare their use of the board with yours based on the same features you have identified in your own practice.

Potential action

1. More systematic use of the board – allocation of areas of the board for specific activities such as recording of new vocabulary.
2. Negotiation with students regarding the types of information they would like to see recorded and left on the board.

Researching the management of affect

Research focus

Ways in which students work with each other in groups. Collaborative activity in the classroom stands or falls on the quality of relationships between students in working groups. Conflict in groups can prevent the achievement of lesson goals unless managed sensitively.

Action research questions (to be adapted as necessary)

- What can I do to help create more productive working relationships between students in groups?
- Can I improve classroom climate by involving students in my action research?

Data generation and analysis (establishing current practices)

In group work, one student is given the task of being an observer and recording events in her group. This material can be reported back to the whole class, or to the teacher only. A simple way of systematically recording data is necessary. For example, a student observation record could look like this:

Things I Liked	Things I Didn't Like

Alternatively, students could decide what they thought it would be useful to observe. After a number of group work sessions, analyse the records to look for patterns in the notes, in terms of likes and dislikes.

Tape recordings of group work, accompanied by more detailed observations of gesture and facial expression – either note-making or video/photography can provide the data. This can assist in identifying further what leads to conflict in groups and what makes for a friendlier and more productive working environment. For example, looking for 'affective markers' in a tape recording of student interaction and how much laughter is generated during group work are valuable indicators of the emotional state of groups.

Ask students individually to list the qualities they would look for in a work companion. Again, these can be collected and trends identified. An alternative is to ask students to share their individual lists in small groups, and ask the groups to make an agreed list. Follow this with a focus group or recorded class discussion aimed at establishing how they responded to a collective task which focused on their own ideas of group behaviour.

Towards understanding

1. Pool the data and identify what the students believe makes for effective group work.
2. Invite discussion with the students on their thoughts about the process of trying to understand working in groups, with an emphasis on establishing what the students believe to be an effective working atmosphere.

Potential action

1. Invite students to generate working rules for group work.
2. Use more group-based activities which explore the affective domain of classroom activity.
3. Carry out a longer-term project which aims to examine the nature of the classroom climate of a learning group, and the effect on it of different activities.

Researching the management of participation

Research focus

Making classroom talk more contingent. Learning groups frequently lack opportunities for more open-ended talk. However, teachers and learners have often created classroom cultures replicating non-contingent interaction. Participation opportunities and practice opportunities are limited because of this. There is a danger that leaving 'safe practices' such as this can arouse opposition from students if they believe that the new practices threaten their chances of success in examinations.

Action research questions
- What can I do to make interaction more contingent in my classroom?
- How can I help students overcome any misgivings they have about reducing certainty in their learning?

Data generation and analysis (establishing current practices)

Recording of lessons (minimum four) to establish the current situation in terms of contingent and less contingent talk. Identification of key episodes of more contingent talk and (a) what initiated them and (b) how they were sustained.

Invite students' metaphors of classrooms. Explore these orally in class time, and ask the students to then write about their metaphors. Record the class session and collect the written accounts for analysis. Look for evidence of the types of participation and talk that the accounts offer or suggest.

Ask students to recall a time when as individuals they felt that they had had a good classroom experience. Ask them to write an account of this experience (in mother tongue if necessary).

Towards understanding
1. Draw up a list of the factors that seem to lead to more contingent interaction in lessons.
2. Hold a focus group discussion with students on 'Participating In Class'. Aim to elicit students' thoughts on effective and ineffective participation patterns, and their preferences.

Potential action
1. Plan lessons which entail open-ended discussion on language issues (language awareness activity, for example). Record them and analyse them fro instances of more contingent talk. Evaluate these sessions with students, eliciting their views on whether or not the discussion offered them opportunities to talk freely.
2. Create a ten-minute slot once a week in which students are invited to initiate a discussion of any points they wish. Invite a student to chair the session.

Do not intervene except as a participant in the discussion. This is best done 'in the round' so that everyone can see each other.

Creating a classroom management portfolio

A longer-term project to research classroom management is a major undertaking, but the rewards are likely to be worth the investment of time and energy. One way of recording one's teaching is via the creation over a term or year of a classroom management portfolio. The basis of the portfolio can be assembled from the following 'raw' components:

- Personal metaphors for the classroom, for teaching and for learning. These can be developed visually and in writing.
- Recordings of lessons, and transcripted extracts which illustrate management of time, space, participation and the affective domain, and combinations of these.
- Observation notes from colleagues who we invite to watch our lessons.
- A teaching log.

Teaching log

Spend about 20 minutes every week writing about your classroom experience. The following prompts can help to focus the writing or trigger thoughts:

Think about the last week

- Recall a time when you felt engaged, excited and conformed as a teacher
- Recall a time when you felt disengaged, bored, or dispirited as a teacher
- Recall a time or period when you experienced anxiety or stress
- Recall a time when you felt surprise of shock or disorientation.
- Recall something you would do differently another time
- Recall your proudest teaching moment during the last week.

Keep these writings in one place – a journal or exercise book is fine, or they can be stored on a computer or in a 'blog' (a web-based diary, or 'weblog').
An alternative is to keep a 'video diary' of your thoughts and observations on teaching, to be edited later.

(adapted from Brookfield 1995)

- Photographs or video clips of your teaching taken by colleagues or students, with notes on why they were taken.
- Recordings of interviews or focus group discussions with students about aspects of classroom life – based for example on themes like order, opportunity and care.

The analysis of this raw data can be done in any way that suits the individual, but with the aim of creating a portrait or profile of classroom management in his or her teaching. The analysis can be brought together with a written commentary which focuses on themes in classroom management. This commentary can also identify potential action research or exploratory teaching projects. If this work is done collaboratively by two or more colleagues who share data and experience, it can be the springboard for development for both.

Summary

This chapter has outlined a selection of the rich array of possibilities for researching aspects of classroom management and classroom life, drawing on a range of data-generation techniques, analytical procedures and theoretical positions. It is hoped that readers are able to follow their own research interests in this rich and often un-explored area of educational practice.

Part 4
Resources

16
Further Resources in Classroom Management

This chapter lists and provides commentary on key sources for teachers, teacher educators and researchers in the field of classroom management. The wide range of classroom management issues and practices and the eclecticism of the literature that informs them is illustrated by Parts 1, 2 and 3. This section provides an overview of the resources available to teachers, teacher educators and researchers wishing to explore further this rich and challenging field.

Books

Most of the key references to classroom management issues have been added at the end of chapters which they best illustrate, and provide a fairly comprehensive picture of the field. A selection of key texts which relate to classroom management, or contain seminal papers are listed below.

Key texts

Arnold, J. (ed.) (1999) *Affect in Language Learning.* Cambridge: Cambridge University Press.

Bailey, K. and D. Nunan (eds) (1996) *Voices From the Language Classroom.* Cambridge: Cambridge University Press.

Bowers, C. A. and D. J. Flinders (1990) *Responsive Teaching: An ecological approach to classroom patterns of language, culture and thought.* New York: Teachers' College Press.

Breen, M. P. and A. Littlejohn (eds) (2000) *Classroom Decision-Making: Negotiation and process syllabuses in practice.* Cambridge: Cambridge University Press.

Briggs, J. B. and P. J. Moore (1993) *The Process of Teaching.* Sydney: Prentice-Hall, 3rd edition.

Candlin, C. N. and N. Mercer (eds) (2001) *The Social Context of Language Teaching.* London: Routledge.

Cazden, C. (1988) *Classroom Discourse: The language of teaching.* Portsmouth, NH: Heinemann.

Coleman, H. (ed.) (1996) *Society and the Language Classroom*. Cambridge: Cambridge University Press.

Dornyei, Z. (2001) *Teaching and Researching Motivation*. Harlow: Longman Pearson.

Eraut, M. (1994) *Developing Professional Knowledge and Competence*. London: Falmer.

Freeman, D. and J. C. Richards (eds) (1996) *Teacher Learning in Language Teaching*. Cambridge: Cambridge University Press.

Hall, D. and A. Hewings (eds) (2001) *Innovation in English Language Teaching*. London: Routledge.

Hargreaves, A. (1994) *Changing Teachers, Changing Times*. London: Cassell.

Holliday, A. (1994) *Appropriate Methodology and Social Context*. Cambridge: Cambridge University Press.

Jacques, D. (1991) *Learning in Groups*. London: Kogan Page (2nd edition).

Jones, V. F. and L. S. Jones (1991) *Comprehensive Classroom Management*. New York: Longman (2nd edition).

Lantolf, J. (ed.) (2000) *Sociocultural Theory and Second Language Learning*. Oxford: Oxford University Press.

Mercer, N. (1995) *The Guided Construction of Knowledge*. Clevedon: Multilingual Matters.

Norton, B. (2000) *Identity and Language Learning: Power and Possibility in Classrooms and Communities*. Harlow: Longman.

Pollard, A. (2000) *Reflective Teaching in the Primary School*. London: Cassell.

Rowland, S. (1993) *The Enquiring Tutor*. London: Falmer.

Van Lier, L. (1996) *Interaction in the Language Curriculum*. Harlow: Longman.

Van Manen, M. (1991) *The Tact of Teaching*. Albany, NY: State University of New York Press.

Wells, G. (1999) *Dialogic Inquiry*. Cambridge: Cambridge University Press.

Wells, G. and G. Claxton (eds) (2002) *Learning for Life in the 21st Century*. Oxford: Blackwell.

Wenger, E. (1998) *Communities of Practice*. Cambridge: Cambridge University Press.

Whitaker, P. (1995) *Managing To Learn: Aspects of practice and experiential learning in schools*. London: Cassell.

Williams, M. and B. Burden (1997) *Psychology for Language Teachers*. Cambridge: Cambridge University Press.

Wragg, E. (1993) *Class Management*. London: Routledge.

Teachers' resources

Classroom activities (selection)

Brandes, D. and H. Phillips (1990) *Gamesters' Handbook No. 2*. London: Stanley Thornes.

Campbell, C. and H. Kryszewska (1992) *Learner-based Teaching*. Oxford: Oxford University Press.

Cross, D. (1995) *Large Classes in Action*. Hemel-Hempstead: Prentice-Hall.

Davis, P. and M. Rinvolucri (1990) *The Confidence Book*. Harlow: Longman.

Davis, P, B. Garside and M. Rinvolucri (1999) *Ways of Doing: Students Explore Their Everyday and Classroom Processes*. Cambridge: Cambridge University Press.

Deller, S. (1990) *Lessons from the Learner*. Harlow: Longman.

Dobbs, J. (2001) *Using* the Board in the Language Classroom. Cambridge: Cambridge University Press.

Dornyei, Z. and T. Murphey (2003) *Group Dynamics in the Language Classroom*. Cambridge: Cambridge University Press.

Dudeney, G. (2000) *The Internet and the Language Classroom*. Cambridge: Cambridge University Press.

Fried-Booth, D. (2002) *Project Work*. Oxford: Oxford University Press (2nd edition).

Griffiths, G. and K. Keohane (2000) *Personalising Language Learning*. Cambridge: Cambridge University Press.

Hadfield, J. (1992) Classroom Dynamics. Oxford: Oxford University Press.

Hess, N. (2001) *Teaching Large Multilevel Classes*. Cambridge: Cambridge University Press.

Painter, L. (2003) Homework. Oxford: Oxford University Press.

Other topics (including activities)

Ayers, H. and F. Gray (1998) *Classroom Management: A Practical Approach for Primary and Secondary Teachers*. London: David Fulton.

Brandes, D. and P. Ginnis (1996) *A Guide to Student-Centred Learning*. London: Stanley Thornes.

McLaughlin, H. J., T. V. Savage, S. Zehm and R. R. Powell (2001) *Management of the Culturally Diverse Classroom: Perspectives on the Social Curriculum*. New York: Pearson.

Salmon, G. (2002) *E-Tivities: The key to active learning online*. London: RoutledgeFalmer.

Salmon, G. (2004) *E-Moderating: The key to teaching and learning online*. London: Routledge and Falmer (2nd edition).

Teacher education resources

Head, K. and P. Taylor (1997) *Readings in Teacher Development*. Oxford: Heinemann.

James, P. (2000) *Teachers in Action*. Cambridge: Cambridge University Press.

Tanner, R. and C. Green (1998) *Tasks for Teacher Education*. Harlow: Longman.

Ur, P. (1996) *A Course in Language Teaching*. Cambridge: Cambridge University Press.

Researchers' resources

Altrichter, H., P. Posch and B. Somekh (1993) *Teachers Investigate Their Work*. London: Routledge.

Burns, A. (1999) *Collaborative Action Research for Language Teachers*. Cambridge: Cambridge University Press.

Freeman, D. (1998) *Doing Teacher Research: From Inquiry to Understanding*. New York: Heinle and Heinle.

Hedge, T. (2000) *Teaching and Learning in the Language Classroom*. Oxford: Oxford University Press.

Holliday, A. (2002) *Doing and Writing Qualitative Research*. London: Sage.

Hopkins, D. (2002) *A Teacher's Guide to Classroom Research*. Milton Keynes: Open University Press (3rd edition).

Pollard, A. (2002) *Reflective Teaching: Effective and Research-based Professional Practice*. London: Continuum.

Richards, K. (2003) *Qualitative Inquiry in TESOL*. Basingstoke: Palgrave Macmillan.

Tripp, D. (1993) *Critical Incidents in Teaching: Developing Professional Judgement*. London: Routledge.

Wallace, M. (1998) *Action Research for Language Teachers*. Cambridge: Cambridge University Press.

Journals

I have listed a selection of journals where relevant articles may sometimes be found. Website addresses are provided where available, but these may change from time to time. Many journals put their abstracts and lists of content online, but most also limit the full text service to subscribers.

ELT Journal
http://www3.oup.co.uk/eltj
ELT Journal is widely read by English Language teaching professionals. Articles are mainly pedagogically-oriented, and there is a good review section and other features like 'Key Concepts' which provide specific information on topics.

Applied Linguistics
http://www3.oup.co.uk/applij/
Occasionally there are classroom-based articles in this publication which is at the 'academic' end of the spectrum of publications available to language teaching professionals.

Prospect
http://www.nceltr.mq.edu.au/prospect/prospect.htm
Journal published by the Australian Migrant English Programme. Wide range of articles on classroom and other topics.

RELC Journal
http://www.relc.org.sg/journal.htm
Journal published by SEAMEO and the Regional English Language center in Singapore (RELC). Articles with a South-East Asian flavour, but with universal interest value.

System
http://www.elsevier.com/locate/system
Theoretical and practical articles can be found in *System*. Both classroom
and Applied Linguistics focus.

TESOL Quarterly
http://www.tesol.edu/pubs/magz/tq.html
The journal of TESOL, the largest association for teachers of English worldwide.
The journal has both theoretical and practical articles.

English Teaching Professional
http://www.etprofessional.com/index.php
Aimed at the practicing teacher. A strong classroom activity focus and useful
position papers on various topics.

English for Specific Purposes
Covers classroom, curriculum and theoretical issues from an ESP perspective.

TESL Canada Journal
http://www.tesl.ca//journal.html
Wide-ranging selection of articles covering full range of activities, from
teaching to research. Published in English and French.

Modern English Teacher
http://www.onlinemet.com/
Practical and classroom-focused.

Language Teaching Research
http://ww.arnoldpublishing.com/journals
Research-oriented journal with a strong classroom orientation.

Teaching and Teacher Education
www.elsevier.com/locate/tate
A wide-ranging selection of articles with an international flavour on all
aspects of educational practice.

Journal of Classroom Interaction
http://www.coe.uh.edu/~coejci/
Specialist journal focused on classroom talk studies.

Educational Action Research
http://ejournals.ebsco.com/direct.asp?JournalID=108422
Broad-based action-research led journal.

Harvard Educational Review
http://ejournals.ebsco.com/direct.asp?JournalID=102010
Occasional articles with a classroom or classroom research focus.
   There are increasing numbers of online journals which are of assistance,
and contain material which has relevance to managing classrooms.

Humanising Language Teaching
http://www.hltmag.co.uk/
Articles on all aspects of language teaching and learning with a strong 'humanistic' orientation.

Compare
http://www.tandf.co.uk/journals/titles/03057925.asp
Net-based journal with authoritative, classroom-based research articles.

Teachers College Record
http://www.trecord
Mainstream US-based journal covering a wide range of theoretical and pedagogic topics. Research-based.

Issues in Educational Research
http://education.curtin.edu.au/iier.html
Australian-based journal devoted to research issues in education.

Teacher Development
http://www.triangle.co.uk/tde/
Online journal devoted to the exploration of teaching.

Research focus

Educational Action Research Online
http://www.triangle.co.uk/ear/
Online journal specializing in action research.

Exploratory Practice
http://www.ling.lancs.ac.uk/groups/epcentre/epcentre.htm
Web pages of the Exploratory Practice Centre at University of Lancaster, founded by Dick Allwright. Papers, links, forum.

ActionResearch.net
http://www.bath.ac.uk/~edsajw/
Extensive site at the University of Bath. Articles, links, forums. Well worth a visit.

Collaborative Action Research Network
http://www.did.stu.mmu.ac.uk/carn/
Good selection of publications and links. Forum for members.

Martyn Ryder
http://carbon.cudenver.edu/~mryder/itc_data/act_res.html
Web pages kept by Martyn Ryder at the University of Colorado at Denver.

PARnet
http://www.parnet.org/
An online action research community. Invites you to share resources.

Scottish Centre for Research in Education
http://www.scre.ac.uk/tpr/index.html
Comprehensive set of online resources and links for educational researchers.

Professional associations

TESOL www.tesol.org
US-based association of teachers of English to speakers of other languages.
Publications, resources, SIGs

IATEFL www.iatefl.org
EFL teachers' association with branches in many countries. Special Interest
Groups available for members, as well as resources and publications.

BAAL www.baal.org.uk
British-based association for applied linguists. Excellent links. Publications.

Local Teachers' Associations. Most countries have a local language teachers'
association. Try a search with 'Language Teachers' Associations'. For
example, the Soros Foundation sponsors a number in Central and Eastern
Europe. www.soros.org/initiatives/english/focus_areas/selp/teachers_associations

JALT www.jalt.org
Japanese association for teachers of English. SIGs. Teachers' resources.

Email lists and bulletin boards

AiTech Links for Teachers
Linguistlist.org
Teacher Education e-List
Sociocultural LISTSERV

Internet sites

There are a great number of websites offering online learning opportunities
for language students and teachers, or with resources. The US has a number
of commercial sites for teachers, with lesson plans and teaching ideas, a lot
of them on the discipline and control aspects of class management. A search
using 'Classroom Management' will find many of these. The selection
offered here is limited, but hopefully targeted for maximum usability.

ECML
http://www.ecml.at/
Website for the European Centre for Modern Languages. Resources for
language teachers, and publications.

CILT (the National Centre for Languages UK)
http://www.cilt.org.uk/
Information and links for language teachers.

Dave Sperling's ESL Café
www.pacificnet.net/~sperling/eslcafe.htm
Very popular English language site. Discussion forums, resources, links.

British Council Resources for Teachers
http://www.teachingenglish.org.uk/
Site for English teachers – resources, lesson ideas, links.

Aardvark's English Forum
http://www.englishforum.com/00/
General resource for teachers and learners of English. Has a teachers' area with forum.

Education Guardian
http://education.guardian.co.uk/tefl
News, articles, resources for teachers.

Other sources (e.g. databases)

ERIC
www.eric.ed.org
Data base and search facilities for a vast number of publications, theses etc.

There are now a number of sites devoted to listing the ever-increasing number of online journals.

Directory of Open Access Journals
http://www.doaj.org

BUBL Link
http://bubl.ac.uk/link

American Educational Research Association
http://aera-cr.asu.edu/links.html

Large Classes
http://www.hywelcoleman.com/learning.htm
Bibliographies on issues related to teaching and learning in large classes are kept by Hywel Coleman. They are the updated residue of the Leeds-Lancaster Project on large classes.

Curricular Resources in English as a Second Language
http://www.cln.org/subjects/esl_cur.html
Links page – access to a number of useful websites offering resources for practitioners.

Internet TESL Journal
http://iteslj.org/links/TESL/
Excellent links page for all aspects of language teaching.

There are now a number of sites devoted to collecting records of online journals, regularly updated. Journals available range from online learning to language teaching, published from several countries.

Directory of Open Access Journals
http://www.doaj.org

BUBL Link
http://bubl.ac.uk/link

American Educational Research Association
http://aera-cr.asu.edu/links.html

EducationLine (service provided by University of Leeds Library)
http://www.leeds.ac.uk/educol

Appropriate Methodology
http://arts-humanities.cant.ac.uk/Language-Studies/bibliography.htm
List of references compiled by Adrian Holliday.

Discussion Groups

Linguist List www.linguistlist.org
TESL-L http://www.hunter.cuny.edu/~tesl-l/

Bibliography

Adendorff, R. D. (1996) The functions of code switching among high school teachers and students in KwaZulu and the implications for teacher education. In K. M. Bailey and D. Nunan (eds).

Allwright, D. (1984) The importance of interaction in classroom language learning. *Applied Linguistics*, 5/2.

Allwright, D. (1989) Interaction in the language classroom: social problems and pedagogic possibilities. *Language Teaching in Today's World*, Vol. 3. Paris: Hachette.

Allwright, D. (1996) Social and pedagogic pressures in the language classroom: The role of socialisation. In H. Coleman (ed.).

Allwright, D. (2001) 'Exploratory Practice': An appropriate methodology for making optimal use of research as a vehicle for language teacher development? Paper delivered at IALS Symposium, Edinburgh. Mimeo: Unpublished.

Allwright, D. (2002) Putting 'quality of life' first: Towards a new view of Exploratory Practice. University of Lancaster. Mimeo: Unpublished.

Allwright, D. (2003) A brief guide to Exploratory Practice: rethinking practitioner research in language teaching. *Language Teaching Research*, 7/2.

Allwright, D. and K. M. Bailey (1991) *Focus on the Language Classroom*. Cambridge: Cambridge University Press.

Altrichter, H., P. Posch and B. Somekh (1993) *Teachers Investigate Their Work*. London: Routledge.

Appel, J. (1995) *Diary of a Language Teacher*. Oxford: Heinemann.

Arndt, V., P. Harvey and J. Nuttall (2000) *Alive to Language*. Cambridge: Cambridge University Press.

Arnold, J. (ed.) (1999) *Affect in Language Learning*. Cambridge: Cambridge University Press.

Arthur, J. (1994) English in Botswana primary classrooms: functions and constraints. In C. M. Rubagumya (ed.) *Teaching and Researching Language in African Classrooms*. Clevedon: Multilingual Matters.

Askew, S. and E. Carnell (1998) *Transforming Learning: Individual and global change*. London: Cassell.

Atkinson, T. and G. Claxton (eds) (2000) *The Intuitive Practitioner*. Buckingham: Open University Press.

Ayers, H. and F. Gray (1998) *Classroom Management: A practical approach for primary and secondary teachers*. London: David Fulton.

Bailey, K. M. (1996) The best-laid plans: teachers' in-class decisions to depart from their lesson plans. In K. M. Bailey and D. Nunan (eds) *Voices from the Language Classroom*. Cambridge: Cambridge University Press.

Bailey, K. M. and D. Nunan (eds) (1996) *Voices from the Language Classroom*. Cambridge: Cambridge University Press.

Banister, P., E. Burman, I. Parker, M. Taylor and C. Tindall (eds) (1994) *Qualitative Research in Psychology: A research guide*. Buckingham: Open Univeristy Press.

Bannink, A. (2002) Negotiating the paradoxes of spontaneous talk in advanced L2 classes. In C. Kramsch (ed.).

Barnes, D. (1969) Language in the secondary school. In D. Barnes, J. Briton and H. Rosen (eds).

Barnes, D. (1976) *From Communication to Curriculum*. Harmondsworth: Penguin.

Barnes, D., J. Briton and H. Rosen (eds) (1969) *Language, The Learner and the School.* Harmondsworth: Penguin.

Benson, P. (2001) *Teaching and Researching Autonomy in Language Learning.* Harlow: Pearson.

Berliner, D. C. (1988) The development of expertise in pedagogy. Paper presented at the meeting of the American Association of Colleges for Teacher Education. New Orleans, LA.

Bernstein, B. (1971) *Class, Codes and Control.* London: Routledge and Kegan Paul.

Bernstein, B. (1996) *Pedagogy, Symbolic Control and Identity: Theory, research and critique.* London: Taylor and Francis.

Biott, C. and J. Nias (eds) (1992) *Working and Living Together for Change.* Buckingham: Open University Press.

Blake, N. and P. Standish (eds) (2000) *Enquiries at the Interface: Philosophical problems of online education.* Oxford: Blackwell.

Bloom, B. (1956) *Taxonomy of Educational Objectives: Book 1, Cognitive Domain.* New York: Longman.

Bolitho, R. and B. Tomlinson (1995) *Discover English.* Oxford: Heinemann (2nd edition).

Bolitho, R., R. Carter, R. Hughes, R. Ivanič, H. Masuhara and B. Tomlinson (2003) Ten questions about language awareness. *ELT Journal,* 57/3.

Booth, M., V. J. Furlong and M. Wilkin (eds) (1990) *Partnership in Initial Teacher Training.* London: Cassell.

Borg, S. (1998) Teacher cognition in second language grammar teaching. Unpublished PhD thesis. University of Exeter.

Bourdieu, P. (1977) *Outline of a Theory of Practice.* Cambridge: Cambridge Univeristy Press.

Bourdieu, P. (1991) *Language and Symbolic Power.* Oxford: Polity.

Bourdieu, P. and J-C. Passeron (1990) *Reproduction in Education, Society and Culture.* London: Sage (2nd edition).

Bowers, C. A. and D. J. Flinders (1990) *Responsive Teaching: An ecological approach to classroom patterns of language, culture and thought.* New York: Teachers College Press.

Bramall, S. (2000) The educational significance of the interface. In N. Blake and P. Standish (eds).

Brandes, D. and H. Phillips (1990) *Gamesters' Handbook No. 2.* London: Stanley Thornes.

Brandes, D. and P. Ginnis (1996) *A Guide to Student-Centred Learning.* London: Stanley Thornes.

Bransford, J. D., A. L. Brown and R. R. Cocking (2000) *How People Learn.* Washington, DC: National Academy Press.

Breen, M. P. (1987) Learner contributions to task design. In C. N. Candlin and D. Murphy (eds) *Language Learning Tasks. Lancaster Practical Papers in English Language Teaching, Vol. 7.* Hemel Hempstaed: Prentice-Hall.

Breen, M. P. (1991) Understanding the language teacher. In R. Phillipson, K. Ellerman, L. Selinker, M. Sharwood-Smith and M. Swain (eds) *Foreign and Second Language Pedagogy Research.* Clevedon: Multilingual Matters.

Breen, M. P. (2001a) The social context for language learning: a neglected situation. In C. N. Candlin and N. Mercer (eds).

Breen, M. P. (2001b) Navigating the discourse: on what is learned in the language classroom. In C. N. Candlin and N. Mercer (eds).

Breen, M. P. (ed.) (2001c) *Learner Contributions to Language Learning.* Harlow: Longman.

Breen, M. P. (2001d) Overt participation and covert acquisition in the language classroom. In Breen (ed.) (2001c).

Breen, M. P. and C. N. Candlin (1980) The essentials of a communicative curriculum in language teaching. *Applied Linguistics* 1/2.

Breen, M. P. and A. Littlejohn (eds) (2000) *Classroom Decision Making: Negotiation and process syllabuses in practice.* Cambridge: Cambridge University Press.

Breen, M. P., B. Hird, M. Milton, R. Oliver and A. Thwaite (2001) Making sense of language teaching: Teachers' principles and classroom practices. *Applied Linguistics,* 22/4.

Briggs, J. B. and P. J. Moore (1993) *The Process of Learning.* Sydney: Prentice-Hall (3rd edition).

Brockbank, A. and I. McGill (1998) *Facilitating Reflective Learning in Higher Education.* Buckingham: Open University Press.

Brookfield, S. (1990) *The Skilful Teacher.* San Francisco, CA.: Jossey-Bass.

Brookfield, S. (1995) *Becoming A Critically Reflective Teacher.* San Francisco, CA.: Jossey-Bass.

Brophy, J. (2001) Teaching Educational Practice Series – 1. International Academy of Education. Available online: http://www.ibe.unesco.org/International/Publications/Educaitonal/Practices/prachome.htm.

Brown, S. and D. McIntyre (1993) *Making Sense of Teaching.* Buckingham: Open University Press.

Brumfit, C. J. (1984) *Communicative Methodology in Language Teaching.* Cambridge: Cambridge University Press.

Brumfit, C. J. (2001) *Individual Freedom in Language Learning.* Oxford: Oxford University Press.

Bruner, J. S. (1966) *Towards a Theory of Instruction.* Cambridge, MA: Belknap Press of Harvard University.

Bruner, J. S. (1979) *On Knowing: Essays for the Left Hand.* Cambridge, MA: Harvard University Press.

Bruner, J. S. (1983) *Child's Talk: Learning to Use Language.* New York: Norton.

Bruner, J. S. (1986) *Actual Minds, Possible Worlds.* Cambridge, MA: Harvard University Press.

Burden, R. (1994) Trends and developments in educational psychology. *School Psychology International.* 15.

Burns, A. (1996) Starting all over again: from teaching adults to teaching beginners. In D. Freeman and J. C. Richards (eds).

Burns, A. (1999) *Collaborative Action Research for Language Teachers.* Cambridge: Cambridge University Press.

Burton, J. (2000) Learning from discourse analysis in the classroom. *TESOL Journal,* 9/4.

Cadorath, J. and S. Harris (1998) Unplanned classroom language and teacher training. *ELT Journal,* 52/3.

Calderhead, J. (ed.) (1988) *Teachers' Professional Learning.* Lewes: Falmer Press.

Campbell, C. and H. Kryszewska (1992) *Learner-based Teaching.* Oxford: Oxford University Press.

Canagarajah, A. S. (1993) Critical ethnography of a Sri Lankan classroom: ambiguities in student opposition to reproduction through TESOL. *TESOL Quarterly,* 27/4. 601–26.

Canagarajah, A. S. (1995) Functions of codeswitching in ESL classrooms: socialising bilingualism in Jaffna. *Journal of Multilingual and Multicultural Development.* 3/3. 173–95.

Canagarajah, A. S. (1999) *Revisiting Linguistic Imperialism in English Teaching.* Oxford: Oxford University Press.

Candlin, C. N. (1998) Problematising professional identities. *TESOL 1998. Colloquium on Identities and language Learning and Teaching*. Seattle, Wa.: Mimeo.

Candlin, C. N. (2001) Introduction to V. Kohonen et al.

Candlin, C. N. and N. Mercer (eds) (2001) *English Language Teaching in its Social Context*. London: Routledge.

Carter, G. and H. Thomas (1986) 'Dear Brown Eyes': experiential learning in a project oriented approach. *ELT Journal*, 40/3.

Carter, K. (1990) Teachers' knowledge and beginning to teach. In W. R. Houston (ed.) *Handbook of Research on Teacher Education*. New York: Macmillan.

Carter, K. (1992) Toward a cognitive conception of classroom management: A case of teacher comprehension. In J. H. Shulman (ed.) *Case Methods in Teacher Education*. New York: Teachers' College Press.

Carter, R. (1999) *Mapping the Mind*. London: Seven Dials.

Carter, R. and M. McCarthy (1995) Spoken grammar: what is it and how can we teach it? *ELT Journal*, 49/3.

Cazden, C. (1988) *Classroom Discourse: The language of teaching and learning*. Portsmouth, NH: Heinemann.

Chick, K. (1996) Safe-talk: collusion in apartheid education. In H. Coleman (ed.).

Choong, K-F. (2001) Projects as instruments of change. The impact of a trainer training project on trainers' professional development in Malaysia – A case study. Unpublished PhD thesis. University of Exeter.

Clark, C. M. (1992) Teachers as designers in self-directed teacher development. In A. Hargreaves and M. Fullan (eds).

Clark, J. (1987) *Curriculum Renewal in School Foreign Language Teaching*. Oxford: Oxford University Press.

Claxton, G. (1984) The psychology of teacher training: inaccuracies and improvements. *Educational Psychology*, 4/2.

Claxton, G. (1999) *Wise Up*. London: Bloomsbury.

Claxton, G. (2002) Education in the learning age: a sociocultural approach to learning to learn. In G. Wells and G. Claxton (eds).

Claxton, G., T. Atkinson, M. Osborn and M. Wallace (eds) (1996) *Liberating the Learner: Lessons for professional development in education*. London: Routledge.

Coleman, H. (1996a) Shadow puppets and language lessons: Interpreting classroom behaviour in its social context. In H. Coleman (ed.).

Coleman, H. (ed.) (1996b) *Society and the Language Classroom*. Cambridge: Cambridge University Press.

Coleman, H. (2002) A Bibliography on Class Size. Section 1: The Learning and Teaching of English in Large Classes. University of Leeds. Mimeo: Unpublished.

Connelly, F. M. and D. J. Clandinin (1988) *Teachers as Curriculum Planners*. New York: Teachers' College Press.

Cook, G. (2000) *Language Play, Language Learning*. Oxford: Oxford University Press.

Cortazzi, M. and L. Jin (1996) Cultures of learning: Language classrooms in China. In H. Coleman (ed.).

Crandall, J. A. (1999) Cooperative language learning and affective factors. In J. Arnold (ed.).

Crichton, J. (2004) Issues of interdiscursivity in the commercialisation of professional practice: The case of English Language teaching. Unpublished PhD Thesis. Macquarie Univeristy, Sydney.

Cross, D. (1995) *Large Classes in Action*. Hemel-Hempstead: Prentice-Hall.

Crystal, D. (1998) *Language Play*. Harmondsworth: Penguin.

Csikszentmihalyi, M. (1990) *Flow: The psychology of optimal experience.* New York: Harper & Row.

Cullen, R. (2002) Supportive teacher talk: the importance of the F-Move. *ELT Journal*, 56/2.

Cunningham, S. and P. Moor (1999) *Cutting Edge – Upper Intermediate.* Harlow: Pearson.

Daloz, L. A. (1986) *Effective Teaching and Mentoring.* San Francisco, CA: Jossey-Bass.

Davis, P. and M. Rinvolucri (1990) *The Confidence Book.* Harlow: Longman.

Davis, P, B. Garside and M. Rinvolucri (1999) *Ways of Doing: Students Explore Their Everyday and Classroom Processes.* Cambridge: Cambridge University Press.

Dawkins, R. (1976) *The Selfish Gene.* Oxford: Oxford University Press.

Deller, S. (1990) *Lessons from the Learner.* Harlow: Longman.

Denscombe, M. (1982) The 'hidden pedagogy' and its implications for teacher training. *British Journal of Sociology of Education*, 3/3.

Dewey, J. (1916) *Democracy and Education. An introduction to the philosophy of education.* New York: Free Press (1966 edn).

Di Giovanni, E. and G. Nagaswami (2001) Online peer review: an alternative to face-to-face. *ELT Journal*, 55/3.

Diamond, P. C. T. (1991) *Teacher Education as Transformation.* Buckingham: Open University Press.

Dillon, J. T. (1994) *Using Discussion in Classrooms.* Buckingham: Open University Press.

Dobbs, J. (2001) *Using the Board in the Language Classroom.* Cambridge: Cambridge University Press.

Donato, R. (1994) Collective scaffolding in second language learning. In J. P. Lantolf and G. Appel (eds).

Dornyei, Z. (2001) *Teaching and Researching Motivation.* Harlow: Pearson.

Dornyei, Z. and A. Malderez (1999) Group dynamics in foreign language learning and teaching. In J. Arnold (ed.).

Dornyei, Z and T. Murphey (2003) *Group Dynamics in the Language Classroom.* Cambridge: Cambridge University Press.

Doyle, W. (1986) Classroom organisation and management. In M. C. Wittrock (ed.) *Handbook of Research on Teaching.* New York: Macmillan (3rd edition).

Drew, P. and J. Heritage (eds) (1992) *Talk at Work.* Cambridge: Cambridge University Press.

Dudeney, G. (2000) *The Internet and the Language Classroom.* Cambridge: Cambridge University Press.

Dunne, R. and G. Harvard (1993) A model of teaching and its implications for mentoring. In D. McIntyre, H. Hagger and M. Wilkin (eds).

Edwards, D. and N. Mercer (1987) *Common Knowledge: The development of understanding in the classroom.* London: Methuen.

Egan, G. (1998) *The Skilled Helper.* Belmont, CA: Wadsworth (4th edition).

Eisner, E. and E. Vallance (1974) *Conflicting Conceptions of Curriculum.* Richmond, CA: McCutchan.

Eken, D. (1999) Through the eyes of the learner: learner observations of teaching and learning. *ELT Journal*, 53/4.

Elbaz, F. (1983) *Teacher Thinking: A study of practical knowledge.* London: Croom Helm.

Elliott, J. (1993) *Action Research and Educational Change.* Buckingham: Open University Press.

Ellis, G. and B. Sinclair (1996) *Learning to Learn English.* Cambridge: Cambridge University Press.

Ellis, R. (2001a) The metaphorical constructions of second language learners. In M. P. Breen (ed.) (2001c).

Ellis, R. (2001b) Second language acquisition: research and pedagogy. In C. N. Candlin and N. Mercer (eds).

Elmhirst, L. K. (1961) *Rabrindranath Tagore: Pioneer in Education*. London: John Murray.

Emmer, E. T. and L. M. Stough (2001) Classroom management: a critical part of educational psychology, with implications for teacher education. *Educational Psychologist*, 36/2.

Engeström, Y., R. Engeström and A. Suntio (2002) Can a school community learn to master its own future? An activity-rheoretical study of expansive learning among middle school teachers. In G. Wells and G. Claxton (eds).

Eraut, M. (1988) Management knowledge: its nature and development. In J. Calderhead (ed.).

Eraut, M. (1994) *Developing Professional Knowledge and Competence*. London: Falmer Press.

Erickson, F. (1982) Classroom discourse as improvisation: relationships between academic task structure and social participation structure in lessons. In L. C. Wilkinson (ed.) *Communicating in the Classroom*. New York: Academic Press.

Erickson, F. (1996) Inclusion into what? Thoughts on the construction of learning, identity and affiliation in the general education classroom. In D. L. Speece and B. K. Keogh (eds) *Research on Classroom Ecologies: Implications for inclusion of children with learning disabilities*. Mahwak, NJ: Erlbaum.

Erickson, F. and J. Shultz (1992) Students' experience of the curriculum. In P. W. Jackson (ed.) *Handbook of Research on Curriculum*. New York: Macmillan.

Fairclough, N. (1991) *Language and Power*. Harlow: Longman.

Fairclough, N. (1992) *Critical Discourse Analysis*. Harlow: Longman.

Feiman-Nemser, S. and R. E. Floden (1986) The cultures of teaching. In M. Wittrock (ed.) *The Handbook of Research on Teaching*. New York: Macmillan (3rd edition).

Fenwick, D. T. (1998) Managing space, energy, and self: junior high teachers' experiences of classroom management. *Teaching and Teacher Education*, 14/6.

Fisher, R. (1990) *Teaching Children to Think*. Cheltenham: Stanley Thornes.

Frawley, W. and J. P. Lantolf (1985) Second language discourse. A Vygotskyan perspective. *Applied Linguistics*, 6/1.

Freeman, D. (1992) Collaboration: constructing shared understandings in second language education. In D. Nunan (ed.).

Freeman, D. (1996) Redefining the relationship between research and what teachers know. In K. M. Bailey and D. Nunan (eds).

Freeman, D. (1998) *Doing Teacher Research: From inquiry to understanding*. New York: Heinle and Heinle.

Freeman, D. and J. C. Richards (eds) (1996) *Teacher Learning in Language Teaching*. Cambridge: Cambridge University Press.

Freire, P. (1972) *Pedagogy of the Oppressed*. Harmondsworth: Penguin.

Fried-Booth, D. (2002) *Project Work*. Oxford: Oxford University Press (2nd edition).

Fullan, M. (1993) *Change Forces*. London: Falmer Press.

Fullan, M. (1999) *Change Forces The Sequel*. London. Falmer Press.

Furlong, V. J. (1990) School-based training: the student's views. In M. Booth, V. J. Furlong and M. Wilkin (eds).

Furlong, V. J. (2000) Intuition and the crisis in teacher professionalism. In T. Atkinson and G. Claxton (eds).

Furlong, V. J. and T. Maynard (1995) *Mentoring Student Teachers. The growth of professional knowledge.* London: Routledge.

Garfinkel, H. (1967) *Studies in Ethnomethodology.* Englewood Cliffs, NJ: Prentice-Hall.

Garton, S. (2002) Learner initiative in the language classroom. *ELT Journal,* 56/1.

Geertz, C. (1973) *The Interpretation of Cultures.* New York: Basic Books.

Gibbons, P. (2001) Learning a new register in a foreign language. In C. N. Candlin and N. Mercer (eds).

Gierlinger, E. (ed.) (1999) *Sharing the European Language Classroom: A project in international classroom research.* Linz: Universitatsverlag Rudolf Trauner.

Gimenez, T. N. (1994) Learners becoming teachers: an explaratory study of beliefs held by prospective and practising EFL teachers in Brazil. Unpublished PhD thesis. University of Lancaster.

Giroux, H. A. (1981) *Ideology, Culture and the Process of Schooling.* London: Falmer Press.

Goffman, E. (1969) *The Presentation of Self in Everyday Life.* Harmondsworth: Penguin.

Goffman, E. (1974) *Frame Analysis: An essay on the organisation of experience.* New York: Harper and Row.

Goffman, E. (1981) *Forms of Talk.* Oxford: Blackwell.

Goleman, D. (1995) *Emotional Intelligence.* London: Bloomsbury.

Goleman, D. (1998) *Emotional Intelligence at Work.* London: Bloomsbury.

Goodfellow, R. (2003) Virtuality and the shaping of educational communities. Mimeo. Unpublished.

Goodfellow, R. (2004) Online literacies and learning: operational, cultural and critical dimensions. *Language and Education,* 18/5.

Goodfellow, R., M. Morgan, M. Lea and J. Petit (2004) Students' writing in the virtual university: an investigation into the relation between online discussion and writing for assessment on two Masters courses. In I. Snyder and C. Beavis (eds).

Goodson, I. (ed.) (1992) *Studying Teachers' Lives.* London: Routledge.

Goodson, I. (2003) *Professional Knowledge, Professional Lives.* Maidenhead: Open University Press.

Gower, R., D. Phillips and S. Walters (1995) *The Teaching Practice Handbook.* Harlow: Longman.

Graddoll, D. (1997) *The Future of English.* London: The British Council.

Graddoll, D. (2004) *The future of language.* Science, 303.

Gray, H. C. (1988) *Management Consultancy in Schools.* London: Cassell.

Gray, J. (1998) *False Dawn.* London: Granta.

Greenfield, P. M. (1984) A theory of the teacher in the learning activities of everyday life. In B. Rogoff and J. Lave (eds).

Greenfield, S. (1998) *The Human Brain: A guided tour.* London: Phoenix.

Griffiths, G. and K. Keohane (2000) *Personalising Language Learning.* Cambridge: Cambridge University Press.

Griffiths, M. and S. Tann (1992) Using reflective practice to link personal and public theories. *Journal of Education for Teaching,* 18/1.

Gumperz, J. J. (1982) *Discourse Strategies.* Cambridge: Cambridge University Press.

Guthrie, G. (1990) To the defense of traditional teaching in lesser-developed countries. In V. D. Rust and P. Dalin (eds) *Teachers and Teaching in the Developing World.* New York: Garland.

Hadfield, J. (1992) *Classroom Dynamics.* Oxford: Oxford University Press.

Hagos, T. G. (2000) Teachers' responses to innovation in ELT methodology in Eritrea. Unpublished PhD thesis. University of Exeter.

Hall, D. and A. Hewings (eds) (2001) *Innovation in English Language Teaching*. London: Routledge.

Hall, E. T. (1966) *The Hidden Dimension*. New York: Anchor/Doubleday.

Hall, E. T. (1984) *The Dance of Life*. New York: Anchor/Doubleday.

Handal, G. and P. Lauvas (1987) *Promoting Reflective Teaching*. Milton Keynes: Open University Press.

Hargreaves, A. (1994) *Changing Teachers, Changing Times*. London: Cassell.

Hargreaves, A. (1998) The emotional practice of teaching. *Teaching and Teacher Education*, 14/8.

Hargreaves, A. (2001) Emotional geographies of teaching. *Teachers College Record*, 103/6.

Hargreaves, A. and M. Fullan (eds) (1992) *Understanding Teacher Development*. London: Cassell.

Hargreaves, D. H. (1993) A common-sense model of the professional development of teachers. In J. Elliot (ed.) *Reconstructing Teacher Education: Teacher Development*. London: Falmer.

Harmer, J. (1991) *The Practice of English Language Teaching*. Harlow: Longman.

Harrison, I. (1996) Look who's talking now: listening to voices in curriculum renewal. In K. M. Bailey and D. Nunan (eds).

Haynes, J. E. (2001) *Children as Philosophers*. London: The Falmer Press.

Head, K. and P. Taylor (1997) *Readings in Teacher Development*. Oxford: Heinemann.

Hedge, T. (2000) *Teaching and Learning in the Language Classroom*. Oxford: Oxford University Press.

Hess, N. (2001) *Teaching Large Multilevel Classes*. Cambridge: Cambridge University Press.

Hilleson, A. (1996) 'I want to talk with them, but I don't want them to hear': an introspective study of second language anxiety in an English-medium school. In K. M. Bailey and D. Nunan (eds).

Hitchcock, G. and D. Hughes (1989) *Research and the Teacher*. London: Routledge.

Holliday, A. (1994) *Appropriate Methodology and Social Context*. Cambridge: Cambridge University Press.

Holliday, A. (1997) Six lessons: cultural continuity in communicative language teaching. *Language Teaching Research*, 1/3.

Holliday, A. (1999) Small cultures. *Applied Linguistics*. 20/2.

Holliday, A. (2002) *Doing and Writing Qualitative Research*. London: Sage.

Holt, J. (1964) *How Children Fail*. Penguin: Harmondsworth.

Hopkins, D. (2002) *A Teacher's Guide to Classroom Research*. Milton Keynes: Open University Press (3rd edition).

Hopkins, D., M. West, M. Ainscow, A. Harris and J. Beresford (1997) *Creating the Conditions for Classroom Improvement: A handbook of staff development activities*. London: Fulton.

Howatt, A. (1984) *A History of English Language Teaching*. Oxford: Oxford University Press.

Hoyle, E. and M. Wallace (2003) Management and teaching: two cultures or one? In R. Sutherland, G. Claxton and A. Pollard (eds).

Hoyle, E. and P. John (eds) (1995) *Professional Knowledge and Professional Practice*. London: Cassell.

Huberman, M. (1993) *The Lives of Teachers*. London: Cassell.

Hubiak, W. and J. H. Banning (1994) The implications of place attachment for campus workplaces. *Campus Ecologist*, 12/3.

Hughes, M. and P. Greenhough (2003) Homework: learning at the interface between two cultures. In R. Sutherland, G. Claxton and A. Pollard (eds).

Illich, I. (1971) *Deschooling Society*. New York: Harper and Row.

Jackson, P. (1968) *Life in Classrooms*. Chicago: Chicago University Press.

Jacobs, G. M. and Ratmaninda (1996) The appropriacy of group activities: views from some Southeast Asian second language educators. *RELC Journal*, 27/1.

Jacques, D. (1991) *Learning in Groups*. London: Kogan Page (2nd edition).

James, P. (2000) *Teachers in Action*. Cambridge: Cambridge University Press.

Jarvis, P., J. Holford and C. Griffin (eds) (2004) *The Theory and Practice of Teaching*. London: Routledge and Falmer (2nd edition).

Jimenez-Arias, I. (1996) Proxemics in the ESL classroom. *Forum*, 34/1.

John, P. D. (1996) Understanding the apprenticeship of observation in initial teacher training: exploring student teachers' implicit theories of teaching. In G. Claxton, T. Atkinson, M. Osborn and M. Wallace (eds).

John, P. D. (2000) Awareness and intuition: how student teachers read their own lessons. In T. Atkinson and G. Claxton (eds).

Jones, V. (1996) Classroom management. In J. Sikula, T. J. Buttery and E. Guyton. (eds) *The Handbook of Research on Teacher Education*. New York: Macmillan (2nd edition).

Jones, V. F. and L. S. Jones (1991) *Comprehensive Classroom Management*. New York: Longman (2nd edition).

Joyce, B., E. Calhoun and D. Hopkins (1997) *Models of Teaching – Tools for Learning*. Buckingham: Open University Press.

Kagan, D. (1992) Professional growth among preservice and beginning teachers. *Review of Educational Research*, 62/2.

Kaikonnen, P. (2001) Intercultural learning through foreign language education. In V. Kohonen, R. Jaatinen, P. Kaikonnen and J. Lehtovaara.

Katz, A. (1996) Teaching style: a way to understand instruction in language classrooms. In K. M. Bailey and D. Nunan (eds).

Keppler, A. and T. Luckman (1991) 'Teaching': Conversational transmission of knowledge. In I. Markova and K. Foppa (eds) *Asymmetries in Dialogue*. Hemel Hempstead: Harvester Wheatsheaf.

Knight, P. (2001) The development of ELT methodology. In C. N. Candlin and N. Mercer (eds).

Kohonen, V. (1992) Experiential language learning: second language learning as cooperative learner education. In D. Nunan (ed.).

Kohonen, V, R. Jaatinen, P. Kaikkonen and J. Lehtovaara (2001) *Experiential Learning in Foreign Language Teaching*. Harlow: Longman.

Kolb, D. (1984) *Experiential Learning as the Science of Learning and Development*. Englewood Cliffs, NJ: Prentice-Hall (3rd edition).

Kolb, D. (2000) Learning places: Building dwelling thinking online. In N. Blake and P. Standish (eds) *Enquiries at the Interface: Philosophical Problems of Online Education*. Oxford: Blackwell.

Kozulin, A. (1998) *Psychological Tools: A sociological approach to education*. Cambridge, MA: Harvard University Press.

Kramsch, C. (ed.) (2002) *Language Acquisition and Language Socialisation: Ecological Perspectives*. London: Continuum.

Kramsch, C. and P. Sullivan (1996) Appropriate pedagogy. *ELT Journal*, 50/3.

Kress, G., C. Jewitt, J. Ogborn and C. Tsatsarelis (2001) *Multimodal Teaching and learning: The rhetorics of the science classroom*. London: Continuum.

Kübler-Ross, E. (1997) *On Death and Dying*. Englewood Cliffs, NJ: Prentice-Hall.

Kumaravadivelu, B. (2001) Toward a post-method pedagogy. *TESOL Quarterly*, 35/4.

Kyriacou, C. (1992) *Essential Teaching Skills*. Hemel Hempstead: Simon and Schuster.

Lambert N. M. (1994) *Seating Arrangements in Classrooms. In The International Encyclopedia of Education*, Volume 2.

Lampert, M. (2000) Knowing teaching: the intersection of research on teaching and qualitative research. *Harvard Educational Review*, 70/1.

Lankshear, C., M. Peters and M. Knobel (2000) Information, knowledge and learning: some issues facing epistemology and education in a digital age. In N. Blake and P. Standish (eds).

Lantolf, J. (2000) (ed.) *Sociocultural Theory and Second Language Learning*. Oxford: Oxford University Press.

Lantolf, J. P. and G. Appel (eds) (1994) *Vygotskyan Approaches to Second Language Research*. Norwood, NJ: Ablex.

Larsen-Freeman, D. (1991) Second language acquisition research: staking out the territory. *TESOL Quarterly*, 25/2.

Lave, J. (1988) The culture of acquisition and the practice of understanding. (Report Nn. IRL 88–0007) Palo Alto, CA: Institute of Research on Learning.

Lave, J. and E. Wenger (1991) *Situated Learning: Legitimate peripheral participation*. Cambridge: Cambridge University Press.

Leask, M. (ed.) (2001) *Issues in Teaching Using ICT*. London: Routledge.

Lee B. H. (1999) A teacher's mind's eye: A study of the congruity between teachers' metaphors and classroom practice. Unpublished PhD thesis. University of Exeter.

Legutke, M. (1995) Redesigning the language classroom. Paper delivered at 29th IATEFL Annual Conference. York. Mimeo: Unpublished.

Legutke, M. and H. Thomas (1991) *Process and Experience in the Language Classroom*. Harlow: Longman.

Lehtovaara, J. (2001) What is it – (FL) teaching? In V. Kohonen, R. Jaatinen, P. Kaikkonen and J. Lehtovaara.

Lemke, J. L. (2002a) Becoming the village: education across lives. In G. Wells and G. Claxton (eds) *Learning for Life in the 21st Century*. Oxford: Blackwell.

Lemke, J. (2002b) Language development and identity: Multiple timescales in the social ecology of learning. In C. Kramsch (ed.).

Leontiev, A. N. (1978) *Activity, Consciousness and Personality*. Englewood Cliffs, NJ: Prentice Hall.

Levinson, S. (1992) Activity types and language. In P. Drew and J. Heritage (eds).

Li, D. (2001) Teachers' perceived difficulties in introducing the communicative approach in South Korea. In D. Hall and A. Hewings (eds).

Lin, A. M. Y. (2001) Doing-English-lessons in the reproduction or transformation of social worlds? In C. N. Candlin and N. Mercer (eds).

Lindh, J. and C-A. Soames (1994) A dual perspective on an online learning course. (available at www.ejel.org).

Littlejohn, A. (1998) The analysis of teaching materials: inside the Trojan Horse. In B. Tomlinson (ed.).

Littlewood, W. (1981) *Communicative Language Teaching*. Cambridge: Cambridge University Press.

Long, M. (1996) The role of the linguistic environment in second language acquisition. In W. C. Richie and T. K. Bhatia (eds).

Lortie, D. C. (1975) *Schoolteacher: A Sociological Study*. Chicago, IL: Chicago University Press.

Loveless, A. and V. Ellis (2001) (eds) *ICT, Pedagogy and the Curriculum: Subject to change*. London: Routledge and Falmer.

Luft, J. (1984) *Group Processes: An introduction to group dynamics*. Palo Alto, CA: Mayfield, 3rd edition.

Lynch, T. (1997) Nudge, nudge: Teacher interventions in task-based learner talk. *ELT Journal*, 51/4.

Machada de Almeida Mattos, A. (2000) A Vygotskian approach to evaluation in foreign language learning contexts. *ELT Journal*, 54/4.

Mackay, R. (1993) Embarrassment and hygiene in the classroom. *ELT Journal*, 47/1.

Mahn, H. and V. John-Steiner (2002) The gift of confidence: A Vygotskyan view of emotions. In G. Wells and G. Claxton (eds).

Markee, N. (2001) The diffusion of innovation in language teaching. In D. Hall and A. Hewings (eds).

Marland, P. (1997) *Towards More Effective Open and Distance Teaching*. London: Kogan Page.

Martin-Jones, M. (2000) Bilingual classroom interaction: a review of recent research. *Language Teaching*, 33.

Mason, R. (1998) Models of online courses. ALN Magazine 2/2 (available at www.al.org/alnweb/magazine/vol2_issue2/masonfinal.htm0).

Maynard, T. and J. Furlong (1993) Learning to teach and models of mentoring. In D. McIntyre, H. Hagger and M. Wilkin (eds).

McGill, I. and L. Beaty (2001) *Action Learning: A practitioner's guide*. London: Kogan Page (2nd edition).

McGuinness, J. (1993) *Teachers, Pupils and Behaviour: A managerial approach*. London: Cassell.

McIntyre, D., H. Hagger and M. Wilkin (1993) (eds) *Mentoring: Perspectives on school-based teacher education*. London: Kogan Page.

McKie, J. (2000) Conjouring notions of place. In N. Blake and P. Standish (eds).

McLaughlin, H. J. (1991) Reconciling care and control: Authority in classroom relationships. *Journal of Teacher Education*, 42/3.

McLaughlin, H. J. (1994) From negation to negotiation: Moving away from the management metaphor. *Action in Teacher Education*, 16/1.

McLaughlin, H. J., T. V. Savage, S. Zehm and R. R. Powell (2001) *Management of the Culturally Diverse Classroom: Perspectives on the social curriculum*. New York: Pearson.

McPake, J., W. Harlen, J. Rowney and J. Davidson (1999) [online] Practices and interactions in the Primary classroom. Scottish Council for Research in Education. Available online at www.scotland.gov.uk/edru

Medgyes, P. and A. Malderez (eds) (1996) *Perspectives on Teacher Education*. Oxford: Heinemann.

Mehan, H. (1979) *Learning Lessons: Social organisation in the classroom*. Cambridge, MA: Harvard University Press.

Mercer, N. (1994) Neo-Vygotskian theory and classroom education. In B. Stierer and J. Maybin (eds) *Language, Learning and Literacy in Educational Practice*. Clevedon: Multilingual Matters.

Mercer, N. (1995) *The Guided Construction of Knowledge*. Clevedon: Multilingual Matters.

Mercer, N. (2000) *Words and Minds*. London. Routledge.

Mercer, N. (2001) Language for teaching a language. In C. N. Candlin and N. Mercer (eds).

Mercer, N. (2002) Developing dialogues. In G. Wells and G. Claxton (eds).

Montgomery, M. (1981) Developing a description of spoken discourse. In M. Montgomery and M. Coulthard (eds) *Studies in Discourse Analysis*. London: Routledge.

Montgomery, M. and M. Coulthard (eds) (1981) *Studies in Discourse Analysis*. London: Routledge.

Moon, J. (1999) *Reflection in Learning and Professional Development*. London: Kogan Page.

Moon, J. (2001) Reflection in higher education learning. *PDP Working Paper 4*. Learning and Teaching Support Network.

Morgan, N. and J. Saxton (1991) *Teaching Questioning and Learning*. London: Routledge.

Murphy, D. R. Walker, G. Webb (eds) (2001) *Online Learning and Teaching with Technology: Case studies, experience and practice*. London: Kogan Page.

Na Ubon, A. and C. Kimble (2003) Exploring social presence in asynchronous text-based online learning communities. Department of Computer Science, University of York. Mimeo.

Naidu, B., K. Neeraja, E. Ramani, J. Shivakumar and V. Viswanatha (1992) Researching heterogeneity: an account of teacher-initiated research into large classes. *ELT Journal*, 46/4.

Nassaji, H. and G. Wells (2000) What's the use of 'triadic dialogue'?: an investigation of teacher-student interaction. *Applied Linguistics*, 21/3.

Newman, D., P. Griffin and M. Cole (1984) Social constraints in laboratory and classroom tasks. In B. Rogoff and J. Lave (eds).

Newman, D., P. Griffin and M. Cole (1989) *The Construction Zone: Working for cognitive change in school*. New York: Cambridge University Press.

Nias, J. (1989) *Primary Teachers Talking: A study of teaching as work*. London: Routledge.

Nolasco, R. and L. Arthur (1988) *Large Classes*. Basingstoke: Macmillan.

North, S. and H. Pillay (2002) Homework: re-examining the routine. *ELT Journal*, 56/2.

Norton, B. (2000) *Identity and Language Learning: Power and possibility in classrooms and communities*. Harlow: Longman.

Norton, B. (2001) Non-participation, imagined communities and the language classroom. In M. P. Breen (2001c).

Nunan, D. (1987) Communicative language teaching: making it work. *ELT Journal*, 41/2.

Nunan, D. (ed.) (1992) *Collaborative Language Teaching and Learning*. Cambridge: Cambridge University Press.

Nunan, D. (1996) Hidden voices: insiders' perspectives on classroom interaction. In K. M. Bailey and D. Nunan (eds).

O'Regan (2003) Emotion and E-learning. *Journal of Asynchronous Learning Networks*, 7/3.

Olson, D. (1996) Introduction to D. R. Olson and N. Torrance (eds) *Modes of Thought*. Cambridge: Cambridge University Press.

Olson, J. (1992) *Understanding Teaching: Beyond expertise*. Milton Keynes: Open University Press.

Ouyang Huhua (2000) One Way Ticket: A story of an innovative teacher in mainland China. *Anthropological and Educational Quarterly*, 31/4.

Painter, L. (2003) *Homework*. Oxford: Oxford University Press.

Pajares, M. F. (1992) Teachers' beliefs and educational research: cleaning up a messy construct. *Review of Educational Research*, 62/4.

Parker, P. (1994) Qualitative research. In P. Banister, E. Burman, I. Parker, M. Taylor and C. Tindall (eds).

Piaget, J. (1929) *The Child's Concept of the World*. London: Routledge & Kegan Paul.

Pica, T. (1994) Research on negotiation: what does it reveal about second-language learning, conditions, processes and outcomes? *Language Learning*, 38.

Pollard, A. (2000) *Reflective Teaching in the Primary School*. London: Cassell.

Pollard, A. (2002) *Reflective Teaching: Effective and research-based professional practice*. London: Continuum.

Pollard, A. and S. Tann (1993) *Reflective Teaching in the Primary School: A handbook for the classroom*. London: Routledge (2nd edition).

Pontecorvo, C. and L. Sterponi (2002) learning to argue and reason through discourse in educational settings. In G. Wells and G. Claxton (eds).

Prabhu, N. S. (1987) *Language Teaching Pedagogy*. Oxford: Oxford University Press.

Prabhu, N. S. (1990) There is no best method. Why? *TESOL Quarterly*. 24/2.

Prabhu, N. S. (1992) The dynamics of the language lesson. *TESOL Quarterly*. 26/2.

Prabhu, N. S. (1995) Concept and conduct in language pedagogy. In G. Cook and B. Seidlhofer (eds) *Principle and Practice in Applied Linguistics*. Oxford: Oxford University Press.

Prophet, R. (1995) Voices from the Botswana Junior Secondary classroom: A case study of a curriculum intervention. *International Journal of Education and Development*, 15/2

Rampton, B. (1999) 'Deutsch' in Inner London and the animation of an instructed foreign language. *Journal of Sociolinguistics*, 3/4

Razianna Abdul Rahman (2003) Learners' understandings of the experiences of learning English: a Malaysian perspective. Unpublished PhD thesis. University of Exeter.

Revans, R. (1988) *The ABC of Action Learning*. London: Lemos and Crane.

Richards, J. C. (2001) Beyond methods. In C. N. Candlin and N. Mercer (eds).

Richards, J. C. and D. Nunan (eds) (1990) *Second Language Teacher Education*. Cambridge: Cambridge University Press.

Richards, K. E. (1997) Staffroom as world. In E. Griffiths and K. Head (eds) *Teachers Develop Teachers Research 2*. Whitstable: IATEFL.

Richards, K. E. (2003) *Qualitative Research for TESOL*. Basingstoke: Palgrave Macmillan.

Richardson, V. and C. Fallona (2001) Classroom management as method and manner. *Journal of Curriculum Studies*, 33/6.

Richie, W. C. and T. K. Bhatia (eds) (1996) *Handbook of Second Language Acquisition*. San Diego: Academic Press.

Rinvolucri, M. (1999) The humanistic exercise. In J. Arnold (ed.).

Roberts, C. and S. Sarangi (1993) 'Culture' revisited in intercultural communication. In T. Boswood, R. Hoffman and P. Tung (eds) *Perspectives on English for Professional Communication*. Hong Kong: City Polytechnic of Hong Kong.

Roberts, J. (1998) *Language Teacher Education*. London: Arnold.

Rogers, A. (1996) *Teaching Adults*. Milton Keynes: Open University Press (2nd edition).

Rogers, C. (1983) *Freedom to Learn for the 80s*. Columbus, OH: Merrill.

Rogoff, B. and J. Lave (eds) (1984) *Everyday Cognition: Its development in social context*. Cambridge, MA: Harvard University Press.

Rowland, S. (1993) *The Enquiring Tutor: Exploring the process of professional learning*. London: The Falmer Press.

Rowntree, D. (1992) *Exploring Open and Distance Learning*. London: Kogan Page.

Salimbene, S. (1981) Non-frontal teaching methodology. *ELT Journal*, 35/2.

Salmon, G. (2000) *E-Tivities: The key to active learning online*. London: Routledge and Falmer.

Salmon, G. (2004) *E-Moderating: The key to teaching and learning online*. London: Routledge Falmer (2nd edition).

Sanger, J. (2001) ICT, the demise of UK schooling and the rise of the individual learner. In A. Loveless and V. Ellis (eds).

Sarangi, S. (1994) Intercultural or not? Beyond celebration of cultural differences in miscommunication analysis. *Pragmatics*. 4/3.

Sarangi, S. and C. Roberts (eds) (1999) *Talk, Work and Institutional Order: Discourse in medical, mediation and management settings*. The Hague: Mouton.

Sarwar, Z. (2001) Adapting individualisation techniques for large classes. In D. Hall and A. Hewings (eds).

Sayer, J. (1988) Identifying the issues. In H. C. Gray (ed.) Management Consultancy in Schools. London: Cassell.

Schegloff, E. A. (1992) Repair after the next turn: the last structurally provided defense of intersubjectivity in conversation. *American Journal of Sociology*, 98.

Schegloff, E. A., I Koshik, S. Jacoby and D. Olsher (2002) Conversation analysis and applied linguistics. *Annual Review of Applied Linguistics*, 22.

Schön, D. A. (1983) *The Reflective Practitioner: How professionals think in action*. San Francisco, CA.: Jossey-Bass.

Schön, D. A. (1987) *Educating the Reflective Practitioner*. San Francisco, CA: Jossey-Bass.

Schön, D. A. and M. Rein (1991) *Frame Reflection: Toward the resolution of intractable policy controversies*. New York: Basic Books.

Schratz, M. (ed.) (1983) *Qualitative Voices in Educational Research*. London: Falmer Press.

Schumann, J. H. (1999) A neurobiological perspective on affect and methodology in second language learning. In J. Arnold (ed.).

Scollon, R. and S. Scollon (1981) *Narrative, Literacy and Face in Interethnic Communication*. Norwood, NJ: Ablex.

Scollon, R. and S. Scollon (1995) *Intercultural Communication*. Oxford: Blackwell.

Seedhouse, P. (1996) Classroom interaction: possibilities and impossibilities. *ELT Journal*, 50/1.

Seedhouse, P. (1997) Combining form and meaning. *ELT Journal*, 51/4.

Seedhouse, P. (1999) Task-based interaction. *ELT Journal*, 53/3.

Senior, R. (1997) Transforming language classes into bonded groups. *ELT Journal*, 55/1.

Senior, R. (2002) A class-centred approach to language teaching. *ELT Journal*, 56/4.

Serpell, R. (1993) *The Significance of Schooling: Life journeys in an African society*. Cambridge: Cambridge University Press.

Shamim, F. (1996a) Learner resistance to innovation in classroom methodology. In H. Coleman (ed.).

Shamim, F. (1996b) In and out of the action zone: location as a feature of interaction in large ESL classes in Pakistan. In K. M. Bailey and D. Nunan (eds).

Shulman, L. (1986) Those who understand: Knowledge growth in teaching. *Educational Researcher*, 15/2.

Sinclair, J. McH. and M. Coulthard (1975) *Towards an Analysis of Discourse: The language of pupils and teachers*. Oxford: Oxford University Press.

Skilbeck, M. (1984) *School-based Curriculum Development*. London: Harper and Row.

Snyder, I. and C. Beavis (eds) (2004) *Doing Literacy Online: Teaching, learning and playing in an electronic world*. Cresskill, NJ: Hampton Press.

Stenhouse, L. (1975) *An Introduction to Curriculum Development and Research*. London: Heinemann.

Stenhouse, L. (1984) Artistry and teaching: the teacher as focus of research and development. In D. Hopkins and M. Wideen (eds) *Alternative Perspectives on School Improvement*. Lewes: Falmer Press.

Stevick, E. (1976) *Memory, Meaning and Method*. Rowley, MA: Newbury House.

Stevick, E. (1980) *Teaching Languages: A way of ways*. Rowley, MA: Newburg House.

Stewart, I. and J. Cohen (1997) *Figments of Reality*. Cambridge: Cambridge University Press.

Stewart, J. (1996) *Managing Change through Training and Development*. London: Kogan Page (2nd edition).

Sullivan, P. (2000) Playfulness as mediation in communicative language teaching in a Vietnamese classroom. In J. P. Lantolf (ed.).

Sutherland, R., G. Claxton and A. Pollard (eds) (2003) *Learning and Teaching: Where worldviews meet*. Stoke-on-Trent: Trentham Books.

Swales, J. (1988) Discourse communities, genres, and English as an international language. *World Englishes*, 4.

Swann, J. (2001) Recording and transcribing talk in educational settings. In C. N. Candlin and N. Mercer (eds).

Szesztay, M. (2001) Professional development through research. Unpublished PhD thesis, University of Exeter.

Tannenbaum, R. and W. H. Schmidt (1958) How to choose a leadership pattern. *Harvard Business Review*, 36.

Tanner, R. and C. Green (1998) *Tasks for Teacher Education*. Harlow: Longman.

Tayeb, M. H. (1996) *The Management of a Multinational Workforce*. Chichester: Wiley.

Tharp, R. G. and R. Gallimore (1988) *Rousing Minds to Life: Teaching, learning and schooling in a social context*. New York: Cambridge University Press.

Tharp, R. G. and R. Gallimore (1991) *The Instructional Conversation: Teaching and learning in social activity*. Santa Cruz, CA: National Centre for Research on Cultural Diversity and Second Language Learning.

Thomas, H. and T. Wright (1999) The role of facilitator training and the development of process competence. *Triangle 15*. Paris: The British Council.

Thompson, G. (1996) Some misconceptions about communicative language teaching. *ELT Journal*, 50/1.

Thornbury, S. (1999) Lesson art and design. *ELT Journal*, 53/1.

Tindall, C. (1994) Personal construct approaches. In P. Banister, E. Burman, I. Parker, M. Taylor and C. Tindall (eds).

Tomlinson, B. (ed.) (1998) *Materials Development in Language Teaching*. Cambridge: Cambridge University Press.

Tripp, D. (1993) *Critical Incidents in Teaching: Developing Professional Judgement*. London: Routledge.

Tsui, A. (1996) Reticence and anxiety in second language learning. In K. M. Bailey and D. Nunan (eds).

Tsui, A. (1998) Awareness raising about classroom interaction. In L. van Lier and D. Corson (eds) *Encyclopedia of Language and Education*, Vol. 6.

Tsui, A. (2003) *Understanding Expertise in Teaching: Case studies of ESL teachers*. Cambridge: Cambridge University Press.

Underhill, A. (1989) Process in humanistic education. *ELT Journal*, 43/4.

Underhill, A. (1999) Facilitation in language teaching. In J. Arnold (ed.).

Ur, P. (1996) *A Course in Language Teaching*. Cambridge: Cambridge University Press.

Vale, D. with A. Fuenteun (1995) *Teaching Children English*. Cambridge: Cambridge University Press.

van Dam, J. (2002) Ritual, face and play in a first English lesson: bootstrapping a classroom culture. In C. Kramsch (ed.).

van Lier, L. (1988) *The Classroom and the Language Learner*. Harlow: Longman.

van Lier, L. (1996a) Interaction in the Language Curriculum: Awareness, Autonomy and Authenticity. Harlow: Longman.

van Lier, L. (1996b) Conflicting voices: language, classrooms, and bilingual education in Puno. In K. M. Bailey and D. Nunan (eds).

van Lier, L. (1998) All hooked up: an ecological look at computers in the classroom. *Studia Anglica Posnaniensia*, 33.

van Lier, L. (2000) From input to affordance: social-interactive learning from an ecological perspective. In J. P. Lantolf (ed.).

van Lier, L. (2001) Constraints and resources in classroom talk: issues of equality and symmetry. In C. N. Candlin and N. Mercer (eds).

van Lier, L. and D. Corson (eds) (1997) *Encyclopedia of Language and Education*, Vol. 6. *Knowledge about Language*. Dordrecht: Kluwer.

van Manen, M. (1991) *The Tact of Teaching*. Albany, NY: State University of New York Press.

Vygotsky, L. (1978) *Thought and Language*. Cambridge, MA: Harvard University Press.

Walker, R. and C. Adelman (1975) *A Guide to Classroom Observation*. London: Methuen.

Wallace, M. (1998) *Action Research for Language Teachers*. Cambridge: Cambridge University Press.

Watkins, C., E. Carnell, C. Lodge and C. Whalley (1996) Effective learning. *SIN Research Matters*, 5. London: Institute of Education, University of London.

Weil, S. W. and I. McGill (eds) (1989) *Making Sense of Experiential Learning*. Buckingham: Open University Press.

Weir, C. (2004) *Language Testing and Validation*. Basingstoke: Macmillan.

Wells, G. (1993) Re-evaluating the value of the IRF sequence: a proposal for the articulation of theories of activity and discourse for the analysis of teaching and learning in the classroom. *Linguistics and Education*. 5. 1–37.

Wells, G. (1999) *Dialogic Inquiry*. Cambridge: Cambridge University Press.

Wells, G. and G. Claxton (eds) (2002a) *Learning for Life in the 21st Century*. Oxford: Blackwell.

Wells, G. and G. Claxton (2002b) Introduction: sociocultural perspectives on the future of education. In G. Wells and G. Claxton (eds).

Wenger, E. (1998) *Communities of Practice: Learning, meaning and identity*. Cambridge: Cambridge University Press.

Wertsch, J. V., N. Minick and F. J. Arus (1984) The creation of context in joint problem-solving. In B. Rogoff and J. Lave (eds).

West, M. (1960) *Teaching English in Difficult Circumstances*. London: Longman.

Whitaker, P. (1993) *Managing Change in Schools*. Buckingham: Open University Press.

Whitaker, P. (1995) *Managing to Learn: Aspects of reflective and experiential learning in schools*. London: Cassell.

Whitaker, P. (1998) *Managing Schools*. London: Butterworth-Heinemann.

Williams, M. and B. Burden (1997) *Psychology for Foreign Language Teachers*. Cambridge: Cambridge University Press.

Wood, J., J. Bruner and G. Ross (1976) The role of tutoring in problem solving. *Journal of Child Psychiatry*, 17/1.

Woods, D. (1996) *Teacher Cognition in Language Teaching*. Cambridge: Cambridge University Press.

Woods, P. (ed.) (1996) *Contemporary Issues in Teaching and Learning*. London: Routledge.

Woods, P. and R. Jeffrey (1996) A new professional discourse? In P. Woods (ed.)

Wragg, E. C. (1993) *Class Management*. London: Routledge.

Wright, T. (1987a) *Roles of Teachers and Learners*. Oxford: Oxford University Press.

Wright, T. (1987b) Instructional task and discoursal outcome in the L2 classroom. In C. N. Candlin and D. Murphy (eds) *Language Learning Tasks*. Lancaster Practical Papers in English Language Teaching, Vol. 7. Hemel Hempstead: Prentice-Hall.

Wright, T. (1990) Understanding classroom role relationships. In J. C. Richards and D. Nunan (eds).

Wright, T. (1992a) Critical moments in the second language classroom: towards an analysis of classroom culture. PhD Thesis. University of Lancaster.

Wright, T. (1992b) L2 classroom research and L2 teacher education: towards a collaborative approach. In J. Flowerdew, M. Brock and S. Hsia (eds) *Perspectives on Second Language Teacher Education*. Hong Kong: City Polytechnic of Hong Kong.

Wright, T. (1999) Teacher development: a personal view. *Caves English Language Teaching*, 25.

Yinger, R., M. S. Hendricks-Lee and S. Johnson (1991) The character of working knowledge. Paper presented at the annual meeting of the American Educational Research Association. Chicago.

Zemblyas, M. (2004) The emotional characteristics of teaching: an ethnographic study of one teacher. *Teaching and Teacher Education*, 20/2.

Name Index

Subject Index